TOWARD A
JUST WORLD ORDER

STUDIES ON A JUST WORLD ORDER

† *Volume 2: International Law and a Just World Order*, edited by Richard Falk, Friedrich V. Kratchowil, and Saul H. Mendlovitz

† *Volume 3: The United Nations and a Just World Order*, edited by Richard Falk, Samuel S. Kim, Donald McNemar, and Saul H. Mendlovitz

Also of Interest

The Myth of Victory: What Is Victory in War? Richard Hobbs

† *Change in the International System*, edited by Ole R. Holsti, Randolph M. Siverson, and Alexander George

U.S. Foreign Policy and the New International Economic Order, Robert K. Olson

† *The Third World and U.S. Foreign Policy: Cooperation and Conflict in the 1980s*, Robert L. Rothstein

† *U.S. Policy in International Institutions: Defining Reasonable Options in an Unreasonable World*, Special Student Edition, Updated and Revised, edited by Seymour Maxwell Finger and Joseph R. Harbert

† *World Power Trends and U.S. Foreign Policy for the 1980s*, Ray S. Cline

† *NATO—The Next Thirty Years: The Changing Political, Economic, and Military Setting*, edited by Kenneth A. Myers

† *The War System: An Interdisciplinary Approach*, edited by Richard A. Falk and Samuel S. Kim

Global Human Rights: Public Policies, Comparative Measures, and NGO Strategies, edited by Ved P. Nanda, James R. Scarritt, and George W. Shepherd, Jr.

How Can We Commit the Unthinkable? Genocide: The Human Cancer, Israel W. Charny

† Available in hardcover and paperback.

About the Book and Editors

STUDIES ON A JUST WORLD ORDER
Volume 1: Toward a Just World Order
edited by Richard Falk, Samuel S. Kim, and Saul H. Mendlovitz

This text is designed to provide students with a solid theoretical and methodological base for understanding how the present international system works, how that system is likely to evolve given current world trends, and what realistically can be done to alleviate the most serious global problems.

Part 1 develops a world order perspective by examining the writings of those who are either victims of oppression or who speak on behalf of the oppressed. This section also thoroughly examines the state system and differing theories and approaches for explaining it. Part 2 applies the world order perspective to major problem areas: militarism and war, poverty, economic underdevelopment, denial of human rights, and ecological decay. The final part explores the nature of global change, how it is likely to occur in the future, and how it is possible to realize the world order values of peace, economic well-being, and sound ecological balance.

Intended for use as a basic text in world order, peace studies, and global issues courses and as a supplementary text in international relations, international organization, and modern history, this collection encourages students to assess their own value positions and the value implications of their own governments' policies and also to look beyond local and national concerns. The seminal articles and original essays make it a valuable resource for scholars, researchers, and libraries as well.

Richard Falk is Albert G. Milbank Professor of International Law and Practice at Princeton University and director of U.S. participation in the World Order Models Project (WOMP). **Samuel S. Kim** is professor of political science at Monmouth College and senior fellow at the Institute for World Order. **Saul H. Mendlovitz** is professor of international law at Rutgers University–Newark, Ira D. Wallach Professor of World Order Studies in the Institute of War and Peace Studies at Columbia University, and director of WOMP for the Institute for World Order.

STUDIES ON A JUST WORLD ORDER

Richard Falk and Saul H. Mendlovitz, General Editors

STUDIES ON A JUST WORLD ORDER

Volume 1

TOWARD A JUST WORLD ORDER

edited by Richard Falk,
Samuel S. Kim, and
Saul H. Mendlovitz

Westview Press / Boulder, Colorado

Studies on a Just World Order

Copyright © 1982 by Westview Press, Inc.

Published in 1982 in the United States of America by
Westview Press, Inc.
5500 Central Avenue
Boulder, Colorado 80301
Frederick A. Praeger, President and Publisher

Library of Congress Cataloging in Publication Data
Main entry under title:
Toward a just world order.
   (Studies on a just world order; v. 1)
   1. International relations. 2. International organization. I. Falk, Richard A. II. Kim, Samuel S., 1935– . III. Mendlovitz, Saul H. IV. Series.
JX1391.T68   327   81-23144
ISBN 0-86531-242-7   AACR2
ISBN 0-86531-251-6 (pbk.)

Printed and bound in the United States of America

10   9   8   7   6   5   4   3   2

CONTENTS

PART ONE
A WORLD ORDER PERSPECTIVE

SECTION 1
Voices of the Oppressed

SECTION 2
The Sovereign State and the World System

PART THREE
TOWARD JUST WORLDS

TOWARD A
JUST WORLD ORDER

GENERAL INTRODUCTION

This volume of readings unabashedly sets forth a just world order approach to the study of international politics. Such an approach is concerned with understanding the extent to which past, present, and future arrangements of power and authority are able to realize a set of human values—including peace, economic well-being, social justice, and ecological balance—for people throughout the globe. At the same time, its primary intention is to sharpen understanding of what is really happening rather than to specify solutions prematurely. At the heart of this particular orientation are two sets of preoccupations: What should we *fear*? What can we *hope*? The responses set forth here are guided by our understanding of world order realism.

This outlook needs to be explained. More conventional students of international politics often deride the world order approach we present here as "idealistic" or "utopian." We do not want to strike a defensive note, but we ask the reader to assess our effort by reference to what he or she regards as "real" and "desirable." Our intention is to provide alternative—and we believe more realistic—tools for understanding the main international challenges and problems as well as to give a clear sense of what might be achieved by way of positive response to the human predicament.

Of course, the prospects of positive global change do not seem very bright at the moment. The arms race deepens and spreads, conflicts over scarce resources pose increasing dangers of general war, world economic stagnancy breeds more nationalistic policies, revolutionary turbulence and transnational terrorism abound, environmental quality continues to erode, impoverished populations continue to expand, water and land are alarmingly scarce in many parts of the world, and constructive negotiations of global issues are in abeyance. Governments are not well attuned to this emergent agenda of world order problems. Instead, their emphasis remains what it has been by tradition: building up national defenses and alliances and confronting the immediate economic challenges.

Since the collapse of the colonial system in the 1950s and 1960s, the state system has expanded greatly in geographical and cultural scope. All parts of the world now have independent states active in global issues. For non-Western peoples, the acquisition of sovereignty has to be understood against a long history of dependence and domination. Statehood is a positive achievement, and the main task of the leadership is to consolidate this achievement, keeping

1

the society truly independent in the face of a variety of pressures. Especially the Third World is suspicious at this time of "globalist" schemes for world order, fearing some overarching framework designed to erode their sovereignty on behalf of Western economic and cultural interests. Henry Kissinger's and Zbigniew Brzezinski's adoption of world order rhetoric gives grounding to these fears, as does the "globalism" of the multinational corporate and banking elite, with borderless maps and catchy phrases such as "the management of interdependence."

It is our intention to provide a framework for inquiry that is neither unduly naive about the dynamics of power and the resilience of statism, nor ready to endorse those world order "claims" that seem designed to keep an unjust structure of privilege and power intact. At the same time, we would point out that this book has been put together by three aspiring "global citizens" living and working in the United States. Our preoccupations and perceptions undoubtedly reflect this aspect of our lives, although our objective is to produce material that is useful and responsive to the struggle to achieve world order values regardless of where that struggle is located. Undoubtedly our presence here unwittingly influences our style, approach to sources, and general pattern of expectations. Despite this constraining influence of time and space, our endeavor is to feel, think, and act as world citizens as well as members of a particular polity. We do not wish to diminish feelings of national patriotism, except to the extent that such feelings assert themselves at the expense of planetary well-being. A complex set of complementary loyalties, undergirded by a vision of the future, represents the profile of benevolent political consciousness.

In part, our conception of world order produces such a global identity. We believe that the world is integrated in such a way—materially, ecologically, and spiritually—as to make the *unity* of the human species the starting point for analysis and prescription. In this sense, a global society has emerged. Yet, we are aware that a global community based on a consensus of shared values seems remote given the divisiveness, strife, and different perceptions of the world that still abound. To some extent also, we are aware that our specific identities as U.S. citizens, as residents of a particular city or community, and as members of a gender, race, or religion shape our understanding of human solidarity. Nevertheless, our adoption of a global identity is an attempt to transcend these differences; it is an exercise of the imagination necessary for the development of global community.

Another feature of our world order approach is its affirmation of values as essential goals of political action. Of course, we know that national leaders more often than not pursue state *interests* (that is, the material and security goals of a given state) even when talking about global *values* (that is, ethically beneficial goals that pertain to humanity as a whole), and that moral claims are often made in a self-serving fashion by geopolitical rivals. Values are implicit in the postulate of human solidarity, especially when account is taken of the actual condition of *oppression*, of *mass poverty*, and of *ecological* and *geopolitical danger* that exists in the world. We favor operational definitions of values that give insight into social costs and benefits (peace in relation to given levels of war-related casualties and costs, economic well-being in relation to minimum income levels and degrees of inequality in wealth and income) so that it becomes possible to assess tradeoffs between values and to tell whether there has been any progress in a given period of international history with respect to the realization of world order values. Our search here, then, is for a more detached or objective appreciation of values as goals.

Finally, our just world order approach emphasizes the possibility and desirability of fundamental changes in the framework of international relations, which is called "system change." For this reason, we also refer to our approach as system transforming, as distinguished from the system-maintaining or system-reforming approaches to world order that see the present state system as inevitable or desirable (see Falk's "Contending Approaches to World Order" in Section 3). This system-transforming outlook reflects the judgment that the existing framework dominated by sovereign states is too fragmented (especially when power is distributed unequally while authority is shared widely among legally equal state entities) to fulfill the requirements of human solidarity or to assure the degree of coordination of wills needed for the realization of world order values. The burdens of fragmentation vary with the level and type of armaments, the degree of industrialization, the level and distribution of population, and the form and success of environmental protection. The case for system change is partly normative and partly empirical, that is, reflecting a mixture of aspirations and trends.

System change does not necessarily mean political integration or centralization at the supranational level, much less "world government." It means a fundamental rearrangement of structure so that a different configuration of actors with different orientations toward power, security, well-being and governance will emerge. System change is *not* necessarily beneficial from the point of view of world order values. A tyrannical world state, for example, would undoubtedly represent a step backward, given our acceptance of world order values as the basis for normative appraisal of world political arrangements.

At the same time, given the apparent inability of the existing system of territorial sovereign states to meet challenges of peace and justice, it seems appropriate to envisage preferred world order systems—that is, frameworks that seem more likely to realize world order values. For this reason, our world order approach depicts images (not blueprints) of plausible alternatives to the present world order system. It is also concerned with *relevant* system change—alternative frameworks that can emerge plausibly from the existing play of social forces active in the world, acknowledging the rich diversity of cultural aspiration that makes it impossible to set forth a unitary image of world order. The social sciences have been slow to build a widely accepted theory of social change, and our understanding of the dynamics of change at the global level is rudimentary at best. We lack dependable predictive capacities, although we can interpret trends, thereby grounding extrapolations and expectations.

It is also evident that history flows in certain broad directions independent of reason or the design of individuals. Nevertheless, individuals sensitive to these flows can help build movements responsive to the range of historical opportunities that exists at any given time. The growth of movements is often sudden and abrupt, sharply altering our conceptions of feasibility. National revolutions seem to happen with little or no warning, befuddling the best of experts; not even Lenin expected the Soviet Revolution to occur as soon as it did under the pressure of events in 1917, and virtually no one as late as 1976 anticipated an Iranian revolution in the decade, whereas only two years later, by the end of 1978, its triumph seemed inevitable. Such uncertainty is, oddly, a source of hope, counseling us not to take our pessimism too literally or to heed the many current voices of doom.

Part of imaging the future is to consider *transition* tactics and pathways. These should not be thought of as predictions, but rather as indications of how system change *could* come about and as recommendations for actions that would embody world order values. The depiction of a transition process cannot be a substitute for a theory of social change, but it is an essential element in a world order approach.

There is also no reason to connect system change and transition prospects with a definite set of future dates. Occasionally world order literature has projected the realization of a preferred system change by a certain specified time. At present, short of some dramatic discontinuity in political behavior by way of catastrophe or spiritual conversion, such specification of dates seems premature, especially given the need for far-reaching modifications. Also, sometimes predictions are made of "imminent collapse unless" or of "utopia or else!" These apocalyptic summonses have turned out to provide, contrary to their tone of urgency, a form of escapism. The state system has managed, so far, to confound pessimistic expectations of a general nuclear war on the heels of World War II. Similarly, it now seems that the Club of Rome's projections that industrial society could not persist much longer were overstated. So far, the state system has proved to be more resilient than its critics have assumed.

However, there are no grounds for complacency. In fact, the nuclear age has had its share of near misses, crises or accidents that easily could have resulted in massive disasters. We do not know adequately how close human activity may be to various precipices of ecological collapse. In an opposite sense, we do not know how much of the transition process that precedes positive types of system change has already taken place. We know, for instance, that disillusionment with war and anxiety about nuclear war are becoming widespread. At what point these feelings might coalesce into a popular movement against war—an abolitionist movement—is almost impossible to tell. The history of earlier social movements—for instance, the struggles against slavery or colonialism—suggests how hard it is to discern the basis for a movement's success until victory is almost at hand. Part of the world order effort is to acquire the mantle of "realism" for a given set of transformative strategies and goals.

The world order approach as presented in this volume has evolved over many years. Three distinct stages of development can be noted, although the successive stages incorporate as well as supplant earlier efforts, and throughout the process one can discern the quest for appropriate politics, a new radicalism built around the world order analysis.

STAGE I

This world order approach concentrated upon developing an image of an orderly world system generally constituted by a core of strengthened international institutions. Institutional centralization would come about through the consent of leading governments, persuaded that such a variant of system change serves their distinct national interests better than the dangerous chaos of the decentralized and laissez-faire management of power by international statecraft. A central feature of the voluntary process of transition implied by this assessment was the relinquishment of warmaking prerogatives and capabilities at the state level and the creation of a world police force at the global level. In effect, this approach looked toward the emergence of a species of world government, but in a form that attempted to preserve the autonomy of states as much as possible.

The most comprehensive and rigorous statement of this approach remains *World Peace Through World Law*, conceived and written by Grenville Clark and Louis B. Sohn, initially published in 1958 and revised twice subsequently. The Clark-Sohn proposals proceed by amending the Charter of the United Nations, thereby transferring some functions, capabilities, and resources from national governments to a tightly knit body of global institutions. Transition prospects rested on the attractiveness of the peace system they proposed as compared with the horrific consequences associated with the continuation of the state system in the nuclear age.

Despite energetic efforts to win the support of world leaders, few converts or advocates could be found. True, a few liberal groups became convinced that the Clark-Sohn approach was the way out. Some other initiatives along a similar line were launched during this period, the most prominent of which was associated with a group of scholars and humanists assembled by Robert Hutchins, then chancellor of the University of Chicago. Their proposals, put forward in the form of a draft world constitution, emphasized regional ordering blocs as the appropriate units for a world government system.

In retrospect, it is clear why such a world order approach failed. First of all, it entrusted transition to the persuasive power of ideas directed at political elites. Second, it arose in the United States, and was heavily influenced by the peculiar historical experience of the United States with its durable federalist structure and prosperous economy; the prospect of a world government system seemed less relevant historically and practically for the rest of the globe. Third, and most fundamentally, nationalism as a passion of peoples and statism as a drive of governments was by no means played out; indeed, these tendencies were, on balance, intensifying, especially in the non-Western world. In essence, there was neither receptivity nor political will to overcome the state system, and no rational scheme could provide a substitute. A scheme, however attractive, is a futile gesture without an implementing political structure.

STAGE II

Reacting to the lack of success with Stage I efforts, a serious attempt was made to overcome some of the difficulties encountered. The World Order Models Project (WOMP) has been the main result. WOMP was organized in 1968 around the idea that an adequate approach to the reform of the state system must be developed through the participation of representatives from the major cultures and ideologies of the world. One of the first results of this transnational participation was to move world order from its focus on war prevention to a more dynamic value framework that includes economic well-being, social justice, and ecological balance, as well as peace.

Agreeing on this broader value framework, participants from different regions embarked on book-length formulations of their approach to world order. Because the values were stated in general terms and were subject to a variety of interpretations, and because participants were free to propose additional values, this framework did not seriously constrain inquiry. These efforts by WOMP resulted in a series of six books: *Footsteps Into the Future*, by Rajni Kothari; *A World Federation of Cultures*, by Ali Mazrui; *Revolution of Being*, by Gustavo Lagos and Horacio Godoy; *The True Worlds: A Transnational Perspective*, by Johan Galtung; *A Study of Future Worlds*, by Richard Falk; and *On the Creation of a Just World Order*, edited by Saul H. Mendlovitz. The series as a whole, published throughout the 1970s, was called "Preferred Worlds for the 1990s."

WOMP's approach was directed at an academic audience, perhaps extended to include those men and women of public affairs concerned about the dangers of the existing world order system. The intention was to challenge those who studied world issues and to provide some ideas about long-range reform prospects. As with Clark-Sohn, however, WOMP also relied heavily on the potential persuasiveness of intellectual discourse. Its mandate included giving attention to the transition problem, but very little substance was set forth in the WOMP books by way of transition guidance for world order activists.

Although the project generated some interest in academic circles, including those outside the West, its overall impact on thought and action has remained rather modest. Mainstream international relations, leavened slightly by a new emphasis on non-Marxist ideas about political economy, held sway powerfully in the English-speaking world. It has proved difficult to challenge this orthodoxy effectively.

During most of the 1970s, WOMP was unable to achieve the sustained, prominent participation of Soviet scholars, or more generally, intellectuals in the Communist world. Also, Third World participation, although active, was complex because it included a constant questioning of the premises of such an undertaking. In this respect, the views of Rajni Kothari, a leading Indian scholar, are quite characteristic. Kothari, while entertaining his own WOMP vision of the future, is still suspicious of the world order enterprise, suspecting that it may be too much a carrier of predominantly Western thinking, a species of cultural imperialism (see his "Toward a Just World" in Section 9).

In essence, WOMP has been hampered by an absence of political will to move even the *study* (much less the *practice*) of politics toward normative goals of societal transformation. Many calmer sensibilities reject the WOMP diagnosis of danger and transformative trends, and concentrate on comprehending the state system and making it work more efficiently, thereby underestimating its structural limitations. Even within WOMP there is some Third World support for regarding global reform as mainly a continuation of the anti-imperial struggle, with emphasis on putting the Third World in a better position in the world economic and political systems.

WOMP's dialogue continues over which world order efforts deserve support. It may exert more influence than now seems evident, partly through its insistence that long-term analysis include normative concerns in a serious way. It must be acknowledged that the diversities within WOMP, let alone within the world as a whole, have not diminished. Except on a very general abstract level (peace, justice, cultural autonomy), no clear image of a preferred future acceptable to the world as a whole has yet emerged. Perhaps stronger universalizing social movements and belief patterns must first emerge to lay the groundwork for a shared global vision of global reconstruction that captures the human imagination.

Despite its proclaimed concern about transition, until now WOMP has not produced a coherent, credible conception of how world order values might be realized in the decades ahead. As such, the images of preferred futures seem just that—images. Hence, the allegation of utopianism has reappeared, despite the abandonment, even in the Western contributions to WOMP, of world government as a solution to the various dangers of world chaos.

Underlying the WOMP process has been dissatisfaction with the tendency to convert humanistic yearnings into political programs by rational explication. A more useful application of the world order approach seems to depend upon a better grasp of social forces—agents of change active in the world, struggling to overcome acute injustice.

STAGE III

Since 1978, WOMP has been moving in this new direction. This series of guided readings is an attempt to make this new emphasis accessible to general students. Instead of diagnosing the global problems that make adjustments in behavior and arrangements necessary, we begin this volume by listening to voices drawn from the ranks of the oppressed so as to discern their relevance to the wider concerns of world order. These active struggles against oppression are carried on largely within national arenas, although some relating to race, sex, and ethnic identity have transnational significance.

Our experience suggests that past approaches to world order have been overly preoccupied with formal organizations and the tension between states

TABLE 1

		VALUES		
	Peace	Economic Well-Being	Social Justice	Ecological Balance
1st SYSTEM (States and MNCs)				
2nd SYSTEM (International institutions, UN)				
3rd SYSTEM (Unofficial initiatives, social movements, popular sector)				

and international institutions, and have not been sufficiently concerned with movements and grassroots initiatives organized within the popular sector. We work here with a framework (see Table 1) that attempts to sharpen these distinctions and that puts the emphasis on what might broadly be conceived of as world order populism. This framework distinguishes between three systems of intersecting politics. The first system is comprised of territorial states—the state system and its supporting infrastructure of corporations, banks, and media. The second system consists of international organizations, including the United Nations and regional international institutions. The third system is represented by people acting individually and collectively through voluntary associations and institutions. This framework is a way of redirecting inquiry into the dynamics of transformation politics; our world order approach is not attempting to convince its audience as much as it is trying to show the extent to which transitional changes are actually being made in various sectors of international society and how these bear on the quest to realize world order values. As indicated in Table 2, these changes can be seen as involving three overlapping stages: first, a period of consciousness raising and exemplary actions, followed by mobilizing acts and movement building, culminating in transforming processes and structures.

Again, our intention is to provide concerned students with an approach that encourages a planetary orientation and that offers an alternative to the persisting paradigm of territorial states and imperial rivalry. By heeding the voices of the oppressed, we hope to encourage actual contact with ongoing political struggles and movements, acknowledging both the extent to which world order values can be promoted now in a variety of contexts and the degree to which system change on a global level is a protracted process entailing struggle and action (as well as thought and contemplation) at every stage.

This cumulative nature of Stage III needs to be stressed. Despite the shifts in emphasis, the world order approach has possessed certain features throughout:

TABLE 2

	TRANSITION		
	Consciousness-raising and Exemplary Actions	Mobilizing Acts and Movement Building	Transforming Processes and Structures
1st SYSTEM			
2nd SYSTEM			
3rd SYSTEM			

- an emphasis on system change
- depiction of preferred world order systems
- a stress on values specifically designated
- authoritative processes and structures
- a concern about transition process and tactics
- a holistic orientation seeking to interpret issues from a global perspective
- a commitment to the aspirations and struggles of the oppressed

The works in this volume will help readers make some sense of the rapidly shifting dimensions of global politics. We believe that more and more people throughout the world are responsive to the call to blend a global perspective with their local involvements. It is also obvious that a local orientation is helpful in giving concreteness to global concerns. The future is here and now, as well as there and later.

SELECTED BIBLIOGRAPHY

Listed below are a few books that provide an orientation to the approach outlined in the General Introduction. More specialized bibliographical suggestions will be made at the end of each section introduction.

To follow current developments we suggest the following: *Alternatives: A Journal of World Policy*, a quarterly published by the Centre for the Study of Developing Societies, Delhi, and The Institute for World Order (777 UN Plaza, New York, NY 10017); the bimonthly *IFDA Dossier* (International Foundation for an Alternative Development, 2 Place du Marche, CH-1260 Nyon, Switzerland); the biannual *Development Dialogue* (Dag Hammarskjold Foundation, Ovre Slottsgatan 2, 752 20, Uppsala, Sweden); and the *SIPRI Yearbook*, the annual volume on armaments from the Swedish Peace Research Institute.

Other useful periodicals include: *Beijing Review* (weekly); *Bulletin of Atomic Scientists* (monthly); *Bulletin of Peace Proposals* (quarterly); *Development Forum* (biannually); *Disarmament Times* (monthly); *Human Rights Quarterly, Journal of Peace Research* (quarterly); *The Nation* (weekly); *Not Man Apart* (News magazine of the Friends of the Earth, monthly); *Review of International Affairs* (Belgrade, weekly); *Third World Quarterly.*

Arguelles, Jose A. *The Transformative Vision*. Berkeley, CA.: Shambala Publications, 1975.

Bergesen, Albert, ed. *Studies of the Modern World System*. New York: Academic Press, 1980.

Boulding, Kenneth E. *The Meaning of the Twentieth Century*. New York: Harper (Colophon ed.), 1964.

Boyd, Gavin, and Charles Pentland, eds. *Issues in Global Politics*. New York: Free Press, 1981.

Bull, Hedley. *The Anarchical Society: A Study of Order in World Politics*. New York: Columbia University Press, 1977.

Camilleri, Joseph A. *Civilization in Crisis: Human Prospects in a Changing World*. New York: Cambridge University Press, 1976.

Clark, Grenville, and Louis Sohn. *World Peace Through World Law*. 2nd edition, revised. Cambridge: Harvard University Press, 1960.

Clark, Ian. *Reform and Resistance in the International Order*. New York: Cambridge University Press, 1980.

Falk, Richard. *A Study of Future Worlds*. New York: Free Press, 1976.

Falk, Richard, and Saul Mendlovitz, eds. *Strategy of Just World Order Series* (4 volumes). New York: World Law Fund, 1966. Vol. 1, *Toward a Theory of War Prevention*; Vol. 2, *International Law*; Vol. 3, *United Nations*; Vol. 4, *Disarmament and Economic Development*.

Frank, Andre Gunder. *Crisis in the World Economy* and *Crisis in the Third World*. New York: Holmes Meiers, 1981.

Galtung, Johan. *The True Worlds: A Transnational Perspective*. New York: Free Press, 1980.

Hoffman, Stanley. *Primacy or World Order: American Foreign Policy Since the Cold War*. New York: McGraw-Hill, 1978.

Kedron, Michael, and Ronald Segal. *The State of the World Atlas*. New York: Pluto Press, 1981.

Kothari, Rajni. *Footsteps Into the Future*. New York: Free Press, 1974.

Lagos, Gustavo, and Horacio Godoy. *Revolution of Being: A Latin American View*. New York: Free Press, 1977.

Mazrui, Ali. *A World Federation of Cultures: An African Perspective*. New York: Free Press, 1977.

Mendlovitz, Saul H., ed. *On the Creation of a Just World Order*. New York: Free Press, 1975.

Mumford, Lewis. *The Transformations of Man*. New York: Macmillan (Collier ed.), 1956.

Nerfin, Marc, ed. *Another Development*. Uppsala, Sweden: Hammarskjold Foundation, 1977.

Roszak, Theodore. *Person/Planet*. New York: Doubleday (Anchor ed.), 1978.

Schumacher, E. F. *A Guide for the Perplexed*. New York: Harper (Colophon ed.), 1977.

Teilhard de Chardin, Pierre. *The Future of Man*. New York: Harper (Torchbook ed.), 1969.

Thompson, William Irwin. *At the Edge of History*. New York: Harper, 1972.

Wager, Warren. *Building the City of Man: Outlines of a World Civilization*. San Francisco: W. H. Freeman & Co., 1971.

PART ONE

A WORLD ORDER PERSPECTIVE

Voices of the Oppressed

INTRODUCTION

A riot is the language of the unheard.
—Martin Luther King, Jr.

As the General Introduction suggests, it is something of a departure to start an investigation of world order by listening to the voices of the oppressed. We believe that in this period of fundamental ferment we can learn much by heeding the voices of those who are victimized by existing arrangements of power and authority. We can learn about motivation, about struggle, and about the visions that animate those fighting to overcome oppression. We can also gain a critical perspective of the world system that traditional scholarly pieces do not provide—a perspective that forces us to constantly consider the human consequences of how the present state system operates.

Our analysis suggests that the destructive effects of social, economic, cultural, and political trends are all-encompassing: There is no escape—even sanctuary on a space colony is a mirage. We are Earth-bound creatures for the indefinite future. Yet, most of us do not grasp the extent to which we are victimized by present geopolitical arrangements, or the extent to which this condition of oppression is itself contingent upon certain arbitrary patterns of behavior that can be challenged and changed. The structure of world order is not rigidly constrained by present patterns, at least not over long time cycles.

Nevertheless, positive forms of transformation depend upon active politics. Any transformation of this sort will result from mass social movements and hard political struggles. This prospect presupposes suitable awareness. Hence, part of our objective in this book is to encourage each reader to grasp his or her situation as conditioned and constrained by world order oppression. This appreciation needs to be more than intellectual. It must be felt in the heart as well as known by the mind.

And so, inevitably, this orientation suggests a concern with action. What can be done? Those who struggle against oppression are essentially hopeful; to them, social, political, and cultural change is possible. They believe in and act upon their own analysis, including its vision of an alternative future. In this section we begin with those who are representatives of ongoing movements of reform and revolution among the visibly oppressed, and then move to those who are trying to articulate an oppression that has not generally entered public consciousness.

The promise of a new world order, as we understand the quest, arises from a central commitment to the realization of a specific set of *humane* values: peace, economic well-being, social justice and ecological balance. These world order values apply to means as well as ends. Thus, not all modes of struggle are acceptable. Indeed, our approach emphasizes the importance of embodying the vision of the future to the extent possible, here and now, starting with the life choices we make as individuals. In the first instance, the most revealing world order statement each of us makes is with his or her life. Again, those who give voice to the situation of oppression are exemplary actors in the struggle for a just world order.

We begin this section with an essay by Ali Shariati, an Iranian who encouraged many Moslems to join in the struggle against the Shah. Shariati's essay is notable because he transcends racial, geographical, and national boundaries to identify with all those who have suffered oppression as a result of slavery and war. He found the inspirational grounds for struggle within his cultural experience and, in particular, in the outlook of Shi'ia Islam, the variety of Islam dominant in Iran. This meditation on oppression stood in contrast to many Iranian radical positions of the day that tried to rally opposition to the Shah by espousing Marxist thought. When the Iranian Revolution swept the Shah from power in early 1979, it did so as a massive, nonviolent movement led by Ayatollah Ruhollah Khomeini on the basis of an appeal to the liberating imperative of Islam. Shariati was one of the heroes of the revolution, although he had died on June 19, 1977, a victim of harassment by the Shah's regime. Of course, the Revolution has produced many disappointments and serious human rights abuses, but its initial victory does suggest how a powerful structure of oppression can be rapidly dismantled without resort to force of arms.

Unlike Iran, the situation in South Africa has not been transformed. In our second selection, Steve Biko asks that victims of apartheid build their struggle around a consciousness of their racial identity. Biko was imprisoned and killed by his South African prison guards. His death on September 12, 1977 was a tragedy that turned many opponents of apartheid away from the path of nonviolence. The oppressor is inclined to quiet the voice of the oppressed, that is, the person whose acts and words dramatize the circumstances of oppression for many others. The voice becomes a leader, and hence a target. To raise one's voice against oppression is to take risks, often without any means of defense. It is a courageous undertaking.

The third selection is a statement from the Czech dissident group Charter 77, which also illustrates exemplary courage in the context of oppression, this time a mixture of Soviet hegemony and Stalinist one-party rule in an East European country. Such victims of oppression are fully aware of their distress; their willingness to challenge openly such an oppressive structure is itself a call for mass resistance. These initiatives of resistance have been recurrent since the extension of Soviet influence to East European countries after World War II. The most recent instance is the remarkable movement of workers' resistance in Poland under conditions of economic hardship as well as political deprivation.

These Czech and Polish voices of the oppressed are, in part, seeking "space" within a general condition of oppression, rather than necessarily struggling, at this time, against the oppressive structure of the Soviet model of authoritarian rule. The structure seems impregnable, but its dynamics can be moderated by resistance within limits; exceeding these limits may lead to Soviet intervention and greater internal oppression. When and where to press and when and where to acquiesce are the essence of the tactical reality faced by opponents of these regimes in their particular struggle against oppression.

In the fourth selection, Awa Thiam presents fundamental claims on behalf of women whose voices have been raised in opposition to patriarchal forms of oppression. The voices are numerous and diverse, reflecting an array of national and cultural circumstances, but there are also important convergences, as this selection suggests. We begin with some voices from francophone Africa, chosen partly to emphasize that, contrary to some contentions (mostly by men), the struggle against the oppression of women extends far beyond the highly industrialized countries of the West. The struggle of women must also be placed in the wider context of overall resistance to oppression at a time of historic upheaval. It may be that our capacity to bring equality into the relations of men and women will necessarily improve our capacities to challenge militarism, social injustice and the excesses of nationalism. In any event, the liberation of women is becoming an important agenda item for world order studies, and it deserves serious treatment in any assessment of the prospects and strategies available for global transformation.

There is a different, yet connected, issue posed by modern warfare waged with weapons of mass destruction. The Hiroshima bomb introduced a new era in human affairs. Civilian victims with no connection to governmental decision processes have had their lives destroyed, their bodies maimed. For some, such effects have always been a part of warfare, but the magnitude of nuclear warfare overwhelms the moral imagination. Indeed, with deterrence doctrine, the idea of "a balance of terror" becomes virtually synonymous with "national security." This background of indiscriminate devastation flies in the face of the historic mission of international law to set limits on the conduct of war. This mission has always been controversial, given the tendency of political leaders to use weapons and tactics that confer a military advantage regardless of their legal and moral status. The tension between normative limits and military necessity reaches its maximum with the use of atomic weapons against modern cities, such as Hiroshima and Nagasaki at the end of World War II.

The reliance on nuclear weapons for deterrence, as Robert J. Lifton has suggested, makes us all, in some fundamental sense, helpless nuclear "guinea pigs." We are dependent on the good will and restraint of leaders who make up their minds in secret about whether and how these awesome weapons shall be tested, deployed, and used. Moreover, nuclear energy facilities release invisible low-level radiation that cannot be seen, felt, or smelled; it only kills, quietly and gradually. Our landscapes are dotted with nuclear missile emplacements and reactors prone to a variety of accidents. And yet, even in democratic societies, what can we do to protect ourselves against such risks? This suggests a dramatic extension of oppressive forms of social reality that directly result from our greatly enhanced technological capabilities.

The next selection, an essay by Richard Falk, carries these themes further. Falk seeks to comprehend our status as "victims" of an oppressive world system that threatens each of us. "Invisible oppression," in its many environmental and cultural forms, is the special circumstance of those societies that seem most privileged in a material sense. Implicit here is the contention that a movement for a just world will depend on the extent to which awareness of this predicament penetrates our social consciousness in a mobilizing way. We do not yet know whether there is, latent in our world society, a powerful (though largely passive) constituency for drastic change—a social force waiting to be activated. The transnational antinuclear movement, present in all democratic industrialized societies, may be a glimmer of the potential for such a movement, as is the growing movement in Western Europe on behalf of nuclear disarmament.

The final work in this section is a brief excerpt from Paolo Freire's influential book, *Pedagogy of the Oppressed*. Freire, an educator who worked with Brazilian peasants, with the people of Guinea Bissau, and in other situations of struggle, presents in these pages a penetrating analysis of the psychology of oppression and liberation. His thesis is that "the great humanistic and historical task of the oppressed [is] to liberate themselves and their oppressors as well." Freire describes how the oppressed often espouse the image of the oppressors as their goal, and thus eventually become oppressors themselves. Understanding that this cripples their efforts for liberation, he articulates a praxis for a genuinely liberating education that should challenge all students, scholars and intellectuals who commit themselves to a just world order.

QUESTIONS FOR DISCUSSION AND REFLECTION

What are the various voices of oppression represented in this section?

How do the demands made by the oppressed relate to the fulfillment of world order values?

Can you think of examples of "invisible oppression," other than those mentioned in the selections, that limit your life experience? Can you imagine the steps that you could take to overcome this oppression? Will you take them? If you will, how? If not, why not?

What does Freire see as the relationship between the oppressed and their oppressors? What does this relationship suggest as a strategy for struggle?

SELECTED BIBLIOGRAPHY

de Beauvoir, Simone. *The Second Sex*. New York: Bantam, 1968.
Biko, Steve. *I Write What I Like*. New York: Harper, 1978.

Boulding, Elise. *The Underside of History: A View of Women Through Time*. Boulder, CO: Westview Press, 1976.

Chinweizu. *The West and the Rest of Us*. London: NOK Publishers, 1978.

Deloria, Vine. *Behind the Trail of Broken Treaties: An Indian Declaration of Independence*. New York: Delacorte Press, 1974.

Douglass, James. *Lightning East to West*. Portland, OR.: Sunburst Press, 1980.

Drinnon, Richard. *Facing West: The Metaphysics of Indian-Hating and Empire-Building*. Minneapolis, MN: University of Minnesota Press, 1980.

Fanon, Frantz. *The Wretched of the Earth*. New York: Grove Press, 1968.

Friere, Paolo. *Pedagogy in Process: The Letters to Guinea-Bissau*. New York: Seabury Press, 1978.

_____. *Pedagogy of the Oppressed*. New York: Herder and Herder, 1970.

Gutierrez, Gustavo. *A Theology of Liberation*. New York: Orbis Books, 1973.

Huston, Perdita. *Third World Women Speak Out*. New York: Praeger, 1970.

Kim, Chi Ha. *Cry of the People and Other Poems*. Brookline, MA.: Autumn Press, 1974.

Lernoux, Penny. *Cry of the People: U.S. Involvement in the Rise of Fascism, Torture and Murder and the Persecution of the Catholic Church in Latin America*. New York: Doubleday, 1980.

Lifton, Robert J. *Death in Life: Survivors of Hiroshima*. New York: Random (Vintage) 1968.

Malcolm X. *Autobiography of Malcolm X*. New York: Ballantine, 1976.

Marcuse, Herbert. *One-Dimensional Man*. Boston: Beacon Press, 1964.

Medvedev, Roy A. *On Socialist Democracy*. New York: Knopf, 1975.

Memmi. *The Colonizer and the Colonized*. New York: Orion, 1965.

Moore, Barrington, Jr. *Reflections on the Causes of Human Misery*. Boston: Beacon Press, 1972.

Neruda, Pablo. *The Heights of Macchu Picchu*. New York: Farrar, Straus & Giroux, 1962.

Nkrumah, Kwame. *Conscientism: Philosophy and Ideology for Decolonization and Development*. New York: Monthly Review Press, 1970.

Panichas, George A., ed. *The Simone Weil Reader*. New York: David McKay Co., 1977.

Rashke, Richard. *The Killing of Karen Silkwood*. Boston: Houghton Mifflin, 1981.

Said, Edward. *Orientalism*. New York: Pantheon, 1979.

Sakharov, Andrei D. *Progress, Co-existence and Intellectual Freedom*. New York: Norton, 1968.

Shariati, Ali. *On the Sociology of Islam*. Berkeley, CA.: Mizan Press, 1979.

Solzhenitsyn, Alexander. *Warning to the West*. New York: Farrar, Straus & Giroux, 1976.

Turner, Frederick. *Beyond Geography: The Western Spirit Against the Wilderness*. New York: Harper, 1980.

Yoder, John Howard. *The Politics of Jesus*. Grand Rapids, MI: Erdmans Publishing Co., 1972.

Zinn, Howard. *A People's History of the United States*. New York: Harper, 1980.

1
REFLECTIONS OF A CONCERNED MUSLIM: ON THE PLIGHT OF OPPRESSED PEOPLES

Ali Shariati

If I confide in you personally, it is because I want to share a personal experience with you. It concerns me because it relates to my class, community, country and history.

I am familiar with the thoughts of educated people. My predecessors, of the remote past where they disappeared in the flow of history, were poverty-stricken people. I, personally, am related to the nobles but not to those whose nobility is the product of silver and gold.

I am deeply interested in human heritage and civilisation. My primary interest has always been to reflect on the works of people who inhabited the earth before us.

In Greece, I saw the temple of Delphi which thrilled me because of its artistic beauty and skill. In Rome, I visited the museum of arts and architecture of temples and great palaces. In the Far East, in China and Vietnam, there are mountains which were shaped by human hands and brains into temples for the gods and their representatives on earth (the religious clergymen). These human legacies are precious to me!

Last summer during my visit to Africa, I decided to see the three Pyramids in Egypt. Because of its vast surroundings, this great monument of civilisation occupied my thoughts. I hastened to see one of the seven wonders of the past—the Pyramids.

Wholeheartedly, I began to listen to the guide's explanations about the structures. We learned that slaves had to bring 800 million blocks of stones from Aswan to Cairo in order to construct six large and three small Pyramids. Eight-hundred million blocks of stones were brought to Cairo from a place which was 980 miles away to construct a building wherein the mummified bodies of the Pharaohs were to be preserved. Inside, the graves are made of five blocks of marble. Four of the blocks are used for the walls and one is used for the ceiling. To imagine the diameter and the weight of the marble blocks used for the ceiling of the grave, it is sufficient to visualise that on this block, millions of blocks of stones were piled on top of each other until the top of the Pyramid was

Reprinted with permission from *Race and Class* 21, Summer 1979. Translated and published by Book Distribution Center, P.O. Box 31669, Houston, Texas 77231.

completed. For the last five thousand years, the ceiling has been supporting this load.

I was amazed by this wonderful work. At a distance of three to four hundred years, I saw some scattered blocks of stones. "What are they?" I asked the guide. He said, "Nothing. Only a few blocks of stones." Of the 30,000 slaves who brought the heavy blocks of stones from hundreds of miles away, on a daily basis, hundreds of them were crushed under the heavy loads. The place I inquired about is where they were buried. So unimportant were they in the system of slavery, that hundreds of them were buried collectively in one ditch. Those who survived had to carry the heavy loads. I told the guide that I would like to see the slaves who were crushed into dust. The guide exclaimed, "There is nothing to see!" He pointed to the graves of the slaves who were buried near the Pyramids by order of the Pharaohs; this was done so their souls could be employed as slaves just as their bodies were.

I requested that the guide leave me alone. I then went to those graves and sat down feeling very close to the people buried in those ditches. It was as if we were of the same race. It is true that each of us came from different geographical areas, but these differences are inconsequential when viewed as a basis for dividing mankind. For out of this phenomenon arose the concepts of strangers and relatives. I was not involved in this system of classification and racial division; therefore, I had nothing but warm feelings and sympathy toward these oppressed souls. I looked back to the Pyramids and realised that despite their magnificence, they were so strange to and distant from me! In other words, I felt so much hatred toward the great monuments of civilisation which throughout history were raised upon the bones of my predecessors! My predecessors also built the great walls of China. Those who could not carry the loads were crushed under the heavy stones and put into the walls with the stones. This was how all the great monuments of civilisation were constructed—at the expense of the flesh and blood of my predecessors!

I viewed civilisation as a curse. I felt a burning hatred for the thousands of years of oppression against my predecessors. I realised that the feelings of all those people buried together in the ditches were once the same as mine. I returned from my visit and wrote one of them a letter describing what had transpired in the past 5,000 years. He was not living in those thousands of years, but slavery existed in one form or another! I sat down and wrote him:

My friend, you have left this world, but we are carrying the loads for the great civilisation, clear victories, and heroic works. They came to our homes at the farms and forced us, as beasts, to build their graves. If we could not carry the stones or complete the task, we were also put into the walls with the stones! Others took the pride and credit for the work that we did. No mention had ever been made of our contributions.

They pushed us forward to fight people whom we did not even know, nor did they know us. We were compelled to kill people whom we did not despise. Some were of our own class, race and destiny. For a long time, our old and helpless parents kept looking for a way to contact us, but their searching eyes never got an answer. According to one thinker, these fights were like wars between two parties who did not know each other but were fighting on behalf of those who knew each other well! They forced us to fight, to massacre, and to be massacred. Our fathers and mothers, as well as their ruined farms, suffered the loss. If victory was achieved, it was others who enjoyed its bounties, not us.

My friend, after you died a great change occurred. The Pharaohs and big powers of history altered their views. This made us happy. Previously, they believed that their souls were eternal; therefore, they believed that if the body was preserved, the soul could maintain a relationship with the body. This was why they made us construct those great yet cruel buildings. However, now they have become wiser. They no longer think about death. We have great news! They have given up those old beliefs. We are spared from transporting 800 million blocks of stones from hundreds of miles away to build graves.

My friend, unfortunately this "good news" proved to be short-lived! After you passed away, they again stepped into our countries to capture us as labourers. Once again, we have to carry loads, but not for their graves; they no longer care about them. This time, it is for their palaces—great palaces, beside which our generation is buried!

We lived in despair, but once again a flash of hope for survival appeared. Great prophets came forth. There was Zoroaster, Buddha the Great and Confucius the philosopher. A gate toward salvation was opened. The "gods" sent their messengers to save us from disgrace of slavery, worship replaced cruelty. Unfortunately, we had bad luck. The prophets, who left their prophetic homes behind and disregarded us, proceeded to the palaces.

We had strong faith in Confucius, the philosopher, because he addressed himself to the question of man and the community. However, he also became a friend of the princes. Buddha, who was a prince, also deserted us. He turned within himself to reach the state of "Nirvana," but we do not know where this state is. Buddha developed many great and ascetic rules. As for Zoroaster, he began his mission from Azerbaijan, Iran. Disregarding our mourning and scars from the lashes inflicted on our bodies by the masters, he continued to Balkh and then to the court of Kashtasib, who was king at that time.

My friend, you were sacrificed for the graves while we were sacrificed for the palaces! Suddenly, besides the Pharaohs and others who employed us as their slaves, there appeared those who claimed to be successors of the prophets and professional spiritual teachers.

From Palestine to Iran, from Egypt to China and throughout all parts of the earth where there was civilisation, we had to carry the loads of stones to construct temples, palaces, and graves. Again in the name of charity, the representatives of the "gods" and the successors of the prophets began to loot us. Again, in the name of holy war, we were pushed into the battlefields. We had to sacrifice our innocent children for the "gods," temples, and idols!

My friend, for thousands of years, our destiny became worse than yours. Three-fifths of the wealth in Iran went to the *Mobedans* [old Persian clergymen] in the name of the gods. We became their servants and slaves. Four-fifths of the wealth in France was taken from us by the clergymen of God. The Pharaoh clergymen and spiritual teachers of religions have always been successful.

My friend, I am living thousands of years after you. Witnessing all the suffering of my friends, I began to feel that the "gods" hated the slaves. Religion seemed to reinforce the slavery system. Even people more intelligent than us, like Aristotle, theorised that, by nature, some people were born to be slaves and others to be rulers. I began to believe that I was born and destined to slavery.

Amidst all of this hopelessness, I learned that a man had descended from the mountains saying, "I have been commissioned by God." I trembled thinking that it possibly involved a new deception or new method of cruelty. He stated, "I have been commissioned by God who has promised to have mercy on slaves and those who are weak on earth." Surprise! I still could not believe it. How could it be true? God was speaking with slaves, giving them good news of being saved, and prosperous, and being heirs of the earth.

I had doubts, thinking that he was also one of those prophets of China, India, etc. His name was Mohammed. I was told that he was an orphan who was a shepherd behind those mountains. I was so surprised. Why did God choose His prophet from among shepherds? I was also informed that his predecessors were prophets; all were chosen from among shepherds. He was the last in that series. With joy and astonishment, I became speechless and trembled. Has God chosen His prophet from among our class?

I began to follow him because I saw my friends around him. Some of those who became leaders of his followers were Bilal, a slave and son of a slave whose parents were from Abyssinia; Salman, a homeless person from Persia owned as a slave; Abu-Zar, the poverty stricken and anonymous fellow from the desert; and lastly, Salim, the slave of the wife of Khudhaifa and an unimportant black alien.

I believed in the prophet Mohammed since his palace was no more than a few rooms constructed of clay. He was among the workers who carried the loads and built the rooms. His court was made of wood and palm-tree leaves. This was everything he had. This was his palace.

I fled from Persia and the ruling system of the *Mobedans* who pushed us as slaves into war to protect their power and rule from their enemies. I escaped and came to the Prophet's country to live with the slaves, the homeless, the helpless, and with him. But when he died, "his eyelids under the heaviness of death, curtained our shining sun." Once more, the situation began to deteriorate.

My friend, again in his name, magnificent temples rose toward the sky. Swords engraved with the Quranic verses on holy war were pointed toward us. His representatives stepped into our homes and took our youth as slaves for the chieftains of their tribes, sold our mothers in distant markets, killed our men in the name of struggle in the way of God, and looted our belongings in the name of charity.

In despair, I could do nothing! A power came into being which, with an appearance of monotheism, really hid idols in the worship palaces of God! Tricky fires (a fire was holy in pre-Islamic Persia) were glowing. In the name of God's vice regency and successorship of the prophets, the faces of the Pharaohs and

those of the false saints joined hands. They began to strike at us in the name of
law. Again, it was the yoke of slavery around our necks which promoted the
construction of the Great Mosque of Damascus. The great contests to build
splendid mosques, magnificent palaces, beautiful houses for the Caliphs in
Damascus and the enactment of a thousand and one nights in Baghdad were
all done at the expense of our blood and lives; but, this time it was pursued in
the name of God! We thought there was no way to safety. Slavery and sacrifice
were our unchangeable destinies!

Who was that man called Mohammed? Was his mission deceitful? Or are he
(the prophet) and we being sacrificed in the system—a system in which we are
decaying in prisons, witnessing the looting and destruction of our possessions
and families, and being massacred?

I do not know where to go! Where should I go? Should I go to the *Mobedans*?
How could I return to those temples which were built to enslave me? Should I
join those who claim to be examples of our national freedom but in essence are
attempting to gain their inhuman privileges of the past? The mosques are no
better than those temples!

I saw the swords which were engraved with verses on holy war. I saw the
places for worship. I saw those who prayed. I saw the saintly faces who spoke in
the name of spiritual leadership, the Caliphs, and the preservation of the Prophet's traditions. Nevertheless, collectively, they took us into SLAVERY! They,
long before my time, put someone to the sword in a mosque. He was Ali, the
son-in-law of that man of God (the prophet Mohammed). He was killed in a
place where God was worshipped. He before me, and his family long before
mine, were, like the suffering slaves of history, all destroyed. In the name of
"charity," his house was looted before ours. The Quran long before it was used
as an instrument to rob and exploit us, was raised on the swords to defeat Ali!

How strange! Five thousand years later, I found a man who spoke of God,
not for the masters but for the slaves. He prayed, but not to reach "Nirvana" or
to deceive people or to unite with God (like the Persians). He prayed for the
welfare and prosperity of mankind. I found a man for the whole world. He was
a man of justice, one who was strong and disciplined enough to make his older
brother the first subject. He was a man whose wife, the daughter of the prophet
Mohammed, worked and suffered deprivation and starvation during her
lifetime as we did. I found a man whose children were the heirs of the red flag
which throughout history belonged to our class.

My friend, I have sought refuge in this house which is built of clay due to my
fears of the temples, pompous palaces that you know and were sacrificed for by
formidable powers. The companions of the prophet are busy. The house is
alone. His wife is dying while he is in the garden of Bani Najjar, working and
telling God all about our misery. Fearing the terrifying temples, palaces and
treasuries that have accumulated through our labour and blood, I have taken
refuge in this house to mourn the sacrifices which were made!

My friend, all those who remained loyal to Ali belonged to our suffering
class. He did not adopt his beautiful sermons (recorded in Nahjul-Balagha) in
order to make excuses for our deprivation or the excesses of those who seek

power. They were adopted to educate and save us. He did not draw his sword to defend himself, his family, his race, nor to defend big powers. It was done to rescue us at all stages. He thinks better than Socrates, not for the sake of demonstrating moral virtues of the noble classes in which slaves have no share, but for the sake of values which we possess. He was not an heir of the Pharaohs or those of similar class. He symbolised thoughts and considerations, not in closed libraries, schools, and academic centres like those who acquire knowledge as an end in itself, living in the world of theories while remaining indifferent to the starving and suffering classes. His thoughts fly high and far. Simultaneously his abstract thoughts and heart are transferred into sympathy at the sadness of an orphan's face. Concurrently, because he realises God's greatness, while praying he does not pay attention to any suffering inflicted on his body by a dagger. However, because of oppression of a Jewish woman, he cries loud saying, "if a person dies because of this disgrace he should not be blamed!" He has excellent abilities to express himself, but never in the manner of one like Ferdowsi (a poet who praised kings) who makes no mention of our class except once in all of his 60,000 couplets.

My friend, at this time and in this community, we desperately need him. He is unlike the thinkers, philosophers and others who are either men of thoughts without action and struggle, or men of action without thoughts, wisdom, and piety. If we imagine someone beside him having all these qualities, perhaps he might not possess the tenderness of feeling, love and pure spirit. Perchance he might lack strong faith in God. He is a man whose essence is extended through all humanitarian dimensions. Like you and I, he works as a labourer. The same hands that recorded the glorious lines of divine guidance merge deep into the soil, tilling and fertilising salty lands. He works for no one! While he makes water gush forth from the ground, his family looks at his work with joy. Before he and his wife rest, he declares, "good news for my heirs, who will not have even one drop from this water as their share." My friend, he has made it a charity for you and me.

We need him. We need leadership like him. The civilisations, educational systems, and religions have made human beings into animals interested only in financial security or selfish and heartless worshippers or men of thought and reason who lack feeling, love and inspiration as well as knowledge, wisdom, and logic. But he is a man who combines all these dimensions in his person. He is a leader of the working class and those who suffer. He is the expressing power who struggles for the well-being of the community. Sincerity, loyalty, patience, steadfastness, and the concepts of revolution and justice were the main features of his daily messages to the masses.

My friend, I live in a society where I face a system which controls half of the universe, maybe all of it. Mankind is being driven into a new stronghold of slavery. Although we are not in physical slavery, we are truly destined with a fate worse than yours! Our thoughts, hearts, and will powers are enslaved. In the name of sociology, education, art, sexual freedom, financial freedom, love of exploitation, and love of individuals, faith in goals, faith in humanitarian responsibilities and belief in one's own school of thought are entirely taken away from within our hearts! The system has converted us into empty pots which accommodate whatever is poured inside them!

Now, we in the name of party, blood, land, and system against system, undergo divisions so that each of us can be easily taken into service. His followers, that is the followers of his school of thought, are pushed to fight against one another. Why, under a global influence, should they consider each other as enemies? One leaves his hands open in prayer while the other folds them together. One prostrates on a piece of clay, the other on a carpet. Fortunately, less differentiation is made now! Our thinkers are driven into exile; they have become guardians.

My friend, knowing that you were a slave, you could identify your master. You could endure the whip-lash on your body. Why, how, and who made you slaves? We are facing the same destiny as you, but unable to know why it exists. Who is making us slaves of this century? From where are we being invaded? Why are we submissive to misleading thoughts? Why are we engaged in worldly worships? Like animals, we have become victims of exploitation—even more so than your era and race!

We work for the systems, powers, machines and palaces which are maintained through our efforts. Riches are accumulated through our hard labour but our share is such a small portion; therefore, we are obliged to work the following day. We are more deprived than you! Cruelty and discrimination are more severe than that of your time!

My friend, Ali sacrificed his life for these considerations: School of Thought, Unity and Justice. It was evident in his twenty-three years of struggles and sacrifices to establish faith in the hearts of barbaric parties. It was evident in his twenty-five years of silence and endurance in order to preserve Islamic unity and save it from the dangers of the Roman and Persian empires. It was evident in his five years of work and suffering to achieve justice, using his sword to destroy hatred and liberate man. Though he was not able to achieve this, he managed to impart to us the meaning of the leadership of mankind and religion. He placed his life and the life of his family on these three slogans: School of Thought, Unity and Justice!

2
BLACK CONSCIOUSNESS AND THE QUEST FOR A TRUE HUMANITY

Steve Biko

It is perhaps fitting to start by examining why it is necessary for us to think collectively about a problem we never created. In doing so, I do not wish to concern myself unnecessarily with the white people of South Africa, but to get to the right answers we must ask the right questions; we have to find out what went wrong—where and when; and we have to find out whether our position is a deliberate creation of God or an artificial fabrication of the truth by power-hungry people whose motive is authority, security, wealth and comfort. In other words, the "Black Consciousness" approach would be irrelevant in a colourless and non-exploitative egalitarian society. It is relevant here because we believe that an anomalous situation is a deliberate creation of man.

There is no doubt that the colour question in South African politics was originally introduced for economic reasons. The leaders of the white community had to create some kind of barrier between blacks and whites so that the whites could enjoy privileges at the expense of blacks and still feel free to give a moral justification for the obvious exploitation that pricked even the hardest of white consciences. However, tradition has it that whenever a group of people has tasted the lovely fruits of wealth, security and prestige, it begins to find it more comfortable to believe in the obvious lie and to accept it as normal that it alone is entitled to privilege. In order to believe this seriously, it needs to convince itself of all the arguments that support the lie. It is not surprising, therefore, that in South Africa, after generations of exploitation, white people on the whole have come to believe in the inferiority of the black man, so much so that while the race problem started as an offshoot of the economic greed exhibited by white people, it has now become a serious problem on its own. White people now despise black people, not because they need to reinforce their attitude and so justify their position of privilege but simply because they actually believe that black is inferior and bad. This is the basis upon which whites are working in South Africa, and it is what makes South African society racist.

The racism we meet does not only exist on an individual basis; it is also institutionalised to make it look like the South African way of life. Although of late there has been a feeble attempt to gloss over the overt racist elements in the system, it is still true that the system derives its nourishment from the existence of anti-black attitudes in society. To make the lie live even longer, blacks have to be denied any chance of accidentally proving their equality with white men. For this reason there is job reservation, lack of training in skilled work, and a tight orbit around professional possibilities for blacks. Stupidly enough, the system turns back to say that blacks are inferior because they have no economists, no engineers, etc., although it is made impossible for blacks to acquire these skills.

To give authenticity to their lie and to show the righteousness of their claim, whites have further worked out detailed schemes to "solve" the racial situation in this country. Thus, a pseudoparliament has been created for "Coloureds," and several "Bantu states" are in the process of being set up. So independent and fortunate are they that they do not have to spend a cent on their defence because they have nothing to fear from white South Africa, which will always come to their assistance in times of need. One does not, of course, fail to see the arrogance of whites and their contempt for blacks, even in their well-considered modern schemes for subjugation.

The overall success of the white power structure has been in managing to bind the whites together in defence of the status quo. By skillfully playing on that imaginary bogey—*swart gevaar*—they have managed to convince even diehard liberals that there is something to fear in the idea of the black man assuming his rightful place at the helm of the South African ship. Thus after years of silence we are able to hear the familiar voice of Alan Paton saying, as far away as London, "Perhaps apartheid is worth a try." "At whose expense, Dr. Paton?," asks an intelligent black journalist. Hence whites in general reinforce each other even though they allow some moderate disagreements on the details of subjugation schemes. There is no doubt that they do not question the validity of white values. They see nothing anomalous in the fact that they alone are arguing about the future of 17 million blacks—in a land which is the natural backyard of the black people. Any proposals for change emanating from the black world are viewed with great indignation. Even the so-called opposition, the United Party, has the nerve to tell the Coloured people that they are asking for too much. A journalist from a liberal newspaper like *The Sunday Times* of Johannesburg describes a black student—who is only telling the truth—as a militant, impatient young man.

It is not enough for whites to be on the offensive. So immersed are they in prejudice that they do not believe that blacks can formulate their thoughts without white guidance and trusteeship. Thus, even those whites who see much wrong with the system make it their business to control the response of the blacks to the provocation. No one is suggesting that it is not the business of liberal whites to oppose what is wrong. However, it appears to us as too much of a coincidence that liberals—few as they are—should not only be determining the *modus operandi* of those blacks who oppose the system, but also leading it, in spite of their involvement in the system. To us it seems that their role spells out the totality of the white power structure—the fact that though whites are our problem, it is still other whites who want to tell us how to deal with that problem. They do so by dragging all sorts of red herrings across our paths. They tell us that the situation is a class struggle rather than a racial one. Let them go to van Tonder in the Free State and tell him this. We believe we know what the problem is, and we will stick by our findings.

I want to go a little deeper in this discussion because it is time we killed this false political coalition between blacks and whites as long as it is set up on a wrong analysis of our situation. I want to kill it for another reason—namely that it forms at present the greatest stumbling block to our unity. It dangles before freedom-hungry blacks promises of a great future for which no one in these groups seems to be working particularly hard.

The basic problem in South Africa has been analysed by liberal whites as being apartheid. They argue that in order to oppose it we have to form nonracial groups. Between these two extremes, they claim, lies the land of milk and honey for which we are working. The *thesis*, the *antithesis* and the *synthesis* have been mentioned by some great philosophers as the cardinal points around which any social revolution revolves. For the liberals, the *thesis* is apartheid, the *antithesis* is nonracialism, but the *synthesis* is very feebly defined. They want to tell the blacks that they see integration as the ideal solution. Black Consciousness defines the situation differently. The *thesis* is in fact a strong white racism and therefore the *antithesis* to this must, *ipso facto*, be a strong solidarity amongst the blacks on whom this white racism seeks to prey. Out of these two situations we can therefore hope to reach some kind of balance—a true humanity where power politics will have no place. This analysis spells out the difference between the old and new approaches. The failure of the liberals is in the fact that their *antithesis* is already a watered-down version of the truth whose close proximity to the thesis will nullify the purported balance. This accounts for the failure of the Sprocas[1] commissions to make any real headway, for they are already looking for an "alternative" acceptable to the white man. Everybody in the commissions knows what is right but all are looking for the most seemly way of dodging the responsibility of saying what is right.

It is much more important for blacks to see this difference than it is for whites. We must learn to accept that no group, however benevolent, can ever hand power to the vanquished on a plate. We must accept that the limits of tyrants are prescribed by the endurance of those whom they oppress. As long as we go to Whitey begging cap in hand for our own emancipation, we are giving him further sanction to continue with his racist and oppressive system. We must realise that our situation is not a mistake on the part of whites but a deliberate act, and that no amount of moral lecturing will persuade the white man to "correct" the situation. The system concedes nothing without demand, for it formulates its very method of operation on the basis that the ignorant will learn to know, the child will grow into an adult, and therefore demands will begin to be made. It gears itself to resist demands in whatever way it sees fit. When you refuse to make these demands and choose to come to a round table to beg for your deliverance, you are asking for the contempt of those who have power over you. This is why we must reject the beggar tactics that are being forced on us by those who wish to appease our cruel masters. This is where the SASO message and cry *"Black man, you are on your own!"* becomes relevant.

The concept of integration, whose virtues are often extolled in white liberal circles, is full of unquestioned assumptions that embrace white values. It is a concept long defined by whites and never examined by blacks. It is based on the assumption that all is well with the system apart from some degree of mismanagement by irrational conservatives at the top. Even the people who argue for integration often forget to veil it in its supposedly beautiful covering. They tell each other that, were it not for job reservation, there would be a beautiful market to exploit. They forget they are talking about people. They see blacks as additional levers to some complicated industrial machines. This is white man's integration—an integration based on exploitative values. It is an integration in which black will compete with black, using each other as rungs up a step ladder leading them to white values. It is an integration in which the black man will have to prove himself in terms of these values before meriting acceptance and ultimate assimilation, and in which the poor will grow poorer and the rich richer in a country where the poor have always been black. We do not want to be reminded that it is we, the indigenous people, who are poor and exploited in the land of our birth. These are concepts which the Black Consciousness approach wishes to eradicate from the black man's mind before our society is driven to chaos by irresponsible people from Coca-Cola and hamburger cultural backgrounds.

Black Consciousness is an attitude of mind and a way of life, the most positive call to emanate from the black world for a long time.

Its essence is the realisation by the black man of the need to rally together with his brothers around the cause of their oppression—the blackness of their skin—and to operate as a group to rid themselves of the shackles that bind them to perpetual servitude. It is based on a self-examination which has ultimately led them to believe that by seeking to run away from themselves and emulate the white man, they are insulting the intelligence of whoever created them black. The philosophy of Black Consciousness therefore expresses group pride and the determination of the black to rise and attain the envisaged self. Freedom is the ability to define oneself with one's possibilities held back not by the power of other people over one but only by one's relationship to God and to natural surroundings. On his own, therefore, the black man wishes to explore his surroundings and test his possibilities—in other words, to make his freedom real by whatever means he deems fit. At the heart of this kind of thinking is the realisation by blacks that the most potent weapon in the hands of the oppressor is the mind of the oppressed. If one is free at heart, no manmade chains can bind one to servitude, but if one's mind is so manipulated and controlled by the oppressor as to make the oppressed believe that he is a liability to the white man, then there will be nothing the oppressed can do to scare his powerful masters. Hence, thinking along lines of Black Consciousness makes the black man see himself as a being complete in himself. It makes him less dependent and more free to express his manhood. At the end of it all he cannot tolerate attempts by anybody to dwarf the significance of his manhood.

In order that Black Consciousness can be used to advantage as a philosophy to apply to people in a position like ours, a number of points have to be observed. As people existing in a continuous struggle for truth, we have to examine and question old concepts, values and systems. Having found the right answers we shall then work for consciousness among all people to make it possible for us to proceed towards putting these answers into effect. In this process, we have to evolve our own schemes, forms and strategies to suit the need and situation, always keeping in mind our fundamental beliefs and values.

In all aspects of the black-white relationship, now and in the past, we see a constant tendency by whites to depict blacks as of an inferior status. Our culture, our history and indeed all aspects of the black man's life have been battered nearly out of shape in the great collision between the indigenous values and the Anglo-Boer culture.

The first people to come and relate to blacks in a human way in South Africa were the missionaries. They were in the vanguard of the colonisation movement to "civilise and educate" the savages and introduce the Christian message to them. The religion they brought was quite foreign to the black indigenous people. African religion in its essence was not radically different from Christianity. We also believed in one God, we had our own community of saints through whom we related to our God, and we did not find it compatible with our way of life to worship God in isolation from the various aspects of our lives. Hence worship was not a specialised function that found expression once a week in a secluded building, but rather it featured in our wars, our beer-drinking, our dances and our customs in general. Whenever Africans drank they would first relate to God by giving a portion of their beer away as a token of thanks. When anything went wrong at home they would offer sacrifice to God to appease him and atone for their sins. There was no hell in our religion. We believed in the inherent goodness of man—hence we took it for granted that all people at death joined the community of saints and therefore merited our respect.

It was the missionaries who confused the people with their new religion. They scared our people with stories of hell. They painted their God as a demanding God who wanted worship "or else." People had to discard their clothes and their customs in order to be accepted in this new religion. Knowing how religious the African people were, the missionaries stepped up their terror campaign on the emotions of the people with their detailed accounts of eternal burning, tearing of hair and gnashing of teeth. By some strange and twisted logic, they argued that theirs was a scientific religion and ours a superstition—all this in spite of the biological discrepancy which is at the base of their religion. This cold and cruel religion was strange to the indigenous people and caused frequent strife between the converted and the "pagans," for the former, having imbibed the false values from white society, were taught to ridicule and despise those who defended the truth of their indigenous religion. With the ultimate acceptance of the western religion down went our cultural values!

While I do not wish to question the basic truth at the heart of the Christian message, there is a strong case for a reexamination of Christianity. It has proved a very adaptable religion which does not seek to supplement existing orders but—like any universal truth—to find application within a particular situation. More than anyone else, the missionaries knew that not all they did was essential to the spread of the message. But the basic intention went much further than merely spreading the word. Their arrogance and their monopoly on truth, beauty and moral judgment taught them to despise native customs and traditions and to seek to infuse their own new values into these societies.

Here then we have the case for Black Theology. While not wishing to discuss Black Theology at length, let it suffice to say that it seeks to relate God and Christ once more to the black man and his daily problems. It wants to describe Christ as a fighting God, not a passive God who allows a lie to rest unchallenged. It grapples with existential problems and does not claim to be a theology of absolutes. It seeks to bring back God to the black man and to the truth and reality of his situation. This is an important aspect of Black Consciousness, for quite a large proportion of black people in South Africa are Christians still swimming in a mire of confusion—the aftermath of the missionary approach. It is the duty therefore of all black priests and ministers of religion to save Christianity by adopting Black Theology's approach and thereby once more uniting the black man with his God.

A long look should also be taken at the educational system for blacks. The same tense situation was found as long ago as the arrival of the missionaries. Children were taught, under the pretext of hygiene, good manners and other such vague concepts, to despise their mode of upbringing at home and to question the values and customs of their society. The result was the expected one—children and parents saw life differently and the former lost respect for the latter. Now in African society it is a cardinal sin for a child to lose respect for his parent. Yet how can one prevent the loss of respect between child and parent when the child is taught by his know-all white tutors to disregard his family teachings? Who can resist losing respect for his tradition when in school his whole cultural background is summed up in one word—barbarism?

Thus we can immediately see the logic of placing the missionaries in the forefront of the colonisation process. A man who succeeds in making a group of people accept a foreign concept in which he is expert makes them perpetual students whose progress in the particular field can only be evaluated by him; the student must constantly turn to him for guidance and promotion. In being forced to accept the Anglo-Boer culture, the blacks have allowed themselves to be at the mercy of the white man and to have him as their eternal supervisor. Only he can tell us how good our performance is and instinctively each of us is at pains to please this powerful, all-knowing master. This is what Black Consciousness seeks to eradicate.

As one black writer says, colonialism is never satisfied with having the native in its grip but, by some strange logic, it must turn to his past and disfigure and distort it. Hence the history of the black man in this country is most disappointing to read. It is presented merely as a long succession of defeats. The

Xhosas were thieves who went to war for stolen property; the Boers never provoked the Xhosas but merely went on "punitive expeditions" to teach the thieves a lesson. Heroes like Makana[2], who were essentially revolutionaries, are painted as superstitious trouble-makers who lied to the people about bullets turning into water. Great nation-builders like Shaka are cruel tyrants who frequently attacked smaller tribes for no reason but some sadistic purpose. Not only is there no objectivity in the history taught us but there is frequently an appalling misrepresentation of facts that sicken even the uninformed student.

Thus, a lot of attention has to be paid to our history if we as blacks want to aid each other in our coming into consciousness. We have to rewrite our history and produce in it the heroes that formed the core of our resistance to the white invaders. More has to be revealed, and stress has to be laid on the successful nation-building attempts of men such as Shaka, Moshoeshoe and Hintsa. These areas call for intense research to provide some sorely-needed missing links. We would be too naive to expect our conquerors to write unbiased histories about us, but we have to destroy the myth that our history starts in 1652, the year Van Riebeeck landed at the Cape.

Our culture must be defined in concrete terms. We must relate the past to the present and demonstrate a historical evolution of the modern black man. There is a tendency to think of our culture as a static culture that was arrested in 1652 and has never developed since. The "return to the bush" concept suggests that we have nothing to boast of except lions, sex and drink. We accept that when colonisation sets in it devours the indigenous culture and leaves behind a bastard culture that may thrive at the pace allowed it by the dominant culture. But we also have to realise that the basic tenets of our culture have largely succeeded in withstanding the process of bastardisation and that even at this moment we can still demonstrate that we appreciate a man for himself. Ours is a true man-centered society whose sacred tradition is that of sharing. We must reject, as we have been doing, the individualistic cold approach to life that is the cornerstone of the Anglo-Boer culture. We must seek to restore to the black man the great importance we used to give to human relations, the high regard for people and their property and for life in general; to reduce the triumph of technology over man and the materialistic element that is slowly creeping into our society.

These are essential features of our black culture to which we must cling. Black culture above all implies freedom on our part to innovate without recourse to white values. This innovation is part of the natural development of any culture. A culture is essentially the society's composite answer to the varied problems of life. We are experiencing new problems every day and whatever we do adds to the richness of our cultural heritage as long as it has man as its centre. The adoption of black theatre and drama is one such important innovation which we need to encourage and develop. We know that our love of music and rhythm has relevance even in this day.

Being part of an exploitative society in which we are often the direct objects of exploitation, we need to evolve a strategy toward our economic situation. We are aware that the blacks are still colonised even within the borders of

South Africa. Their cheap labour has helped to make South Africa what it is today. Our money from the townships takes a one-way journey to white shops and white banks, and all we do in our lives is pay the white man either with labour or in coin. Capitalistic exploitative tendencies, coupled with the overt arrogance of white racism, have conspired against us. Thus, in South Africa now it is very expensive to be poor. It is the poor people who stay furthest from town and therefore have to spend more money on transport to come and work for white people; it is the poor people who use uneconomic and inconvenient fuel like paraffin and coal because of the refusal of the white man to install electricity in black areas; it is the poor people who are governed by many ill-defined restrictive laws and therefore have to spend money on fines for "technical" offences; it is the poor people who have no hospitals and are therefore exposed to exorbitant charges by private doctors; it is the poor people who use untarred roads, have to walk long distances, and therefore experience the greatest wear and tear on commodities like shoes; it is the poor people who have to pay for their children's books while whites get them free. It does not need to be said that it is the black people who are poor.

We therefore need to take another look at how best to use our economic power, little as it may seem to be. We must seriously examine the possibilities of establishing business cooperatives whose interests will be ploughed back into community development programmes. We should think along such lines as the "buy black" campaign once suggested in Johannesburg and establish our own banks for the benefit of the community. Organisational development amongst blacks has only been low because we have allowed it to be. Now that we know we are on our own, it is an absolute duty for us to fulfil these needs.

The last step in Black Consciousness is to broaden the base of our operation. One of the basic tenets of Black Consciousness is totality of involvement. This means that all blacks must sit as one big unit, and no fragmentation and distraction from the mainstream of events [should] be allowed. Hence we must resist the attempts by protagonists of the Bantustan theory to fragment our approach. We are oppressed not as individuals, not as Zulus, Xhosas, Vendas, or Indians. We are oppressed because we are black. We must use that very concept to unite ourselves and to respond as a cohesive group. We must cling to each other with a tenacity that will shock the perpetrators of evil.

Our preparedness to take upon ourselves the cudgels of the struggle will see us through. We must remove from our vocabulary completely the concept of fear. Truth must ultimately triumph over evil, and the white man has always nourished his greed on this basic fear that shows itself in the black community. Special Branch agents will not turn the lie into truth, and one must ignore them. In a true bid for change we have to take off our coats, be prepared to lose our comfort and security, our jobs and positions of prestige, and our families, for just as it is true that "leadership and security are basically incompatible," a struggle without casualties is no struggle. We must realise that prophetic cry of black students: "Black man, you are on your own!"

Some will charge that we are racist, but these people are using exactly the values we reject. We do not have the power to subjugate anyone. We are merely responding to provocation in the most realistic possible way. Racism does not only imply exclusion of one race by another, it always presupposes that the exclusion is for the purposes of subjugation. Blacks have had enough experience as objects of racism not to wish to turn the tables. While it may be relevant now to talk about black in relation to white, we must not make this our preoccupation, for it can be a negative exercise. As we proceed further toward the achievement of our goals let us talk more about ourselves and our struggle and less about whites.

We have set out on a quest for true humanity, and somewhere on the distant horizon we can see the glittering prize. Let us march forth with courage and determination, drawing strength from our common plight and our brotherhood. In time we shall be in a position to bestow upon South Africa the greatest gift possible—a more human face.

NOTES

1. Study Project on Christianity in an Apartheid Society. Set up by S.A. Council of Churches and Christian Institute in 1968. Editor's note.

2. Early nineteenth-century Xhosa prophet, sentenced to life imprisonment on Robben Island and drowned while escaping in a boat. Refusal by blacks to accept the truth of his death led to the mythical hope of his eventual return. Editor's note.

3
CHARTER 77: CZECH GROUP'S PLEA FOR HUMAN RIGHTS

Law No. 120 of the Czechoslovak Collection of Laws, published October 13, 1976, includes the text of the International Covenant on Civil and Political Rights, and the International Covenant on Economic, Social and Cultural Rights, both signed on behalf of our Republic in 1968 and confirmed at the 1975 Helsinki Conference. These pacts went into effect in our country on March 23, 1976; since that date our citizens have had the right, and the State has had the duty, to abide by them.

The freedoms guaranteed to individuals by the two documents are important assets of civilization. They have been the goals of campaigns by many progressive people in the past, and their enactment can significantly contribute to a humane development of our society. We welcome the fact that the Czechoslovak Socialist Republic has agreed to enter into these covenants.

Their publication, however, is at the same time an urgent reminder of the many fundamental human rights that, regrettably, exist in our country only on paper. The right of free expression guaranteed by Article 19 of the first pact, for example, is quite illusory. Tens of thousands of citizens have been prevented from working in their professions for the sole reason that their views differ from the official ones. They have been the frequent targets of various forms of discrimination and chicanery on the part of the authorities or social organizations; they have been denied any opportunity to defend themselves and are practically the victims of apartheid. Hundreds of thousands of other citizens have been denied the "freedom from fear" cited in the Preamble to the first pact; they live in constant peril of losing their jobs or other benefits if they express their opinions.

Contrary to Article 13 of the second pact, guaranteeing the right to education, many young people are prevented from pursuing higher education because of their views or even because of their parents' views. Countless citizens worry that if they declare their convictions, they themselves or their children will be deprived of an education.

Exercising the right to "seek, receive and impart information regardless of frontiers and of whether it is oral, written or printed," or "imparted through art"—Point 2, Article 13 of the first pact—can result in persecution not only outside the court but also inside. Frequently this occurs under the pretext of a criminal indictment (as evidenced, among other instances, by the recent trial of young musicians).

Freedom of speech is suppressed by the government's management of all mass media, including the publishing and cultural institutions. No political, philosophical, scientific, or artistic work that deviates in the slightest from the narrow framework of official ideology or esthetics is permitted to be produced. Public criticism of social conditions is prohibited. Public defense against false and defamatory charges by official propaganda organs is impossible, despite the legal protection against attacks on one's reputation and honor unequivocally afforded by Article 17 of the first pact. False accusations cannot be refuted, and it is futile to attempt rectification or to seek legal redress. Open discussion of intellectual and cultural matters is out of the question. Many scientific and cultural workers, as well as other citizens, have been discriminated against simply because some years ago they legally published or openly articulated views condemned by the current political power.

Religious freedom, emphatically guaranteed by Article 18 of the first pact, is systematically curbed with a despotic arbitrariness: Limits are imposed on activities of priests, who are constantly threatened with the revocation of government permission to perform their function; persons who manifest their religious faith either by word or action lose their jobs or are made to suffer other repressions; religious instruction in schools is suppressed, et cetera.

A whole range of civil rights is severely restricted or completely suppressed by the effective method of subordinating all institutions and organizations in the State to the political directives of the ruling Party's apparatuses and the pronouncements of highly influential individuals. Neither the Constitution of the CSSR nor any of the country's other legal procedures regulate the contents, form or application of such pronouncements, which are frequently issued orally, unbeknown to and beyond the control of the average citizen. Their authors are responsible only to themselves and their own hierarchy, yet they have a decisive influence on the activity of the legislative as well as executive bodies of the State administration, on the courts, trade unions, social organizations, other political parties, business, factories, schools and similar installations, and their orders take precedence over the laws.

If some organizations or citizens, in the interpretation of their rights and duties, become involved in a conflict with the directives, they cannot turn to a neutral authority, for none exists. Consequently, the right of assembly and the prohibition of its restraint, stemming from Articles 21 and 22 of the first pact; the right to participate in public affairs, in Article 25; and the right to equality before the law, in Article 26, all have been seriously curtailed. These conditions prevent working people from freely establishing labor and other organizations for the protection of their economic and social interests, and from freely using their right to strike as provided in Point 1, Article 8 of the second pact.

Other civil rights, including the virtual banning of "wilful interference with private life, the family, home and correspondence" in Article 17 of the first pact, are gravely circumscribed by the fact that the Interior Ministry employs various practices to control the daily existence of citizens—such as telephone tapping and the surveillance of private homes, watching mail, shadowing individuals, searching apartments, and recruiting a network of informers from the ranks of the population (often by illegal intimidation or, sometimes, promises), etc. The Ministry frequently interferes in the decisions of employers, inspires discrimination by authorities and organizations, influences the organs of justice, and even supervises the propaganda campaigns of the mass media. This activity is not regulated by laws, it is covert, so the citizen is unable to protect himself against it.

In the cases of political motivated persecution, the organs of interrogation and justice violate the rights of the defendants and their counsel, contrary to Article 14 of the first pact as well as Czechoslovakia's own laws. People thus sentenced to jail are being treated in a manner that violates their human dignity, impairs their health, and attempts to break them morally.

Point 2, Article 12 of the first pact, guaranteeing the right to freely leave one's country, is generally violated. Under the pretext of "protecting the State security," contained in Point 3, departure is tied to various illegal conditions. Just as arbitrary are the procedures for issuing visas to foreign nationals, many of whom are prevented from visiting Czechoslovakia because they had some official or friendly contact with persons who had been discriminated against in our country.

Some citizens—privately at their places of work, or through the media abroad (the only public forum available to them)—have drawn attention to these systematic violations of human rights and democratic freedoms and have demanded a remedy in specific cases. But they have received no response, or have themselves become the objects of investigation.

The responsibility for the preservation of civil rights naturally rests with the State power. But not on it alone. Every individual bears a share of responsibility for the general conditions in the country, and therefore also for compliance with the enacted pacts, which are as binding for the people as for the government.

The feeling of this coresponsibility, the belief in the value of civic engagement and the readiness to be engaged, together with the need to seek a new and more effective expression, gave us the idea of creating Charter 77, whose existence we publicly announce.

Charter 77 is a free and informal and open association of people of various convictions, religions and professions, linked by the desire to work individually and collectively for respect for human and civil rights in Czechoslovakia and the world—the rights provided for in the enacted international pacts, in the Final Act of the Helsinki Conference, and in numerous other international documents against wars, violence and social and mental oppression. It represents a general declaration of human rights.

Charter 77 is founded on the concepts of solidarity and friendship of people who share a concern for the fate of ideals to which they have linked their lives and work.

Charter 77 is not an organization; it has no statutes, permanent organs or registered membership. Everyone who agrees with its idea and participates in its work and supports it, belongs to it.

Charter 77 is not intended to be a basis for opposition political activity. Its desire is to serve the common interest, as have numerous similar organizations of civic initiative East and West. It has no intention of initiating its own programs for political or social reforms or changes, but it wants to lead in the sphere of its activity by means of a constructive dialogue with the political and State authorities—and particularly by drawing attention to various specific violations of civil and human rights, by preparing their documentation, by suggesting solutions, by submitting various more general proposals aimed at furthering these rights and their guarantees, by acting as a mediator in the event of conflict situations which might result in wrongdoings, etc.

By its symbolic name, Charter 77 stresses that it has been established on the threshold of what has been declared the year of political prisoners, in the course of which a meeting in Belgrade is to review the progress—or lack of it—achieved since the Helsinki Conference.

As signatories of this declaration we designate Dr. Jan Patocka, Dr. Vaclav Havel and Professor Jiri Hajek to act as spokesmen for Charter 77. These spokesmen are authorized to represent Charter 77 before the State and other organizations, as well as before the public at home and throughout the world, and they guarantee the authenticity of its documents by their signatures. In us and other citizens who will join Charter 77, they will find their collaborators who will participate in the necessary negotiations, who will accept partial tasks, and will share the entire responsibility.

We trust that Charter 77 will contribute to making it possible for all citizens of Czechoslovakia to live and work as free people.

4
THE WORD TO BLACK WOMEN

Awa Thiam

It is not necessary to be a feminist to notice the universality of oppression that women suffer past and present in the most diverse forms, from the most subtle to the most cruel. . . . The genocide or witch hunts that were staged in Europe from the 14–17th centuries as their power threatened that of the church and of men; the foot binding that the Chinese practised which continued for centuries until Mao Tse Tung; the seclusion and segregation of millions of women robbing them of all their rights of freedom and education from the day of puberty to menopause goes on all over the Near East. These are just some of the more spectacular examples of the domination of the bodies and spirits of women. . . .

In many countries there are men who denounce the abuse of power and political repression. But it is a curious fact that when it comes to women one covers up the reality with a veil of shame. It is treated as if the injustice women suffer has nothing to do with oppression but rather that it is just the way each culture deals with putting women "in their place" in society. . . .

Justice is never conferred from heaven. The powerful, the privileged and those of influence, no matter who they are or where—whether inherited by acquisition, by color of skin, or by sex—they have never and nowhere spontaneously shared their privileges. Each freedom, each right has to be fought for piece by piece. In many countries the women have not yet begun that battle. Because in order to fight for their independence women must first realize their dependence. And without doubt this is the most difficult stage.

From the Preface by Benoite Groult

There were some important African women in history who made important decisions, who ruled and who fought. Women must again take the word—the word which at present is usurped by the privileged males, and they have every intention to keep their privileges; they have already attacked women, for instance in Senegal. What does it mean to have a few token women in the government when polygamy is institutionalized? The figures by UNESCO [of] who gets an education speak for themselves.

The Black Africans have for a long time mystified the lives of their women. This campaign to conceal the facts must cease. The problems of African

Translated excerpts and preface summary by Fran Hoskin from *La Parole aux Négresses* by Awa Thiam. Paris: Denoel/Gonthier, 1980. Reprinted by permission from *Women's International Network News* (Lexington, MA).

women have always been hidden by African men, by the men in the African governments, by the intellectual reactionaries, and by the pseudorevolutionaries.

It is no longer a question of abstract problems and even less the one that is posed most frequently: that the liberation of the black peoples is much more important than the liberation of women. We want to stress here that we are concerned with the terrible condition of the Black African woman who is of the same black race as men vis à vis other races. It is also a fact that the Black African woman is a human being if we leave out the factors of race. Finally, if we dispose of social classes, we end up with two categories of people: men and women who are in opposing positions—the men who rule and the women who are oppressed.

It is often argued that men and women are in a "complementary" position. Who has defined this position? The men who have imposed it. This system allows them every kind of oppression and exploitation that the patriarchal system has imposed on women for no other reason than sex, in the family, at the work place, everywhere. It is high time that this condition must be looked at and redefined.

It is time that women take the word themselves and begin to act. It is now time that they claim their rights and start the all-important task to put an end to their miserable conditions as producers and reproducers, as the super exploited by the capitalists, patriarchate and government chiefs.

We must take the word to turn things around. Take the word to say we refuse, we revolt. Word and Action. The Word is to resist, the Word is to Act, and to Act in practice and implementing as we go and changing everything.

But who are the Black African women? Much has been written about their customs but rarely with objectivity. The African authors have ignored women except as sex objects, as suffering mothers, or in their relationships with whites—but their reality has been ignored.

It is known that in the patriarchal societies the woman has never spoken for herself—she has been subjected to institutionalized polygamy, to forced marriage, to excision and infibulation; she is seldom paid for her productive activities but grows the food and takes care of all the household tasks. . . . She works hard from dawn to dusk, carries the water and wood, prepares the food with the most primitive tools. . . . What can be done? What are the possibilities for action, given these heavy tasks?

First of all, we must rid ourselves of the myths of the matriarchal Black African society. It is a grave error to believe for one moment that the woman has any power because she does the subsistence farming or housework and decides in part the marriages of her children. The same error is to believe that the matrilinear system is a matriarchate. When a woman does not have the right to have no rights, it is certain that she has no rights whatever.

She has a pseudo right as long as she does not make any demands on her husband or the capitalist system—she is allowed to exist. All the decisions are made by men without the slightest regard for women. The Black African male disposes not only over his life but also that of his wife, especially in the African

Moslem societies where a woman can go to paradise only through the intervention of her husband.

Does the Black African woman agree? Does she complain about her situation? Does she revolt? Does she blindly agree with everything that the
"God—her husband" does? We want to find out and therefore we want to listen
to our African sisters, to learn their stories, to share a bit of their lives briefly,
and to learn to know them and thus to know ourselves.

SOME OF THE WOMEN'S OWN STORIES

Yacine

"My father is a naturalized Senegalese from Mali. I was married at 18 to a
man from the Ivory Coast. My husband was a small businessman who travelled
between Abidjan, Bamako and Ouagadougou. We lived in Abidjan in a small
room in Treichville, the quarter where most Senegalese live. . . .

"We had two children, however we always lived in the same small room. One
day my husband came back from a business trip with a young woman. 'Here is
my new wife; she is called X . . . ,' he said. 'This evening you and your children
will sleep on the mat in the corner. I shall take the bed.'

"That was all. What could I do? I was four months pregnant with my third
child and had no place to go and no money. It was difficult to live that way
with the two children in a single room, the children, myself, and my husband
and his new wife. I suggested to my husband that a screen should be put between myself and my children and himself and his new wife. He agreed. I had to
pay for it and install it myself.

"I did not know what to do. I knew no one in Abidjan who could help me
and I had to listen each night to my husband and his new wife on our bed.

"After I had the baby I decided I could not go on this way. There was no
sense in making a scene; I sold my jewelry and bought a ticket to Bamako
where my mother lived. I told my husband before I left but he did not take it
seriously because he knew I had no money. I returned with my children to my
mother, who cried.

"He wrote a letter to my mother and later to me but we did not reply. Finally
he sent a friend because it usually costs a great deal of money to effect a reconciliation and my mother told his emissary that he would have to pay the support of the children and my support before I would think of rejoining him. It is
now three years and he has done nothing. . . ."

(*Editor's Note*: Polygamy is prohibited officially in the Ivory Coast, the only
West African country that has such legislation.)

Coumba (Senegal)

"I am married to a man who works in the same factory as I do, where we met.
We are married six years and have two children. Since last year our marriage is
no longer monogamous since my husband brought another wife home. Until
then we had no financial problems but since then we have had both the water

and the electricity cut off. Our salaries are not sufficient to support a polygamous household. My co-wife is a very young woman of 17 who does not work. She is pregnant and depends entirely on my husband and spends a great deal of money. After the 20th of each month we have nothing left (*Editor's Note*: Salaries are paid monthly in Senegal). I do not have enough to feed my children. I do not know how we can go on this way unless my husband finds a way to pay for a polygamous household. Either I will get a divorce or he will have to divorce his other wife. We did very well but my husband has created all these problems. . . ."

Mouna (married to a Moslem religious leader)

"I have been married since I was 16—I am now 43. I have given my husband 12 children, 2 died as infants. I am the first wife of my husband and have had 13 co-wives over the years and of all different ages. The youngest one is 20 now that my husband is in his fifties. Some of the wives did not live in the same house or even town. But at present all 4 of us live together—according to the wishes of my husband. He travels frequently.

"Since I have been with him longest—though I hardly see him now—I know all that has happened. Each time a new wife comes she is the center of attention of my husband. After a while she finds herself neglected either because of the arrival of another wife or because of another voyage. This kind of married life is impossible: no matter how we try to please, how well we behave . . . my co-wives and I are always abandoned in favor of another wife. I did not dare to do what some of the others did—take a lover or get a divorce—because I was afraid for my children. My youngest is only three.

"Each time my husband left, some of his wives took a lover, and then he divorced them when he returned. The second to the last wife had a child by another man after my husband married yet another; he baptized the child as his own. I do not speak against my co-wives—they are young and they cannot stand being neglected and ignored when another woman takes their place. I am already a grandmother: my oldest son is more than 10 years older than the recent co-wife.

"When one cannot get a divorce there is nothing else to do but to be resigned to one's fate. The Moslem religion is strict in this respect. There is no solution."

Medina

"I had the bad luck to be born into a very traditional family. This is how it happened that I got married to a distant cousin who was studying in Saudi Arabia.

"I was in the second year of high school when my grandfather, a marabout (a Moslem holy man) who is considered as a father-god by many people, asked me to see him. He had complete authority over all his children, grandchildren, nephews, and nieces and everybody in his environment. Nobody questioned his decisions.

"My mother and father accompanied me to the meeting. He told them, 'You have a nice daughter and she will be given in marriage next Wednesday to her cousin. He is studying in Saudi Arabia. You do not know him but he is a very nice boy and very well educated. He will stay in Saudi Arabia to finish his studies and after that your daughter will come to live with him in Saudi Arabia. . . .'

"I was completely astounded. No one questioned this decision. I did not know how to refuse or even raise the question in front of my grandfather, such a religious man. Of course it was agreed although I was never asked. . . .

"As arranged, I was married the next Wednesday although my husband was not there. That is the custom in Black Africa: the marriage of the young people is contracted in the absence of one or sometimes both by the parents and grandparents. I went back to school, where I stayed. I did not know what to do.

"When the vacation started and I returned home I was told that my husband was soon to arrive and that the marriage would then be consummated. I wanted to marry another boy whom I had met at school and we both knew and liked each other very much. I told my oldest brother, who said he would tell my parents. I did not dare to tell my father. I decided to go on a hunger strike. When my father heard about this he called me into his room. 'How dare you refuse to eat.' He started to beat me. 'I shall kill you if you do not eat.' I screamed and ran out of the room and went to the house of friends next door. My mother sent somebody after me but I would not come back. Finally, my mother and I had a quiet talk. 'Your father insists that he will kill you and then will kill himself if you do not do what your grandfather wishes,' she said.

"I was persuaded also by my mother and all my friends to go and apologise to my father, whom I loved very much. The marriage day finally arrived. An enormous number of people came from the entire family. Not a single one of my friends was invited. I had never been asked about this marriage at all; I was simply an object that was being disposed of.

"After this great celebration I was given to the man whom I had never seen before. I was a virgin. The next morning my family exhibited the sheet with my blood with pride to all the people around to prove that I had been a virgin. Thus the honor of the family was saved.

"Since that wedding night I have never again been near my husband. The man was not satisfied with this situation and a few days after the festival of the marriage he asked for a divorce. . . ."

5
ON INVISIBLE OPPRESSION AND WORLD ORDER

Richard Falk

The mobilization of a movement for value change depends upon an active political consciousness. Such a condition does not seem to exist at the present time in relation to world order issues among most people throughout the world. Our thesis in this book is that the present world order system, by its structural imperative, is oppressive, threatening people everywhere with nuclear devastation, ecological decay, and economic stagnancy or collapse, as well as with less dramatic, but quite real (and avoidable) threats to health and developmental well-being. At the same time, the tradition of protest and opposition is mainly associated with reforms and transformations at the national level. It is true that some transformative movements, such as Marxism-Leninism, are conceived transnationally, that is, as a revolution that can spread from society to society, one by one. It is this prospect that inspires fear on the part of counterrevolutionary forces, producing such images as "falling dominoes."

On the global level, leaders of less privileged societies have articulated demands about global reform, generally centering on a fairer world economic system. Leaders of all states bemoan war and talk vaguely of the desirability of peace and justice. Such talk has become common diplomatic currency in the nuclear era, and yet for years nothing much has been done to take serious account of these concerns. The natural effect is to make world order concerns seem like so much "globaloney," cheap and soothing appeals to conscience not supported by any willingness to alter the dangerous patterns of behavior. This debasement of our normative currency makes it difficult even to formulate in a convincing fashion the case for global reform. Bad language drives out good causes; hence, the case for a new world order is no longer taken seriously (even as compared to the 1920s or 1940s and 1950s). As a result, the case for global reform has been almost reduced despite the continuing deterioration of the international situation.

Indeed, the normative trends in recent years are mainly adverse. It seems sensible to suggest that there is transpiring in the present decade a phenomenon of

---

The content of this selection reflects collaborative work with Samuel Kim, Saul Mendlovitz, and Sherle Schwenninger.

normative regression: a decline in stature of the United Nations; a new tolerance of or resignation to aggressive war (consider international reactions to Iraq's attack on Iran, China's attack on Vietnam, and Tanzania's attack on Uganda); a new set of interventionary politics associated with nondefensive uses of force (e.g., the Soviet invasion of Afghanistan and the threat by the United States to intervene to arrest hostile developments in the Caribbean and Persian Gulf regions); a waning of such relatively benign managerial notions as interdependence, détente, and arms control; a drop in levels of assistance given to poorer countries.

And yet, despite these dangers and trends, the citizenry in most countries is not aroused or outraged. The dynamics of oppression associated with the workings of world order remain largely latent and invisible, and as such they remain at the margins of feasibility, if not beyond. It is the persisting political invisibility, not the intractable character of the real world challenges, that gives world order thinking its reputation for pipe-dreaming and utopianism. As long as social problems remain invisible—not seen as problems to be solved or solvable—it seems almost futile to propose positive responses.

Invisibility in the sense used here takes several forms. First of all, a given social arrangement may be seen as inevitable or in the nature of things. Such was the case for centuries with respect to slavery and various types of lesser servitude. So long as the structure is believed to be in the nature of things, it seems foolish to mount a challenge. Secondly, some realities seem so painful, so pervasive, and so powerful, that rather than confront our helplessness we deny their existence. This denial is obviously a defense mechanism. We have all heard about people who refuse to move from the base of an active volcano, but do we know about people who acquiesce in their predicament as ecological guinea pigs and nuclear hostages? The world gets properly outraged when a handful of innocent people are seized as hostages, but what about the billions held hostage by the perils of nuclear weapons strategy? In these settings, there is additionally an oppressiveness that relates to the absence of accountability. Quite literally, a few men, at most, decide in secret whether and under what conditions nuclear war will be waged. Their decision is not even based on guidelines accepted in advance by the citizenry. This greatest delegation of authority imaginable has been made "invisibly," thereby impairing seriously the effective domain of democracy.

There is a third type of invisibility, a literal failure "to see." In some contexts this failure has a physical explanation: the colorless, odorless character of low-level radioactivity released by nuclear plants and accidents. We are beginning to discover that our secure "back yards" contain a variety of invisible hazards of an extreme character. Ultratoxic chemical dumps are spread around the country, evidently seeping into ground waters and endangering health. The furor over Love Canal near Buffalo, New York, is only one instance of an invisible hazard rising all at once to a level of dramatic and frightening visibility.

Many instances of injustice are invisible, sometimes because information is kept secret or merely because it seems unimportant given prevailing cultural criteria. The condition of untouchables in rural India is so deeply embedded in

Hindu tradition that even liberal Indians who reject the caste ethos are completely unaware of the extent to which their relations to servants embodies attitudes that dehumanize all parties. In other situations, information is held back, either deliberately or unwittingly, as when minorities are persecuted within a state and have no constituency outside that will speak on their behalf. The Bangsa-Moro people in the Philippines, the Timorese in Indonesia, and the Kurds in Iran, Iraq, and Turkey are examples of victimized groups whose vulnerability is greater because they lack effective ties to extranational opinion makers. Their oppression is ignored in the literal sense. It is virtually not reported by the media. It is, therefore, not seen by most people and remains invisible to them. Many North Americans are not able to see the extent to which the Indian nations in our midst continue to be oppressed, not as a matter of unfortunate early history, but as an aspect of continuing social policy. For instance, Indian communities in a number of regions have been and are being exposed to uranium mining to extents that produce high incidences of radiation sickness and genetic defects. Why don't we know? We have a free press. Secrecy and deception are only part of the story; more fundamental are the engrained habits of "not-seeing."

Often the initial phases of a struggle against oppression center on a quest for visibility. Making people aware of oppression involves more than dissemination of facts, although information is essential. Becoming visible means *feeling* for the victims, associating our dignity with their liberation. Martin Luther King, Jr., created visibility of this character by dramatizing the reality that black Americans experienced in their daily lives. The women's movement, at least in the West, has started to have this kind of impact. Millions of men are beginning to feel for women as victims of multidimensional oppression, although the reality of these oppressive male/female structures remain obscure, or even invisible, for the majority.

We can sometimes discern the existence of invisible oppression of an intense kind in the form of signs of societal disintegration. The defensive mechanisms of denial take their toll through drug and alcohol addiction, divorce, mental illness, suicide, cynicism, and a sense of low political efficacy. Such phenomena suggest only that societal arrangements are not working, that life has lost its sustaining purpose for many citizens, a loss that is bewildering because its effects do not normally register in this form upon our consciousness. Indeed, this loss of meaning saps the inner strength of a polity and makes it vulnerable to all kinds of spurious social and cultural phenomena. Religious cults, the "Moral Majority," endless fads relating to diet, health, and personal relationships are among the manifestations of this cultural emptiness that is one main consequence of invisible oppression in a prosperous, developed country. One large unacknowledged expression of invisible oppression is a direct outgrowth of world order deficiencies, especially relating to the continuous threat to our lives, to our society and civilization, and even to our species, in the form of catastrophic nuclear war. The enormity of the peril and our helplessness in relation to its prospect lead us to block our awareness of the danger, but not completely. We are immobilized on the level of action, haunted on the level of dream. As a result, there is a lack of psychic integration as well as an unhealthy receptivity to escapist paths. A process results that psychohistorian Robert Jay Lifton dubbed "psychic numbing," a protective refusal to feel in relation to threats that seem beyond our power to remove.

The emerging enterprise of global reform is committed to shifting oppressive structures of world order into the domain of visibility for millions of people. Such shifting encounters resistance. Claims of alarmism are made by defenders of the status quo, and often it is necessary to break through resistance by shock tactics. Civil disobedience plays a role here. Those individuals who learn to see invisible oppression and to feel with its victims have a special mission to awaken others. World order education in this spirit intends to set off an alarm in the sensibilities of students. And yet, of course, it is not nearly enough to become worried—in fact, a bleak vision by itself is numbing and demobilizing. The positive side of awakening people to the realities of invisible oppression is to illuminate paths of transition to alternative worlds without oppression.

Finally, the leaders who officially represent us are likely to be the last ones to see what is happening. The struggle of the oppressed in the context of world order studies cannot be left to educational efforts designed to edify elites, whose vested interests in "not-seeing" are generally strong. Our confidence in the future is primarily a belief in enlightenment from below. Such an orientation flies in the face of mainstream politics of either left or right, whether it takes refuge in notions of "vanguards of the proletariat" or "a creative minority" of enlightened aristocrats.

The pervasiveness of invisible oppression threatens our humanity, breaking contact with the forces that contravene our values and interests. Governmental uses of secrecy (in the name of national security) often make it evident that it is leaders' distrust of citizens, not fear of foreign enemies, that explains the withholding of information. During President Nixon's "secret" campaign of bombing Cambodia in the early 1970s, it was obvious that the people targeted were aware of what was being done. Secrecy was for the sake of inhibiting criticism and protest, extending even to misrepresentations by the White House to ensure that Congress would not know the realities. This instance is blatant, but there are many more subtle interferences with seeing that impair our capacity as purposive human beings to act for our own sake or on behalf of others. The world order perspective is designed to make a massive assault on the overall politics of invisibility.

6
PEDAGOGY OF THE OPPRESSED

Paulo Freire

While the problem of humanization has always, from an axiological point of view, been man's central problem, it now takes on the character of an inescapable concern.[1] Concern for humanization leads at once to the recognition of dehumanization, not only as an ontological possibility but as an historical reality. And as man perceives the extent of dehumanization, he asks himself if humanization is a viable possibility. Within history, in concrete, objective contexts, both humanization and dehumanization are possibilities for man as an uncompleted being conscious of his incompletion.

But while both humanization and dehumanization are real alternatives, only the first is man's vocation. This vocation is constantly negated, yet it is affirmed by that very negation. It is thwarted by injustice, exploitation, oppression, and the violence of the oppressors; it is affirmed by the yearning of the oppressed for freedom and justice, and by their struggle to recover their lost humanity.

Dehumanization, which marks not only those whose humanity has been stolen, but also (though in a different way) those who have stolen it, is a *distortion* of the vocation of becoming more fully human. This distortion occurs within history; but it is not an historical vocation. Indeed, to admit of dehumanization as an historical vocation would lead either to cynicism or total despair. The struggle for humanization, for the emancipation of labor, for the overcoming of alienation, for the affirmation of men as persons would be meaningless. This struggle is possible only because dehumanization, although a concrete historical fact, is *not* a given destiny but the result of an unjust order that engenders violence in the oppressors, which in turn dehumanizes the oppressed.

Because it is a distortion of being more fully human, sooner or later being less human leads the oppressed to struggle against those who made them so. In order for this struggle to have meaning, the oppressed must not, in seeking to regain their humanity (which is a way to create it), become in turn oppressors of the oppressors, but rather restorers of the humanity of both.

This, then, is the great humanistic and historical task of the oppressed: to liberate themselves and their oppressors as well. The oppressors, who oppress, exploit, and rape by virtue of their power, cannot find in this power the strength to liberate either the oppressed or themselves. Only power that springs from the weakness of the oppressed will be sufficiently strong to free both. Any attempt to "soften" the power of the oppressor in deference to the weakness of the oppressed almost always manifests itself in the form of false generosity; indeed, the attempt never goes beyond this. In order to have the continued opportunity to express their "generosity," the oppressors must perpetuate injustice as well. An unjust social order is the permanent fount of this "generosity," which is nourished by death, despair, and poverty. That is why the dispensers of false generosity become desperate at the slightest threat to its source.

True generosity consists precisely in fighting to destroy the causes which nourish false charity. False charity constrains the fearful and subdued, the "rejects of life," to extend their trembling hands. True generosity lies in striving so that these hands—whether of individuals or entire peoples—need be extended less and less in supplication, so that more and more they become human hands which work and, working, transform the world.

This lesson and this apprenticeship must come, however, from the oppressed themselves and from those who are truly solidary with them. As individuals or as peoples, by fighting for the restoration of their humanity they will be attempting the restoration of true generosity. Who are better prepared than the oppressed to understand the terrible significance of an oppressive society? Who suffer the effects of oppression more than the oppressed? Who can better understand the necessity of liberation? They will not gain this liberation by chance but through the praxis of their quest for it, through their recognition of the necessity to fight for it. And this fight, because of the purpose given it by the oppressed, will actually constitute an act of love opposing the lovelessness which lies at the heart of the oppressors' violence, lovelessness even when clothed in false generosity.

But almost always, during the initial stage of the struggle, the oppressed, instead of striving for liberation, tend themselves to become oppressors, or "suboppressors." The very structure of their thought has been conditioned by the contradictions of the concrete, existential situation by which they were shaped. Their ideal is to be men; but for them, to be men is to be oppressors. This is their model of humanity. This phenomenon derives from the fact that the oppressed, at a certain moment of their existential experience, adopt an attitude of "adhesion" to the oppressor. Under these circumstances they cannot "consider" him sufficiently clearly to objectivize him—to discover him "outside" themselves. This does not necessarily mean that the oppressed are unaware that they are downtrodden. But their perception of themselves as oppressed is impaired by their submersion in the reality of oppression. At this level, their perception of themselves as opposites of the oppressor does not yet signify engagement in a struggle to overcome the contradiction;[2] the one pole aspires not to liberation, but to identification with its opposite pole.

In this situation the oppressed do not see the "new man" as the man to be born from the resolution of this contradiction, as oppression gives way to liberation. For them, the new man in themselves become oppressors. Their vision of the new man is individualistic; because of their identification with the oppressor, they have no consciousness of themselves as persons or as members of an oppressed class. It is not to become free men that they want agrarian reform, but in order to acquire land and thus become landowners—or, more precisely, bosses over other workers. It is a rare peasant who, once "promoted" to overseer, does not become more of a tyrant towards his former comrades than the owner himself. This is because the context of the peasant's situation, that is, oppression, remains unchanged. In this example, the overseer, in order to make sure of his job, must be as tough as the owner—and more so. Thus is illustrated our previous assertion that during the initial stage of their struggle the oppressed find in the oppressor their model of "manhood."

Even revolution, which transforms a concrete situation of oppression by establishing the process of liberation, must confront this phenomenon. Many of the oppressed who directly or indirectly participate in revolution intend—conditioned by the myths of the old order—to make it their private revolution. The shadow of their former oppressor is still cast over them.

The "fear of freedom" which afflicts the oppressed,[3] a fear which may equally well lead them to desire the role of oppressor or bind them to the role of oppressed, should be examined. One of the basic elements of the relationship between oppressor and oppressed is *prescription*. Every prescription represents the imposition of one man's choice upon another, transforming the consciousness of the man prescribed to into one that conforms with the prescriber's consciousness. Thus, the behavior of the oppressed is a prescribed behavior, following as it does the guidelines of the oppressor.

The oppressed, having internalized the image of the oppressor and adopted his guidelines, are fearful of freedom. Freedom would require them to eject this image and replace it with autonomy and responsibility. Freedom is acquired by conquest, not by gift. It must be pursued constantly and responsibly. Freedom is not an ideal located outside of man; nor is it an idea which becomes myth. It is rather the indispensable condition for the quest for human completion.

To surmount the situation of oppression, men must first critically recognize its causes, so that through transforming action they can create a new situation, one which makes possible the pursuit of a fuller humanity. But the struggle to be more fully human has already begun in the authentic struggle to transform the situation. Although the situation of oppression is a dehumanized and dehumanizing totality affecting both the oppressors and those whom they oppress, it is the latter who must, from their stifled humanity, wage for both the struggle for a fuller humanity; the oppressor, who is himself dehumanized because he dehumanizes others, is unable to lead this struggle.

However, the oppressed, who have adapted to the structure of domination in which they are immersed, and have become resigned to it, are inhibited from waging the struggle for freedom so long as they feel incapable of running the risks it requires. Moreover, their struggle for freedom threatens not only the oppressor, but also their own oppressed comrades who are fearful of still greater repression. When they discover within themselves the yearning to be free, they perceive that this yearning can be transformed into reality only when the same yearning is aroused in their comrades. But while dominated by the fear of freedom they refuse to appeal to others, or to listen to the appeals of others, or even to the appeals of their own conscience. They prefer gregariousness to authentic comradeship; they prefer the security of conformity with their state of unfreedom to the creative communion produced by freedom and even the very pursuit of freedom.

The oppressed suffer from the duality which has established itself in their innermost being. They discover that without freedom they cannot exist authentically. Yet, although they desire authentic existence, they fear it. They are at one and the same time themselves and the oppressor whose consciousness they have internalized. The conflict lies in the choice between being wholly themselves or being divided; between ejecting the oppressor within or not ejecting him; between human solidarity or alienation; between following prescriptions or having choices; between being spectators or actors; between acting or having the illusion of acting through the action of the oppressors; between speaking out or being silent, castrated in their power to create and re-create, in their power to transform the world. This is the tragic dilemma of the oppressed which their education must take into account.

This book will present some aspects of what the writer has termed the pedagogy of the oppressed, a pedagogy which must be forged *with*, not *for*, the oppressed (whether individuals or peoples) in the incessant struggle to regain their humanity. This pedagogy makes oppression and its causes objects of reflection by the oppressed, and from that reflection will come their necessary engagement in the struggle for their liberation. And in the struggle this pedagogy will be made and remade.

The central problem is this: How can the oppressed, as divided, unauthentic beings, participate in developing the pedagogy of their liberation? Only as they discover themselves to be "hosts" of the oppressor can they contribute to the midwifery of their liberating pedagogy. As long as they live in the duality in which *to be* is *to be like*, and *to be like* is *to be like the oppressor*, this contribution is impossible. The pedagogy of the oppressed is an instrument for their critical discovery that both they and their oppressors are manifestations of dehumanization.

Liberation is thus a childbirth, and a painful one. The man who emerges is a new man, viable only as the oppressor-oppressed contradiction is superseded by the humanization of all men. Or to put it another way, the solution of this contradiction is born in the labor which brings into the world this new man: no longer oppressor nor longer oppressed, but man in the process of achieving freedom.

This solution cannot be achieved in idealistic terms. In order for the oppressed to be able to wage the struggle for their liberation, they must perceive the reality of oppression not as a closed world from which there is no exit, but as a limiting situation which they can transform. This perception is a necessary but not a sufficient condition for liberation; it must become the motivating force for liberating action. Nor does the discovery by the oppressed that they exist in dialectical relationship to the oppressor, as his antithesis—that without them the oppressor could not exist[4]—in itself constitute liberation. The oppressed can overcome the contradiction in which they are caught only when this perception enlists them in the struggle to free themselves.

The same is true with respect to the individual oppressor as a person. Discovering himself to be an oppressor may cause considerable anguish, but it does not necessarily lead to solidarity with the oppressed. Rationalizing his guilt through paternalistic treatment of the oppressed, all the while holding them fast in a position of dependence, will not do. Solidarity requires that one enter into the situation of those with whom one is solidary; it is a radical posture. If what characterizes the oppressed is their subordination to the consciousness of the master, as Hegel affirms,[5] true solidarity with the oppressed means fighting at their side to transform the objective reality which has made them these "beings for another." The oppressor is solidary with the oppressed only when he stops regarding the oppressed as an abstract category and sees them as persons who have been unjustly dealt with, deprived of their voice, cheated in the sale of their labor—when he stops making pious, sentimental, and individualistic gestures and risks an act of love. True solidarity is found only in the plenitude of this act of love, in its existentiality, in its praxis. To affirm that men are persons and as persons should be free, and yet to do nothing tangible to make this affirmation a reality, is a farce.

Since it is in a concrete situation that the oppressor-oppressed contradiction is established, the resolution of this contradiction must be *objectively* verifiable. Hence, the radical requirement—both for the man who discovers himself to be an oppressor and for the oppressed—that the concrete situation which begets oppression must be transformed.

To present this radical demand for the objective transformation of reality, to combat subjectivist immobility which would divert the recognition of oppression into patient waiting for oppression to disappear by itself, is not to dismiss the role of subjectivity in the struggle to change structures. On the contrary, one cannot conceive of objectivity without subjectivity. Neither can exist without the other, nor can they be dichotomized. The separation of objectivity from subjectivity, the denial of the latter when analyzing reality or acting upon it, is objectivism. On the other hand, the denial of objectivity in analysis or action, resulting in a subjectivism which leads to solipsistic positions, denies action itself by denying objective reality. Neither objectivism nor subjectivism, nor yet psychologism is propounded here, but rather subjectivity and objectivity in constant dialectical relationship.

To deny the importance of subjectivity in the process of transforming the world and history is naïve and simplistic. It is to admit the impossible: a world without men. This objectivistic position is as ingenuous as that of subjectivism, which postulates men without a world. World and men do not exist apart from each other, they exist in constant interaction. Marx does not espouse such a dichotomy, nor does any other critical, realistic thinker. What Marx criticized and scientifically destroyed was not subjectivity, but subjectivism and psychologism. Just as objective social reality exists not by chance, but as the product of human action, so it is not transformed by chance. If men produce social reality (which in the "inversion of the praxis" turns back upon them and conditions them), then transforming that reality is an historical task, a task for men.

Reality which becomes oppressive results in the contradistinction of men as oppressors and oppressed. The latter, whose task it is to struggle for their liberation together with those who show true solidarity, must acquire a critical awareness of oppression through the praxis of this struggle. One of the gravest obstacles to the achievement of liberation is that oppressive reality absorbs those within it and thereby acts to submerge men's consciousness.[6] Functionally, oppression is domesticating. To no longer be prey to its force, one must emerge from it and turn upon it. This can be done only by means of the praxis: reflection and action upon the world in order to transform it. "Hay que hacer al opresión real todavía mas opresiva añadiendo a aquella la *conciéncia* de la opresión haciendo la infamia todavía mas infamante, al pregonarla."[7]

Making "real oppression more oppressive still by adding to it the realization of oppression" corresponds to the dialectical relation between the subjective and the objective. Only in this interdependence is an authentic praxis possible, without which it is impossible to resolve the oppressor-oppressed contradiction. To achieve this goal, the oppressed must confront reality critically, simultaneously objectifying and acting upon that reality. A mere perception of reality not followed by this critical intervention will not lead to a transformation of objective reality—precisely because it is not a true perception. This is the case of a purely subjectivist perception by someone who forsakes objective reality and creates a false substitute.

A different type of false perception occurs when a change in objective reality would threaten the individual or class interests of the perceiver. In the first instance, there is no critical intervention in reality because that reality is fictitious; there is none in the second instance because intervention would contradict the class interests of the perceiver. In the latter case the tendency of the perceiver is to behave "neurotically." The fact exists; but both the fact and what may result from it may be prejudicial to him. Thus it becomes necessary, not precisely to deny the fact, but to "see it differently." This rationalization as a defense mechanism coincides in the end with subjectivism. A fact which is not denied but whose truths are rationalized loses its objective base. It ceases to be concrete and becomes a myth created in defense of the class of the perceiver.

Herein lies one of the reasons for the prohibitions and the difficulties designed to dissuade the people from critical intervention in reality. The oppressor knows full well that this intervention would not be to his interest. What *is* to his interest is for the people to continue in a state of submersion, impotent in the face of oppressive reality. Of relevance here is Lukács' warning to the revolutionary party: "Il doit, pour employer les mots de Marx, expliquer aux masses leur propre action non seulement afin d'assurer la continuité des expériences révolutionnaires du prolétariat, mais aussi d'activer consciemment le développement ultérieur de ces expériences."[8] In affirming this necessity, Lukács is unquestionably posing the problem of critical intervention. "To explain to the masses their own action" is to clarify and illuminate that action, both regarding its relationship to the objective facts by which it was prompted, and regarding its purposes. The more the people unveil this challenging reality which is to be the object of their transforming action, the more critically they enter that reality. In this way they are "consciously activating the subsequent development of their experiences." There would be no human action if there were no objective reality, no world to be the "not I" of man and to challenge him; just as there would be no human action if man were not a "project," if he were not able to transcend himself, to perceive his reality and understand it in order to transform it.

In dialectical thought, world and action are intimately interdependent. But action is human only when it is not merely an occupation but also a preoccupation, that is, when it is not dichotomized from reflection. Reflection, which is essential to action, is implicit in Lukács' requirement of "explaining to the masses their own action," just as it is implicit in the purpose he attributes to this explanation: that of "consciously activating the subsequent development of experience."

For us, however, the requirement is seen not in terms of explaining to, but rather dialoguing with the people about their actions. In any event, no reality transforms itself,[9] and the duty which Lukács ascribes to the revolutionary party of "explaining to the masses their own action" coincides with our affirmation of the need for the critical intervention of the people in reality through the praxis. The pedagogy of the oppressed, which is the pedagogy of men engaged in the fight for their own liberation, has its roots here. And those who recognize, or begin to recognize, themselves as oppressed must be among the developers of this pedagogy. No pedagogy which is truly liberating can remain distant from the oppressed by treating them as unfortunates and by presenting for their emulation models from among the oppressors. The oppressed must be their own example in the struggle for their redemption.

NOTES

1. The current movements of rebellion, especially those of youth, while they necessarily reflect the peculiarities of their respective settings, manifest in their essence this preoccupation with man and men as beings in the world—preoccupation with *what* and *how* they are "being." As they place consumer civilization in judgment, denounce bureaucracies of all types, demand the transformation of the universities (changing the rigid nature of the teacher-student relationship and placing that relationship within the context of reality), propose the transformation of reality itself so that universities can be renewed, attack old orders and established institutions in the attempt to affirm men as the Subjects of decision, all these movements reflect the style of our age, which is more anthropological than anthropocentric.

2. As used throughout this book, the term "contradiction" denotes the dialectical conflict between opposing social forces.—Translator's note.

3. This fear of freedom is also to be found in the oppressors, though, obviously, in a different form. The oppressed are afraid to embrace freedom; the oppressors are afraid of losing the "freedom" to oppress.

4. See Georg Hegel, *Phenomenology of Mind* (New York, 1967), pp. 236–237.

5. Analyzing the dialectical relationship between the consciousness of the master and the consciousness of the oppressed, Hegel states: "The one is independent, and its essential nature is to be for itself; the other is dependent, and its essence is life or existence for another. The former is the Master, or Lord, the latter the Bondsman." *Ibid.*, p. 234.

6. "Liberating action necessarily involves a moment of perception and volition. This action both precedes and follows that moment, to which it first acts as a prologue and which it subsequently serves to effect and continue within history. The action of domination, however, does not necessarily imply this dimension; for the structure of domination is maintained by its own mechanical and unconscious functionality." From an unpublished work by José Luiz Fiori, who has kindly granted permission to quote him.

7. Karl Marx and Friedrich Engels, *La Sagrada Familia y otros Escritos* (Mexico, 1962), p. 6. Emphasis added.

8. Georg Lukács, *Lénine* (Paris, 1965), p. 62.

9. "The materialist doctrine that men are products of circumstances and upbringing, and that, therefore, changed men are products of other circumstances and changed upbringing, forgets that it is men that change circumstances and that the educator himself needs educating." Karl Marx and Friedrich Engels, *Selected Works* (New York, 1968), p. 28.

The Sovereign State and the World System

INTRODUCTION

Attitudes toward the sovereign state are crucial to the formation of a just world order perspective. There is no doubt that the territorial state has been the dominant political actor on the international stage for several centuries. Where doubt enters concerns the appraisal of the state's role in relation to world order values and with respect to the durability of the state's dominance. These doubts were first raised during World War I, when many individuals began to insist that alternatives to the state were both necessary and possible. The emphasis on alternative forms of world order has been highlighted more recently, of course, by the threat of nuclear war.

Yet the issue is confusing for students and citizens alike. It is true that the state is under attack as obsolete and dangerous in an interdependent world of nuclear armaments and ecological stress, but it is also true that nationalism continues to increase in most non-Western countries, where the vast majority of the world's population live. In fact, state-building is the ideal of these societies, reacting to centuries of dependence and beset by a variety of internal divisions. Surely, nationalism was a powerful force in the anticolonial struggle of these societies. Globalist positions are viewed by political leaders in the Third World with suspicion, as means to reestablish in new guises some form of imperial control. Such a crosscurrent of experiences and preoccupations colors discussions of the state and the state system.

There is also the confusion between state and nation. The state confers nationality by granting citizenship and acting on behalf of its "nationals" in international relations. Yet nationality is also a matter of felt identity arising out of shared experience and ethnic differences of appearance, language, and tradition. Most modern states are multinational in this sense. Often the apparatus of the state is dominated by one ethnic group that discriminates against another in a manner that amounts to a severe abuse of human rights. The unhappy situation of the Kurds in Iran, Iraq, and Turkey is but one example of a nationality trapped within the confines of the state. It is a severe failing of the current world order system (dominated by First System actors) that dependent nationalities often exist without any protection. Their plight is virtually invisible unless it coincides with transnational concerns. How many readers, for instance, realize that the Bangsa Moro people of the southern Philippine Islands, numbering more than four million, live under severe persecution, with genocidal overtones, at the hands of the Ferdinand Marcos regime in Manila? The Bangsa Moro people are Moslem, and their tragedy is better known in Islamic circles than elsewhere.

These issues are not just "foreign." How many of us know the realities that bear on the claims of American Indian groups to be "nations" entitled to respect and autonomy? There has been continuous interference with Indian land tenure and settlement patterns since the first Europeans arrived on this continent. Yet the Indian has been subject to the policies and laws enacted by and for the whites. In many instances, the state does not represent the interests of a component nation within its broader statist boundaries.

What does seem evident in our era is *the spread of the state system to a global scale.* As indicated in the General Introduction, virtually every part of the world is now organized on the basis of states and networks of states. These states participate directly in international society via diplomatic relations, membership in international organizations like the United Nations, and by way of negotiations for new global arrangements such as a new law of the seas. This globalization of the state system is a new reality of relatively recent origin, with its largest expansion coming in the first two decades of the post-war period.

At the same time, in this period we find the growth of nonstate actors. The assessment of this growth is controversial, especially in terms of whether such actors as international financial organizations (e.g., International Monetary Fund and the World Bank) or multinational corporations should be perceived primarily as instruments of the dominant state or as emergent competitors to its dominance.

From our world order perspective, the main concern is with trends and values. In this respect, the focus is upon the capacity of the state system to realize world order values under contemporary conditions. This concern can be expressed by reference to a "global human interest," as Robert Johansen discusses in Section 3. The state system is organized around the interaction of individual states each pursuing its national interests, usually conceived in short-run terms. Our system transforming approach to world order believes that statecraft oriented around short-term concerns is incapable of preventing nuclear war, conserving resources, regulating population growth, achieving human rights, protecting the environment, or securing a healthy world economy. Statists, including those who embrace system-maintaining and system-reforming approaches to world order, retort that the state system is the best prospect we have to achieve world order values, that nuclear war has not taken place, that deterrence can keep the peace, and that international procedures for cooperation are being developed to protect global interests at stake. Furthermore, statists argue that alternative futures are a pipe dream lacking any political basis and that thinking in such futurist terms distracts us from the real world order task of making the state system work better. Finally, statists contend that world order activists generally favor world government and that such a centralization of authority could easily degenerate into a global tyranny enslaving all peoples.

Of course, just world order advocates have many lines of response. First of all, there are the trends themselves. The era of state autonomy seems to be giving way in the face of increasing complexity and vulnerability. Failure to regulate the transfer of nuclear technology encourages proliferation of weapons of mass destruction, but economic self-interest favors sales, especially if others are willing to sell. *Some sort of global mechanism or process is necessary to protect the human interest* in these cases, but this does not necessarily mean a world government system.

Furthermore, statism seems unable to protect us against the waste and risks of arms rivalry. Alternative forms of security seem better suited to conserve resources, uphold national and international security, and reconcile the interests of a given society with those of the world as a whole. *Statism is a conditional arrangement that arose at a certain point in history when it seemed responsive to the ordering needs of its era.* It should and can be displaced by other conditional arrangements of power and authority when it becomes less responsive to those needs.

Finally, just world order advocates are sensitive to the potential dangers of some alternatives to the state system. The focus is upon the design and promotion of preferred alternatives by reference to world order values. Increasingly, this sensitivity leads to skepticism about governmental solutions to world order. To conceive of alternatives to the state system, as we shall see in later chapters, means to explore visions of the future considerably different than that of a world state. Yet statists frequently use world government as "a straw man" in their argument against world order, consciously or unconsciously failing to recognize that this image of a world order solution no longer corresponds to the convictions or expectations of those working on behalf of drastic global reform.

Against this background, we examine a range of views on the state and the state system. We begin with a traditionalist account by Hedley Bull, a well-known Australian specialist in international relations and now Montague Professor of International Relations at Oxford University. Bull vigorously expounds the case for the state system, maintaining that it is preferable to other alternatives and is almost certain to persist indefinitely. His assessment rests on a positive view of the balancing consequences of a competitive order of states, relying on the dynamics of self-determination to overcome the internal failure of particular national governments that repress their own peoples. He rejects any globalist claims in favor of the decentralist autonomy of state entities.

We follow with a short essay by Eqbal Ahmad that emphasizes the degree to which the modern state in the Third World has become an instrument of domestic abuse. Ahmad connects this *deformation of the state* to international as well as domestic factors. He contends, in effect, that the collapse of colonialism should not be confused with the end of imperialism. New modes of informal and indirect control by the powerful, rich Western world shape the polities of many Third World countries despite the attainment of formal independence. Thus, Ahmad makes us think about *the connections between world order values*, and *the persisting structure of international hierarchy* that is embodied in the functioning of the state system. The realization of world order values depends on mitigating this hierarchy, as well as on building an alternative framework of transnational institutions. Such a prospect depends primarily on national revolution, not on reforms in the global arena. Less interventionary policies by dominant states is also relevant against a reality shaped largely within domestic political arenas.

The third work in this section provides the provocative interpretation by Stanley Diamond, a distinguished anthropologist, that the basic denial of human values is implicit in the very organization of societies into units governed by state-like institutions. In formulating his argument, Diamond accepts the Marxist analysis of the state as an instrument of class rule, and traces the process back to ancient and premodern times when priests and warriors established the basis for legitimation of coercive rule serving the few by exploiting the many. Diamond's argument is that *the deep structure of the state is inconsistent with humane governance*, and must be transformed to achieve a preferable mode of world order. As with Ahmad, Diamond declares that the primary arena of struggle is domestic, with the global dynamics being treated as derivative and subordinate.

In the next selection, Johan Galtung shifts the focus to the structure of the state system itself. Galtung contends that long-term trends are increasing the role of nonterritorial actors (international governmental and nongovernmental, including multinational corporations) in ways that are reshaping the world political system. He sees positive achievements arising out of this trend, including the erosion of statist dominance of the competitive framework. An open question is whether such an interpretation is too sanguine about nonterritorial actors in relation to their cumulative growth, their independence from statist control, and their dedication to the promotion of world order values.

We end this section with an essay by Immanuel Wallerstein that illustrates the "world system" approach to the study of international politics. Wallerstein, in developing a structural view of the world economy, points to the relationships among three categories of states: core, periphery, and semiperiphery. He argues that all political relationships are derived from the distinct relations these states have to global modes of production and their related economic functions. The outlook is at once Marxist and humanist. It envisages that the capitalist organization of international society will remain dominant for some decades, but that it is in the process of being superseded by socialist modes of production. As a consequence, Wallerstein argues that *a socialist world government will ultimately come into being* through the process of conflict and struggle. As such, Wallerstein construes the future of world order by way of interpreting historical tendencies heavily weighted toward changing modes of production and ownership of capital goods. His essay, then, is not merely an explanatory and prescriptive assessment of the state system, it is a predictive one as well.

QUESTIONS FOR DISCUSSION AND REFLECTION

What are the basic assumptions of the state system? Why and how have these assumptions been called into question in recent decades?

To what extent is the oppressive internal nature of the state an issue of world order? How do struggles against such oppressiveness contribute to a constructive response to the global agenda of world order issues? Can a reformed state system provide a world order solution for our times?

Are there emerging more hopeful alternatives than the state system?

Is it useful and possible to think globally while still remaining a loyal citizen of a sovereign state? Is global allegiance compatible with national citizenship?

SELECTED BIBLIOGRAPHY

Brucan, Silviu. *The Dialectics of World Politics*. New York: Free Press, 1978.

Bull, Hedley. *The Anarchical Society: A Study of Order in World Politics*. New York: Columbia University Press, 1977.

Camps, Miriam. *The Management of Interdependence*. New York: Council on Foreign Relations, 1974.

Carneiro, Robert L. "A Theory of the Origin of the State." *Science* 169, 1970, pp. 733–38.

Donelan, Michael, ed. *The Reason of States*. London: Allen & Unwin, 1978.

Hass, Ernst B. *Beyond the Nation-State: Functionalism and International Organization*. Stanford: Stanford University Press, 1968.

Herz, John. *The Nation-State and the Crisis of World Politics*. New York: McKay, 1976.

Hinsley, F. H. *Power and the Pursuit of Peace*. New York: Cambridge University Press, 1978.

Kissinger, Henry A. *A World Restored*. New York: Houghton Mifflin, 1964.

Kohr, Leopold. *The Breakdown of Nations*. New York: Dutton, 1978.

Mansbach, Richard W., W. H. Ferguson, and D. E. Lamport. *The Web of World Politics*. Englewood Cliffs, NJ: Prentice-Hall, 1976.

Miliband, Ralph. *The State in Capitalist Society*. New York: Basic Books, 1969.

Modelski, George, ed. *Transnational Corporations and World Order*. San Francisco: W. H. Freeman & Co., 1979.

Nye, Joseph, and Robert Keohane. *Transnational Relations and World Politics*. Cambridge: Harvard University Press, 1972.

Pettman, Ralph. *State and Class*. New York: St. Martin's, 1979.

Skocpol, Theda. *States and Social Revolutions*. New York: Cambridge University Press, 1979.

Tucker, Robert W. *The Inequality of Nations*. New York: Basic Books, 1977.

Vernon, Raymond. *Sovereignty at Bay*. New York: Basic Books, 1971.

Wallerstein, Immanuel. *The Modern World System*. New York: Academic Press, 1974.

Wight, Martin. *Systems of States*. Leicester, England: Leicester University Press, 1977.

7
THE STATE'S POSITIVE ROLE
IN WORLD AFFAIRS

Hedley Bull

We are constantly being told, at least in the Western world, that the state (and along with it, the system of states) is an obstacle to the achievement of a viable world order. First, the state is said to be an obstacle to peace and security: while the world continues to be organized politically as a system of states, war will remain endemic—a condition of affairs that could be tolerated before the advent of nuclear weapons but can be no longer. Second, the state is said to stand in the way of the promotion of economic and social justice in world society. It is the sovereign state that enables the rich peoples of the world to consume their greedy, mammoth portions of the world's resources, while refusing transfers to poor countries; and it is the sovereign state, again, that makes it possible for the squalid and corrupt governments of many poor (and some not so poor) countries to ignore the basic needs of their own citizens and to violate their human rights. Third, the state is held to be a barrier to man's grappling effectively with the problem of living in harmony with his environment. The connected issues of the control of the world's population, the production and distribution of food, the utilization of the world's resources, and the conservation of the natural environment, it is said, have to be tackled on a global basis, and this is prevented by the division of mankind into states.

Those who see the problem of world order as one of getting "beyond the state" (or the sovereign state or the nation-state) are not necessarily agreed as to what form of universal political organization should replace the system of states, or what combination of suprastate, substate, or transstate actors should deprive the state of its role. But they all feel that there is some basic contradiction between, on the one hand, the unity or interconnectedness of the global economy, the global society, the global polity, and, on the other, the system under which each state claims exclusive jurisdiction over a particular area of the earth's surface and of the human population. Thus political economists tell us that we must transcend the state in order to manage "the economics of interdependence," lawyers sound the clarion call of an advance "from international law to world law," and political scientists speak of the need to disavow

Reprinted by permission from *Daedalus* 108, Fall 1979.

the "states-centric paradigm."[1] The term "statist" is applied in a new, pejorative sense to describe those unable to free themselves from the bad old ways.

No doubt the system of sovereign states, when compared with other forms of universal political organization that have existed in the past or might come to exist in the future (e.g., a world government, a neo-medieval order in which there is no central authority but in which states are not "sovereign," or an order composed of geographically isolated or autarchic communities) does have its own particular disadvantages. But the attack on the state is misconceived.

In the first place it seems likely that the state, whether we approve of it or not, is here to stay. If this is so, the argument that we can advance the cause of world order only by getting "beyond the state" is a counsel of despair, at all events if it means that we have to begin by abolishing or subverting the state, rather than that there is a need to build upon it. Of course, the state is not the only important actor on the stage of world politics: nonstate groups and movements of various kinds play a role, as do individual persons. There never was a time in the history of the modern international system when this was otherwise: in eighteenth and nineteenth century Europe, too, states shared the stage with chartered companies, revolutionary and counterrevolutionary political parties, and national liberation movements. Indeed, it is difficult to believe that anyone ever asserted the "states-centric" view of international politics that is today so knowingly rejected by those who seek to emphasize the role of "the new international actors."[2] What was widely asserted about European international relations from the time of Vattel in the mid-eighteenth century until the end of the First World War was the *legal fiction* of a political universe that consisted of states alone, the doctrine that only states had rights and duties in international law. But assertion of such a doctrine does not imply that the actual course of international political events can be understood in terms of this fiction rather than in terms of the actions of actual persons and groups of persons, such as are set out in any history of the period.

It is sometimes suggested that in recent decades "other actors" have increased their role in world politics at the expense of that of the state, but even this—although it may be so—is difficult to establish conclusively because of the impossibility of reducing the question to quantitative terms.[3] It is true that international governmental and nongovernmental organizations have multiplied visibly, that multinational corporations have had a dramatic impact on the world economy, and that vast networks of contact and intercourse have grown up at the transnational level. But the state's role in world politics has been growing dramatically also.

There has been a geographical spreading of the state, from Europe outward. Two centuries ago most of the non-European world lay beyond the boundaries of any sovereign state, in the sphere of the Islamic system or of Oriental empires or of tribal societies. Today the sovereign state is established throughout the world. No doubt the multiplication of states—the United Nations began with 51 member states and now has 151—has been accompanied by an increase in heterogeneity among them. There has been a certain debasing of the currency of statehood as a consequence of the growth of ministates and microstates, and many of the non-European ones—to which Michael Oakeshott contemptuously refers as "imitation states"—are imperfectly established and unlike the originals in important respects.[4] But for the first time the sovereign state is the common political form experienced by the whole of mankind.

At the same time the role of the state in world affairs has expanded functionally. Whereas a few decades ago states in their dealings with one another confined themselves to diplomatic and strategic issues and allowed economic, social, and ideological relations among peoples to be determined for the most part by the private sector, today the state has extended its tentacles in such a way as to deprive businessmen and bankers, labor organizations and sporting teams, churches and political parties of the standing as international actors independent of state control that they once enjoyed. It has been said that the growth of transnational relations has deprived traditional interstate politics of its previous autonomy.[5] But what is rather the case is that the growth of state involvement in trade, in exchange and payments, in the control of migration, and in science and culture and international sporting events has brought an end to the autonomy of transnational relations.

It is difficult to see evidence of the decline of the sovereign state in the various movements for the regional integration of states that have developed in the post-1945 world, such as the European Economic Community, the Organization of African Unity, the Organization of American States, or the Association of South East Asian Nations. It is not merely that the EEC, which provides the most impressive example of progress toward a goal of regional integration, has not in fact undermined the sovereignty of its member states in the sense of their legal independence of external control. Nor is it merely that the very considerable achievements of the Community in promoting peace, reconciliation, prosperity, and cooperation in Western Europe have depended more upon intergovernmental cooperation than on Community institutions bypassing the constituent states. It is that the movement for European integration has been led from the beginning by the conception that the end goal of the process is the creation of a European superstate, a continental United States of Europe—a conception that only confirms the continuing vitality of "statist" premises.

Nor is there much evidence of any threat to the state as an institution in the attempts—sometimes successful, sometimes not—of nationalist separatist groups to bring about the disintegration of existing states, as in Nigeria, Pakistan, Yugoslavia, Canada, the United Kingdom, or Iraq, to name only a few. For if we ask what have been the goals of the separatist Biafrans, East Bengalis, Croats, Quebecois, Scots, or Kurds, the answer is that they have been trying to create new states. While the regional integrationists seek to reduce the number of states in the world, and the nationalist separatists seek to increase it, both are as committed as the defendants of existing states to the continuation of the state as an institution. It might be thought that a serious challenge to the position of the state lies in the tendency of Socialist and Third World states to accord rights and duties in international law to nations that are not states; and that, in particular, national liberation movements—most notably, the Palestine Liberation Organization—have achieved a degree of recognition in the United

Nations and elsewhere that in some way sounds the death knell of the state, or at all events brings to an end its claims to a privileged position among political groups in the world today. But again, what we have to notice is that the thinking both of the national liberation groups and of the states that lend support to them is confined within statist logic. What national liberation movements seek to do is to capture control of existing states (as in Eritrea or Nagaland), or to change the boundaries of states (as in Ireland). In seeking recognition of their claims in international society, the starting point of their argument is the principle that nations ought to be states, and the strongest card they have to play is that they represent nations that seek to be states.

It is not a matter for celebration that regional integrationists and nationalist disintegrationists are as unable as they appear to be to think beyond the old confines of the states-system. There are other ways in which their aspirations might be satisfied than by seeking to control sovereign states.

One may imagine, for example, that a regional integration movement, like that in the countries of the European Community, might seek to undermine the sovereignty of its member states, yet at the same time stop short of transferring this sovereignty to any regional authority. If they were to bring about a situation in which authorities existed both at the national and at the European level, but no one such authority claimed supremacy over the others in terms of superior jurisdiction or its claims on the loyalties of individual persons, the sovereign state would have been transcended. Similarly, one may imagine that if nationalist separatist groups were content to reject the sovereignty of the states to which they are at present subject, but at the same time refrained from advancing any claims to sovereign statehood themselves, some genuine innovation in the structure of the world political system might take place.

We may envisage a situation in which, say, a Scottish authority in Edinburgh, a British authority in London, and a European authority in Brussels were all actors in world politics and all enjoyed representation in world political organizations, together with rights and duties of various kinds in world law, but in which no one of them claimed sovereignty or supremacy over the others, and a person living in Glasgow had no exclusive or overriding loyalty to any one of them. Such an outcome would take us truly "beyond the sovereign state" and is by no means implausible, but it is striking how little interest has been displayed in it by either the regional integrationists or the subnationalist "disintegrationists."

In the second place, those who say that what we have to do is get "beyond the states-system" forget that war, economic injustice, and ecological mismanagement have deeper causes than those embodied in any particular form of universal political organization. The states-system we have today is indeed associated with violent conflict and insecurity, with economic and social inequality and misery on a vast scale, and with failures of every kind to live in harmony with our environment. But this is no reason to assume that a world government, a neo-medieval order of overlapping sovereignties and jurisdictions, a system of isolated or semi-isolated communities, or any other alternative global order we might imagine would not be associated with these things also. Violence, economic injustice, and disharmony between man and nature have a longer history than the modern states-system. The causes that lead to them will be operative, and our need to work against them imperative, whatever the political structure of the world.

Let us take, for example, the central "world order goal" of peace. It is true that the states-system gives rise to its own peculiar dangers of war, such as those that have been stressed by exponents of "the international anarchy" (C. Lowes Dickinson), "the great illusion" (Norman Angell), "the arms race" (Philip Noel-Baker), or "the old game, now forever discredited, of the balance of power" (Woodrow Wilson). It is true that war is endemic in the present states-system, not in the sense that it is made "inevitable" (particular wars are avoidable, and even war in general is inevitable only in the sense of being statistically probable), but in the sense that it is institutionalized, that it is a built-in feature of our arrangements and expectations. We may agree also that nuclear weapons and other advanced military technology have made this state of affairs intolerable, if it was not so before.

But the idea that if states are abolished, war will be abolished, rests simply on the verbal confusion between war in the broad sense of armed conflict between political groups and war in the narrow sense of armed conflict between sovereign states. Armed conflicts, including nuclear ones, will not be less terrible because they are conducted among groups other than states, or called police actions or civil uprisings. The causes of war lie ultimately in the existence of weapons and armed forces and the will of political groups to use them rather than accept defeat. Some forms of universal political organization may offer better prospects than others that these causes can be controlled, but none is exempt from their operation.

Of course, it is possible to imagine a world government or other alternative form of universal political organization from which war, economic injustice, and ecological mismanagement have been banished. But so is it possible to imagine a states-system so reformed that it has these utopian features: a world of separate states disciplined by the arts of peace, cooperating in the implementation of an agreed universal standard of human welfare and respectful of a globally agreed environmental code. It is a perfectly legitimate exercise to compare these different utopias and to consider whether some are more feasible than others. What is not acceptable—but what critics of the states-system commonly do—is to compare a utopian vision of a world central authority, or of whatever other alternative universal political order they favor, with the states-system, not in a utopian form but as it exists now.

In the third place, the critics neglect to take account of the positive functions that the state and the states-system have fulfilled in relation to world order in the past. The modern state—as a government supreme over a particular territory and population—has provided order on a local scale. To the extent that Europe, and at a later stage other continents, were covered by states that actually maintained their authority and were not constantly breaking down as a result of internal or external conflicts, local areas of order have been sustained by states over vast areas of the world. Most of our experience of order in modern times derives from these local areas of order established by the authority of states; and the chief meaning that we have been able to give to the concept of world order before very recent times is that it has been simply the sum of the local areas of order provided collectively by states.

States, moreover, have cooperated with one another in maintaining a structure of interstate, or international, order in which they confirm one another's domestic authority and preserve a framework of coexistence. For all the conflict and violence that have arisen out of their contact and intercourse with one another, they have formed not only an international system, but also a rudimentary international society. They have sensed common interests in preserving the framework of coexistence that limits and restrains the rivalry among them; they have evolved rules of the road that translate these common interests into specific guides to conduct; and they have cooperated in working common institutions such as international law, the diplomatic system, and the conventions of war that facilitate observance of the rules. Experts on "the international anarchy" will tell us, and rightly so, how precarious and imperfect this inherited structure of international order is, and exponents of "spaceship earth" will show how inadequate it is to meet the needs of the present time. But it does represent the form of universal political order that has actually existed in modern history, and if we are to talk of extending the scope of order in world affairs, we need first to understand the conditions under which there is any order at all. The critics of the states-system contrast it with the more perfect world order they would like to see; but the historical alternative to it was more ubiquitous violence and disorder.

We associate states with war: they have claimed, and still claim, a legal right to resort to it and to require individual citizens to wage it in their name. They dispose of most of the arms and armed forces with which it is waged, and notwithstanding the large role played in modern war by civil factions of one kind or another and by so-called barbarian powers beyond the confines of European international society, states have been the principal political groups actually engaged in war. But if we compare war among modern states with other historical violence or with future violence that we can readily enough imagine, we have to note that, with all its horrors, it has embodied a certain normative regime, without which violence has been and might be more horrible still.

Thus states when they go to war have recognized a need to provide one another and international society at large with an explanation in terms of a common doctrine of just causes of war, at the heart of which there has always been the notion that a war is just if it is fought in self-defense. No doubt there is great ambiguity and much disagreement about the meaning of this rule; other causes have been thought to be just in addition to that of self-defense. It is only in this century that limitations on the right of a state to go to war have been clearly expressed in legal terms, and the limitations are in any case observed more in the breach than in observance. Yet the conception that resort to war requires an explanation in terms of rules acknowledged on both sides is a mark of the existence at least of a rudimentary society; it imparts some element of stability to the expectations independent political communities can have about one another's behavior. Where—as in the encounter between political communities that do not belong to a common states-system or international society—war can be begun without any feeling of a need for an explanation, or the explanation felt to be necessary derives from rules accepted on one side only and not on the other—as in Europe's belief in its civilizing mission, or the Mongols' belief in the Mandate of Heaven, or in the conception of a crusade or holy war—no such element of stability can be achieved.

Modern states, moreover, wage war under the discipline of the belief that some means are legitimate in war and some are not, a belief expressed sometimes in a doctrine of morally just means in war, sometimes in a body of laws of war, sometimes simply in an unthinking acceptance of what Michael Walzer calls "the war convention."[6] At the heart of this is the notion that the soldiers or military agents of the enemy state are legitimate objects of the use of force and that others are not. On the one hand, this notion sanctifies a particular kind of killing and maiming, breaking down the ordinary civil prohibition of taking life and causing physical injury; on the other hand, it establishes boundaries between the kinds of killing and injury that are part of war and the kinds that are not. On the basis of these boundaries, states have built up rules to limit the force they employ against one another, to distinguish belligerents and neutrals and thus contain the spread of conflict, and to uphold standards of humanity and protect the innocent. Of course, it is not only in the special case of war in the strict sense, war between states, that war takes place in a normative framework: such a framework sometimes surrounded the armed conflicts of primitive, feudal, and oriental societies also. But in modern times there has been a sophisticated body of rules that are held to apply to war between states but not to armed conflicts in which one or both parties is a nonstate group, such as a civil faction or a "barbarian" power. These rules for the conduct of war are notoriously prone to be disregarded, and in the twentieth century they have been subject to special strain, but they are part of the heritage that has been bequeathed to us by the states-system.

More important even than the conceptions of legitimate ends and of legitimate means in war has been the notion that war to be legitimate must be begun, as Aquinas put it, on the proper authority. Cardinal to the distinction between war and mere brigandage or private killing is the idea that the former is waged by the agents of a public authority, which is recognized to be entitled to resort to force against its adversaries, and signifies that it has done so by issuing a declaration of war or in some other way. In the modern states-system it has been held that states alone have this authority: deeply divided though they have been, states have usually been united in maintaining that they are entitled to a monopoly of the legitimate use of force, both domestically and across state frontiers. Of course, they have not always been successful in preserving their monopoly, which has been broken from time to time by civil factions, by "barbarian" powers, and by pirates. States also experience difficulty in maintaining a united front on the issue: the Socialist and Third World countries at present, for example, uphold the right of national liberation groups to resort to force internationally, and in the Second World War both the Western powers and the

Soviet Union supported partisan groups in their struggle against Germany. Nevertheless, the idea that the right to engage in war should be confined to certain public authorities and should not be generally available to self-appointed political groups of all kinds is one of the most vital barriers we have against anarchy, and the modern states-system has passed on to us a rule embodying this idea that has proved workable.

At present, of course, the state's monopoly of the legitimate use of force is under some challenge, especially from national liberation groups. This is not new or unusual, and the challenge is mitigated to the extent that these groups are themselves would-be states whose claims to legitimacy and recognition rest in large measure upon the belief of their supporters that they should be states. Neither national liberation groups themselves nor their supporters in the Socialist countries and the Third World (they enjoy in some cases considerable support in the West also) put forward any general attack upon the state's monopoly position or advocate a wide or indiscriminate license to resort to force. We do, however, find that some Western critics of the states-system put forward a general attack on the state's monopoly position, as if the attempt of states to confine to themselves the right to use force were some unwarranted attempt to cling to an unfair privilege, to be opposed in the same spirit in which men opposed the Big Trusts or the propertied franchise. We are told that the "elite claims" of states are inappropriate now that there is "a rich diversity of authorized participants in the processes on international law."[7] The suggestion seems to be that "a rich diversity" of actors in world politics should be entitled to maintain "private armies" and go to war to support their demands, so long as these demands measure up to certain policy criteria ("world order with human dignity") drawn up in New Haven or elsewhere.

This kind of talk is not only dangerous in an era of frequent resort to force by small armed groups with no claims to representative status of any kind, and widespread availability of destructive weapons; it is also shallow in overlooking the difference between a modern state, endowed with authority as well as mere power and exercising rights to the use of force recognized by the domestic and international legal order, and a mere political cabal or party that has chosen to turn itself into an armed band. No doubt there are illegitimate governments and insurgent or vigilante groups with just causes. But in the absence of authority to resort to force across international boundaries, possession of a just cause should be regarded as totally irrelevant. International society does not maintain that groups within a state have no right of revolution against an illegitimate government. It does, however, seek to protect itself against the use of force by civil factions across state boundaries. The convention we have restricting the use of force across international boundaries to states accomplishes this. The rule confining the right to the international use of force to states is readily recognizable and widely accepted, even if it is sometimes violated. A rule that confers this right upon any political group with a cause we regard as just is one that imposes no barrier at all.

We associate states not only with war but also with sovereignty—which in internal affairs connotes supremacy, the supreme jurisdiction of the state over citizens and territory, and in external affairs connotes independence, freedom from external control. The claims of the state to a right of external sovereignty or independence are sometimes taken to imply rejection of all moral or legal authority other than that of the state, and indeed such claims have sometimes been put forward in its name. When they are (as by Hegel or Treitschke), they are a menace to internal order. A state's rights to sovereignty, however, are not asserted against the international legal order but conferred by it (from which it follows that they can be qualified by it, and even taken away). A state's right to sovereignty or independence is not a "natural right," analogous to the rights of individuals in Locke's state of nature: it is a right enjoyed to the extent that it is recognized to exist by other states. So far from it being the case that the sovereignty of the state is something antithetical to international order, it is the foundation of the whole edifice.

The order provided by the states-system, founded upon the exchange of recognition of sovereignty, is rightly said to be inferior to that provided within a properly functioning modern state. Within the states-system there is still no authoritative legislature, empowered to make laws, amend and rescind them in accordance with the will of the community; no independent judicial authority to which the impartial interpretation and application of the laws is entrusted; no central authority commanding a monopoly of force to ensure that the law will prevail. It is this perception of the contrast between the more perfect order enjoyed by individual persons in domestic political systems and the less perfect order enjoyed by states in international society that provides the impulse behind the desire to create a central world authority that will reproduce the conditions of domestic society on a universal scale. The states-system does, however, provide an imperfect and rudimentary form of order that holds anarchy at bay. It provides external support to the internal order created by states in areas where their writs run. And it maintains among states a regime of mutual tolerance and forbearance that limits conflict, sustains intercourse, and provides the conditions in which cooperation can grow.

The case for the states-system as it has operated in the past is that it is the form of universal political organization most able to provide minimum order in a political society in which there is not a consensus broad enough to sustain acceptance of a common government, but in which there is a consensus that can sustain the coexistence of a plurality of separate governments. When independent political communities have little or no intercourse with one another—as between European communities and pre-Columbian American communities, or between the former and China before the nineteenth century—a states-system is not necessary. Where such intercourse exists but consists of almost unmitigated hostility, as between Europe and Islam during much of the history of their encounter, a states-system is not possible. But in relation to European political society from, say, the sixteenth to the early twentieth centuries, a strong argument was put forward to the effect that the attempt to create strong central authorities, or to restore and develop the central authorities that had existed in the past, would lead only to division and disorder; whereas there could be fashioned—out of the surviving rules and practices inherited from

Christendom and the new body of precedent emerging from the experience of secular Europe—a decentralized form of interstate society. The question now is how far this argument is still valid in relation to the decentralized interstate society of today, now expanded to encompass the whole globe and inevitably diluted and modified in the process.

Today, order in world affairs still depends vitally upon the positive role of the state. It is true that the framework of mere coexistence, of what is sometimes called "minimum world order," inherited from the European states-system, is no longer by itself adequate. The involvement of states in economic, social, cultural, and communications matters has led us to judge the international political system by standards which it would not have occurred to a nineteenth century European to apply. We now expect the states-system not only to enable independent political communities to coexist, but also to facilitate the management of the world economy, the eradication of poverty, the promotion of racial equality and women's rights, the raising of literacy and labor standards, and so on. All of this points to a universal political system that can promote "optimum world order," a system that can sustain not only coexistence but cooperation in the pursuit of a vast array of shared goals.

If one believed that states were inherently incapable of cooperation with one another and were condemned—as on the Hobbesian theory—to exist permanently in a state of war, there would be no escape from the conclusion that the requirements of world order in our time and the continued existence of states are in contradiction of one another. In fact, states can and do cooperate with one another both on a regional and on a global basis. So far is it from being the case that states are antithetical to the need that we recognize to inculcate a greater sense of unity in human society, that it is upon the states-system that our hopes for the latter, at least in the short run, must principally depend. It is the system of states that is at present the only political expression of the unity of mankind, and it is to cooperation among states, in the United Nations and elsewhere, that we have chiefly to look if we are to preserve such sense of common human interests as there may be, to extend it, and to translate it into concrete actions. We do not live in a world in which states are prepared to act as agents of the international community, taking their instructions from the UN or some such body; but we do have to restore the element of consensus among states, without which appeals for a sense of "spaceship earth" are voices crying in the wilderness.

In the fourth place, there is no consensus in the world behind the program of Western solidarists or global centralists for "transcending the states-system." In the Socialist countries and among the countries of the Third World there is no echo of these views. From the perspective of the two weaker sections of the world political system, the globalist doctrine is the ideology of the dominant Western powers. The barriers of state sovereignty that are to be swept away, they suspect, are the barriers that they, the weaker countries, have set up against Western penetration: the barriers that protect Socialist countries from capitalism and Third World countries from imperialism. The outlook of the Western globalist does indeed express, among other things, an exuberant desire to reshape the world that is born of confidence that the economic and technological power to accomplish it lies at hand. One senses in it a feeling of impatience that the political and legal obstacles ("ethnocentric nationalism," "the absurd political architecture of the world," "the obsolete doctrine of state sovereignty") cannot be brushed aside. It is also notable that the prescriptions they put forward for restructuring the world, high-minded though they are, derive wholly from the liberal, social-democratic, and internationalist traditions of the West, and take no account of the values entertained in other parts of the world, with which compromises may have to be reached.

For the Soviet Union and other Socialist countries the state is not an obstacle to peace but the bulwark of security against the imperialist aggressors; not an obstacle to economic justice but the instrument of proletarian dictatorship that has brought such justice about; not a barrier to the solution of environmental problems, for these exist only in capitalist countries. It is true that the Socialist countries are heirs to a profoundly antistatist ideology. Classical Marxism looks forward to the withering away of the state and hence of the states-system, while also (although the point is less clear) treating the nation as a transitory phenomenon; it is neither interstate nor international but class struggle that provides the main theme of world history. But the outlook of the Socialist countries is shaped less by ideology than by practical interest: finding themselves a minority bloc of states in a world dominated by the military power, the industrial, commercial, and managerial enterprise, and the scientific and technological excellence of the capitalist countries, they have had a greater need than the West to avail themselves of the rights of states to sovereignty, equality, and noninterference. In a period when Western leaders have talked of expanding the role of the United Nations, of accepting the implications of increased international "interdependence," or of the need for a unified, global approach to the environment, the Soviet Union has seemed to stand for a dogged defense of the entrenched legal rights of sovereign states. Of course, where the entrenched legal rights in question have been those of colonialist or white supremacist states, the Soviet Union had been willing enough to attack them. So also the Soviet Union was willing to proclaim the subordination of the sovereignty of Socialist states to the higher law of "proletarian internationalism" in intervening against Czechoslovakia in 1968. But in responding to the aggressive challenge of American globalism—as in rejecting the Baruch Plan in the 1940s or the UN's Korean action in the 1950s or the Congo action in the 1960s, the Soviet Union and its Socialist allies have adopted a conservatively statist position.

Among the Third World countries the idea that we must all now bend our efforts to get "beyond the state" is so alien to recent experience as to be almost unintelligible. Because they did not have states that were strong enough to withstand European or Western aggression, the African, Asian, and Oceanic peoples, as they see it, were subject to domination, exploration, and humiliation. It is by gaining control of states that they have been able to take charge of their own destiny. It is by the use of state power, by claiming the rights due to them as states, that they have been able to resist foreign military interference, to protect their economic interests by excluding or controlling multinational corporations, expropriating foreign assets, planning the development of their economies, and bargaining to improve the terms of trade. It is by insisting upon their privileges of sovereignty that they are able to defend their newly won independence against the foreign tutelage implicit in such phrases as "basic human needs," "the international protection of human rights," or (more sinister still) "humanitarian intervention."

Of course Third World countries have not displayed the same solicitude about the sovereign rights of Western countries with which they have been in conflict that they have shown for their own. Like the Socialist countries, they have been strong champions of interference in the domestic affairs of colonialist and white supremacist states, which they have seen not as interference but as assistance to peoples who are victims of aggression. While they insist on the right of developing states to have wealth and resources transferred to them, it is the *duty* of the advanced countries to transfer these resources that they are insistent upon, rather than any corresponding rights—as emerges from the Charter of Economic Rights and Duties of States, which the UN General Assembly endorsed in 1974.

In the controversy over establishment of an International Seabed Authority controlled by the developing countries—where it is the advanced countries whose deepsea mining operations will be subject to the Authority's control, and the developing countries that will gain from distribution of the rewards—the Third World countries are the champions of subordinating sovereignty to a common effort to preserve "the common heritage of mankind."

Finally, those in the West who disparage the states-system underestimate the special interests the Western countries themselves have in its preservation and development. We have noted that distrust of the state and the states-system appears to flourish especially in Western societies. A number of factors account for this. The liberal or individualist political tradition, so much more deeply rooted in the West than elsewhere, has always insisted that the rights of states are subordinate to those of the human beings that compose them. Loyalties that compete with loyalty to the state—allegiances to class or ethnic group or race or religious sect—can be openly proclaimed and cultivated in Western societies and often cannot be elsewhere. Moreover, it is only in the West that it has been possible to assume that if the barriers separating states were abolished, it would be our way of life and not some other that would be universally enthroned.

It is the last point that is the crucial one. We in the West have not had—to the same degree as the Socialist countries and the Third World—a sense of dependence on the structure of the states-system. We assume that if the division of the world into separate states were to come to an end, and a global economy, society, and polity were allowed to grow up, it would be our economies, our ways of doing things, our social customs and ideas and conceptions of human rights, the forces of modernization that we represent, that would prevail. On the one hand, we have not had the feeling of vulnerability to "nonstate actors" shaping us from outside that Socialist countries have about Western libertarian ideas, or that developing countries have about Western-based multinational corporations, or that Islamic countries have about atheistic materialism. On the other hand, we have believed that our impact on the rest of the world does not depend merely on the exercise of state power. Our ways of doing things attract the peoples of Socialist countries even without efforts by our governments to promote them, and the withdrawal of Western governors, garrisons, and gunboats from the Third World countries has not brought the processes of Westernization at work in these countries to an end. Socialist and Third World states have sought to combat our influence—by withdrawing from the international economy, by excluding or controlling foreign investment, by building walls around their frontiers, by suppressing the flow of ideas—and the designs of Western globalists or "one-worlders," as we have noted, are designs to remove these obstacles. But Socialist and Third World states are in part in league with us. For while Socialist states seek to remain untainted by capitalism, Third World states to be free of imperialism, and both to diminish the West's dominant power, both are also seeking to become more modern; and because they cannot fail to recognize in the societies of North America, Western Europe, and Japan specimens of modernity more perfect than themselves, are compelled to imitate and to borrow. In Western attitudes toward the rest of the world there is still the belief, more deep-seated perhaps than that of the heirs of Marx and Lenin who rule the Soviet Union today, that the triumph of our own ways is historically inevitable.

There is some question whether this belief is well-founded. In the 1970s there has occurred a shift of power against the West and toward the Soviet Union and certain of the Third World countries. It has become more apparent that the revolt against Western tutelage that has played so large a part in the history of this century is a revolt not only against Western power and privilege, but also in large measure against Western values and institutions. Although the evidence is contradictory (consider, for example, the contrary cases at the present time of China and Iran) and we cannot now foresee what the outcome of the process will be, there are many signs in the extra-Western world of a conscious rejection of Western ways, not merely of capitalism and liberal democracy but even of modernity itself. In many parts of the world there is under way an attempt to revert to indigenous traditions, to restore institutions to the condition in which they were before they became contaminated by contact with the West, or at least to create the illusion that they have been restored. Just as the Western powers for more than a decade have found themselves a beleaguered minority in the United Nations, so they are coming to see themselves as forming a redoubt in a hostile world. There is a new attitude of defensiveness, even of belligerence, in Western attitudes toward the Soviet Union; and the countries of the Third World, until recently regarded as weak and dependent states in need of our help, are increasingly viewed as alien, hostile, and in some cases powerful and competitive states against which we need to defend ourselves.

At all events, the preservation of world order is not a matter of removing state barriers to the triumph of our own preferred values and institutions, but rather a matter of finding some *modus vivendi* as between these and the very different values and institutions in other parts of the world with which they will have to coexist. In thinking about world order it is wrong to begin, as the critics of the states-system do, by elaborating "goals" or "relevant Utopias" and drawing up plans for reaching them. This is how the "policy-scientist's" mind works but it is not what happens in world politics. It is better to begin with the elements of world order that actually exist, and consider how they might be cultivated. This must lead us to the state and the states-system, without which there would not be any order at all.

NOTES

1. See, for example, Miriam Camps, *"First World Relationships": The Role of the OECD* (Paris: Atlantic Institute for International Affairs; New York: Council on Foreign Relations, 1975) and Joseph Nye and Robert Keohane, *Transnational Relations and World Politics* (Cambridge, Mass.: Harvard University Press, 1972). Also Richard A. Falk, *This Endangered Planet* (New York: Random House, 1971), and *A Study of Future Worlds* (New York: Free Press, 1975).

2. See especially Nye and Keohane, *Transnational Relations.*

3. See, for example, Richard W. Mansbach, Yale H. Ferguson, and Donald E. Lamport, *The Web of World Politics. Non-state Actors in the Global System* (Englewood Cliffs, N.J.: Prentice-Hall Inc., 1976).

4. Michael Oakeshott, *On Human Conduct* (New York: Oxford University Press, 1975).

5. Nye and Keohane, *Transnational Relations*, Introduction.

6. Michael Walzer, *Just and Unjust Wars. An Argument with Historical Illustrations* (New York: Basic Books, 1977).

7. Michael Reisman, "Private Armies in a Global War System," in *Law and Civil War in the Modern World*, John Norton Moore (ed.) (Baltimore: Johns Hopkins University Press, 1974), p. 257.

8
THE NEO-FASCIST STATE:
NOTES ON THE PATHOLOGY OF POWER
IN THE THIRD WORLD

Eqbal Ahmad

Through the 1960s and 1970s, while our attention was focused on the Indo-Chinese war, there was occurring in the Third World an ominous development. These two decades witnessed the emergence and/or maturing of regimes which one may describe, for lack of a better term, as neo-fascism or perhaps developmental fascism. Some of these countries—for example South Korea, Iran, and Nicaragua—were already in the 1950s authoritarian states, whose survival required widespread repression of political opposition and social institutions—such as religious, educational and professional associations, and labour and peasant organizations—outside state control. The 1960s and 1970s witnessed the hardening of the authoritarian arteries of these states, the systematization of terror, the 'modernization' and 'rationalization' of their repressive institutions. Other states—for example Brazil, Indonesia, Greece, the Philippines, Uganda, Zaire, Uruguay, and Chile—changed in the mid-1960s and early 1970s from being democratic, proto-democratic, or radical authoritarian regimes to becoming militarist states. In the second half of the 1970s the ranks of these states continued to be swelled: Argentina and Thailand were among the new members. However, with the possible exception of Brazil, none of these states had consolidated their tyrannies; that is, they had not acquired the economic wherewithal to sustain themselves without continued external support, and they had not forged meaningful political links with significant sectors of the civil society.

At the same time the second half of the 1970s revealed, first in Greece, then in Iran and Nicaragua, these neo-fascist regimes to be extremely vulnerable and brittle; when faced with a major challenge they collapsed totally and with a speed which surprised most observers. This paper attempts to summarize (1) the characteristics of this type of regime in the Third World; (2) the roots of neo-fascism; and (3) the vulnerability of these regimes and the sources of resistance to them.

Reprinted by the author's permission from *IFDA Dossier* 19, September–October 1980. Copyright © 1980 by the author.

GENERAL CHARACTERISTICS OF NEO-FASCIST STATES

Some variations among them notwithstanding, the following are the common characteristics of the neo-fascist state:

A fundamental shift in the use of organized terror: They are by far the most blatant contemporary violators of human rights in both substantive and procedural matters. Most of them have developed highly sophisticated and complex machineries of repression. They are ever experimenting with new methods of terrorizing the people and eliminating their opposition while reducing the "visibility" of their excesses. Increasingly, people are tortured in "safe houses," in civilian quarters rather than identifiable prisons or concentration camps. Actual and potential dissenters disappear more often than they are imprisoned. The lucky prisoner who, because of international pressures on his behalf, gets released from captivity often becomes unusually and fatally accident-prone. Thus in 1976-77 there were in Argentina some 8,500 members of the opposition and independent bodies such as labour unions who were officially acknowledged to be missing; officially too 600 were killed and 15 wounded in "combat." Amnesty International, on the other hand, established some 15,000 persons to have disappeared; 8,000 to 10,000 were in known, official prisons, that is, the figure did not "include the secret detention camps." Argentinians and foreign journalists widely believed that some 15,000 people had been killed between the *coup d'état* of March 1976 and early 1978. Similar figures—and discrepancies between official and independent body-counts—can be cited for the other countries in this category. The scales of violence exercise credulity. Some 350,000 people are established to have gone through the torture chambers of the Shah of Iran. An estimated 500,000 to one million alleged communists were killed in Indonesia after the coup of 1965; 750,000 people were arrested by official count; of these it is doubtful that few if any were brought to trial, and Amnesty International did not find a single case of acquittal. Martin Ennals, the head of Amnesty International, reported that "about 30,000 people have disappeared in the last ten years in Latin America after being seized by official security forces or their sympathizers."[1]

What is striking about these gruesome violations of human rights is not only the increase in their scale but a qualitative shift in their administration and purpose. As Amnesty International's *Report on Torture* of 1974 put it, "there is a marked difference between traditional brutality stemming from historical conditions, and the systematic torture which has spread to many Latin American countries within the past decade." More importantly, the purpose of governmental coercion appears to have shifted from punishment to prevention. For example, torture is increasingly administered not so much to obtain information or punish a member of the opposition but literally to discourage people from linking with each other politically and socially; its purpose is to prevent a political process and the formation of relationships among people.

There is an historical irony to the emergence of these regimes; it occurred in a period when elsewhere in the world the margins of procedural freedoms and of substantive human rights had started to widen. In Spain and Portugal, for example, the fascist states had begun since the early 1960s to experience a process of liberalization, and by the mid-1970s they had changed into social democratic polities. Since the start of de-Stalinization in Eastern Europe and the Soviet Union, too, the margins of procedural freedom had been widening significantly—although not enough to warrant satisfaction. For example, the 1974 Amnesty International *Report on Torture* noted that "although prison conditions and the rights of the prisoners detained on political charges in Eastern Europe and the Soviet Union may still be in many cases unsatisfactory, torture as a government-sanctioned, Stalinist practice, has ceased." By contrast, the same report noted that torture had "shown phenomenal growth in Latin America"; it explained further that "institutional violence and high incidence of political assassinations has tended to overshadow the problem of torture."

It is noteworthy also that the neo-fascist states mark a qualitative as well as a quantitative shift towards the worse in the area of human rights. Violations of human rights had been occurring—and still occur—in other Third World systems of power.[2]

Yet in these other countries the practice of terror is neither as systematized nor as wide-spread, nor does repression constitute the mainstay of the regime. Furthermore, in some of those states (e.g., in the radical authoritarian, and the Marxist-socialist systems) the margins of substantive freedoms (e.g., improvement of health, education and nutrition) have widened for the population at large; hence these regimes enjoy a measure of legitimacy which correspondingly diminishes the need for repression. Similarly the regimes that belong in the ascriptive-palace or the pragmatic-authoritarian systems enjoy a measure of ascriptive and/or historical legitimacy, and a lingering traditional style of government and conflict resolution. They too violate human rights, sometimes excessively, but repression has not quite become the mainstay of these regimes. By contrast, the neo-fascist states command, at best, the support of a microscopic, generally praetorian, minority. As such, they enjoy no title to authority and must depend on organized state terror as the primary means of staying in power.

Fascism and neo-fascism: The neo-fascist state shares several characteristics with conventional fascism as witnessed in Europe in the 1920s and 1930s. These include: a repressive terrorist state apparatus; state control over the economy and labour; and its origins in petit bourgeois and propertied classes. But it differs from the classic model in many ways: unlike conventional fascism, the neo-fascist state in the Third World evinces but little ideological nationalism. To the contrary, it appears largely as a product of dependence and is sustained by its symbiotic relationship to the external metropolis. Unlike Nazism, neo-fascism is not anti-semitic; the only exception is Argentina where the junta's pronouncements were explicitly anti-semitic during its most brutal years. To the contrary, almost all the neo-fascist states, including Argentina, maintain close links to Israel—a phenomenon which underlines their common links with imperialism and the United States. Neo-fascist states are remarkable also for their inability to produce the "charismatic leader" capable of achieving any degree of mass mobilization, or of invoking popular support. Further more, while the neo-fascist state exercises totalitarian powers, unlike the historical fascist system, it is unable to perform the political functions of aggregation, communication, and socialization. Above all, unlike Germany and Japan—where low wages, combined with restraint on consumption, produced high rates of gross national investment and industrialization—the economies of the neofascist states are based primarily on extraction, and are characterized by growing dependence on the multi-national corporations. As such, these states are not the instruments of "modernization" which liberal social scientists often describe them to be. It is true that they produce a measure of uneven industrialization; but at the same time they dislocate and disinherit the majority rural population, lower the living standards of the working classes, mortgage the country's future to foreign investors and debtors, and generally produce economic ruin. Iran under the Shah, Brazil since 1964, and Indonesia since 1965 are examples.

Ideological base of the neo-fascist state: While the neo-fascist state lacks a consistent and pronounced ideology, its origins lie in, and its existence is defined by, a pervasive ideological environment which favours the national security state. The doctrine of national security has its roots in the ideas, institutions and policies associated with the Cold War. Ironically, it is nourished at the same time by the seemingly opposing heritage of modern nationalism and colonialism. It views the state as absolute, the individual as unimportant. It emphasizes a continual war between communism and freedom, stability and subversion, national security and anarchy. Instead of seeking mass manipulation and public control through political institutions such as parties, youth and labour organizations, it posits the armed forces to be, as Nelson Rockefeller put it, "a major force for constructive social change." Next to the armed forces, secret police organizations—SAVAK, DINA, KCIA, etc.—permeate the society. Their highest officials rank among the country's most powerful men.

The ideological underpinnings of these states lie in the ideas and institutions associated with the Cold War. What A. J. Langguth says of Latin America holds true of practically every neo-fascist state:

> The main exporter of Cold-War ideas, the principal source of the belief that dissent must be crushed by every means and by any means, has been the United States. Our indoctrination of foreign troops provided a justification for torture in the jail cells of Latin America. First in the Inter-American Police Academy in Panama, then at the more ambitious International Police Academy in Washington, foreign policemen were taught that in the war against international communism they were the "first line of defense." The US training turned already conservative men into reactionaries.[3]

Predominant among the leaders of the neo-fascist system are military officers who have been trained in the counterinsurgency academies and programmes run by the United States Government: Generals Papadopoulous of Greece, Pinochet and Leigh of Chile, Geisel of Brazil, Massera of Argentina, Zia ul Haq of Pakistan, are among the many examples. These training programmes invariably steeped the officers under training in the anti-communist dogma that subversives and infiltrators could be anywhere, and these latter undermine national security in a variety of ways, through student protest, labour strikes, and peasant demands. Deep fear of and hostility to populist movements and expressions of popular demands are, therefore, basic to the national security outlook.[4] The concept of national security, then, completely transcends military considerations; it is enmeshed with political, economic and social issues, and constitutes the basis for the armed forces' broad, all-pervasive mission. Furthermore, there exists a negative correlation between the perceived security problems of a country and its actual power and privileges on an international scale, to wit: the more powerful and the richer the state, the less secure it is believed to be by the ruling élite.

A *"model" of development:* Closely related to the idea of national security are the ideologically rigged notions of "development" and "modernization." Typically, the neo-fascist state is deeply committed to economic development; this is the reason for suggesting at the beginning of this essay that alternatively we might describe this system as "developmental fascism." It views "development" in terms of rates of growth. "Growth" involves the concentration of wealth and of power, for both are necessary to the required rate of capital formation. Thus, profit equals investment equals growth equals power. The preferred development model favours return to the "free market." But the return is always selective; it does not involve curtailment of monopoly power or of untrammeled investment incentives, but it does entail strict controls over wages, labour unions, and prohibition of strikes. A cheap labour force is offered as a primary incentive to capital; the internal market does not expand except for luxury goods. The economy becomes increasingly export-oriented; raw materials, including fancy food products, become the primary export items.[5] Income inequality multiplies. Any resistance to corporate and foreign interests is treated *ipso facto* as a police problem; anyone questioning this model of development is viewed as a subversive, a terrorist.

Hunger stalks the impoverished people while Western economic experts and institutions extol the "economic miracles" of their allies and clients. Thus a decade after coming to power the government of Suharto had turned Indonesia, formerly self-sustaining in rice, into the worlds' number one rice importer; and famine broke out only a few miles from Jakarta, the capital. Similarly, in Brazil the real incomes of the lowest 80 percent of the Brazilian population had dropped steadily during the decade following the *coup d'état* of 1964, despite "the tripling of the GNP to $80 billion."[6] In May 1973, eighteen Catholic Bishops of north-east Brazil issued a heart-rending statement which informed, among other things, that "hunger in the north-east has taken on the characteristics of an epidemic"; the statement noted that infants (that is, the half who survived mortality before age five) and children were the primary victims of malnutrition which had contributed to an alarming rate of feeblemindedness among those who lived.[7] Social services seriously declined while prestige projects—such as communications satellites and domestic communications networks, to which Indonesia allocated $840 million in 1978 alone—are added on to the benefit of foreign contractors and native contractors. Poor peasants are hurt or wiped out by agribusiness and large landed proprietors. State monopolies provide fiefdoms for the powerful; in every neo-fascist state a dozen or so family names become hated household words signifying the corruption, the callousness, and the brutality of the system. If there exists in a country an excludable minority people (e.g., Amazon Indians, Baluchis, the Aches, Timouris, etc.) the regime follows a policy of dispossession, and even genocide.[8] These realities add up to a sordid picture of substantive denials and violations of human rights, in comparison to which the better publicized procedural violations appear insignificant.

Symbiotic external ties: Almost without exception these regimes began as clients of the United States and, with the exception of Uganda and Ethiopia, remain tied to the Western metropolis economically, strategically, and psychologically. The largest and the richest of them (e.g., Iran, Brazil, Indonesia, South Korea) were among the Nixon/Kissinger doctrine's original choices for leading the regional constellations of pro-Western power—a strategy and preference which remained, with minor adjustments, United States policy under the Carter administration. They are also the objects of corporate concentration as "export-platform countries" of the Third World. They are attractive to American policy makers and international corporations for obvious reasons. Their strategic locations and natural resources are highly valued. More to the point is the fact that these economic-growth seeking tyrannies tend to be extremely hospitable to foreign capital. The denial of distributive justice under these regimes secures a high rate of profit. Their repressiveness assures stable, low wages for a quiescent labour force. By enriching a small but highly consumptive indigenous bourgeoisie, they provide lucrative markets for Western consumer products as well as the transfer of "excess capital" to the financial institutions of the West.

There exists, then, as Noam Chomsky and Edward Herman have pointed out, a "systematic positive relationship between United States aid and human rights violations." Using ten selected countries as examples, Chomsky and Herman show a remarkable correlation in this regard. A typical example is Brazil, where "overall aid and credits by the United States and multinational lending organizations went up 112 percent . . . in the three years following the coup (1964) as compared with the three years preceding the coup." From the ten examples they rightly conclude that "for most of the sample countries United States-controlled aid has been positively related to investment climate and inversely related to maintenance of a democratic order and human rights."[9] Similarly, Michael Klare has shown that during 1973-78 the ten worst violators at the top of the lists of such human rights organizations as Amnesty International were the primary recipients of US economic and military aid. During this period they received economic aid of over $2 billion, and military aid and credits of $2.3 billion; they were sold armaments in excess of $18 billion, and

12,723 military officers from these countries had been trained in American schools and programmes. In his well-documented study, Klare concluded that the United States stood "at the supply end of the pipeline of repressive technology."[10]

THE ROOTS OF NEO-FASCISM

The roots of neo-fascism can be understood by reference to the following basic points.

First, almost all the neo-fascist states have succeeded populist and reformist governments, most of them belonging in the radical authoritarian category discussed in an earlier paper.[11] The emergence of the neo-fascist regimes was premised on the nature of the post-colonial state, its symbiotic relationship to the national bourgeoisie which was predominantly a state bourgeoisie, and the expansion of this bourgeoisie under populist and reformist slogans. In the previous paper I argued that:

1. The contemporary Third World state was a colonial creation designed to serve the imperial metropolis. In it the process of modern state formation was reversed: far from being the creation of an ascendant national bourgeoisie, the colonially-created state gave birth to a native class of civil servants and soldiers—the national bourgeoisie. From the beginning the development of the modern state in the Third World involved the imposition of a well-developed military bureaucratic superstructure of power over an under-developed infrastructure of participation.

2. After formal decolonization the less developed civic political class tended to be overthrown or bypassed by the state bourgeoisie when it became an impediment to oligarchic growth, and/or sought the reinforcement of popular institutions and the exercise of popular power.

3. The overthrow of the civic, generally parliamentary, system was effected by the state-related power elite which legitimized itself on the basis of populist, reformist and nationalist slogans. Yet it was in the nature of these regimes that they should vastly expand the powers and the membership of their class (state employees) without being able to improve the welfare of the masses. Ultimately, it had to face a disillusioned and expectant mass. And when that moment of truth arrived, the most powerful and privileged group within that class carried out the proto-fascist "counterrevolution."

Hence, in almost all cases, the neo-fascist system emerged in reaction to organized popular demands for fundamental economic and social change. In Iran, Guatemala, Brazil, the Dominican Republic, Chile, Zaire, and Indonesia, for example, the counterrevolutionary *coup d'état* occurred at a time when popular discontent was becoming vocal and visible. These coups also followed a trend towards the institution of desired reforms concerning taxes, profit repatriation, and nationalization of national resources—steps taken in response to popular pressures. In some cases the praetorian reaction occurred after expressions of institutional threats against international vested interests. For example, the 1972 *coup d'état* in the Philippines followed the Supreme Court's ruling against foreign ownership of land; the Brazilian coup of 1964 coincided with a major dispute over mineral concessions to the Hanna Mining Company; the nationalization of Iranian oil in 1953 was followed by the overthrow of Mohamed Mossadegh; and, of course, the story of Allende's Chile is well known.

It is noteworthy that the neo-fascist system has emerged in societies which have developed a measure of economic stratification and class consciousness. The initial move of the praetorian putschists was often successful because it was able to rally the forces of order—particularly among the petite bourgeoisie, the conservative landed and the foreign corporate sectors—against the working class, peasants, and their progressive political allies. In this respect the neo-fascist states bear some resemblance to European fascism. Yet its differences with European fascism are more significant: the Third World non-state bourgeoisie which initially supports the praetorian reaction is more commercial than industrial, more comprador than indigenous, and thus different in character from its European counterpart. Similarly the state bourgeoisie is somewhat more autonomous of the civil society because it is linked with and sustained by the foreign metropolis; as such, it is less dependent on the civil society and has fewer incentives to maintain meaningful links with any part of it; and in fact tends ultimately to lose its erstwhile allies. At the same time, in conjunction with foreign corporations, it exercises greater control over the nation's economic resources. Thus it becomes easily and completely isolated from the civil society while it becomes symbiotically linked and identified with foreign vested interests.

The ascension of the neo-facsist system then does not involve the reestablishment of the power of a pre-colonial, indigenous class which, under colonialism, was either destroyed or weakened and reduced to a peripheral status. Nor does it mean the accession to power of an indigenous entrepreneurial class, for the dependent and underdeveloped economy remains dominated by the metropolis and subject to continued penetration by the transnational corporations. The advent of neo-fascism entails merely an enlargement of the colonial, national-security bourgeoisie whose power was based on its control over the modern state, and its managerial and military skills. In other words, the social roots of the neo-fascist states are quite different from those of European fascism. To the contrary, it is correct to say that European fascism was produced by severe limitations on colonial expansion while the neo-fascist of the Third World is a product of colonialism and neo-colonialism.

RESISTANCE AND INSTABILITY

In the United States and Europe the neo-fascist state was generally viewed as promising stability in an unstable Third World. By the end of the 1970s this myth of stability had exploded. During the Greco-Turkish war over Cyprus the remarkably quick collapse of the US-supported Greek junta should have led to a closer examination of the extreme vulnerabilities of these regimes. But the event was ignored and no examination of the assumed stability of these regimes was undertaken until after the Shah went down in Iran. The Nicaraguan revolution followed closely on the heels of Iran; the regimes in South Korea and El Salvador are badly shaken. A more detailed analysis underlying the weaknesses of these regimes is needed; here we briefly mention the possible lines of inquiry.

First, the neo-fascist state, more than any other in the Third World, is characterized by what A. Sivanandan has aptly described as "disorganic development." The economic model which it follows superimposes on a Third World country a capitalist economy "unaccompanied by capitalist culture or capitalist democracy." The result is an economic system "at odds with the cultural and political institutions of the people it exploits," a system "not mediated by culture or legitimated by politics."[12] Political power and civil society, far from complementing and linking with each other, exist in a relationship of fundamental conflict. Since political institutions are severely repressed, culture and religion provide the strongest expressions of resistance. Hence the revolutions that emerge in such societies, as in Iran, are not necessarily class-oriented revolutions. They are mass movements that cut across class lines, and contain within them elements of cultural and religious affirmations.

Secondly, the apparatus of the state in the neo-fascist system grows more rapidly than the society's capability to sustain it. Since the superstructure of the state bears little logical, much less organic, relationship to the infrastructure of the society, it has no capacity to serve society's needs, accommodate its demands, or even keep pace with the changes within it. It was thus that the Pahlavi state became too heavy and dry a burden for the Iranian people to carry; hence Khomeini's call for overturning it obtained a national consensus quite unparalleled in history.

Thirdly, the specific contradictions of the neo-fascist model of development should be noted:

1. Being highly centralized and involving the state as the link between foreign corporations and a microscopic local elite, it focuses mass discontent on the state and the governing elite.
2. The economic model which favours collaboration of state and international capital relegates the local business class to a secondary position in times of expansion; it produces their socio-economic deterioration in periods of economic downturn. Thus the increasingly marginalized indigenous business class joins in the forefront of the opposition's demand for democracy—a phenomenon observable both in Iran and Nicaragua.
3. The ruling elites in these states are remarkable for narrowing, rather than broadening, their base; an increasingly clannish exercise of power and concentration of privileges ultimately alienates a broad array of even the propertied classes. These, too, end up abandoning their erstwhile allies when the latter are faced with a serious challenge.

NOTES

1. Martin Ennals, *The Boston Globe*, 26 November 1978.
2. These were:

   1. The elective-parliamentary system (e.g., India, Ceylon, Malaysia, Jamaica, Singapore).
   2. The ascriptive-palace system (e.g., Morocco, Nepal, Saudi Arabia, Kuwait).
   3. The dynastic-oligarchic system (e.g., Nicaragua [Somoza], Haiti, Paraguay).
   4. The pragmatic-authoritarian system (e.g., Ivory Coast, Senegal, Tunisia, Zambia, Cameroon, Egypt under Sadat).
   5. The radical-authoritarian system (e.g., Algeria, Tanzania, Mexico, Iraq, Syria, Somalia, Libya).
   6. The Marxist-socialist system (Cuba, Mozambique, Guinea-Bissau, Vietnam).
   7. The neo-fascist system (e.g., Brazil, Indonesia, Chile, Uruguay, Argentina, Iran under the Shah, Zaire).

See: "Post-Colonial Systems of Power". *Arab Studies Quarterly*, Vol 2, #4 (Fall 1980), pp. 350–363.

3. Jacques Langguth, "The Mind of a Torturer", *Nation* (24 June 1978). See also A.J. Langguth, *Hidden Terrors* (New York: Pantheon, 1978).

4. On this point see Frederick Nunn, "Military Professionalism and Professional Militarism in Brazil", *Journal of Latin American Studies* (vol. IV, no. 1, 1972); Jeffrey Stein, "Grad School for Juntas", *Nation* (21 May 1977); Michael Klare, *Supplying Repression: US support for authoritarian regimes abroad* (Institute for Policy Studies, Washington, D.C., 1977); and Noam Chomsky and Edward Herman, *The Washington Connection and Third World Fascism* (Boston: South End Press, 1979).

5. See Frances Moore Lappé and Joseph Collins, *Food First: Beyond the myth of scarcity* (Boston: Houghton Mifflin Co., 1977), especially chapters 5, 6, 8.

6. *Business Week* (28 April 1975) p. 8.

7. *I have heard the cry of my people* (unpublished, 6 May 1973).

8. Shelton H. Davis, *Victims of the Miracle* (Cambridge University Press), and N. Chomsky and E. Herman, *op. cit.*, pp. 109–118.

9. N. Chomsky and E. Herman, *op. cit.*, p. 44. See especially tables I, II, pp. 43, 45.

10. M. Klare, *op. cit.*, p. 9.

11. Eqbal Ahmad, "Post Colonial Systems of Power", *op. cit.*, second of three summary essays for the International Foundation for Development Alternatives.

12. A. Sivanandan, "Imperialism and disorganic development in the Silicon Age" *Race and Class*, V-1. XXI, no. 2 (Autumn 1979).

9
CIVILIZATION AND PROGRESS

Stanley Diamond

Civilization originates in conquest abroad and repression at home. Each is an aspect of the other. Anthropologists who use, or misuse, words such as "acculturation" beg this basic question. For the major mode of acculturation, the direct shaping of one culture by another through which civilization develops, has been conquest. Observe, for example, the Euro-American "influence" on the South Vietnamese, or the fact that white Protestant Anglo-Saxons who settled in New England learned a few things from the aboriginal Indian peoples (of which the writers of history for civilized children make so much), and that black slaves "contributed" African rhythms to southern American music. In all these instances, one group was dominant and the other subordinate. Such examples of the diffusion of cultural traits suggest the struggles that have taken place within various societies. When—as generally happens—this diffusion is traced as an abstract exchange, somehow justified by the universal balance sheet of the imperial civilization, the assault by civilized upon primitive or traditional societies is masked, or its implications evaded. The propagation of basic elements of ancient Egyptian culture along the eastern Mediterranean strip was, for example, a precipitant of political and economic conquest. The politically "weaker" peoples were confronted with a single set of alternatives, rooted in the Egyptian experience. This historical fact is then reflected as a law of development; as civilization accelerates, its proponents project their historical present as the progressive destiny of the entire human race. The political component is obscured by deterministic arguments from natural law, natural history and natural science. Anthropology as a civilized discipline has, despite the pretentious relativism of many of its practitioners, "reluctantly" shared these ethnocentric notions of historical inevitability. Political decisions, however, are rather more existential in their nature. They can be literally decisive; they are implicated with problems of will and authority. For popular—as opposed to imposed—politics is people in groups deciding to act in order to reject, create or maintain a given form of social life. Civilized peoples and civilized disciplines have, therefore, been particularly sensitive to political action on the part of "backward" peoples, which created the possibility of

Published by permission of Transaction, Inc. From *In Search of the Primitive*. Copyright © 1974 by Transaction, Inc.

autonomous societies and alternative cultures. In the mind of the imperialist, the world is small, and loss of control in one area threatens the whole. The fabric of world culture, our oral or inscribed literary, esthetic and religious inheritance, may be, as anthropologists are prone to put it, a "multicolored fabric"; but since the rise of civilization that fabric has been woven on a political loom.

No matter how far we range in time and space, from Teotihuacan to Angkor Vat the tale is always the same. No matter what distinctions we encounter in language, art, religion, cultural style or social structure, the history of civilization repeats itself not as farce, which Marx supposed to be the fate of all historical repetitions, but as tragedy. In the shadow of this tragedy, the achievements of civilization are reduced to their proper proportions. They were intended for the use and pleasure of the very few at the expense of the skill and labor of the many.

The original crimes of civilizations, conquest and political repression, were committed in silence and that is still their intention, if not always their result. For most of the victims, through most of human history, could not and cannot read or write. It is sometimes said that they had no history. That is a complex opinion—false, yet profoundly true in a way not intended. It is false because it assumes that history is a matter of documents. Conventional historians, who live by documents and, therefore, consider them sacrosanct, would deny authentic history to most of the human race for the greater period of time on this planet. The opinion of H. Trevor-Roper, Regius Professor of History at Cambridge University, is typical: "Perhaps in the future there will be some African history to teach. But at present there is none. There is only the history of Europeans in Africa. The rest is darkness. . . ."

Africa along with all other areas inhabited by human beings has both a "prehistory" and a "history" recorded in the migrations of people, the artifacts found in the earth, the connections traceable among myriad languages, and the oral traditions of indigenous societies. Africa is the locus of predominantly unwritten, deeply self-conscious human experiences, the ensemble of which constitute the only authentic definition of history. Even so, documents exist; in the Western Sudan, for example, the Kano chronicle provides information about events ten centuries old. Of course, that kind of "history" is necessarily skewed by the official attitudes of invading groups; the distortions are probably of the same magnitude as the information that has come to us, filtered through the scribes, priests and courtiers of eleventh-century England, or, for that matter, the journalists and closet academicians of the twentieth century. But Trevor-Roper is, in a sense that he would not admit, perfectly correct; most men, whether Africans, medieval Europeans, or working-class Englishmen, have lived in the "darkness" to which they have been confined by those who record and rationalize the career of civilization. For their histories, in Africa, for example, were of no use to the European historian—not being reified, they could not be endlessly mined for the sake of either the academic specialist or the establishment he represented. When Trevor-Roper claims, therefore, that Africa has no history, he means that Africa has no history that *he can use*.

Those people who *could* write, the scribes and priests of Egypt, Babylonia or China, were rarely disposed to record the attitudes of those they taxed, subordinated and mystified. Writing itself was initially used to keep tax, census and other administrative records; it was, in short, an instrument for the recording of official histories, invented by bureaucrats. The oral tradition, the ceremony, the round of daily life, the use and manufacture of tools by the people at large did not depend on writing, nor did they need to be reflected in writing. The compulsive rite of civilization is writing, and the compulsions of the official concept of reality are both experienced and expressed in the exclusive mode of cognition signified by writing. This fixation on one-dimensional realities is particularly evident in the attitude of the ethnologist whose civilized insistence on recording the exact and proper form of a ritual, the exclusive mode of marriage or descent, the precise code of behavior, may reveal his own motivation and certain shortcomings of scientism, but fails to resonate with the variety and flexibility of primitive social usages. The connection between Malinowski's insistence on word-perfect magic among the Trobriand Islanders and his clinically compulsive personality, as reflected in his diary—"a diary in the strict sense of the term"—is a case in point.

Writing was one of the original mysteries of civilization, and it reduced the complexities of experience to the written word. Moreover, writing provides the ruling classes with an ideological instrument of incalculable power. The word of God becomes an invincible law, mediated by priests; therefore, respond the Iroquois, confronting the European: "Scripture was written by the Devil." With the advent of writing, symbols became explicit: they lost a certain richness. Man's word was no longer an endless exploration of reality, but a sign that could be used against him. Sartre, the Marxist existentialist, understands this; it is the hidden theme of his autobiography, *Words*. For writing splits consciousness in two ways—it becomes more authoritative than talking, thus degrading the meaning of speech and eroding oral tradition; and it makes it possible to use words for the political manipulation and control of others. Written signs supplant memory; an official, fixed and permanent version of events can be made. If it is written in early civilizations, it is bound to be true.

History, then, has always been written by the conqueror: the majority of people have traditionally remained silent, and this is still largely the case. It is the civilized upper class who, conceiving their positions as determined by God, talent or technology, create the facts of history and the deterministic theories which justify both the facts and their own pre-eminence. Thus, we have no conventional way of knowing what the "ordinary" peasant in Bronze Age China or early dynastic Egypt felt, thought or suffered. Even Shakespeare found it necessary to deal with kings and nobles when exploring the human soul. The Greek novelist Kazantzakis tells us that he was not impressed by the ideologues when he visited Russia shortly after the Revolution. Rather, standing in Kremlin Square, he shuddered at the snarl of rage that rose from the endless parade of peasants, soldiers, workers and urban riffraff. This is the sound that is rarely recorded. It is, rather, the chain of conventional historical chronicles that defines the "mainstream of civilization," and makes us certain that history as we know it is somehow inevitable, and must be the record of the fittest survivors.

In the beginning, conquest and domestic oppression were indistinguishable. As the earliest societies that began to consolidate as states expanded territorially, local peoples were conquered and incorporated as lower-class subjects or slaves into the evolving polity. We find this pattern everywhere—in the Nile Valley some 5,000 years ago; in England following the Norman invasion; among the Incas of the Peruvian highlands; in the valley of Mexico prior to the Spanish conquest; in the coastal forests of West Africa in the sixteenth century. Imperialism and colonialism are as old as the state; they define the political process. In Dahomey for example, any person born within the territory claimed by the emerging "king" was, by right of conquest, a Dahomean subject. His ultimate obligations to the nascent state, the political definition of his humanity, took precedence at least abstractly over his local, kin-mediated, social existence.

After the initial consolidation of the state, as V. Gordon Childe relates, the ancient Egyptians colonized the eastern Mediterranean littoral and that, along with their economic imperialism and punitive expeditions, stimulated state-building among local peoples. This archetypal imperial process is worth examining. The importation of raw materials, needed for the development of Egyptian industries as well as for funerary ceremonies, was financed from the royal revenues. Copper and turquoise were mined in the Sinai. Expeditions equipped by the state, escorted by royal soldiers, were periodically dispatched across the desert for this purpose. Similarly, cedarwood and resins were imported from North Syria. Ships bound for Byblos were equipped and provided with trade goods by the state; government officials led expeditions to the upper Nile and brought back gold and spices.

The major purpose of this traffic was to secure luxuries and magic substances or raw materials; while peasants and laborers still used stone tools in the fields and quarries, soldiers were armed with metal weapons. This trade also helped sustain new classes—merchants, sailors, porters, soldiers, artisans and clerks were supported from the surplus revenues collected by the pharaoh. More specifically, the effects of the imperial trade on Byblos were as follows: the Egyptians needed cedarwood for tombs, boats and furniture; they obtained it from Lebanon, and shipped it from the port of Byblos, close to Beirut. Before the rise of civilization in Egypt, Byblos had been the site of a neolithic town. As early as 3200 B.C., the Giblites had been self-sufficient fishermen and farmers. But the consolidation by conquest of the Egyptian state from a series of neolithic villages strung out along the banks of the Nile turned Byblos into a primary supplier of raw materials for the use of the Egyptian upper classes. In satisfying the Egyptian demands, Byblos abandoned the economic self-sufficiency of its neolithic structure, and came to depend upon a foreign market. One is reminded of Rousseau's observation: "Alexander, desiring to keep the Ichthyophay dependent on him, forced them to give up fishing and to eat foodstuffs common to other peoples." Moreover, Egyptian traders and officials settled there in order to secure their interests, and the Eygptians "instructed" the Giblites in the administration of the city and the management of their money, establishing what was in effect a protectorate. A stone temple was built in the city, decorated by immigrant Egyptian craftsmen and the Giblites learned the Egyptian script, the language of commerce.

As time went on, Byblos became a pre-industrial city, a market for raw materials, and a further center for the diffusion of the new social economy. But it should be noted that the imposed elements of Egyptian civilization tended to remain static in Byblos. The Imperium changed the nature of the indigenous society, which retained certain of its cultural traits by adapting them to the new structure, but Byblos, in the classic colonial mode, did not and could not keep pace with further developments in Egypt. While the Egyptians improved their script, for example, the Giblites maintained for a millennium the archaic characters which they had originally adopted. The imperial process, then, increased the affluence of the Egyptian upper classes, and converted Byblos into a little Egypt through the direct effect of the division of labor needed to supply raw materials for the related tasks of administration and defense. This, in turn, led to the impoverishment and dependence of the majority of people engaged in fishing and farming.

A similar chain of events was set in motion by the imperial thrust of Mesopotamia, which resulted, after 2500 B.C., in the breakup of the neolithic communities and their replacement by urban civilization. Here again the "secondary centers" remained provincial, compared to the "dynamic" metropolitan powers. But self-replication, which is both the need and the desire of the imperialist center, was not always accomplished so directly. The nomads of Sinai, for example, those "wretched Bedouins," refused to mine copper for the Egyptians in return for manufactured trinkets. Workers from Egypt, under the eye of the royal army, had to do the job. And in other areas, such as Nineveh, the primitive farming settlements were forcibly converted into imperial towns. Eventually these archaic civilizations (Egypt, Sumer, India), through direct or indirect conquest, reproduced themselves throughout the ancient world. "Initially, on the borders of Egypt, Babylonia, and the Indus Valley—in Crete and the Greek Islands, Syria, Assyria, Iran and Baluchistan, and further afield on the Greek mainland, the Anatolian Plateau, South Russia, villages were converted to cities and self-sufficient food producers became commercially specialized." Only those who lived in the most remote areas could escape this process; only the nomads of the desert denied its reality. Like the primitives who flee civilization, they refuse to cooperate or to alter their image of themselves, as imperialism invests each secondary and tertiary center.

More than 2,000 years after the inception of archaic imperialism, the same imperatives are constantly at work. In 416 B.C., the Athens of Plato and Socrates, then at war with Sparta, refused to recognize the right of the inhabitants of Melos to remain neutral. Thucydides reports, truthfully in spirit if not in fact, a dialogue between the Melians and the Athenean envoys in which the latter reject all reasonable and humane argument. Power, they say, is what counts in this world; and it would be better for Athens to be defeated by Sparta than to reveal so damaging a weakness to other subject peoples by accepting the friendship of defenseless Melos. The Melians insist on their independence and reject the honor of becoming an Athenean colony. The Atheneans then attack Melos, kllling the mature men and selling the women and children into slavery. Thereafter they colonized Melos themselves. This was the same Athens that condemned Socrates as a traitor a few years later. The two events taken together—the one externally imperialistic, the other internally repressive—remind us of the still more ancient association between this twin dynamic of the state, which converges to a single process at the origins of civilization itself. And it is always useful to remember that in Athens, at the height of its cultural achievement, there were at least three slaves to every free man. This fact is reflected in the classic utopian projections of civilization, as instanced in the work of Thomas More, where it is assumed that a special class of the disenfranchised will engage in "black labor." And in Plato's *Republic*, that prototypical apology for the state, the workers and farmers constitute lower orders of being.

Civilization has always had to be imposed, not as a psychodynamic necessity or a repressive condition of evolved social life, as Freud supposed, and not only in terms of the state's power securing itself against its own subjects, but also with reference to the barbarian or primitive peoples who moved on the frontiers. Native communities were the ground out of which the earliest, class-structured, territorially defined civilizations arose. Internally, these native peoples were transformed into the peasant and proletarian "masses" who supported the apparatus of the state. No matter how "necessary" the political structure of civilization may have been initially, the progessive degradation of the independent native communities remains a truth of history. No rationalization for the existence of the early state can alter the fact that the majority of the people were always taxed in goods and labor far more than they received from the state in the form of protection and services.

Even if we acknowlege the necessity—due to population pressure, scarcity of land, water and other resources—for political constraints in the earliest stages of state formation, there is no inherent reason for it to have taken the oppressive form that it did—except for the burgeoning anxiety of those removed from direct production about their economic and political security. That security seems to have been all the more problematic when we assume along with Marx, Morgan, Engels, Radin, Childe and Redfield that primitive societies are proto-democratic and communalistic, and further, that the character of the neolithic communities that immediately preceded the rise of the earliest civilizations could be similarly defined. For primitive customs and habits so long in their formulation would hardly have been transformed without very great resistance. The consequent struggle between the state—the civil authority—and the constituent kin or quasi-kin units of society is the basic social struggle in human history. It is still reflected in local attitudes and institutional buffers against the center even where distorted.

Their anxiety about not being self-supporting, along with the anticipation of such resistance, seems to constitute the motive for the upper classes' elaborate extortion of wealth from the direct producers. But even if we accept the necessity of the political transformation of society and agree that no state could survive unless "surplus" wealth created by the emerging peasants and workers was appropriated for the support of the classes not directly engaged in production, this does not account for the accelerating inequalities in the distribution of wealth. The widening gap between the rich and poor as ancient civilizations developed could not have been due simply to scarcity, or to the need for supporting specialists removed from subsistence activity. Rather, it was due to increasing expropriation. For as Marshall Sahlins has pointed out, the richer a society, the greater the distance between its classes, and the greater the concentration of wealth at the summit. Nor was the archaic concentration of wealth a function of its presumably rational reinvestment. Not only were the uses of wealth irrational, inflating the tautology of power, but redistribution in the form of public works or services eventually increased, rather than lessened, the gap between classes. The dynamics of archaic civilization reveal the pathology of wealth—wealth as power, or luxury as "well-being"—and the inadequacy of the distribution of wealth. By 3000 B.C. in the Middle East, such rationalizations for the state, which also apply to monopoly capitalism, are apparent. As Marx understood, the processes of state formation and function are generalizable beyond the specific form of the state.

The critical question, then, is that of the socioeconomic exploitation and the concomitant loss of the cultural creativity and autonomy of the vast majority of human beings. Conspicuous extortion from worker and peasant was a confirmation of power; but power, so reified, not only confirmed social status, it also displaced anxiety about the actual powerlessness of the privileged, which was a result of the loss of their direct command of the environment. The sheer accumulation of wealth, the antithesis of primitive customary usage, was thus compensatory, a sign of the fear of impotence. It is a response of the alienated in pursuit of security; the manipulation of people is substituted for the command of things. As civilization spreads and deepens, it is ultimately man's self, his species being, which is imperialized.

But according to the evolutionary determinists, the support of emerging artisans, soldiers, bureaucrats, priests by workers and peasants, a division of labor and class which presumably insured greater productivity in a given area subject to an accelerating population-resource ratio was rational, if not spontaneous. Specialization of function is supposed to maximize economic results (but the political question is always "for whom"); it breaks down the multi-dimensional functioning of the person in the primitive neolithic community, and leads to the institutionalizing of the division of labor, as not only determined, but socially desirable. The division of labor provides, in turn, the internal logic and coherence of class-structured society. Markets, middlemen, administrators became necessary because property had to be guarded and regulated, and exchange values established; thus the mutually dependent relations of the basic producers to the middlemen and the rulers are "completed" (mystified) in the structure of the state. The state appears as the inevitable sum of its social parts; its ideology is the projection of a unity by the "naturally" differentiated. If the process of civilization had unfolded in this way, as simply an adaptive machine, then all social ills can be ascribed to inadequate technology or "geometric" increases in population; correlatively, scarcity, and hence competition for scarce goods and services, could be put forward as the major factor in the growth of the state. Scarcity may even be conceived as a meta-principle, an existential condition of the human race which, satiated in one area, will find reason to compete in another. Thus, scarcity is conceived as a natural, not a social phenomenon.

The point is that the capitalist social dynamic and consequent logic of scarcity and the abstract rage to consume (the other side of the coin of affluence), combined with the positivism of Protestant culture, have rationalized the dynamics of civilization as rooted in human nature. Human nature is conceived as a system of reflexes tuned to detect and overcome scarcity. Society, not to speak of civilization, is conceived of as *ab initio* the visible structure of the struggle for what is scarce—food, women, land, material resources, power. It is only when the positivist mind abreacts under the influence of drugs or alcohol that a more spacious view of the human past and potential appears, and then its images tend to be mechanical, dissociated, admittedly unreal. But ordinarily, the positivist spirit abandons the contingencies of history for the constricted certainties of evolution. Law is its touchstone, or as Tylor put it, "if there is law anywhere, it is everywhere"—and civilization is accepted as a rational contract negotiated by sane men aware of their limitations. So goes the capitalist view of the nature of civilization, which reflects the accumulating 7,000-year-old myth of the state. But even at its best, in the form of a liberal ameliorative rationalism, its proponents will call on the power of the state when tried by the prospect of radical change. The capitalist view is only a minor deviation from the aristocratic conception which accepts the received class and occupational structure qua structure as rational, but wants to put the right people in the right places. Some, it seems, are leaders, and others followers by virtue of their birth, talent, training, capacity. Where the emphasis is on talent, the aristocratic rationale for the state, as in the *Republic*, dissolves into a meritocratic view. And the latter, in turn, is always in danger of dissolving into racism, which feeds back into the argument of birth, sometimes refined to a genetic point.

None of these conceptions is correct. Yet they remain the only possible explanations for the existence of civilization, if we do not ground ourselves in the converse existence of primitive society, and in a theory of exploitation which can only be based on the latter. In primitive cultures, wrote Malinowski, "there are no rich people and paupers, no people of great power; nor yet people who are oppressed; no unemployed, and no unmarried." And further, "before the advent of military pursuits and political power, which appear late in human evolution, there occurred no taxation, no confiscation of private property by chiefs or other tribal potentates."

Exploitation, then, is the hidden process which contradicts all totalitarian or amelioristic rationalizations for state power. All revolutionary theory is based on this civilizational process. Marx, in particular, identified exploitation as the appropriation of a surplus—initially, in the earliest civil societies, in the direct form of tribute and labor service. Its modern, monetized and ultimate form is surplus value—that is, the appropriation of a certain portion of the labor power of the worker by the capitalist, expressed as an inadequate wage. In Marxism, all "private" profits flow from surplus value, although the organs of the state maintain the ancient, more direct forms of expropriation—taxation, conscription, the right of eminent domain, etc. The point is that the theory of surplus appropriation, including that of surplus value, is the critical issue for revolutionaries: any doctrine of social change which omits this is reduced to the effort to modify the distribution of wealth within a bureaucratic state, conceived as essentially rational and necessary, and when cruel, inescapably so.

The opportunity for exploitation is obscured by the emphasis on the obligation to serve; the bureaucrat is said to be a civil servant, the monarch is said to serve his people, and so on. The case for the unity of the state is no more than a mystification of exploitation.

From the beginning, that *sine qua non*, the continuous production of a "surplus" in support of the State apparatus, was not spontaneous; it required the mediation of political authority. As Robert McC. Adams has maintained, there was no imminent logic in surplus production. The fact that primitive cultivators can produce a surplus does not mean that they will; or put another way, the occasional use of a surplus for ceremonial, symbolic and reciprocal exchange purposes is of a different order than the routine production of a surplus in support of other classes and occupational groups. But this classic statement of the problem is inadequate. The terms must be refined if we are to begin to understand the process. The imposition of tribute in kind on local communities in, say, the Nile Valley, cannot be understood as drawing on a productive base which is somehow divided into a "subsistence" segment (supporting and reproducing customary functions of the group), and a "surplus" segment (set aside for the tax collector, or otherwise directed to the support of non-producers). Surplus production is not an abstract economic category. It is, rather, the portion of goods and services expropriated from the direct producer in support of other classes or occupations. But that expropriation cuts directly into so-called subsistence production; it reduces the share of the direct producer in his own product; it represents the alienation of his labor power. Subsistence production among primitive peoples should be understood, then, as the economic effort required to reproduce society as a whole, a society in which the individual participates fully.

But with the advent of the state, production is more or less rapidly depressed, to the point where the merely biological functions of the cultivator are replicated, within a constricted range of social functions. This is true *subsistence* production, whereas the conventional use of the term with reference to stateless societies implies, or should imply, no more than the absence of specialized cash cropping for commercial marketing. The production of a surplus conceived as merely an increase in production over that needed to reproduce the traditional society of a local group is a politically-inspired economic myth.

The occupational and class division, which depends on the basic producers, does not, of course, happen all at once. In the earliest stages of state formation, the peasant was also an artisan, echoing primitive usage. Analogously, in the aboriginal state of Dahomey, every man was supposed to be able to roof a house, build a wall and cut a field. And most people in the major Yoruba "towns" in West Africa work as farmers, as did many of the inhabitants of the largest communities in ancient Sumer and prehispanic Mexico. An "appreciable proportion" of the inhabitants of Islamic Middle Eastern cities have also been farmers, cultivating adjacent fields. The point is that the expropriation of labor power was initially a process of *relative* impoverishment; it was limited by the immaturity and relative weakness of the early state, and by the consequent recognition of the emerging peasant-artisan as the source of all wealth.

The separation of functions between peasant and artisan was accelerated by the direct confiscation of the artisan's labor time, indeed of the artisan himself, by the civil power; the carpenter or potter was, literally, "in his majesty's service." Artisans may become further specialized in the manufacture of military equipment and that, in turn, reinforces emerging class distinctions. But it was the ostentation of royal courts, with their thousands of retainers, which most effectively subordinated the artisan to the civil power. At Susa, the palace staff in the Early Dynastic Three Period numbered about 950 people; but after Mesopotamia was unified by Sargon I, over 5,000 men are reported to have eaten daily in the royal palace.

As the peasant evolved from the primitive cultivator, the artisan became differentiated from the peasant so that, even as separate persons, they were not necessarily confined to the same household. At the same time, the traditional barter market allowed for the confiscation of goods by the civil power, thus fixing the artisan more firmly in his identity as an artisan. As the part-time specialist wandered from market to market, from group to group, offering his services in order to pay his taxes and find food, he also diminished his connection with the land. The point is that the division of labor, like the production of a "surplus," required the mediation of political power; the humanity of both the producers and the consuming classes is gradually sacrificed. Poverty, political imposition and social degradation reduced the life of the toiler to an economic imperative, to a question of sheer subsistence; the symbolic content and the social meaning of labor progressively declined. Even the everyday tools and implements of the lower classes, which are usually manufactured by craftsmen in order to produce a wide range of goods, can be distinguished from the elite artifacts produced by specialists who concentrate on a narrow range of work. A Berber housewife may tan her own skins, but the production of Morocco leather in Fez demands 20 consecutive operations, each performed by a different, highly trained work group. The result is that the poor were increasingly deprived of superior tools, while their esthetic and inventive impulses declined. The implications of this process, which begins with civilization, will be understood if one recalls that the primary inventions on which civilization itself depended were the work of primitive neolithic cultivators. At the same time, the specialized artisans, divided into their guilds and under the command

of the royal court, create their objects in a craft rather than a human environment, and in response to an external, specialized and conspicuous demand.
This may and can lead to the efflorescence of certain styles—"a master carver
may design and add the finishing touches to a piece of work"—but it also leads
to boredom; as the reputation of the master is inflated, so the specialized ap-
prentice is relegated to chiseling out the design.

This degradation of the artisan's life for the sake of the object is also basically
economic; like all assembly-line procedures, it cuts costs. But cost-cutting,
which is one of the rationalizations for the division of labor, is a political, not
an intrinsically "economic" process. For the efficiency and high technical skills
supposedly involved do not reward the majority of artisans, nor do their goods
reach the majority of consumers. The mobilization of the artisans simply made
their products available to the upper classes at the prices and in the quantity
that they found socially desirable.

But if the lower classes were degraded, and the artisans in effect imprisoned,
the nonlaboring classes were only free in fantasy—their dissociated dependence
on the work of others was, as we have seen, a pathological condition; at the
same time their symbolic lives were deformed by their partial and fanciful functioning in the world. This growing division between classes and occupations,
and their consequent reification, is the social basis for the split in human consciousness which civilization institutionalizes. The potential integrity of the
person remains unrealized; only society as a whole seems to have this integrity,
and the conception of the person as a social reflex becomes credible because it
reflects social reality. The related breach between mental and manual labor to
which Marx alludes is both a symptom of and a cause for the alienation of persons from themselves, reflected in the mind-body dualisms with which civilization conjures; and that in turn is epitomized in the rise of academic philosophy.

These dualities, which reflect the class structure and the division of labor in
archaic civilizations, were classically evident in northwestern Cambodia. For
an indeterminate period, up to about 800 A.D., a number of societies that were
just then becoming centralized existed along the Mekong River. They have
been described as "kingdoms, loosely held together . . . with chieftains . . .
villages . . . [or] village communities." The peasantry remained relatively free,
labor relatively undifferentiated, authority relatively traditional, within the
autonomous local groups. But with the development of "irrigation agriculture,"
a new state, religion and ruling class became possible and were, in fact, created.
As irrigation led to the multiplication of crops and increased population, the
peasant became specialized as a mere laborer on the land. On this productive
base there developed a strongly centralized state, signified by an emperor cult,
"the divine king on the mountain." The consolidation of royal authority here,
as elsewhere, was inherently contradictory—the more the king was objectified
as a political fetish, the more circumscribed were his actions, and the more
powerless he became in actuality. Compared to the old chiefs of the late
neolithic villages that preceded the rise of the state, he was impotent, bound by
the existing order, otiose and remote, after the pattern of civilized gods. The
Cambodian state was actually run by aristocrats and theocrats. As they grew

richer and more alienated, the villagers sank to the level of a working force, and when mentioned by name in the priestly inscriptions they are called "dog," "cat," "loathsome," "stinking brute," etc. As the population continued to increase, the surplus—that is, the confiscation of the fruits of local labor—also grew while the people, incapable of reproducing their traditional social lives, "fell into ever greater misery." And all the while, the "immense dams glittered in the sunlight," and "rice paddy upon rice paddy" stretched "away to the horizon." As their localities were denuded of art and artisanship, "the temples," suborning the skill of the artisans, "rose ever more vast and beautiful." Angkor Vat was, and remains, the material evidence for the monumental alienation of a whole people. Those who built it and those whose labor paid for its construction, neither planned nor commanded the finished product; the Temples of Angkor Vat towered over an oppressed peasantry; they had no place in what remained of the local community. And the ruling oligarchy manipulated the meaning of these monuments as symbols of power. As for the artisans, such structures were no longer their work, the expression of their human being, but merely edifices to which they were compelled to contribute their labor.

These ceremonial centers of power and tribute were, of course, common in the ancient world. The administrators, soldiers, landlords and artisans who populated the *Ch'eng*, the traditional Chinese administrative center, were supported by tribute, in rent or taxes, imposed on the peasantry of the hinterland. In the valley of Mexico, Tenochtitlán was the annual tributary center for luxuries of all kinds, clothing, and over 50,000 tons of food—borne on the shoulders of porters. The inflated wealth of imperial Rome, and the Mongol capital of Karakorum were similarly based. In each case, the monarch was able to redistribute periodically a certain portion of the tribute to the inhabitants of the capital city. And this had the classic imperial effect of binding the ruled to the ruler (a tenuous bond) within the metropole, in a common enterprise. But, we must remember along with Marx, that to the degree men are socially determined, they are irresponsible agents of history; the revolutionary perspective, not to speak of the imperatives of revolutionary conflict, does not include moral condemnation.

It is likely, for example, that the ancient peasants and workers collaborated in their own exploitation. Once the structure of the original community had been weakened or transformed, the sheer need to keep body and soul together, meet domestic obligations, confront police and military coercion, along with the hope of individual reward, priestly mystification and other familiar factors, would have served well enough to inhibit men from acting on or even recognizing their own, more fully human interests. But that, of course, does not inhibit them from rebelling. On the other hand, sufficient autonomy was preserved by the local groups which produced the resources for the support of the state to make the system viable; the priestly-military-bureaucratic oligarchies could not destroy the basis of their own sustenance without destroying themselves. The state, then, permitted what it could not command. As civilization evolves, the central authority permits less, commands more; and states grow more, not less totalitarian.

We must conclude that the development of the early civilizations as instruments of oppression was the result, not of some environmental or technical
imperative, but of the new possibilities of power which men in certain positions
found it necessary to cultivate and legitimate. As Starobinski has pointed out,
the idea of liberty as a human possibility was not to be invented until the
French Revolution. "Reinvented" is a more accurate term, for as Boas and
Marx understood, freedom as a concept does not exist among primitive peoples
because society is not perceived as oppressive. Exploitation, like the idea of
liberty, is a complex social-economic-psychological invention diffusing with
civilization itself. In this sense, the grossly inegalitarian aspects of civilization
are contingent, not predetermined. This view, of course, implies a good deal
about human nature—mainly that, given the opportunity and driven by certain needs, some men will compound their profit and seek an illusory freedom,
based on the exercise of power, at the expense of others. In reality, of course,
they are bound to those whom they exploit.

On the other hand, there is ample historical evidence that the great majority
of people have always been suspicious and resentful of political power as such.
The only fully participant societies have been primitive; they lack explicit
political structures and, subsequently, exploitation, in the basic, civilized definition of the term. Whatever else we may say about men as political beings, it is
clear that the great majority of them have viewed the exercise of political power
as either irrelevant to, or destructive of their daily concerns.

Yet we have no way of knowing how many abortive rebellions may have
been launched by slaves or peasants exasperated by taxes and labor service, or
by artisans commanded to work for the ruling class in ancient civilizations. We
do know, for example, that in Polynesia, during the earliest intimations of state
formation, when the big chiefs failed to redistribute the goods of the community according to custom, local uprisings resulted. In traditional China, many
landlords lived in the walled towns because their garrisons were a defense
against peasant rebellions. And there is a rare Egyptian document dated about
2000 B.C.—"the story of the eloquent peasant"—which attacks the extortionate
behavior of the bureaucrats. Another document, dated some centuries later, in
the form of a letter to the correspondent's son, advises him in the most
dramatic terms to become a scribe so that he may escape a manual laborer's or
a peasant's life of degradation.

For 5,000 years peasants have rebelled, by evading the imposition of the central power, or by directly attacking its representatives. But only in this century
has the peasantry become a revolutionary force. In the West, peasants have
been liquidated as a social class since the rise of commercialism and industrialism. The proportion of people on the land constantly diminished—in
both the United States and the United Kingdom, for example, currently about
4 percent of the people live on the land—and those remaining are, of course,
not peasants but itinerant laborers, full-fledged farmers or corporate
agricultural workers. Therefore, the problem of the peasant qua peasant has
solved itself, albeit within a capitalistic framework. But this is not true
elsewhere. The processess of urbanization and industrialization linked to the

revolutionary ascendancy of the bourgeoisie in most of Europe quickly reduced the ranks of the peasantry, and cash-cropping businessmen-farmers emerged while the new technology converted the countryside into an extension of the city. This has not happened among the ancient peasantries of Africa, Asia, Latin America, or the Near and Middle East. There, the peasants, in some areas declining to rural proletariats, either have the potential to become restive or are already revolutionary. Their emergence in new rural forms, their relationship to the national institutions and to the urban populations, their actual and potential political weight are central to any projection of the future conceived on a global scale. Unlike the Western "self liquidating" peasantry, the existent peasantries of most of the world will not wither away through social and economic attrition. Their intolerable living conditions, steadily worsening since the upper neolithic period, and their self-consciousness, will not wait upon the blind processes of urbanization and industrialization which changed the social contours and demography of Europe. The peasants are there; they constitute most of the world's population, the link between archaic and modern civilizations. They are the poor who are getting poorer, both intranationally and internationally, as the Western world gets richer.

10
THE NONTERRITORIAL SYSTEM: NONTERRITORIAL ACTORS

Johan Galtung

Ultimately, as often said, the world consists of human beings, of individuals. But individuals are organized in collectivities that become actors and form systems. The total, the *world* system, can be split into two: the *territorial system* (T) and the *nonterritorial system* (NT)—which, one hopes, do not add up to TNT.

Actors in the territorial system are organized on the basis of *contiguity* of territorial units, actors in the nonterritorial system on the basis of *similarity* (in associations) or *interaction* (in organizations).[1] This works like Chinese boxes: inside a territorial actor, e.g., a country, there are associations and organizations (parties, trade unions, farms, factories, firms); inside a nonterritorial actor there may be states, for states also form associations (like the Francophone countries) or organizations (like the sphere of influence of a hegemonial power).[2] The basic point remains clear, however: membership in a territorial actor is based on location in *geographical space*; membership in a nonterritorial actor on location in some *sociofunctional space*, defined by similarity and/or interaction. In the first case *vicinity* is the guiding principle, in the second case *affinity*.[3]

One misunderstanding should now be cleared up. A truly nonterritorial actor is, of course, geographically *universal*. Thus, no Nordic association is a nonterritorial actor in the sense discussed here; it is only a component in a regional territorial actor (the Nordic countries) or a part of a truly nonterritorial actor (the corresponding world association, if there is any). Since our primary focus here is the world, our attention is focused on nonterritorial actors that are not regional, that do not recognize any territorial borderline at all. They may in fact not have members all over the world, but in principle they might have; they are open to all, as no Nordic association is.

Let us then go more deeply into "nonterritoriality." What kinds of units may be members of the "international organizations" that constitute nonterritorial actors? By and large there seem to be three answers, on a scale of increasing nonterritoriality:

From *The True Worlds: A Transnational Perspective*. Reprinted by permission of The Free Press, a Division of Macmillan Publishing Co., Inc., New York, 1980.

1. Members are national governments, and the organization is *intergovernmental* (IGO);
2. Members are other national organizations or associations, and the organization is *internongovernmental* (INGO);
3. Members are individuals, and the organization is *transnational nongovernmental* (TRANGO).

I prefer not to use the term "international" for any one of these, for that term, in my view, does not imply any organization or actor at all. The "international" system is simply the system of nations (actually the system of states, or countries), in cooperation and conflict – nothing more, nothing less. For that reason I interpret IGO to mean intergovernmental (and not international, governmental), INGO to mean internongovernmental (and not international, nongovernmental), and I add to this well-known distinction the transnational (or, really, transnongovernmental) organization, the TRANGO, which relates directly to individuals wherever they are found. In the TRANGO there are no "national chapters" or similar arrangements controlling the direct relation between individuals, possibly absorbing the loyalty between the individual and the nonterritorial organization.[4]

There exists a vitally important case of the INGO: the *business* internongovernmental organization (BINGO). It links together nongovernmental business organizations in various countries and is known today as the "multinational corporation." However, the latter is an unfortunate term for at least four reasons. First, "multi" connotes more than two nations, but often there are only two.[5] In the case of an organization drawing on only two states the term "cross-national" may be preferred to "multinational."[6] Further, the term "multinational" conceals how asymmetric these corporations are, with one country often dominating them. Then, "corporation" may not be broad enough, for there may be many other ways of organizing international business than in corporations. (Incidentally, one of these ways would be governmental, as an IGO, which in that case could be termed a BIGO.[7]) Finally, these organizations are entities of their own kind, *sui generis*, not just a multiple of companies. They are very often Business-TRANGO, for which reason the recent term "transnational corporation" (TNC) fits better.

The significance of the distinction just made between IGOs, INGOs, and TRANGOs has to do with two important phenomena located at the interface between the territorial and the nonterritorial systems. These two systems are by no means unrelated, particularly since one, the territorial, preceded the other by thousands of years and consequently must have set its stamp on the latecomer, however efficiently the latter makes use of transportation and communication.[8] The two phenomena characterizing the relation between the two systems are *isomorphy* and *homology*. The propositions are simple:

1. The nonterritorial actors tend to be isomorphic with the territorial system.

2. The nonterritorial actors tend to induce homology between territorial actors.
3. Propositions 1 and 2 are most valid for intergovernmental organizations (usually), less for internongovernmental organizations, and (almost) invalid for transnational organizations.

It is characteristic of the two most weakly nonterritorial of the nonterritorial actors, the IGOs and the INGOs, that the *world territorial structure, the state structure, is still entirely visible*. NT is a mirror reflection of T. When governments are members this is obvious, but it also applies to the typical international organization built as an association of national associations (e.g., an association of national associations of dentists, longshoremen, stamp collectors), and even to the multinational corporation. An association or organization at the national level becomes a "national chapter" or a "mother," "sister," or "daughter" company, depending on its position in the hierarchy of the nonterritorial actor.[9] Not only the *elements* of the territorial system, but also the *relations* between them can usually be rediscovered among the nonterritorial actors, which is why the term "isomorphy" is used. Relations of power (both in terms of resources and structures) and interaction frequency are often mirrored faithfully. The most powerful chapter is located in the most powerful country, in terms of location of the organization's headquarters, recruitment of staff, general perspective on world affairs, and so on.[10] Frequencies of interaction in the territorial system are mirrored in frequencies of interaction in the organization, and so on.[11] In other words, the territorial system is reproduced inside the nonterritorial actor, which for that reason is not truly nonterritorial.

This way of thinking carries us quite far analytically. Nonterritorial actors with national components—governmental or nongovernmental—can be seen as governed primarily by the principle of isomorphy. This is the baseline, as implemented in the United Nations when the major victors among the "united nations," the Allies fighting against the Axis powers, appointed themselves to permanent Security Council positions. Isomorphy is called "realism" in the plain language of power. It means that to those who have power in the territorial system, power shall also be given in the nonterritorial system. And it is probably partially true that the more an intergovernmental organization departs from this isomorphy, the less attention will be paid to it, because its decisions will be seen as not reflecting the "real world," meaning the territorial system with its bilateral relations, particularly among the strong, to which decisions will then be referred.[12]

But this is only a partial truth. A nonterritorial actor that is 100 percent isomorphic with the territorial system is in a sense only a replication of that system, except that it makes multilateral interaction possible. Some deviations from strict isomorphy will of course take place since countries are represented by persons with their idiosyncrasies, making these organizations a medium in which the smaller powers can more easily express themselves, can be listened to, and can have some impact on the territorial system. This medium is not merely one in which they can be more easily bossed.

But then there is the opposite view, that this is precisely the medium in which the territorial system of yesterday can be kept alive and even reinforced. For instance, Nationalist China had for a long time a power excess because of its position in the UN Security Council. The argument would be, however, that this is the result not of too much isomorphy but of a lack of isomorphy, because the UN served to freeze the past. One might also extend that argument to the case of the United Kingdom and France, and even to the United States, for all practical purposes defeated by what it often referred to as a "fifth-rate power," Vietnam.[13]

Imagine the United Nations brought up to date, in an effort to mirror the territorial system. The argument against it would then be that any distinction between veto and nonveto is too sharp, too absolute relative to the power distinctions in the much more subtle and complicated territorial system. Moreover, if prowess in war is used to decide who has the veto, then the United States and Vietnam should at least be on par, with Vietnam viewed as an effective challenger of the former heavyweight champion.[14]

Of course, over time the internal workings of a nonterritorial actor will acquire facets never contemplated by its social architects, the lawyers. There will be informal structures in addition to the formal ones. But existing power differentials may actually be magnified rather than reduced in an intergovernmental organization.[15]

In the INGO all this becomes much less important. Nongovernments may feel less obliged to act in the name of the "national interest" and more free to find the pattern of action and interaction that fits the values of the organization. Thus, one would assume in general that INGOs have national elements—by definition—but the relations between them are different, for instance, much more egalitarian. The world has come to accept the idea of a big-power veto in the United Nations, whether this adequately reflects or even exaggerates territorial power, but it would hardly accept it in an international philatelic association. Needless to say, all shades and gradations can be imagined here.[16]

When it comes to transnational organizations, isomorphy breaks down almost completely: there are neither the territorial elements nor the relations of the territorial system. Transnational ties uniting individuals across territorial borders would be stronger than common citizenship. The classical example here is, of course, *membership in a nationality* as opposed to *state citizenship*. The nation, defined as a group of human beings having in common some characteristics referred to as ethnic, is the most important of all transnational organizations. (Here the unfortunate consequences of the double meaning of "nation" become particularly obvious!) Time and again nationality proves to be more important than territorially defined state citizenship, but the two are often confused because the nation-state is taken as the norm and sometimes is also a fact in our world. Thus, Jews formed such a transnational group,[17] although a much better expression would be "transgovernmental"—a TRAGO—since they are found under the protection (or abuse) of various governments. The extent to which Jews would identify themselves as "Soviet"

Jews, "American" Jews, and so on would be a test of the extent to which this grouping is an INGO or a TRANGO. In some years the same reasoning may apply to women and to age groups—obviously TRANGOs in the making.

More recent examples would be international scientific unions where the dissolution of national emphasis has gone quite far.[18] Of course, people in the same discipline from the same country may know each other better, and their interaction is usually facilitated by their speaking the same language, but the search for significant colleagues, for meaningful persons with whom to work, to converse, and to exchange ideas will not be restricted by such borders. Only few and particularly repressive countries would imagine organizing their citizens to force them to speak with one voice in a transnational scientific organization.

Then there are, of course, the political parties and pressure groups that are transnational, such as the World New Left and the Vietnam solidarity movement.[19] The fact that there may also be cooperation at subnational and national levels does not detract from the transnational character of such world movements, for national identities are usually successfully washed out. A good case in point is the world hippie movement—or any movement for new life styles in defiance of the various versions of model II society, the vertical, success-oriented, power-oriented society.[20]

For these reasons I see the transnational organizations as the nonterritorial actors of the future. Only they can deserve the epithet "global actors," since only they are both based on individuals as their unit and are global in their scope.

To summarize: the idea of isomorphy can be split in two: the presence of territorial *elements*, states in nonterritorial actors, and the presence of territorial *relations* in these actors. In this regard we find the three types shown in Table 1.

Let us then turn to the problem of *homology*, to see how nonterritorial organizations act as giant mechanisms for making all states as similar to each other as possible. Just as a state tries to find its appropriate place (often called its "natural" position) in a nonterritorial organization, so a nonterritorial organization is a vehicle facilitating the search for one's *opposite number* inside other states. Whether members are governments, nongovernmental associations, organizations, or simply individuals, any international organization will try to bring together like-minded or like-positioned elements in all states around the world. For that is their task: *to organize all of their kind*, wherever they can be found. Where their kind do not exist they can be created by, for instance, inviting observers to international conferences who then return to their country with one message imprinted on their minds: *"Solch ein Ding müssen wir auch haben"* (We must have that too). But international organizations may become giant mechanisms through which people in the stronger states that started these organizations can imprint a message on the people of weaker states: "You must have this ministry and that profession, this hobby and sports association and that ideological movement, you must produce this and that—in order to be full-fledged members of the World." Active membership in international organizations is taken as an indicator of how deeply embedded the country is in

TABLE 1. Three types of nonterritorial actors

Territorial elements	Territorial relations	Nonterritoriality
present	present	low (IGOs, many BINGOs)
present	absent	medium (INGOs)
absent	absent	high (TRANGOs)

the world system, without questioning too much who started all these organizations, on what social basis, for what purpose, in what image.[21]

Thus, international conferences become giant markets where isomorphy and homology can be tested, the former vis-à-vis interstate characteristics, the latter vis-à-vis intrastate characteristics. They become giant reproduction mechanisms. Power relations in the nonterritorial organization will be compared to power relations in the territorial system, to see to what extent T is reflected in NT. And individuals from various countries will compare notes to find to what extent that particular NT is reflected in their part of T—whether it is present at all, and whether their government pays as much attention to it in terms of subsidy and deference as other governments, and so on.

This entire presentation may now gain in depth if it is . . . used to develop a typology of such organizations (see Figure 1). In Figure 1 the little dots at the top of each circle represent the governments, the nuclei of the centers. Obviously, the IGOs connect these dots in various ways. The INGOs do not necessarily connect only the centers of nations; they may also tie periphery elements together. But chances are that the masses are tied to their territorial units, *that the whole concept of nonterritoriality is fundamentally an elite concept.* Even such grandiose concepts as "Europe" and even the nation-state are very much elite concepts. Why? Because such means for developing consciousness as literacy, reading beyond primary school, access to transportation and communication, and knowledge of foreign languages are badly distributed. Hence, without having really good data on national participation in the types of associations and organizations that also are multinationally organized, we can at least say that those individuals who participate internationally in conferences and in secretariats and the like generally belong to the elite (or the counterelite). These are the individuals who serve as links between nations, not the nonparticipant members and the even less-participant nonmembers, hidden behind the nation-state screen.[22]

Thus, if nonterritorial actors (including the transnational ones) essentially link governments and other elite groups together, then there are, in principle and in reference to the figure, four types of international organizations:

1. Those connecting Center countries (horizontal lines, top);
2. Those connecting Center and Periphery countries in the same bloc (vertical lines);

FIGURE 1. Nonterritoriality as an elite concept

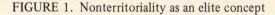

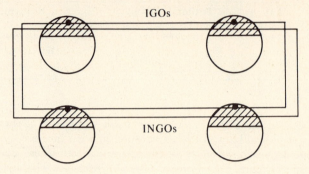

3. Those connecting Periphery countries (horizontal lines, bottom)
   (a) in the same bloc,
   (b) in different blocs;
4. Universal organizations (the whole rectangle).

The first three may be referred to as "regional" organizations (as long as we keep in mind the distinction between horizontal and vertical regions) and are not really nonterritorial actors.

In the real world, however, a particular organization is often too complex to permit classification in any single one of these types.[23] The secretariat of an organization for instance, may often be different from the rest of the organization, being transnational even when the rest is intergovernmental or inter-nongovernmental. Much of the history of the big intergovernmental organizations is the story of how the secretariat has tried to transnationalize the national delegates (meeting in conferences and assemblies, in councils or in executive boards), teaching them "to think in terms of the world as a whole" (the "world" usually meaning the organization as conceived of by the secretariat) *and* of how the national delegates try to internationalize the secretariat by such methods as secondment, short tenure, return to governmental posts rather than a career in another transnational secretariat, and so on.[24]

The net conclusion is that the two systems, T and NT, are not independent of each other, nor should one expect them to be. The NTs of today are mainly instruments in the hands of the territorial units who know how to use them, and that does not include only the big powers.[25] But this is less true for the transnational organizations, since they are not organized in national chapters and since loyalty in them is directed to the world level and the individual level, not to the intermediate nation-state level. These members are not so concerned with "organizing something similar at home" after they have been exposed to patterns in other nations through the medium of transnational conferences. For them an institution found or founded in one country is already a world institution, not something to be used in and for one country and copied elsewhere.

But what this means is that one cannot naively assume that nonterritorial actors are on the side of the good—peace, for instance—while territorial actors are on the other side.[26] The whole matter is much more complex. In fact, it may be argued that nonterritorial actors in the broad sense are probably the most dangerous vehicles of structural violence. Territorial actors can also exercise structural violence internationally, in the form of colonialism, although it now is outmoded. What territorial actors can still do of a destructive nature is to fight wars. In fact, wars are based on territorial concepts, since most weaponry we know, from catapults and arrows to atomic weapons, destroys territorially contiguous units. They are based on the assumption that there is a high concentration of enemies (with a low concentration of friends) at the point of impact. Wars between nonterritorial actors are conceivable, but less easily fought, at least with the present military technology.[27]

In conclusion, some words about the transnational corporations (TNCs). I have deliberately chosen not to devote a special section to an analysis of this phenomenon, partly because an extensive and very fine literature exists on the subject and partly because analytically this literature does not offer much that is really new.[28] *Basically the TNCs are the carriers of economic imperialism.* The latter is inconceivable without large-scale economic cycles in which capital, labor, raw materials, semimanufactured goods, and manufactured goods are moved and shuffled around. The administrator of that process, including all stages of financing, exploration, research and development, extraction, processing, marketing, consumption, and reinvestment at any point, is a corporation. When the cycle crosses international borders, the obvious organizational solution is the transnational corporation. The interesting analytical foci would be not only the *domain* ("In which countries does the corporation operate?") but also the *scope* ("How much of the total economic cycle does it control; does it have its own financial institutions? its own facilities for consumption?"). In general I assume that TNCs will tend to become universally monopolistic *and to control the total cycle*—and I find this last problem not sufficiently researched and more important than the problem of the size of the assets controlled (quite well researched, it seems).[29] However, it is unnecessary for one single TNC to control everything; it can do so in cooperation with others, forming some kind of loose federation among TNCs.[30] Some of them may be highly informal, like the organizations that manage to transport "guest workers" from Africa to France, for instance. To focus too much on the individual transnational corporation is to miss the point; the total system is what counts.

Much of the debate about the TNCs has been focused on their size (measured in assets and, incorrectly, compared to the GNPs of countries), the conclusion being that they have become too big, too powerful, *and potentially too autonomous.* Autonomy is not necessarily objectionable. If a TNC is autonomous it must be somewhat independent of the territorial system, and that system has not proven itself so capable of satisfying human needs that there is no space for the emergence of new actors free from some of the constraints of the territorial system, and in addition possessing resources. After all, many would like to see the United Nations endowed with these characteristics. The problem is what

effect the TNCs have, on balance. It is also important to know to what extent
they are autonomous, to know, for example, whether a TNC can act against the
interests (as articulated by the government) of a country in which it has headquarters. The general assumption is that there is a very pronounced harmony
of interest here; but to obtain that harmony the government may have to yield,
not the TNC, which is of course a sign of some kind of TNC autonomy. But
about this too little is known at present, it seems.[31]

We now list five major objections to TNCs,[32] all stemming from the assumption that they are not nonterritorial enough, but are in fact fundamental ar-
ticulations of the territorial system. Two of these objections fall under the
heading of "isomorphy" and two under "homology," and a fifth is even more
closely linked to the territorial system itself.

From the point of view of isomorphy:

[1] *The TNCs serve to maintain, probably even to reinforce, a vertical division of
labor.*[33] The sophisticated parts of the cycle are carried out by the headquarters
in the Center (research and development, difficult aspects of finance and administration, some of the most sophisticated manufacture), the simpler parts by
the daughter companies in the Periphery (extraction, simple processing, processing according to existing blueprints, marketing, local consumption). It may
well be that production (for the world market, incidentally) has been moved to
where many of the factors are found (particularly the raw materials and cheap
labor), and even most of the consumers – a wise move when costs of transportation and insurance are considered. But the division of labor in terms of differential spin-off effects ("externalities") is still there, all the more so because the
TNCs may serve as a conveyor belt for the brain drain, getting "young talent"
from the periphery to the center in its most creative period. Thus, general C–P
relations are replicated within the TNC, reinforced by the ease with which
blueprints can flow within the corporation, obviating any need for self-reliance.

[2] *Through the TNCs, net transfer of capital from the Periphery to the Center is
facilitated.* The point is, of course, that the TNC can trade with itself, fixing all
the costs to the extent it covers all aspects of the cycle, including transportation, letting profits show up where taxation is most lenient, and so on.[34]
Hence, TNCs can serve both types of exploitation, the in-change and the exchange varieties.

From the point of view of homology:

[3] *Through the TNCs a certain mode of production is propagated, particularly one
that is capital-intensive and research-intensive.* The TNCs produce and communicate a way of producing that is developed in the industrialized countries.
The methods are generally capital-intensive rather than labor-intensive, except
when local labor is used for simple operations. Such methods have a well-
known structural impact on the local economy, dividing it into sectors of very
high and very low productivity (ultimately leading to what is known as a
"population problem" in the latter sector). Moreover, the methods usually have
a high research component built into them, making it "unnecessary" for locals
to do their own research. This process is referred to, generally, as "transfer of

technology," but it can also be seen as a way of depriving others of the chance to develop through their own efforts.

[4] *Through the TNCs certain products are propagated that are not necessarily needed in other countries.* Particularly, I am thinking of the extremely poor showing of the TNCs when it comes to satisfying fundamental needs: whether in food, clothing, shelter, health, or education, the TNCs cannot be said to have made a positive contribution to those most in need. In other words, what is wrong with a TNC like Coca-Cola is not only the division of labor between countries (probably not so important in this case, as the spin-offs from the recipe cannot be that extensive), the transfer of profits, or the high productivity *but the product itself* — the forgotten dimension in so much research on TNCs. It should be possible to produce a nutritious, highly positive drink from the point of view of health. Instead, a product that is questionable from both points of view is marketed all over the world. Even when products are at least neutral in their consequences, the argument still remains that production factors are steered away from fundamental needs satisfaction and toward the satisfaction of other needs for more privileged groups of people. Think of the amount of capital, labor, and building materials that go into a Hilton or Intercontinental hotel and imagine allocating it to the slums of the cities over which such hotels tower, and the point is made.[35]

And then there is the last point:

[5] *The TNCs will tend to try to maintain this type of international structure and to support those local groups that think likewise.* It is enough to mention the case of ITT in Chile: whether it is an extreme or a typical case, research later in this century may be able to tell us.[36] But it brings up the point about autonomy again: to the extent that the TNCs are autonomous the experience so far seems to be that they overrepresent rather than underrepresent the territorial system, being among its most eager proponents. We do not hear about TNCs that turn the division of labor upside down, produce a net transfer of profits in the opposite direction, go in for labor-intensive methods based on local creativity, and in addition put fundamental needs for the masses first. The reason is simple: all of that would be contrary to the logic of capitalism, and the TNCs are the most important instruments of capitalism of our time, ultimately pointing to a world capitalist system, *sui generis*, to succeed the international one.[37]

Something has to be done about the transnational corporations, but it is not obvious that the measures often contemplated under the heading "code of conduct" will be anything like sufficient. To the extent that such a code can be gleaned from the principles expressed in the New International Economic Order and the Charter of Economic Rights and Duties of States[38] it would mainly be directed against the foregoing points 2 and 5. It would not come to grips with the problems of vertical division of labor, the intensiveness of capital and research, and whether the products are wanted or needed at all.[39] As part of a process, control of the transfer of capital is important, even crucial; but chances are that the TNCs will be flexible enough to understand that they should yield on this point in order to retain the more subtle forms of power built into the other three points.[40]

A proposal that goes far beyond the codes of conduct so far contemplated will be developed in a discussion of a world central authority.[41] Unless something profound is done to change the very structure of these corporations they will probably be able to regroup and to devise counterstrategies to nullify the impact of any code of conduct, given the human, capital, and research resources they have at their disposal.

Hence, there is room for much new thinking in this field, not necessarily because these corporations are big and do not obey orders from states. The problem is to destroy them as vehicles of structural violence, as carriers of isomorphy with a false territorial system, and to make them serve the needs of those most in need, turning them into one of the many world cementing forces needed as a barrier against direct violence.

NOTES

References to *Essays* are to Johan Galtung, *Essays in Peace Research*, 5 vols. (Copenhagen: Ejlers, 1975–1980) (Atlantic Highlands, N.J.: Humanities Press).

1. For further development of this theme, see Galtung, "A Structural Theory of Integration," *Essays* IV, 11.

2. Let T, A, and O stand for territorial, associational, and organizational integration respectively, and TAO, for instance, for a territorial unit built around associations of organizations. TO might be a proper way of looking at Japan, as a country built around economic organizations; TA might be a perspective on Norway, where the basic unit seems to be associations (trade unions, professional associations, political parties, value-oriented associations of all kinds), and TT or T^2 would be the appropriate perspective on a federal country. All nine combinations are empirically meaningful, but AT and OT perhaps less so than the others as the territorial focus is so predominant that there is much less integration between than within territorial units.

3. The word-pair is taken from the former Israeli foreign minister, Abba Eban. It should be noted that there are two kinds of affinity, though, A and O.

4. Anyone who has tried to organize a conference, or anything else for that matter, with Soviet citizens knows what this means in practice. The whole idea of a transnational organization presupposes that state borders are penetrable both ways, between individuals within and organizations without. This condition does not obtain in the Soviet Union, nor in many other countries.

5. For imperialism to function, two parties are sufficient, one Center and one Periphery country—e.g., the United States and Canada.

6. For some terminology of this kind, see Galtung, "On the Future of the International System," *Essays* IV, 18; also published as the first chapter in Jungk and Galtung, eds., *Mankind 2000* (Oslo, 1968).

7. And this is one of the highly underresearched areas in the world economic system: the role played by the Soviet state enterprises abroad. One hypothesis might be that a key role is to negotiate long-term deals with raw materials and unprocessed agricultural products flowing into the Soviet Union for resale on the world market when prices improve (sugar from Cuba, cocoa from Ghana, gas from Iran, possibly wheat from the United States).

8. Thus, I would maintain that the most important aspect of the industrial revolution was not mass manufacture—that had happened before, e.g., the famous pottery factories in Arezzo—but increasingly rapid and efficient communication and transportation, making the mobility of all production factors (capital, labor, raw materials) and the products themselves possible over ever-expanding areas, ending up with the modern transnational corporations and their *global reach*—the excellent title of the equally excellent book on them by R. J. Barnet and R. E. Müller (New York, 1975). The real watershed in recent history can be spelled out in such terms, in addition to the concentration of power over capital, including capital goods (means of production). See the UN report on these matters: "Report of the Group of Eminent Persons to Study the Role of Multinational Corporations on Development and on International Relations" (E/5500/Add.1, Parts I and II); the group was established by an ECOSOC resolution of 2 July 1972 (1721–LIII). See also Document E/5500 of 14 June 1974.

9. It is interesting to note how many sinister phenomena operate under the guise of such female terms as "mother," "sister," and "daughter" company, etc.

10. For some data on this, see Galtung, "Nonterritorial Actors and the Problem of Peace," in Saul H. Mendlovitz, ed., *On the Creation of a Just World Order* (New York: Free Press, 1975), or Galtung and Skjelsbaek, "Nonterritorial Actors: The Invisible Continent," *Essays* IV, 12, and Anthony J. N. Judge and Kjell Skjelsbaek, "Transnational Associations and Their Functions," in A.J.R. Groom and Paul Taylor, eds., *Functionalism: Theory and Practice in International Relations* (London: University of London Press, 1973).

11. On the other hand, there will always be some discrepancies. After all, it is easier for the Periphery to interact inside an organization, particularly during conferences and conventions. See Chadwick F. Alger, "Non-resolution Consequences of the United Nations and Their Effect on International Conflict," *Journal of Conflict Resolution* (1961), pp. 128–45.

12. For some data on the extent to which bilateral contact in the territorial system follows the principle of first big with big, then big with small, and finally small with small, see Galtung, "East-West Interaction Patterns," *Essays* IV, 7. Typically, so-called disarmament negotiations have also been taken out of the General Assembly to forums, usually Geneva-based, with a higher proportion of the big, and tend to end up in bilateral negotiations between the super-powers, e.g., the SALT talks.

13. It is ironical to think of all those defense intellectuals, no doubt rating themselves as first-rate intellectuals, who talked about that fifth-rate power. They proved to be fifth-rate intellectuals talking about a first-rate power, because their thinking about power was so primitive (in my view a failure to understand the role of autonomy power in addition to conventional balance power, power-over-oneself as opposed to power-over-others).

14. In international politics it is, fortunately, not the round-robin method with everybody competing with everybody that is used; the system is more similar to the way champions emerge in boxing (by challenging the champion).

15. One reason for this is that everything is so transparent and so explicit. Although it is fashionable to have people from small countries as chairmen and presidents, it is hard to imagine an intergovernmental organization without all or most big powers on the board, if they are members at all. In a transnational organization no such position would come automatically. Of course, it is possible for the small to meet behind their backs, but organizations have formalized procedures for decision making that usually are seen as having to be acceptable to big powers to be "realistic"—an assumption that fortunately has been challenged quite often in the United Nations recently. The territorial system does not have a similar system (if it had, it would be an IGO); it relies instead on a

complex web of bilateral pressures and occasional eruptions of more naked power.

16. Such gradations are often introduced in functionally specific organizations, e.g., that contemplated for the seabed, defining functionally specific big powers (according to length of coastline, shipping tonnage, importance of fisheries, etc.).

17. I say "formed" with some qualification. Since the creation of a Jewish nation-state, Israel, it is doubtful whether Jews differ very much from others in this regard, except insofar as a great proportion live outside the borders of that state. One Jewish argument was, of course, "Why should we be different from others, why should it fall on us to be some kind of cementing force in a world of states?" The argument is highly understandable, and yet the day may perhaps come when the nation-state program is given up by most nations in favor of a nations-world, possibly with some small territory for each nation, a shrine like Vatican City, but otherwise mixing with each other all over the world.

18. In two such associations particularly known to me, the International Peace Research Association and the World Future Studies Federation, some national identities are, of course, still discernible because the topics—peace and the future—have not been universalized in the way mathematics and chemistry have been. National interests and styles are reflected to some extent. And yet correlations with national background are remarkably low, as also applies to Pugwash—with the possible exception of the Soviet participants, who are remarkably uniform in their presentations. Their papers look identical, as if they are produced by the same national secretariat, and names are allocated at random to comply with Western models in the TRANGO direction (according to the best sources this is exactly what happened some years ago).

19. 1968 was a remarkable year in this sense. Suddenly it became obvious how little in terms of organization is needed to constitute such movements. In all continents students revolted; but they were successful only in China—if one assumes that the Cultural Revolution was a part, *partly*, of the same phenomenon. Obviously modern mass media do, unpaid, more to coordinate such groups by making them and their actions mutually visible than they would ever have been able to do themselves, and in a homogenizing world (because of industrialism and various forms of capitalism) problems are similar enough to make their experiences mutually relevant.

20. This would constitute a more conscious type of revolt than the more ubiquitous "revolts" that are merely efforts to obtain adjustments within a model II society. This is where the Chinese part from fellow student revolutionaries in many other countries. "On the Cultural Revolution," chapter 3 in Galtung and Fumiko Nishimura, *Learning from the Chinese People* (Oslo, 1975).

21. And who started all these organizations. That we know something about, and it is more than clear what message is conveyed through that channel: the northwestern corner of the world (see the references cited in note 10).

22. In other words, among these are the people who, often unwittingly, are necessary conditions for imperialism to function at all. In saying so, however, I am of course not thinking of all kinds of international organizations. Obviously, economic imperialism is above all carried by the BINGOs (the MNCs, or TNCs as the name would be now); political imperialism by IGOs and by the internationals of the parties (better organized on the left than on the right because the latter have the whole BINGO complex to back them up); military imperialism by all the military alliances and international cooperative systems with their special kind of daughter companies known as bases; social imperialism by the latter two but also by all kinds of experts belonging to international or regional professional communities, shaping societies in their image; cultural imperialism mainly by INGOs, but also to a large extent by the culture agencies run by governments to

propagate the national culture abroad; and communication imperialism by the news agencies and the like.

23. Very often an organization wants to become universal, and may even pretend to be so, but in fact ends up connecting Center countries only—if for no other reason than that the resources of the world are so distributed that only they can afford to participate. Another reason may be added, though: most Westerners fail to contemplate how utterly Western is the entire idea of detachable individuals leaving their home context to exchange experiences and views in an abstract, theoretical form in a conference. The difficulty in getting Chinese participants to Western-style conferences is related to this: how can any one individual represent collective Chinese reality, and how can any reality be represented in words alone?

24. The Soviet Union is particularly famous for this in the United Nations. As it is itself a Western country, I prefer to interpret it as control over individuals rather than as a rejection of the Western organization model.

25. On the contrary, there are some indications that NTs are particularly well used by the smaller, Western, capitalist countries. Thus, if we look at the number of INGOs per capita, eight of the ten top countries on the list fall into this category (but not for IGOs per capita, because all countries have to be members of a certain number, so the size of the population pushes a number of Third World countries up on the top of the list). As to number of international officials per capita, however, the capitalist northwest dominates. See the references cited in note 10.

26. This error is, I hope, avoided in the present chapter and in the following chapters, as well as in my essay "Nonterritorial Actors and the Problem of Peace" in Saul H. Mendlovitz, ed., *On the Creation of a Just World Order* (New York: Free Press, 1975). However, I readily admit to much more skepticism about the NTs than I had some years ago, perhaps seeing better the role they play. What remains is the idea that they can be changed and therefore constitute a tremendous potential, for peace and development.

27. On the other hand, a recourse to cloak-and-dagger techniques, singling out special individuals rather than territories for destruction, is conceivable, even with "modern" technology—e.g., some kind of mini-rocket steered by homing devices placed surreptitiously on those designated as victims.

28. In addition to Barnet and Müller's *Global Reach* I recommend Louis Turner's *Invisible Empires* (London: Hamilton, 1970). Both have excellent bibliographies. In some years the UN research center on transnational corporations will no doubt be a major source of insight and information in this field. Their guide to research in the field is already useful: *Survey of Research on Transnational Corporations* (New York: United Nations, 1977); based on questionnaires to researchers and institutes.

29. These three propositions would follow from the expansionist nature of capitalism: to try to cover the whole world and to cover it alone—not only to control the prices, but because expansionism is built into the capitalist production process. The tendency to control the total cycle is, of course, not new; it is also found in the plantation economy, and others, but the scale is new. It is no longer merely a question of forcing workers to buy in the company stores but of controlling the consumption patterns of entire populations.

30. Japan can be seen as one such cooperative federation when operating abroad. There is not only the individual *zaibatsu*; all of Japan is a *zaibatsu*.

31. Take the case of Exxon, reputed not to have supplied fuel to the U.S. Sixth Fleet in the Mediterranean during the Yom Kippur war in October 1973 for fear of offending the Arabs. It looks as if this disharmony of interest between a U.S. corporation and the U.S. government was solved in the direction of the former.

32. This is inspired by a discussion of multinational corporations in the third week of the World Future Models course at the Inter-University Centre, Dubrovnik, January 1975. I am indebted to the organizer of the seminar, Professor Nasrollah Fatemi, and to Mr. F. Reinauer-Second for particularly important criticism.

33. This point was repeatedly made by the late Stephen Hymer, whose premature death was a great loss to the critical research in this field.

34. This is a basic point in the critique of the TNCs, but of the five on the list I tend to rank it last in real significance.

35. "But nobody would invest in a slum" is the answer, which is true within short-run capitalist rationality. In the long run the use of the social surplus for such purposes would liberate the population from the shackles of poverty, thereby increasing production and productivity—provided that the economy would permit the absorption of more labor in more creative capacities. The truth is, of course, that the capitalist economy in the Periphery in general would not allow this, being based on uneven development inside the country. As a consequence the combination of luxury hotels and slums is an essential, not an accidental part of the system.

36. One of the lasting achievements of the late Salvador Allende will be his UN speech on transnational corporations in general and on the ITT in particular—showing the power of the United Nations as an articulation forum. From the report in the *International Herald Tribune*, 5 December 1972: "Mr. Allende also harshly criticised the large, multinational corporations, which he accused of 'economic aggression' against Chile. He attacked in especially strong terms International Telegraph and Telephone and Kennecott Copper Corp., which he said 'had driven their claws deep into my country, [and] proposed to manage our political life.'"

37. Immanuel Wallerstein's monumental study *The Modern World System*, with the first volume covering 1450 to 1640 (New York and London: Academic Press, 1975), is of course the key work in this field today.

38. For a critique, see Galtung, "Self-reliance and Global Interdependence: Some Reflections on the New International Order," *Papers*, no. 55, Chair in Conflict and Peace Research, University of Oslo, 1976; also CIDA (Ottawa, 1978).

39. One reason for this may be that the Third World elites drafting such resolutions want/need products themselves, another that this type of criticism would be even more resented because it goes deeper. One thing is to criticize somebody for exploitation, even for cheating; quite another is to intimate that the entire production process is based on a major fallacy, that most of the products are in the "pink toilet paper category" and are the consequence of wrong priorities in a distorted system. My own impression from many meetings of that kind is that non-Western elites often are extremely tactful and polite and prefer less contentious dimensions of argument, not only for political reasons.

40. Which is the point that can be made about the Lomé Convention; see "The Lomé Convention and Neo-capitalism," *Africa Today* (1976).

41. See Johan Galtung, *The True Worlds* (New York: Free Press, 1980), pp. 341–81.

11
THE RISE AND FUTURE DEMISE
OF THE WORLD CAPITALIST SYSTEM:
CONCEPTS FOR COMPARATIVE ANALYSIS

Immanuel Wallerstein

The growth within the capitalist world-economy of the industrial sector of production, the so-called "industrial revolution," was accompanied by a very strong current of thought which defined this change as both a process of organic development and of progress. There were those who considered these economic developments and the concomitant changes in social organization to be some penultimate stage of world development whose final working-out was but a matter of time. These included such diverse thinkers as Saint-Simon, Comte, Hegel, Weber, Durkheim. And then there were the critics, most notably Marx, who argued, if you will, that the nineteenth-century present was only an antepenultimate stage of development, that the capitalist world was to know a cataclysmic political revolution which would then lead in the fullness of time to a final societal form, in this case the classless society.

One of the great strengths of Marxism was that, being an oppositional and hence critical doctrine, it called attention not merely to the contradictions of the system but to those of its ideologists, by appealing to the empirical evidence of historical reality which unmasked the irrelevancy of the models proposed for the explanation of the social world. The Marxist critics saw in abstracted models concrete rationalization, and they argued their case fundamentally by pointing to the failure of their opponents to analyze the social whole. As Lukacs put it, "it is not the primacy of economic motives in historical explanation that constitutes the decisive difference between Marxism and bourgeois thought, but the point of view of totality."[1]

In the mid-twentieth century, the dominant theory of development in the core countries of the capitalist world-economy has added little to the theorizing of the nineteenth-century progenitors of this mode of analysis, except to quantify the models and to abstract them still further, by adding on epicyclical codas to the models in order to account for ever further deviations from empirical expectations.

What is wrong with such models has been shown many times over, and from

Reprinted with permission from *Comparative Studies in Society and History* 16, September 1974.

many standpoints. I cite only one critic, a non-Marxist, Robert Nisbet, whose very cogent reflections on what he calls the "Western theory of development" conclude with this summary:

> [We] turn to history and only to history if what we are seeking are the actual causes, sources, and conditions of overt changes of patterns and structures in society. Conventional wisdom to the contrary in modern social theory, we shall not find the explanation of change in those studies which are abstracted from history; whether these be studies of small groups in the social laborabory, group dynamics generally, staged experiments in social interaction, or mathematical analyses of so-called social systems. Nor will we find the sources of change in contemporary revivals of the comparative method with its ascending staircase of cultural similarities and differences plucked from all space and time.[2]

Shall we then turn to the critical schools, in particular Marxism, to give us a better account of social reality? In principle yes; in practice there are many different, often contradictory, versions extant of "Marxism." But what is more fundamental is the fact that in many countries Marxism is now the official state doctrine. Marxism is no longer exclusively an oppositional doctrine as it was in the nineteenth century.

The social fate of official doctrines is that they suffer a constant social pressure towards dogmatism and apologia, difficult although by no means impossible to counteract, and that they thereby often fall into the same intellectual dead-end of ahistorical model-building. Here the critique of Fernand Braudel is most pertinent:

> Marxism is a whole collection of models. . . . I shall protest . . . more or less, not against the model, but rather against the use to which people have thought themselves entitled to put it. The genius of Marx, the secret of his enduring power, lies in his having been the first to construct true social models, starting out from the long term (la longue durée). These models have been fixed permanently in their simplicity; they have been given the force of law and they have been treated as ready-made, automatic explanations, applicable in all places to all societies. . . . In this way has the creative power of the most powerful social analysis of the last century been shackled. It will be able to regain its strength and vitality only in the long term.[3]

Nothing illustrates the distortions of ahistorical models of social change better than the dilemmas to which the concept of stages gives rise. If we are to deal with social transformations over long historical time (Braudel's "the long term"), and if we are to give an explanation of both continuity and transformation, then we must logically divide the long term into segments in order to observe the structural changes from time A to time B. These segments are however not discrete but continuous in reality; *ergo* they are "stages" in the "development" of a social structure, a development which we determine however not *a priori* but *a posteriori*. That is, we cannot predict the future concretely, but we can predict the past.

The crucial issue when comparing "stages" is to determine the units of which the "stages" are synchronic portraits (or "ideal types," if you will). And the fundamental error of ahistorical social science (including ahistorical versions of Marxism) is to reify parts of the totality into such units and then to compare these reified structures.

For example, we may take modes of disposition of agricultural production, and term them subsistence-cropping and cash-cropping. We may then see these as entities which are "stages" of a development. We may talk about decisions of groups of peasants to shift from one to the other. We may describe other partial entities, such as states, as having within them two separate "economies," each based on a different mode of disposition of agricultural production. If we take each of these successive steps, all of which are false steps, we will end up with the misleading concept of the "dual economy" as have many liberal economists dealing with the so-called underdeveloped countries of the world. Still worse, we may reify a misreading of British history into a set of universal "stages" as Rostow does.

Marxist scholars have often fallen into exactly the same trap. If we take modes of payment of agricultural labor and contrast a "feudal" mode wherein the laborer is permitted to retain for subsistence a part of his agricultural production with a "capitalist" mode wherein the same laborer turns over the totality of his production to the landowner, receiving part of it back in the form of wages, we may then see these two modes as "stages" of a development. We may talk of the interests of "feudal" landowners in preventing the conversion of their mode of payment to a system of wages. We may then explain the fact that in the twentieth century a partial entity, say a state in Latin America, has not yet industrialized as the consequence of its being dominated by such landlords. If we take each of these successive steps, all of which are false steps, we will end up with the misleading concept of a "state dominated by feudal elements," as though such a thing could possibly exist in a capitalist world-economy. But, as André Gunder Frank has clearly spelled out, such a myth dominated for a long time "traditional Marxist" thought in Latin America.[4]

Not only does the misidentification of the entities to be compared lead us into false concepts, but it creates a non-problem: can stages be skipped? This question is only logically meaningful if we have "stages" that "co-exist" within a single empirical framework. If within a capitalist world-economy, we define one state as feudal, a second as capitalist, and a third as socialist, then and only then can we pose the question: can a country "skip" from the feudal stage to the socialist stage of national development without "passing through capitalism"?

But if there is no such thing as "national development" (if by that we mean a natural history), and if the proper entity of comparison is the world-system, then the problem of stage-skipping is nonsense. If a stage can be skipped, it isn't a stage. And we know this a posteriori.

If we are to talk of stages, then — and we should talk of stages — it must be stages of social systems, that is, of totalities. And the only totalities that exist or have historically existed are mini-systems and world-systems, and in the nineteenth and twentieth centuries there has been only one world-system in existence, the capitalist world-economy.

We take the defining characteristic of a social system to be the existence within it of a division of labor, such that the various sectors or areas within are dependent upon economic exchange with others for the smooth and continuous provisioning of the needs of the area. Such economic exchange can clearly exist without a common political structure and even more obviously without sharing the same culture.

A mini-system is an entity that has within it a complete division of labor, and a single cultural framework. Such systems are found only in very simple agricultural or hunting and gathering societies. Such mini-systems no longer exist in the world. Furthermore, there were fewer in the past than is often asserted, since any such system that became tied to an empire by the payment of tribute as "protection costs"[5] ceased by that fact to be a "system," no longer having a self-contained division of labor. For such an area, the payment of tribute marked a shift, in Polanyi's language, from being a reciprocal economy to participating in a larger redistributive economy.[6]

Leaving aside the now defunct mini-systems, the only kind of social system is a world-system, which we define quite simply as a unit with a single division of labor and multiple cultural systems. It follows logically that there can, however, be two varieties of such world-systems, one with a common political system and one without. We shall designate these respectively as world-empires and world-economies.

It turns out empirically that world-economies have historically been unstable structures leading either towards disintegration or conquest by one group and hence transformation into a world-empire. Examples of such world-empires emerging from world-economies are all the so-called great civilizations of premodern times, such as China, Egypt, Rome (each at appropriate periods of its history). On the other hand, the so-called nineteenth-century empires, such as Great Britain or France, were not world-empires at all, but national-states with colonial appendages operating within the framework of a world-economy.

World-empires were basically redistributive in economic form. No doubt they bred clusters of merchants who engaged in economic exchange (primarily long-distance trade), but such clusters, however large, were a minor part of the total economy and not fundamentally determinative of its fate. Such long-distance trade tended to be, as Polanyi argues, "administered trade" and not market trade, utilizing "ports of trade."

It was only with the emergence of the modern world-economy in sixteenth-century Europe that we saw the full development and economic predominance of market trade. This was the system called capitalism. Capitalism and a world-economy (that is, a single division of labor but multiple polities and cultures) are obverse sides of the same coin. One does not cause the other. We are merely defining the same indivisible phenomenon by different characteristics.

How and why it came about that this particular European world-economy of the sixteenth century did not become transformed into redistributive world-empire but developed definitively as a capitalist world-economy I have explained elsewhere.[7] The genesis of this world-historical turning-point is marginal to the issues under discussion in this paper, which is rather what conceptual apparatus one brings to bear on the analysis of developments within the framework of precisely such a capitalist world-economy.

Let us therefore turn to the capitalist world-economy. We shall seek to deal with two pseudo-problems, created by the trap of not analyzing totalities: the so-called persistence of feudal forms, and the so-called creation of socialist systems. In doing this, we shall offer an alternative model with which to engage in comparative analysis, one rooted in the historically specific totality which is the world capitalist economy. We hope to demonstrate thereby that to be historically specific is not to fail to be analytically universal. On the contrary, the only road to nomothetic propositions is through the historically concrete, just as in cosmology the only road to a theory of the laws governing the universe is through the concrete analysis of the historical evolution of this same universe.[8]

On the "feudalism" debate, we take as a starting-point Frank's concept of "the development of underdevelopment," that is, the view that the economic structure of contemporary underdeveloped countries is not the form which a "traditional" society takes upon contact with "developed" societies, not an earlier stage in the "transition" to industrialization. It is rather the result of being involved in the world-economy as a peripheral, raw material producing area, or as Frank puts it for Chile, "underdevelopment . . . is the necessary product of four centuries of capitalism itself."[9]

This formulation runs counter to a large body of writing concerning the underdeveloped countries that was produced in the period 1950–70, a literature which sought the factors that explained "development" within non-systems such as "states" or "cultures" and, once having presumably discovered these factors, urged their reproduction in underdeveloped areas as the road to salvation.[10]

Frank's theory also runs counter, as we have already noted, to the received orthodox version of Marxism that had long dominated Marxist parties and intellectual circles, for example in Latin America. This older "Marxist" view of Latin America as a set of feudal societies in a more or less pre-bourgeois stage of development has fallen before the critiques of Frank and many others as well as before the political reality symbolized by the Cuban revolution and all its many consequences. Recent analysis in Latin America has centered instead around the concept of "dependence."[11]

However, recently, Ernesto Laclau has made an attack on Frank which, while accepting the critique of dualist doctrines, refuses to accept the categorization of Latin American states as capitalist. Instead Laclau asserts that "the world capitalist system . . . includes, *at all level of its definition*, various modes of production." He accuses Frank of confusing the two concepts of the "capitalist mode of production" and "participation in a world capitalist economic system."[12]

Of course, if it's a matter of definition, then there can be no argument. But then the polemic is scarcely useful since it is reduced to a question of semantics. Furthermore, Laclau insists that the definition is not his but that of Marx, which is more debatable. Rosa Luxemburg put her finger on a key element in

Marx's ambiguity or inconsistency in this particular debate, the ambiguity which enables both Frank and Laclau to trace their thoughts to Marx:

> Admittedly, Marx dealt in detail with the process of appropriating non-capitalist means of production [N.B., Luxemburg is referring to primary products produced in peripheral areas under conditions of coerced labor—I.W.] as well as with the transformation of the peasants into a capitalist proletariat. Chapter XXIV of *Capital*, Vol. 1, is devoted to describing the origin of the English proletariat, of the capitalistic agricultural tenant class and of industrial capital, with particular emphasis on the looting of colonial countries by European capital. Yet we must bear in mind that all this is treated solely with a view to so-called primitive accumulation. For Marx, these processes are incidental, illustrating merely the genesis of capital, its first appearance in the world; they are, as it were, travails by which the capitalist mode of production emerges from a feudal society. As soon as he comes to analyze the capitalist process of production and circulation, he reaffirms the universal and exclusive domination of capitalist production [N.B., that is, production based on wage labor—I.W.].[13]

There is, after all, a substantive issue in this debate. It is in fact the same substantive issue that underlay the debate between Maurice Dobb and Paul Sweezy in the early 1950s about the "transition from feudalism to capitalism" that occurred in early modern Europe.[14] The substantive issue, in my view, concerns the appropriate unit of analysis for the purpose of comparison. Basically, although neither Sweezy nor Frank is quite explicit on this point, and though Dobb and Laclau can both point to texts of Marx that seem clearly to indicate that they more faithfully follow Marx's argument, I believe both Sweezy and Frank better follow the spirit of Marx if not his letter[15] and that, leaving Marx quite out of the picture, they bring us nearer to an understanding of what actually happened and is happening than their opponents.

What is the picture, both analytical and historical, that Laclau constructs? The heart of the problem revolves around the existence of free labor as the defining characteristic of a capitalist mode of production:

> The fundamental economic relationship of capitalism is constituted by the *free* [italics mine] labourer's sale of his labour-power, whose necessary precondition is the loss by the direct producer of ownership of the means of production. . . .
>
> If we now confront Frank's affirmation that the socio-economic complexes of Latin America have been capitalist since the Conquest Period . . . with the currently available empirical evidence, we must conclude that the "capitalist" thesis is indefensible. In regions with dense indigenous populations—Mexico, Peru, Bolivia, or Guatemala—the direct producers were not despoiled of their ownership of the means of production, while extra-economic coercion to maximize various systems of labour service . . . was progressively intensified. In the plantations of the West Indies, the economy was based on a mode of production constituted by slave labour, while in the mining areas there developed disguised forms of slavery and other types of forced labour which bore not the slightest resemblance to the formation of a capitalist proletariat.[16]

There in a nutshell it is. Western Europe, at least England from the late seventeenth century on, had primarily landless, wage-earning laborers. In Latin

America, then and to some extent still now, laborers were not proletarians, but slaves or "serfs." If proletariat, then capitalism. Of course. To be sure. But is England, or Mexico, or the West Indies a unit of analysis? Does each have a separate "mode of production"? Or is the unit (for the sixteenth–eighteenth centuries) the European world-economy, including England *and* Mexico, in which case what was the "mode of production" of this world-economy?

Before we argue our response to this question, let us turn to quite another debate, one between Mao Tse-Tung and Liu Shao-Chi in the 1960s concerning whether or not the Chinese People's Republic was a "socialist state." This is a debate that has a long background in the evolving thought of Marxist parties.

Marx, as has been often noted, said virtually nothing about the post-revolutionary political process. Engels spoke quite late in his writings of the "dictatorship of the proletariat." It was left to Lenin to elaborate a theory about such a "dictatorship," in his pamphlet *State and Revolution*, published in the last stages before the Bolshevik takeover of Russia, that is, in August 1917. The coming to power of the Bolsheviks led to a considerable debate as to the nature of the regime that had been established. Eventually a theoretical distinction emerged in Soviet thought between "socialism" and "communism" as two stages in historical development, one realizable in the present and one only in the future. In 1936 Stalin proclaimed that the U.S.S.R. had become a socialist (but not yet a communist) state. Thus we now had firmly established *three* stages after bourgeois rule: a post-revolutionary government, a socialist state, and eventually communism. When, after the Second World War, various regimes dominated by the Communist Party were established in various East European states, these regimes were proclaimed to be "peoples' democracies," a new name then given to the post-revolutionary stage one. At later points, some of these countries, for example Czechoslovakia, asserted they had passed into stage two, that of becoming a socialist republic.

In 1961, the 22nd Congress of the CPSU invented a fourth stage, in between the former second and third stages: that of a socialist state which had become a "state of the whole people," a stage it was contended the U.S.S.R. had at that point reached. The Programme of the Congress asserted that "the state as an organization of the entire people will survive until the complete victory of communism."[17] One of its commentators defines the "intrinsic substance (and) chief distinctive feature" of this stage: "The state of the whole people is the first state in the world with no class struggle to contend with and, hence, with no class domination and no suppression."[18]

One of the earliest signs of a major disagreement in the 1950s between the Communist Party of the Soviet Union and the Chinese Communist Party was a theoretical debate that revolved around the question of the "gradual transition to Communism." Basically, the CPSU argued that different socialist states would proceed separately in effectuating such a transition whereas the CCP argued that all socialist states would proceed simultaneously.

As we can see, this last form of the debate about "stages" implicitly raised the issue of the unit of analysis, for in effect the CCP was arguing that "communism" was a characteristic not of nation-states but of the world-economy as a whole. This debate was transposed onto the internal Chinese scene by the ideological debate, now known to have deep and long-standing roots, that gave rise eventually to the Cultural Revolution.

One of the corollaries of these debates about "stages" was whether or not the class struggle continued in post-revolutionary states prior to the achievement of communism. The 22nd Congress of the CPSU in 1961 had argued that the U.S.S.R. had become a state without an internal class struggle, there were no longer existing antagonistic classes within it. Without speaking of the U.S.S.R., Mao Tse-Tung in 1957 had asserted of China:

> The class struggle is by no means over. . . . It will continue to be long and tortuous, and at times will even become very acute. . . . Marxists are still a minority among the entire population as well as among the intellectuals. Therefore, Marxism must still develop through struggle. . . . Such struggles will never end. This is the law of development of truth and, naturally, of Marxism as well.[19]

If such struggles *never* end, then many of the facile generalizations about "stages" which "socialist" states are presumed to go through are thrown into question.

During the Cultural Revolution, it was asserted that Mao's report "On the Correct Handling of Contradiction Among The Peoples" cited above, as well as one other, "entirely repudiated the 'theory of the dying out of the class struggle' advocated by Liu Shao-Chi. . . ."[20] Specifically, Mao argued that "the elimination of the system of ownership by the exploiting classes through socialist transformation is not equal to the disappearance of struggle in the political and ideological spheres."[21]

Indeed, this is the logic of a *cultural* revolution. Mao is asserting that even if there is the achievement of *political* power (dictatorship of the proletariat) and *economic* transformation (abolition of private ownership of the means of production), the revolution is still far from complete. Revolution is not an event but a process. This process Mao calls "socialist society"—in my view a somewhat confusing choice of words, but no matter—and "socialist society covers a fairly long historical period."[22] Furthermore, "there are classes and class struggle throughout the period of socialist society."[23] The Tenth Plenum of the 8th Central Committee of the CCP, meeting from September 24-27, 1962, in endorsing Mao's views, omitted the phrase "socialist society" and talked instead of "the historical period of proletarian revolution and proletarian dictatorship, . . . the historical period of transition from capitalism to communism," which it said "will last scores of years or even longer" and during which "there is class struggle between the proletariat and the bourgeoisie and struggle between the socialist road and the capitalist road."[24]

We do not have directly Liu's counter-arguments. We might however take as an expression of the alternative position a recent analysis published in the U.S.S.R. on the relationship of the socialist system and world development. There it is asserted that at some unspecified point after the Second World

War, "socialism outgrew the bounds of the one country and became a world system. . . ."[25] It is further argued that: "Capitalism, emerging in the 16th century, became a world economic system only in the 19th century. It took the bourgeois revolutions 300 years to put an end to the power of the feudal elite. It took socialism 30 or 40 years to generate the forces for a new world system."[26] Finally, this book speaks of "capitalism's international division of labor"[27] and "international socialist co-operation of labor"[28] as two separate phenomena, drawing from this counterposition the policy conclusion: "Socialist unity has suffered a serious setback from the divisive course being pursued by the incumbent leadership of the Chinese People's Republic," and attributes this to "the great-power chauvinism of Mao Tse-Tung and his group."[29]

Note well the contrast between these two positions. Mao Tse-Tung is arguing for viewing "socialist society" as process rather than structure. Like Frank and Sweezy, and once again implicitly rather than explicitly, he is taking the world-system rather than the nation-state as the unit of analysis. The analysis by U.S.S.R. scholars by contrast specifically argues the existence of *two* world-systems with two divisions of labor existing side by side, although the socialist system is acknowledged to be "divided." If divided politically, is it united economically? Hardly, one would think; in which case what is the substructural base to argue the existence of the system? Is it merely a moral imperative? And are then the Soviet scholars defending their concepts on the basis of Kantian metaphysics?

Let us see now if we can reinterpret the issues developed in these two debates within the framework of a general set of concepts that could be used to analyze the functioning of world-systems, and particularly of the historically specific capitalist world-economy that has existed for about four or five centuries now.

We must start with how one demonstrates the existence of a single division of labor. We can regard a division of labor as a grid which is substantially interdependent. Economic actors operate on some assumption (obviously seldom clear to any individual actor) that the totality of their essential needs—of sustenance, protection, and pleasure—will be met over a reasonable time-span by a combination of their own productive activities and exchange in some form. The smallest grid that would substantially meet the expectations of the overwhelming majority of actors within those boundaries constitutes a single division of labor.

The reason why a small farming community whose only significant link to outsiders is the payment of annual tribute does not constitute such a single division of labor is that the assumptions of persons living in it concerning the provision of protection involve an "exchange" with other parts of the world-empire.

This concept of a grid of exchange relationships assumes, however, a distinction between *essential* exchanges and what might be called "luxury" exchanges. This is to be sure a distinction rooted in the social perceptions of the actors and hence in both their social organization and their culture. These perceptions can change. But this distinction is crucial if we are not to fall into the trap of identifying *every* exchange-activity as evidence of the existence of a system.

Members of a system (a mini-system or a world-system) can be linked in limited exchanges with elements located outside the system, in the "external arena" of the system.

The form of such an exchange is very limited. Elements of the two systems can engage in an exchange of preciosities. That is, each can export to the other what is in *its* system socially defined as worth little in return for the import of what in its system is defined as worth much. This is not a mere pedantic definitional exercise, as the exchange of preciosities *between* world-systems can be extremely important in the historical evolution of a given world-system. The reason why this is so important is that in an exchange of preciosities, the importer is "reaping a windfall" and not obtaining a profit. Both exchange-partners can reap windfalls simultaneously but only one can obtain maximum profit, since the exchange of surplus-value within a system is a zero-sum game.

We are, as you see, coming to the essential feature of a capitalist world-economy, which is production for sale in a market in which the object is to realize the maximum profit. In such a system production is constantly expanded as long as further production is profitable, and men constantly innovate new ways of producing things that will expand the profit margin. The classical economists tried to argue that such production for the market was somehow the "natural" state of man. But the combined writings of the anthropologists and the Marxists left few in doubt that such a mode of production (these days called "capitalism") was only one of several possible modes.

Since, however, the intellectual debate between the liberals and the Marxists took place in the era of the industrial revolution, there has tended to be a *de facto* confusion between industrialism and capitalism. This left the liberals after 1945 in the dilemma of explaining how a presumably non-capitalist society, the U.S.S.R., had industrialized. The most sophisticated response has been to conceive of "liberal capitalism" and "socialism" as two variants of an "industrial society," two variants destined to "converge." This argument has been trenchantly expounded by Raymond Aron.[30] But the same confusion left the Marxists, including Marx, with the problem of explaining what was the mode of production that predominated in Europe from the sixteenth to the eighteenth centuries, that is before the industrial revolution. Essentially, most Marxists have talked of a "transitional" stage, which is in fact a blurry non-concept with no operational indicators. This dilemma is heightened if the unit of analysis used is the state, in which case one has to explain why the transition has occurred at different rates and times in different countries.[31]

Marx himself handled this by drawing a distinction between "merchant capitalism" and "industrial capitalism." This I believe is unfortunate terminology, since it leads to such conclusions as that of Maurice Dobb who says of this "transitional" period:

> But why speak of this as a stage of capitalism at all? The workers were generally not proletarianized: that is, they were not separated from the instruments of production, nor even in many cases from occupation of a plot of land. Production was scattered and decentralized and not concentrated. *The capitalist was still predominantly a*

merchant who did not control production directly and did not impose his own discipline upon the work of artisan-craftsmen, who both laboured as individual (or family) units and retained a considerable measure of independence (if a dwindling one).[32]

One might well say: why indeed? Especially if one remembers how much emphasis Dobb places a few pages earlier on capitalism as a mode of *production*—how then can the capitalist be primarily a merchant?—on the concentration of such ownership in the hands of a few, and on the fact that capitalism is not synonymous with private ownership, capitalism being different from a system in which the owners are "small peasant producers or artisan-producers." Dobb argues that a defining feature of private ownership under capitalism is that some are "obliged to [work for those that own] since [they own] nothing and [have] no access to means of production [and hence] have no other means of livelihood."[33] Given this contradiction, the answer Dobb gives to his own question is in my view very weak: "While it is true that at this date the situation was transnational, and capital-to-wage-labour relations were still immaturely developed, the latter were already beginning to assume their characteristic features."[34]

If capitalism is a mode of production, production for profit in a market, then we ought, I should have thought, to look to whether or not such production was or was not occurring. It turns out in fact that it was, and in a very substantial form. Most of this production, however, was not industrial production. What was happening in Europe from the sixteenth to the eighteenth centuries is that over a large geographical area going from Poland in the northeast westwards and southwards throughout Europe and including large parts of the Western Hemisphere as well, there grew up a world-economy with a single division of labor within which there was a world market, for which men produced largely agricultural products for sale and profit. I would think the simplest thing to do would be to call this agricultural capitalism.

This then resolves the problems incurred by using the pervasiveness of *wage-labor* as a defining characteristic of capitalism. An individual is no less a capitalist exploiting labor because the state assists him to pay his laborers low wages (including wages in kind) and denies these laborers the right to change employment. Slavery and so-called "second serfdom" are not to be regarded as anomalies in a capitalist system. Rather the so-called serf in Poland or the Indian on a Spanish *encomienda* in New Spain in this sixteenth-century world-economy were working for landlords who "paid" them (however euphemistic this term) for cash-crop production. This is a relationship in which labor-power is a commodity (how could it ever be more so than under slavery?), quite different from the relationship of a feudal serf to his lord in eleventh-century Burgundy, where the economy was not oriented to a world market, and where labor-power was (therefore?) in no sense bought or sold.

Capitalism thus means labor as a commodity to be sure. But in the era of agricultural capitalism, wage-labor is only one of the modes in which labor is recruited and recompensed in the labor market. Slavery, coerced cash-crop production (my name for the so-called second feudalism), share-cropping, and tenancy are all alternative modes. It would be too long to develop here the conditions under which differing regions of the world-economy tend to specialize in different agricultural products. I have done this elsewhere.[35]

What we must notice now is that this specialization occurs in specific and differing geographic regions of the world economy. This regional specialization comes about by the attempts of actors in the market to avoid the normal operation of the market whenever it does not maximize their profit. The attempts of these actors to use non-market devices to ensure short-run profits makes them turn to the political entities which have in fact power to affect the market—the nation-states. (Again, why at this stage they could not have turned to city-states would take us into a long discursus, but it has to do with the state of military and shipping technology, the need of the European land-mass to expand overseas in the fifteenth century if it was to maintain the level of income of the various aristocracies, combined with the state of political disintegration to which Europe had fallen in the Middle Ages.)

In any case, the local capitalist classes—cash-crop landowners (often, even usually, nobility) and merchants—turned to the state, not only to liberate them from non-market constraints (as traditionally emphasized by liberal historiography) but to create new constraints on the new market, the market of the European world-economy.

By a series of accidents—historical, ecological, geographic—northwest Europe was better situated in the sixteenth century to diversify its agricultural specialization and add to it certain industries (such as textiles, shipbuilding, and metal wares) than were other parts of Europe. Northwest Europe emerged as the core area of this world-economy, specializing in agricultural production of higher skill levels, which favored (again for reasons too complex to develop) tenancy and wage-labor as the modes of labor control. Eastern Europe and the Western Hemisphere became peripheral areas specializing in export of grains, bullion, wood, cotton, sugar—all of which favored the use of slavery and coerced cash-crop labor as the modes of labor control. Mediterranean Europe emerged as the semi-peripheral area of this world-economy specializing in high-cost industrial products (for example, silks) and credit and specie transactions, which had as a consequence in the agricultural arena share-cropping as the mode of labor control and little export to other areas.

The three structural positions in a world-economy—core, periphery, and semi-periphery—had become stabilized by about 1640. How certain areas became one and not the other is a long story.[36] The key fact is that given slightly different starting-points, the interests of various local groups converged in northwest Europe, leading to the development of strong state mechanisms, and diverged sharply in the peripheral areas, leading to very weak ones. Once we get a difference in the strength of the state-machineries, we get the operation of "unequal exchange"[37] which is enforced by strong states on weak ones, by core states on peripheral areas. Thus capitalism involves not only appropriation of the surplus-value by an owner from a laborer, but an appropriation of surplus of the whole world-economy by core areas. And this was as true in the stage of agricultural capitalism as it is in the stage of industrial capitalism.

In the early Middle Ages, there was to be sure trade. But it was largely either "local," in a region that we might call the "extended" manor, or "long-distance," primarily of luxury goods. There was no exchange of "bulk" goods, of "staples" across intermediate-size areas, and hence no production for such markets. Later on in the Middle Ages, world-economies may be said to have come into existence, one centering on Venice, a second on the cities of Flanders and the Hanse. For various reasons, these structures were hurt by the retractions (economic, demographic, and ecological) of the period 1300–1450. It is only with the creating of a *European* division of labor after 1450 that capitalism found firm roots.

Capitalism was from the beginning an affair of the world-economy and not of nation-states. It is a misreading of the situation to claim that it is only in the twentieth century that capitalism has become "world-wide," although this claim is frequently made in various writings, particularly by Marxists. Typical of this line of argument is Charles Bettelheim's response to Arghiri Emmanuel's discussion of unequal exchange:

> The tendency of the capitalist mode of production to become worldwide is manifested not only through the constitution of a group of national economies forming a complex and hierarchical structure, including an imperialist pole and a dominated one, and not only through the antagonistic relations that develop between the different "national economies" and the different states, but also through the constant "transcending" of "national limits" by big capital (the formation of "international big capital," "world firms," etc. . . .).[38]

The whole tone of these remarks ignores the fact that capital has never allowed its aspirations to be determined by national boundaries in a capitalist world-economy, and that the creation of "national" barriers—generically, mercantilism—has historically been a defensive mechanism of capitalists located in states which are one level below the high point of strength in the system. Such was the case of England vis-à-vis the Netherlands in 1660–1715, France vis-à-vis England in 1715–1815, Germany vis-à-vis Britain in the nineteenth century, the Soviet Union vis-à-vis the U.S. in the twentieth. In the process a large number of countries create national economic barriers whose consequences often last beyond their initial objectives. At this point in the process the very same capitalists who pressed their national governments to impose the restrictions now find these restrictions constraining. This is not an "internationalization" of "national" capital. This is simply a new political demand by certain sectors of the capitalist classes who have at all points in time sought to maximize their profits within the real economic market, that of the world-economy.

If this is so, then what meaning does it have to talk of structural positions within this economy and identify states as being in one of these positions? And why talk of three positions, inserting that of "semi-periphery" in between the widely-used concepts of core and periphery? The state-machineries of the core states were strengthened to meet the needs of capitalist landowners and their merchant allies. But that does not mean that these state-machineries were manipulable puppets. Obviously any organization, once created, has a certain autonomy from those who pressed it into existence for two reasons. It creates a stratum of officials whose own careers and interests are furthered by the continued strengthening of the organization itself, however the interests of its capitalist backers may vary. Kings and bureaucrats wanted to stay in power and increase their personal gain constantly. Secondly, in the process of creating the strong state in the first place, certain "constitutional" compromises had to be made with other forces within the state-boundaries and these institutionalized compromises limit, as they are designed to do, the freedom of maneuver of the managers of the state-machinery. The formula of the state as "executive committee of the ruling class" is only valid, therefore, if one bears in mind that executive committees are never mere reflections of the wills of their constituents, as anyone who has ever participated in any organization knows well.

The strengthening of the state-machineries in core areas has as its direct counterpart the decline of the state-machineries in peripheral areas. The decline of the Polish monarchy in the sixteenth and seventeenth centuries is a striking example of this phenomenon.[39] There are two reasons for this. In peripheral countries, the interests of the capitalist landowners lie in an opposite direction from those of the local commercial bourgeoisie. Their interests lie in maintaining an open economy to maximize their profit from world-market trade (no restrictions in exports and access to lower-cost industrial products from core countries) and in elimination of the commercial bourgeoisie in favor of outside merchants (who pose no local political threat). Thus, in terms of the state, the coalition which strengthened it in core countries was precisely absent.

The second reason, which has become ever more operative over the history of the modern world-system, is that the strength of the state-machinery in core states is a function of the weakness of other state-machineries. Hence intervention of outsiders via war, subversion, and diplomacy is the lot of peripheral states.

All this seems very obvious. I repeat it only in order to make clear two points. One cannot reasonably explain the strength of various state-machineries at specific moments of the history of the modern world-system primarily in terms of a genetic-cultural line of argumentation, but rather in terms of the structural role a country plays in the world-economy at that moment in time. To be sure, the initial eligibility for a particular role is often decided by an accidental edge a particular country has, and the "accident" of which one is talking is no doubt located in part in past history, in part in current geography. But once this relatively minor accident is given, it is the operations of the world-market forces which accentuate the differences, institutionalize them, and make them impossible to surmount over the short run.

The second point we wish to make about the structural differences of core and periphery is that they are not comprehensible unless we realize that there is a third structural position: that of the semi-periphery. This is not the result merely of establishing arbitrary cutting-points on a continuum of characteristics. Our logic is not merely inductive, sensing the presence of a third category from a comparison of indicator curves. It is also deductive. The semi-periphery is needed to make a capitalist world-economy run smoothly. Both kinds of world-system, the world-empire with a redistribute economy and the world-economy with a capitalist market economy, involve markedly unequal distribution of rewards. Thus, logically, there is immediately posed the question of how it is possible politically for such a system to persist. Why do not the majority who are exploited simply overwhelm the minority who draw disproportionate benefits? The most rapid glance at the historic records shows that these world-systems have been faced rather rarely by fundamental system-wide insurrection. While internal discontent has been eternal, it has usually taken quite long before the accumulation of the erosion of power has led to the decline of a world-system, and as often as not, an external force has been a major factor in this decline.

There have been three major mechanisms that have enabled world-systems to retain relative political stability (not in terms of the particular groups who will play the leading roles in the system, but in terms of systemic survival itself). One obviously is the concentration of military strength in the hands of the dominant forces. The modalities of this obviously vary with the technology, and there are to be sure political prerequisites for such a concentration, but nonetheless sheer force is no doubt a central consideration.

A second mechanism is the pervasiveness of an ideological commitment to the system as a whole. I do not mean what has often been termed the "legitimation" of a system, because that term has been used to imply that the lower strata of a system feel some affinity with or loyalty towards the rulers, and I doubt that this has ever been a significant factor in the survival of world-systems. I mean rather the degree to which the staff or cadres of the system (and I leave this term deliberately vague) feel that their own well-being is wrapped up in the survival of the system as such and the competence of its leaders. It is this staff which not only propagates the myths; it is they who believe them.

But neither force nor the ideological commitment of the staff would suffice were it not for the division of the majority into a larger lower stratum and a smaller middle stratum. Both the revolutionary call for polarization as a strategy of change and the liberal encomium to consensus as the basis of the liberal polity reflect this proposition. The import is far wider than its use in the analysis of contemporary political problems suggests. It is the normal condition of either kind of world-system to have a three-layered structure. When and if this ceases to be the case, the world-system disintegrates.

In a world-empire, the middle stratum is in fact accorded the role of maintaining the marginally-desirable long-distance luxury trade, while the upper stratum concentrates its resources on controlling the military machinery which can collect the tribute, the crucial mode of redistributing surplus. By providing, however, for an access to a limited portion of the surplus to urbanized elements who alone, in pre-modern societies, could contribute political cohesiveness to isolated clusters of primary producers, the upper stratum effectively buys off the potential leadership of coordinated revolt. And by denying access to political rights for this commercial-urban middle stratum, it makes them constantly vulnerable to confiscatory measures whenever their economic profits become sufficiently swollen so that they might begin to create for themselves military strength.

In a world-economy, such "cultural" stratification is not so simple, because the absence of a single political system means the concentration of economic roles vertically rather than horizontally throughout the system. The solution then is to have three *kinds* of states, with pressures for cultural homogenization within each of them—thus, besides the upper stratum of core-states and the lower stratum of peripheral states, there is a middle stratum of semi-peripheral ones.

This semi-periphery is then assigned as it were a specific economic role, but the reason is less economic than political. That is to say, one might make a good case that the world-economy as an economy would function every bit as well without a semi-periphery. But it would be far less *politically* stable, for it would mean a polarized world-system. The existence of the third category means precisely that the upper stratum is not faced with the *unified* opposition of all the others because the *middle* stratum is both exploited and exploiter. It follows that the specific economic role is not all that important, and has thus changed through the various historical stages of the modern world-system. We shall discuss these changes shortly.

Where then does class analysis fit in all of this? And what in such a formulation are nations, nationalities, peoples, ethnic groups? First of all, without arguing the point now,[40] I would contend that all these latter terms denote variants of a single phenomenon which I will term "ethno-nations."

Both classes and ethnic groups, or status-groups, or ethno-nations are phenomena of world-economies and much of the enormous confusion that has surrounded the concrete analysis of their functioning can be attributed quite simply to the fact that they have been analyzed as though they existed within the nation-states of this world-economy, instead of within the world-economy as a whole. This has been a Procrustean bed indeed.

The range of economic activities being far wider in the core than in the periphery, the range of syndical interest groups is far wider there.[41] Thus, it has been widely observed that there does not exist in many parts of the world today a proletariat of the kind which exists in, say, Europe or North America. But this is a confusing way to state the observation. Industrial activity being disproportionately concentrated in certain parts of the world-economy, industrial wage-workers are to be found principally in certain geographic regions. Their interests as a syndical group are determined by their collective relationship to the world-economy. Their ability to influence the political functioning of this world-economy is shaped by the fact that they command larger percentages of the population in one sovereign entity than another. The form their organizations take has, in large part, been governed too by these political boundaries. The same might be said about industrial capitalists. Class analysis is perfectly capable of accounting for the political position of, let us say, French skilled workers if we look at their structural position and interests in the world-economy. Similarly with ethno-nations. The meaning of ethnic consciousness in a core area is considerably different from that of ethnic consciousness in a peripheral area precisely because of the different class position such ethnic groups have in the world-economy.[42]

Political struggles of ethno-nations or segments of classes within national boundaries of course are the daily bread and butter of local politics. But their significance or consequences can only be fruitfully analyzed if one spells out the implications of their organizational activity or political demands for the functioning of the world-economy. This also incidentally makes possible more rational assessments of these politics in terms of some set of evaluative criteria such as "left" and "right."

The functioning then of a capitalist world-economy requires that groups pursue their economic interests within a single world market while seeking to distort this market for their benefit by organizing to exert influence on states, some of which are far more powerful than others but none of which controls the world-market in its entirety. Of course, we shall find on closer inspection that there are periods where one state is relatively quite powerful and other periods where power is more diffuse and contested, permitting weaker states broader ranges of action. We can talk then of the relative tightness or looseness of the world-system as an important variable and seek to analyze why this dimension tends to be cyclical in nature, as it seems to have been for several hundred years.

We are now in a position to look at the historical evolution of this capitalist world-economy itself and analyze the degree to which it is fruitful to talk of distinct stages in its evolution as a system. The emergence of the European world-economy in the "long" sixteenth century (1450–1640) was made possible by an historical conjuncture: on those long-term trends which were the culmination of what has been sometimes described as the "crisis of feudalism" was superimposed a more immediate cyclical crisis plus climatic changes, all of which created a dilemma that could only be resolved by a geographic expansion of the division of labor. Furthermore, the balance of inter-system forces was such as to make this realizable. Thus a geographic expansion did take place in conjunction with a demographic expansion and upward price rise.

The remarkable thing was not that a European world-economy was thereby created, but that it survived the Hapsburg attempt to transform it into a world-empire, an attempt seriously pursued by Charles V. The Spanish attempt to absorb the whole failed because the rapid economic-demographic-technological burst forward of the preceding century made the whole enterprise too expensive for the imperial base to sustain, especially given many structural insufficiencies in Castilian economic development. Spain could afford neither the bureaucracy nor the army that was necessary to the enterprise, and in the event went bankrupt, as did the French monarchs making a similar albeit even less plausible attempt.

Once the Hapsburg dream of world-empire was over — and in 1557 it was over forever — the capitalist world-economy was an established system that became almost impossible to unbalance. It quickly reached an equilibrium point in its relations with other world-systems: the Ottoman and Russian world-empires, the Indian Ocean proto-world-economy. Each of the states or potential states within the European world-economy was quickly in the race to bureaucratize, to raise a standing army, to homogenize its culture, to diversify its economic activities. By 1640, those in northwest Europe had succeeded in establishing themselves as the core-states; Spain and the northern Italian city-states declined into being semi-peripheral; northeastern Europe and Iberian America had become the periphery. At this point, those in semi-peripheral status had reached it by virtue of decline from a former more pre-eminent status.

It was the system-wide recession of 1650–1730 that consolidated the European world-economy and opened stage two of the modern world-economy. For the recession forced retrenchment, and the decline in relative surplus allowed room for only one core-state to survive. The mode of struggle was mercantilism, which was a device of partial insulation and withdrawal from the world market of *large* areas themselves hierarchically constructed—that is, empires within the world-economy (which is quite different from world-empires). In this struggle England first ousted the Netherlands from its commercial primacy and then resisted successfully France's attempt to catch up. As England began to speed up the process of industrialization after 1760 there was one last attempt of those capitalist forces located in France to break the imminent British hegemony. This attempt was expressed first in the French Revolution's replacement of the cadres of the regime and then in Napoleon's continental blockade. But it failed.

Stage three of the capitalist world-economy begins then, a stage of industrial rather than of agricultural capitalism. Henceforth, industrial production is no longer a minor aspect of the world market but comprises an even larger percentage of world gross production—and even more important, of world gross surplus. This involves a whole series of consequences for the world-system.

First of all, it led to the further geographic expansion of the European world-economy to include now the whole of the globe. This was in part the result of its technological feasibility both in terms of improved military firepower and improved shipping facilities which made regular trade sufficiently inexpensive to be viable. But, in addition, industrial production *required* access to raw materials of a nature and in a quantity such that the needs could not be supplied within the former boundaries. At first, however, the search for new markets was not a primary consideration in the geographic expansion since the new markets were more readily available within the old boundaries, as we shall see.

The geographic expansion of the European world-economy meant the elimination of other world-systems as well as the absorption of the remaining mini-systems. The most important world-system up to then outside of the European world-economy, Russia, entered in semi-peripheral status, the consequence of the strength of its state-machinery (including its army) and the degree of industrialization already achieved in the eighteenth century. The independences in the Latin American countries did nothing to change their peripheral status. They merely eliminated the last vestiges of Spain's semi-peripheral role and ended pockets of non-involvement in the world-economy in the interior of Latin America. Asia and Africa were absorbed into the periphery in the nineteenth century, although Japan, because of the combination of the strength of its state-machinery, the poverty of its resource base (which led to a certain disinterest on the part of world capitalist forces), and its geographic remoteness from the core areas, was able quickly to graduate into semi-peripheral status.

The absorption of Africa as part of the periphery meant the end of slavery world-wide for two reasons. First of all, the manpower that was used as slaves was now needed for cash-crop production in Africa itself, whereas in the eighteenth century Europeans had sought to *discourage* just such cash-crop production.[43] In the second place, once Africa was part of the periphery and not the external arena, slavery was no longer economic. To understand this, we must appreciate the economics of slavery. Slaves receiving the lowest conceivable reward for their labor are the least productive form of labor and have the shortest life span, both because of undernourishment and maltreatment and because of lowered psychic resistance to death. Furthermore, if recruited from areas surrounding their workplace the escape rate is too high. Hence there must be a high transport cost for a product of low productivity. This makes economic sense only if the purchase price is virtually nil. In capitalist market trade, purchase always has a real cost. It is only in long-distance trade, the exchange of preciosities, that the purchase price can be in the social system of the purchaser virtually nil. Such was the slave-trade. Slaves were bought at low immediate cost (the production cost of the items actually exchanged) and none of the usual invisible costs. That is to say, the fact that removing a man from West Africa lowered the productive potential of the region was of *zero* cost to the European world-economy since these areas were not part of the division of labor. Of course, had the slave trade totally denuded Africa of all possibilities of furnishing further slaves, then a real cost to Europe would have commenced. But that point was never historically reached. Once, however, Africa was part of the periphery, then the real cost of a slave in terms of the production of surplus in the world-economy went up to such a point that it became far more economical to use wage-labor, even on sugar or cotton plantations, which is precisely what transpired in the nineteenth-century Caribbean and other slave-labor regions.

The creation of vast new areas as the periphery of the expanded world-economy made possible a shift in the role of some other areas. Specifically, both the United States and Germany (as it came into being) combined formerly peripheral and semi-peripheral regions. The manufacturing sector in each was able to gain political ascendancy, as the peripheral subregions became less economically crucial to the world-economy. Mercantilism now became the major tool of semi-peripheral countries seeking to become core countries, thus still performing a function analogous to that of the mercantilist drives of the late seventeenth and eighteenth centuries in England and France. To be sure, the struggle of semi-peripheral countries to "industrialize" varied in the degree to which it succeeded in the period before the First World War: all the way in the United States, only partially in Germany, not at all in Russia.

The internal structure of core-states also changed fundamentally under industrial capitalism. For a core area, industrialism involved divesting itself of substantially all agricultural activities (except that in the twentieth century further mechanization was to create a new form of working the land that was so highly mechanized as to warrant the appellation industrial). Thus whereas, in the period 1700–40, England not only was Europe's leading industrial exporter but was also Europe's leading agricultural exporter – this was at a high point in the economy-wide recession – by 1900, less than 10 percent of England's population were engaged in agricultural pursuits.

At first under industrial capitalism, the core exchanged manufactured products against the periphery's agricultural products – hence, Britain from 1815 to 1873 as the "workshop of the world." Even to those semi-peripheral countries that had some manufacture (France, Germany, Belgium, the U.S.), Britain in this period supplied about half their needs in manufactured goods. As, however, the mercantilist practices of this latter group both cut Britain off from outlets and even created competition for Britain in sales to peripheral areas, a competition which led to the late nineteenth-century "scramble for Africa," the world division of labor was reallocated to ensure a new special role for the core: less the provision of the manufactures, more the provison of the machines to make the manufactures as well as the provision of infra-structure (especially, in this period, railroads).

The rise of manufacturing created for the first time under capitalism a large-scale urban proletariat. And in consequence for the first time there arose what Michels has called the "anti-capitalist mass spirit,"[44] which was translated into concrete organizational forms (trade-unions, socialist parties). This development intruded a new factor as threatening to the stability of the states and of the capitalist forces now so securely in control of them as the earlier centrifugal thrusts of regional anti-capitalist landed elements had been in the seventeenth century.

At the same time that the bourgeoisies of the core countries were faced by this threat to the internal stability of their state structures, they were simultaneously faced with the economic crisis of the latter third of the nineteenth century resulting from the more rapid increase of agricultural production (and indeed of light manufactures) than the expansion of a potential market for these goods. Some of the surplus would have to be redistributed to someone to allow these goods to be bought and the economic machinery to return to smooth operation. By expanding the purchasing power of the industrial proletariat of the core countries, the world-economy was unburdened simultaneously of two problems: the bottleneck of demand, and the unsettling "class conflict" of the core states – hence, the social liberalism or welfare-state ideology that arose just at that point in time.

The First World War was, as men of the time observed, the end of an era; and the Russian Revolution of October 1917 the beginning of a new one – our stage four. This stage was to be sure a state of revolutionary turmoil but it also was, in a seeming paradox, the stage of the *consolidation* of the industrial capitalist world-economy. The Russian Revolution was essentially that of a semi-peripheral country whose internal balance of forces had been such that as of the late nineteenth century it began on a decline towards a peripheral status. This was the result of the marked penetration of foreign capital into the industrial sector which was on its way to eliminating all indigenous capitalist forces, the resistance to the mechanization of the agricultural sector, the decline of relative military power (as evidenced by the defeat by the Japanese in 1905). The Revolution brought to power a group of state-managers who reversed each one of these trends by using the classic technique of mercantilist semi-withdrawal from the world-economy. In the process of doing this, the now U.S.S.R. mobilized considerable popular support, especially in the urban sector. At the end of the Second World War, Russia was reinstated as a very strong member of the semi-periphery and could begin to seek full core status.

Meanwhile, the decline of Britain which dates from 1873 was confirmed and its hegemonic role was assumed by the United States. While the U.S. thus rose, Germany fell further behind as a result of its military defeat. Various German attempts in the 1920s to find new industrial outlets in the Middle East and South America were unsuccessful in the face of the U.S. thrust combined with Britain's continuing relative strength. Germany's thrust of desperation to recoup lost ground took the noxious and unsuccessful form of Nazism.

It was the Second World War that enabled the United States for a brief period (1945–65) to attain the same level of primacy as Britain had in the first part of the nineteenth century. United States growth in this period was spectacular and created a great need for expanded market outlets. The Cold War closure denied not only the U.S.S.R. but Eastern Europe to U.S. exports. And the Chinese Revolution meant that this region, which had been destined for much exploitative activity, was also cut off. Three alternative areas were available and each was pursued with assiduity. First, Western Europe had to be rapidly "reconstructed," and it was the Marshall Plan which thus allowed this area to play a primary role in the expansion of world productivity. Secondly, Latin America became the reserve of U.S. investment from which now Britain and Germany were completely cut off. Thirdly, Southern Asia, the Middle East and Africa had to be decolonized. On the one hand, this was necessary in order to reduce the share of the surplus taken by the Western European intermediaries, as Canning covertly supported the Latin American revolutionaries against Spain in the 1820.[45] But also, these countries had to be decolonized in order to mobilize productive potential in a way that had never been achieved in the colonial era. Colonial rule after all had been an *inferior* mode of relationship of core and periphery, one occasioned by the strenuous late-nineteenth-century conflict among industrial states but one no longer desirable from the point of view of the new hegemonic power.[46]

But a world capitalist economy does not permit true imperium. Charles V could not succeed in his dream of world-empire. The Pax Britannica stimulated its own demise. So too did the Pax Americana. In each case, the cost of *political* imperium was too high economically, and in a capitalist system, over the middle run when profits decline, new *political* formulae are sought. In this case the costs mounted along several fronts. The efforts of the U.S.S.R. to further its own industrialization, protect a privileged market area (eastern Europe), and force entry into other market areas led to an immense spiralling of military expenditure, which on the Soviet Side promised long-run returns whereas for the U.S. it was merely a question of running very fast to stand still. The economic resurgence of western Europe, made necessary both to provide markets for U.S. sales and investments and to counter the U.S.S.R. military thrust, meant over time that the west European state structures collectively became as strong as that of the U.S., which led in the late 1960s to the "dollar and gold crisis" and the retreat of Nixon from the free-trade stance which is the definitive mark of the self-confident leader in a capitalist market system. When the cumulated Third World pressures, most notably Vietnam, were added on, a restructuring of the world division of labor was inevitable, involving probably in the 1970s a quadripartite division of the larger part of the world surplus by the U.S., the European Common Market, Japan, and the U.S.S.R.

Such a decline in U.S. state hegemony has actually *increased* the freedom of action of capitalist enterprises, the larger of which have now taken the form of multinational corporations which are able to maneuver against state bureaucracies whenever the national politicians become too responsive to internal worker pressures. Whether some effective links can be established between multinational corporations, presently limited to operating in certain areas, and the U.S.S.R. remains to be seen, but it is by no means impossible.

This brings us back to one of the questions with which we opened this chapter, the seemingly esoteric debate between Liu Shao-Chi and Mao Tse-Tung as to whether China was, as Liu argued, a socialist state, or whether, as Mao argued, socialism was a *process* involving continued and continual class struggle. No doubt to those to whom the terminology is foreign the discussion seems abstrusely theological. The issue, however, as we said, is real. If the Russian Revolution emerged as a reaction to the threatened further decline of Russia's structural position in the world-economy, and if fifty years later one can talk of the U.S.S.R. as entering the status of a core power in a *capitalist* world-economy, what then is the meaning of the various so-called socialist revolutions that have occurred in a third of the world's surface? First let us notice that it has been neither Thailand nor Liberia nor Paraguay that has had a "socialist revolution" but Russia, China, and Cuba. That is to say, these revolutions have occurred in countries that, in terms of their internal economic structures in the pre-revolutionary period, had a certain minimum strength in terms of skilled personnel, some manufacturing, and other factors which made it plausible that, within the framework of a capitalist world-economiy, such a country could alter its role in the world division of labor within a reasonable period (say 30–50 years) by the use of the technique of mercantilist semi-withdrawal. (This may not be all that plausible for Cuba, but we shall see.) Of course, other countries in the geographic regions and military orbit of these revolutionary forces had changes of regime without in any way having these characteristics (for example, Mongolia or Albania). It is also to be noted that many of the countries where similar forces are strong or where considerable counterforce is required to keep them from emerging also share this status of minimum strength. I think of Chile or Brazil or Egypt—or indeed Italy.

Are we not seeing the emergence of a political structure for *semi-peripheral* nations adapted to stage four of the capitalist world-system? The fact that all enterprises are nationalized in these countries does not make the participation of these enterprises in the world-economy one that does not conform to the mode of operation of a capitalist market-system: seeking increased efficiency of production in order to realize a maximum price on sales, thus achieving a more favorable allocation of the surplus of the world-economy. If tomorrow U.S. Steel became a worker's collective in which all employees without exception received an identical share of the profits and all stockholders were expropriated without compensation, would U.S. Steel thereby cease to be a capitalist enterprise operating in a capitalist world-economy?

What then have been the consequences for the world-system of the emergence of many states in which there is no private ownership of the basic means of production? To some extent, this has meant an internal reallocation of consumption. It has certainly undermined the ideological justifications in world capitalism, both by showing the political vulnerability of capitalist entrepreneurs and by demonstrating that private ownership is irrelevant to the rapid expansion of industrial productivity. But to the extent that it has raised the ability of the new semi-peripheral areas to enjoy a larger share of the world surplus, it has once again depolarized the world, recreating the triad of strata that has been a fundamental element in the survival of the world-system.

Finally, in the peripheral areas of the world-economy, both the continued economic expansion of the core (even though the core is seeing some reallocation of surplus internal to it) and the new strength of the semi-periphery has led to a further weakening of the political and hence economic position of the peripheral areas. The pundits note that "the gap is getting wider," but thus far no-one has succeeded in doing much about it, and it is not clear that there are very many in whose interests it would be to do so. Far from a strengthening of state authority, in many parts of the world we are witnessing the same kind of deterioration Poland knew in the sixteenth century, a deterioration of which the frequency of military coups is only one of many signposts. And all of this leads us to conclude that stage four has been the stage of the *consolidation* of the capitalist world-economy.

Consolidation, however, does not mean the absence of contradictions and does not mean the likelihood of long-term survival. We thus come to projections about the future, which has always been man's great game, his true *hybris*, the most convincing argument for the dogma of original sin. Having read Dante, I will therefore be brief.

There are two fundamental contradictions, it seems to me, involved in the workings of the capitalist world-system. In the first place, there is the contradiction to which the nineteenth-century Marxian corpus pointed, which I would phrase as follows: whereas in the short-run the maximization of profit requires maximizing the withdrawal of surplus from immediate consumption of the majority, in the long-run the continued production of surplus requires a mass demand which can only be created by redistributing the surplus withdrawn. Since these two considerations move in opposite directions (a "contradiction"), the system has constant crises which in the long-run both weaken it and make the game for those with privilege less worth playing.

The second fundamental contradiction, to which Mao's concept of socialism as process points, is the following: whenever the tenants of privilege seek to co-opt an oppositional movement by including them in a minor share of the privilege, they may no doubt eliminate opponents in the short-run; but they also up the ante for the next oppositional movement created in the next crisis of the world-economy. Thus, the cost of "co-option" rises even higher and the advantages of co-option seem ever less worthwhile.

There are today no socialist systems in the world-economy any more than there are feudal systems because there is only *one* world-system. It is a world-economy and it is by definition capitalist in form. Socialism involves the creation of a new kind of *world*-system, neither a redistributive world-empire nor a capitalist world-economy but a socialist world-government. I don't see this projection as being in the least utopian but I also don't feel its institution is imminent. It will be the outcome of a long struggle in forms that may be familiar and perhaps in very new forms, that will take place in *all* the areas of the world-economy (Mao's continual "class struggle"). Governments may be in the hands of persons, groups or movements sympathetic to this transformation but *states* as such are neither progressive nor reactionary. It is movements and forces that deserve such evaluative judgments.

Having gone as far as I care to in projecting the future, let me return to the present and to the scholarly enterprise which is never neutral but does have its own logic and to some extent its own priorities. We have adumbrated as our basic unit of observation a concept of world-systems that have structural parts and evolving stages. It is whithin such a framework, I am arguing, that we can fruitfully make comparative analyses—of the wholes and of parts of the whole. Conceptions precede and govern measurements. I am all for minute and sophisticated quantitative indicators. I am all for minute and diligent archival work that will trace a concrete historical series of events in terms of all its immediate complexities. But the point of either is to enable us to see better what has happened and what is happening. For that we need glasses with which to discern the dimensions of difference, we need models with which to weigh significance, we need summarizing concepts with which to create the knowledge which we then seek to communicate to each other. And all this because we are men with hybris and original sin and therefore seek the good, the true, and the beautiful.

NOTES

1. George Lukacs, "The Marxism of Rosa Luxemburg," in *History and Class Consciousness* (London: Merlin Press, 1968), p. 27.

2. Robert A. Nisbet, *Social Change and History* (New York: Oxford University Press, 1969), pp. 302–3. I myself would exempt from this criticism the economic history literature.

3. Fernand Braudel, "History and the Social Sciences," in Peter Burke (ed.) *Economy and Society in Early Modern Europe* (London: Routledge and Kegan Paul, 1972), pp. 38–39.

4. See André Gunder Frank, Ch. IV (A), "The Myth of Feudalism" in *Capitalism and Underdevelopment in Latin America* (New York: Monthly Review Press, 1967), 221–242.

5. See Frederic Lane's discussion of "protection costs" which is reprinted as Part Three of *Venice and History* (Baltimore: Johns Hopkins Press, 1966). For the specific discussion of tribute, see pp. 389–390, 416–420.

6. See Karl Polanyi, "The Economy as Instituted Process," in Karl Polanyi, Conrad M. Arsenberg and Harry W. Pearson (eds.), *Trade and Market in the Early Empire* (Glencoe: Free Press, 1957), pp. 243–270.

7. See my *The Modern World-System: Capitalist Agriculture and the Origins of the European World-Economy in the Sixteenth Century* (New York: Academic Press, 1974).

8. Philip Abrams concludes a similar plea with this admonition: "The academic and intellectual dissociation of history and sociology seems, then, to have had the effect of deterring both disciplines from attending seriously to the most important issues involved in the understanding of social transition." "The Sense of the Past and the Origins of Sociology," *Past and Present*, No. 55, May 1972, 32.

9. Frank, op. cit., p. 3.

10. Frank's critique, now classic, of these theories is entitled "Sociology of Development and Underdevelopment of Sociology" and is reprinted in *Latin America: Underdevelopment or Revolution* (New York: Monthly Review Press, 1969), 21–94.

11. See Theontonio Dos Santos, *La Nueva Dependencia* (Buenos Aires: s/ediciones, 1968).

12. Ernesto Laclau (h), "Feudalism and Capitalism in Latin America," *New Left Review*, No. 67, May–June 1971, 37–38.

13. *The Accumulation of Capital* (New York: Modern Reader Paperbacks), 364–365. Luxemburg, however, as is evident, lends herself further to the confusion by using the terminology of "capitalistic" and "non-capitalistic" modes of production. Leaving these terms aside, her vision is impeccable: "From the aspect both of realising the surplus value and of producing the material elements of constant capital, international trade is a prime necessity for the historical existence of capitalism—an international trade which under actual conditions is essentially an exchange between capitalistic and non-capitalistic modes of production." *Ibid.*, 359. She shows similar insight into the need for recruiting labor for core areas from the periphery, what she calls "the increase in the variable capital." See *ibid.*, p. 361.

14. The debate begins with Maurice Dobb, *Studies in the Development of Capitalism* (London: Routledge and Kegan Paul, 1946). Paul Sweezy criticized Dobb in "The Transition from Feudalism to Capitalism," *Science and Society*, XIV, 2, Spring 1950, 134–157, with a "Reply" by Dobb in the same issue. From that point on many others got into the debate in various parts of the world. I have reviewed and discussed this debate *in extenso* in Chapter I of my work cited above.

15. It would take us into a long discursus to defend the proposition that, like all great thinkers, there was the Marx who was the prisoner of his social location and the Marx, the genius, who could on occasion see from a wider vantage point. The former Marx generalized from British history. The latter Marx is the one who has inspired a crucial conceptual framework of social reality. W. W. Rostow incidentally seeks to refute the former Marx by offering an alternative generalization from British history. He ignores the latter and more significant Marx. See *The Stages of Economic Growth: A Non-Communist Manifesto* (Cambridge: at the University Press, 1960).

16. Laclau, *op. cit.*, 25, 30.

17. Cited in F. Burlatsky, *The State and Communism* (Moscow: Progress Publishers, n.d., *circa* 1961), p. 95.

18. *Ibid.*, p. 97.

19. Mao Tse-Tung, *On The Correct Handling of Contradictions Among The People*, 7th ed., revised translation (Peking: Foreign Languages Press, 1966), pp. 37–38.

20. *Long Live The Invincible Thought of Mao Tse-Tung!*, undated pamphlet, issued between 1967 and 1969, translated in *Current Background*, No. 884, July 18, 1969, 14.

21. This is the position taken by Mao Tse-Tung in his speech to the Work Conference of the Central Committee at Peitaiho in August 1962, as reported in the pamphlet, *Long Live . . .*, p. 20. Mao's position was subsequently endorsed at the 10th Plenum of the 8th CCP Central Committee in September 1962, a session this same pamphlet describes as "a great turning point in the violent struggle between the proletarian headquarters and the bourgeois headquarters in China." *Ibid.*, 21.

22. Remarks made by Mao at 10th Plenum, cited in *ibid.*, 20.

23. Mao Tse-Tung, "Talk on the Question of Democratic Centralism," January 30, 1962, in *Current Background*. No. 891, Oct. 8, 1969, 39.

24. "Communiqué of the 10th Plenum Session of the 8th Central Committee of the Chinese Communist Party," *Current Background*, No. 691, Oct. 5, 1962, 3.

25. Yuri Sdobnikov (ed.), *Socialism and Capitalism: Score and Prospects* (Moscow: Progress Publ., 1971) p. 20. The book was compiled by staff members of the Institute of World Economy and International Relations, and the senior contributor was Prof. V. Aboltin.

26. *Ibid.*, p. 21.

27. *Ibid.*, p. 26.

28. *Ibid.*, p. 24.

29. *Ibid.*, p. 25.

30. See Raymond Aron, *Dix-huit leçons de la société industrielle* (Paris: Ed. Gallimard, 1962).

31. This is the dilemma, I feel, of E. J. Hobsbawm in explaining his so-called crisis of the seventeenth century. See his *Past and Present* article reprinted (with various critiques) in Trevor Aston (ed.), *The Crisis of the Seventeenth Century* (London: Routledge and Kegan Paul, 1965).

32. Maurice Dobb, *Capitalism Yesterday and Today* (London: Lawrence and Wishart, 1958), p. 21. Italics mine.

33. *Ibid.*, pp. 6–7.

34. *Ibid.*, p. 21.

35. See my *The Modern World-System, op. cit.*, Chap. 2.

36. I give a brief account of this in "Three Paths of National Development in the Sixteenth Century," *Studies in Comparative International Development*, VII, 2, Summer 1972, 95–101.

37. See Arghiri Emmanuel, *Unequal Exchange* (New York: Monthly Review Press, 1972).

38. Charles Bettelheim, "Theoretical Comments" in Emmanuel, *op. cit.*, 295.

39. See J. Siemenski, "Constitutional Conditions in the Fifteenth and Sixteenth Centuries," *Cambridge History of Poland, I.* W. F. Reddaway et al. (eds.), *From the Origins to Sobieski (to 1696)* (Cambridge: At the University Press, 1950), pp. 416–440; Janusz Tazbir, "The Commonwealth of the Gentry," in Aleksander Gieysztor et al., *History of Poland* (Warszawa: PWN–Polish Scientific Publ., 1968), pp. 169–271.

40. See my fuller analysis in "Social Conflict in Post-Independence Black Africa: The Concepts of Race and Status-Group Reconsidered" in Ernest W. Campbell (ed.), *Racial*

Tensions and National Identity (Nashville: Vanderbilt Univ. Press, 1972), pp. 207–226.

41. Range in this sentence means the number of different occupations in which a significant proportion of the population is engaged. Thus peripheral society typically is overwhelmingly agricultural. A core society typically has its occupations well-distributed over all of Colin Clark's three sectors. If one shifted the connotation of range to talk of style of life, consumption patterns, even income distribution, quite possibly one might reverse the correlation. In a typical peripheral society, the differences between a subsistence farmer and an urban professional are probably far greater than those which could be found in a typical core state.

42. See my "The Two Modes of Ethnic Consciousness: Soviet Central Asia in Transition?" in Edward Allworth (ed.), *The Nationality Question in Soviet Central Asia* (New York: Praeger, 1973), pp. 168–175.

43. A. Adu Boahen cites the instructions of the British Board of Trade in 1751 to the Governor of Cape Castle (a small British fort and trading-settlement in what is now Ghana) to seek to stop the local people, the Fante, from cultivating cotton. The reason given was the following: "The introduction of culture and industry among the Negroes is contrary to the known established policy of this country, there is no saying where this might stop, and that it might extend to tobacco, sugar and every other commodity which we now take from our colonies; and thereby the Africans, who now support themselves by wars, would become planters and their slaves be employed in the culture of these articles in Africa, which they are employed in in America." Cited in A. Adu Boahen, *Topics in West Africa History* (London: Longmans, Green and Co., 1966), p. 113.

44. Robert Michels, "The Origins of the Anti-Capitalist Mass Spirit," in *Man in Contemporary Society* (New York: Columbia University Press, 1955), Vol. 1, pp. 740–765.

45. See William W. Kaufman, *British Policy and the Independence of Latin America, 1804–28* (New Haven: Yale University Press, 1951).

46. Cf. Catherine Coquéry-Vidrovitch, "De l'impérialisme britannique à l'impérialisme contemporaine—l'avatar colonial," *L'Homme et la société*. No. 18, Oct.–Nov.–Dec. 1970, 61–90.

Approaches to World Order

INTRODUCTION

Our understanding of world order is deeply influenced by our orientation to the subject matter. Orientation encompasses both ideology and methodology. With respect to ideology, the emphasis is upon a more or less coherent set of beliefs, interests, and values that shape one's perspective toward social and political reality. In the context of this book, the question of ideology pertains especially to attitudes toward the state system and world order values. Our concern is to depict the contours of an ideology appropriate for the realization of world order values as well as for a sustaining constitutional and institutional framework. Such an ideology for drastic social change, as we have argued, emphasizes the catalytic role of the oppressed. However, given our analysis of the menace of nuclear war, ecological collapse, and cultural regression, we believe that the entire human race is, in the most genuine sense, oppressed. Hence, the only qualification for participating as a revolutionary element in a movement for global renewal is the activated consciousness of oneself as a victim of the present world order system.

This ideological focus is far less particularistic than that of other main radical perspectives that specify their conception of "the oppressed" by reference to a *part* (e.g., class, race, religion, gender, party) of the social order that is victimized by existing arrangements of power and privilege. To illustrate simplistically, a Marxist tends to believe that class identity decisively shapes our political consciousness, and that the most vital issue of world order involves augmenting the struggle against the class rule of bourgeois states. Lenin's vision of a benevolent world society is one in which all or most states have already undergone a successful socialist revolution.

This particular world order ideology seems less and less tenable as our experience with socialist revolution accumulates. First, we have the experience of repressive governance within socialist societies, initially justified to some extent by the demands of defending the socialist victory in Russia against its internal and external enemies. With time, however, the revelations of Stalinist abuse—the incredible gulag story—and their continuation in post-Stalinist Soviet life has weakened the Marxist/Leninist moral claims, especially since this disillusionment with Soviet experience has been generally confirmed by the character of communist rule elsewhere.

In external relations, also, the initial promise of socialist internationalism has not held up. The Sino-Soviet conflict is only the most dramatic instance refuting the assertion that socialist rule provides a solid basis for international solidarity. Factors connected with nationalism and racial identity are at least as important in determining international relations as are the class ownership of the means of production or control of the apparatus of the state. Furthermore, Soviet foreign policy has not shown itself free from hegemonic ambitions, as confirmed by its invasion of Afghanistan in late 1979.

There are other ideologies prevalent in today's world, especially those associated with capitalism, nationalism, liberalism, and humanism. Each accepts as durable the state system, although each draws somewhat different tactical lessons therefrom. Each conceives international order as a product of "balance" and "power"; otherwise, competitive rivalry would produce conflict and war. Under such a view of international order, there are no self-imposed limits on expansive energies; aggression is checked by countervailing power. This struggle is waged by state leaders who, at most, represent their peoples, and often act on behalf of only some fragment (either class, race, region, or religion) of their own overall polity; the avowal of a foreign policy based on "the national interest" is itself an overstatement. In this kind of world, the military dimension is critical. The most realistic kind of world order is conceptualized by statists as a balanced one in which rival state actors feel neutralized. Such a dynamic has produced frequent wars, has encouraged a constant testing of limits, and has led to a notorious "balance of terror" as well as to an unending arms race.

Our world order ideology rejects these alternatives in some, but not all, basic respects. It emphasizes, as we have said, the prospects for *system change*, both as a trend and as a goal. It also places stress upon a normative orientation, the creed constituted by a set of posited values, and it challenges the utility and even the viability of the war system in the nuclear age. At the same time, it draws from the Marxist/Leninist tradition the importance of analyzing the *structure* of power and of understanding that *policies* and *tactics* are dependent upon the struggles of the oppressed. It accepts from liberalism ideas about the need to limit state power by a constitutional order of checks and balances. Forming a coherent ideology of wide applicability in a variety of cultural circumstances is one of the objectives of world order studies.

The question of an appropriate approach is also important, although subordinate to the matter of ideology. Adopting an approach to the politics of the future requires tools for analysis, understanding, and, possibly, persuasion. Our world order approach is set forth in the General Introduction of this volume. It emphasizes structure, assesses data in relation to specified values and goals, and provides some insight into the dynamics of system change, or transition. As such, this world order approach seeks to provide a *critical* foundation for perceiving developments within the state system and a *futurist* frame of reference for conceiving and assessing alternative world order systems.

We can grasp the character of any approach by the way it uses *data*, confirming and contradicting generalizations about the real world, and by its key *concepts*, delimiting the subject matter to serve the purposes of inquiry. In this section, we explore some of the global policy implications of various world order positions and offer examples of different ideological orientations toward world order.

The first selection, an essay by Richard Falk, attempts to survey and encompass "the approaches debate." Its inquiry focuses on the basic stance taken toward the state system, distinguishing system-maintaining, system-reforming, and system-transforming perspectives from this viewpoint. Such a classificatory scheme, in the global humanist tradition, is concerned about world order values rather than about the relations of dominance and dependence within the world capitalist system.

The Falk analysis also argues the case for a transdisciplinary orientation toward world order studies. At issue in the context of system change is an implicit controversy about human nature and human potential bearing especially on the balance between conflictual and cooperative propensities. To get at this issue, it is necessary to consider human experience in light of philosophical, theological, anthropological, and psychological learning, as well as in light of political science, economics, and history. The world order approach proposed by Falk is anti-reductionist—that is, it rejects the idea that any one feature of human nature is decisive for adequate explanation of the past or anticipation of the future. As such, it rejects, in particular, the claims often associated in political thought with Thomas Hobbes that "man (that is, the human being) is inherently selfish or aggressive or materialistic." The complexity and plasticity of human nature, emphasizing the importance of political and normative context (including education and religion), is one of the central foundations of hope for the future.

The second selection is by Roy Preiswerk, former Director of the Institute of Development Studies and a member of the faculty at the Graduate Institute of International Studies in Geneva, Switzerland. Preiswerk emphasizes the extent to which traditional modes of inquiry into the world political system have neglected the concerns of the world's peoples. Preiswerk argues that the abstraction of statism, with its preoccupations with alliances, geopolitical trends, international crises, and the like, leaves the human being virtually out of account. His article is a plea for humanist reorientation that also illustrates the extent to which methodology embodies ideology and leads in a given substantive direction.

The final selection, by Robert Johansen, is taken from the first chapter of his recently published book, *The National Interest and the Human Interest*. In this chapter, Johansen confronts directly the issue of whether the state system, operating through the interaction of elites in terms of what they consider to be the national interest of their own societies, is capable of responding to the challenges of war, poverty, social injustice, and ecological collapse. His argument is that the state system as it presently operates endangers human survival and exhibits an incapacity to achieve world order values. Johansen's interpretation can be read as a direct response to Hedley Bull's position in Section 2 with its positive argument for the state system. Johansen presents what he labels "a globalist-humanist frame of reference" for evaluating the foreign policy of the United States and, by implication, the foreign policies of every state. In reviewing the rise of the state system from the Peace of Westphalia, Johansen argues that the "tragedy of the commons," an image of the effects of the market in circumstances of scarcity in which individual units serving their own interests produce serious harm to the general interests of society, is now applicable to the political organization of international society. His use of the globalist-humanist paradigm for exploring five alternative world order systems is especially helpful in understanding the variety of orientations and perspectives that any inquiry into a just world order should bear in mind at all times.

QUESTIONS FOR DISCUSSION AND REFLECTION

What are the main alternative methods of conceiving of the world system? What are the distinct global policy implications of these alternatives?

What assumptions about human nature seem most helpful and persuasive in approaching the broad question of the limits of global reform?

How does one contrast global humanist and world system perspectives (e.g., those of Robert Johansen on the one hand and of Immanuel Wallerstein on the other) on world order? In turn, how do these perspectives contrast with nonstructural views of global society that stress the durability and continuity of the state system?

What would be an ideal educational foundation for world order studies? Can this be achieved within the curriculum of your present university or college environment?

SELECTED BIBLIOGRAPHY

Angell, Robert C. The Quest for World Order. Ann Arbor, MI.: University of Michigan Press, 1979.

Falk, Richard A. A Global Approach to National Policy. Cambridge: Harvard University Press, 1975.

Galtung, Johan. The True Worlds: A Transnational Perspective. New York: Free Press, 1980.

Haas, Ernst; Mary Pat Williams; and Don Babai. Scientists and World Order. Berkeley: University of California Press, 1977.

Hoffman, Stanley. Primacy or World Order: American Foreign Policy Since the Cold War. New York: McGraw-Hill, 1978.

Johansen, Robert C. The National Interest and the Human Interest. Princeton: Princeton University Press, 1980.

Keohane, Robert O., and Joseph S. Nye, Jr., eds. Transnational Relations and World Politics. Cambridge: Harvard University Press, 1972.

Kim, Samuel. *China, the United Nations, and World Order*. Princeton: Princeton University Press, 1979.

Kuhn, T. S. *The Structure of Scientific Revolutions*. Chicago: University of Chicago Press, 1970.

Morgenthau, Hans J. *Politics Among Nations*. 5th ed. New York: Knopf, 1973.

Mumford, Lewis. *The Story of Utopias*. New York: Viking Press, 1962.

Pirages, Dennis. *The New Context for International Relations: Global Ecopolitics*. North Scituate, MA: Duxbury Press, 1978.

12
CONTENDING APPROACHES TO WORLD ORDER

Richard Falk

The topic "contending approaches" calls for a mixture of description and appraisal. In the first sections of this chapter an attempt will be made to depict the contours of this emergent academic field of "world order" which is rapidly also becoming a fashionable term of art for political leaders. This descriptive account seeks to be informative, for the most part, and will draw some distinctions that seem helpful in discerning the various tendencies sheltered beneath the broad umbrella of world order.

Part 4 of the chapter, which proceeds from an affinity with system-changing approaches to world order, acknowledges that a minimum realization of normative goals on a planetary scale requires profound changes in political culture and structure. I do not argue the case for this approach, but discuss some intellectual developments that are emerging at its frontiers, developments that strengthen its analysis and provide a more sensitive understanding of social forces at work in the world.

The overall consideration of world order, at this stage, regards it as a principal development in the North American intellectual context, and therefore, it should be complemented by related studies of peace research, conflict resolution, and alternative political futures being carried on elsewhere in the world.[1] The United States, of course, is a global presence, whose intellectual fashions, for better or worse, exert great influence even as they arouse antagonism elsewhere. In this regard, the global spread of world order studies and the suspicions engendered by its point of origin together help shape the context of inquiry.

1. LEGITIMATING "WORLD ORDER"

It is less than a decade since "world order studies" began to be taken seriously as an academic focus for teaching and research, and throughout this recent period, its acceptance has been fitful and controversial. As is often the case, this resistance is expressive of a variety of concerns, some acknowledged, some not.

Reprinted by permission from the *Journal of International Affairs* 31, Fall-Winter, 1977.

One characteristic ground of opposition has maintained that a world order focus invariably politicized the learning process, as it substituted advocacy for analysis. In an uphill battle, now largely won, academics promoting a world order outlook sought to display analytic credentials within a framework of explicit values. Those who proposed a world order outlook essentially argued that an element of study appropriate to higher education involved understanding the place of values in the political process. They concluded that anyone who insisted that objectivity excluded normative considerations endorsed, wittingly, or not, the status quo. In other words, an academic inquiry could never be a neutral one.

Another major criticism of the world order approach is its concentration upon an alleged commitment to world government as a solution for the problems of international life.[2] In this context, critics consistently underscore "the utopian" and sterile character of the position, because they argue that its very unattainability makes the serious assessment of such a political solution a waste of time. This sort of criticism implicitly restricts "valuable" inquiry to those possibilities for political development that seem relevant, given the conventional wisdom on what it is plausible to expect. At times these critics combine their dismissal of world order as something fanciful with the opposite allegation that its very outlook is pernicious, as it exchanges the diverse character of relatively autonomous sovereign states for the brave new world of global tyranny. This particular argument against world order studies is explicitly ideological, but as most current world order specialists point out, the target is largely misconceived. Even among those world order specialists who favor "system-change" most are, by now, wary of centralizing solutions of the sort implied by world government, and increasingly favor design conceptions of political futures that stress the potentiality for decentralizing shifts in the arrangements of power. It is probably a greater mistake these days to associate world order studies with world federalism than with libertarian anarchism, or more aptly, both of these opposed political traditions should be treated as part of the ideological heritage of the world order focus. The world order approach, in fact, does not simply imply a specific configuration of political power and authority at the global level, but moves towards a comparative systems approach on such matters. Alternative political systems discernible at earlier stages in international history are, in effect, compared with both the present world order system built around sovereign states, and with a variety of possible future systems which range from highly centralized images of a world state, to federal and nonfederal conceptions of planetary governance, as well as to various regionalist conceptions. This comparison extends, also, to encompass a variety of decentralizing images drawn from utopian writings, in addition, attention is given to feudalist forms of organization, anarchist writing, communitarian socialism and ethnic separatist movements.[3]

There is also a strong cultural criticism present which, from a different perspective, rejects world order approaches for their naive rationalism including the conviction that solutions can be found by intellectuals for the dangers and tragedies of the world through a combination of analysis and good will.[4] The contention of these critics is that world order approaches are largely irrelevant because they generally proceed from an inadequate conception of human nature. Specifically, world order analysts are accused of overlooking the role of unconscious motivation in human behavior. This deficiency, in turn, is connected with the widespread failure in world order literature to appreciate the role of evil and irrationality in all spheres of human affairs, including politics. An adequate appreciation of human nature would either clarify the notion that "peace and justice" were unattainable because of the foibles of human nature or base transformative hopes on the expectation that the deepest levels of human motivation could be influenced. In either event, the political/economic preoccupations of world order studies are scorned as virtually irrelevant. Such a foreshortened sense of human character can yield either a pessimistic or an optimistic judgment about the future. Where the pessimistic view tends to reinforce standard approaches to international relations based on "balance of power," "deterrence," and "prudence," the optimistic view is hopeful about the long-distance religious and cultural potentialities of human society.[5]

World order studies have been vulnerable to this anti-rationalist line of criticism. Though the rest of the social sciences share this vulnerability, such criticism is more telling in this global context, where analysis often emphasizes the necessity for drastic change. It is impossible to fashion a convincing account of change unless coupled with an adequate conception of human nature. It is for this reason that world order theorizing has, in my view, been unsuccessful in its attempts to explain how to proceed from here to there, or, to employ more recent terminology, in its attempt to solve "the transition problem." In their defense, it is true that system changing world order approaches are becoming more aware of the relevance that culture, myth, religion, and value-change have for their central political preoccupation with alternative political futures.[6]

An opposite threat to world order perspectives than that posed by critics, but by no means a trivial one, arises from their superficial apparent adoption by political leaders as a mainstream prescription for foreign policy analysis. At the time of his inauguration, President Jimmy Carter addressed these words to foreign nations: "I want to assure you that the relations of the United States with the other countries and peoples of the world will be guided during my own Administration by our desire to shape a world order that is more responsive to human aspirations. The United States will meet its obligation to help create a stable, just, and peaceful world order."[7] On the one hand, the espousal of "world order politics" by the President of the United States is certainly an acknowledgement of the case of fundamental international adjustments carried out within a normative framework of widely shared values.[8] At the same time, however, the espousal, unaccompanied by modifications of traditional statecraft, reinforces the view that world order thinking is merely verbiage, and even worse, is an expression of the status quo ideological insistence that "orderly" procedures of adjustment can satisfy claims for change in international life. It is for this reason, therefore, that many who believe change will occur only as a consequence of a militant social movement from below, now regard the rhetoric of world order studies as a contemporary opiate of the people, functioning virtually as an imperial ideology designed to quiet down emergent discontent. The extent to which world order studies has been generated from the United States should also be noted, as it is perceived elsewhere as a managerial "fix" for global issues that merely represents a new geopolitical strategy for perpetuating global economic, political and cultural hegemony. Such an attempt by those at a geopolitical pinnacle to define the terms of conflict and resolution is correctly regarded with suspicion by those in more dependent positions.

Along related lines is the concern that world order advocacy by statesmen and their intellectual cadre falsely reassures the public about the capacity of elites and official institutions to meet the new agenda of international challenges. It is up to the world order studies movement to distance itself from official rhetoric in order to avoid getting swallowed up by it. Such avoidance is not easy, and it is always tempting to assuage ivory tower insecurities by invoking supportive statements of "hard-headed" practical men and women of affairs to demonstrate the acceptance and acceptability of world order concerns. In the last analysis, I think, we must acknowledge a definite split within the ranks of world order studies between system-maintainers, who seek to appropriate world order rhetoric for marginal reforms instituted by official elites, and system-transformers, who seek a populist style involving militant challenge to carry forward their demands for fundamental reform.

A related objection to the world order approach is associated with its apparent emphasis upon order as the missing ingredient in an acceptable world system. Though the word "order" has repressive connotations which are evident in the phrase "law and order," it implies that strict enforcement of legal rules is the essence of world order. Such a static image is especially inappropriate for those world perspectives that advocate a process of transformation to realize minimum goals. In this respect the emphasis on "order" seems deceptive and overly static. In theory, the concept of "world order" could be treated as satisfied by any stable arrangement of parts, including tyrannical and exploitative arrangements. Some academics, therefore, are abandoning the earlier label "world order" in favor of more *dynamic* and *value-laden* terminology such as "a movement for a just world," "just world order," or "human world order." In contrast, however, those who are primarily concerned with stability and managerial efficiency view the central imagery of "order" as an asset, which partly accounts for its acceptability to current political leaders. As is often the case, then, the battle over definitions hides a deeper battle over substance.

A final issue of perspective reflects the division between idealists and realists as to the agenda of global reform. Critics of world order studies mount both lines of attack, accusing world order thinking of being simultaneously "idealistic" in its conception of human potentiality, even as it is "morbid" in its prophetic insistence on mounting dangers of planetary catastrophe. Two responses in the world order literature can be noted. System-maintenance world order approaches deny the charge, rejecting apocalyptic diagnosis and making clear their commitment to gradualism that can over time improve the quality of order in world affairs without undermining current modes of stability. System-transformers tend to accept the charge with the proviso of claiming for their position the imprimatur of "realism," arguing that unless positive potentialities for global reform are quickly realized, international trends and risks will produce the decline and, eventually, the collapse of civilization. Their faith in positive potentialities may not be very strong, but their perceptions do lead them to the conclusion that it is necessary to try by all available means to act as though a peaceful and just world is, indeed, a possibility and that without it we will face the virtual inevitability of gruesome apocalypse.

It is possible, of course, to downplay this upsurge of concern with the future of the world. Perhaps, as some claim, this concern is nothing more durable than an elaborate pyschic preparation for the advent of the year 2000. After all, as the year 1000 approached, we know there was much speculation about the end of the world, as well as about its imminent salvation. It is probably beneficial to condition world order inquiry by such realizations to encourage greater modesty of tone, and humility of expectations. Part of what has given "world order" a bad name in some circles is undoubtedly its tendency to cry "wolf" about the immediate future seeking a hearing by the shrill insistence that the human race has only a decade or so to set things straight. Such literal warnings are simply not credible. I think this lesson is being slowly learned, and that world order projects and studies, as a consequence, are increasingly aware that transformation of the world system presupposes a long, ambiguous struggle dependent on the emergence of a robust global social movement.[9] There is no "quick-fix" in the offing, only the slim hope that there will be enough time for a global learning process among elites and masses to evolve in such a way as to be able to encourage a series of political adjustments in the world that gradually shift the weight of behavior in directions that are humane and ecologically sensitive.

2. TOWARD A DEFINITION OF WORLD ORDER

Reporting on a widely publicized symposium, held at Bellagio, Italy in 1965, and devoted to "Conditions of World Order," Stanley Hoffmann notes that from the outset discussion was muddled by conference participants who tended to use world order in distinct, inconsistent ways. Hoffmann praises the conference chairman, Raymond Aron, for providing "the composers with a key for their symphony" by first discerning five possible meanings for the term "world order" and then selecting one of these as the basis for further discussion. According to Hoffmann these five meanings were distinguished as follows:

> Two of the meanings were purely descriptive: order as any arrangement of reality, order as the relations between the parts. Two were analytical—partly descriptive, partly normative: order as the minimum conditions for existence, order as the minimum conditions for coexistence. The fifth conception was purely normative: order as the conditions for the good life.[10]

Aron then proposed that the conferees adopt the fourth variant and concentrate their discussion ". . . under what conditions would men (divided in so many ways) be able not merely to avoid destruction, but to live together relatively well in one planet."[11]

A procedure along these lines also meant that the frame of reality is the political experience of the planet as a whole (i.e., the world), constituted by states as principal actors and shaped both by the character and diversity of domestic structures of authority, as well as by a variety of transnational actors and forces.

More recently, however, Hedley Bull has articulated, with greater precision and elegance, a similar conception of world order: "By world order I mean those patterns or dispositions of human activity that sustain the elementary or primary goals of social life among mankind as a whole."[12] Such a position acknowledges the fact that a range of ordering options exists to determine how world order might be achieved, but supports the primacy of the state in relation to individuals and the state system in relation to collectivities. Bull draws a sharp distinction between the role of government as the principal source of domestic order and the more primitive forms of order operative in what he regards as the anarchical setting of international society, anarchy being conceived in the technical sense of the absence of government.

Bull maintains that the achievement of order can be assessed only by reference to the realization of "elementary goals of social life" identified as common interests of all peoples: "Thus the facts of human vulnerability to violence and proneness to resort to it lead men to the sense of common interests in restricting violence. The fact of human interdependence for material needs leads them to perceive a common interest in ensuring respect for agreements. The facts of limited abundance and limited human altruism lead them to recognize common interests in stabilizing possession."[13] Rules as incorporated in international law are generally regarded as beneficial for the clarification and preservation of these common interests, but are not effective in relation to fundamental security for the state. For international society, which lacks governmental capacities and is composed of members with a weak perception for common interests, order is obtained principally by such mechanisms as "balance of power" and "deterrence," encouraging mutual restraint in a manner compatible with the perceived separate interests of governments: "Within international society, however, as in other societies, order is the consequence not merely of contingent facts such as this [i.e., balance of power], but of a sense of common interests in the elementary goals of social life; rules prescribing behaviour that sustain these goals; and institutions that help to make these rules effective."[14]

Bull regards "order" of this character as valuable in itself and as "the condition of the realization of other values," including the pursuit of justice.[15] At the same time, however, Bull regards the demands for justice as relating, in a profound way, to the search for acceptable forms of order. If the parties can agree on just results, or if a consensus on an international level can be achieved, then order and justice can be reconciled. It is when there is disagreement among states as to the character of just results that the more fundamental ordering goals of international society on which agreement can be presumed suggest, to Bull, the need to accord priority to considerations of order as against the claims of justice.

Finally, Bull considers alternatives to the present reliance on the state system for the achievement of order and justice on a global scale. He concludes that the state system is durable, despite its defects and vulnerabilities, and superior to any alternative conception of world order that can be plausibly presented at this stage of human experience.[16]

A feature of this Aron-Bull approach to world order, surely the dominant orientation in academic and governmental circles, is its hostility toward "normative" conceptions of world order that stress the pursuit of valued goals as the object of inquiry. Aron calls for the abandonment of such an emphasis because it only leads "to platitudes and to an acrimonious reproduction of the conflicts of values that exist in the world."[17] Bull acknowledges the appropriateness of studying the pursuit of justice as seriously as the pursuit of order, but he believes it is a "corrupting" trait to introduce policy recommendations into the study of world political activity: "The search for conclusions that can be presented as 'solutions' or 'practical advice' is a corrupting element in the contemporary study of world politics, which properly understood is an intellectual activity and not a practical one. Such conclusions are advanced less because there is any solid basis for them than because there is a demand for them which it is profitable to satisfy."[18] Bull closes his book and concludes his argument with this admonition: "The fact is that while there is a great desire to know what the future of world politics will bring, and also to know how we should behave in it, we have to grope about in the dark with respect to the one as much as with respect to the other. It is better to recognize that we are in darkness than to pretend that we can see the light."[19]

The Bellagio meeting also affirms Hedley Bull's muddling-through-with-the-state-system view of the future both as a prediction and prescription. This approach is aptly treated as a world order approach because it is concerned with the conditions for a satisfactory persistence of the present state system, as well as with comprehending its operating dynamics. Its normative contribution is to make these conditions explicit so that policy-makers and power-wielders will be more likely to perform in an intelligent manner. At the core of this approach is a neo-Machiavellian type of advice to the prince, in effect, a counsel of prudence given a spirit of urgency in an era of global politics beset by the pervasive menace of nuclear warfare.

Another quite different approach to world order is a curious blend of ideology and behavioral methodology. The ideology associates world order with degrees of centralization of political authority, while the behavioral methodology measures this tendency by reference to quantifiable elements of international politics. Martin Rochester structures his inquiry by taking note of what he calls "[a] favorite pastime of observers of international relations . . . to speculate on how much progress has been made toward 'world order' and how much progress can be expected in the future." Rochester contends that this speculation has concentrated on "the evolving role of international institutions" and has tended to be flawed by being "normative, impressionistic, and unstructured."[20] His conception of world order seems to reduce to the question of how much measurable institutionalization of behavior occurs in international life. This focus leads Rochester to undertake such empirical exercises as the comparison of the roles of the Permanent Court of International Justice, operative between World War I and World War II, and the International Court of Justice, operative since World War II, so as to assess whether recourse to international judicial settlement procedures is rising or falling.[21] The central tenet of Rochester's view is that if states are using these judicial facilities more frequently and regularly to resolve their disputes with one another, then it is proper to conclude that a growth of world order has taken place. Political context is ignored. Only the criteria of institutional roles, which include salience and resources, are discussed; there is no mention of the intervening experiences of ideological rivalry (East-West), of decolonialization, and of technological innovation as affecting whether or not institutional facilities will be used and for what.

Such a conception of world order is, of course, absurdly restricted. It implicitly endorses governmental solutions of a supranational character and identifies the growth of world order, presumably something beneficial with the elaboration of international institutional capabilities. This approach is an empirically oriented extension of world government thinking about world order, as it confines alternatives for the state system to a single model of political development on the global level. Such an emphasis also takes into account the rise of functional pressures which tend to foster increased international cooperation. It implicitly rejects the earlier view regarding a constitutional convention by government actors as a necessary step in the process of building a consummated system of world order. Another implication of Rochester's viewpoint is that the state system *per se*, however well it keeps order in the Bull sense, is nevertheless inherently incapable of qualifying as a world order system because it is insufficiently centralized. As far as Rochester is concerned, world order is dynamic in a structural and not in a normative sense because it involves the movement toward institutional centralization. Except by implication we have no perception that a centralized system will be more efficient in realizing a set of world order values than the current system.

A more sophisticated extension of this perspective, but one that avoids creating normative misimpressions that might derive from the explicit adoption of world order terminology, is the currently fashionable tendency of international relations specialists to study "interdependence." "Measurable interdependence," indeed, makes an effort to combine the objectivity of analysis with behavioral criteria of assessment (that which can be quantified), while not remaining oblivious to changes in behavioral features of international life, which include the rise of transnational phenomena of many kinds.[22] Such an emphasis is transactional and does not view politics from the outlook of "the world," nor does it assess performance of global political systems from the standpoint of normative criteria, or values.

Admittedly, normative approaches to world order usually proceed from specific agendas of concerns and on the basis of a definite program of goals. Saul Mendlovitz and Thomas Weiss define world order as "the study of international relations and world affairs that focuses on the manner in which mankind can significantly reduce the likelihood of international violence and create minimally acceptable conditions of worldwide economic well-being, social justice, ecological stability, and participation in decision-making processes. In short, a student of world order seeks to achieve and maintain a warless and more just world to improve the quality of human life."[23] Implicit in such a view of world order is the quest for a new system of power/authority. It is not surprising, therefore, that Mendlovitz and Weiss assert that "[a] world order inquiry involves the use of relevant utopias culminating in the statement of the investigator's preferred world." From this conviction that a new system of world order is necessary, there follows the generalized depreciation of the state as an instrument of order or justice. Non-state actors, ranging from international institutions to multinational corporations, consequently, are looked upon with favor and a concerted effort is made to depict a plausible, minimally violent path of transition to the model or utopia. In the words of Mendlovitz and Weiss, "a concrete behavioral statement of transformation from the present system and to the projected model is necessary."[24]

Gerald and Patricia Mische believe that two types of world order must be distinguished on normative grounds. The first, which they reject, "is the order that presently exists on the planet, an order of dependent relationships between allegedly independent sovereignties that are dominated by raw economic, monetary and military power rather than by law." The second, which they endorse, "envisions an order of relationships determined by law and based on universal social justice for all persons; an order whose operative principles embrace the centrality and sovereignty of the human person."[25] In contrast to Bull, the Misches do not regard the state as a minimally adequate agent for the realization of human dignity, and world order in their normative sense means a diminished role for the state and an end of the state system. Their vision of the future is specified in ideological terms as involving a mix of functional centralization ("e.g., peace-keeping, transnational ecological protection, regulation of world trade and of an integrated monetary system, regulation of the uses of the seas, and some global taxation") and political decentralization via dismantling of the national security roles of the state. Here again the idea of world order is associated with a relevant utopia whose attainability by education and struggle is affirmed as the sole alternative to catastrophic global destiny.

Unlike the analytical approaches, a normative approach necessarily includes tendering practical advice for activists. It seeks to shape and inspire a world movement for systemic change, and is not content with understanding how the present system operates. At the same time, however, the search for an integrated vision of a preferred future specified in terms that suggest attainability within a reasonable time period (combining considerations of utopian quest and political feasibility) does not necessarily prejudge the character of a solution. So long as the values posited can be realized, any structure will do, although the implications seem to call for some buildup of international institutions in a deliberate fashion to carry out some of the activities now administered at the state level.

In this respect, there is an apparent similarity to Rochester's approach, although for normative approaches such a tendency is one feature of an emergent alternative system rather than an expression of the essence of what world order is concerned about. The advice implicit in radically normative approaches to world order, as compared to Aron and Bull, is directed towards those who would join in the struggle to build support for distinct and oppositional conceptions of security and well-being rather than support those characteristics of the war-oriented, sovereignty-inclined state system. Mendlovitz, Weiss and the Misches, in effect, are saying that the evolution of the state system inclines the world toward destruction; that no way to arrest these self-destructive tendencies is implicit in the traditional forms of statecraft, and, consequently, that a movement for global reform is needed as soon as possible.

My approach to world order combines analytic, empirical, ideological, and normative concerns in its definition. Such a conception of world order involves studying the extent to which a given past, present, or future arrangement of power and authority is able to realize a set of human goals that are affirmed as beneficial for all people and apply to the whole world, and achieve some objectivity by their connection with a conception of basic human needs, as required for the healthy development of the human person. The set of human goals, or values, can be specified in a variety of testable and semi-testable ways. Past and future systems can be compared with the present system to the extent that relative goal realization can be determined in measurable terms. The role of the state and other international actors is left open, as are the contours of a satisfactory future world order system.

This definition of world order does not assume an ideological stance, as such, because in this sense it is an instance of an analytic definition. Underlying my assessment of the historical situation, however, is also my conviction that the state system is not capable of a satisfactory performance in relation to the goals set forth, and that contained within its main operating dynamic are excessive risks of thermonuclear, ecological, economic, and cultural deterioration, and even of collapse. For these reasons, my approach to world order does entail the construction of relevant utopias, as well as the depiction of transition paths. However, the role of the state, as distinct from the state system, is uncertain in a transformed system. This conception is also a normative one, to the extent that it advocates reliance on "central guidance" mechanisms in response to the functional imperatives of interdependence and decentralization in response to ethical imperatives of humane patterns of governance. My relevant utopia, as such, is similar in its broad conception to the one outlined by Gerald and Patricia Mische, although it considers the domestic arenas of states as the most critical context for world order transformation and is correspondingly skeptical of direct approaches to global reform by way of strengthening the United Nations and the like.

3. DELIMITATION OF WORLD ORDER STUDIES

There are, I believe, two broad and rather dissimilar endeavors being carried forward beneath the rubric of world order studies at the present time. The first endeavor involves the narrower effort to reorient international relations away from its purely Machiavellian orientation. Mainstream international relations seeks to explicate how the system works under evolving circumstances; it associates statesmanship and even political virtue with adapting to the logic of interstate relations in a prudent, yet unsentimental, fashion.[26] In this vein Henry Kissinger and Chou En Lai can be viewed as master practitioners because they exhibited such a successful command over the dynamics of the system for the sake of securing national advantage. In contrast, a world order approach to international relations is relatively disinterested in manipulative skills and stresses, and tries, instead, to elevate normative, futurist, and structural concerns. To be more specific, world order approaches focus on the character of world order problems and on goals and values as tests of whether the system is working, and for whom. A world order approach of this variety envisions positive and negative scenarios based on interpreting trends and tendencies, converting the future into a present concern of urgent character; as well, structural features of the existing system of world order based on sovereign states are appraised, especially to undergird a critique and to guide the search for, and design of more acceptable world order systems based on an innovative combination of actors and orientations.[27]

The second type of world order studies cuts a broader path that flows from an initial diagnosis of the present world situation rather than from the political system that had evolved over past centuries. The world situation, increasingly, generates a variety of challenges and poses a vast array of social problems that seem to cluster around war/peace issues, economic well-being concerns, human rights, and ecological balance. In addition, the interactions between population growth, political repression, and economic development strategies suggest that the problems posed are not susceptible to *separate* treatment, but must be dealt with in a *systemic* or *organic* way. This systemic way of problem-solving crystallizes into an ecological orientation in some formulations, ecology being conceived as the study of how to sustain the quality of life in *total* systems. A holistic outlook leads ecological types of world order studies to stress synthesis as well as analysis in the educational process, and, as such, works toward building up integrated patterns of understanding.

This ecological type of world order studies is inclined to undertake various kinds of model-building exercises to examine the reality and extent of integrative patterns, assessing global policy options of states or regions from the standpoint of the whole. Such global models are inter-disciplinary and give varying degrees of attention to the workings of international relations, while attempting to construct a viable future in defiance of the main governmental centers of power and authority.[28] The models can assume any character, of course, and it is only now that beginnings are being made to emphasize the urge to be simultaneously normative, futurist, and structural, as well as to integrate economic and political assessments of potentiality. The Latin American model of the Fundacion Bariloche, with its focus on the capital reallocations required to achieve a development path where most of the population would achieve an income sufficient for basic needs, is illustrative.[29] These global models are beginning to combine the rigor of their methodology with the inclusion of "softer" considerations bearing on political effects, such as authoritarian outputs of growth maximization and equalization inputs in a variety of Third World contexts.

The point taken here is that interdisciplinary research and teaching teams are starting to explore and redesign the potentialities of political systems at all levels of societal generalization. These potentialities will remain inert, however, unless actualized by a social movement of support. They already constitute a species of "dangerous knowledge," because they show that technocratic modes of analysis and projection can be adapted to promote quite different societal goals than the ones being pursued by an existing leadership that partly bases its claim of legitimacy on the objectivity and necessity of its economic development program.[30]

These types of world order studies share a combination of normative, futurist, and structural concerns explored in relation to a disciplined framework of inquiry. Despite this common orientation that justifies the extension of the term world order, there are some critical distinctions with respect to goals and expectations. The diversities can be discussed in the following terms:

- system-maintaining approaches;
- system-reforming approaches;
- system-transforming approaches.

Reality, of course, does not divide as neatly as our analytic categories suggest, and a given undertaking may partake of more than one of these outlooks on global reform. What is emphasized here, however, is that attitudes toward change, with respect to the depth and extent of global reform, are the essence of the world order endeavor.

System-Maintaining Approaches

Those who control the dominant institutions of government and business seek above all else to discover the means to sustain the system. Their search is for stability under constantly changing conditions. The intellectual outlook of system-maintaining approaches to world order is closely associated with sustaining particular positions and privilege in the status quo. The Trilateral Commission, founded in 1973 at the initiative of David Rockefeller, epitomizes a system-maintaining perspective on world order.[31] The Trilateral Commission was formed as a private initiative designed to link elites in North America, Western Europe, and Japan, especially encouraging consensus formation around issues of international economic policy. As has been widely noticed a surprising number of its American members and consultants have moved into positions of policy-making prominence in the Carter Administration.[32] That is, there is an easy flow between playing official roles in policy formation within the existing system and the kind of image of global reform associated with Trilateral type of thinking. This is exemplified by Zbigniew Brzezinski's shift from his role as intellectual mentor of the Trilateral Commission to his current job as chief foreign policy advisor to President Carter. The essence of Brzezinski's views is that world economic arrangements shaped after World War II served well until recently, but now need to be significantly recast by cooperative action on the part of the governments of the advanced industrial countries, i.e., the Trilateral sector of the world economy. With post-war European reconstruction having been completed, with colonialism fully destroyed, and with the rise in prominence of OPEC, a new more pluralistic situation will require more pluralistic economic arrangements so as to encourage a healthy economic dynamic. This interpretation of world requirements leads to an emphasis on trade, money, international financial institutions, and energy policy.[33] In the conceptual frame of world order analysis two observations are relevant: first, the system-maintaining propensities of principal governments and elites; secondly, the priority attached to coordination of economic policy as the basis for an improved world order.

A system-maintaining perspective tends to emphasize the strengthening and further creation of specialized international institutions which handle economic issues. Daniel Bell, for instance, in a typical statement of this outlook, writes the following: "The problem, then, is to design effective international instruments—in the monetary, commodity, trade, and technology areas—to effect the necessary transitions to a new international division of labor that can provide for economic and, perhaps, political stability."[34] An interesting feature of system-maintaining approaches to world order is the stress placed upon *technical* solutions and the corresponding disregard of the political or normative. One searches virtually in vain through the writings of the Trilateral Commission and kindred perspectives for positive proposals on the United Nations or analyses of the dangers of warfare and ecological decay.

The dominant preoccupation of Trilateralists and their allies is to keep the world economy growing in the face of three sets of threats: rivalry with Communist powers, the challenge from the Third World, and the deepening competition among the Trilateral countries themselves. On the level of prescription this assessment of the world scene leads to military preparedness in relation to Communism, and to superficial concessions and accommodationism in relation to the Third World.[35] Internal conflict within the Trilateral sector is most difficult to handle, partly because it creates a tension between the competitive pressures that are escalating in a period of economic stagnancy, inflation, and unemployment, and partly because such tensions imperil a geopolitical partnership on matters of security, a partnership reinforced by a shared outlook on cultural and many other global policy issues.[36] At the present time, a frantic effort is underway to avoid a repetition of trade wars by reconciling nationalist insistence on protectionism with internationalist pressure for openness. This appreciation of danger induces an intense desire to tinker with the world order system to avoid further deteriorations. Among the elements of the situation that provoke concern are a heavy debt burden being borne by a variety of Third World and European countries, an intensifying struggle for export outlets as productive capacity seems to grow beyond demand in a whole series of product areas, an awareness that OPEC leverage on prices and supply makes the industrial countries vulnerable, and a related awareness that new sources of energy are both necessary and problematical. The cumulative effect is to create a fear that the world economic system could unravel, producing grave domestic crises and heightening international tensions in alarming respects. In this regard, the Trilateral Commission seeks to moderate these dire prospects by devising mutually acceptable arrangements that can "manage interdependence."

Another quite different dimension of Trilateralist thinking explores the conviction that international tensions reflect the excesses of democratic patterns of governance that produce behavior inconsistent with elite interests; for instance, protectionist demands by certain labor and business interests to safeguard jobs and profits in noncompetitive sectors of domestic industry. It is not surprising, therefore, to discover Trilateral sponsorship of studies lamenting the "excesses" of democracy and affirming the importance of inculcating public respect for authority structures.[37] Among these excesses in democratic societies is the alleged tendency of intellectuals to withdraw their commitment to the legitimacy of the present order.[38]

Such a system-maintaining perspective currently dominates the foreign policy debate. On the future of the Panama Canal, for instance, the pro-treaty advocates are "rational imperialists" arguing that imperial prerogatives are preserved in a manner acceptable to the Panamanians; on the other hand, the anti-treaty, "sentimental imperialists" believe that any symbolic renunciation of prerogatives weakens the United States' claim on canal facilities. Since both positions insist that the interventionary prerogatives be safeguarded, neither addresses the core question of imperialist legitimacy. Given the dynamic of self-determination, why should use and access to the canal be entrusted to the unilateral discretions of a single great power? In anticipation of this question, a system-reforming position would propose Panamanian sovereignty over the canal, whereas a system-changing position would entrust the canal to some supranational control arrangement designed on the basis of global community considerations to assure peaceful use for all and belligerent use for none.

"System-maintaining" approaches to world order can be associated with governing groups and their supporting elites in the most powerfully constituted states. The organizing objective is to assure efficient economic performance, as measured by economic growth and calculated by GNP increases. Whatever means facilitate such growth are positive and should be encouraged; whatever means interfere, even if it is the exercise of democratic rights themselves, are negative and should be curtailed. The international distribution of power, wealth, and prestige is relevant only to the extent that it poses managerial challenges. The state system, with its reliance on war as the ultimate arbiter of conflict, is accepted as inevitable, and the ecological dangers engendered by industrial-technological pressures are viewed as containable.

System-Reforming Approaches

A wider range of initiatives can be associated with a system-reform focus. The critical feature, in this instance, is the realization that structural modifications over a broad series of subject matters will be required to satisfy both interests and values, but that these modifications are not so fundamental as to call into question the basic ordering of international relations around the role and predominance of the sovereign state. The 1980's Project of the Council on Foreign Relations is a good example of a system-reformist perspective. As Richard Ullman, the architect and director of the undertaking, writes: "The 1980's Project is based upon the belief that serious effort and integrated forethought can contribute—indeed, are indispensable—to progress in the next decade toward a more humane, peaceful, productive, and just world."[39] The pretension of The 1980's Project, despite its sponsorship by an elite American institution like the Council on Foreign Relations, is to study the future in a universalistic spirit of ideological neutrality and policy pluralism; in Ullman's words: "It is not the Project's purpose to arrive at a single or exclusive set of goals. Nor does it focus upon the foreign policy or national interests of the United States alone. Instead, it seeks to identify goals that are compatible with the perceived interests of most states, despite differences in ideology and in level of economic development."[40]

Another feature of reformist thinking is a concentration of speculative analysis on a period long enough to be independent of current contexts of choice, but short enough to engage the concerns of policy-makers. Thus, The 1980's Project starts from the premise "that many of the assumptions, policies, and constitutions that have characterized international relations during the past 30 years are inadequate to the demands of today and foreseeable demands of the period between now and 1990 or so."[41] It is interesting to note that the treatment of time, the historical as well as the futurist aspect, is balanced in such a way as to encompass the span of past experience (30 years) as the basis for thinking ahead.

The 1980's Project has definitely broken new ground in its attempt to construct an integrated picture of policy choices for the years ahead. It also has opted for a global, as distinct from an American, perspective, although the identity of the Council on Foreign Relations, as well as the main body of participants and their early proposals make it doubtful whether the influence of its American auspices/orientation can be overcome. The globalist aspiration, nevertheless, is significant in itself and expresses some awareness that the expanding planetary agenda must be handled in as cooperative a manner as possible. Furthermore, The 1980's Project is normative in a system-reforming manner, acknowledging the need for normative adjustments in international relations, but failing to question the basic structure of a state-centric system. The ambitious scale and august sponsorship of The 1980's Project is, in any event, a revealing acknowledgement that world order approaches in the basic sense of normative, futurist, and structural studies of the global situation are relevant even for those whose primary orientation is managerial.

System-Transforming Approaches

The distinguishing characteristic of system-transforming approaches to world order is the acceptance of the need to transform the structure of international relations by diminishing the role of sovereign states in some decisive respects.

Even more so than with advocates of system-reform, those who propose system-transformation seek an integrated strategy of change guided by certain values and aiming toward the construction of a coherent new system of world order.

The World Order Models Project (WOMP) of the Institute for World Order provides an example of a system-transforming perspective. WOMP, initiated in 1968, is constituted by groups of scholars associated with principal regions and/or actors of the world (Latin America, Africa, Japan, Europe, Soviet Union, India, United States, with indirect representation for China and for the network of transnational actors). The WOMP group, through periodic interaction, evolved a framework of world order values which were general enough to command consensus and yet distinctive enough to establish an identity. The values agreed upon as suitable criteria for world order appraisal were as follows: minimization of collective violence; maximization of economic well-being; maximization of social and political justice; and maximization of ecological quality.[42] There was discussion at WOMP meetings as to whether the goal of democratizing participation in authority structures within states and in the world system should be emphasized through the device of formulating a fifth value of participation or by being incorporated in the interpretation of the agreed four. In essence, the issue was left unresolved with each author free to proceed as he or she wished. It was also understood that the affirmation of a series of values could not be fully reconciled with the concrete realities of social choice where value tradeoffs must generally be made. The varying ways of ranking priorities brought great diversity to the substance of WOMP manuscripts despite the agreement on a common framework of inquiry. This diversity is most evident in relation to the proposals made for global reforms, especially the contours of a transformed world order system that could be projected as attainable by the end of the century.

In the first phase of WOMP, each distinct group usually represented by one or two of its members, evolved its own version of "a relevant utopia." This took the form of a comprehensive schema for a positive rearrangement of power, wealth, and prestige on a world scale, together with a transition plan for reaching the promised land. WOMP has published a series of books that explore and analyze these diverse perspectives on what form of drastic global reform seems desirable and attainable by the 1990's.[43]

Despite its American auspices, WOMP has sought, and largely achieved a transnational context for its work. Having engendered diverse conceptions of world order solutions attainable, though not assured, by the 1990's, WOMP is now embarking on a series of continuation studies. First of all, an attempt is being made to link the present to the future through a group of studies of global policy issues that are currently engaging the attention of governmental leaders and public opinion. These studies, essentially, are centered around nonproliferation and nuclear power; human rights; satisfying basic needs; and the new international economic order. The objective of these studies is to demonstrate, in the realistic terms of policy discourse, the distinctiveness of an approach developed from the WOMP set of world order values. An additional

goal is to clarify these values in specific and controversial enough ways to avoid
the danger of allowing world order advocacy to degenerate into a pious series of
platitudes, endorsed by all because of their apolitical character and respected by
no one struggling for change because of their failure to be defined in relation to
ongoing struggles. To help inspire a movement for global reform depends on
WOMP finding ways to mobilize a variety of groups working in widely
disparate arenas for peace and justice, often in opposition to official state
policy.

The second line of WOMP's current work is concentrated on building a more
ambitious transnational consensus as to the direction and shape of an acceptable world order solution among those who endorse the values and accept the
need for system-change as a prerequisite to their realization. The early work of
WOMP restricted itself to the agreed values framework and the conceptual
commitment to consider system-change, to depict a relevant utopia, and to
devise a transition strategy. To proceed from this agreed methodology to an
agreement on substance may prove difficult, even impossible, given the diversity of outlooks represented in WOMP, but even a partial failure will be illuminating to the extent that it sharpens the limits of consensual approaches to
consciousness-raising on a transnational basis at this time.

WOMP as a system-changing perspective also takes a political stance that is
more populist than is characteristic of system-maintainers or system-reformers.
It seeks to inspire, or to take part in, a movement for a just world order, and it
regards most political élites, especially those with a stake in the existing system,
as likely to resist shifts in values, behavior, and structures. This transnational
group of scholars, therefore, is committed to the search for peace with equity,
and seeks to evolve a globalist ideology that draws on liberalism to check the
abuse of state power in the relations between governments and people, on
socialism to depict a humane set of economic relationships based on societal
well-being, on ecological humanism to reorient the relations between human
activity and nature, and on global modeling to put complex interactions of
societal processes at various levels of organization into a dynamic, disciplined
framework. It may be too early in the difficult work of constructing a world
order ideology to give it a label distinct from these antecedents and attitudes.

The real test of the WOMP perspective will be whether or not it can take
roots in the imaginings, cravings, and activities of peoples diversely situated in
various parts of the world. The quasideterminist claim that makes WOMP
more predictive than prescriptive is its assurance that a global integrative process is proceeding in any event, and the zone of freedom is limited to influencing its normative content. We can ask over what time span, with what structure, for whose sake, and by reference to what values, norms and guidelines is
this global integrative process likely to follow under a series of likely patterns of
development. WOMP seeks to shift these historical developments away from
what appears to be their technetronic and political destiny—a mixture of tyrannical structures and catastrophic occurrence on the plane of conflict and
ecological decay. Instead WOMP seeks to promote an ethical and ecological
flourishing in a political setting that joins solidarity of sentiment to diffusion of
structure and power.

4. AT THE FRONTIERS

Posing "The Political Question"

The rhetoric and inquiry associated with world order are evolving in response to new perceptions of what is needed to make the world work; that is, to evolve, as a dynamic political system, in a manner consistent with a general attitude of hope about the future. System-maintaining modes tend to be very traditionalist in their inquiry as their major goal is to provide policy guidance for exceedingly short time intervals. More than anything else these modes identify bargaining space capable of damping down intergovernmental conflicts, especially those conflicts that bear on global economic issues.

System-reforming modes, which are somewhat bolder in scale and ambitious in scope, seek major adjustments to reflect shifts in value/power configurations, adjustments that may require decades for actualization. The distinguishing substantive feature of these approaches is their assumption that the political framework of world order is durable. In more concrete terms this means that a vision of reform that is expected to unfold in conformity with a distribution of power and authority to territorially sovereign governments. Any changes in relative circumstances within or between these governments would have to evolve without benefit of a new pattern of relations among non-state actors. Most normative modeling initiatives fall into the system-reforming category of world order approaches. Sometimes these models can be used to persuade elites that they could attain their proclaimed goals (e.g., full employment, better distribution of income) by altering their priorities (e.g., investment patterns, tax structure). At other times these models can be useful to expose the failure of the political leadership to carry out the policies it purports to favor (e.g., alleviation of poverty at home and abroad).[44] Most model-building exercises seek to increase their influence by proceeding as rigorously as possible, using empirical data, computerized modes of analysis, and reinforcing their policy goals by numerical results. There is little doubt that such an approach may maximize its impact on prevailing political sensibilities and may even entrust a powerful weapon of persuasion to more progressively inclined individuals and groups in positions of control. The limits of this kind of approach to knowledge in the world order field are two-fold: first, a foreshortening of inquiry through the acceptance of a framework that seems outmoded, and second, a related failure to pose "the political question" of how to get a hearing for a position, no matter how persuasive its rationale, antithetical to the perceived interests of dominant elites.

System-transforming approaches may also suffer, as mentioned earlier, by a touchingly irrelevant belief that rational argument suffices because global reform is, essentially, a rational adjustment process. The world federalist tradition, with its abiding faith in the inevitability of world government, is the most glaring case of a program of action that would become plausible only after decades of struggle, or possibly only after the breakdown of the existing structures of world order in a terrible, traumatic manner. The avoidance of "the political question" involves, to some extent, the acceptance of the legitimacy of the status quo, it also involves attributing to existing political leaders the disposition to make those changes necessary to protect the public interest. Such an expectation seems woefully naive. So long as the key élite clusters of the world are diversely situated in its hierarchy, and are primarily responsive to particularized interests within their own society, and not to the society as a whole, there is no chance that voluntarist adjustment patterns can initiate and sustain a transition process on such a grand scale.

In the past, successful responses to "the political question" have presupposed an integrated vision of global reform. One modern instance is associated with the Marxist tradition, especially as developed by Lenin and Trotsky. Non-violent militancy of the sort associated with the efforts of Martin Luther King, Jr., and Mahatma Gandhi is always alive to the universalizing potential of con-crete, isolated acts and activities. These responses to the political question, adapted to concrete realities, inspired by charismatic leadership, and achieved by perseverance at the tactical level, only sought to accomplish change at the state level. The more global vision, espoused by Trotsky, Hitler, or Tanaka, failed at the enactment stage because the forces of resistance were too strong. It was unclear for some time whether or not the Chinese Revolution was attempt-ing a system-changing role; as of now, at least in this early post-Mao phase, it seems apparent that the vision of global liberation has been superceded by the drive for the full fruits of national autonomy and a quest for status within the existing framework of international society. Dreams of world conquest and unification have haunted Chinese (and other) political leaders over the centuries. To date no strategy has succeeded beyond that of ephemeral empire-building; the cycle of growth and decay has been evident everywhere as such leading macro-historians as Toynbee and Spengler demonstrate. In effect, no one has, as yet, answered "the political question" on a global scale.

In world order studies the political question is being posed in terms of "transi-tion" to a new system. To date, however, the attempts have been unconvinc-ing. There is little insight into a credible process of guided change, especially as non-violence as an orientation is stressed, rationalist approaches are scorned, and a general appreciation prevails that politically entrenched elites will remain unreceptive. How does one encourage a positive transition process (i.e., toward preferred world order values) without merely sitting back and waiting (hoping?!) for the apocalypse?

Some flickers of a credible response to such questions are emergent at the frontier. The global interdependence phenomenon is gradually having an im-pact on political consciousness in a way that may have real potential. Even those who endorse the system-reform track acknowledge this development as a "social fact" and attribute significance to it. In a recent article published in *Foreign Affairs*, for instance, its editor, William Bundy, noted the following: "something beyond nationalism is slowly taking root in the world . . . the signs of a developing sense of common human destiny *are* present. Such a sense can-not substitute for a careful focus on the present and pressing problems that can only be met through nations. But world affairs will have a very dim future if this universal sentiment fails to show a steady increase from now."[45] Along the same lines, Ervin Laszlo's Club of Rome major study on the goals of mankind gives a central place to "a solidarity revolution," as the basis for hope about the future.[46]

The translation of this latent possibility into politically effective form is, of course, an enormous challenge. At the same time, however, ideas about leverage in the transition process are beginning to take shape. The rise of ethnic nationalism, which poses serious challenges to the authority and legitimacy of sovereign states is an example of militant politics with a global reform potential as yet untested. In addition, more systematic and longer range economic planning at the global level is beginning to occur, spurred on by fears of a slide into economic warfare and by the various vulnerabilities associated with the interdependence problematique. The functional issues of control and management, whether they are in relation to nuclear capabilities, energy supplies, ocean resources, or environmental protection are also building an awareness that "central guidance" of some structured kind is the only alternative to chaos, as is the realization that functional bargains (e.g., law of the oceans; trade and monetary reform) cannot be reached or sustained unless they have an equity dimension built into them.

Technological innovations have made us all more aware of developments elsewhere. This awareness includes, at present, concern about the spread of authoritarian politics and repressive methods. Emphasis on human rights is a multifaceted response to this concern. Among other motives and effects is its contribution to the formation of a global constituency, persons who complement their national citizenship with an identity as planetary citizen. Such an expansion of identity and loyalty patterns is critical for transition to a humane system of world order. In fact, acquisition of a planetary outlook and its embodiment in thought, feeling, and action is what system-transforming types of world order is about at this stage of international history. Multiple identity patterns are quite consistent with this imperative. Thus, one can add a planetary identity to national, ethnic, religious, local, and family identity; each can be vivid and intense. More and more nongovernmental transnational actors (Amnesty International, International Commission of Jurists, and International League of Human Rights) are becoming primary actors in this human rights sphere, manifesting their primary allegiance to world order values with no territorial constraints.

These factors establish a context where, at long last, a system-transforming movement and an ideology become a realistic possibility. Such a possibility has never existed earlier, almost inevitably making earlier system-transforming visions into utopography. And the occasional claim that the utopia could be realized by good faith argumentation only made such positions seem ridiculous, depriving them of even their role as enchantments for the imagination. In recent years, however, I believe this new possibility offers system-transforming approaches a rich opportunity to take steps to found a movement, formulate an ideology, and build bridges between thought and action in the realm of global reform.

Enriching the Inquiry

The drift of scholarly inquiry has been in accord with the wider pattern of the division of labor. As a consequence, technical mastery and specialization have become increasingly valued. In intellectual terms, thought analysis has grown sharper, with the focus being placed on ever smaller segments of reality, but at the cost of its progressive detachment from a sense of the whole. A unified feature of all types of world order thinking is to work against this tendency and to seek a holistic understanding of the world political system. Such an understanding is not yet assisted very much by modern social science. Oddly enough, it is from engineering approaches to complex decision-making and the modeling of whole systems that ways are being found to reconcile the scientific temper of the times with the widely acknowledged importance of comprehending planetary politics as a whole, or to study some national or regional segment to discern how the national or regional part fits into the whole; it would also be helpful to specify the impact which the whole has on the part.

In addition, some efforts are being made in system-transforming approaches to world order to examine the role of culture in generating a range of alternative political futures. Many students of world order look more to the humanities and to religious thought than to the social sciences for intellectual help. Macro-history, the story of the rise and fall of religious movements, cultural criticism, along with works of the literary imagination are valued resources of the world order scholar. In this regard, novels such as Ursula LeGuin's *The Dispossessed* or Doris Lessing's *Briefing for a Descent into Hell* and *Memoir of a Survivor* are world order "texts" in the quite literal sense of being used in courses. Such works appear to transmit a better overall interpretation of what is happening to erode earlier systems of order and what kinds of future alternatives there are than is derived by studying facts, trends, and proposals of a more traditional reforming intellectual variety. In effect, world order studies needs the synthetic discipline of the novelist more than the analytic discipline of the social scientist.

To overcome the dualisms of the rational/scientific tradition, so dominant in the West, it is necessary to create a more unified sense of the inner/outer sensibilities that are sometimes differentiated in Freudian terms. This calls for the separation of the conscious intellect of the superego from the subconscious and unconscious realms of ego and id. Whatever the metaphor, the point remains that behavior cannot be understood in any purely rational reductionist interpretation that limits its observations to external planes of existence. Marxist and liberal interpretations of human endeavor, with their exclusive reference to external relationships, are jointly flawed by their attempt to explain the failure of societal arrangements. Marxists base their explanation of failure on a primary reference to exploitative relations arising out of the productive process that converts any social order into classes of rulers and victims,[47] liberals mount their explanations by reference to the insufficiency of productive output, and scarcity that can be overcome, in time, by technological innovation. Marxists await revolution as the dynamic in which victims seize the means of production so as to reorganize society along non-exploitative lines. Liberals, on the other hand, seek only to institutionalize moderation in the state so that abundance can serve as the dynamic providing everyone with sufficiency needed for life, liberty, and happiness. Both outlooks are overly optimistic, secular, materialistic, and rationalistic, awaiting societal fulfillment in historical time without inner transformation or divine intervention. Both underestimate the religious or spiritual dimension of human personality.

The effort to sustain these hopeful, but automatic outlooks on societal liberation in the face of all the evidence, exerts an immense strain on the polity, draining it of authentic confidence and making hope depend on banal bravado.[48] The more authentic documents of interpretation flowing out of these traditions, especially in the North, are filled with foreboding and despair, not necessarily because the apocalypse is around the next corner, but because various forms of Stalinism have discredited socialist claims, while a variety of ecological constraints have drawn into question liberal expectations based on a modernizing world.[49]

The impact which these realizations have on world order studies is to underscore the need for a *deeper* and *wider* conception of knowledge than is customary according to rationalist canons of higher education. Spiritual traditions and insights become relevant, especially as they shape cultural potentialities that draw on neglected aspects of national and civilizational heritage and posit a sound basis for forms of cultural renewal supportive of economic and political reforms that correspond to ethical and functional imperatives of organizing life humanely on a crowded planet running out of some critical resources.[50] The evolutionary studies of biological time also suggest, in a contrasting way, adaptive possibilities—mutations—but on a time scale that exceeds the horizons of secular action-oriented sensibilities. It is these subject-matter areas, rather than the world order heartland of politics and economics, that provide for hope given the currently dismal course of secular trends and prospects.

Some indication of what an enriched inquiry would encompass is suggested by Table 1. This table is designed to identify some boundaries and to suggest the kind of coverage needed. What is left out of such an image is the integrating sensibility that gives coherence to insights drawn from a variety of sources. Without such an integrative effort, the extended inquiry will not lead anywhere. Whether anyone has the capacity to carry out such an ambitious program of study is also to be considered. Perhaps it will require decades of "preparation" until a genius of integration can unfold a generally acceptable conception of world order studies. It took centuries to produce St. Thomas Aquinas, who gave satisfying coherence to the doctrine and teaching of the Catholic Church.

World order studies of the most traditional variety have confined their inquiry to level III, with some superficial attention to levels II and IV. A sophisticated integration of II, III, and IV would be an important contribution to the orientation of world order values around the related postulates of either system-reform or system-transformation. What I have argued in this section is

TABLE 1
Scope of World Order Inquiry

LEVEL	PERSPECTIVE	UNIT OF ANALYSIS	EXPLANATORY FOCUS
I	Religion Culture	Civilization	Beliefs, Symbols Myths, Values Consciousness
II	History	Nation-state Region World	Events Patterns, "laws" Narrative line
III	Politics	Polity-State State System	Power, Authority Influence Legitimacy Leadership
IV	Economics	Society Market Class	Wealth, trade Ownership Productive Process Capital Accumulation Process
V	Psychology	Person Group Species	"inner man" motivation behavioral patterns
VI	Biology	Species	Evolutionary patterns
VII	Anthropology	Tribe Species	Alternative societal forms
VIII	Ecology	Ecosystem biosphere	Nature, ecological principles
IX	Astrophysics	Stars, planets, Solar system Galaxies Universe	Physical laws and relations

the need to bring level I and VII into play in an explicit way[51] so as to develop a richer sense of tradition and to grasp the potentialities for various kinds of development. To get beneath the rationalist/bureaucratic superstructure it is, of course, necessary to consider levels V and VII. Longer run potentialities for change can be understood by reference to levels VI, VIII, and IX, as well as to constraining elements on what is possible. Looking into the distant past creates a context for a more searching, less time-bound inquiry into the future because it liberates, even as it conditions, the imagination.

State, War, and Revolution

System-maintaining and system-reforming approaches have, for the most part, taken the state for granted as the principal structural ingredient of international political life. System-transforming approaches have tended to build their image of a future world on the basis of a substantially weakened state entity. What does seem evident is the evolving character of the state and its uneven relationship, as measured in time and space, to the realization of world order values. A more sophisticated and differentiated conception of the state as actor is required for all varieties of world order studies, especially to clarify the position of system-transformers.

This need for clarification is reinforced by the inadequacy associated with the main ideological perspectives on the modern state. Both liberal and Marxist theory underestimated the autonomous role of the state as an actor with its own set of interests distinct from those of the general population or its division by class, ethnic identity, region, or religion. Bureaucratism is a modern phenomenon that alters both role and expectations regarding the state. Furthermore, notions of the minimal or weak state, as well as those of the neutral state, seem to underestimate, in decisive respects, the social services and economic interventionary role that a modern citizenry expects from the leadership of a modern state. Circumstances of expanding population accentuate this tendency to assign more and more functions to the state, which in turn generates expanding fiscal requirements. These functions include a need to sustain economic growth and aspire to full employment without fostering inflation, a need that encourages ever-expanding regulatory undertakings. These tendencies toward bureaucratic expansion are further heightened by the complex, hazardous, and vulnerable character of modern technology in which the state simultaneously becomes entrepreneur (supplying capital), promoter, and custodian. These roles are difficult to reconcile, as is evident in the relation to the balance between promotional and protective governmental roles in the context of nuclear technology; this balance is further complicated by countervailing pressure groups of unequal capabilities, such as those of the nuclear industry versus those generated by the general public. Pressures on the state arising from the spread of terrorism also encourage an expansion of bureaucratic claims to interfere with a wide range of activities previously regarded as falling within a protected private sphere.

In the international context the role of the state has often been conceived in simplistic terms as the *bête noire* of world order. Such a view concludes that the only obstacle to a just and peaceful world is the demonic preoccupation of states with their military prowess. The state also functions to achieve autonomy for territorial units, and a strong state mechanism, especially in Latin America, Africa, and Asia whose countries have endured various degrees of hegemony for centuries, seems closely associated with the successful prosecution of the struggle against imperialism, assuring a given society the fruits of political independence after its liberation has been formally achieved. The postcolonial state therefore, has emerged in the southern hemisphere both as guardian of independence and as an agency of drastic repression in a growing variety of situations where a governing coalition in a particular country is unable or unwilling to satisfy the expectations of important components of the society. The outlook of the state is shaped by the perceived domestic interests and affinities of its governing coalition, although the international rhetoric of Third World solidarity may coexist with a set of official policies designed to perpetuate the social, economic, and cultural norms associated with colonial or even pre-colonial patterns of relations.

What is required for world order studies is a definite appreciation of these various facets of statism and an appraisal of their normative consequences. On the basis of such an appraisal, it will then be possible to formulate some valid generalizations about the state system, including its links with all forms of violence and warfare in human experience. There is no doubt that status, wealth, and power seem closely correlated with military prowess, and that this correlation pervades the virtual entirety of international relations. It is also apparent that technological innovation applied to war is quickly spreading the capacity to inflict mass destruction all around the planet, that the waste of talent and resources on military activities is on the rise, and that the strategic arms race between the superpowers continues above and beyond thresholds of stability and restraint in the direction of "first strike" postures.

Does the state, as a political institution, lead to this kind of militarized approach to security as a matter of necessity, or is it possible to envision a set of conditions that would induce a counter-dynamic of demilitarization? Is the state an entity that is conditioned by the reality of other states competing for ill-defined shares of the fixed stock of planetary patrimony, and therefore dependent on a "structure of peace" which rests on abiding, mutual exchanges of mortal, genocidal threats, all wrapped in the antiseptic doctrinal language of "deterrence"? These kinds of questions go to the essence of state power, and foreshadow the extent to which the ruling coalitions of states themselves can play a positive role in promoting world order values in consistent fashion. In other words, the fundamental issues posed by the inadequacies of the state system to cope with the intertwined trends associated with violence, crowding, scarcities, misery, and environmental decay can be stated succinctly: Is global revolution necessary? If necessary, is it possible? If possible, then what form will it take and over what time period? What are the connections between revolutionary politics on the national and the global level?

World order approaches need to confront their relationship to revolutionary tactics, strategies, and thinking. The revolution we consider here, of course, has to do with reconstituting the basis of governance, and with creating a context for humane governance throughout the planet. Such a revolutionary goal may involve drastic changes in cultural outlook, prevailing values, and it may require prolonged struggle, sacrifice, and anguish. Certainly, the character of revolution contemplated here is not centered on the seizure of state power by means of armed struggle, although it may include this meaning in particular national circumstances (e.g., South Africa, Iran, the Philippines, and the Soviet Union). The underlying challenge is to transform the exercise of state power in such a way that it will initiate a wider process of transformation that enhances the quality of life throughout the world. It is essential, and seems appropriate, therefore, for system-transforming world order approaches to explore the various facets of this revolutionary possibility.

Planetary Citizenship

Changing patterns of individual and group loyalty and identity play a critical role in periods of political transition. System-transforming approaches to world order emphasize the importance of treating the planet as a whole, which in turn implies recognizing the wholeness of the human race. Such recognition goes against the tradition of partial loyalty (to self, family, tribe, class, nation, region, race, religion, language group) that has dominated political life on the planet heretofore. Increasingly, in the present period, exemplary individuals and associated spiritual groups, while affirming their separate identity, are proclaiming a commitment to an emergent conception and reality of planetary citizenship. Feeling, thinking, and acting from a planetary perspective is what world order politics is increasingly about. The substance of such a perspective centers on the task of establishing humane patterns of goverance at all levels of social interaction, from the self to the world.

Initially, at least, one can expect the energy for such a shift in political consciousness to take hold among individuals and non-governmental organizations, especially those with religious and humanitarian missions. The balance of power and wealth will remain heavily concentrated in governments, corporations, and banks that retain a vested interest in primary loyalty to the part rather than to the whole, whether the part be defined in terms of state, class, or region. A multinational corporation or a world bank may have a planetary outlook in a territorial sense, but its operating logic is based on maximizing profits for its shareholders rather than benefits for the global community. As such, its planetary identification is deficient, and should not be confused with that of a citizen or group dedicated to the well-being of the whole.

The genuine planetary citizen will tend not to look to official institutions or dominant economic actors, at least not at first, for support. If the global situation further decays, then public opinion may achieve access to power for those who are by temperament and commitment dedicated to the realization of political community on a global scale. We have no reason to expect such a development in the near future, unless a major catastrophe generates mass support for the case for drastic global reform. Short of this, populist critiques of official institutions and oppositional politics rather than reorientations of governing style will be the main political activity of planetary citizens.

NOTES

For sensitive comments helpful in revision, I want to thank both Mark Blasius and R.B.J. Walker.

1. This broad terrain of intellectual endeavor is usefully surveyed in Juergen Dedring, *Recent Advances in Peace and Conflict Research*, Beverly Hills, Calif., Sage Library of Social Research, Vol. 27, 1976; also helpful is L. Gunnar Johnson, "Conflicting Concepts of Peace in Contemporary Peace Studies," Sage Professional Papers, International Studies Series, Vol. 4, 02-046, 1976.

2. See, e.g., Tom Farer, "The Greening of the Globe: A Preliminary Appraisal of the World Order Models Project," *International Organization*, Vol. 31 (1977) pp. 129–147.

3. For a presentation of this range of plausible alternative systems of world order see Falk, *A Study of Future Worlds*, New York, Free Press, 1975, esp. pp. 174–220.

4. William Irwin Thompson, *Evil and World Order*, New York, Harper and Row, 1976.

5. In effect, either the flaws of human character are integral to the potentialities for politics, or these flaws can in time be removed so as to establish far brighter potentialities for political behavior than now seems plausible.

6. For one major attempt to project an alternative future based upon cultural factors see Ali A. Mazrui, *A World Federation of Cultures*, New York, Free Press, 1976; see also important earlier work by F.S.C. Northrop, *The Meeting of East and West*, New York, Macmillan, 1946.

7. "Address by President Carter to People of Other Nations," Dept. State Bull., Vol. LXXVI, Feb. 14, 1977, p. 123.

8. For a mainstream discussion of these possibilities, alive to the contradictory pulls of domestic and international forces, see Stanley Hoffmann, "No Choices, No Illusions," *Foreign Policy*, Winter 1976–77, 25:97–140.

9. Saul Mendlovitz in his role as General Director of the World Order Models Project and President of the Institute for World Order has been seeking to initiate such a movement in recent years.

10. Stanley Hoffmann, "Report of the Conference on Conditions of World Order — June 12–19, 1965, Villa Serbelloni, Bellagio, Italy," *Daedalus*, Spring 1966, pp. 455–478, at 456.

11. *Ibid.*

12. Hedley Bull, *The Anarchical Society: A Study of Order in World Politics*, New York, Columbia, 1977, p. 20.

13. *Ibid.*, pp. 53–4.

14. *Ibid.*, p. 65.

15. *Ibid.*, pp. 96–7.

16. *Ibid.*, pp. 233–256.

17. View attributed to Aron in Hoffmann, note 10, at p. 456.

18. Bull, note 12, pp. 319–320.

19. *Ibid.*, p. 320.

20. J. Martin Rochester, "International Institutions and World Order: The International System as a Prismatic Polity," *Sage Professional Papers, International Relations Series*, Vol. 3, 02-025, 1974, p. 5.

21. William Coplin and Rochester, "The PCIJ, ICJ, League and UN: A Comparative Empirical Survey," *Amer. Pol. Sci. Rev.*, Vol. 62, pp. 529–550.

22. Robert O. Keohane and Joseph Nye, *Power and Interdependence: World Politics in Transition*, Boston, Little-Brown, 1977. See also Miriam Camps, "The Management of Interdependence: A Preliminary View," New York, Council on Foreign Relations, 1974; Richard Rosecrance and others, "Whither Interdependence?" *International Organization*, Vol. 31, Summer 1977, pp. 425–472.

23. Mendlovitz and Weiss, "The Study of Peace and Justice: Toward a Framework for Global Discussion," in Louis René Beres and Harry Targ, ed., *Planning Alternative Futures*, New York, Praeger, 1975, pp. 148–174, at 157.

24. *Ibid.*, p. 158.

25. Gerald and Patricia Mische, *Toward A Human World Order*, New York, Paulist Press, 1977, p. 64.

26. See, e.g., Raymond Aron, *Peace and War: A Theory of International Relations*, New York, Doubleday, 1966; Henry Kissinger, *American Foreign Policy*, New York, Norton, expanded ed., 1974; Hans J. Morgenthau, *Politics Among Nations*, New York, Knopf, 5th ed., 1973.

27. For inquiry along these lines see Falk, note 3.

28. For useful survey and evaluation see Sam Cole, "Global Models and the International Economic Order," Elmsford, N.Y., Pergamon Press, 1977.

29. A. Herrera and others, *Catastrophe or New Society?* IDRC, Ottawa, Conn., 1976; see also G. Chichilnisky's article in this symposium, pp. 275–304.

30. For a discussion of "dangerous knowledge" along these lines see Falk, "A New Paradigm for International Legal Studies: Prospects and Proposals," *Yale Law Journal*, Vol. 84, pp. 969–1021, at 1009–1012.

31. For description of Trilateral Commission see pamphlet entitled "The Trilateral Commission" issued at its inception and seasonal accounts of activities in newsletter issued quarterly under title Trialogue. See also *Trilateral Commission Task Force Reports 1-7*, New York, New York University, 1977.

32. For a full account of impact on Carter presidency see Craig S. Karpel. "Cartergate: The Death of Democracy," *Penthouse*, Nov. 1977, pp. 69–74, 90, 104–6, 130.

33. For Brzezinski's views on these issues see "Recognizing the Crisis," *Foreign Policy* 17:63–74, Winter 1974–75.

34. Bell, "The Future of World Disorder," *Foreign Policy* 27:109–136, Summer 1977, at p. 134.

35. E.g., Tom J. Farer, "The United States and the Third World: A Basis for Accommodation," *Foreign Affairs*, Vol. 54, Oct. 1975, pp. 79–95.

36. See Zbigniew Brzezinski, "U.S. Foreign Policy: The Search for Focus," *Foreign Affairs*, Vol. 57, July 1973, pp. 708–727, see also gentle critique by Richard H. Ullman, "Trilateralism: 'Partnership' for What?" *Foreign Affairs*, Vol. 55, Oct. 1976, pp. 1–19.

37. Michael Crozier, Samuel P. Huntington, and Joji Watanuki, *The Crisis of Democracy: Report on the Governability of Democracies to the Trilateral Commission*, New York, New York University Press, 1975.

38. *Ibid.*, at pp. 6–7.

39. For representative statement by Ullman see "Forward: The 1980's Project" in F. Hirsch and M. Doyle and Edward L. Morse, *Alternatives to Monetary Disorder*, New York, McGraw-Hill, 1977, at p. xi.

40. *Ibid.*, p. x.

41. *Ibid.*, p. ix.

42. For background and rationale of WOMP see Saul Mendlovitz and Tom Weiss

"Toward Consensus: The World Order Models Project of the Institute for World Order," in *Introduction to World Peace Through Law*, Chicago, World Without War Publications, 1973, pp. 74–97; see also Mendlovitz's Introduction to Mendlovitz, ed., *On the Creation of a Just World Order*, New York, Free Press, 1975, pp. vii–xvii; on the specification of the values see Falk, note 3, pp. 11–39. See also Fouad Ajami, " 'World Order': The Question of Ideology" (mimeographed WOMP II paper, 1977).

43. So far published: Mendlovitz, note 42; Mazrui, note 6; Falk, note 3; Rajni Kothari, *Footsteps into the Future: Diagnosis of the Present World and a Design for an Alternative*, New York, Free Press, 1974.

44. For different methodological and normative treatments of this theme see Wassily Leontief et al., *The Future of the World Economy*, New York, Oxford University Press, 1977; Jan Tinbergen, coordinator, *Reshaping the International Order*, New York, E. P. Dutton, 1976; Roger Hansen, "Major U.S. Options on North-South Relations: A Letter to President Carter," in James Sewell and staff, *The United States and World Development: Agenda 1977*, Overseas Development Council, New York, Praeger, 1977; see also Herrera and Chichilnisky references in note 29.

45. William P. Bundy, "On Power: Elements of Power," *Foreign Affairs*, Vol. 56, Oct. 1977, pp. 1–26, at 26.

46. See Ervin Laszlo et al., *Goals for Mankind: A Report to the Club of Rome on the New Horizons of Global Community*, New York, E. P. Dutton, 1977, esp. pp. 415–424; on p. 415: "The achievement of world solidarity is the great imperative of our era."

47. For a stimulating account of pre-industrial exploitative relations and their link to present societal distortions see Stanley Diamond, *In Search of the Primitive*, New Brunswick, N.J., Transaction Books, 1974, esp. pp. 1–48.

48. E.g. Herman Kahn and others, *The Next 200 Years: A Scenario for America and the World*, New York, Morrow, 1976.

49. E.g. Robert Heilbroner, *The Human Prospect*, New York, Norton, 1974; Donella Meadows et al., *The Limits to Growth, A Report for the Club of Rome's Project on the Predicament of Mankind*, New York, Universe, 1972; Barry Commoner, *The Closing Circle*, New York, Knopf, 1971; Edward Goldsmith and others, *A Blueprint for Survival*, Boston, Houghton Mifflin, 1972; Richard Falk, *This Endangered Planet: Prospects and Proposals for Human Survival*, New York, Random House, 1972.

On the more specific theme of the value consequences of various developmental paths see Peter Berger, *Pyramids of Sacrifice: Political Ethics and Social Change*, New York, Basic Books, 1974; Barrington Moore, Jr., *Reflections on the Causes of Human Misery*, Boston, Beacon, 1972; Victor Ferkiss, *The Future of Technological Civilization*, New York, Braziller, 1974; Falk, "Militarization and Human Rights in the Third World," *Bull. Peace Proposals* 3:220–232 (1977).

50. See Theodore Roszak, *Unfinished Animal: The Aquarian Frontier and the Evolution of Consciousness*, New York, Harper and Row, 1975; also Falk, "Political Prospects, Cultural Choices, Anthropological Horizons," *The Journal of the New Alchemists*, Vol. 4, pp. 138–148 (1977).

51. For examples of authors who approach global issues with these perspectives see William Irwin Thompson, note 4, *At the Edge of History*, New York, Harpers (1971); *Passage About Earth*, New York, Harpers (1974); see also Diamond, note 47, Northrop, note 6.

13
COULD WE STUDY
INTERNATIONAL RELATIONS
AS IF PEOPLE MATTERED?

Roy Preiswerk

When we study international relations we are often quite remote from social reality. This sounds provocative, but it is necessary regularly to re-examine the nature and purpose of our work in a rapidly changing world.

There are enough studies to demonstrate how many things have gone wrong with the development of mankind. Some say we are on a dangerous path. I would go one step farther and submit that mankind's development has taken a pathological direction. Perhaps just one example would suffice to illustrate the point. According to the 1976 Yearbook of the Stockholm International Peace Research Institute, the nuclear equipment of the world now amounts to 50,000 megatons, which is about 15 tons for each one of us and 60 tons for each inhabitant of a NATO or Warsaw Pact country. Between 1945 and 1975, the world has spent 7,000 billion dollars on military expenditure. No other species in nature, no species of the category of animals which the French call *bêtes* (synonymous with stupid) has ever invested such a proportion of its resources in means of mutual destruction while so many of the same species are dying of hunger every minute. During the same period only 200 billion dollars, or 3 percent of the above amount, were spent on development aid.

We will not present an inventory of all aspects of mankind's madness. What we must ask ourselves is whether anything can be done to make the social sciences in general and the study of international relations in particular less irrelevant to the solution of the most acute contemporary social problems.

I. SOCIAL SCIENCE IN GENERAL: FOUR REMINDERS

We now come to a brief series of generalizations which may sound unfair to those social scientists who occasionally reflect on professional ethics and who sincerely try to tackle fundamentals. What follows is valid if, as I think is the case, it is applicable to at least 51 percent of social science research.

First published by Graduate Institute of International Studies, *International Relations in a Changing World*, Geneva, 1977. Reprinted by permission of the author.

1. Social Science Is Dehumanized

The dehumanization of social sciences is parallel to the dehumanization of social life, particularly in the industrial societies. K. William Kapp epitomizes this in one sentence: "Neither in science nor in society are the concrete human beings and their interests at the centre of interest."[1] Let us make it clear that we are not speaking of the concern with the individual in the sense that this term has assumed in Western individualistic societies. The concern is with people, with the human being as a social being.

Social science in general takes little interest in the lives of human beings when it deals with institutions, processes, or events as if people were molecules which do not matter as such, but are noticed to the extent that they function as members of institutions, heroes or victims of processes and participants in events. The average social scientist treats people as objects, as sources of information, and he uses more and more technological hardware to achieve highly specialized and often esoteric results. Actually this kind of professional ethics (the more specialization the better) runs parallel to the interest of the ruling power (the more specialization, the weirder the language becomes for the layman, consequently no one can use the specialists' findings to question the established system). Thus, the consumers of social science are not people, but other social scientists (who admittedly are also people, but in very small numbers), governments or corporations. The question remains open for the moment, what these other social scientists or institutions do with the knowledge obtained.

We submit that many social scientists become alienated from their own societies, or from the societies they study, largely because of dominant thinking about what are supposed to be serious academic standards and research methods.

This may be a good occasion to point out that Western scientists could here and now learn something from other civilizations. Joseph Needham, a biochemist and embryologist, who came into close contact with engineering and medicine, says: "Of one thing I feel certain, namely that China will not produce those types of utterly inhuman scientists and engineers who know little, and care less, about the needs and desires of the average man and woman".[2]

2. Fragmented Social Sciences Can Be Useless or Counterproductive

The dehumanization of the social sciences is partly the result of their fragmentation. Fragmentation prevents an understanding of what man is all about. To narrow the sphere of observation is considered a sign of seriousness in academic circles. Specialization is necessary, but leads to abuses if there is no awareness of the ideological and ethical presuppositions of knowledge.[3] In a different form, Alfred Sauvy highlights this when he says: "Science has indeed succeeded in making men live longer and worse."[4]

Fragmented social sciences can be useless, because they only provide information on minute issues, because other researchers often cannot build on the findings of their colleagues and because the degree of comparability across classes, nations, and cultures is low. It is simply absurd to invent a *homo oeconomicus*, a *homo psychologicus*, or a *homo sociologicus* and then refuse to relate these analytical abstractions to the totality of the real human beings.

Quite a few social scientists find themselves at peace with their conscience when they say things such as: "The arms race is none of my business, I'm dealing with human rights." Or: "I'm specializing in balance-of-payments problems, I can't find the time to look into income inequalities." Or worse still: "It's for the economists to solve the problem of hunger, I'm looking at political systems in the Third World." Tom Lehrer, former Harvard professor in mathematics, who became a rather cynical songwriter, once imagined an interview with Wernher von Braun, in the course of which he speculated about the moral implications of building rockets which were generously sprinkled over the British population during World War II. The answer was this: "Once the rockets are up, who cares where they come down—that's not my department, says Wernher von Braun."

Fragmented social sciences can be counter-productive because they make us lose sight of mankind's development, they blur the pathological direction of that development and prevent an understanding of real forces at work. They also make it easier for technocrats and autocrats to manipulate society with knowledge which has the blessing of so-called scientists.

Fragmentation, incidentally, is not only a problem within the social sciences. It is becoming increasingly difficult to separate the social and the natural sciences. Some of the most disturbing questions today are: What are the social and psychological consequences of the continuing exploitation of nature? What type of energy production corresponds to a social structure we desire? What kind of socio-psychological problems arise from the means of self-destruction that the physicists are providing us with? How far will the chemical manipulation of peoples' minds go? The significance of these questions is dawning upon an increasing number of natural scientists, ecologists and physicists in particular.

3. If Presumed To Be Separate from Ethics and Ideology, Social Science Can Be Irrelevant or Dangerous

Science, at this stage of our development, probably creates as many problems as it solves. In fact, many "scientists" spend their time denying that our present development *is* pathological. Others specialize in setting up some kind of coherent interpretation which makes this very pathology look acceptable.

Science can be useful, but it is not sufficient. If scientists say that X thousands of people die of hunger every day, or that nuclear weapons can exterminate mankind X times, is that enough? Such information is useful and necessary, but if nobody has the courage to draw a conclusion other than that "mankind" is synonymous with "madness," then we might as well dispense with scientists. More people must come forward, even if they are—in a derogatory sense—termed "ideologues," to say that hunger is scandalous (therefore we must redistribute wealth) and that preparing an "overkill" is simply idiotic (therefore we must stop the race towards mutual annihilation). The "ideologues" are thus a disturbing factor: they express anxiety which others want to ignore, they ask for change which implies an effort and a commitment that others are reluctant to accept.

In fact, it is false to oppose science to ideology. There is no science without ideology. Whoever refuses to admit this elementary truth is either naive or completely unaware of his implicit ideological position. In some cases, however, he is a shrewd calculator who manages to hide his ideology behind some esoteric vocabulary or mathematical formula. Science is in the midst of politics. In many societies, those who agree with the established power and values stand a good chance of being considered as scientists, while those who disagree and demand social change are easily discredited by the label of "ideologues."[5]

The present dilemma does not arise from the fact that we have insufficient knowledge about social problems. It stems from the fact that self-styled "neutral" scientists do not know who will do what with their findings. To discover something and let public or private power structures use that knowledge in unethical ways is a totally irresponsible attitude on behalf of scientists.

One contribution we can all make immediately is to claim less often that what we are asserting has "scientific" value. Today, we are in a phase of the development of the sciences which is largely determined by positivistic standards. This is a school of thought which is particularly limited in finding instruments to deal with human problems.

The value-neutrality of science is a stubborn myth. Let us take one example. It is being stated over and over again that the functioning of the market system is a process which is linked with no particular ideology. This statement is false in four respects: ideologically, culturally, ecologically, and ethically. The market is a place where the purchasing power of those who have money, rather than the essential needs of *all* people, determines the distribution of goods. The products available on the market are an expression of the income inequalities within the population. The satisfaction of demand is not the same thing as the satisfaction of needs. In almost every Third World country, you can buy egg shampoo to wash your hair with, while a large proportion of the population cannot afford to buy eggs to eat. In poor societies, the market system guarantees access of the privileged few to luxury goods. In rich societies, the market system can be seen as a way to fight simultaneously capitalist monopolies and excessive State interference in private spheres. All of this has something to do with *ideology*, with choices made by human beings concerning who gets what, when, how, where and why. There is no law of nature saying that there must be a market. The distribution of goods can be organized in various ways.

Western economists and anthropologists have noticed that there are societies without a market system. This has usually been considered, in the ethnocentric tradition, as a sign of backwardness. But the introduction of trade based on a monetary economy has led to much confusion, to the dislocation of entire societies, to the destruction of distributive systems which made it possible, in many parts of the world, to assure the survival of every member of a group. The market system is the product of a specific type of *culture*. Once again, it is not a law of nature.

The market system puts a price on everything, but the very low-priced factor of production is nature; probably because it cannot scream, publish pamphlets, or organize a trade union. The fact that the resources of nature, particularly the sun, air and water, to some extent have no price at all, has led to the most disastrous abuses with which economic theory has acquainted us under the powerful umbrella of "science." The market system, in reality, is not value-free in terms of *ecology* either.[6]

There is a dreadful concept in economics which is called the "labour market." In fact, we are talking here about the price of human beings, although not exactly in the same terms as the slave traders were able to do. The labour market is an inhuman concept, because it means pricing the value of people according to their (more or less accidentally acquired) qualifications and to the circumstances prevailing at a particular time and place. It is also an irrational concept when one thinks that the demand on this particular "market" must always be met, just to satisfy the needs of production, whether it be for food or for arms. The market concept, consequently, is not neutral in *ethical* terms either.

This is just one example, among many thousands we could find in the so-called social "sciences," of intellectual constructs based on either naivety or dishonesty. Let us, then, proceed to think what social science, and the study of international relations in particular, could be if we stopped talking about what may seriously be regarded as scientific and instead started to think realistically about the world we are living in.

Realism is a big word, particularly when it makes claims to "scientific" evidence. It is used widely to discredit those who find something wrong with the present international system. The kind of realism we are propagating today may result in widespread famine, growing inequalities, and World War III (which, incidentally, will destroy the supermonsters and leave a number of peripheral and "primitive" peoples quite undisturbed, nuclear fall-out notwithstanding). If we accept the arms race, poverty, racism, and other charming attributes of the present system, we are being "realistic." There is something weird about a human mind capable of producing the contemptuous assertion that those who denounce these phenomena are idealists, ideologues, or dreamers. The term "realism" should be given a new meaning: not to conform with what is happening, but to be able to see what our present options mean, what could result from them, and what changes we have to envisage, drastic as they may be.

The antinomy of science versus ideology and ethics is beautifully abolished by the physicist Victor Weisskopf, when he says: "Human existence depends upon compassion, and curiosity leading to knowledge, but *curiosity-and-knowledge without compassion is inhuman*, and compassion without curiosity-and-knowledge is ineffectual."[7]

4. Social Science Often Creates Obstacles to Knowledge

It may sound absurd that the official knowledge-producers in society may actually turn out to be the knowledge-hiders. But the problem is a real one. Let us take two examples. In *development economics*, we have accumulated tons of learned writings over the past thirty years. Two approaches are dominant: a more theoretical one, which usually extrapolates from the experience of industrial societies to formulate proposals concerning growth, productivity, and other marvels. There is also a more pragmatic approach, defended by those who descend on some Third World village and use their "common sense," telling the natives what they have to do about irrigation, fertilizers, and other down-to-earth matters. Both approaches have led to visible or measurable signs of "success" (buildings, plantations, growth rates, etc.), but have failed in two ways: first, they cannot free themselves of the idea that their own society is superior to all others and their "science" the only possible source of any conceivable change. Today it is becoming clear that different civilizations move in different directions and that the social sciences offered by industrial societies have not discovered much to explain the diversity of developing processes. Second, the social sciences were unable to warn us that the development strategies adopted after 1945 would lead to a deterioration of living conditions in many parts of the world. The large majority of development economists obscured our vision for three decades, pretending that the world was "progressing." In 1977, we find more hunger, misery, and unemployment than thirty years ago. Those who were the first to say this publicly were rarely academics, and when they were, as in the case of Gunnar Myrdal or René Dumont, for example, they were frowned upon by most of their colleagues, unable to cope with so much unorthodoxy. But can we be taken seriously when we produce splendid studies on balance-of-payments adjustments, Special Drawing Rights, transfers of technology, capital accumulation and growth rates, only to realize at the end, that every day more human beings in the poor countries see their living conditions deteriorate while in rich countries profound feelings of alienation from our way of life are spreading rapidly?

Another example is that of *history*. Our libraries are stacked with "World History" books. A recent study of thirty school textbooks from eight different countries reveals enormous distortions in our knowledge of other civilizations.[8] Anyone who really takes the trouble to examine these distortions must agree with the statement that some ways of systematizing knowledge under the label of "objective science" constitute a veritable obstacle to knowledge. But the striking element in the situation is the exclusion of human beings. All these thousands of pages concentrate on invasions, catastrophes, royal weddings, "discoveries," and various other events, mostly sad ones. Except for a few heroes (Christopher Columbus or Winston Churchill), villains (Ghengiz Khan or Adolf Hitler), hero-villains (King Chaka, Cortez, or Pizarro) and distinguished aristocrats (all the kings of France, for instance, even the most feeble-minded), there is no reference to the fact that history ought to have something to do with people. We are quite often treated to the most gruesome details about ever more sophisticated techniques which heroic warriors have been using on every occasion to slice each other up. However, there is not a word about how the common man throughout these thousands of years went through his daily life, struggled for the survival of his family, or suffered within his natural and social environments.[9]

These are brief illustrations, but there is enough evidence that similar distortions of knowledge through science are widespread.[10]

II. INTERNATIONAL RELATIONS IN PARTICULAR: FOUR EXAMPLES

Our purpose is to reach constructive proposals as quickly as possible. Therefore this section will be extremely brief and go no further than pointing out a few of the difficulties we face when studying international relations.

1. The State-Centric Approach

"The objective of International Relations is to study relations among States." How many times have we been given this simplistic definition of the scope of our field of study? Of course, the definition represents a pragmatic and realistic view; after all, the State alone holds military and police power and is entitled to sovereignty. But this definition is unacceptable for two reasons: it limits the scope of investigation (States related to States) and presents almost as a law of nature what is merely a man-made system (problem pertaining to epistemology). It also covers up an elaborate network of power relationships which are often based on extreme inequalities and injustices (problem pertaining to ethics and ideology).

Contemporary international law consolidates a system based on the supremacy of the State. In recent years it was said that the state-system is being eroded by various forces. Some analysts see three such forces: international organizations, transnational corporations, and liberation movements. In our view none of these are eroding forces; on the contrary, international organizations are based on the state-system and contribute to its consolidation. It is extremely difficult to give power to an inter-state agency dealing directly with people without passing through governments. The only important exceptions are the European Communities and the European Commission on Human Rights.[11] Transnational corporations are, it is true, more powerful and richer than many States. The annual turnover of the largest corporations is greater than the Gross National Product of a majority of States in the Third World. In comparison to these states, the corporation can indeed be considered as an eroding factor. But at the same time, they are strengthening the power of their home base and are thus contributing to growing inequalities within a state based international system.[12] Finally, liberation movements may indeed question the legitimacy of a particular State, be it a colonial power or a State made up of different ethnic groups. But they only aim at the creation of new States which will become parties to the already established international system. If the Bretons, the Basques, the Occitans, the Alsatians, and the Corsicans all manage a revolution against France, one and indivisible as the Constitution says, setting up five more nation-states, and taking their seats at the United Nations, they will merely contribute to the consolidation of a state-based international system.

The state-based international system raises the crucial question of the way people are represented at the world level. We argue that dominant elites, not populations, are in fact represented. Behind the walls of sovereignty and non-interference in domestic affairs, ruling elites are protected and left quite free to practice domestic colonization, to advance the interests of a small minority and to resort to almost any method of repression. The New International Economic Order, adopted at the United Nations on 1 May 1974, and so vigorously defended by Third World diplomats, illustrates this eloquently. Only States can act, no State can be questioned about its domestic situation. And what the "representatives" of the Third World are asking for, is to obtain the means to consolidate *their* power: more money, more technology, in short, more of what we have seen in the past, despite obvious failures, when we look at the situation of the majority of the people. Critics of this approach in rich countries are now accused of a new paternalism towards Third World leaders. It is convenient for conservative elements in rich countries to say what the progressives were saying twenty years ago: do not interfere with the choices made by the newly independent countries. When, in 1975, the question was raised in Switzerland whether technical co-operation should be initiated between people rather than governments, one prominent businessman replied: "Poverty of the masses is a matter lying within the domestic jurisdiction of a country." The implication of this argument is that we are to be concerned with famine, malnutrition, disease, and other evils which, in various ways, affect at least half of the world's population only when *governments* allow us to do so. But how many of these governments have been looking seriously into such questions? 1977 is not 1947, when aid programmes were launched, or 1960, when many of us hoped that independence would lead to a better life for the populations of the former African colonies. If those who, today, are deeply concerned about the deteriorating situation must be labelled "paternalists," then let them be proud of it.

It is true that we now have a lot of those "soft states" that Gunnar Myrdal has been talking about when it comes to questions of administrative inefficiency in the field of economic development. But most of these same States are also becoming "tough states" through militarization and improvements in their capacity to suppress any forces contesting the rights of privileged minorities to continue to ignore the basic needs of the people. It is true then, for all of these reasons, that the State is here to stay for some time, but students of international relations should not merely acknowledge this fact: they should start trying to imagine an alternative system which eliminates the inhuman aspects of a state-based international system.

2. Fragmentation and Isolation

It is quite obvious, and needs no undue elaboration, that the study of international relations reproduces the fragmentation of the social sciences in general. It remains multidisciplinary, a juxtaposition of separate disciplines

jealously guarding their precarious identity. Sometimes it claims to be interdisciplinary, an objective which it usually fails to attain. It is never
transdisciplinary.

Isolation results from arbitrary decisions on what is included or excluded
from the study of international relations. There is no reason, advanced by
either God, Thucydides, or contemporary epistemologists for legal, economic,
or historical aspects of international relations to be given priority, while social
psychology or political anthropology are left out. Furthermore, there is no valid
argument why the natural sciences should not be part of the study of international relations. Why not call upon ecologists, nutritionists, or nuclear
physicists to teach international relations?

3. On Hiding Values

There is an enormous fraud in contemporary science which allows the
credibility of the "scientist" to increase at the same rate as he manages to hide
his value judgements, personal preferences, and political attitudes. The
technical term for this is positivism. The non-technical word for it is dishonesty. Somehow, although we "internationalists" are outside of the spectrum of
established academic disciplines, we have not overcome this problem, because
we do not realize that a good portion of positivistic epistemology leads us right
into intellectual dishonesty. Dishonesty in a very small way, perhaps. If we do
not announce our ideology, we are probably more acceptable in the society.
Also, we probably do not know to what extent our academic upbringing has
brainwashed us into the positivistic mould.

4. On Forgetting Basic Human Needs

In Freudian terms it is called scotomization, more simply it means disregarding what deeply disturbs us. It could be inequality, poverty, torture, unemployment or the arms race. What is really expected of us? That we describe in depth
the processes taking place in diplomatic gatherings and the deliberations of
some international court which has no power to change anything whatsoever
in the international power game? Or are we to think of the fact that what
human beings need is food, fresh air and water, habitat, and a few other essential things? If international relations is to remain a relevant discipline, these
problems will have to be given top priority. Otherwise we may soon be
associated with stamp collectors, mountain climbers, or numismatists as far as
our impact on society is concerned.

Two dangers of immense significance are involved in forgetting about basic
human needs. One is to indulge in retrospection while neglecting contemporary and future worlds. This is unacceptable from a merely cognitive point
of view. The other is that of sacrificing half of this generation, condemning
them to a state of underprivileged existence, and putting an enormous burden on future generations. The preoccupation with basic needs has a totality
to it: today's inequalities are linked with tomorrow's injustices: the exploitation of man by man runs parallel to the domination exerted by man over
nature.

III. ALTERNATIVE THINKING: EPISTEMOLOGY AND METHODOLOGY

If we have a grain of optimism left, we must agree with E. Boulding that "ways can be found to transform the whole international system into something less costly economically and less outrageous morally."[13]

Before indicating areas of research which should be given priority, some remarks on epistemology and methodology are necessary. This is very simple: the question has to be asked again *who* studies *what, why, how,* and *for whom?* In other words: who are the producers of knowledge (researcher, observer), what is the object of their research (observed reality), what are the motives, the ideology, the value system behind the research, which method is applied, and who is the consumer of knowledge, the public to which the producer addresses himself?

1. What Has Been Done?

More than a decade ago, a growing group of social scientists started to look for what T. Kuhn would call a new "paradigm."[14] Peace research, world society studies, world order studies, world future studies all have attempted to overcome the "statocracy" approach and widen the spectrum of inquiry. From the narrow perspective of interstate relations, they have moved to intergroup, intersocietal or intercultural relations, taking into consideration the role of units left outside of the classical study of international relations mainly because such units have no status as recognized actors under present international law.

The most important contribution of the new approaches is not to have widened the scope of levels and units of analysis. It lies in the qualitative transformation of the researchers' motivations. Let us take the example of hunger. It is no longer sufficient to be descriptive (how many people are dying every day), nor to be explanatory (what are the causes of hunger), or even predictive (how many people will die of hunger by the year 2000). What is required is an explicit ideology, which in this case means an extension into the normative domain (what kind of world do we want to live in) with prescriptive substance (how are we going to prevent increasing hunger).

At present, a very fundamental change is occurring in the new approaches to the study of contemporary and future world problems. So far, various groups have been trying to establish new schools of thought in the hope that they might be recognized as giving *the* answer to the inadequacy of classical international relations studies. Now we notice a movement towards the convergence of these approaches. A first example: peace research and world order studies converge when the following methodology is proposed: first, state values, second, analyse forecasts, third, devise a design, fourth, clear up contradictions and incompatibilities, fifth, propose transitional strategies.[15] Another example: peace research and development studies find a common objective when development ceases to be seen as a "problem" afflicting poor countries and becomes a process taking place in all countries with important connections being revealed between the poverty of the former and the affluence of the latter.[16] If a complete convergence between peace studies, development studies, and future studies can be achieved, we will have a formidable coalition to confront the classical study of international relations. We will then have teams of people working simultaneously for the elimination of war, poverty, social injustice, ecological imbalance, and mass alienation. In positive terms, they will produce ideas for the achievement of peace, economic well-being, social justice, ecological stability, and participation, in all parts of the world, both for present and future generations.[17]

2. What Should Happen

What the social sciences can do to contribute to the goals just stated depends on the willingness to recognize a few fundamental principles of an epistemological and methodological nature.

(a) The Acceptance of Utopian Thinking. / "A map of the world that does not include Utopia is not worth even glancing at . . .," says Lewis Mumford.[18] But Mumford also reminds us of an important differentiation which Sir Thomas More makes regarding the etymology of the word. Outopia is "no place," it is a vain dream of a land never to exist. Eutopia is "the good place." It arises out of a real environment and is part of an effort to reshape man's condition according to some ideal standards. It is about Eutopia that we are talking. This is not to be confused with an idealistic view of history. Even if infrastructures or productive forces are decisive in man's history, human thought and inventiveness going beyond existing structures also have something to do with the shaping of history. Those Marxists who have not forgotten about dialectics (there are a few who have) would agree with this.

Utopias, incidentally, are not simply mental constructs aimed at bringing about a better world. A lot of what is considered "realistic" thinking about mankind's present development, contained in many forecasts, is utopian. The most widespread utopia, using the word in the negative connotation which most "realists" tend to give to it, is that exponential economic growth must and *can* continue.

(b) The Integration of Knowledge. / As long as knowledge remains fragmented, as we have said before, it contributes to the dehumanization of society. Specialization in one particular discipline is necessary, but not sufficient. Many scientists have managed to break out of the narrow field of study which the university has defined for them. The demand for "generalists" is increasing in national governments, business enterprises, and international organizations. This is an indication that to be even a perfect specialist will be increasingly considered as valid in academic circles alone, while people and institutions of public interest will develop a different view.

The integration of knowledge has at least these four fundamental facets: transdisciplinary concepts (e.g., structure or culture used in all disciplines), structural isomorphisms (the same hypotheses tested in all disciplines), globalism (the interrelations of problems in different parts of the world made evident), and totality (the interrelations of problems attributed to different disciplines made explicit).

Two remarks are necessary about the integration of knowledge. The first is that all those, and they are a vast majority in the academic world, who adhere to the cult of specialization, get off too lightly when they call the generalists dilettantes. Modesty obviously has to be the prime quality of the generalist. K. William Kapp, an economist who has written one of the path-breaking works on the integration of knowledge, says: "Inasmuch as we proceed to elaborate the tentative conceptual frameworks of man and culture, we are dealing with concepts and findings of disciplines outside our narrow speciality. This was unavoidable and no one is more aware of the hazards of such an enterprise than the author."[19]

The second remark has to do with a more profound dilemma. Transdisciplinarity is more than interdisciplinarity; it has to be achieved within the conceptual work of a researcher instead of merely bringing together specialists of various disciplines who politely listen to each other without budging from their original positions. A good number of so-called interdisciplinary exercises taking place today actually reinforce specialization, each person involved finding it necessary to draw more precise lines between "his" field and that of the others.[20]

(c) The Humanization of Knowledge. / Social scientists have to rediscover that their prime task is to put the human being and his essential needs back into the centre of attention. As we have pointed out earlier, the dehumanization of social science is parallel to the dehumanization of society.[21] So we are facing one of these famous chicken-and-egg questions again. Do we have to wait for society to change in order to change science? In my view, it is in the true nature of dialectic thinking, and not an expression of philosophical idealism, to affirm that scientists can modify their behaviour as social actors and begin to help changing the society. Social change has never been the exclusive result of anonymous forces. The dissident thought of social analysts also makes its impact. One clear example is the profound transformation of development objectives at the present time, as compared to the first two United Nations Development Decades. Certainly, those who began to put basic needs into the centre of the debate were inspired by a deteriorating situation among the poorest segments of the world's population. Someone however had to come along, not only to see this phenomenon occur, but to represent a value system within which such a situation is intolerable. It is the combination of an objective situation with a subjective (personal, ideological, affective, etc.) valuation that leads to action for social change.

Humanization is, of course, closely interrelated with the other aspects of a new social science epistemology. It means being value-oriented and transdisciplinary. The Japanese economist Shigeto Tsuru expresses it in this way for his discipline:

> Economists are called upon to extend their inquiry in two directions: (1) to be prepared to make normative judgements, and (2) to widen the scope of their enquiry to encompass what were once regarded as externalities. The former task requires specifying the processes through which a normative judgement can be derived from

social consensus, and the latter task implies replacing the idea of economics as being a closed equilibrium system with that of it being an open-ended discipline having symbiotic contact with neighbouring disciplines.[22]

Another economist, Kurt Dopfer, goes a little further than "symbiotic contact" when he claims that a holistic approach has to take the place of interdisciplinarity. His hope is that a study of economics which covers ecology will contribute to human well being.[23] The interesting point here is that taking a much broader view, thereby arriving at a considerable degree of abstraction, including such methods as systems analysis, may bring us closer to an understanding of basic human needs. Paradoxical as it may sound, the humanization of science will not be achieved through the simplification of problems, the repudiation of such basically inhuman gadgets as the computer, or a return to non-scientific approaches. Empirical data-gathering, conceptualization, and theorizing on a very large scale are still necessary.

(d) *Responsibility of the Scientist.* / The three preceding points inevitably lead to a more general one in the field of the professional ethics of the knowledge-producer. Once we accept the demand for the humanization of knowledge, we have to admit two further principles: social science must be committed to the reduction of social inequalities in today's world and must concern itself with the well-being of future generations. In abstract terms these are the principles of equity and intertemporal distribution. They are not new in peace research or future studies. They have found their way into development thinking through, among other things, the Cocoyoc Declaration.[24] Unfortunately they are neglected in positivistic social science.

A third type of responsibility, which has not been underlined as much as the other two, is the one that the social scientist ought to have with regard to the natural sciences. It is truly surprising how little attention is paid to the sociocultural consequences of food technology, genetic manipulation or nuclear energy. In a broader definition of the field of international relations, such questions are a matter of concern simply because they are not confined to particular territories. The influence exerted by some States on others in the field of science and technology is enormous. It affects relations between industrial States, but probably has more profound implications in relations between industrial and nonindustrial societies.

The responsibility of the scientist with regard to equity, intertemporal distribution, and natural sciences can only be achieved if he is prepared to examine the value of utopias (or to create some), and to contribute to the integration and humanization of knowledge.

(e) *Respect for the Diversity of Intellectual Styles.* / A new social science epistemology has to take into account cultural diversity and the diversity of modes of thinking that goes with it. International relations studies are deeply affected by the lack of concern with this very problem.[25] Whether we analyse negotiations, conflicts, or decolonization, we will always be handicapped if we disregard the significance of cultural diversity.

Unfortunately there is no encyclopedia of intellectual styles. Probably it is beyond the capacity of any living human being to produce such a source of information, because no one has been brought up with the idea that this is a worthwhile exercise to undertake.[26] A modest beginning would be to examine the ways in which Western societies, with the enormous military and economic power they exert over the world, "grasp" non-Western worlds. The study of international relations would greatly benefit from it in this polycentric, multicultural world. Just to give a hint: Western thought is deeply anthropocentric (man is outside and above nature), dichotomous (good and bad, body and soul, civilized and savage, etc.), unilinear (progress from here to eternity), and compartmentalized (fragmentation and hyper-specialization as discussed above). To be aware of this and to know that these structures of knowledge might be different in other societies is absolutely indispensable.

These are just a few dimensions of a new epistemology for social science, and consequently for the study of international relations. What we also have to reflect upon are the concrete research areas which ought to be given priority in the future.

IV. ALTERNATIVE THINKING: AREAS FOR FURTHER RESEARCH

General statements regarding epistemology, methodology, and the professional ethics of the scientist can be translated into concrete proposals for alternative thinking on the study of international relations. Broadly speaking, there are two directions in which such thinking can lead, the two being in no way exclusive, but clearly interdependent.

1. New Units and Other Actors

The first question which arises is that of people's participation in decision-making processes at the international level. A new world model taking this into account must be based on a critical appraisal of the representatives of State officials in international organizations. Nongovernmental organizations (trade unions, women's movements, youth groups) which sometimes have a membership of dozens of millions, must be given the right to be more than mere observers in international gatherings.[27] Instead of a Security Council and a General Assembly, both based on State representation, a future United Nations might have two Houses, one representing States, the other NGOs. It is also possible to improve participation procedures outside established international organizations. Amnesty International is an excellent example of an organization run by citizens to combat the abuses committed by State power in all parts of the world. Its success in obtaining the liberation of political prisoners, in fighting political repression, physical and mental torture, and various forms of violation of the private sphere is outstanding.

A second area of concern which should be given priority by students of international relations is transnationalism. By this we mean the study of "contacts, coalitions and interactions across state boundaries that are not controlled by the central foreign policy organs of governments."[28] This may include institutions such as NGOs or transnational corporations as well as informal relations through student exchanges or tourism. A word of caution is needed here. We must not be made to believe that transnational interaction is by definition good for people because it erodes State power or interstate coalitions. The opposite is in fact possible: "Without transnational *participation*, transnational *power* remains elitist and parochial social reality remains untempered."[29]

A somewhat different field for concern, although not totally separate from the preceding one, is the study of intercultural relations. Instead of looking at the interaction of States, let us examine how cultural units at various levels (micro- as well as macro-cultures) interact.[30] This is revealing in many ways: we learn about ethnic groups communicating across cultural boundaries, about cognitive styles of different cultures which are confronted in interstate relations or about movements trying to bring together groups of States on the grounds of cultural similarity. One model for a future world based on a system of macro-cultures instead of States has already been proposed.[31]

A further approach lies in the creation of functional, cross-boundary entities. In Africa, such entities exist on an informal basis, because the frontiers acquired with independence are usually too artificial to keep neighbouring populations from having closer relations across frontiers than within frontiers. In Europe, the need for institutionalized crossboundary co-operation seems rather acute. To give an example: a movement launched many years ago in Basle under the name of "Regio basiliensis," with the objective of establishing co-operative relations between French, German, and Swiss living in the area around Basle, has a significant role to play. There is proof of this in the fact that the separate decisions of the three countries to establish nuclear power stations on their respective territories near Basle is now generally recognized by specialists, and more so even by the population of Basle, as dangerous and irresponsible. It would mean the highest concentration of nuclear power stations in the whole world. Effective regional entities dealing with this type of problem, thereby reducing exclusively national prerogatives, are a necessity for the well-being of the populations concerned.[32]

All of this may sound reasonably acceptable and open up many avenues for international relations research, but the underlying problem which we have to face takes us back to utopia, in the sense of eutopia: it has to do with the inequalities of the size and power of States. H. Simons goes all the way in his analysis of the "overgrown nation states" when he says: "These monsters of nationalism and mercantilism must be dismantled, both to preserve world order and to protect internal peace."[33] And another economist, Leopold Kohr, well known for his life-long struggle against the large State, puts it even more dramatically: "The great powers, those monsters of nationalism, must be broken up and replaced by small states; for, as perhaps even our diplomats will eventually be able to understand, only small states are wise, modest and, above all, weak enough, to accept an authority higher than their own."[34]

What we have said earlier about the trend of liberation movements only to create more states must now be qualified. It is futile to strive for some world State or federation comprising the present units with all the inequalities existing between them, while the already weaker members are further sub-divided. Kohr's utopia is probably the one that could, if we had any sense, lead to an alternative world order. In his logic, the super-monsters called USA and USSR should be the first to be dismantled, preferably by dividing them into at least fifty units each. It has often been said, occasionally by people who prefer to live in the nineteenth century, that the unification of multiple small units into nation-states constituted a progress (e.g., Germany, Italy). Two world wars in the twentieth century should have taught us a lesson. With larger units, the danger of mutual destruction is merely elevated to a higher degree. If the USA and the USSR were split up, there would be ample opportunity for the smaller units to quarrel among themselves and leave the rest of the world alone.

It may well be that the dismantlement of the super-monsters is impossible without war. But what are students of international relations to do: discard the utopia and wait for the war to come?

2. New Priorities in International Relations Research

Rather than concentrating on units and actors, one can also redefine the scope of the study of international relations by indicating problem areas which need to be given special attention. What follows can, of course, not be an ex-haustive catalogue of predominant themes of interest. It derives essentially from a preoccupation with the relationship between rich and poor segments in various societies.

(a) Basic Human Needs. / The dichotomy between developed and under-developed societies is being slowly overcome. One reason is that all societies are in a process of development or underdevelopment. The other is that global relationships are beginning to be perceived in a way that shows how the overdevelopment of some is linked to the underdevelopment of others. Maldevelopment is now the accepted term for this global process.[35]

What is also becoming generally accepted, after a few decades of discussions on "development," is that we are not solving anything with power dams, steel plants, or banana plantations as long as at least three basic human needs are not satisfied in all parts of the world: nutrition, health, and habitat. As simple as that. But it is usually the simple things that take time to be discovered.

One preoccupation of international law has been to determine a minimum standard guaranteed to individuals sojourning abroad. This was linked to an international economic system in which private property and the security of merchants were of prime importance. Perhaps it is time to determine the minimum standards of human existence in terms of the fulfilment of basic needs. Private property would then be a relevant criterion only to the extent that it serves to meet such needs. Parallel to the determination of a minimum standard, research must lead us to the determination of a maximum standard, one that will prevent social costs (such as investment in health care) resulting from over-consumption.

The complexity of this undertaking is readily apparent. If we want to liberate ourselves from a state-centric approach, pay attention to transnational rela-tions, and deal with basic human needs, we have to determine levels of significance in what we are studying. To give one example: for whom are the transnational corporations producing food? What are the distribution patterns and the effects of consumption in different cultural settings? How does the industrial mode of food production affect different social structures? If we want to give serious answers to these questions we have to evaluate the relative contributions made by state actors and non-state actors. It is not enough to say that X numbers of multinationals have a turnover which is higher than the GNP of Y countries in the world. The relevant question is what these corporations are doing to meet basic needs as compared to States? Are state-owned and state-run corporations doing better than private ones? We will probably discover that some transnational corporations have done more for the satisfaction of basic needs than the governments of Haiti, Paraguay, or similar countries. A really careful examination of *who* does *what for whom* is still awaited.

As a brief reminder: if the study of international relations deals with basic human needs, problems such as those of energy, natural resources, science and technology will become its main preoccupation.

(b) Determining the Causes of Growing Inequalities. / As Robert McNamara has kept pointing out regularly since 1972, income inequalities of three kinds have been growing while the so-called development process has been taking place: between the rich and poor countries, within the group of poor countries, and between the richer and poorer segments of the populations in poor countries.[36] Sometimes it is in countries where the growth rate of the GNP is highest that the growth rate of inequality is also high. To give one example in the domain of internal inequalities: between 1960 and 1970, the growth rate of the Chinese GNP was 0.3 per cent per annum. Nevertheless, the country succeeded in reducing inequalities and fulfilling basic needs. During the same period, the Soviet GNP grew probably more than twenty times faster, and yet the country reached a stage of incapacity to feed its entire population. Denis de Rougemont predicted as far back as 1956 that NATO countries would one day have to come to the rescue of the Soviet Union to preserve it from serious internal strife.[37] Not feeding one's population means both not fulfilling basic needs and accepting inequalities.

International relations students should be concerned with growing internal inequalities, because these most certainly are caused partly by the nature of external relations conducted by the countries concerned. Many recent studies on dependence, centre-periphery relations, structural violence, and imperialism provide us with conceptual frameworks for more research in this direction.[38]

A fruitful field for research is trans-boundary comparisons of production and consumption of vital resources and goods. It is important to know, for instance, what quantity of fertilizers is used in different countries to arrive at the same level of nutritional satisfaction. An example: Switzerland imports annually 1.4 million tons of wheat and feeds 1 million to animals for meat production. The meat thus produced contains a quantity of proteins equivalent to only 0.2 million tons of wheat. With the 0.8 million tons lost in the process, 6 million people could be fed for a year in other parts of the world.[39] Another example: 15 per cent of US consumption of fertilizers is used for growing lawns, cultivating golf courses, and adorning cemeteries. In absolute quantity, this is the amount of fertilizers at the disposal of all the farmers of India.[40] Transboundary comparisons highlight existing inequalities and inequities and, if they are put to good use, may lead the way out of global maldevelopment into a newly defined and for once real global development.

(c) *New International Economic Order or Self-Reliance.* / Since the Sixth Special Session of the UN General Assembly passed its resolution on a New International Economic Order (NIEO) on 1 May 1974, this theme has been at the centre of debates in a wide variety of institutions all over the world. What is amazing is that the envisaged order is not all that new to deserve so much attention. The right to nationalization and better prices for raw materials may be important. Measures in this direction can be taken overnight, look dramatic, and yet leave the entire international economic structure intact. The "new" order, when closely examined, looks more like an intensification of the old one: more transfers of capital and technology, increased trade, and a reaffirmation of national sovereignty. The approach is profoundly state-centric. In their annual pilgrimage to New York and Geneva, Third World elites obtain Charters, Declarations, and Resolutions affirming their right to sovereignty, independence, and non-interference in domestic affairs, though everyone knows that the big powers safeguard their interests through the use of force, regardless of any written or spoken words or treaties. Hungary, the Dominican Republic, Czechoslovakia, Vietnam, Chile, Angola: do we need more examples for just the period between 1956 and 1976?

A good example in the economic sphere is the question of the seabed. According to UN resolutions and to the Cocoyoc Declaration, the resources of the seabed should be exploited by a supranational agency to benefit the poorer countries of the world. From the sea could come some of the resources that are now flowing out of the Third World into the industrial countries. Less food would go to the overfed. Poor countries would become less dependent on aid. But according to the American journalist Jack Anderson, who has published explosive news before now, the Oceanography Committee of the US House of Representatives proposed, on 15 March 1976, to counter Third World proposals on the exploitation of the seabed by setting up special military units to protect the activities of US private corporations: "If the legislation clears both the House and the Senate, the US will give physical protection for the US mining consortiums. . . . Should any nation seek to prevent the operation . . . US planes and warships would intervene under the legislation."[41]

If that became true, what was the use of the UN's adopting a Charter of Economic Rights and Duties of States with its repetitious demands for the respect of State sovereignty or economic cooperation?

Many Third World representatives at international gatherings find it deeply unjust to minimize the importance of the NIEO (however quite a few Third World militants agree with our position). The NIEO, if implemented at all, will create more dependence and more inequalities. What has happened to the first two Development Decades and to the Pearson Report may well happen to the NIEO: the discovery, ten years hence, that the Third World has once more been fed on words, this time at the request of its own leaders.

The NIEO has been praised as an achievement due to the "collective self-reliance" of the Third World. The term is misleading. What is really meant is increased bargaining power through Third World solidarity. Self-reliance has a deeper meaning: to rely on one's own forces at a local level whenever possible and to use inputs from the national, regional, or world levels only when local resources or knowhow are missing. Local self-reliance needs to be protected or at least tolerated by national governments. But if the representatives of these governments jointly ask for more foreign inputs, their action is counterproductive to self-reliance, not an expression of it. Studies of the feasibility of self-reliance as a development strategy, or as a new definition of development, must take a central place in international relations research.[42]

(d) *Alternative Ways of Life.* / The introduction of the concept of maldevelopment and the replacement of the dichotomy of developed versus developing countries by a distinction between *over* and *under*developed areas all over the world leads to the question: are we capable of inventing new ways of life for the overdeveloped?

In a satirical plea for "aid for the overdeveloped," G. Kocher brings out a few revealing figures. In the overdeveloped countries (10 per cent of the world's population), we find the following indicators: 98 per cent of the world's psychopharmacological consumption, 56 per cent of impotency and frigidity, 86 per cent of telephone calls, 80 per cent of suicides, 75 per cent of television consumption, 74 per cent of heart attacks, etc.[43] The World Health Organization has established that the USA and the USSR have the same percentage of schizophrenics in their populations: 0.9 per cent. That is over 4 million people in the two major industrial countries of the world!

This is not the place to draw up a list of evils afflicting the overdeveloped countries. Nor at this stage can we adequately summarize the thinking which is devoted to inventing an alternative society. At this very moment, however, many things are happening in Europe and North America which should be of some concern to the specialist in international relations.[44] Ways of life are not confined to national boundaries. They are exported and imported. If the population of one particular country asks for change, external forces will come into action. Political or business interests will begin to manifest themselves across State frontiers. Again, a whole new vital area is open to us for research.

(e) *Making the Protection of Human Rights Effective.* / The number of human rights conventions is increasing at a slower rate than the production of technical gadgets suited for undermining human rights. At this stage, we only have one effective human rights convention in the world: the European Convention supervised by the Council of Europe in Strasbourg. Any detainee in a European prison may address himself directly to the European Human Rights Commission. Prison authorities have no right to stop or alter letters. No fees have to be paid for the inquiries carried out by the Commission; possibly the Commission will even provide legal counsel. The treatment of offenders, their rehabilitation and resocialization are the object of many Council of Europe resolutions. Other fields, such as the recognition of diplomas, youth policy, public health (facilities for war cripples, establishment of a European blood bank) are concerns of an international organization which obviously deals with human beings.[45]

Some specialized agencies of the United Nations have the same objective, but their problem usually is that they do not have the same powers. When the ILO sets standards about working conditions of women and children or when the FAO determines minimum standards of nutrition, they are contributing to the satisfaction of basic needs. The concept of human rights must be given a broader connotation to include all of these activities and students of international relations must provide answers to the crucial question of the implementation of such broadly defined rights.

Just two more points on human rights. One significant endeavour would be to study the absence of conflict. Some societies get along without too much internal strife or external conflict, but preoccupation usually lies with conflict situations. Perhaps knowledge about less conflictual social behaviour may reveal ways and means of improving the human condition. The other line of thought concerns the participation of citizens in the effective protection of human rights. Amnesty International has been mentioned as an example of possible action. Many other organizations are mushrooming in various parts of the world. Their impact on the protection of human rights may be particularly significant in countries which have not committed themselves through interstate conventions.

CONCLUSION

The purpose of this inquiry has been to propose constructive avenues for international relations research. New fields must be explored and new methods applied. Merely descriptive, or even explanatory and predictive approaches will only describe, explain, and predict mankind's pathological development without any chance of contributing to change.

One condition for this is that people should not simply be considered as objects of knowledge but as knowledge-producers. Let us conclude therefore with this statement by Johan Galtung: A less exploitative system of knowledge production implies that we are not content with doing "research on people, but together with people, not to act as a stimulus and registrar of responses, but to enter dialectically in a dialogue with the 'researched.' In that case, they would, in fact, no longer be researched people but be part of a team, of an effort to explore some aspect of the social condition of humankind together."[46]

With this in mind, we can begin to hope that the scope and methods of the study of international relations will expand to include a preoccupation with basic human needs more so than in the past.

NOTES

The title of this chapter is obviously inspired by E. F. Schumacher's book *Small Is Beautiful: A Study of Economics as if People Mattered*. London, Sphere Books, 1974. The author is particularly grateful for comments on a first draft of Part I to Johan Galtung,

Ekkehart Müller-Rappard, Peter O'Brien, Denis de Rougemont, Rolf Steppacher, Albert Tevoedjre, Monica Wemegah, and especially Noa Zanolli.

1. K. W. Kapp, "Zum Problem der Enthumanisierung der 'Reinen Theorie' und des gesellschaftlichen Realität, *Kyklos*, vol. 20, 1967, p. 329 (hereafter K. W. Kapp, "Zum Problem").

2. J. Needham, "History and Human Values: A Chinese Perspective for World Science and Technology," *The Centennial Review*, vol. 20, 1976, p. 27.

3. E. F. Schumacher, *Small is Beautiful*, p. 76.

4. A. Sauvy, *La fin des riches*, Paris, Calmann-Lévy, 1975, p. 19.

5. See also J. Habermas, *La technique et la science comme "idéologie*," Paris, Gallimard, 1973.

6. More precisely, what is meant is that air or sunshine are not calculated in terms of monetary costs, but of course the use and abuse of air or water resources present a problem of social costs. See K. W. Kapp, *The Social Costs of Private Enterprise*, Cambridge, Mass., Harvard University Press, 1950. We must remember also that public enterprise may create similar social costs, a fact that representatives of East European countries have sometimes attempted to deny at the Stockholm Conference on the Environment.

7. V. F. Weisskopf, *Physics in the Twentieth Century: Selected Essays*, Cambridge, Mass., Harvard University Press, 1972, p. 364. Italics added.

8. R. Preiswerk and D. Perrot, *Ethnocentrism and History: Africa, Asia and Indian America in Western Textbooks*. New York: Lagos NOK Publishers, 1978.

9. There are, of course, other approaches. See UNESCO, *Histoire du développement culturel et scientifique de l'humanité*, Paris, Laffont, 1967, 9 vols.

10. See, for instance, F.S.C. Northrop and H. Livingstone, *Cross-Cultural Understanding: Epistemology in Anthropology*, New York, Harper and Row, 1964. Also the interesting debate between M. Herskovits and F. Knight, in M. Herskovits, *Economic Anthropology*, 2nd ed., New York, Norton, 1960, appendix. For similar problems in intercultural psychology, see R. Preiswerk, "Jean Piaget et l'étude des relations interculturelles," in G. Busino (ed.), *Les sciences sociales avec et après Jean Piaget*. Geneva, Droz, 1976.

11. We will subsequently present a more balanced picture as far as the role of international organizations is concerned, particularly with regard to the ILO, WHO, and FAO. See Part IV.

12. The converse is sometimes true, as R. J. Barnet and R. E. Müller show in *The Global Reach: The Power of the Multinational Corporations*, New York, Simon and Schuster, 1974.

13. Quoted by M. Banks, "The Relationship between the Study of International Relations, Peace Research and Strategic Studies," paper presented to UNESCO Advisory Meeting of Experts on UNESCO's Role in Developing Research on Peace Problems, Paris, July 1969, pp. 5–6.

14. T. S. Kuhn, *The Structure of Scientific Revolutions*, Chicago, University of Chicago Press, 1970.

15. M. S. Soroos, "A Methodological Overview of the Process of Designing Alternative Future Worlds," in L. R. Beres and H. R. Targ (eds.), *Planning Alternative Futures*, New York, Praeger, 1975, pp. 3–27.

16. For instance, Hessische Stiftung für Friedens- und Konfliktforschung, *Friedensanalysen*, Schwerpunkt Unterentwicklung, Frankfurt, Suhrkamp, 1976.

17. See the contribution of Saul Mendlovitz in the volume edited by Beres and Targ quoted in note 15.

18. L. Mumford, *The Story of Utopias*, New York, Viking Press, 1962 (1st ed. 1922).

19. K. W. Kapp, *Toward a Science of Man in Society*, The Hague, Nijhoff, 1961, pp. ix–x.

20. See J. Piaget, *Epistémologie des sciences de l'homme*, Paris, Gallimard, 1976, and the article on Piaget mentioned in note 10, p. 510.

21. See K. W. Kapp, "Zum Problem."

22. S. Tsuru, "Towards a New Political Economy," in K. Dopfer (ed.), *Economics in the Future*, London, Macmillan, 1976, p. 112.

23. *Ibid.*, p. 9.

24. Published in *Development Dialogue*, no. 2, 1974, pp. 88–96.

25. R. Preiswerk, "The Place of Inter-Cultural Relations in the Study of International Relations," *The Yearbook of World Affairs*, London, 1978.

26. There are, of course, quite a few attempts. See, for instance, F.S.C. Northrop, *The Meeting of East and West*, New York, Macmillan, 1946. This book is stimulating but also to be read sceptically because of its marked dichotomy between East and West. See also J. Galtung, *Deductive Thinking and Intellectual Style: An Essay on Teutonic Intellectual Style*, Oslo, Chair in Conflict and Peace Research, 1976, no. 2.

27. J. Galtung, "Nonterritorial Actors and the Problem of Peace," in S. Mendlovitz (ed.), *On the Creation of a Just World Order, Preferred Worlds for the 1990's*, New York, Free Press, 1975.

28. R. O. Keohane and J. S. Nye, *Transnational Relations and World Politics*, Cambridge, Mass., Harvard University Press, 1972, p. xi.

29. J. Harrod, "Transnational Power," *The Yearbook of World Affairs*, London, 1976, p. 115.

30. See Chapter I in the publication quoted in note 25.

31. A. Mazrui, "World Culture and the Search for Human Consensus," in S. Mendlovitz (ed.), *op. cit.*

32. See D. de Rougemont, *L'Europe des régions*, Geneva, Centre européen de culture, 1976. Also L. Kohr, *The Breakdown of Nations*, London, Routledge and Kegan Paul, 1957, pp. 191–192.

33. H. C. Simons, *Economic Policy for a Free Society*, Chicago, Chicago University Press, 1948, p. 125.

34. L. Kohn, *The Breakdown of Nations*, p. 187.

35. See J. Galtung et al., *Measuring World Development*, Oslo, Chair in Conflict and Peace Research, 1974. Paper no. 11. Also Commission des organisations suisses de coopération au développement, *Maldéveloppement Suisse-Monde*, Geneva, CETIM, 1975.

36. See in particular the speech delivered on 14th April 1972, before the UNCTAD meeting at Santiago de Chile.

37. D. de Rougemont, *L'aventure occidentale de l'homme*, Paris, Albin Michel, 1957, p. 255.

38. See in particular J. Galtung, "A Structural Theory of Imperialism," *Journal of Peace Research*, vol. 8, 1971, pp. 81–118, and the case study on Switzerland by R. Gerster, "Schweizerisches Volkseinkommen und Dritte Welt." *Aussenwirtschaft*, vol. 30, 1976, pp. 33–71.

39. Calculations prepared by Rudolf Strahm and the "Déclaration de Berne." See also *Leserzeitung*, Zurich, 18 May 1976.

40. L. Brown, "Allons-nous aussi avoir faim?" *Tribune de Genève*, 17 February 1975, p. 21.

41. J. Anderson, "Mining the Ocean Floor," *New York Post*, 30 March 1976.

42. See J. Galtung, P. O'Brien and R. Preiswerk (eds.), *Self-Reliance, A Strategy for Development*, London: Bogle-L'Ouverture, 1980.

43. G. Kocher, "Die Hilfe an Die überentwickelten Länder," *Tages-Anzeiger Magazin*, 22 May 1976.

44. See the chapter on an alternative way of life for Sweden in *What Now?* the special

edition of *Development Dialogue* edited in 1975 for the Seventh Special Session of the UN General Assembly. In the 1976, no. 1 edition of this periodical is an article by J. Galtung on alternative life styles and a commentary on the reactions of the Swedish public concerning the proposals made.

45. See in particular Council of Europe, *Man in a European Society*, Strasbourg, April 1974, Doc. 3420.

46. J. Galtung, "Is Peaceful Research Possible? On the Methodology of Peace Research," in *Peace: Research, Education, Action*, Copenhagen, Christian Ejlers, 1975, p. 273.

14
THE ELUSIVENESS OF A HUMANE WORLD COMMUNITY

Robert Johansen

CHALLENGES TO HUMANITY'S FUTURE

The Westphalian System in a Post-Westphalian Era

If profound [global] problems with historic consequences are not resolved, is this due to unwise foreign policies? If so, then foreign policy could be corrected by getting additional information to officials, improving the policy-making machinery, or selecting new leadership in Washington. Alternatively, one may conclude that global challenges are unmet because the international system is poorly structured to meet present political and economic needs. If that is true, then fundamental structural changes are required to overcome the threats to survival and to preferred values. The difficulty may be a combination of unwise policies and structural defects, in which case the necessary changes are even more risky to undertake and difficult to bring about.

To increase our understanding of these questions, it is useful to consider the present international system in historical perspective.

The Limits of Decentralized, Territorially-based Authority. / The Peace of Westphalia at the conclusion of the last of the great religious wars of Europe is a convenient benchmark for noting the major shift in European political organization which produced the current international system. Although the selection of any particular date to note systemic changes is somewhat arbitrary, the political changes symbolized by the Peace of Westphalia of 1648 stand in sharp contrast to the political organization of the Middle Ages before the religious wars. In medieval society the Christian commonwealth was hierarchically organized and subject to the authority of the Pope and the Holy Roman Empire. The Roman Catholic Church and its appointed representatives exercised centralized authority across the territorial boundaries of feudalism. Although subunits throughout Europe exercised some power, it was on behalf of and subject to the authority of Pope and Emperor. This continental system gradually changed as authority, power, wealth, and loyalties shifted to a subcontinental or state level. The Peace of Westphalia acknowledged the development of independent, secular, sovereign states, no longer subject to the centralized authority of the Pope or Emperor.[1]

In the Westphalian model, political authority was decentralized on the continent and based on territory, thus making boundaries very important. National governments were all-powerful within their boundaries; no outside authority could legally intrude within each national shell. As the Pope's influence declined and there was no overreaching political authority to regulate conduct between sovereigns, there could be no prohibition of war. Because authority was tied to territory, there was little possibility of establishing sovereignty over the oceans.

The existing international system corresponds to the Westphalian model of a decentralized system of independent states, each exercising dominant authority within its territorial domain. However, mounting evidence of social interpenetration, such as that presented earlier, indicates that we are living during a period pregnant with possibilities for system change. These are similar in significance to the structural transformation registered at Westphalia. This era is marked by rising needs to transform the nation-state or Westphalian system into a new system of order that is in some ways reminiscent of two principal attributes of medieval society. (Of course, one should not assume that the changing world order either should or will develop an authority structure similar to that of the Holy Roman Empire.) First, there is the need to establish a transnational structure of power and authority with increased capacity at the center for coordinating policy and enforcing it on national governments. Second, there is a need for a new structure of authority not limited to a piece of territory for either its sources of legitimacy or the domain of its directives. It must be global in scope and extend its authority even to outer space.

In the emerging system, national boundaries are becoming less important than they were in the nineteenth century. This is illustrated by the growth of multinational corporations and the international regulation of travel, commerce, and communication. The need for additional forms of central guidance is reflected in negotiations about regulating the use of the oceans and the seabed. Incipient supranational institutions are perhaps present in the European economic community. Although governments tenaciously guard their sovereignty, they also advance occasional claims that international organizations may have the right to intervene, such as against apartheid, in areas of traditionally national jurisdiction. In the League of Nations and the United Nations, governments made their first modern effort, although without major success, to control and prohibit aggressive war. The need for international guarantees against war reflects the decline of the invulnerable, impermeable state in the nuclear age.[2]

Yet, the systemic transition now under way reveals a sharp asymmetry. Industrialization and advanced technology have made the earth a post-Westphalian functional unit, but the world remains politically fragmented by Westphalian national divisions of the planet and of human loyalties. Threats

posed by the pollution of the atmosphere and oceans, the instability in the supply of food and oil, and the all-encompassing consequences of nuclear war are
feebly confronted by a system of sovereign states that recognize no coordinating authority above their national governments.

The Tragedy of the Commons. / The unprecedented scope of the foreign
policy problems facing Washington emerges from the incongruity between the
functional unity and the *political disunity* of the globe. Serving human needs requires cooperative efforts based upon a recognition of the unity of the
ecosystem and the universal impact of some political decisions. The
Westphalian disunity of political organization encourages self-seeking, competitive efforts. The consequences of this incongruity were illustrated by
biologist Garrett Hardin in his well-known discussion of the "tragedy of the
commons." He pictured a pasture held in common by a village of cattle herdsmen. As rational beings, the herdsmen seek to maximize their gains from
pasturing their animals. Each herdsman asks himself: "What is the utility *to me*
of adding one more animal to my herd?" This utility, Garrett explained, has
one negative and one positive component. The positive component is nearly
+ 1 because of the increment of one animal; the negative component is a function of the additional overgrazing created by one more animal. Excessive
overgrazing can lead to severe soil erosion and eventual destruction of the
pasture. However, unlike the positive component which accrues entirely to the
owner, the negative effect of overgrazing is shared by all the herdsmen. As a
result, the negative utility for any particular herdsman is only a small fraction
of -1. After adding the utilities of the positive and negative components, the rational herdsman concludes that the most sensible course for him to pursue is to
add another animal to the herd. Following the same calculation, a second is
added—and then a third, fourth, and so on. The same conclusion is reached by
all rational herdsmen sharing the commons. It makes little sense for any one of
them to exercise self-restraint and not add to his herd because the pasture will
eventually be destroyed anyway due to the overgrazing by others. As Hardin
concluded: "Therein is the tragedy. Each man is locked into a system that com-
pels him to increase his herd without limit—in a world that is limited. Ruin is
the destination toward which all men rush, each pursuing his own best interest
in a society that believes in the freedom of the commons. Freedom in a commons brings ruin to all."[3]

A similar problem was raised much earlier by Jean-Jacques Rousseau.[4] He
described a primitive hunting party in which a small group of hungry men attempted to catch a deer to satisfy their appetites. If, during the hunt, one man
noticed a hare which would satisfy the man's hunger, he would pursue it even if
his action would provide no food for the rest of the group and would allow the
deer to escape because he had left his post. By this simple example, Rousseau
demonstrated his belief in a natural inclination to put self-interest above
mutual, general interest. Rousseau did not elaborate upon his story but we
might speculate about the alternatives the hunter faced.[5] He might have
thought that rational self-interest dictated that he remain faithful to his hunting partners and refuse to pursue the hare. This would be especially true in the

long run, because it would establish a precedent for securing future meals. He could have predicted that, by pursuing the hare, his abandonment of the group would enable the deer to escape. He would have regretted that result, but he also knew that if he did not pursue the hare, it would be possible that the second hunter would see the hare, make calculations similar to his own, and then catch the hare for his own meal. In that case also, the deer would escape, leaving many empty stomachs, including that of the first hunter. With these thoughts in mind, the first hunter then left the hunting party to catch the hare.

The story demonstrates that, in the absence of a central administrative system to help coordinate human behavior and make it more dependable, even a sincere, rational actor fails to engage in otherwise desirable cooperation. This is true even though the rational person at first is willing to cooperate to satisfy common needs as basic as food itself. If a central authority existed and required that the captured hare be divided equally among all hunters, then the hunters would ignore the hare as long as there was a reasonable chance of catching the deer.

Today's slow movement toward central, worldwide administration of some aspects of life, such as carried out by multinational corporations and international regulatory organizations controlling transnational air transportation and electronic communication, suggests that the question no longer is: Will there be a worldwide system of order? Instead, the sobering issue has become: What will be its nature? This is true despite the failure of a majority of the world's people to recognize that a global system is in the making. If one acknowledges that, barring nuclear suicide or ecological collapse, the economic and political structures of the world are becoming enmeshed with one another on a global basis, an issue of high importance is to assess whether the incipient system serves the values that one believes are most worthy of support. Given the value orientations of the dominant actors in today's world, it is possible that new forms of inequity or exploitation may be established.

Because the developing system is global in scope, it is especially important that avoidable errors be averted, since there will be no sanctuaries to which to flee should the evolving system prove tyrannical or inhumane. Therefore, it is imperative to construct a normative basis for international transactions to insure that through inadvertence or moral callousness we do not create a system that eventually destroys our highest values.

In summary, citizens in one state or group of states have no way of assuring that actions of other governments will not be harmful to or catastrophic for the lives of all. Means do not exist to insure that various national interests will harmonize with the human interest. The international structures of power and authority and the prevailing criteria for selecting foreign policies are unable (1) to satisfy the security and survival requirements that a prudent foreign policy must, and (2) to implement the preferred values that a just foreign policy should. The apparent need to establish a system of policy coordination commensurate with the global dimensions of modern human behavior poses two remaining questions: First, what are the most useful standards for assessing whether foreign policies are helping to achieve a more secure and humane global community? These standards will be discussed in the remainder of the present chapter. Second, are U.S. foreign policies in fact implementing the values and transforming the structures without which survival will be in question and human dignity indefinitely denied? The answer to this question is pursued in subsequent chapters [of my book], which contain detailed analyses of four case studies of U.S. foreign policy.

A GLOBAL HUMANIST RESPONSE

In developing a framework around which to build a foreign policy capable of moving safely into the 1990s, it is useful to begin by clarifying the values that one wants to realize. Of course, one's fundamental values are chosen or assumed, not proven. To be sure, students and practitioners of foreign policy frequently justify one particular policy or another by saying that the national interest "requires" it. A certain policy, they say, is "necessary." This language conveys the false impression that the policy is a direct outgrowth or an empirical expression of what *is*, rather than a statement of what someone thinks the policy *ought* to be. A policy is "required" or "necessary" only in the sense that its proponents believe it is necessary for serving certain other values which are usually not stated explicitly. The highly acclaimed concept of the national interest is not scientifically determined. It is a cluster of goals and strategies derived from more fundamental values. Traditionally, foremost among these is the preservation of the security and prosperity of the government and its supporters. This includes maintaining sovereign control over a defined territory and population. The competitive accumulation of military power and, secondarily, of economic resources are the principal means for pursuing the values of security and prosperity.

If one chooses to depart from traditional definitions of the national interest, one is not less scientific or less empirically oriented than the defenders of traditional definitions. An untraditional orientation may simply mean that one endorses a slightly rearranged hierarchy of values.

An Alternative Framework for Decision Making

The earlier discussion of mounting foreign policy problems called into question the capacity of national societies to provide security and reasonable opportunities for the fulfillment of humanitarian values as long as governments continue acting in accordance with traditional diplomatic precepts. The challenge for policymakers now and in the future will be to bring policies, which in the past have served the national interest as traditionally defined, into harmony with the human interest in abolishing war and poverty and in halting gross denial of human rights and ecological decay. These four problems can also be stated as world order values: peace without national military arsenals (V_1), economic well-being for all inhabitants on the earth (V_2), universal human rights and social justice (V_3), and ecological balance (V_4).[6] It is imperative to make progress in achieving these values if we seek to insure the long-range survival of the species and to improve the quality of human life for all people.

Although these values may appear uncontroversial, they provide a different set of standards for policymaking than are found in traditional understandings of the national interest. Three clarifying principles will establish points of difference between the two approaches. First, the value framework proposed here rests upon the assumption that the human race is the important constituency to consider in policymaking. The world's people should benefit from policy decisions. The traditional approach gives priority to the people of one nation. It also provides more benefits for the governmental elite and its supporters within the nation than for the national population in general. Thus my proposed emphasis on the human interest differs in two ways from traditional diplomacy. First, the scope of human identity extends across national boundaries rather than remaining confined to people within them. Second, human identity expresses bonds of community between those at the top and at the bottom of the class structure. Compared to the traditional foreign policy approach, human community is expanded horizontally to include all nations and vertically to encompass all classes.

A second idea that undergirds the proposed value framework is that the service of human needs should be the guiding principle for major economic and political decisions, rather than the maximization of national power or corporate profit. This does not mean that nationhood or profit are excluded, but only that they should rank lower in the hierarchy of values than service to basic human needs. A corollary of this value orientation is that human transactions based on cooperation and a sense of human solidarity would increase, while transactions that are competitive and based on a denial of community would decrease. Competitiveness among large social groups is less useful when the human race is the subject of concern than when only a national group is the focal point for protection, production, and consumption. If fulfilling human needs is to become the guiding principle for policymaking, then those most in need should be the first to receive attention. A politics of liberation, which the fourfold value framework is designed to advance, is like the practice of medicine at its best: to help first those people who are most in need. It differs sharply from theories of politics that call for triage, the lifeboat ethic, or the trickle-down theory of development.

Third, the *entire* planet, the atmosphere around it, and the high seas are of prime concern. They are to be protected and conserved for both present and unborn generations. In contrast, the exponents of the national interest place the exercise of sovereignty over one *part* of the planet's territory at the top of their hierarchy of values. They are concerned with securing advantages for "their" segment of the planet and of the human race, and they pay little attention to the needs of future generations.

The four preferred world order values and the three clarifying principles provide the value framework that I call *global humanism* in the course of this analysis. The *human interest* is the collection of goals and strategies that are consistent with and will advance the values of global humanism. The term *humane world community* is used to mean a universal human identity or all-inclusive sense of human solidarity combined with social norms and institutions that aim at achieving a life of dignity for all through an equitable sharing of decision-making powers, opportunities, and resources. *Global populism* refers both to (1) the emphasis on a citizens' movement to mobilize and empower the poor and politically weak and (2) the introduction of structural reforms inspired by the preferred values and designed to help the dispossessed.

In the course of this study, U.S. foreign policy is evaluated by the extent to which it implements or is designed to implement the values of global humanism.[7] In earlier discussion, I have argued that a foreign policy informed by such a value framework is necessary to insure human security and is desirable to achieve other values on which there is a high degree of consensus in our own society. To assess the impact of U.S. foreign policy upon the prospects for preferred world order reform, a representative case study has been selected to illustrate U.S. performance in each of the four value areas. This performance cannot be understood merely by comparing officially professed values with the values of global humanism. As in any political system, a wide gap often exists between rhetoric and reality. To account for this possible discrepancy, the analyses below will distinguish *professed values* from *implicit values*. The former are the goal values expressed in official statements about U.S. foreign policy. Implicit values are the unspoken value preferences that are embedded in actual political behavior and revealed in the value impact of the policy.

With these definitions in mind, the effort to explain the global meaning of U.S. foreign policy will proceed as follows: The first section of each case study consists of an empirical description of U.S. policy, with an emphasis on revealing the professed and implicit values of U.S. policy. The analysis clarifies whether the real value impact was consistent with the goals proclaimed in the rhetoric. Next, the implicit values are juxtaposed against the values of global humanism to determine whether U.S. policy was helping to realize a humane world community. Fourth, the global humanist value framework is used to develop specific recommendations for future policy in the area of each case study. Finally, some indicators of world order progress are provided in order to enable scholars or political activists to check on future progress in realizing the preferred values.

One purpose of this analysis is to provide a fresh global framework by which to examine the wisdom and utility of U.S. foreign policies. This framework ideally should transcend both the idiosyncracies of this historical era and one's own political culture. I doubtless have been unable to accomplish that fully; thus the framework should be viewed as tentative and subject to refinement and modification.

Before examining U.S. policy itself, it will be useful to look at some implications and applications of the value-centered approach proposed here. We turn now to that discussion.

The Utility of a Value-Centered Approach

This study of foreign policy is a value-centered approach. It delineates the values that guide decision makers in their policy choices and that are expressed in official behavior.[8] A value-centered approach to foreign policy analysis is admittedly a break with the prevailing intellectual tradition. Most foreign policy analysis falls into one of two categories. Some authors treat foreign policy as history. They emphasize a chronological description of events. In contrast, behavioral scientists focus on the processes by which policy is made, negotiated, or executed. They discuss the interactions of officials, the effects of policymaking machinery, the politics of bureaucratic bargaining, or occasionally the psychological origins of policy. In both of these approaches, past scholarship has usually focused on the use of power, without giving much attention to the value impact of policy and to who benefits or should benefit from policies. Traditional approaches have impoverished reality and discouraged use of the imagination by excessive emphasis on the way things are and by inattention to the way they ought to be. In contrast, when a value-centered approach incorporates a rigorous empiricism with explicit attention to values embedded in policy, it yields several advantages.

In the first place, one's understanding of political events is enhanced if international politics is viewed as a value-realizing process. The observer's focus shifts away from examining the processes of political interaction by themselves and from viewing policy consequences merely as discrete events. For example, the values of officials as expressed in several policies may be compared to the global humanist values that this analysis suggests are useful guides for political action. The value impacts of specific foreign policies then provide intellectual handles by which one may grasp the normative direction in which a changing system of world order is moving.

Moreover, if observers examine foreign policy as a value-realizing process, they are able to see more clearly the recurring values that apparently idiosyncratic policies often are advancing. If similar values are repeatedly served by political leaders, one can extrapolate from this the structure of interests or the classes that benefit from the ruling group's policies. This is particularly important in attempting to define the nature of a more just world polity and in developing strategies to attain one. By assessing the desirability and consequences of political action in light of a set of explicit norms, a value-centered approach facilitates a structural analysis of social problems and remedies. This in turn helps to identify both the structures that need reform and the people who can be expected to resist or to support such change.

Whenever a state executes foreign policy, some values are advanced and others are negated. Every major policy issue contains within it a moral issue. Practitioners of foreign policy often disguise the moral code that a state follows in order to obscure the real beneficiaries of acts by the state. A value-centered approach directly attacks this problem by clarifying the implicit values of the ruling group. This provides information essential for the practice of self-government. Because many ordinary citizens implement the leadership's political values by paying taxes or sacrificing their own lives in war, they understandably want not to be deceived about the value impact of their own government's policies.

A value-centered approach also is useful for establishing preferred goals for future behavior. It encourages imaginative thinking about the possibility of change in the international system. Because a value-centered approach explicitly emphasizes human preferences, it helps chart action to reform the existing system. If in making foreign policy officials react to crises as they arise, they are unlikely to think about changing the structure of international relations. If instead they ask themselves how to implement preferred values, they would be more likely to develop alternative visions of future world order systems.

Political leaders seldom follow this approach, but when they do the results stand out boldly against the backdrop of routine diplomacy. For example, when Adlai E. Stevenson was U.S. Representative to the United Nations, he once delivered a speech entitled "Working Toward a World Without War." In it he said, "We do not hold the vision of a world without conflict. We do hold the vision of a world without war—and this inevitably requires an alternative system for coping with conflict. We cannot have one without the other."[9]

To emphasize values does not mean that one must proceed with an idealistic or optimistic view of the future. A value-centered approach may lead to a pessimistic assessment of the prospects for world order reform. One might conclude that the prevailing value perspective of officials departs widely from one's own value preferences. In such a case, the tendency of the actors within the system would be to make the future worse than the present in terms of preferred value realization.

Of course, no process of value clarification can eliminate arbitrariness or subjectivity in selecting preferred values. But this approach underscores the need to make deliberate choices and tradeoffs in the interaction of different values. In the short run at least, some preferred values may conflict with others; all cannot be grasped without the right hand knowing what the left hand is doing. To maximize food production, for example, one may need to use chemical fertilizers or pesticides that pollute. An approach that does not emphasize values obscures the choice among conflicting goals.

Moreover, value clarification can diminish unintended consequences of government behavior. The more explicit and accurate a value impact statement is, the more possible it becomes to make behavior implement value preferences. Without a clear statement of the value impact of a given policy, the possible gap between governmental rhetoric and political reality may go unnoticed. Such a condition could lead citizens to support policies that in practice negate a preferred value that officials have embraced only rhetorically. This could produce citizen behavior that in practice resisted rather than encouraged a desirable change.

A value-centered approach also helps overcome the level-of-analysis problem. That is, by adopting a value framework that can be deliberately constructed so as to reflect planetary rather than strictly national concerns, it is easier to avoid the trap of looking at international relations from a parochial nation-state view. Officials can then give adequate attention to both the total world system and the subsystems within it. Sensitivity to double standards is enhanced by this approach because explicit norms can be universally applied.

It is instructive to examine one example of the level-of-analysis problem that is a central issue in this study and that traditional approaches have seldom clarified. From the nation-state vantage point, diplomacy should protect the interests of the state, usually measured in terms of power. But that is a laissez-faire approach to the interests of the *planet*. The nation-state vantage point is the international variant of the "invisible hand" of classical capitalism. Proponents of this doctrine assumed that separate people or businesses each maximizing their private economic advantages would produce desirable results for the entire society. Likewise, proponents of serving national interests assume that separate nations maximizing their national advantages will produce desirable results for world society. Such an approach is sensitive to the needs of the nation but indifferent to the interests of the planet. It oversimplifies reality by assuming that what is good for the nation is good for the world.

The weakness of the laissez-faire approach is evident in both economics and international relations. There is often a fundamental contradiction between the pursuit of private profit and the service of human needs. Some things that are profitable ought not to be done; some things that ought to be done are not profitable. Similarly, there is often a fundamental contradiction between the pursuit of national advantage of separate states and the service of global human needs. For example, taking fertile land out of production in Kansas or Iowa may be good for U.S. farmers who want to sell wheat or corn at a higher price, but not for malnourished south Asians who want to buy grain at low cost. By using preferred world order values for assessing national policies we are sensitized to this possible contradiction.

Finally, a value-centered approach also holds promise for deepening our understanding and improving the quality of decisions made in the context of a presently inescapable lack of knowledge. For example, no one knows the risks of war that are inherent in the strategy of nuclear deterrence. No one knows whether Indians are more or less secure because their government conducted one nuclear explosion in 1974. No one knows the range of values that would be sacrificed or fulfilled by a deliberate U.S. decision to disarm. When there is little knowledge available for calculating the consequences of decisions, value presuppositions become more important in the choice of behavior. In such cases values determine the outcome of decisions at a more primitive stage. The less certain we are about how to achieve our ends, the more we let our values influence the means we select for immediate action. Thus it is extremely important for policy analysts and citizens to know whether national officials value, say, national power or human life more highly.

To clarify this point, consider the following example of a dearth of knowledge. If U.S. citizens knew that the U.S. nuclear arsenal would eventually involve the United States in a nuclear war that would kill 100 million Americans and leave an additional 50 million with radiation sickness or genetic damage, presumably there would be more intense public pressure to disarm. National power or sovereignty might even be restricted in order to protect human lives. But in the absence of dependable knowledge about the risks inherent in using nuclear deterrence as a means to prevent war, the public prefers to protect national power through augmenting the nuclear arsenal. This preference may take priority over other values, including the value of human life. But the nuclear priority does not *appear* to sacrifice the value of human life because uncertain knowledge about negative consequences enables us to hope for indefinite postponement of nuclear war. The lack of knowledge about risks makes this hope plausible, although the probability of avoiding war permanently may in fact be very remote.

In contrast, abundant knowledge clarifies the relationship between means and ends. In such cases, the means chosen to implement policy must conform to the terminal values one professes to serve, or else the inappropriateness of the means can be quickly shown. For example, if a man living in Chicago values a reunion with friends in Long Island, when making travel plans he would not select a flight to San Francisco. If he did, a travel agent could quickly demonstrate the inappropriateness of the action. On the other hand, lack of knowledge lets a decision maker choose *any* means which his or her value system may prefer, because no one can show that the means selected will not lead to the end professed. (Without dependable information, a flight to San Francisco appears as good as a flight to New York for one's trip to Long Island.)

Thus on foreign policy issues where imponderables abound, alarming results can occur. Decision makers are most likely to choose means that serve their vested interests. If the way to peace is seen as uncertain, then policies might as well benefit the leadership's interests while they pursue peace. Yet an elite's vested interests seldom are congruent with the global human interest, either in its domestic or global manifestations. In this example, the policy decisions might be based on a desire to protect power and wealth for national decision makers and their group of supporters within the nation, not to achieve peace or a humane world community. Who benefits most from the worldwide growth of armaments and the accumulation of U.S. power overseas? A political and economic elite? All U.S. citizens? Humanity? A plausible case could be made that the value impact of additional armaments contributes more certain and immediate benefits to the power and wealth of decision makers than to the achievement of security for the human race in the long run. Until the contrasting values—privileges for national security managers or security for ordinary people—are clear, intelligent policy for world order reform is impossible. A value-centered approach helps reveal the occasionally vested nature of the values being realized.

The Application of a Global Humanist Framework
to Alternative Images of World Order

In addition to the benefits of a value-centered approach listed above, both citizens and officials could use the four values of global humanism to construct a range of future world order options, to compare the value-realizing potential of each, and to select the foreign policies most likely to achieve the preferred values. In contrast to the waning Westphalia system, one might envisage at least four types of future world order systems:[10] a concert of great powers, a concert of multinational corporate elites, world government, and global humanism.[11]

Concert of Great Powers. / One possible future system of world order is a slightly remodeled version of the existing system, with new emphasis on cooperation among the great powers. This could be thought of as a global, twentieth-century equivalent of Metternich's effort to achieve a concert of European great powers after the Congress of Vienna in 1815. The United States, the Soviet Union, Western Europe, Japan, and China could lower tensions among themselves and together administer many of the economic and political affairs of the rest of the world. Because such a system would be hierarchical and inequitable, it would doubtless be exploitative. It probably would not attack worldwide poverty, political repression, or ecological decay. It would flourish with client states and sphere-of-influence politics. It would also work to repress terrorism, to stabilize the world economy, and to exploit ocean resources.

If United States policy aimed to implement this option for achieving international stability, it would give priority to protecting or enhancing its power position vis-à-vis the other great powers, to seeking consensus among the great powers while ignoring the grievances of smaller powers, to defending the dollar in the world monetary system, and to developing strategies to insure access to vital raw materials from foreign markets. The government would be unconcerned about Third or Fourth World countries except insofar as liberation movements or political instability might jeopardize the opportunities for U.S. corporations to invest, buy, or sell abroad, and insofar as the former's political orientation might bear upon the power of the United States within the concert of great powers. When threats to U.S. power would arise, counterrevolutionary intervention by the United States would be likely after seeking concurrence from, or at least neutralizing the opposition of, the Soviet Union or any other relevant great powers.

Concert of Multinational Corporate Elites. / A second variant of future world order is global, private government by multinational corporations. In this model, corporate elites act together to maximize profit and economic growth, to secure worldwide markets, and to protect the wealth and privilege of relatively few owners and managers against the protests of the poverty-stricken masses. Multinational corporate elites managing global resources would probably lead toward dampened international political conflict, increased transnational class conflict, rapid but uneven economic growth in the private sector, use of resources to maximize profit rather than the service of human needs, and relative unconcern about environmental and humanitarian issues. The Trilateral Commission, a group of wealthy, influential business people from North America, Japan, and Western Europe, illustrates this possibility. Its purposes include a transnational effort to adapt corporate capitalism to changing economic and political forces to insure capitalism's future in a nonterritorially-oriented economy facing possible conflicts with territorially-based national governments or dispossessed classes.

Multinational corporations may have some advantages over states in the approaching play of social forces leading to a new system of world order. For the first time in history, managerial skills and technology make the management of

the globe as an integrated unit a genuine possibility.[12] Multinational corporations, as private agencies, can respond with more flexibility and speed to the
functional unity of the globe than many national governments, which are
restrained by nationally-oriented ideological and political inertia. Markets and
the field for investment, after all, are nonterritorial and include the planet,
whereas national governments still operate from a territorial base. The nonterritorial perspective of corporate managers maximizing profits may put them at
odds with the national government ruling the territory in which the corporation is primarily based. For example, when the price of crude oil increases, this
may be much less objectionable to U.S.-based multinational oil corporations
than to the United States government, representing a constituency territorially
more limited in scope than the oil companies themselves. Multinational corporations place less emphasis than national governments on the interests of
one state in the system or the well-being of its domestic population.

U.S. foreign policy could serve this image of world order by facilitating the
movement of capital abroad, by allowing corporations to escape the domain of
any national government's effective regulation, by not restricting high profits
on the corporate provision of vital resources, and by declining to insure that
the major corporations scrupulously respect the environment or serve the
general public rather than private interest. If large corporations are able to influence governmental policies sufficiently, either through the placement of
members of the business elite in positions of political decision making or
through financial support and control of government officials recruited from
outside the business elite, the government itself will serve the interests of
multinational corporations more directly, meanwhile giving less attention to
national interests more traditionally defined as territorially-based security and
prosperity.

World Government. / The prescriptions favored by most traditional advocates of world government are contained in *World Peace Through World Law* by
Grenville Clark and Louis Sohn. They described a greatly strengthened United
Nations with modified voting procedures, world disarmament, and world
federation on a sufficient scale to prevent future military buildups. This model
aims to create "an effective system of *enforceable* world law in the limited field of
war prevention."[13] It gives less attention to the other values of global
humanism.

If U.S. policy were to aim at achieving this option, policymakers would seek
to amend the UN Charter in order to democratize the voting procedures and
qualify the veto principle. In addition, after accepting enhanced decision
making and enforcement authority for the UN, the United States would need
to undertake substantial arms reductions. Until an effective strategy is
developed for implementing this vision, its very low political feasibility makes it
unrealistic in the foreseeable future. Its implementation rests on agreement
among national governments to restrict their sovereignty voluntarily. This is
unlikely given present political attitudes and institutions.

Global Humanism. / A system based on global humanism can be illustrated
by the image of world order developed by the North American team of

participants in the World Order Models Project. Richard A. Falk has elaborated this model in *A Study of Future Worlds*.[14] It calls for drastic changes in the existing configuration of power, wealth, and authority during the next thirty years. The transition strategy calls for widespread education, attitudinal changes, and populist mobilization to realize substantial gains in preferred values without recourse to violence and without the traumas that would attend nuclear war, widespread famine, or ecological collapse.

This model, slightly revised by the present author, is described here in greater detail than the other models because it provides a tentative vision of how the world might look if global humanist values were pursued in U.S. foreign policies.

One particularly appealing feature of the model is that it avoids merely a transferal of state power and authority to a unified world government. Instead, authority and power are dispersed in *two* directions from the national level: "downward" toward provincial or local governments as well as "upward" toward a central guidance agency. The happy result is a form of policy coordination that increases the capacity for global administration without increasing the overall bureaucratic presence in human life at various levels of social organization. Two countervailing organizational tendencies would be present: (1) *centralization* of functional control and planning to enable more equitable allocation of scarce resources, to protect endangered values in the "commons," and to enforce provisions for disarmament; and (2) *decentralization* of political structures combined with localization of identification patterns. The focus of human identity, now pinpointed upon national symbols, would be dispersed to include global human solidarity on the one hand, and increased subnational identification and participation in political and economic decisions on the other.

This model avoids the hierarchical centralization implicit in most classical schemes for world government. It seeks to create global policy coordination with wide dispersion of authority and distribution of power among various actors, such as global and regional intergovernmental organizations, national governments, local or provincial governments, and transnational coalitions of people or private organizations acting in the global arena without going through their respective national governments.

In general, this constitutional structure would tolerate less efficiency to achieve diverse, equitable participation and to inhibit the abuse of concentrated powers. Proposed governing machinery might include the following:

1. A world assembly would set general policy respectful of global humanist values. It would be organized to represent peoples, nongovernmental organizations, states, and regional groups.

2. A smaller council would apply the policy of the assembly and act in its place during emergencies.

3. Supporting administrative agencies would assure that directives of the former bodies are carried out by other actors in the system. It would also provide feedback useful for tailoring policies to fulfill the values of global

humanism. Agencies for implementation would be organized around the
following four functions.

a. A world security system would include a transnational peace force, a
world disarmament service, and a world grievance system. The latter
would insure that all states could respond to policy decisions. It would
also facilitate peaceful change to avoid the danger that a global system
did not merely enforce a peace of the status quo. Individuals and
nongovernmental organizations, as well as governments and intergovernmental organizations, could forward complaints to this body.

b. A world economic system would include agencies for economic planning, equity, world monetary policy, taxing authority, and development. This cluster of agencies would facilitate economic development
aimed at insuring economic well-being for all, promoting intergroup
and intragroup economic equity and achieving balance between human
activity and ecological capacities for disposal and resource use.
Economic policies would be tailored to curtail wasteful growth and to
encourage growth aimed at fulfilling human needs.

c. A human rights commission and court would enhance the prospects for
respecting human dignity and human rights. Any person or group
could take grievances to these bodies.

d. A global environmental authority would establish procedures to
monitor pollutants, to set and enforce waste disposal standards, and to
conserve and allocate scarce resources fairly. The authority would seek
to implement a humane transition from a growth orientation to an
equilibrium orientation respectful both of nature and of human needs.
An effort would be made to establish an index of Gross National Quality to highlight the qualitative rewards that may compensate for the
quantitative decline in Gross National Product which some wealthy
societies may encounter during the effort to equalize world incomes and
to avoid injury to the environment.

The benefits from this system, as well as the strategy for achieving it, are consistent with populism in a global context. This image of world order seeks to
avoid both the multinational corporate elite's tendency to put corporate profit
and growth above human needs and conservation, and the national governmental elite's tendency to impose nationalist advantages and values upon
major political and economic activity, with little regard for global implications.

In contrast to the world government approach, the populist image places
greater emphasis on the likelihood of political conflict with entrenched elites in
the process of transforming the existing system, and on the need to mobilize
support among dispossessed peoples presently not influential in government
processes. The global humanist perspective emphasizes values that transcend
the limits of class and national boundaries and that anticipate the emergence of
a system of nonterritorial central guidance. This perspective is based on an
understanding that the outcome of the present transition period will be deter-

mined by the interplay of statist, business, and populist social forces. This approach reflects a belief that the most beneficial future world order system will be responsive to populist demands for peace, economic equity, social and political dignity, and ecological balance.

The global humanist vision offers a humane alternative to the neo-Darwinian trend in the establishment of a concert of great powers or multinational corporate elites. This trend is encouraged by resource scarcity and political or economic competition, in which both national governmental and corporate elites seek to accumulate more power and prosperity for their respective national or corporate constituencies, neither of which represents humanity at large. The global humanist option seeks to reorient institutions so they will serve the needs of all people rather than the wants of a privileged minority.

Images of the Future and the Content of Foreign Policy

The preceding four images of alternative futures help us understand the present. With an awareness of several alternatives it is easier to appraise the meaning of contrasting foreign policies for the future of humanity. Without some reflection about alternative futures, policymaking is little more than tactical calculation to maintain an unsatisfactory status quo or to gain a short-range advantage in an otherwise aimless drift on the expansive, uncharted waters of the future. Or even worse, some narrowly based but powerful elites may seek to implement an image of the future that the majority of people would oppose if the future world prospects were openly exposed.

The preceding models also enable one to take steps toward the particular future that one desires. Of the four options discussed, world government seems politically unfeasible, and the concerts of great powers or corporate elites are deficient in realizing one or more important values. Therefore, the global humanist image of world order will be used to assess the performance of U.S. policy in the remainder of this study.

The political attractiveness of a vision of world order based on an open, self-correcting understanding of the values of global humanism could be critically important in determining which of several alternative models of the future will in fact become reality. What people implicitly believe about how the world functions and will function in the future contributes to making it function that way in the present as well as in the future. It is commonplace to say that past events influence or determine the present, but growing evidence suggests it is no less accurate to say that one's image of the future determines the present.[15] For example, when a foreign policy bureaucracy views the present international system as continuing indefinitely into the future, that bureaucracy constructs policy in ways that prevent another future from being realized.

In making decisions, an official must extend lines of action into the future and select among alternatives according to his or her expectations about future events.[16] An official's image of the immediate future, even if not explicitly stated, influences current governmental behavior. That behavior opens some doors and closes others for the future. As sociologists Wendell Bell and James

Table 1   A Summary Comparison of Alternative World Order Systems, 1980–2000[a]

Leadership	Westphalian nation-state system	Concert of great powers	Concert of multinational corporations	World government	Humane world community
Basic aspirations	Sovereign independence, unregulated governmental behavior	Geopolitical stability, political and economic inequity	Unregulated economic growth, profit maximization, capital intensive technology, high consumption	Enforced disarmament, strengthened international institutions	Dependable peace, economic well-being for all, respect for human rights and social justice, ecological balance
Strategy for fulfillment of aspirations	Competitive power-seeking in decentralized international system	Consensus of dominant governments, stratified inter-governmental system, regional spheres of influence	Consensus among privileged elites, stratified transnational system	Negotiations among national governments	Global populist movement, major attitudinal and value change
Performance in implementing global humanist values:					
Peace	Low	Medium	High	High	High
Economic well-being	Low	Low	Low	Medium	High
Social justice	Low	Low	Low	Low	High
Ecological balance	Low	Medium	Low	Medium	High
Performance in achieving human solidarity:					
Vertical (transclass) identity	Medium	Medium	Low	Medium	High
Horizontal (transnational) identity	Low	Low	High	Medium	High

[a] Several of the categories in this table are adapted from Richard A. Falk, "A New Paradigm for International Legal Studies," p. 1001.

A. Mau have correctly warned: "Today's images of the future need elaboration, refinement, and revision; the actual future is rolling over people and whole societies before they are prepared; the possibilities of a better life are not being fulfilled as adequately as they could be."[17]

NOTES

1. For a more comprehensive treatment of these themes, see Richard A. Falk, "The Interplay of Westphalia and Charter Conceptions of the International Legal Order," in Richard A. Falk and Cyril E. Black, eds., *The Future of the International Legal Order*, vol. 1 (Princeton: Princeton University Press, 1969), pp. 32–70. See also Richard A. Falk, "A New Paradigm for International Legal Studies," *Yale Law Journal* 84 (April 1975), pp. 978–987.

2. John Herz discussed the demise of the territorial state in *International Politics in the Atomic Age*. He revised his assessment of the end of territoriality in "The Territorial State Revisited," *Polity* 1 (September 1968), pp. 11–34.

3. Garrett Hardin, *Exploring New Ethics for Survival* (Baltimore: Penguin, 1972), p. 254.

4. "On the Origin and Foundation of the Inequality of Mankind," translated by G.D.H. Cole, *The Social Contract and Discourses* (London: J. M. Dent, 1913), p. 194. Kenneth Waltz discusses this passage in *Man, the State and War* (New York: Columbia University Press, 1954), pp. 167–168.

5. Waltz in part suggests this reasoning, *Man, the State and War*, p. 169.

6. This fourfold value framework was first suggested by a transnational group of scholars representing all major regions of the world and participating in the World Order Models Project. Their purpose has been to develop models of a preferred world order for the 1990s. In the early stages of their efforts, they agreed to focus upon these four value areas to provide a basis for studying strategies of world order reform. For an early statement of the objectives of this project, see Ian Baldwin, "Thinking About a New World Order for the Decade 1990," *War/Peace Report* 2 (January 1970), pp. 3–7. For a more recent statement, see Saul H. Mendlovitz and Thomas G. Weiss, "Towards Consensus: The World Order Models Project of the Institute for World Order," in Grenville Clark and Louis B. Sohn, eds., *Introduction to World Peace Through World Law* (Chicago: World Without War Publications, 1973), pp. 74–97. The important products of this project to date are a series of books on "Preferred Worlds for the 1990s," published by the Free Press. See Falk, *A Study of Future Worlds*; Johan Galtung, *The True Worlds*; Rajni Kothari, *Footsteps Into the Future*; Gustavo Lagos and Horacio H. Godoy, *Revolution of Being*; Ali A. Mazrui, *A World Federation of Cultures*; Saul H. Mendlovitz, *On the Creation of a Just World Order*.

7. The values of global humanism could, of course, be used as yardsticks to measure the foreign policy behavior of any government at various points in time. Such indicators could also be used to judge the relative merits of differing policies advocated by competing sets of leadership within a single country at the same time.

8. For the role of values as guides for decision making, see Milton Rokeach, *The Nature of Human Values* (New York: Free Press, 1973), p. 12.

9. The text of this speech of November 15, 1961 was reprinted in United States Arms Control and Disarmament Agency, *Disarmament* (Washington, D.C.: Government Printing Office, 1962), p. 18.

10. The typology and following analysis of alternative models of world order are drawn in part from the ground-breaking scholarship of Richard A. Falk, especially "A New Paradigm," pp. 999–1017.

11. The political structures of each type of system could vary somewhat. A range of normative orientations is also possible in the first three models, although their structures limit the extent to which they could realize the preferred values. The prospects are most severely limited in the first two examples. The models are described in what the author calculates are their most likely manifestations.

12. See Richard Barnet and Ronald Mueller, *Global Reach* (New York: Simon and Schuster, 1974).

13. Clark and Sohn, *World Peace Through World Law* (Cambridge: Harvard University Press, 1960), p. xv. (Italics in original.)

14. Falk, *A Study of Future Worlds*, pp. 224–276.

15. In some cases, development of socially destructive values has correlated more closely with a person's expectation for future conflicts than with the subject's background and experience. For example, Arthur L. Stinchombe found that different images of the future in part determined whether young people rebelled: "the future, not the past, explains adolescent rebellion, contrary to the hypothesis that deviant attitudes are the result of distinctly rebel biographies." *Rebellion in High School* (Chicago: Quadrangle Books, 1964), p. 6, noted in Wendell Bell and James A. Mau, eds., *The Sociology of the Future*, p. 33.

16. Bell and Mau, *Sociology of the Future* (New York: Sage, 1971), p. 18; Harold Lasswell, *The Analysis of Political Behavior: An Empirical Approach* (London: Routledge and Kegan Paul, 1948), and "The Changing Image of Human Nature: The Socio-cultural Aspect, Future-oriented Man," *American Journal of Psycho-Analysis* 26 (1966), pp. 157–166; Heinz Eulau, "H. D. Lasswell's Developmental Analysis," *Western Political Quarterly* 2 (1958), pp. 229–242.

17. Bell and Mau, *Sociology of the Future*, p. 14.

PART TWO

ANALYSIS OF WORLD ORDER VALUES

Peace

INTRODUCTION

The pursuit of peace by preparing for war is perhaps the clearest manifestation of humankind's maladaptive behavior in the present nuclear-ecological era. In 1980, the world's governments spent over $500 billion on arms and armies; if present trends continue, world military expenditures will easily exceed $600 billion in 1982. Even though the superpowers and their alliances account for 80 percent of this spending, the most dramatic increases in military expenditures in recent years have occurred among developing countries. Fueled by increasing arms sales, military assistance programs, and the development of indigenous armament manufacturing in Third World countries, the war system has spread to every corner of the globe, bringing with it previously unanticipated regional arms races and conflicts. It is no longer only the superpowers who are able and willing to use military force. In the period 1977–1981, for example, eleven international conflicts broke out, all of them in the Third World; two of them involved the major use of force among socialist states, i.e., Vietnam and Kampuchea, and China and Vietnam.

These realities of militarization stand in sharp contrast to the efforts of the past century to delegitimize war as an instrument of modern statecraft. On a formal authoritative level at least, the legitimacy of war has been increasingly questioned. The conduct of aggressive wars, for example, has been outlawed in a series of international agreements, including the League of Nations Covenant, the Kellogg Briand Pact (1928), the United Nations Charter, the acceptance in 1954 by the UN General Assembly of the International Law Commission's Codification of the Nuremberg and Tokyo principles with regard to aggression and crimes against humanity, and most recently in the 1974 U.N. Consensus Definition of Aggression adopted by the General Assembly. As well, there have been numerous resolutions calling for arms reduction and other forms of disarmament. The 1980 session of the General Assembly alone passed a record number of 44 disarmament resolutions. Yet despite these normative initiatives, militarism has grown largely unchecked.

Militarism seems to be deeply ingrained in our thinking about international politics in general and national security in particular. Despite the dangers and

219

costs associated with modern warfare, the world's political elites still cling to a Clauswitzian conceptualization of war as an integral part of international politics. Even the development of nuclear weapons has not fundamentally altered this anachronistic concept; military power is still regarded as an important instrument of international diplomacy, necessary for exerting influence in the world as well as for ensuring national security. The doctrine of deterrence is illustrative of the futility and wastefulness of this concept. A seemingly permanent, ever-spiraling nuclear arms race has resulted from a mutually felt need on the part of the two superpowers to deter each other by possessing the capability of delivering an unacceptable level of destruction; as one has increased its capability, so has the other. A similar dynamic seems to be operating in conventional arms races in various regions throughout the world.

There is also a popular belief that war is inevitable. According to this view, violence is inherent in human nature. This Hobbesian reductionism of describing war as a natural, inevitable and universal condition of human life surely stands in the way of public consciousness about the hazards of militarism. Yet, this notion rests on shaky historical and empirical grounds. One leading study has concluded that nation-states have varied so much in the frequency of their participation in wars in modern times such that "none can be properly characterized as inherently belligerent or inherently pacific" (Richardson, 1970:x, 176). Further, a multivariate analysis of 652 primitive societies (taken from A Study of War by Quincy Wright) by Broch and Galtung (1966) shows that only 33 percent of states were "belligerent" in the sense that they were found to have engaged in aggressive warfare for economic and political exploitation. Even more revealing is that the level of belligerency increased with decreasing primitiveness (i.e., increasing civilization). Moreover, there is no conclusive empirical evidence to suggest that human aggression must result in organized warfare. Human society existed for thousands of years before the institution of war arose. Nonetheless, the still prevailing Hobbesian school encourages a fatalistic sense among potential popular forces that a disarmament movement is futile, and reinforces elite acceptance of the "rational" management of the war system rather than pushing for its abolition.

Our world order approach looks beyond this simplistic notion of war as inevitable to consider the deeper structural and systemic explanations for militarism. It rejects one single explanation for war and instead probes deeply into the relationship of war to economic and social justice, to the dynamics of the state system, as well as to prevailing conceptions of national security and international hierarchy. It also avoids a too narrowly conceived definition of peace—that is, peace defined solely in terms of order or stability. Such a definition would appear to suggest a freezing of the status quo at the expense of those struggling to transform the present inequitable system. Traditional peace thinking tended to be preoccupied with negative peace, that is, with the absence of direct violence. Our perspective is concerned with negative peace and with positive peace, which is the absence of structural violence resulting from hunger, poverty, and social injustice.

Our world order approach in turn takes account of the impact that the war system has on the values of economic well-being, social justice, and ecological balance. The threat of war not only presents a clear and present danger to human survival, it also claims and diverts resources from a more humane and just allocation of goods and services at a time of acute resource scarcity and ecological deterioration. There is evidence, as well, linking arms to repression domestically and to the maintenance of dominance internationally. Understanding the relationship and interaction among the world order values is one of our central concerns throughout this book.

The first work in this section, by Kenneth E. Boulding, presents a sophisticated interpretation of the evolution of war. Boulding observes that organized warfare did not arise until the advent of cities, thus challenging the widely held view referred to above that war is the inevitable consequence of human aggression. Boulding cogently argues that war has already become dysfunctional and that it now stands as the most serious obstacle in the transition from civilization to postcivilization. He contends that the abolition of war is primarily a problem of social learning. Boulding's concern centers on learning rational ways and means of conflict management, not of conflict elimination, to avoid the dangerous war trap. For Boulding, "conflict is not a bad thing in itself;" in fact, it is "an essential element in that creative process by which evolution proceeds." But as Boulding notes, conflicts tend to get out of hand, and thus institutions of third-party intervention to control conflict on a world scale are needed.

The prevention of nuclear war, however, may be structurally more complicated and difficult than Boulding suggests. Proposals for conflict management and disarmament have abounded for years, with no results. Like Hedley Bull (1977), Boulding also seems to betray a privileged Western bias by defining "peace" in terms of maintaining the stability of the existing international order. One may also question Boulding's suggestion that decolonization has created a new threat to world order by giving birth to so many Third World countries whose international behavior is "immature and pathological." Such "hegemonic" peace thinking has been institutionalized in the norms and rules of the present nonproliferation regime, which allows a few countries to possess nuclear weapons while denying this right to all others. In maintaining that the greatest dangers to the world arise from those states that do not possess such weapons, the nuclear superpowers have diverted attention from the dangers resulting from their own nuclear arsenals and geostrategic games.

In the second selection, Dieter Senghaas avoids the normative traps of traditional peace thinking by presenting a macro-structural theory of contemporary international society. Senghaas conceptualizes conflict formations in contemporary world politics as a function of new domination structures, not as the outbreak of random processes. Peace is conceptualized not merely as an avoidance of war or violence but as a dynamic development of social justice, an emphasis that Senghaas says is justified because "those conflicts which arise under conditions of gross social injustice (*structural violence*) have in the past ten years even become more frequent than the classical type of war between states." Senghaas advances what may be called "a struggle theory of just peace," presenting a counterargument to Boulding's conventional peace thinking. The underdevelopment of the Third World is seen as a constituent part of the ongoing historical process dominated by the capitalist metropoles.

From this nonconventional macro-analysis of international structures of domination, Senghaas suggests an equally nonconventional prescription for peace: "Because other channels of social change have been foreclosed," Senghaas argues "that revolution . . . to overcome social injustice must be integrated into a concept of peace promotion." Does Senghaas shift too much of the attention from "world peace" to "world justice," or can such a broadened conception of "peace" be operationalized without any value tradeoffs?

The third selection, by Leo Tolstoy, presents an eloquent testimonial of the extent to which our consciousness has been corrupted by the inhumane logic of the nation-state system. Tolstoy also reminds us of the extent to which Christianity also has been corrupted in the service of national interests by providing justifications for deliberately killing human beings. Inspired by the heroism of the young Dutch conscientious objector van der Meer, Tolstoy declares that killing even in war is a crime, and thus lays the moral and intellectual basis for the "crime against humanity" articulated in the Nuremberg and Tokyo trials of 1945. Tolstoy's essay is a powerful and poetic sermon for the transformation of our consciousness. It also suggests how individual heroism wedded to the highest moral cause of serving humanity can serve as a catalyst for a wider social movement to abolish the war system.

In the next work, Robert Johansen graphically illustrates the failures of existing security policies and presents a cogent case for a series of specific system-changing strategies for building an alternative security system. In contrast with the technological and managerial orientation of mainstream scholarship in the field of arms control and disarmament, this monograph is an expression of "world order realism." Johansen argues that "the very nature of the system of sovereign states encourages armed rivalry between governments." Because "security" is a central *raison d'être* of the state, there is no escape from a self-perpetuating arms race as long as the militarized conception of security remains unchanged and the present security system remains untransformed.

At the same time, Johansen does not succumb to fatalistic determinism. Instead, he undertakes an exercise in positive peace thinking by sketching out scenarios for overcoming the age-old scepticism about system change and by proposing ways and means of building an appropriate alternative security system. The reader may, of course, wish to take issue with some specific proposals for system change as being undesirable, infeasible or unworkable, but it is such a dialogue on system-changing strategies that enlivens and energizes the development of world order studies as part of a global populist movement to demilitarize world society.

The last piece in this section is a third-system document on the war/peace problematique. It was issued on the occasion of the International Workshop on Disarmament, held in New Delhi, 27–31 March 1978; eighty-seven scholars and activists from different parts of the world draw attention to the normative and structural linkage between nuclear hegemony and social injustice in the present militarized world order. This document is historic in declaring that the possession and manufacture as well as the use and threat of use of nuclear weapons are crimes against humanity. (It should be noted that the UN General Assembly adopted a similar but more limited resolution [35/152D] on December 12, 1980, declaring, *inter alia*, that the use of nuclear weapons is "a crime against humanity.")

The New Delhi Declaration is also notable because it specifies a set of different but mutually complementary prescriptive tasks for various groups to undertake as part of a global coalition for a demilitarized world order. Governments are prodded to sign a proposed Nuclear Disarmament Treaty; the peoples of the world are called upon to seize the initiative in working toward an alternative security system; and scientists, technologists and intellectuals are challenged to abandon their complicity in the war system and join instead the peoples of the world in the service of peace. As an alternative security system that would unite the rich and the poor, the nuclear haves and have-nots, and the young and the old, the Declaration proposes the establishment of a World Commission for Disarmament and Development.

QUESTIONS FOR DISCUSSION AND REFLECTION

What are the main causes of the arms race? Who gains and who loses most in this arms race? What are the social costs or benefits of the arms race?

What are the main obstacles to disarmament? Who would gain or lose most with disarmament? What would be the societal costs or benefits in such a disarmed world?

How do you respond to the perennial debate and tension between "order" and "justice?" Is it possible to eliminate war without eliminating the most grievous forms of structural violence?

What does national security mean in this period of nuclear weapons and ecological constraints? Do you think there is a difference between the security needs of ruling elites and those of the people? Do armaments represent the best means for providing people's security?

What alternative security systems can you imagine? Is the world security organization Johansen suggests a desirable and realistic alternative?

Based on your own criteria of desirability, feasibility, and workability, what specific elements in the New Delhi Declaration make sense and which ones do not? Why?

SELECTED BIBLIOGRAPHY

Beer, Francis A. *Peace Against War: The Ecology of International Violence.* San Francisco: W. H. Freeman & Co., 1981.

Beres, L. R. *Apocalypse: Nuclear Catastrophe in World Politics.* Chicago: University of Chicago Press, 1980.

Brock, T., and J. Galtung. "Belligerence Among the Primitives: A Re-Analysis of Quincy Wright's Data," *Journal of Peace Research*, Vol. 3 (1966), pp. 33–45.

Calder, Nigel. *Nuclear Nightmares*. New York: Viking Press, 1979.

Caldicott, Helen. *Nuclear Madness: What Can We Do?* Brookline, MA.: Autumn Press, 1979.

Falk, Richard, and Samuel Kim, eds. *The War System: An Interdisciplinary Approach*. Boulder, CO.: Westview Press, 1980.

Frank, Jerome D. *Sanity and Survival: Psychological Aspects of War and Peace*. New York: Random House, 1967.

Gandhi, Mohandas. *Nonviolence in Peace and War*. New York: Garland, 1971.

Gompert, David C., et al. *Nuclear Weapons and World Politics*. New York: McGraw-Hill, 1977.

Herz, John H. *International Politics in the Atomic Age*. New York: Columbia University Press, 1959.

Keys, Donald, and Ervin Laszlo. *Disarmament: The Human Factors*. New York: Pergamon, 1981.

Melman, Seymour. *The Permanent War Economy: American Capitalism in Decline*. New York: Simon & Schuster, 1974.

Myrdal, Alva. *The Game of Disarmament*. New York: Pantheon, 1976.

Nelson, Keith L., and Spencer C. Olin, Jr. *Ideology, Theory and History*. Berkeley, CA.: University of California Press, 1979.

Richardson, Lewis F. *Statistics of Deadly Quarrels*. Pittsburgh: The Boxwood Press, 1960.

Shawcross, William. *Side-Show: Kissinger, Nixon and the Destruction of Cambodia*. New York: Simon & Schuster, 1979.

Singer, J. David, and Melvin Small. *The Wages of War 1816–1965*. New York: John Wiley & Sons, 1972.

Sivard, Ruth Leger. *World Military and Social Expenditures 1980* (Annual). Leesburg, VA.: World Priorities, 1980.

Walzer, Michael. *Just and Unjust Wars: A Moral Argument with Historical Illustrations*. New York: Basic Books, 1979.

Wright, Quincy. *A Study of War*. Chicago: University of Chicago Press, 1965.

15
THE WAR TRAP

Kenneth Boulding

I have suggested earlier that although the great transition from civilization to postcivilization is now under way in many parts of the world, there is no guarantee that it will be completed successfully. I have identified at least three traps which may either delay or prevent the accomplishment of this transition and may even lead to irretrievable disaster and to a total setback to the evolutionary process in this part of the universe. The three traps may be labeled briefly war, population, and entropy. Any one of them could be fatal. Not one of them has to be fatal. And the more self-consciously aware we are as a human race of the nature of the traps that lie before us the better are the chances of avoiding them.

The war trap is the most immediate and urgent. The movement in technology in this area is so rapid that a strong case can be made that this is a problem which must be solved in this generation, for consequences of failure may be fatal. The reason is of course that the scientific revolution and even more the revolution in organized research and development have had a concentrated effect in the field of military technology and weaponry. There has been an enormous increase in man's powers of destruction—at least in the rapidity with which he can employ these powers—and a spectacular increase in the range and deadliness of his deadly missiles. This has created a revolution in the art of war which makes the whole existing political structure of the world dangerously obsolete, and makes the consequences of political breakdown much more serious for mankind than they used to be. A major nuclear war at the present time would certainly be a massive setback, and in view of our ignorance of its ecological consequences it is at least possible that it might be an irretrievable disaster. Furthermore, the process of research and development in weaponry which has produced the present situation continues in spite of the nuclear test ban. Most of the major powers are putting resources into research and development of chemical and bacteriological weapons which may easily exceed in ultimate deadliness the more spectacular nuclear weapons. If research and development in weaponry and the means of destruction continue at the rate of

From *The Meaning of the Twentieth Century* by Kenneth Boulding. Volume 34 of the World Perspectives Series edited by Ruth Nanda Anshen. Copyright © 1964 by Kenneth E. Boulding. Reprinted by permission of Harper & Row, Publishers, Inc.

the last twenty years, the process would almost certainly lead to the development of what Herman Kahn[1] calls the "doomsday machine," which will have the power to end all life on earth. Under these circumstances the search for stable peace takes on an urgency and an intensity which it has never had before in the history of mankind.

It is probably true, as Toynbee suggests, that war has been the downfall of all previous civilizations. These disasters in the past, however, have been essentially local in character. In some local areas such as Crete or Carthage the setbacks were so severe that the region never fully recovered. For mankind as a whole, with some minor ups and downs, the spread of civilization from its sources in Mesopotamia, the Indus Valley, and Shang China has represented an almost continuous geographical expansion. In spite of barbarian conquests and the destruction by war of many cities, it is doubtful whether the total number of people living in cities has ever declined absolutely for more than a century or two at a time. The character of war has changed so drastically in the last generation, however, that we may well regard the Second World War as the last of the "civilized" wars in spite of the airplane and the A-bomb. The destruction which it caused was largely repaired in less than a generation.

A strong case can be made for the proposition that war is essentially a phenomenon of the age of civilization and that it is inappropriate both to precivilized and postcivilized societies. It represents an interlude in man's development, dated 3000 B.C. to, say, 2000 A.D. It is particularly associated with the development of cities by the expropriation through coercion of the food surplus from agriculture. It is significant that the neolithic villages which preceded the development of cities, in which agriculture was practiced but the surplus from agriculture was not yet collected into large masses to feed urban organization, seem to have been very peaceful. Most neolithic villages, as far as we can judge from the archaeological remains, were unwalled and undefended. Between the invention of agriculture about 8000 B.C. and the first cities of about 3000 B.C. we have the world-wide spread of a remarkably uniform neolithic agricultural culture from its origins in the hills above Mesopotamia west to the extremities of Europe, and east into Asia and the Americas, with Africa south of the Sahara and Australia as the last refuge of the paleolithic hunter. We can hardly doubt that there were many violent encounters between the neolithic farmers and the paleolithic hunters and food gatherers whom they so largely displaced, but these were not organized as war.

With the coming of civilization we have quite a new picture. It is true that by reason of its remoteness the civilization of Harappa and Mohenjo-daro in the Valley of Indus seems to have enjoyed many centuries of peace. These, however, were the remote provincial outposts, and in the center of civilization in Mesopotamia the cities were walled almost from the start. Indeed even before Sumer, Jericho, which may reasonably be claimed to be the oldest city in the world, was a warlike city and itself was destroyed many times. Sometimes as in Egypt an initial period of internal war is followed by the unification of a country cut off from the outside world and a long period of internal peace follows. As contact with the outside world increases, however, the incidence of war once again rises.

This association of war with the urban revolution is no accident. I have suggested that the urban revolution itself is the result of the imposition of a threat system on a society possessing a surplus of food from agriculture. The collection of food from large numbers of farmers and its concentration in the cities is not at first so much the result of exchange as the result of coercion. As suggested earlier, in the first instance the coercion was probably spiritual, and the first city-states seem to have been theocracies. The farmer is threatened with the spiritual disaster if he does not turn over a proportion of his food to the priestly caste. The king, however, soon succeeds the priest as the main organizer of the threat system. Indeed, it was on the alliance of king and priest—that is, of temporal and spiritual coercion—that the urban revolution mainly rests. The concentrated food surplus then enabled the king to organize armies. An army is essentially a movable city. It is an organization quite distinct from mere banditry, raiding, and casual violence, and war is a matter of the interaction of organized armed forces. It requires as its prerequisite the urban revolution—that is, a surplus of food from agriculture collected in one place and put at the disposal of the single authority. Where that single authority is unchallenged from outside, as in favorable situations such as the Indus Valley or the Nile Valley, it might be that a stable system of threat on the part of the ruler and submission on the part of the ruled could be established which would last for many centuries. In more open, less protected, or more thickly populated countries like Mesopotamia the coercion system soon degenerated into war.

The reason for this is very simple. It is due to the fundamental principle that the ability of a threatener to carry out his threat diminishes the farther away from the seat of authority one travels. This is simply because it costs something to transport violence and the means of violence, or even more subtle instruments of doing harm. Like goods, "bads" have a cost of transport. The principle of "the further the weaker" (one should add "beyond a certain point") is an iron law of all organization. The king and the priest can therefore set up a very effective coercive apparatus within the home territory. As they go away from the center, however, eventually they get to the point where their capability of carrying out threats is so diminished that the possibility arises of an independent locus of power. Another king or priest can then arise with a system of counterthreats. Submission is no longer necessary for those beyond the range of the old centers, and so defiance becomes possible. We then get a rival center of power, and the relation between the two power centers is almost inevitably that of counterthreat or deterrence.

A counterthreat system is one in which each party says to the other, "If you do something nasty to me I will do something nasty to you." Such a system may be fairly stable for short periods. But it has a fatal instability. Its stability depends on the mutual credibility of the threats. The credibility of threat is a curious and highly subjective variable of social systems, for it is the credence which I attach to your threat and you to mine that is significant, and this may depend as much on the character of the threatened as on the character of the threatener. Furthermore, the credibility of a threat may be only loosely related to the capability of carrying it out, even though there is undoubtedly a relationship of some sort between the two. It is quite possible, however, for one party to be capable of damaging another and for the other not to believe it, or alternatively, I may believe that you have a capability of threatening me which in fact you do not possess. What is clear, however, is that if threats are not carried out their credibility gradually declines. Credibility, as it were, is a commodity which depreciates with the mere passage of time.

In the old days—that is, in civilized societies—capability also frequently depreciated if it was not used. Armed forces, for instance, had a certain tendency to degenerate during peacetime and were re-formed and strengthened during war. This latter phenomenon is less true today in an age of research and development than it was in a cruder and more empirical age. If the credibility of threats in a counterthreat or deterrence system depreciates, however, the time eventually comes when the threats are no longer credible enough to keep the system stable. One party or the other decides that it believes so little in the threats of its potential opponent that it can defy them. When this happens the system experiences crisis. If one threatener is defied the next move in the system is up to him; ordinarily he sees only two choices, either to carry out the threat, which will be costly to him as well as to his defier, or not to carry it out—in which case his future credibility is likely to be impaired. There are possible exceptions to this rule. The failure to carry out a threat the first time it is defied may induce the belief that the threat is more likely to be carried out after a second act of defiance. At some points in this process, however, the threatener is always faced with the grim choice of carrying out the threat or of seeing the whole organization which is based on the threat system collapse, and if he sees nothing to take its place he is likely to carry out the threat at whatever cost to himself or to the defier.

War, therefore, is peculiarly a property of a system of deterrence under urban—that is, civilized—conditions. The cyclic character of war is clearly a product of a system of deterrence which, as we have seen, will be stable for a while but will eventually break down into war. Even from its earliest days, however, the object of war was peace—that is, the re-establishment of a workable and at least temporarily stable system of deterrence again. There are of course a number of different kinds and outcomes of war. There is the limited war characteristic of some periods of history which represents, as it were, the trying out or testing of threat capabilities and the re-establishment of a somewhat revised system of credibilities without much fundamental change in the structure of existing states. The wars of Europe in the eighteenth century, war in almost any feudal age, the wars of the Greek cities before Alexander—or perhaps it would be safer to say before the fall of Athens—were limited war systems.

Sometimes, however, the deterrence system becomes too unpleasant to be stable, and we find wars of conquest and consolidation in which states are actively eliminated. There are also wars of super conquest, such as those of

Alexander or of the Roman Empire, which have as their objective the establishment of a world state or at least a state with no challengers. A state which experiences a long series of successes in limited wars may easily get ambitions to
be a world state, and if at the same time it comes into the exclusive possession
of a superior military technology this aim may be accomplished. In the age of
civilization, however, world states were fundamentally unstable, mainly
because of the high cost of transportation which constantly permitted the
establishment of rival centers of power. The empires of great personal conquerors, Alexander, Alaric, Genghis Khan, and the like, have fallen apart immediately on the death of the conqueror himself. Empires of organization like
the Roman Empire have been able to resist the tendency to fall apart over
longer periods, as organization can to some extent diminish the cost of
transport of military power. But even the Roman Empire was too large for the
techniques of its day and eventually gave way to a large number of succession
states, as did the Turkish Empire which eventually succeeded it. The instability
of empire, the instability of peace, and the cyclical stability of war compose the
constant theme of the whole age of civilization from 3000 B.C. to the present
time.

I have said earlier, however, that civilization is passing away, and that this is
the meaning of the twentieth century. The technical changes introduced by the
scientific revolution are so great that we are passing into a new state of man. In
this condition stable peace becomes necessary. A world state becomes possible
though not necessary, and war becomes so costly and inefficient as a means
either of gaining or preserving values that its abandonment is progressively
organized. The crucial element in this revolution lies not so much in the increased destructiveness of particular weapons, important as this is, as in the increase in the range of deadliness and the general decline in the cost of transport
of the means of violence. The destructiveness of modern weapons is so great
and so spectacular that we are apt to exaggerate its importance. The limit of
destructiveness is total destruction, and this was reached a long time ago.
Babylon, Nineveh, Carthage, and Jerusalem were destroyed just as completely,
indeed probably more completely, than Hiroshima or Nagasaki, or even Hamburg and Tokyo. The destruction of cities did not begin with nuclear weapons
nor even with high explosives and airplanes. We can now destroy them more
rapidly than we used to do, but certainly no more completely.

What is different in the present situation is that we can effect total destruction at much longer range than we used to be able to do. A system of deterrence will develop, as we have seen, if the capability and the credibility of the
threatener diminish rapidly enough with increase in distance from his center so
that at some point, say x miles away, a new center of threats can be established
and a counterthreat system set up. The question is how far is x. When weapons
consisted of battle axes, spears, and bows and arrows in the hands of casual and
unorganized tribesmen, their threat capability might decline very rapidly as
they moved away from their headquarters. Under these circumstances the city-
states could prosper, and the wall around the city reduced the threat capability
of potential enemies to negligible proportions within the city boundaries. Even

the city-state, however, proved to be unstable the moment the organized army (a guided missile on legs) was invented, even though city-states constantly reappear for short periods in the ebb and flow of military organizations. It is not quite clear who invented the organized army, but it is plausible at any rate to credit Sargon as the first builder of empire and the welder of city-states into an imperial domain.

Even the organized army, however, had its limits. The farther it got from home the harder it was to feed and organize. Even in the Second World War this principle was important. As Hitler's armies moved into Russia their lines of communication became longer, they became harder to supply, and they became weaker. As the Russians moved back, their lines of communication became shorter and they became stronger. At Stalingrad, at Leningrad, and before Moscow an equilibrium was reached temporarily in a long line where the Germans and Russians were of equal strength. Then the Germans overstrained the resources of the Reich, and German armies were rolled right back into Germany and destroyed. It is clear, however, that any increase in the effective range of the means of violence, whatever these are, is likely to increase the minimum size of the viable state and to diminish the number of such which can coexist.

A further complication in the situation is the existence of projectiles – that is, instruments of destruction which are not carried by hand but are shot to take effect at a distance from the organized armed force. If a state is to be viable in the military sense it must be able to dominate an area around its essential heartland equal in width to the range of the enemy's deadly projectile. Otherwise the enemy can squat within the range of the essential values and shoot at them without ever occupying the territory in person. An increase in the range of the projectile has revolutionized warfare and political relations of states almost as dramatically as an increase in the range of the armies. Thus the invention of the crossbow had a profound effect upon personal warfare, and the invention of firearms an even more striking effect. It has often been remarked that gunpowder destroyed the feudal system even though its foundations had no doubt been weakened by economic factors. Both the feudal castle and the walled city were useless in the face of gunpowder, and new forms of social organization had to be developed to take their place. This is largely a result of the increase in the range of the projectile.

The significance of the military revolution of the twentieth century is that there has been an enormous increase in the range of the deadly projectile and a very substantial diminution in the cost of transportation of organized violence of all kinds, especially of organized armed forces. The range of the deadly projectile, which covered only a few feet or at most a few yards in the days of arrows and spears, a few hundred yards in the early days of gunpowder, a few miles in the beginning of the twentieth century, and a few hundred miles by the time of the Second World War, is now rapidly approaching twelve and a half thousand miles – that is, half the circumference of the earth. This is the end of a long historic process. It cannot go any further than this and be significant. This means, however, that no place on earth is out of range, and the missile and the nuclear warhead have potentially made the conventional national states as obsolete as gunpowder made the feudal baron and the walled city. By the time of the Second World War it was clear that national states the size of France and Germany were no longer what I call unconditionally viable, as they probably had been even in the early twentieth century. In the Second World War it was clear that the Soviet Union and the United States alone perhaps of all the states of the world retained their unconditional viability, in the sense that they were both large enough for each to be stronger than the other or any likely combination of states at home. France and Germany could be overrun. The Soviet Union could not.

But the developments of the last twenty-five years have profoundly changed the picture. Both the United States and the Soviet Union have the power to do unacceptable damage to each other, and each from points well within their own boundaries. Under these circumstances it is reasonable to assume that unconditional viability has disappeared from the earth and that if we are to retain a world of national states we must all learn to live at each other's mercy. This is not an unprecedented situation. We have in fact had to learn to do this in our personal relations, certainly since the invention of firearms—which had much the same impact on personal viability that the nuclear missile has on national viability. The invention of firearms and perhaps, even earlier, of the crossbow—it is significant that gentlemen never wore crossbows, only swords—led with surprising rapidity to personal disarmament over a very large range of human life and society. Indeed in the modern world a personal threat system backed up by a personal armament survives only in criminal and juvenile delinquent cultures or in remote and undeveloped parts of the world. It is reasonable to suppose that the development of the nuclear missile will have much the same effect on international relations and that it will lead to the abandonment of large-scale organized warfare as an instrument of national policy just as firearms led to personal disarmament and the abandonment of the use of weapons in personal relations.

It is easy to see that only a system of national disarmament which is close to universal and complete can ensure stability or even national defense in a world such as we have today. It is not so easy to see the dynamic steps which will lead to such a system, nor are we sure what the institutions will have to be to ensure stability of such a system once we have arrived at it. The system of general and complete disarmament will be stable if it pays no one to break it—that is, if it pays no one to rearm. Two conditions may generate such a situation. The first is where the pay-offs to peaceful activity are so great that the possible pay-offs of developing even a one-sided threat system do not look attractive by comparison. The second is the existence of an apparatus of law and government which can diminish the pay-offs to one-sided threats through the invoking of punishment.

The first condition has certainly been an important factor in personal disarmament. For most of us the gains which we might have obtained by armed robbery or enslavement seem very uncertain and meager as compared with the rewards of participating in the business of peaceful economic development. The second condition—the policeman and the law—reinforces the first, especially in cases where the first breaks down.

The same is undoubtedly true these days for nations. There may have been some economic pay-offs to military adventure in the sixteenth, seventeenth, and eighteenth centuries. By the nineteenth century, however, the scientific revolution was so far under way that it began to be apparent that one could get a lot more out of the knowledge of nature than one could out of the exploitation of man. In the twentieth century it is even more apparent that countries which stay home and mind their own business well will get rich, whereas military adventure has a strongly negative rate of return, as the cases of Germany and Japan indicate. Even empire, which is the result of the past military adventure, has become a burden rather than a benefit to the imperial country. Indeed the imperial powers have been getting rid of their empires as fast as they can, with the single exception of poor obsolete Portugal. On the other hand the absence of an effective international policeman and government presents grave dangers where national policymakers have unrealistic images or are emotionally disturbed, so that the first condition is not enough.

The general conclusion of this argument is that man is now faced with the problem of getting rid of war, and this is a unique and unprecedented problem peculiar to the twentieth century. In the age of civilization war was a stable social institution, and for mankind as a whole, a tolerable one. In the twentieth century the system of international relations which was based on unilateral national defense has broken down because of the change in the fundamental parameters of the system, and war has therefore become intolerable. There are many serious thinkers who believe that man is not capable of solving this problem, and that hence he is literally doomed to extinction.

The argument of this chapter, however, permits at least a modest optimism. We have to concede to the pessimists that the probability of irretrievable disaster for mankind within the next few decades, or certainly within a next few centuries, is a positive number. We do not know how large a number this is and one hopes that it is fairly small. As long as it is a positive number, however, no one can feel really secure about the future of himself or of his descendants. We may dramatize the present world situation by saying that every day the hand of fate dips into a bag containing one black ball amid many white balls: the black ball of nuclear disaster. Up to now, every day, fate has brought up a white ball, and the world goes on, but the black ball is still in the bag, and as long as it remains there no one can feel very secure about his future.

On the optimistic side of the picture, however, we have a chance of getting the black ball out of the bag through a learning process. The problem of the abolition of war is essentially a problem in social learning. I know of no theorem which says that man is incapable of this process. As long as he is capable of it, there is also a positive probability that in the future we shall get the black ball of disaster out of the bag of fate. It is this race between learning and disaster which makes the present age so exciting and of such unique significance.

The field of social learning which is relevant to this problem is the process by which man learns to manage his conflicts. It is important to notice that it is the management of conflict and not the elimination of conflict which is the essential problem. If the future of mankind depended on the elimination of conflict the outlook would be black indeed. As long as there is life, there is almost bound to be conflict. Furthermore, conflict is not a bad thing in itself. It is indeed an essential element in that creative process by which evolution proceeds. Conflict, however, has a strong tendency to get out of hand and to become destructive. There are well-recognized dynamic processes in the interaction of individuals, organizations, or the states by which conflict becomes intensified. These are the processes involved in arms races, price wars, and mounting tensions and quarrels. These are now better understood than they used to be, thanks in part to the pioneering work of Lewis Richardson in his book *Arms and Insecurity* (Chicago, Quadrangle Press, 1960).

An expression of the same kind of instability in conflict situations is found in game theory under the delightful title of the "prisoner's dilemma." This can be illustrated in terms of the problem of armaments. Suppose we have two countries, A and B. Each can be either armed or disarmed. If both are disarmed both will be better off; call this position 1. They will be richer and more secure than under any other conditions of the system. Unfortunately, however, this happy situation may be unstable. If one country remains disarmed it will pay the other country to arm; call this position 2. Even though this reduces total welfare the armed country may enforce a distribution of this smaller total in its favor, so that it is absolutely better off than before. Either country may take the initiative in this. If, for instance, A arms while B is disarmed (position 2a) then A may be better off than if both are disarmed, but B will be much worse off. In this situation, however, it may pay B to arm, leading to position 3, with both armed. The total welfare will be less than in the second situation, but B may redistribute this diminished total toward himself and so will be better off than he is when he is disarmed and A is armed, although both parties will be worse off when they are both armed (position 3) than when they are both disarmed (position 1). This presents an almost universal problem in social life, and a great many social institutions have been devised to try to push the system back into the most favorable position (1) and keep it there. The institutions of government, law, police, education, and religion can all be interpreted partly in this light.

Putting the problem in the form of the prisoner's dilemma reveals immediately that there are two lines of attack on its solution. The first is to change the behavior of the parties to conflict themselves, so that they come to take long views and learn to be realistic about the ultimate consequences of their behavior. In the prisoner's dilemma situation, suppose each party is longsighted so that each realizes that arming unilaterally will benefit him only for a while, and will eventually make him worse off because of the reaction of the other party. Then the initial step from position 1 to position 2 will never be taken. The building in of resistance to short-run temptations because of a long-run point of view is one of the major objectives of moral education, and it is an important element in the whole learning process. Without this, indeed, society would be impossible. The apparatus of law, for instance, would be quite helpless in the face of the widespread individual action to violate it. Law and police operate only at the fringes of society. Unless there is a solid center in which people refrain from taking the short-run advantages of immoral behavior because they have learned to internalize a value system which is based on long-run consequences, the social system could not operate at all. We have seen examples indeed at certain times and places in which the social system has disintegrated into banditry and universal violence, in a Hobbesian war of all against all. In such a situation the mere formal institutions of law, order, and government cannot prevail or even come into being, unless there is a widespread process of moral learning among the individuals of the society by which they learn to moderate their own behavior by social values.

An important and much neglected aspect of the dynamics of a system of this kind is the problem of how a system which moves from position 1 to position 2, in which one party is armed while the other is still disarmed, can be moved back into position 1 instead of going to position 3 of mutual armament. Going back to the terminology of the first part of this chapter, we might say that this problem involves the creative response to threat by which a learning process is set up in the whole system which will eventually restore it to the first position. There are many historical records, for instance, in which the "saint" has overcome the "bandit" and restored him to a place in society. This is perhaps an extreme case, but even at more humdrum level we have developed a large number of techniques which might be described generally as "disarming." The whole history of the rise of politeness needs to be written in the light of this view of social dynamics. The handshake, the bow, the polite form of speech, and the "soft answer that turneth away wrath" constitute a vital part of the techniques of conflict management, yet to my knowledge they have never been recognized as such or given the importance in human history which they deserve.

It is significant that the word civility and the word civil derive from the same root as the word civilization. The age of civilization is characterized not only by conquest, military ruthlessness, and the predominance of the threat as an organizer. It is also characterized by the development of elaborate integrative systems of religion, politeness, morals, and manners. The dynamics of this process whereby the rough feudal baron was turned into a "gentleman"—again the literal meaning of the word is highly significant—is a process that has never been adequately studied, yet it may well be the most important single process in a whole dynamics of the age of civilization, for it is the process which permitted the rise of civil society, without which science would have been impossible. There is a subtle combination of submission and defiance to threat which undermines the threat system itself because it unites the threatener and the threatened in a single integrative social system. This is an art which man has practiced without self-consciousness for thousands of years. It might well be that one of the significant things that is happening in the twentieth century is that man is becoming self-conscious about this process and hence may be able to conduct it more efficiently than hitherto. If this is so it is a genuine source for optimism, for it means that we can set about in a rational and conscious way the elimination of the international threat system which propagates and perpetuates war, and put in its place a genuine system of world integrative relationships.

At the political level this argument may seem strange to us, although it is interesting to see the already enormous development in the twentieth century of what might be called integrative elements in the foreign policies of states—such things, for instance, as cultural exchange, information agencies, even propaganda. As these things are institutionalized they cannot fail to have a profound effect on the behavior of the states themselves. Even propaganda that is initially conceived as an adjunct to the threat system, and that is deliberately and cynically designed to deceive its unwary recipient, may react back on the propagandist, who may eventually come to believe even his own propaganda. Something like this may have happened, for instance, with the massive peace propaganda which has been put out by the Communist countries in the last twenty years. Something which may start off as a hypocritical instrument of national power ends by taking on a life of its own and profoundly affecting the value systems of those who have propagated it. Similarly in the United States, as Gunnar Myrdal pointed out in *The American Dilemma*, the great moral principles of the nation as enshrined in the Declaration of Independence, the Constitution, and the Gettysburg Address have acted with unrelenting pressure in the society to emancipate the Negro and to bring him toward full citizenship. Wherever the professed ideals of a society diverge from its realities, even though these ideals may be conceived sentimentally and used cynically, a constant long-run pressure is set up to bring the reality closer to the ideal.

The ideal of what might be called mature conflict behavior on the part of both individuals and states, or other organizations, is more important in the modern world than many have recognized, though the concept has never received a powerful literary expression. In the case of individual behavior, especially in a society moving toward a universal middle class, the ability to manage conflict without overt violence and even without undue tension or emotions of hatred is an important part of the training of the child and the young adult. The same pattern can be observed in the businessman, the corporation executive, the governmental official, or the professional man of the United States, the equivalent "salary man" of Japan, the manager and commissar of the socialist countries, and indeed the middle class everywhere. It is a style of life in which bravado, braggadocio, violence, and even violent emotion are severely frowned upon and lead to rapid demotion. It is a very different style of life from either that of the aristocrat or of the genuine proletariat—both of whom are social species well on the way to extinction in advanced societies. It is therefore not unreasonable to suppose that the learning process which can take place in the individual can also take place in the image of the nation. The ideal of a world of middle-class, nonaggressive, polite states is implied in the behavior of all the more mature countries.

Perhaps one of the greatest short-run dangers to the world at the moment arises out of the fact that the achievement of maturity and political realism on the part of the developed countries has led to the abandonment of empire and hence to the creation of a large number of new countries. Many of these new countries are already exhibiting signs of immature and pathological international behavior. We may therefore have a very difficult period to go through while the new countries "grow up" into political maturity. In this sense, political development may be an even more urgent task than economic development.

This leads to further consideration of the second element in conflict management which is the development of third-party intervention. We cannot always rely on the learning process or on the dynamics of interaction among the parties to conflict themselves. If the parties in the prisoner's dilemma are in fact shortsighted it may be impossible to prevent a deterioration of conflict into a perverse or malign dynamic in the absence of any third parties. The third party may play a number of different roles. It may act simply as a mediator and a teacher, facilitating the learning process by which the actual parties to the conflict come to manage it themselves. Third-party intervention, however, usually involves the manipulation of the pay-offs, so that penalties are imposed on any party which moves unilaterally from position 1 to position 2. A good example of resolution and management of conflict by means of third-party intervention is to be found in any hierarchy. One of the main tasks of a person in a superior rank in hierarchy is to resolve the conflicts among his subordinates. He is able to do this partly because he can act as a teacher, partly because he is part of an integrative system in which he has status and respect and in which his words will therefore be listened to and his advice followed, and also partly because he can employ sanctions—that is, he can make the offending party actually worse off and so change the pay-offs to the point where it does not pay any party to move from position 1 to position 2.

This is one of the main functions of the apparatus of law and police. The criminal by breaking the social contract is in effect moving society from position 1 to position 2. The apparatus of police and law is set up in order to create a situation in which crime does not pay. The fact that crime persists in all societies indicates that this attempt is not universally successful. Nevertheless law and police are usually successful in confining crime to a small subculture of the society, and if they did not exist we might find that the criminal elements would grow so large as to threaten the stability of the society itself.

A successful process of the third-party intervention almost inevitably involves all these different aspects. Unless the third party is a teacher in the sense that he affects the behavior and values of the parties to conflict themselves, his attempt to change the pay-offs is likely to be only partially successful. On the other hand the lesson of mature, long-sighted behavior may be too hard to learn or may not even be true. It may be difficult for these two functions to be performed by the same body, which perhaps is one reason why we have developed a large number of para-legal institutions such as arbitration, marriage counseling, social work, psychiatric care, and the like. It seems that this aspect of third-party intervention will increase even more in the future.

The abolition of war then requires a twofold learning process, one whereby the values and behavior states themselves change toward long-sightedness, toward accurate reality testing of power systems, and toward a value system which lays stress on the welfare of all mankind. The other is a learning process whereby we develop the institutions of third-party intervention on a world scale. The United Nations and its surrounding organizations furnish an example. The advocates of world government have a strong case when they claim that the United Nations is not effective enough as a third-party organization, and that there must be a world organization at least sufficiently powerful to police disarmament and to change the pay-offs of international behavior in such a way as to make an aggression on the part of any nation obviously unprofitable. We can then think of the learning process in international systems proceeding to some threshold on the far side of which we have a system of stable peace in which the black ball of disaster has been removed from the bag of fate, and on the near side of which we have unstable peace and a positive probability of irretrievable disaster. It seems clear that we are not yet over this threshold or watershed. Nevertheless, we may be closer to it than we now think. It is uphill all the way to a watershed, and it has been uphill so long to this one that we may be excused if we think that the human road goes on uphill forever. There are, however, watersheds in social systems, and I believe we are close to this one. It will therefore be unspeakably tragic if like Sisyphus mankind falls down the hill again to disaster when he is so close to the top of this particular divide.

A large part of the solution of any problem is the identification of the system where the problem lies. In this case we can put the problem in the form of a change in the "noösphere," to use a concept of Pierre Teilhard de Chardin's. The noösphere is the total body of knowledge as it exists in the three billion minds of the human race spread over the surface of the earth. The existing noösphere is almost certainly not consistent with human survival in the long run, or even in the next few decades. We believe too many things which are not true, we do not know things that are true, and we have values (which are also a part of noösphere) which are inconsistent with the successful management of conflict or the process of human development. We should not, however, relapse into pessimism on this account, because the noösphere is capable of change and even of rapid change. An important segment of society which we are coming to call the knowledge industry is indeed specifically directed to changing the noösphere, even though a large part of this activity must be directed toward simple replacement of the knowledge which is lost by death. In our day, however, we have a knowledge industry with a capacity far beyond the mere requirements of replacement, and hence we can invest in changing the noösphere. This is a process indeed that has been going on with great rapidity. More people know more things today than at any other period of man's history.

The difficulty here is that we do not know in which direction we want to change the noösphere, and there are many voices urging change in different directions. The Communist wants us all to learn Marxism and the planned economy. A liberal wants us to learn one thing, a conservative another. In this babel of voices and confusion of conflicting remedies the surprising thing is that we make as much progress as we do.

It is at this point that one hopes that the social sciences can be of great assistance in the years to come. I have no illusions about the ability of the social sciences to resolve all conflicts, to reconcile divergent value systems, or to give surefire recipes for salvation. Nevertheless, in so far as the social sciences can provide improved methods of reality testing in the field of social systems, their influence is exerted in the direction of what I will call the survival change that has to take place in the noösphere. The removal of conflict from the area of folk knowledge to the area of scientific knowledge has a stabilizing, one is tempted to say a sterilizing, effect. The hum of the calculator is a great soother of emotions, and calculation, even bad calculation, is the enemy of the irrational. If ideological struggles can be transformed even partially into conflicts of scientific theory, we have a much better chance for their resolution. The whole idea of research in social systems is therefore a stabilizer, and makes actively for successful conflict management.

If I were to nominate the activity which is now open to mankind and which would increase most dramatically the probability of his survival, I would nominate a massive intellectual effort in peace research—that is, in the application of the social sciences to the study of conflict systems and especially of conflict systems in their international aspect. This will be a major part of that self-conscious effort toward the accomplishment of the great transition which is the major task of man in this period of his history.

NOTE

1. Herman Kahn, *On Thermonuclear War*. Princeton: Princeton University Press, 1961.

16
CONFLICT FORMATIONS IN CONTEMPORARY INTERNATIONAL SOCIETY

Dieter Senghaas

INTRODUCTION: SOME METHODOLOGICAL AND SUBSTANTIVE CONSIDERATIONS

For decades, international society has been analyzed by concepts which stress the lack of mandatory legal norms (within a highly unstable order in inter-state relations) as a *structural* element of the international system.[1]

In these investigations the classical nation-state is characterized by just the opposite: sovereign force, restrained by general legal standards as well as by the bonds of loyalty of the citizens. This nation-state is then considered — in theory, but on the average also in reality — as a guarantee of *social peace* within its own frontiers — *a peace defined as the absence of arbitrary rule by individual social groups and by the containment of collective violence.*[2] It is assumed that if the rules of the game — e.g., those of a parliamentary system — are considered as binding for everyone, *social conflicts* seem to be amenable (in principle at least) to peaceful settlement, whereas *international conflicts*, including war, time and again demonstrate the inescapable basic characteristics of *international* society: an anarchic and potentially eruptive structure frequently permeated by *overt violence*. If conflicts of interest within a civil society, even those of a principle and antagonistic nature, may be stripped of their explosive character within the frame of the nation-state and channelled into 'peaceful' directions by various institutional and legally binding arrangements (for avoiding recourse to the open use of force), conflicts of interest in *international* society have been interpreted as the social basis from which a kind of open violence might emerge, a violence far more difficult to contain and to counteract in this setting than within the nation-state. If such violence breaks out, there is usually no decisive preventive intervention by a superior and sovereign institution within the international setting which could thus secure 'peace' in a manner conforming to our traditional understanding. (Cf. Hoffmann, 1965.)

That is why in many theories and public statements, international society is regarded as a social order deficient in many respects. It is assumed deficient with respect to its inadequate basis in law and loyalty; deficient as far as ability to regulate

---

Reprinted by permission from the *Journal of Peace Research* No. 3, 1973.

conflicts is concerned (in the sense that these conflicts of interest ought to be solved without involving violence); deficient also with respect to ability to adjust cognitively and organizationally to changed power configurations and dynamic developments provoked particularly by technological progress. In recent decades, this technological progress has caused doubt as to the viability of the traditional order of international society, and it has jeopardized the latter in a principal sense. This is particularly true for the military area and with respect to international information and communication potentials, as is well known. These have increasingly made the idea of national sovereignty fictitious. (Cf. Falk, 1971.) This international society is seen as deficient also as far as the disparities prevailing in it are concerned: production, income distribution, and welfare measures are much more unequal—for reasons to be investigated later—than in most highly developed national and industrial societies. (Cf. Sprout, 1972.)

If we take the average nation-state as an ideal, or at least apply a certain idealized image of it to the analysis of international society, then the latter may be characterized rather as a structure of disorder and of chaos; at best as a fragile system, potentially always at the point of collapse. It certainly does not represent a particularly viable organization. Even *traditional* efforts to strengthen and secure this deficient social order, aimed at improving its viability and its potential for autonomous change, seem instead to strengthen the *existing* basic structure or have only a marginal impact on it. The alleged *strengthening* of social order on the basis of conventional military security policies leads, today as never before, to international arms races, sometimes to open warfare within the context of organizationally petrified friend/enemy fixations. The second, *marginal changes*, may occasionally be observed in the case of international organizations through which, according to the general understanding, cooperative elements should be incorporated into this deficient social order. These elements consist of psychological and institutional bonds of loyalty supposedly transcending the nation-state (integration processes); they consist further in provisions for conflict regulation on the basis of supra- and international organizations designed to contribute either to solving conflicts of interest before these become virulent, or as devices of conflict mediation if these have already escalated to actual use of violence. In present-day international society there do exist privileged zones where such instruments intended to promote cooperation have overcome the traditional basic structure outlined above. However, this has been confined to certain regions only (e.g., the Scandinavian countries)[3] without replacing this fundamental worldwide structure of international society.

The comparison of the *civil order* organized within the framework of the nation-state with an *international society* based on nation-states with sometimes questionable sovereignty frequently gives rise to a thesis that—due to the deficiencies cited above—the development of *international* society as such is much more uncertain than the developments *within* nation-states. The reason given is that social change within the first context is much less predictable and far more permeated with random processes than is social change within the latter, where developments are considered more foreseeable and reliably controlled by organs of the nation-state (legal system, political system, socialization processes, etc.). This theory implies that, due to the lack of structure and because of political processes that do not seem oriented towards clear-cut goals, the basic structure of *international* society is much less amenable to analytical elucidation than are domestic social orders, with their comparatively stable subsystems (politics, economics, law, socialization, etc.) and their relatively rigid societal interaction patterns.[4]

However, this theory appears to be, generally speaking, wrong. If we disregard for a moment so-called "high politics" (that area of international politics generally reflected in mass media headlines) it may be demonstrated that *contemporary international society is based on a structure much firmer and subject to much more calculable changes than we are usually aware, even though diplomatic configurations may change and power shifts occur.* Such relatively rigid patterns, to be analyzed in the rest of this paper, make it only possible to talk about *structure* as contrasted with *random processes* with respect to international society. . . .

This methodical differentiation between *structure* and *processes* needs to be stressed. In politics, daily events generally exert a great fascination. In view of the continuously changing content of communications about events in international society, and the increasing volume of information, this fascination leads to an image of our environment which bears little resemblance to reality. Indeed, it frequently provokes an image of chaos, as we observed at the beginning of this paper.

The *lack of reality-testing*, together with the comparative *cognitive remoteness* of international society to the citizens of most nation-states, strengthens the tendency of individuals and states to adopt *egocentric self-images* and *self-centered images of the world* particularly characterized by their amorphous content. This can be observed despite the growing amount of information available nowadays. Individuals are then receptive to disjointing information, particularly to news of a spectacular nature (e.g., the political news offered in television). They do not possess cognitively and affectively structured, flexible interpretation patterns which could bring some structure into daily events and which would be able to delineate the context out of which they emerge.[5]

It must be a task of peace research to make such structures transparent in order to dissolve analytically such chaotic impressions and images about international society. From psychology we know that an environment regarded as chaotic encourages misperception as well as the suggestibility of people to irrational behavior. Today such cognitive and affective errors on the part of governments or collectives may even be fatal, in view of the incomparably destructive potentials and the inability of nation-states to insulate themselves from the rest of the world. For this reason, it is vital to criticize publicly the powerful images of international society wherever they obstruct the view for reality or offer inadequate explanations about partial aspects of this international society. (Cf. Deutsch & Senghaas, 1972.)

Of course, international society is not a nation-state writ large. Its *relatively* loosely patterned organization and interaction structure cannot straight-away be compared with the tremendously dense inner societal networks of the nation-state.[6] However, international society is based on structures and built out of elements which, as a whole, demonstrate a high degree of *regularity*. The history of the past 400 years shows, however, that its dynamics time and again result in serious crises and the outbreak of violence—seemingly justifying the image of the chaotic. If we want to term the international society as *anarchic*, this should only be done to the extent that its structure is permeated by *antagonistic contradictions* which traditionally rather provoke (rather than preclude) conflicts involving use of force.[7]

CONFLICT FORMATIONS IN CONTEMPORARY INTERNATIONAL SOCIETY

After these initial considerations we now turn to *the analysis of some predominant conflict formations in present-day international society*. We begin by presenting some basic structural features.

Capitalism and Globalization of International Politics

The history of international society is identical with the development of modern capitalism and worldwide anti-capitalist movements on a world scale provoked by the existence of capitalism. That we here promulgate such a formulation does not mean we have adopted an eurocentric view. The *globalization of international politics* has, however, undoubtedly emerged from the classical nation-states of Europe, and their dynamics caused by the development of capitalism. What appears today to be a *worldwide interdependency* is to no small extent due to colonialism, imperialism, and neo-colonialism. The dynamic poles of this development have always been the leading metropoles of Europe, which themselves have competed among each other for leading positions since the 16th century.[8]

By the beginning of this century, the inroads of these European capitalist metropoles, including the US, into the continents which we today term *Third World* had not yet been concluded. At the same time, *anti-capitalist* and *anti-imperialist* movements made themselves increasingly felt, registering their first and most important permanent success in 1917 in Russia. In 1949, China followed, and its dissociation from the capitalist world economy has contributed considerably to the institutionalization of a *worldwide system-antagonism*. In turn, *the globalization of the socio-economic antagonism between capitalism and socialism has clearly promoted the globalization of international politics*. Third World areas which still constituted spheres of influence of individual European metropoles after the imperialist conflicts of the last century and at the beginning of this century have increasingly been drawn into new antagonistic struggles after 1917 and particularly after 1945—whereby their own weight in international politics has been increased many times. Also, during its fight for political emancipation, the *Third World* began—albeit in a restricted sense—to constitute itself as a *new subject in international politics*. (Cf. the classical work by Emerson, 1960.) We shall explain later why the Third World does not constitute a collectively acting subject.

Thus, since the 15th or 16th century, modern international society has become a reality more than ever before. It is built on specific structural patterns that we will have to delineate later. Today it can be understood only as a *totality* which is undergoing a process of rapid development. As to terminology, we are deliberately speaking of *international society* and not just of a system of *international relations* or even of *international politics.* The degree of *inter-dependence* and *inter-penetration* is much better expressed by the first term than by the latter. The rapid development of communications and information technology, and increased chances of contact and penetration have created the objective basis for a structure which, despite continuing differences with domestic social orders, is increasingly assuming the character of a *society.*

What are the essential *structural characteristics* of this international society, and why does this structure constitute a *totality?*

Inter-Capitalist Conflict Formation

Just as centuries ago—although today this is much more subject to political controversy than even a few decades ago—a *dynamic pole* of international society from which decisive development impulses have emerged is situated in the *capitalist metropoles.* The overwhelming part of the world economy—still *essentially organized according to capitalist principles*—is being directed from such centers. (Cf. particularly Palloix, 1971.) This is primarily because, since the industrial revolution, technological progress has been more organized and advanced in these centers. This has led to a considerable rise in the forces of production and in technological achievements. (See Landes, 1969; Kuznets, 1966; Mandel, 1972.)

However, compared to the history of international relations up to the end of World War II, these capitalist metropoles are today not only tied together by multiple transactions like trade, investment, etc., but also by *organizations of joint interests.* Even though there still exist, as during the time of classical imperialism, genuine conflicts about power and market positions in international politics and the international economy, today these conflicts are rather channelled through joint organizations. Open warlike conflict between the capitalist powers may be considered highly improbable. . . .[9]

These *inter-capitalist relation patterns* are characterized by an *interaction density* unparalleled in international relations. True, this interaction density is slight compared with the manifold transactions that occur *within* societies. However, compared with the worldwide average in inter-state relations, it is far above the mean. This dense interaction pattern may be observed particularly in the economic field. The flow of trade and capital organized within the framework of the capitalist world economy today circulates primarily between the highly industrialized countries of the capitalist West. This also holds true for the international banking system, for the flows of patents and licences. (As a case study cf. Wolff, 1971.) International communications, traffic and information systems have been built up to an incomparable density, particularly *between* these capitalist metropoles. No other region in the world knows so many joint supranational (governmental and nongovernmental) organizations intended to bring about mutual adjustment of interests (e.g., the OECD, the Common Market). While these organizations each exercise a special function, their basic structure is similar. More essential, their political goals are highly synchronized. (See Senghaas-Knobloch, 1972.)

This organizational basis and the institutional superstructure of the actual relations between the capitalist metropoles is relatively new, something practically unknown in world politics prior to 1945. It is also true that prior to 1945, or even prior to 1914, the most highly developed industrial nations generally exchanged, statistically speaking, much more among each other than with their colonies. However, at that time they never succeeded in creating *joint* supranational organizations to represent their interest.

Thus, the remarkable factor about this permanent dynamic pole in international society is not so much the incomparable density of interaction between the industrial countries—something that might be expected due to sheer size—but an *institutional grid system to secure their common interests*—something of decisive importance for the evaluation of potential conflicts *between* capitalist centers. Today power politics and economic conflicts that still exist between the capitalist metropoles are smoothed out by the institutions established within this grid of interest with the aim to articulate and settle such conflicts. The danger of renewed basic *inter-capitalist* conflicts has furthermore been essentially restricted by a continuing worldwide socio-economic antagonism between East and West. The challenge presented to the capitalist powers by the Soviet Union, China, Eastern Europe, and individual Third World socialist countries like Cuba, leads the Western metropoles to the defense of *joint* capitalist positions, i.e., *of the general capitalist interest*, and it demands that these interests be granted priority over narrow national ones.[10]

Though capitalist countries pursue a strategy designed to resolve by force conflicts in areas *outside* their own territory (as in the case of Vietnam), there is a real chance that within this scope of modern international society, *inter-capitalist* conflicts will *not* lead to military acts of force within their own area.

There is also a chance that mutual adjustments may resolve more profound structural conflicts such as those manifested in the instability of the world currency system.[11] This also applies to the development in which in the Common Market and Japan, major powers are rising next to the United States, gradually establishing new power spheres of political and economic interest. *These will be subject to hard struggles* (investment and trade 'wars'), *but in inter-capitalist conflicts this will not result in the overt use of force with all its consequences*, such as mobilization of the military machinery. Recalling that only a few decades ago, *inter-capitalist (imperialist)* conflicts gave rise to two world wars, some may regard our assessment as a too optimistic prognosis. However, the rationally defined *overall capitalist self-interest* will probably preclude a repetition of such developments, today and in the foreseeable future. The organizations in which the joint capitalist interest is represented (OECD, Common Market, etc.) and other institutions governed by the capitalist metropoles (World Bank, etc.) serve this *collective* policy to the advantage of the general capitalist interest.[12]

West-East Conflict Formation

However, the perpetuation of the *West-East conflict formation* which by its structure and content in reality represents *the first North-South conflict formation in recent history*, can be regarded as highly probable. (Cf. Gantzel, 1972; Galtung, 1972; Willms, 1972.) Since the Soviet Union has accepted the tremendous arms race with the West (which no doubt deliberately encouraged this policy), and since in the military field *quasi*-bipolar-structures attract all our attention, the fact that socialist countries like the Soviet Union have intentionally excluded themselves from the capitalist world economy in the pursuit of an *anti-capitalist strategy* (the North-South element in the West-East conflict formation) has been pushed into the background of most people's minds in the West. In the consciousness of these Western nations this has created a distorted and rigid image of the socio-economic antagonism between the systems on the world scale which actually represents far more than a quasi-bipolar arms race pattern. (Cf. Schmiederer, 1973.)

Since this dissociation of Russia (1917), China (1949), and the Eastern European countries (after 1945 in association with the Soviet Union) laid the foundation for a general though incomplete, autonomous *socialist development*, this process has established and institutionalized a firm structure of an *antagonism in nuce* inherent in international society since the onset of the capitalist world system. Once we consider the double task of *such anti-capitalist counter-organization* that had to be solved simultaneously, we can easily understand that this socio-economic system antagonism, pursued with the classical means of inter-state confrontations, has led to a deformation of socialism in these societies. They have had to assure their own survival against various attempts at renewed penetration from the side of the capitalist centers, while at the same time speeding up industrial development to be able to catch up with the West. Moreover, this had to be accomplished in countries where initial conditions for socialism were not optimal. Despite extreme difficulties (boycott, invasion, etc.) and contrary to expectations based on traditional evaluations and views still accepted in the Dulles era, these socialist societies have proved viable. They have consolidated themselves during the past decade in which the hectic era of the cold war gradually gave way to a sober and realistic rather than purely ideological Western evaluation of socialism as it exists in the two major powers, the Soviet Union and China.

The breakup of the relationship between the Soviet Union and China, a relationship which had never been very profound, has again increased the realm of manoeuver of western metropoles. However, this manoeuvering ability is not large enough to enable the capitalist West to regain a new foothold in order to finally exert effective control over the infrastructure of socialist societies. Of course, there is a technological gradient from the leading capitalist countries to the two most important socialist societies: the Soviet Union (including Eastern

Europe) and China. Of course, this West-East slope leads almost inevitably to *asymmetrical penetration in the case of increased interaction* (through asymmetrical flows of investment and transfers of technology, transfer of consumption patterns, etc.).[13] However, the fact that despite all their objective internal difficulties the socialist societies today are relatively *self-centered*[14] increases the chance that external influences exerted by the capitalist powers may be controlled selectively. Thus, these countries would not be faced with total foreign domination, as they were prior to the revolutions which removed them from the scope of the world capitalist system. This is of course not guaranteed. The gradient between West and East (despite some exceptions such as in armaments which rather promote a convergence) (Senghaas, 1972h) is still so great that a loss of autonomy of socialist societies which would facilitate foreign domination may be expected to develop with the gradual rise of the development level of the socialist societies within such an international context. This is so because after elementary needs have been satisfied (abolition of hunger and of illiteracy and the establishment of a modern infrastructure), Western capitalist consumption patterns and standards serve as an attractive standard of comparison, regardless of the different socio-economic premises on which they are based, and present a temptation for imitation.

Despite increased efforts to find a *modus vivendi* of peaceful coexistence, the West-East conflict formation will maintain its *basically antagonistic character*. We are faced not only with a power conflict and incompatible interests between the two major powers and their allies, but also with a *fundamental antagonism*: the challenge to, and the defense of, the capitalist metropoles in international society where these metropoles are still predominant, even though their rule has suffered considerable restriction within the world economy they dominate.

To the extent to which the militarized security policies developed during the last 20 years — as manifested in the *arms race between East and West* — may be partially abandoned for various reasons (costs, overkill capacities, etc.) by the power elites, and to the extent that a system competition as manifested in the *escalation of militarism* would gradually be overcome (for which there are no particular reasons to expect this now), the *socio-economic* aspects of this system antagonism will become more distinct. The persistence of traditional security and armament policies, demonstrated in the face of general efforts for relaxation of tensions between East and West, should not only be ascribed to factors inherent in armament policies, although their importance should not be underestimated. Such persistence should also be attributed to the danger envisaged by power elites to the end *that the policy of relaxation of tension might have spillover effects into the socio-political field* — effects which might jeopardize power structures built up and consolidated during the cold war and its armament policies, structures that were accepted unquestioningly for a very long time. (Möller and Vilmar, 1972.) Under this perspective, armament policies impose restrictive conditions on a policy of detente within the West-East-conflict formation — a detente which in turn is only pursued as a politically tamed one. (See Senghaas, 1972h.)

In this context, a further observation should be stated. The *dynamics of the arms race between East and West,* which still most strikingly documents the antagonism between the systems, will be determined in the foreseeable future by the essentially *qualitative* character of contemporary armament policies. Today this arms race is less the result of an *action-reaction* process (less a race *between* the protagonists in the struggle) and more *a race of each party with itself.* This *self-centeredness of armament policies* is not so surprising if we consider the scope of contemporary armament policy, its security premises (deterrence), its interest basis within societies and military alliances, its technological impulses, and the resulting organizational imperatives essential for an efficient military policy. Such autodynamic growth patterns (Eigendynamik) should be stressed since powerful security doctrines and ideologies still propagate different rationales for armament policies, based on assumptions that armament policies are imposed by the potential opponent, i.e, that they are determined by external, not internal, forces. (Senghaas, 1972h.) The dangers which result from the arms race continue to be major ones; and we must consider that these dangers result from the military potential itself and also, indirectly, from the *opportunity costs of armament policies* (particularly from the pauperization of infrastructures, etc.). The conventional *arms control policy,* more and more advocated in recent years, does not live up to contemporary armament dynamics. This can be clearly shown by the results of the conventional arms control policy within the last ten years *since armament dynamics is redundantly caused and since there are many cumulative reasons for the perpetuation of the West-East conflict.* (Senghaas, 1972d.)

On this basis we might project that despite all the apparent "cooperation euphoria" in central Europe and between East and West in general, it will be difficult to develop a solid basis for genuinely peaceful cooperation. What can be observed today as *cooperation* (contractual agreements about territorial status quo, technology transfer, joint ventures, increased trade flows, etc.) will certainly relax the cold war confrontation: but this will not result in a real breakthrough. For the foreseeable future, the antagonistic conflict formation between West and East will remain a genuine factor in modern international society. The militarized competition between the systems will also not be overcome easily, because the power elites regard it as a reliable guarantee of international *and* social stability. Inroads into the military apparata, e.g., with the goal of *numerical* limitation of armaments, are possible and probable—*provided these measures do not restrict the qualitative development of the existing apparata and do not prevent further innovation processes in military technology.*[15] Major economic exchange is also possible, although there are certain limits to this, particularly if the so-called *integration race* continues on both sides.[16] Instead of promoting cooperation, the following factors rather prevent the further deepening of *joint* undertakings: the quasi-autarchy of both systems, differences in economic and management practices, problems of currency exchange, political implications of further cooperation, social spillover effects, etc.[17]

Despite such an evaluation of the situation, the chances of preventing warfare between the two antagonists are today better than at any time since the end of World War II. Efforts to bring about a *Conference on Security and*

Cooperation in Europe and similar meetings, which in contrast to the fifties and the sixties can no longer be avoided (despite what traditional diplomacy may do in the way of pulling and hauling) may contribute considerably to stabilizing a comparatively fragile overall situation. (Albrecht et al., 1972; Senghaas et al., 1973.) *These measures will at least reduce the probability of a sudden setback into the situation of the cold war from which a war-like situation could result at any time.*[18]

It can be assumed that the differentiation between *fundamental (antagonistic) incompatibilities of interest and solvable particular conflicts of interest* will have a moderating impact on this conflict formation. Although specific criteria for *antagonistic* and *non-antagonistic* imcompatibilities of interest have not been explicitly elaborated in Eastern and Western doctrines, there is hope that with the further elaboration of such a differentiation the *doctrine of peaceful coexistence* can be further developed.[19]

The So-called North-South Conflict Formation

The socialist states have succeeded in dissociating themselves from the capitalist-ruled world economy and have also successfully coped with the typical basic problems (hunger, illiteracy, etc.) of developing countries. With the exception of Cuba, the countries of the Third World have not achieved this goal so far. To assess the so-called *North-South conflict formation* adequately, the *structural* situation of the Third World within the international society has to be described. Although embedded in a situation similar to that of the West-East conflict formation, the position of these countries hardly resembles the latter in any respect.

We have described the interaction of the *capitalist* metropoles with each other as an institutional *grid of dense exchange and communication processes* to secure overall capitalist interests. On the other hand, relations between the *capitalist* and the relatively self-centered *socialist* states are characterized by *structural dissociation* and *political confrontation* counteracted only by a few actual transactions. (In any event, there are fewer exchanges than would normally be expected on the basis of the size of the parties involved).[20] *The infrastructure of the Third World or region and the pattern of its relation with the rest of the international society represent the exact opposite of both the structural patterns mentioned above.*

Since the penetration of Latin America, Africa, and Asia by the colonialism and imperialism of Europe and the United States, these continents have lost their independence and have been integrated into an *international division of labor* enforced upon them by the capitalist metropoles.[21] In past centuries, from the days of uninhibited robbery colonialism to the present-day rapid growth of multinational corporations, *relations of deep dependency* were created which today characterize the situation of the Third World.[22] Nowhere in international society are *domination structures* so gross and so transparent as in the relationship between the capitalist *centers* and their *"peripheries"* in the three continents of the South. Not only did the *capitalist penetration* during past centuries destroy the more or less organic social structures which had been existing there and replace them with new ones created at the drawing boards of European cabinets or as a result of military conflicts carried out in the countries themselves: *the colonies thus created were forcibly also oriented towards their metropoles in a manner that left little chance for an articulation and organization of solidarity among themselves against the metropoles.* This goal was achieved by destroying the channels of communication and transaction between the various areas of the Third World (where in some instances, prior to the arrival of the Europeans, regional trade had thrived) or through the *systematic prevention of the buildup of a modern regional infrastructure* which would have made such exchanges possible, enhancing also the *structural* basis for political solidarity. Quite to the contrary, the metropoles involved, which were the dominant dynamic poles of this penetration, kept a monopoly of information, communication, political power, and of the instruments of rule (troops for military intervention, etc.). At the same time—in different regions at different times and with different methods—they tried to build up in the colonies reliable *bridgeheads* consisting of the members of old or new elites, in order to establish their rule through a political division of labor, thus stabilizing their influence. It would be completely wrong to assume that this system of *divide et impera,* which was designed in different variations by the capitalist metropoles, existed only as a super-structure in the colonies, or that it was concentrated only in the area of political administration. Actually, this political structure of foreign rule still exists today, even though the accents are set differently, *and it still mirrors the profound penetration of the dependent areas by the outside centers.* This asymmetrical penetration of the dominating centers into the dependent peripheries took place—even though in individual cases in various combinations and with different accentuations—in all the essential social fields. This was done by controlling socialization processes in the widest sense of the word (*cultural imperialism*); by controlling the media of communication (*communication imperialism*), as well as the political, military and legal systems (*political imperialism*), and—rather more important—by orienting economic reproduction in the peripheries towards the requirements of the metropoles (*economic imperialism and dependent reproduction*). *Without accepting an economic and thus monistic theory, we may state that the enforced integration of the economies of the Third World into the economy of the metropoles through the capitalist-dominated world economic system (which was established during the past centuries) developed in stages and still represents the core of an explanation of the present situation of the Third World.*[23]

As mentioned above, this integration was based on a worldwide *division of labor,* according to which the Third World had to specialize in the production and export of *raw materials* and/or *agricultural products.* Lately this has also included the production of industrial goods with a *low* degree of processing, whereas the industrial nations made *manufactured goods* and exported them to their peripheries. If such a division of labor is maintained for decades, or as in this case for centuries, a gap *necessarily* develops between the industrial nations and the suppliers of nonprocessed or only slightly processed goods, a gap that becomes an established structure.[24] This is so because processing is based on modern infrastructures and in turn promotes their growth and differentiation in production, distribution, training, technology, etc. The dependent socioeconomic structures are not granted a comparable chance of such relative *autonomy* and *self-directed development*; rather, they are characterized by *dependent and deformed reproduction* (mono-culture, export orientation, marginalization, etc.), as *a result of their integration into the division of labor of the capitalist world economy.* (Senghaas, 1973.) They did not choose their specialization themselves. They were instead forcibly geared into the need patterns of the metropoles. (Mandel, 1972.) In a historical analysis of the Third World, this fact becomes strikingly evident. A history of the *political* and *social* structures of the Third World may be sketched as a function of the external penetration—this history cannot, by any means, be explained in terms of domestic conditions alone.

Of course, this integration of the Third World into the capitalist world economy did not proceed without resistance or friction. Today the instruments used to rule and exploit the Third World are not as spectacularly brutal—with considerable exceptions like Vietnam—as they were just a few decades or even centuries ago. Capital investment, development aid, technology transfer, cultural indoctrination etc. today represent more elegant media of rule than the pirate colonialism, slave trade, military intervention, overt political repression, etc. However, even today, despite formal political independence, relations between the capitalist metropoles and their peripheries are those of *unequal exchange*, of *exploitation*, and of *a division of labor* which, by its very nature, *systematically* works in favor of the dominating metropoles and *systematically* against the ruled or dependent peripheries.[25]

The conclusions to be drawn from this may be formulated in a thesis which is of fundamental importance for understanding the situation as it prevails in the Third World:

> *The underdevelopment of the Third World is not a transitory stage on the way towards self-directed development as it prevailed in the history of the industrialization or modernization of European societies. Rather, underdevelopment is a constituent part of the historical process of the international society dominated by the capitalist metropoles. The development of these metropoles and the history of the underdevelopment of the Third World are complementary processes connected through the international economic system.*[26]

An adequate analysis of the situation of the Third World may therefore not be restricted to finding out whether a certain capital investment made it possible to reap extra profits for the metropoles—profits that could not have been realized in the metropoles themselves; nor is it sufficient to analyze whether the terms of trade can be stabilized, etc. Rather, the *totality* or the *systematic character of the asymmetrical structure of the relation between the metropoles and the peripheries has to be analyzed.*[27] In other words, an *international structure of rule and domination* has to be made transparent, a structure which *systematically* encourages the flow of riches towards one pole (and thus a speeded-up capital accumulation process) and the relative, in some cases even the absolute, pauperization of the dominated.[28]

However, the picture presented here requires further essential details which characterize this structure of domination, *details which make an enormous difference*. The view as developed up to now *suggests* a confrontation between North and South, just as it is popular today to talk about a North-South *conflict*. In reality, this image of the dichotomy of a worldwide polarized structure, characterized by a distinct ruling and upper group in the metropoles and a distinct subject and exploited group in the peripheries, is contradicted by the fact that the ruling classes and privileged strata in the peripheries themselves—i.e., a minority of the population—have attained a standard of living and of consumption which in almost every respect corresponds to that in the capitalist metropoles. These classes and strata operate not only as the local bridgeheads of the metropoles; as a privileged class they are also integrated into the core of the capitalist world economy. On the second (sub-imperialist) level or on lower levels of this over-all system they play a role of political agents for these metropoles. (Cf. the paradigmatic article by Marini, 1972.) The existence of this privileged and fully *internationalized core* within the Third World countries (the centers of the peripheries) is being veiled by the usual statistics, for example by the comparison of per capita income data, a method still popular in the mass media in the metropoles. In reality, the per capita income of the *privileged* strata in the peripheries is in some places higher than the average per capita income in the highly developed industrial nations. It is therefore not surprising that these persons have pledged allegiance to the existing order—they have much to lose by even small changes.

The existence of such *internationalized bridgeheads* (see also Sunkel, 1972) recruited from the local population may also help explain why up to now, despite 500 years of dependency and exploitation, there has been no *collective* confrontation between the Third World and the metropoles. Of course, the difference in the level of development plays an overall role. The relation of forces seems too unequal to dare provoke a conflict. Certainly the system of *divide et impera*, which successfully split up the Third World and prevented it from becoming an *active* political subject, precluded solidarity actions against the overwhelming power of the colonial masters right from the beginning. The decisive aspect, however, is that this international domination structure was supported locally within the Third World by recruited and organized bridgeheads working on behalf of the capitalist metropoles; in the final analysis, this order was defended by them and was rarely attacked. Thus, as a rule there was *no social basis for an individual and collective confrontation, and the necessary sociological platform for such action was lacking*. The overall structure of the capitalist world economy has also caused the ruling strata in the Third World to integrate themselves into this system as privileged sub-centers *(transnational capitalist integration)*. This has exposed their social system to a growing disintegration and denationalization process up to the recent takeover of national industries by the multinational corporations of the metropoles *(national disintegration)*. Thus the formation of a self-conscious national bourgeoisie in the Third World countries comparable to that of Europe in the 16th to the 19th centuries is therefore rather improbable. (Cf. Cardoso, 1971.) The *proletariat* in the Third World also remains split between those parts that have assumed the status of *worker aristocracies* and those who continue their miserable existence on or below the bare minimum based on chronic unemployment, underemployment, and marginal employment, whether in the urban centers or in the country. The latter make up the majority of the masses of the population, but objective difficulties preclude their organizing as a *collective* political subject. These difficulties are greater than those with which the traditional European workers' movements of the 18th and 19th centuries were confronted. (On this see the fundamental article by Quijano, 1970.)

At this point we should like to stop the presentation of some elements of the so-called North-South conflict formation. This is not a conflict among equals, as was the case in the classical inter-imperialist conflicts of the past century (England versus France, etc.). Instead, this relationship rather resembles that of *master and servant (Herr und Knecht)*. In more detail, it is characterized by *gradual stages of dependency* and by *dependency chains* maintained by specific mechanisms of domination and rule (division of labor, bridgehead, etc.). Since the victory of the Chinese revolution (1949) and despite the political decolonizing processes of the fifties and sixties, this conflict formation has up to now not assumed a virulence which would have escalated it to the level of *overt* conflict. There are exceptions like Cuba and Vietnam, the importance of which becomes apparent only if we at the same time look at the overall structure as we have outlined it, as well as at the security and precaution measures against changes built into that structure. That the Third World can no longer be controlled and steered without problems, as was the case still a few decades ago (despite the occasional eruptions and military confrontations that even existed then) is clearly demonstrated by the *rapid increasing use of instruments of repression to safeguard law and order* within the last two decades. With respect to that type of policy, labelled as *counter-insurgency*, the United States was a particularly prominent pacemaker.[29]

Our analysis further reveals that the *image* of peacefully cooperating capitalist metropoles is questionable unless complemented by the statement that *this* peace—defined as the absence of the use of force between states—also includes the historically grown systematic exploitation pursued by the capitalist metropoles through a capitalist-dominated world economy (i.e., by *a worldwide organization of injustice*). Beyond that, this so-called peace—which is rather best described as *organized peacelessness*—has also been characterized in the last 20 years by a vehement armaments policy. This evaluation holds also true, indeed perhaps particularly true, for the European Community which has now been able to consolidate, for the time being, the general structure described in this chapter by means of association agreements with parts of the Third World.[30]

Further Conflict Formations: Inter-Socialist; Inter-Third World;
Formations of Structural Violence

Our considerations up to this point have not been intended to give a *complete* review of the present important conflict formations within international society.

Particularly, this presentation must be supplemented by an analysis of the *conflict formation between socialist states.* Here a characterization of the conflict between the Soviet Union and China is particularly required.

This formation is of great relevance because it shows that a socialist social order within a nation-state framework per se is not a reliable guarantee for peaceful external relations, particularly if these socialist social orders are on present-day development levels as in the USSR and in China. That each of these two nations claims to embody "true" socialism whereas the other is characterized as "revisionist" seems a propagandistic diversion. There can be no doubt that in their principles both societies differ more from capitalist social orders than from each other despite *development differentials* among themselves. This conflict formation shows, in a paradigmatic manner, which influences in addition to socio-economic factors (which typically characterize *specific* societies) should be attributed to such parameters as historically grown *socio-psychological fixations* and the *state* as a frame of policy. Also in the socialist context, these factors are powerful enough to mobilize the loyalties of the masses. This can be done particularly easily in the absence of effective democratic controls of decisionmaking processes—which, in the area of security policies, are highly centralized also in socialist countries. (On the role of state organizations see Krippendorf, 1971.)

The conflict between the Soviet Union and China is also important since it closely resembles, in its most basic structure, the conflict formation as it developed between the U.S. and the Soviet Union after 1943. Of course capitalism and socialism are not the main issue in this conflict formation between the Soviet Union and China. If one follows the propaganda issued in Moscow against China, Chinese society is considered as a *petty bourgeois social order* in which a *power clique* rules which is in opposition to genuine socialism; and China in its propaganda against the Soviet Union considers this nation as a kind of *social imperialist power* which has taken a step back from socialism to state capitalism. Here, we are not interested in these invectives but rather in the fact that both nations do not have transactions of any importance (in the area of economic change, technology transfer, communications, etc.) with each other, whereas their negative affective fixations towards each other (friends/enemy images) have been escalating tremendously in the past few years, deliberately promoted by the state and party propaganda apparata. Parallel to the escalation of these invectives, the military apparata have been escalating on both sides as the backbone for an otherwise "word politics." The conflict formation between the Soviet Union and China has thus developed into a typical case of *autistic* conflict on the basis of which, very similar to the conflict between West and East, there are certain perceived incompatibilities of political interest.[31] The latter particularly refer to the strife for an uncontested leading position in the international socialist movement to which both powers aspire.

There exists yet another similarity on this conflict formation to the West-East-conflict formation. In both cases, the structure is highly *asymmetric*; and in both cases *the dominating power acts as a peacemaker of the dispute* particularly in concrete armaments programs and military policies—in the case of the

West-East confrontation, the U.S.; and in the case of the Soviet-Chinese conflict, the Soviet Union.

The escalation which we can observe today between the Soviet Union and China follows classical patterns of power politics. If both powers pursued a rationally calculated policy of detente, their strategy towards each other would be just the opposite of what it is today: *Instead of a policy of over-reaction, a policy of under-reaction unilaterally initiated by those powers would have to be pursued.* So there exists a tremendous danger that a new axis of the international arms race will be built up further, and that this arms race may develop in a similar pattern as the one within the West-East conflict formation, always with the danger that word politics may switch over into a violent military confrontation.

Nor have we exposed sufficiently all the *conflict formations within the Third World* which, as a kind of late heritage of colonialism, are today being carried on by the politically "sovereign" states within the three Southern continents. This colonial heritage should be stressed because in most specific cases the results of the policy pursued by Europeans during past centuries have predetermined those conflicts which today manifest themselves as *inter-state conflicts* and/or *civil wars.* (The rationales of European policy have been objects like the creation of arbitrary borders, the separation of ethnic groups, the allocation of privileges to some groups at the expense of others as a special trick to secure domination, etc.)

These cases, too, are of general importance and cannot solely be ascribed to local and regional idiosyncrasies. This is not only because, as a rule, the metropoles of the West and the anti-centers of the socialist states frequently take part in curious alliances and counter-alliances—as demonstrated in the recent war between India and Pakistan about Bangla Desh. In fact, this is the old, expectable policy of intervention—and therefore nothing new. The general relevance of these conflicts within Third World societies lies in the fact that *in general their structures correspond well to the North-South conflict formation* which we have outlined above. (See Misra, 1972.) Such conflicts also break out in the metropoles themselves (as in the black ghettos in the U.S., in Northern Ireland, and elsewhere). Statistics show that those conflicts which arise under conditions of gross social injustice (*structural violence*) have in the past 10 years even become more frequent than the classical type of war between states. In Vietnam and Bangla Desh one could see that these conflicts in the Third World typically contain elements of both inter-state conflict *and* civil war.

The purely numerical increase of such conflicts should be regarded as a signal. It shows that, at least in the local, and possibly even in the regional context, there are growing chances for mobilizing and organizing people in such social situations with the attempt to overcome their political apathy. Gross social injustice and exploitation (*structures implying violence which kills people by social order*) (on "structural violence" see Galtung, 1971) are no longer being borne by the potential victims of such violence as patiently as has been the case for decades, even centuries. Tolerance for unjust suffering due to structural violence has—fortunately—been considerably reduced in recent years. *This in itself is a hopeful sign for peace if it is understood as a dynamic development of social justice*. But, at the same time we must state that the road towards just and humane living conditions for most people in the world, and even the road to conditions in which most people would simply *physically* survive, will be more permeated by force, the more ossified the traditional political and social orders are. Once the legitimate basis of such petrified social structures starts gradually eroding and once the political and social economic status quo starts driving people—*with no alternatives at hand*—to use violence as a means of communication, such violence may be kept in bounds by the use of police and armed forces. However, that type of conflict can not be solved by a *law-and-order* policy as supported by legalistic arguments throughout the world, nor can such a law-and-order policy be justified with reference to the alleged maintenance of peace—whatever that formula means for the contemporary establishments and the administrators of the status quo. (Cf. Senghaas, 1972c; Narr, 1973; Coser, 1972.)

ON THE PROBLEMS OF PEACE AND SOCIAL JUSTICE IN INTERNATIONAL SOCIETY

In view of the structure of international society and its conflict formations as we have discussed them in this study, we would like to make some additional general remarks on peace and social justice. This will be done in the following short theses:

1. In view of the conflict formations and the conflict potentials inherent in them as these exist in international society, there is no panacea for one single peace policy, no uniform practical instruction for political action which could be applicable to all specific situations. *Our search therefore has to be directed towards strategies for the resolution of conflicts, addressed to specific conflict formations or to a specific conflict*—strategies which have to be varied according to the stage a specific conflict has reached. (Cf. Senghaas, 1972g.)

2. *The traditional concepts of how to secure peace*, oriented towards a peace defined as the absence of violence, *today prove inadequate*. This is particularly true if, as it happens frequently, attempts are made to apply them to all conflict formations and to whatever specific conflicts regardless of their structure. (Cf. contributions by Schmid, Galtung, and Dencik in Senghaas, 1972e.) This inadequacy, even danger, is shown wherever a security policy based on traditional slogans ("si vis pacem, para bellum") with all its consequences is being pursued. *In antagonistic situations, such attempts to secure peace provoke arms races.* (Cf. Senghaas, 1972b part I; Senghaas, 1972h.) In conflicts *within* a society based on structural violence, this kind of peace policy, carried out under the slogan of *law and order*, leads to the further repression of discriminated social strata or entire populations, *thus turning this concept into a focus of peacelessness.*

3. This is why a *more comprehensive concept of peace promotion* has to be formulated. Essentially it must be oriented towards three typical conflict formations:

a) Conflicts involving relatively *equal parties:* i.e., in which *symmetrical* rather than asymmetrical structures exist. This would apply to the intercapitalist conflict formation and—with considerable reservations—also to the capitalist-socialist conflict formation between East and West.

This strategy for promoting peace may be oriented towards two goals: *integration,* by which the confrontation will be superceded; and *association,* by which the infrastructure of such formations is changed (like between Germany and France after 1950). (Cf. Senghaas-Knobloch, 1969; Galtung, 1970.)

However, integration and association cannot be regarded as generally valid principles for action within a peace policy, or as peace-policy blank checks, which in such frames of reference might generally be regarded as proper concepts for peace promotion. They have to be examined in their specific context. Thus the existence of the European Community makes the use of force *between* its principal center members practically impossible. Whether this organization promotes peace beyond this, however, can only be decided by an analysis which determines *its contribution to the promotion of social justice* in domestic matters and in its foreign relations.[32]

b) The concept of peace promotion is to be oriented towards those situations in which the traditional concept is useful: where the prevention of the use of force and of the further escalation of force represents a first, preliminary, step towards the solution of conflicts. This has been the case in some, by far not all, third party interventions.

c) Finally, the concept has to be oriented towards conflicts of an *asymmetrical* structure (North-South conflicts; configurations implying structural violence etc.). Here the peace promotion strategy has to promote the *accentuation* of the conflict in varying intensity in favor of the dependent and discriminated. Their awareness of their own interests should be raised and improved; the articulation and organization of the interests of such groups and states should be built up with the goal of creating a real counterpoise against the other party to the conflict which in the initial situation is the dominant and superior.[33] Thus, in this context, *polarization* cannot be understood as an arbitrary incitement of a specific conflict. Rather is it required for the promotion of peace in order to establish a *conscious* and *sociologically* founded basis for the outlawed, the discriminated, the exploited, and the dependent populations and states by enabling these strata to promote their own interests. On such a basis, there would be a chance for successfully breaking out of discriminating social roles assigned to them within the existing status quo.

This means *that revolutions attempting to overcome social injustice, because other channels of social change have been foreclosed, must be integrated into a concept of peace promotion.* (Dencik, 1972; Galtung, 1973b.) That this consideration is not very popular in the latitudes of highly industrialized countries is easily explained by the privileged situation maintained by this group of states within international society. Such an assessment from the part of the privileged changes nothing in social reality as it exists for most people in this world, nor does it change anything in their fate and suffering to which our considerations refer.[34]

One might have different conceptualizations of such a concept of peace promotion in details. Every specific case to which this concept is applied will inexorably lead to political disputes; the concept *promotion of peace* is a *scientific* yet at the same time a highly *political* concept whose impulse cannot be depoliticized by definitions and semantics. The decisive question which will always have to be put would be: *does the analysis and praxis promoted by peace research also promote social justice for those involved?* This question points to more general problems of social theory and moral philosophy. From an academic point of view, one might approach more and more adequate formulations, but the problems can be solved only in practice. This makes peace and conflict research a non-academic, albeit seriously scientific, discipline *whose ideas have to turn into actual interests of concrete people.* For this reason it represents a nuisance for many—a fact that, in view of the contemporary world situation, has not only to be accepted, but even provoked.

CONCLUDING REMARKS ON THE FOUNDATIONS OF A STRUCTURAL THEORY OF INTERNATIONAL SOCIETY

In the present paper we have developed some systematic observations on contemporary international society and its historical development. While such an analysis has to be short in the context of a brief paper, we nevertheless attempted to give something more than an overview. We have quite deliberately talked about *conflict formations* since that notion seems very appropriate to characterize *general* and at the same time *concrete* structures of international society.

We speak about *general* structures since out of them *concrete conflict potentials* emerge, out of which in turn *specific conflicts* develop. What is generally labelled as the East-West conflict is today a general conflict formation with many concrete political, ideological, socio-economic and, last not least, military conflict potentials (like the 20-year long dispute on the consolidation of the post World War II status quo in central Europe). Such general conflict formations also provoke concrete conflict potentials and conflicts in areas outside their immediate realm which is a result of the globalization of international politics. (On this conflict formation see Willms, 1972 and Krippendorff, 1972.) Such concrete conflict potentials then manifest themselves in *concrete conflicts* (like the Berlin crises) where concrete *conflict attitudes* and *conflict behavior* can be observed and systematically analyzed.

A *structural theory of international society* has to elaborate its constitutive components both under a *diachronic* and under a *synchronic* perspective. In such a procedure, *theoretical reflection* and *concrete analysis* have to be interconnected with the aim of formulating *a concrete-general theory*. We deliberately emphasize the oscillation between *theoretical reflection* (in which already a lot of empirical experience has to go in if it should not be in a very bad sense abstract) and *empirical analysis* (which itself would be empiricist without theoretical foundation), since only a permanent feedback between theory and empirical reality will, within specific analytical issue areas, promote a concrete-general theory. Under working perspectives, a so called *progressive-regressive method* is of utmost importance in this context. (Cf. Schmidt, 1971; Sartre, 1967.)

We do not believe that there exists a special method in social science for the analysis of the international society. Rather we assume that one has to put into such an analysis whatever available social science methodology, and this is a reason why we would only hint at certain procedural aspects of the process of formulating such a theory. The following six prerequisites for a formulation of such a theory cannot be separated one from the other, but are highly interlocked with many feedbacks among themselves:

1. Comprehensive elaboration of empirical reality and the analysis of the material surface appearances in its historically relevant details.

2. Analytical differentiation of this material into its constitutive abstract components *(the step from the concrete to the abstract)*.

3. Investigation of the decisive interdependencies between these components, with the aim of formulating, on a certain level of abstraction, the basic patterns and the moving principles of that segment of empirical reality to which one's analysis is related.

4. Discovering decisive linkages between the essences and the surface appearances *(the step from the abstract to the concrete*; the analytical reproduction of the concrete as a unity of manifold determinants).

5. Practical empirical verification of the analysis in face of concrete historical developments.

6. Discovering new and empirically relevant data and new interdependencies, thanks to the application of theoretical and empirical results in concrete practical actions within a highly complex reality. (These six points are quoted from Mandel, 1972, pp. 14–15.)

Such a *concrete-general* theory, which can be built up only gradually, is vital for the understanding of international society, since this society is not characterized by the coexistence of self-encapsulated socio-economic formations qua subsystems (to use the language of systems analysis here): instead, *international society is a highly antagonistic and contradictory totality*. We must emphasize this *totality* as a basic characteristic of international society, since most researchers are still accustomed to interpreting international society as an *international system* with *subsystems* as its components. Formally such a conceptual approach is possible, of course, but the development of the theory of international politics and the international system in the last fifteen years has shown that this approach is a highly sterile one.[35] Even though, on a very formal basis, system analysis can come to some preliminary understanding of the architecture of the international society, and even though certain useful research has been inspired by such approaches (for example transaction studies), *this approach has, in the past fifteen years, not been able to come to grips with the causes of the development dynamics of international society*. It is characteristic for systems analysis that it, often more implicitly than explicitly, assumes *dynamic* forces like power politics, *disregarding the particular development stage of international society and disregarding concrete conflict formations*. Necessarily, international politics then looks like the recurrence of the ever-similar, which is not the case in reality.

If international society and its development is conceived as an *antagonistic totality*, then there is an immediate challenge to elaborate in detail those *causes of the development dynamics* of international society. In this respect, the established disciplines of *international politics* and *international relations* as they have developed in the last 20 years in the West (and as they seem to be developing also in socialist countries) are of no particular help. This is so because neither in these disciplines nor in most of contemporary peace and conflict research has international society been understood as *a totality of production relations and their exchange relations on a world scale*. (A first, and very perspicacious analysis is Bucharin, 1929.) If at all, then these disciplines looked into exchange relations under the perspective of descriptive statistics, or dealt with problems of the conventional bourgeois economy (the theorem of comparative costs, etc.). In reality, international society (and by implication also the world economy) is characterized by a *graduated structure of productivity differentials as the result of an unequal and combined development of regions, states, production branches, and even firms.* (Mandel, 1972, p. 96. Italics mine.) It constitutes an *integrated unity,* but *an integrated unity of nonhomogenous parts in which the lacking homogeneity serves as a prerequisite of unity.*

In this context, within the concluding remarks of our paper, we can only state *that the political economy of international society must become the very focus of a structural theory of this society.* The structure, the dynamics, the extent, and the distribution patterns of *accumulation on a world scale*—to use the notion in the sense of the critique of political economy—will be the analytical take-off point for theoretical reflection and empirical analysis. Only under such a perspective will it be possible to cope with processes of *metropolization* and processes of *peripherization* over time. This problem refers particularly to the rise and fall of new and old metropoles (up to the status of a metropole, or down to the status of a periphery), including an analysis of those peripheries which had never achieved in history the status of a metropole (like most countries in the Third World today). This perspective will also make it possible to analyze the simultaneity of social economic formations of unequal development levels *as unequal but combined formations.* And finally, it will be possible to conceptualize and analyze concretely the mechanisms of exploitation on a world scale. (See particularly Amin, 1971 and Novack, 1966; also Dos Santos, 1972; Bambirra, 1972.)

NOTES

1. The notes and references are restricted essentially to some information about the most recent international literature. This is justified by the fact that the *macro*-discussion on the international society has only begun very recently.

2. Compare the majority of contributions in Deutsch & Hoffman, 1968.

3. On this area see Deutsch, 1971, particularly Chapt. 15, as well as Senghaas-Knobloch, 1969, and Senghaas-Knobloch, 1972.

4. Many formulations by the so called realistic school (Morgenthau) come very close to such a thesis.

5. Some further theoretical reflections are to be found in Senghaas, 1972b, part II.

6. On the theory of the nation state see the classical work by Deutsch, 1966.

7. Such a notion of *anarchic* comes very close to the one used by Marx with reference to capitalism. It refers to a structure whose dynamics regularly produce crises. A critique of those characterizations of the international society to which I referred in the first part of this paper can be found in Luhmann, 1971, particularly pp. 1–10.

8. On this see the classical literature by Weber and Sombart as well as the brilliant essay by Hintze, 1964. See also the comprehensive descriptions in Kulischer, 1971; Nef, 1963; Dobb, 1970; as well as Krippendorff, 1972; Krippendorff, 1973; and now particularly Mandel, 1972.

9. On the inter-capitalist community of interests cf. Jalée, 1971; on conflict potentials between the capitalist metropoles see Neusüss, 1972.

10. The interlinkages between the *general* capitalist *interest* and *particular* capitalist *interests* have not yet been dealt with in serious theoretical reflections.

11. Cf. Altvater, 1969; Neusüss et al., 1971; Busch/Schöller/Seelow, 1971, as well as Neusüss, 1972. On classical imperialism and those conflict potentials which characterized the classical period see Wehler, 1970; Mommsen, 1971; Boulding & Mukerjee, 1972.

12. In making such an assessment, one must not forget that this development has been accompanied by a tremendous militarization by the Western societies, particularly the U.S. Asbjörn Eide (Oslo) has in a critique of a previous version of this paper explicitly called my attention to this fact (see his paper: "De-escalation and Prevention of Escalation," Vienna, Institut für den Frieden, December 1972). On U.S. imperialism and militarism see the studies in Fann & Hodges, 1971.

13. This danger has explicitly been analysed by Galtung, 1972 as well as by Lodgaard, 1972.

14. I am using here this notion as a contrast term to "*dependent reproduction*" as it is used in the Latin American literature on "*dependencia.*"

15. See my argumentation in Senghaas, 1972d.

16. Galtung has used this notion in this article on Europe; see Galtung, 1972.

17. See the literature mentioned in note 14.

18. Cf. also the result of a study group under the direction of Johan Galtung, Galtung et al., 1972.

19. This differentiation is part of the official semantics in socialist states, although the specific contents vary.

20. On this see the model on autistic processes in such areas in Senghaas, 1972a.

21. On the following cf. my introduction to and the contributions in Senghaas, 1972f. Furthermore, the following works are of particular interest to that area: Amin, 1971; Palloix, 1972; Cardoso & Faletto, 1971; Garcia, 1970; Gonzáles Casanova, 1970; Dos Santos, 1970; Frank, 1968; Furtado, 1969; Marini, 1969; Hinkelammert, 1970; Sunkel & Paz, 1970. See also Martins, 1972, and Lagos, 1963.

22. On the development and function of multinational corporations see Kindleberger, 1970; Vernon, 1971; and various studies by Hymer, 1972.

23. On this topic see Khalatbari, 1972; Baran, 1966; Schuhler, 1968; Rhodes, 1970; and the very informative study by Jalée, 1969.

24. Johan Galtung has explicitly referred to this phenomenon in his theorem of differential spinoff effects in his contribution on imperialism. See Galtung, 1971.

25. Besides the literature already quoted in note 22, see Emmanuel, 1969; Mandel, 1972, particularly chap. 11.

26. This is one fundamental result of the so-called *dependencia* discussion in Latin America within the last 10 years. Extensive references to the *dependencia* literature which go beyond the ones mentioned in note 22 can be found in the bibliography in Senghaas, 1972f, pp. 386–399. See particularly the work by Dos Santos, Celso Furtado, as well as Osvaldo Sunkel in this book. A good review in Peña, 1971.

27. Armando Cordova in an unpublished paper.

28. On the political economy of this problem see Weisskopf, 1972. For the pauperization effects of aid see Mende, 1972.

29. As is well known, the counter-revolutionary strategy of *"counter insurgency"* was revitalized about 15 years ago, though not invented at that time, and has been translated into new weapon programs.

30. Cf. Galtung, 1972, as well as the very instructive article by Hveem & Holthe, 1972. On the concept of organized peacelessness, see Senghaas, 1972a.

31. On the theory of autistic escalation processes see Senghaas, 1972b, part II. Which misinterpretation, conditioned by fixated political interests, science can bring forth is clearly demonstrated in the evaluation of the Soviet-Chinese conflict by Soviet scientists in a most recent publication supposed to be representative of Soviet thinking on international conflicts. Cf. the article of W. I. Gantmann on types, content, structure, and development phases of international conflicts in the book edited by Zurkin & Primakov, 1972. In this article one can read the following: "It is not excluded that the development of particular (even relatively stable and very sharp) international conflict situations can be observed in those cases where in the leading circles of a socialist country, nationalist, chauvinist, anti-Soviet movements prevail under particular conditions, as is now the case in China. These emotions are able to deform the class nature and the aims of foreign policy, and lead to conflicts with other socialist states. Such a development is, however, not typical for socialist foreign policy. Under the perspective of a scientific assessment they should not be discussed within the frame of a typology. Each case of such extraordinary conflict situations should be subject to a particular concrete analysis." (p. 36.)

32. With respect to its external relations Johan Galtung has most recently correctly analysed the imperialist character of the growing superpower EEC, see Galtung, 1972. Unfortunately there is still no cost-benefit analysis of the EEC, as it would have to be related to the different payoffs of this integration process for different social strata and classes.

33. This step process is very aptly analyzed by Dahrendorf, 1957. See particularly also the studies initiated and carried out by Ebert, 1970, and Dencik, 1972.

34. The increasing critical self-assertions even by establishment organizations like the Church, scientific organizations within the Third World speak for themselves.

35. I do not go here into a deeper critique of this since it seems to be more important to work on a new productive beginning than to criticize once again the deficiency of old contributions.

REFERENCES

Albrecht, U., et al. 1972: Is Europe to demilitarize? Some analytical suggestions and practical recommendations, *Instant Research on Peace and Violence*, No. 4.

Altvater, E. 1969: *Die Weltwährungskrise*. Frankfurt.

Amin, S. 1971: *L'accumulation à l'échelle mondiale*. Paris.

Bambirra, V. 1972: Integracíon monopolica mundial e industrializacíon: sus contradicciones, *Sociedad y Desarrollo*, No. 1, pp. 53–80.

Baran, P. 1966: *Politische Ökonomie des wirtschaftlichen Wachstums*. Neuwied and Berlin.

Bhagwati, N. (ed.). 1972: *Economics and world order*. New York.

Boulding, K., & T. Mukerjee (eds.). 1972: *Economic imperialism*. Ann Arbor.

Bucharin, N. 1929: *Imperialismus und Weltwirtschaft*. Vienna.

Busch/Schöller/Seelow. 1971: *Weltmarkt und Weltwährungskrise*. Bremen.

Cardoso, F. H. 1971: *Ideologías de la burguesía industrial en sociedades dependientes*. Mexico.

Cardoso, F. H., & Faletto Enzo 1971: *Dependencia y desarrollo en América Latina*. Mexico.

Coser, L. (ed.). 1972: *Collective violence and civil conflict*. Special Issue of the *Journal of
Social Issues* 28, No. 1.

Dahrendorf, R. 1957: *Soziale Klassen und Klassenkonflikt in der industriellen Gesellschaft*.
Stuttgart.

Dencik, L. 1972: Plädoyer für eine revolutionäre Konfliktforschung, pp. 247–270 in
Senghaas, 1972e.

Deutsch, K. W. 1966: *Nationalism and social communication*. Cambridge.

———— . 1971: *Analyse internationaler Politik*. Frankfurt.

Deutsch, K. W., & S. Hoffman (eds.). 1968: *The relevance of international law*. Cambridge.

Deutsch, K. W., & D. Senghaas. 1972: Die brüchige Vernunft von Staaten, pp. 105–63
in Senghaas, 1972d.

Dobb, M. 1970: *Entwicklung des Kapitalismus. Vom Spätfeudalismus bis zur Gegenwart*.
Cologne.

Dos Santos, T. 1970: *Dependencia y cambio social*. Santiago.

———— . 1972: Contradicciones del imperialismo contemporáneo, *Sociedad y Desarrollo*,
No. 1, pp. 9–34.

Ebert, T. 1970: *Gewaltfreier Aufstand. Alternative zum Bürgerkrieg*. Frankfurt.

Emerson, R. 1960: *From empire to nation. The rise to self-assertion of Asian and African
peoples*. Boston.

Emmanuel, A. 1969: *L'échange inégal*. Paris.

Falk, R. 1971: *This endangered planet. Prospects and proposals for human survival*. New
York.

Fann, K. T., & D. Hodges (eds.). 1971: *Readings in US imperialism*. Boston.

Frank, A. G. 1968: *Kapitalismus und Unterentwicklung in Lateinamerika*. Frankfurt.

Furtado, C. 1969: *La concentracion del poder económico en los Estados Unidos y sus reflejos en
la América Latina*. Buenos Aires.

Galtung, J. 1969: Violence, peace, and peace research, *Journal of Peace Research* 6,
pp. 167–191.

———— . 1970: A theory of peaceful cooperation, pp. 9–20 in J. Galtung (ed.): *Cooperation in Europe*. Oslo and Assen.

———— . 1971: A structural theory of imperialism, *Journal of Peace Research* 8,
pp. 81–118.

———— . 1972: Europe: bipolar, bicentric, or cooperative? *Journal of Peace Research* 9,
pp. 1–26.

———— . 1973a: *The European Community: a superpower in the making*. Oslo and London.

———— . 1973b: Eine strukturelle Theorie der Revolution, pp. 121–167 in M. Jänicke
(ed.): *Herrschaft und Krise*. Cologne.

Galtung, J., et al. 1972: Some institutional suggestions for a system of security and
cooperation in Europe, *Bulletin of Peace Proposals* 3, No. 1, pp. 73–88.

Gantzel, J. 1972: Zur herrschaftssoziologischen Problembereichen von Abhängigkeits-
beziehungen in der gegenwärtigen Weltgesellschaft, pp. 105–120 in Senghaas, 1972f.

García, A. 1970: *La estructura del atraso en la América Latina*. Buenos Aires.

Gonzáles Casanova, P. 1970: *Sociología de la explotacíon*. Mexico City.

Hinkelammert, F. 1970: *El subdesarollo latino-americano: un caso del desarrollo capitalista*. Buenos Aires.

Hintze, O. 1964: Wirtschaft und Politik im Zeitalter des modernen Kapitalismus, pp. 427–452 in *Soziologie und Geschichte*. Göttingen.

Hoffman, S. 1965: *The state of war*. New York.

Hveem, H., & O. K. Holthe. 1972: EEC and the Third World, *Instant Research on Peace and Violence*, No. 2, pp. 73–85.

Hymer, S. 1972: Multinationale Konzerne und das Gesetz der ungleichen Entwicklung, pp. 201–238 in Senghaas, 1972f.

Jalée, P. 1969: *Die Dritte Welt in der Weltwirtschaft*. Frankfurt.

————. 1971: *Das neueste Stadium des Imperialismus*. Munich.

Khalatbari, P. 1972: *Ökonomische Unterentwicklung. Mechanismus, Probleme, Ausweg*. Frankfurt.

Kindleberger, C. (ed.). 1970: *The international corporation*. Cambridge.

Krippendorff, E. 1971: The state as a focus of peace research. *Papers, Peace Research Society (International)* 16, pp. 47–60.

Krippendorff, E. (ed.). 1972: *Probleme der internationalen Beziehungen*. Frankfurt.

————. 1973: *Internationale Beziehungen*. Cologne.

Kulischer, J. 1971: *Allgemeine Wirtschaftsgeschichte des Mittelalters und der Neuzeit*. Darmstadt.

Kuznets, S. 1966: *Modern economic growth. Rate, structure, and spread*. New Haven.

Lagos, G. 1963: *International stratification and underdeveloped countries*. Chapel Hill.

Landes, D. 1969: *The unbound Prometheus*. Cambridge.

Lodgaard, S. 1972: Political changes and economic reorientation in Europe. The role of industrial cooperation, *Instant Research on Peace and Violence*, No. 3, pp. 145–157.

Luhmann, N. 1971: Die Weltgesellschaft, *Archiv für Rechts- und Sozialphilosophie* 57, pp. 1–35.

Mandel, E. 1968: *Die EWG und die Konkurrenz Europa-Amerika*. Frankfurt.

————. 1972: *Der Spätkapitalismus*. Frankfurt.

Marini, R. M. 1969: *Subdesarrollo y revolucíon*. Mexico City.

————. 1972: Brazilian subimperialism, *Monthly Review* 23, No. 9, pp. 14–24.

Martins, L. 1972: *Amérique Latine. Crise et dépendence*. Paris.

Mende, T. 1972: *De l'aide à la récolonisation. Les leçons d'un échec*. Paris.

Misra, K. P. 1972: Intra-state imperialism. The case of Pakistan, *Journal of Peace Research* 9, pp. 27–40.

Möller, W., & F. Vilmar. 1972: *Sozialistische Friedenspolitik für Europa*. Reinbeck.

Mommsen, W. (ed.). 1971: *Der moderne Imperialismus*. Stuttgart.

Narr, W. D. 1973: Gewalt und Legitimität, *Leviathan* 1, No. 1, pp. 7–41.

Nef, J. U. 1963: *Western civilization since the Renaissance. Peace, war, industry and the arts*. New York.

Neusüss, C. 1972: *Imperialismus und Weltmarktbewegung des Kapitals*. Erlangen.

Neusüss, C. et al. 1971: Kapitalistischen Weltmarkt und Weltwährungskrise, *Probleme des Klassenkampfes*, No. 1, pp. 5–116.

Novack, G. 1966: *Uneven and combined development in history*. New York.

Palloix, C. 1971: *L'économie mondiale capitaliste*. Paris.

Peña, S. de la. 1971: *El anti-desarrollo en América Latina*. Mexico.

Quijano, A. 1970: *Redefinicíon de la dependencia y de la marginalizacíon en América Latina*. (Unpublished.)

Rhodes, R. (ed.). 1970: *Imperialism and underdevelopment*. New York.

Rowthorn, R. 1971: Imperialism in the seventies: unity or rivalry. *New Left Review* 69, pp. 31–54.

Sartre, J. P. 1967: *Kritik der dialektischen Vernunft.* Hamburg.

Schlupp, F., et al. 1973: Zur Theorie und Ideologie internationaler Interdependenz. Special Issue No. 5 of *Politische Vierteljahresschrift.* Ed. by Jürgen Gantzel. Cologne and Opladen.

Schmidt, A. 1971: *Geschichte und Struktur. Fragen einer marxistischen Historik.* Munich.

Schmiederer, U. 1973: Systemkonkurrenz als Strukturprinzip der internationalen Politik. In Special Issue No. 5 of *Politische Vierteljahresschrift.* Ed. Jürgen Gantzel. Cologne and Opladen.

Schuhler, C. 1968: *Zur politischen Ökonomie der armen Welt.* Munich.

Senghaas, D. 1972a: *Abschreckung und Frieden. Studien zur Kritik organisierter Friedlosigkeit.* Frankfurt.

————. 1972b: *Rüstung und Militarismus.* Frankfurt.

————. 1972c: *Aggressivität und kollektive Gewalt.* Stuttgart.

————. 1972d: *Aufrüstung durch Rüstungskontrolle. Über den symbolischen Gebrauch von Politik.* Stuttgart.

————. (ed.). 1972e: *Kritische Friedensforschung.* Frankfurt.

————. (ed.). 1972f: *Imperialismus und strukturelle Gewalt.* Frankfurt.

————. 1972g: Friedensforschung. Theoretische, Fragestellungen und praktische Probleme, *Jahrbuch für Friedens- und Konfliktforschung* 2, pp. 10–22.

————. 1972h: Dynamique de la course aux armements, condition restrictive de la politique de détente Est l'Ouest, *Politique Etrangère* 37, pp. 765–782.

————. (ed.). 1973: *Abhängigkeit und strukturelle Theorie der Unterentwicklung.* Frankfurt.

Senghaas, D., et al. 1973: MBFR: *Aufrüstung durch Rüstungskontrolle?* (Unpublished manuscript.)

Senghaas-Knobloch, E. 1969: *Frieden durch Integration und Assoziation.* Stuttgart.

————. 1972: Internationale Organisationen, pp. 103–136 in Krippendorff (ed.), 1972.

Sombart, W. 1913: *Krieg und Kapitalismus.* Munich and Leipzig.

Sprout, H., & M. Sprout. 1972: *Towards a politics of the planet Earth.* New York.

Sunkel, O. 1972: Transnationale kapitalistische Integration und nationale Desintegration: Der Fall Lateinamerika, pp. 258–315 in Senghaas, 1972f.

Sunkel, O., & P. Paz. 1970: *El subdesarrollo latinoamericano y la teoría del desarrollo.* Mexico.

Vernon, R. 1971: *Sovereignty at bay. The multinational spread of US enterprises.* New York.

Weber, M. 1967: *Wirtschaft und Gesellschaft.* Tübingen.

Wehler, H.-U. (ed.). 1970: *Imperialismus.* Cologne.

Weisskopf, T. 1972: Capitalism, underdevelopment, and the future of poor countries, pp. 43–77 in Bhagwati, 1972.

Willms, B. 1972: *Entwicklung und Revolution. Grundlagen einer dialektischen Theorie der internationalen Politik.* Frankfurt.

Wolff, R. 1971: Die US Banken und das expandierende US Imperium, pp. 219–246 in *Kapitalismus in den siebziger Jahren.* Frankfurt.

Zurkin, V. V., & E. M. Primakov (eds.). 1972: *Mezdunarodnye konflikty* ("International conflicts"). Moscow.

17
THE BEGINNING OF THE END

Leo Tolstoy

During last year, in Holland, a young man named Van der Veer was called on to enter the National Guard. To the summons of the commander, Van der Veer answered in the following letter:

"Thou Shalt do no Murder."

To M. Herman Sneiders, *Commandant of the National Guard of the Middelburg district.*

Dear Sir—Last week I received a document ordering me to appear at the municipal office, to be, according to law, enlisted in the National Guards. As you probably noticed, I did not appear, and this letter is to inform you, plainly and without equivocation, that I do not intend to appear before the commission. I know well that I am taking a heavy responsibility, that you have the right to punish me, and that you will not fail to use this right. But that does not frighten me. The reasons which lead me to this passive resistance seem to me strong enough to outweigh the responsibility I take.

I, who, if you please, am not a Christian, understand better than most Christians the commandment which is put at the head of this letter, the commandment which is rooted in human nature, in the mind of man. When but a boy, I allowed myself to be taught the trade of soldier, the art of killing; but now I renounce it. I would not kill at the command of others, and thus have murder on my conscience without any personal cause or reason whatever.

Can you mention anything more degrading to a human being than carrying out such murder, such massacre? I am unable to kill, even to see an animal killed; therefore I became a vegetarian. And now I am to be ordered to shoot men who have done me no harm; for I take it that it is not to shoot at leaves and branches of trees that soldiers are taught to use guns.

But you will reply, perhaps, that the National Guard is besides, and especially, to keep civic order.

M. Commandant, if order really reigned in our society, if the social organism were really healthy—in other words, if there were in our social relations no

Reprinted from *Tolstoy's Writings on Civil Disobedience and Non-Violence* by permission of Humanities Press, Inc. Atlantic Highlands, New Jersey.

crying abuses, if it were not established that one man shall die of hunger while another gratifies his every whim of luxury, then you would see me in the front ranks of the defenders of this orderly state. But I flatly decline to help in preserving the present so-called "social order." Why, M. Commandant, should we throw dust in each other's eyes? We both know quite well what the "preservation of order" means: upholding the rich against the poor toilers who begin to perceive their rights. Do we not know the role which the National Guard played in the last strike at Rotterdam? For no reason, the Guard had to be on duty hours and hours to watch over the property of the commercial houses which were affected. Can you for a moment suppose that I should shoot down working-people who are acting quite within their rights? You cannot be so blind. Why then complicate the question? Certainly, it is impossible for me to allow myself to be molded into an obedient National Guardsman such as you want and must have.

For all these reasons, but especially because I hate murder by order, I refuse to serve as a National Guardsman, and ask you not to send me either uniform or arms, because I have a fixed resolve not to use them.—I greet you, M. Commandant,

J. K. Van der Veer.

This letter, in my opinion, has great importance. Refusals of military service in Christian states began when in Christian states military service appeared. Or rather when the states, the power of which rests upon violence, laid claim to Christianity without giving up violence. In truth, it cannot be otherwise. A Christian, whose doctrine enjoins upon him humility, non-resistance to evil, love to all (even to the most malicious), cannot be a soldier; that is, he cannot join a class of men whose business is to kill their fellow-men. Therefore it is that these Christians have always refused and now refuse military service.

But of true Christians there have always been but few. Most people in Christian countries count as Christians only those who profess the doctrines of some Church, which doctrines have nothing in common, except the name, with true Christianity. That occasionally one in tens of thousands of recruits should refuse to serve did not trouble the hundreds of thousands, the millions, of men who every year accepted military service.

Impossible that the whole enormous majority of Christians who enter upon military service are wrong, and only the exceptions, sometimes uneducated people, are right; while every archbishop and man of learning thinks the service compatible with Christianity. So think the majority, and, untroubled regarding themselves as Christians, they enter the rank of murderers. But now appears a man who, as he himself says, is not a Christian, and who refuses military service, not from religious motives, but from motives of the simplest kind, motives intelligible and common to all men, of whatever religion or nation, whether Catholic, Mohammedan, Buddhist, Confucian, whether Spaniards or Japanese.

Van der Veer refuses military service, not because he follows the commandment, "Thou shalt do no murder," not because he is a Christian, but because he holds murder to be opposed to human nature. He writes that he simply abhors all killing, and abhors it to such a degree that he becomes a vegetarian just to avoid participation in the killing of animals; and, above, all, he says, he refuses military service because he thinks "murder by order," that is, the obligation to kill those whom one is ordered to kill (which is the real nature of military service), is incompatible with man's uprightness.

Alluding to the usual objection that if he refuses others will follow his example, and the present social order will be destroyed, he answers that he does not wish to preserve the present social order, because it is bad, because in it the rich dominate the poor, which ought not to be. So that, even if he had any other doubts as to the propriety of serving or not serving, the one consideration that in serving as a soldier he must, by carrying arms and threatening to kill, support the oppressing rich against the oppressed poor would compel him to refuse military service.

If Van der Veer were to give as the reason for his refusal his adherence to the Christian religion, those who now join the military service could say, "We are no sectarians, and do not acknowledge Christianity; therefore we do not see the need to act as you do."

But the reasons given by Van der Veer are so simple, clear, and universal that it is impossible not to apply them each to his own case. As things are, to deny the force of these reasons in one's own case, one must say:

"I like killing, and am ready to kill, not only evil-disposed people, but my own oppressed and unfortunate fellow-countrymen, and I perceive nothing wrong in the promise to kill, at the order of the first officer who comes across me, whomever he bids me kill."

Here is a young man. In whatever surroundings, family, creed, he has been brought up, he has been taught that he must be good, that it is bad to strike and kill, not only men, but even animals; he has been taught that a man must value his uprightness, which uprightness consists in acting according to conscience. This is equally taught to the Confucian in China, the Shintoist in Japan, the Buddhist, and the Mohammedan. Suddenly, after being taught all this, he enters the military service, where he is required to do the precise opposite of what he has been taught. He is told to fit himself for wounding and killing, not animals, but men; he is told to renounce his independence as a man, and obey, in the business of murder, men whom he does not know, utter strangers to him.

To such a command, what right answer can a man of our day make? Surely, only this, "I do not wish to, and I will not."

Exactly this answer Van der Veer gives. And it is hard to invent any reply to him and to those who, in a similar position, do as he does.

One may not see this point, through attention not having been called to it; one may not understand the import of an action, as long as it remains unexplained. But once pointed out and explained, one can no longer fail to see, or feign blindness to what is quite obvious.

There may still be found men who do not reflect upon their action in entering military service, and men who want war with foreign people, and men who would continue the oppression of the laboring class, and even men who like murder for murder's sake. Such men can continue as soldiers; but even they cannot now fail to know that there are others, the best men in the world—not only among Christians, but among Mohammedans, Brahmanists, Buddhists, Confucians—who look upon war and soldiers with aversion and contempt, and whose number grows hourly. No arguments can talk away this plain fact, that a man with any sense of his own dignity cannot enslave himself to an unknown, or even a known, master whose business is killing. Now just in this consists military service, with all its compulsion of discipline.

"But consider the consequences to him who refuses," I am told. "It is all very well for you, an old man exempted from this exaction, and safe by your position to preach martyrdom; but what about those to whom you preach, and who, believing in you, refuse to serve, and ruin their young lives?"

"But what can I do?"—I answer those who speak thus:

"Because I am old, must I therefore not point out the evil which I clearly, unquestionably see, seeing it precisely because I am old and have lived and thought for long? Must a man who stands on the far side of the river, beyond the reach of that ruffian whom he sees compelling one man to murder another, not cry out to the slayer, bidding him to refrain, for the reason that such interference will still more enrage the ruffian? Moreover, I by no means see why the government, persecuting those who refuse military service, does not turn its punishment upon me, recognizing in me an instigator. I am not too old for persecution, for any and all sorts of punishments, and my position is a defenseless one. At all events, whether blamed and persecuted or not, whether those who refuse military service are persecuted or not, I, whilst I live, will not cease from saying what I now say; for I cannot refrain from acting according to my conscience." Just in this very thing is Christian truth powerful, irresistible; namely, that, being the teaching of truth, in affecting men it is not to be governed by outside considerations. Whether young or old, whether persecuted or not, he who adopts the Christian, the true, conception of life, cannot shrink from the claims of his conscience. In this is the essence and peculiarity of Christianity, distinguishing it from all other religious teachings; and in this is its unconquerable power.

Van der Veer says he is not a Christian. But the motives of his refusal and action are Christian. He refuses because he does not wish to kill a brother man; he does not obey, because the commands of his conscience are more binding upon him than the commands of men. Precisely on this account is Van der Veer's refusal so important. Thereby he shows that Christianity is not a sect or creed which some may profess and others reject; but that it is naught else than a life's following of that light of reason which illumines all men. The merit of Christianity is not that it prescribes to men such and such acts, but that it foresees and points out the way by which all mankind must go and does go.

Those men who now behave rightly and reasonably do so, not because they follow prescriptions of Christ, but because that line of action which was pointed out eighteen hundred years ago has now become identified with human conscience.

This is why I think the action and letter of Van der Veer are of great import.

As a fire lit on a prairie or in a forest will not die out until it has burned all that is dry and dead, and therefore combustible, so the truth, once articulated in human utterance, will not cease its work until all falsehood, appointed for destruction, surrounding and hiding the truth on all sides as it does, is destroyed. The fire smolders long; but as soon as it flashes into flame, all that can burn burns quickly.

So with the truth, which takes long to reach a right expression, but once that clear expression in word is given, falsehood and wrong are soon to be destroyed. One of the partial manifestations of Christianity—the idea that men can live without the institution of slavery—although it had been included in the Christian concept, was clearly expressed, so it seems to me, only by writers at the end of the eighteenth century. Up to that time, not only the ancient pagans, as Plato and Aristotle, but even men near to us in time, and Christians, could not imagine a human society without slavery. Thomas More could not imagine even a Utopia without slavery. So also men of the beginning of this century could not imagine the life of man without war. Only after the Napoleonic wars was the idea clearly expressed that man can live without war. And now a hundred years have gone since the first clear expression of the idea that mankind can live without slavery; and there is no longer slavery in Christian nations. And there shall not pass away another hundred years after the clear utterance of the idea that mankind can live without war, before war shall cease to be. Very likely some form of armed violence will remain, just as wage-labor remains after the abolition of slavery; but, at least, wars and armies will be abolished in the outrageous form, so repugnant to reason and moral sense, in which they now exist.

Signs that this time is near are many. These signs are such as the helpless position of governments, which more and more increase their armaments; the multiplication of taxation and the discontent of the nations; the extreme degree of efficiency with which deadly weapons are constructed; the activity of congresses and societies of peace; but above all, the refusals of individuals to take military service. In these refusals is the key to the solution of the question. You say that military service is necessary; that, without soldiers, disasters will happen to us. That may be; but, holding the idea of right and wrong which is universal among men today, yourselves included, I cannot kill men to order. So that if, as you say, military service is essential—then arrange it in some way not so contradictory to my, and your, conscience. But, until you have so arranged it, do not claim from me what is against my conscience, which I can by no means disobey.

Thus, inevitably, and very soon, must answer all honest and reasonable men; not only the men of Christendom, but even Mohammedans and the so-called heathen, the Brahmanists, Buddhists, and Confucians. Maybe, by the power of inertia, the soldiering trade will go on for some time to come; but even now the question stands solved in the human conscience, and with every day, every hour, more and more men come to the same solution; and to stay the movement is, at this juncture, not possible. Every recognition of a truth by man, or rather, every deliverance from an error, as in the case of slavery before our eyes, is always attained through a conflict between the awakening conscience and the inertia of the old condition.

At first the inertia is so powerful, the conscience so weak, that the first attempt to escape from error is met only with astonishment. The new truth seems madness. Is it proposed to live without slavery? Then who will work? Is it proposed to live without fighting? Then everybody will come and conquer us.

But the power of conscience grows, inertia weakens, and astonishment is changing to sneers and contempt. "The Holy Scriptures acknowledge masters and slaves. These relations have always been, and now come these wiseacres who want to change the whole world"; so men spoke concerning slavery. "All the scientists and philosophers recognize the lawfulness, and even sacredness, of war; and are we immediately to believe that there is no need of war?"

So men speak concerning war. But conscience continues to grow and to become clear; the number increases of those who recognize the new truth, and sneer and contempt give place to subterfuge and trickery. Those who support the error make slow to understand and admit the incongruity and cruelty of the practice they defend, but think its abolition impossible just now, so delaying its abolition indefinitely. "Who does not know that slavery is an evil? But men are not yet ripe for freedom, and liberation will produce horrible disasters"—men used to say concerning slavery, forty years ago. "Who does not know that war is an evil? But while mankind is still so bestial, abolition of armies will do more harm than good," men say concerning war today.

Nevertheless, the idea is doing its work; it grows, it burns the falsehood; and the time has come when the madness, the uselessness, the harmfulness, and wickedness of the error are so clear (as it happened in the sixties with slavery in Russia and America) that even now it is impossible to justify it. Such is the present position as to war. Just as, in the sixties, no attempts were made to justify slavery, but only to maintain it; so today no man attempts any longer to justify war and armies, but only tries, in silence, to use the inertia which still supports them, knowing very well that this cruel and immoral organization for murder, which seems so powerful, may at any moment crumble down, never more to be raised.

Once a drop of water oozes through the dam, once a brick falls out from a great building, once a mesh comes loose in the strongest net—the dam bursts, the building falls, the net unweaves. Such a drop, such a brick, such a loosed mesh, it seems to me, is the refusal of Van der Veer, explained by reasons universal to all mankind.

Upon this refusal of Van der Veer like refusals must follow more and more often. As soon as these become numerous, the very men (their name is legion) who the day before said, "It is impossible to live without war," will say at once that they have this long time declared the madness and immorality of war, and they will advise everybody to follow Van der Veer's example. Then, of wars and armies, as these are now, there will remain only the recollection.

And this time is coming.

18
TOWARD A DEPENDABLE PEACE: A PROPOSAL FOR AN APPROPRIATE SECURITY SYSTEM

Robert Johansen

OUR PRESENT INSECURITY

We can no longer escape an alarming fact of life: the global arms buildup is out of control. At the present time, nobody can regulate it. No one can anticipate the human consequences of new weapons technology rapidly being deployed by the militarily strong and spreading soon thereafter to many other governments.

Most experts agree that if present trends continue they will eventually lead to catastrophe. Despite almost continuous rounds of arms control negotiations[1] since World War II, more deadly weapons exist in the arsenals of more national governments who are spending greater amounts of money for instruments of more frightening destruction than at any time in history.

Can nothing be done? Are there no alternatives to massive armaments or surrender? Are there no practical steps to be taken toward a more secure, less violent world? The purpose of this chapter is to address these questions from the perspective of a planetary citizen, yet with a focus on the United States role in global peacemaking.

THE FAILURE OF PRESENT POLICIES

The limits of the present approach to reversing the arms buildup are clear. Military expenditures, destructive capability, and the ability to produce nuclear weapons have expanded dangerously over the past three decades of arms control negotiations.

Despite prolonged arms control negotiations, the world's governments have spent more than $6 trillion for armaments since World War II. Since 1948, world military expenditures in real terms have increased at an average annual rate of 4.5%. More than twice as large a portion of the world's total output now goes to military uses as did either before World War I or during the period

Reprinted with permission from *Bulletin of Peace Proposals*, 1979, 2. This is an abridged version of an essay published by the Institute for World Order, New York, 1978.

between World Wars I and II. In 1978 alone, the world's governments spent roughly $400 billion for military purposes. Annual military expenditures equal the total income of the 2 billion people in the poorest half of the world's population. Governments spend approximately as much in preparation to destroy human beings as they spend annually to educate them.

The pace for these expenditures is set by the United States and Soviet Union, which spend two-thirds of all military outlays. The Warsaw and North Atlantic Treaty Organizations account for about 80% of the world total. Yet, the global pattern of spending has been gradually changing.

Third World countries have been increasing their military purchases faster than even the richest of the industrialized countries. All the developing countries together spent about 18% of the world total in 1975, compared to 9% in 1960. The most extreme case has occurred in the Middle East, where real military expenditures in 1975 were thirteen times higher than in 1960.

In brief, the prevailing approach to arms reductions is failing, as ample evidence demonstrates:

- Total expenditures are enormous.
- They are rising.
- The pattern of spending is shifting toward the militarization of the entire planet, whereas previously only the industrialized states purchased large arsenals.
- Despite the decline in the percentage of the world total that is spent by the industrial powers, even the most heavily armed are not decreasing their spending in absolute terms.

These data mean that a vast amount of natural resources, capital, and brainpower is unavailable to meet pressing human needs. In addition, the military-related people and their financial strength together constitute a formidable political force that resists conversion to non-military purposes. This force increases steadily.

The ability to destroy entire societies has also grown enormously while negotiations for arms control have proceeded. The most intense recent negotiations to control the arms race have been the Strategic Arms Limitation Talks (SALT) between the United States and the Soviet Union. During the period of time from the opening of the talks until one year after the Vladivostok Accord (1969–75), the number of deployed strategic launch vehicles increased by one-third.

Despite *detente* and "success" in the SALT treaty of 1972 and the Accord of 1974, immediately after these accomplishments the US Department of Defense announced plans to increase its destructive capability by proceeding with efforts to develop:

- the enormous Trident submarine with 24 missile tubes;
- the long-range Trident missile;
- a maneuverable reentry vehicle (MaRV) with pinpoint accuracy;

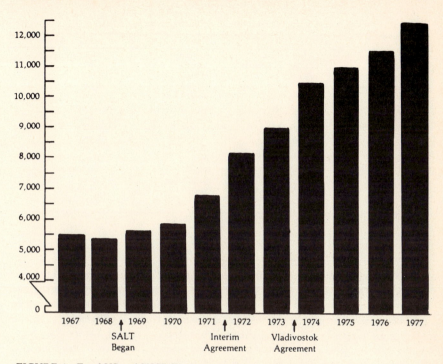

FIGURE 1. Total US and USSR Warheads on Strategic Delivery Vehicles

- additional missile capability, to provide greater yield, accuracy, and throw weight for land- and submarine-based ballistic missiles;
- new techniques for rapid firing from Intercontinental Ballistic Missile (ICBM) silos;
- the Command Data Buffer System, permitting the Minuteman III to be retargeted remotely and rapidly;
- the M-X, an entirely new, mobile ICBM;
- the cruise missile, which can maneuver and target itself after being launched from a submarine, ship, aircraft, or mobile land base;
- sophisticated guidance and command technologies, such as the Advanced Ballistic Reentry System (ABRES), which gives warheads increased maneuverability, penetrability, and terminal guidance;
- a totally new reentry vehicle capable of carrying a higher yield warhead;
- a worldwide communication satellite system, called NAVSTAR Global Positioning System, designed to give pinpoint accuracy even to Submarine Launched Ballistic Missiles (SLBM's).

The Soviet Union has pushed forward with similar research and development in many of the same areas. (See Figure 1.)

TABLE 1. Countries with technical capability of detonating a nuclear device

Now	Within 1 to 2 years	Within 3 to 6 years	Within 7 to 10 years
China	Canada	Argentina	Bulgaria
France	Fed. Rep. of Germany	Australia	Chile
India	Israel	Austria	Cuba
Soviet Union	Italy	Belgium	Egypt
United Kingdom	Japan	Brazil	Finland
United States	South Africa	Czechoslovakia	Hungary
	Sweden	Denmark	Indonesia
	Switzerland	German Dem. Rep.	Iran
	Taiwan	Netherlands	Libya
		Norway	Mexico
		Pakistan	Portugal
		Poland	Romania
		South Korea	Turkey
		Spain	Venezuela
			Yugoslavia

The Spread of Nuclear Weapons

As far as is publicly known, from 1945 until 1977 six governments have exploded a total of 1,081 nuclear devices. More than half of all nuclear tests have occurred since the 1963 Test Ban Treaty was signed. The average yearly number of tests during the thirteen years since the treaty is 68% *higher* than the average number of tests during the eighteen years of testing before the agreement. The nuclear-weapons powers continue to modernize their weapons and to gain prestige and diplomatic leverage from them. In doing so, they whet the appetites of countries without nuclear weapons technology for acquiring it. (See Table 1.)

The apprehensive concern about the spread of nuclear weapons to additional countries can divert attention away from the alarming growth occurring in the already massive arsenals of the superpowers. Despite the genuine dangers of horizontal proliferation, it is important to understand that there is no reasonable means to prevent the spread of nuclear weapons to more countries without drastic changes in the policies of the present nuclear-weapons powers themselves. The poor and presently less powerful states will not be inclined to give up access to nuclear weapons permanently as long as the nuclear-weapons countries claim a right to retain such weapons indefinitely.

THE NEED FOR SYSTEM CHANGE

The history of efforts to control arms reveals not only the failure to reduce them, but also the failure of the international political system to provide the security that all societies need and deserve.

Consider how poorly the present security system functions. Although the United States is the most powerful nation on earth, we have no way to protect ourselves against a nuclear attack. Given the continuation of the trends noted above, our security will decline further in the future, even in the face of continuing efforts to maintain a very high level of military preparedness.

Although any single national government may believe that its security is increased if it accumulates more and more advanced weapons, for world society as a whole both the likelihood and the destructiveness of future wars are increased by the steady expansion of military arsenals and military influence around the world.

The frequence of conventional war may also be increasing. More than 100 international and civil wars have been fought from 1945 to 1975. The total duration of this collective violence exceeds 350 war-years. The armed forces of 81 different states, composed predominantly of young people, have killed more persons in these wars than died during all of World War II. From 1945 through 1976, not a day passed in which at least one war was not being waged somewhere on our planet.

The very nature of the system of sovereign states encourages armed rivalry between governments. Because the system provides no impartial, dependable way to prevent one government from violently coercing another, governments seek arms as a means of self-help. Regardless of who is in the White House or the Kremlin, and whether the perceived threat is one "ism" or another, arms buildups will continue indefinitely—unless this system is fundamentally changed. As long as arms are allowed to be useful, they will be acquired and used, either to gain advantage in diplomacy or in combat.

The Military Habit

The perspectives and attitudes that prevent the creation of a more desirable security system are learned—they are not innate or determined by human nature. If learned, they can be changed. Yet we, and the institutions we have created, tend to behave as changeless creatures of habit. Faced with new technologies of warfare and more interdependent social relations, old habits that once made sense no longer do so. Historically, civilizations have collapsed when unable to change fast enough to adapt to new conditions. Today old diplomatic habits practiced within the existing international system do not take account of new conditions. As a result, lengthy negotiations fail to halt the arms race, leaving many people of good-will both frustrated and puzzled by the lack of results.

Yet, the reason for diplomatic failure is quite simple. Diplomats seek to reduce armaments (new behavior required by new technology) while at the same time they want to retain the war-system in which governments depend upon arms for power and security (traditional behavior to satisfy old habits and vested interests). Officials cannot abolish weapons at the same time that they rely upon them. Increasing military power is a culturally-approved way of feeling more secure when under international tension. Yet despite the real threats that may push us toward these habits, they easily become self-destructive. This is true even though resort to the habit-forming behavior *at first seemed the only solution*. Arms that once may have solved security problems now threaten our security.

If one genuinely wants to reverse the arms buildup, one must make a commitment to fundamental changes that will enable one to break the military habit completely. This means a decision at the outset to work for abolishing both national military arsenals and the war system which brought them into being.

Some social beliefs—like the idea that there is no feasible alternative to the present system—are so widely held that few people question them. One person confirms another person's belief, even though their common belief has little basis in reality. For example, for one thousand years after the astronomer Claudius Ptolemy's influential writings, people confirmed one another's belief that the earth was the center of the universe, with the sun revolving around it. Religious and political authorities, supported by a larger population in general, harassed and even killed heretics who suggested that the earth was not the center of the universe. Such people were considered mad or subversive. For a time, it was conventional wisdom that the earth was flat. Similar beliefs, often supported by religious authorities of the time, for centuries have held women and certain races to be inherently inferior.

These erroneous beliefs are matched today by the socially validated notion that human nature and our honor require us to participate in a war-system. Because habit influences thought and behavior, many people erroneously believe that there is no better, feasible security system. As in similar cases in the past, people who now advocate an alternative view of the world and who say that a global society is possible without a war-system are usually dismissed as unrealistic.

The following conclusions emerge from the preceding analysis. Although arms control agreements may stabilize certain armaments momentarily, they have not halted the arms buildup any more successfully than a large rock, placed in the middle of a river, halts the flow of the stream. No water moves through the rock, but the river swirls around it on both sides, with the volume undiminished. There are two reasons why arms control agreements fail to stop the arms race in general. First, they do not restrict the overall military programs of governments. Second, arms control policies fail to plan—as realistic policies for major arms reductions must—for substantial changes in people's beliefs and in the structure of the international political system. Nothing less can provide security without national arsenals.

Therefore, the time has come (1) to advocate comprehensive arms reductions rather than to aim only for arms control, and (2) to advocate system change rather than to cling either to the military habit or to the unrealistic hope that disarmament can occur without system transformation.

THE NEED FOR A SOCIAL MOVEMENT

In their speeches, officials sometimes acknowledge that the time is right for behaving as if disarmament were a serious goal. President Carter, for example, spoke in his Inaugural Address of steps toward "the elimination of all nuclear weapons from this earth." Meanwhile, in their actions, officials reject the policies and institutions that could establish a new peace system. Although aware of the dangers of the present direction, they cannot bring themselves to break the military habit.

One reason for this gap between word and deed is that, even with good intentions, leaders have difficulty resisting the rewards and punishments offered by the present system. Leaders' actions are guided by a psychological attachment to power, which is reinforced by the benefits of money and influence that accompany large military expenditures. The governmental power to reverse the arms buildup is generally held by those who benefit most from arming. Where power is most concentrated, change is most needed.

That is why change must be initiated by ordinary people, with whom power is now least concentrated. To move toward a more appropriate security system we must first understand that most major governments, if left to their own pursuits, will not lead the way to a better security system. Those who hold the reins of national military power do not want to relinquish them. Those with wealth do not want to share it more equitably. If they did, they could do it quite quickly. The fact that they have not should make us skeptical of mere rhetoric to the contrary.

To expect the world's most powerful governments, without outside pressure, to build a new security system where those states now militarily weak would gain influence relative to the states now militarily strong, is like expecting a divine-right king to lead the revolution for democracy and for abolition of the throne.

The single most difficult task in creating a security system appropriate for our time is convincing people to join a movement that aims to abolish war. We are reluctant to try to create such a system because of our belief that it cannot happen. An erroneous but socially validated belief that a certain change is not possible makes it impossible. Take slavery as an example. It has existed in some form or another throughout human history, and during the 1800s in our own society the institution was closely linked to a belief in the racial inferiority of the slaves. Most people thought abolition was unrealistic. But because the opponents of slavery stubbornly insisted on nothing less, it was abolished.

Now, slowly, we are beginning to ask: Should there be a war-system? Must there be a war-system? The age-old skepticism about system change is being challenged by a new awareness of planetary limits, interdependency, and the need for global policy coordination. The potential for mobilizing a broadly based popular movement is increasing because of the growth of planetary consciousness, instant global communication, and the formation of political coalitions among people impressed with the interlocking relationship between militarism, unemployment, poverty, resource shortages, denial of human rights, and ecological decay.

Throughout the world there are literally millions of people who now hold the values that are necessary for building a global community in which the serving of human needs takes highest priority—not for the benefit of any national group at the expense of the rest, but for the benefit of all people riding on the planet together. There are probably millions more ready to join a movement for change when it looks like it might have a chance of succeeding.

A STRATEGY FOR SYSTEM CHANGE

A movement for a more appropriate security system can begin among concerned individuals on all continents of the world. The suggestions below apply to US citizens. In other societies complementary actions should be designed to take into consideration local cultural and political conditions. Those leading the effort might be called planetary citizens: defined simply as people who live according to the understanding that politically, ecologically, and morally their well-being and that of their nation are inseparable from the rest of humanity. To assure a system change of global proportions, the movement must be transnational, committed to abolition of the warfare system, and dedicated to firm, nonviolent, citizen action. It would be unwise for such a movement to adopt the idea that a few revolutionaries can or should seize power for themselves in order to usher in a new age. Until there has been widespread attitudinal change, there would be insufficient political support for a humane implementation of the desired changes in institutions, even in the unlikely event that one could capture power.

If concerned individuals and groups make intense efforts to educate and organize for a demilitarized planet, it might be possible within the next twenty-five years to have a process well underway to abolish the war-system. Although it is impossible to predict the pace at which changes may occur, for analytical convenience we can distinguish five different stages, each of five years' duration, for building an appropriate security system:

Phase One: The first five years include vigorous educational and lobbying activities to raise public consciousness and to begin changing government priorities. The balance of political forces in the United States and several other states, where there is already dissatisfaction with wasteful military spending, turns against the perpetuation of the arms buildup.

Phase Two: The United States, the Soviet Union, and many other states commit themselves to annual reductions in military expenditures. These continue throughout the remaining phases. They are coupled to some particular force reductions and a pledge to stop the testing and deployment of all new strategic delivery systems and warheads. A world security organization, whether entirely new or based upon a remodeled United Nations, verifies reductions. National means for verification could also continue.

Phase Three: Both the United States and the Soviet Union move to a minimal nuclear deterrent. Annual budget reductions continue. All middle-range powers are brought within the system of verified, military cutbacks.

Phase Four: Budget cuts proceed at a quickened pace of 20% each year. By the end of this stage the nuclear powers dismantle their remaining nuclear weapons. All fissionable materials are regulated by a global authority. Any small states not yet participating are brought into the phased arms reductions.

Phase Five: Conventional arms reductions continue. At the end of this phase military spending and production are permanently prohibited. The global security organization, previously in place, prevents any effort at rearmament.

Regular Reductions of Military Budgets

This strategy makes budget cuts, coupled with subsequent ceilings for specific weapons systems, the central feature of the disarming process. In the long run, military expenditures provide a useful general measure of military capability. Budget reductions restrict a total military effort more effectively than agreements on single weapons systems.

A second merit of this approach is the high degree of flexibility that budget restrictions allow. Participating governments may select the precise mix of forces that they need. Land-locked states, for example, might want to retain far different residual forces during the transition than would sea powers. In short, budgetary reductions provide the most comprehensive yet flexible approach to arms reductions.

Moreover, the budgetary approach is attractive because of its simplicity—an essential quality in selecting the most effective strategy for public education, political mobilization, and legislative lobbying. The public may lack time and information to unravel the complexities of whether the United States should have 1,320 MIRV's or only 1,000, but the public can insist on a 10% reduction in expenditures each year.

One problem with this approach is the difficulty of verifying reductions. Obviously, many military expenditures could be made without including the items explicitly in a public budget. As a result, verification of budget cuts will depend upon a global monitoring system that would, through use of satellite surveillance, electronic telecommunication, and other means, make an annual estimate of the expenditures of each nation. Equivalent monetary values would be assigned to comparable components in each state's equipment and military forces, and an overall estimate then made. Because states occasionally would dispute the figures for their own or a rival's expenditures, the agency monitoring expenditures should provide opportunity for presentation of evidence by an interested national government, perhaps from its own intelligence estimates. The final judgment about expenditure levels would have to reside with the global authority, similar to a court of last resort in domestic legal proceedings. With appropriate efforts and the use of advanced technology for monitoring, the problems of verification could be overcome.

Budget Reductions. / As soon as the planetary citizens movement has mobilized sufficient political strength in the United States, the US government will announce its intention to build an alternative security system. Toward that end, it also will commit itself to cut military expenditures annually by 10%. It will ask the Soviet Union to reciprocate. Even if the Soviet Union at first does not, the cuts can be safely undertaken and probably should be continued for three successive years. Time is needed for reluctant governments to witness the economic advantages present in a society no longer burdened by increasing military expenditures.

In addition, several years of an arms reversal program would be required for those governments supporting the new initiatives to establish transnational verification and preliminary enforcement agencies. These agencies' effective operations and their obvious refusal to become instruments of any single nation state would provide reassurance to governments at first reluctant to join in arms reductions.

Three years of reductions would not jeopardize US security even within the present international system based on military prowess. The cuts proposed here would enable the United States to retain a nuclear deterrent capable of assured destruction of the Soviet Union until *after* full Soviet participation.

Of course, cutting the budget by a given percentage each year would *not* mean cutting strategic weapons by an identical percentage. The size of weapons reductions would depend upon the particular mix of strategic weapons, tactical weapons, troops, and other conventional forces that the President, Joint Chiefs of Staff, and Congress might choose.

Budgetary cutbacks should be accompanied by some explicitly announced reductions of specific weapons. The budget cuts will then carry more precise meaning and communicate clearer intent to reverse the arms buildup. The following procedure probably would be the most efficient means for implementing such reductions. The United States or another country could announce a specific arms reduction at the time it is made. Like the continuing budget cuts, an arms reduction would occur without specific diplomatic negotiations preceding it. *Afterwards*, the precedent-setting state should seek to transform its own initiative into a legal obligation for other states.

As the transition toward an appropriate security system gains momentum, any states "holding out" would have to be brought under the prescribed norm. The greater the global consensus, the more likely that sanctions against such a state would be effective.

The Politics of Reductions. / In considering specific arms reductions, there is no magic formula for calculating what should be done first. But, in general, these guidelines apply:

1. Any given reduction by a national government should *precede* the effort to universalize the reduction through conclusion of a formal treaty.

2. Once written, a treaty establishing a new norm for restricting arms should take effect immediately among those nations ratifying it. Norms would then begin to take shape under the influence of the most progressive states, rather than be the product of the lowest common denominator of agreement.

3. Verification of each reduction should be carried out by a global agency, which could include representatives of states not at first agreeing to the reduction.

The first of these guidelines deserves further explanation. Reductions should precede negotiations in order to avoid the following negative consequences that occasionally accompany diplomatic efforts:

- Arms control negotiations focus attention on inequalities in weapons deployed by two sides, so that the inferior side usually steps up its efforts to become equal, while the superior side tries to move further ahead in order to be able to negotiate from a position of strength.
- Weapons that might never have been deployed, or that might not have been deployed so soon, are quickly developed in order to have bargaining chips to "negotiate away" during arms control talks. However, weapons begun as bargaining chips often are later deployed in expanded arsenals. This expansion is then imitated by the rival power.

- The domestic vested interests that favor military expenditures are so powerful that often only cosmetic agreements, formalizing what the governments would have done without any agreement, are possible.
- If an agreement is eventually reached, the Department of Defense often can be moved to accept a treaty only by promising it something in return, such as the right to develop a more advanced and more destructive weapon.
- Negotiations sometimes increase international tension and anxiety because critics of a potential agreement are always eager to claim either that the other side will get the best part of the bargain or else that it has cheated on its past promises.
- Ongoing arms control negotiations encourage the informed public to believe, mistakenly, that the government is doing all that can be done to end the arms buildup. If a limited agreement is reached, the public is led to believe that eventually there may be major reductions, although significant reductions of destructive capability in fact have never occurred in the past thirty years. If no agreement is reached, the public is encouraged to believe that the opponent is insincere, aggressive, and troublesome, and that our side should keep up its guard and deploy even more weapons. Arms control negotiations discourage people from looking for more basic flaws in the security system that perpetuates the arms spiral.

Because the arms competition is driven mainly by international political conflicts or by domestic pressures for weapons expenditures, it is not likely that arms can be reduced by focusing mainly on negotiations for arms reductions themselves. Substantial reductions will occur only when a sufficient number of people press their governments for decreased expenditures and transformation of the international system in which military power plays a role in settling disputes. Negotiations will not produce this shift in citizens' attitudes and values.

Until a coalition of planetary citizens and other sympathetic groups has the political strength to get the US government to make reductions *without* prior negotiations with its rivals, the arms buildup will not really be reversed. If officials or the public insist that negotiations precede reductions, pro-military vested interests—in both the United States and the Soviet Union—will have an easy opportunity to stall and suffocate the arms reversal effort.

Time after time, arms control negotiations have provided the basis for pro-military officials to enlist the support of anti-military or neutral forces on the side of new weapons development. Arms *opponents* have voted money *for* research and development of new weapons in order to give bargaining power to US diplomats negotiating for arms reductions. This effect can be avoided only if the public demands reductions first, with negotiations coming later to formalize a precedent rather than to prepare the way to make one.

The Problem of Soviet Reciprocation

The remaining question is the one that most troubles US citizens. What can be done if the United States and other sympathetic states carry out budget cuts but the Soviet Union does not reciprocate? In order to avert this possibility, from the very beginning the United States and other supporting governments should attempt to provide economic, trade, and political incentives to the Soviet Union, as well as to China, France, and other major powers, to cooperate.

A firm US commitment to create a peace system would have a profound impact upon Soviet leaders. Their decision whether or not to initiate reductions will depend upon their assessment of how to maximize Soviet interests. The same competition that now propels the arms buildup could eventually encourage reciprocation of budgetary cuts. The failure of one superpower to divert spending from needless overkill weapons to humane growth could lead to competitive disadvantages for the arming country. When it becomes clear to the Soviet leadership that it is not militarily threatened by the intentions or capabilities of any other state, and that it is economically or diplomatically harmful for Soviet society to continue weapons procurement, it is reasonable to expect Soviet leadership to join the process.

As is well-known, deterrence is based on the assumption that one's opponents will be rational enough to avoid behavior that will bring destruction of their own society. If the leaders were sensitive to avoiding destruction in the long run, they would probably reciprocate with budget reductions. If they were not that sensitive, long-range security for the United States can hardly be assured even with a competitive arms buildup. Yet, irrational behavior is more likely to be corrected by creating a non-threatening political environment than by making nuclear threats against the people behaving irrationally. Peaceful policies are reassuring and conducive to more rational action.

The point here is not to belittle the tragic consequences of a superpower's chronic refusal to proceed toward an appropriate security system. Nor is it to overlook human greed and the arrogance of power. The point is simply that, even if a superpower refused to move toward an appropriate security system, the human race would not be more secure by reverting to a new arms race than it would be if it were to search for a new stategy aimed at eventually abolishing the warfare system.

THE CHALLENGE

The preceding pages have shown that:

- the continued expansion of military arsenals, coupled with their obvious inability to serve human and environmental needs, makes us less secure with each passing month;
- present governmental approaches to control armaments have failed—not because of any official's bad intentions but because current policies do not aim at replacing the war-system with a peace system;
- the advocates of keeping the United States militarily "number one" in the arms buildup are in reality advocates of unilateral initiatives that will, in the long run, leave the people of the United States and world insecure and susceptible to nuclear destruction;

- a more secure, less violent global system can be created;
- this preferred system can provide not only peace but far greater social justice, economic well-being, and ecological security than the present, highly militarized international system;
- the most important *missing* ingredient for creating an appropriate security system is the willingness of ordinary people to work with determination and tireless dedication to abolish war and to build a better system.

That system can be built if enough people believe in its feasibility and act for its realization. Many persons are inactive because they genuinely doubt that major arms reductions are possible. These people need to consider what they can do to weaken the link between arms and security and to forge a new link between disarmament and security. For those who share the positive vision of a world without war, of a world with local communities of people seeking lives of dignity, participation, mutual cooperation, and genuine freedom, now is the time to join the effort for a new peace system.

NOTES

Dr. Robert C. Johansen is a participant in the World Order Models Project and President of the Institute for World Order.

1. *"Arms control"* normally is used to refer to international agreements aimed at *stabilizing* levels of armaments. Such agreements may specify that arms be modestly reduced, increased, or maintained at existing levels. *"Disarmament"* refers to measures aimed at *reducing* arms to a point where only sufficient arms are retained to enable internal police forces to maintain domestic tranquility. Usually disarmament measures mean large reductions, but they may also refer to small reductions if they are a part of a process leading toward general and complete disarmament. These definitions are followed in this essay.

19
DISARMAMENT FOR A JUST WORLD: DECLARATION OF PRINCIPLES, PROPOSAL FOR A TREATY, AND CALL FOR ACTION

Possessed by a deep sense of crisis facing humanity in the present nuclear era, and committed to the goal of disarmament in a just world, we hold the following as self-evident.

Much of the basis for the perpetuation of injustice in the world is to be found in an international system dominated by a small group of nations. They maintain power disproportionate to their populations or their needs and contrary to all sense of justice and decency. They do this by means of their control of resources, technology, information-flows and the diffusion of culture. At the heart of these structures of domination is their possession of nuclear weapons and their manipulation of the nuclear threat.

An overwhelming majority of the world's peoples do not possess or desire nuclear arms. They understand that the possession of these weapons is a means to domination, not defence. The nuclear war system protects the vested interests of the ruling elites of a few states but does not provide security for peoples anywhere. It is an umbrella for imperialist interventions in the Third World and an instrument for blackmailing the weak. It deepens and lends permanence to a system of oppression and exploitation and to the denial of true national sovereignty and independence to a majority of the nations of the world.

Initiated and led by the West, the nuclear arms race defines the expanding boundaries of destructive technology. It impels the development of satellite systems which are designed to perpetuate imperial hegemony, spurs the export of not only military arsenals but also the doctrines and technology of repression and, through these measures, augments the capability of the few to terrorize the majority of humanity.

As long as a few governments hold the world hostage to their possession of nuclear weapons, it will be extremely difficult to achieve a new economic order, or equitable North-South relations, or liberation for the occupied and oppressed peoples of the world, or human rights. We solemnly declare the possession and threat of the use of these weapons to be a crime against humanity.

In the nuclear weapon countries, the never-ending quest for advanced

---

Issued on the occasion of the International Workshop on Disarmament, 27–31 March 1978, New Delhi.

weaponry has produced a culture of war and violence, of arms race and militarism, of stimulated fear and false security. The results are economies marked by misallocated resources and distorted growth. The escalating investment in highly capital-intensive military hardware has added to this an inflationary spiral and an employment crisis in the United States and countries allied to it, the effects of which are felt throughout the world. Similarly, although Soviet entry in the nuclear arms race was a defensive reaction, the heavy military expenditures in the Soviet Union and other socialist countries have sharply limited improvement in their standards of living.

Elsewhere, the existence of the war system based on nuclear weapons and technological imperialism has distorted the development process. Inflation, pollution, technologies of repression, maladies that originate in the industrialized countries, are exported through the global arms race to the developing countries which do not possess the means to defend themselves against these. The insecurity engendered by both the global arms race and its deliberate export to other regions induces the latter to increase their armament expenditures and military establishments, with serious consequences for their economic and political development. The bottling up of capital resources in militarism everywhere, the so-called transfer of technology and the consequent failure to invest in alternative technologies and alternative sources of energy have obstructed the developing countries in removing the sources of dependence, inequity and destitution. This has accentuated the gap between the haves and the have-nots.

The doctrine of "deterrence," which ostensibly regards nuclear war as unthinkable, has permitted the transformation of the mammoth coercive capacities into instruments of domination over the rest of the world. The result is a war system which integrates nuclear weapons with the so-called conventional weapons, and shifts great power confrontation to the battlefields of the Third World. Peace in the nuclear age has meant continuous warfare by proxy. Large stocks of armaments from the military-industrial machine of the North are transferred to the South. The richer among the Third World elites are enticed into acquiring such armaments which make them dependent on the imperialist powers; by being cast in the role of regional security managers, they are also encouraged to indulge in their own expansionist fantasies and to oppress their populations.

By stimulating the arms race, the nuclear weapon powers have managed to thwart a major challenge to their power that decolonization, economic development and better oil and commodity prices might have heralded. An increasing number of developing countries have been infected by militarism. They have suffered repressive regimes and witnessed the erosion of indigenous cultures and traditions. Much of the human misery and degradation in our time can be traced to the war system as it has evolved along with the nuclear arms race.

Given these self-evident facts, it is at once sanctimonious and futile to lecture to the Third World countries on future proliferation when actual proliferation is taking place through the actions of the nuclear powers themselves. Fissionable material has been clandestinely diverted to Israel and nuclear technology to South Africa. The counterforce weapon systems, now about to be deployed by the United States and the Soviet Union (cruise-missile, MX, Trident, neutron bomb, SS-20, etc.), make it self-evident that the arms race is out of control. Indeed, the world is now entering the most dangerous period in the entire history of the nuclear arms race. A miscalculation by the superpowers or their allies in such a time of rising tension would trigger a world-wide holocaust threatening human life and civilization everywhere.

Such then is the emerging scenario of danger, domination and duplicity facing the world. It is a scenario that needs to be reversed and reversed quickly.

PROPOSAL FOR A TREATY

The most urgent task facing humanity today is to delegitimize nuclear weapons, to dismantle the hierarchical international order that supports the war system of which nuclear weapons represent the most dangerous and unacceptable component, and to replace it by an alternative security system based on the acceptance of equal sovereignty of all nations.

The first step in this task is for peoples everywhere to denounce nuclear weapons, to denounce not only their use and threat of use but also all planning for their potential use under any circumstances. The entire world must be made a nuclear weapon-free zone.

To this end, the UN General Assembly should declare the use and threat of use of nuclear weapons of any kind as crimes against humanity, and their manufacture and possession as grave dangers to human survival.

An international Nuclear Disarmament Treaty should be negotiated to give effect to this proclamation. The Treaty should contain the following provisions.

Affirming that the use and threat of use of nuclear weapons are crimes against humanity, and the manufacture and possession of these constitute grave dangers to human survival, *The Preamble* of such a Treaty should call upon:

- nuclear weapon states to submit to the General Assembly, or to a machinery set up by it, plans for the progressive reduction and early final elimination of nuclear weapon stockpiles, and for discontinuation of further manufacture, testing, development, and research on new nuclear weapons;
- nations allied to nuclear weapons states to cease any support for nuclear warfare, including cancellation of permission to stockpile nuclear weapons on their soil, provision of facilities for nuclear weapons transit and communication to nuclear weapons carriers and cancellation of plans for participating in contingency planning for nuclear war;
- the UN General Assembly to establish a monitoring and inspection system to check on the cessation of nuclear weapon production, on the progressive elimination of nuclear stockpiles, and on the demilitarization of nuclear weapon production facilities.

The operative part of the Treaty should contain undertakings:

- to renounce the possession and use of nuclear weapons forever and to join in a common effort to promote all measures to eliminate all nuclear weapon stockpiles;
- to secure from the nuclear weapon states plans for the progressive reduction and early final elimination of their nuclear weapon stockpiles, and for the discontinuation of further manufacture, tests, development, and research on new nuclear weapons;
- not to engage in production of nuclear weapons, singly or in partnership with others;
- not to permit the stationing of nuclear weapons on their soil;
- not to allow facilities of transit and communication to nuclear weapon carriers, including passage through straits which fall within the territorial waters of the signatory countries;
- not to transfer any nuclear raw material to nations possessing nuclear weapons or those who in any way assist nuclear weapon nations to produce or deploy nuclear weapons;
- to commit an appropriate percentage of their annual budgets for promoting the cause of disarmament.

As for the system of implementation, the State Parties to the Treaty should:

- establish an international monitoring and inspection system to supervise compliance with the Treaty. The agency established for this purpose should consist of persons drawn solely from the State Parties to the Treaty;
- prohibit in domestic law, under sanction of punishment, acts by individuals consisting of
  (a) advocacy of nuclear war doctrines or preparation for nuclear war,
  (b) direct participation in planning for the use of nuclear weapons, and
  (c) participation in research and development directly related to the production of nuclear weaponry or their use,
- give, in their national legislation on these issues, effect also to acts specified above committed outside their territory.

CALL FOR ACTION

Covenants to deal with situations of crisis and catastrophe often reflect the collective consciousness of humanity. Today, the vast majority of the peoples of the world, to be free of the terrors of nuclear domination and war, demand a just world in which development becomes possible. This growing consciousness must now be embodied in a process of regeneration and reconstruction. This task cannot be left to governments alone. What is needed is a global coalition of enlightened governments, the scientific community of peoples' movements to press for disarmament for a just world.

Today, we live in a world where the most powerful are at once the most insecure. Such insecurity leads to repression of the weak, which in turn arouses resistance that reinforces the insecurity of the powerful. Only a historic and international gathering of popular pressure can end this spiral. The Treaty which we have proposed is intended to achieve this end. Universal mobilization in support of the Treaty will help the formation of a global community dedicated to using the resources of this planet and space for solving the global evils of pollution, energy shortage, unequal distribution and ecological degeneration which face humanity today.

The peoples of the world, including those in the countries possessing nuclear weapons, can no longer leave it to the governments of the nuclear weapon states to take steps towards genuine disarmament and a just international order. These states have amply demonstrated their unwillingness to put the interests of the people ahead of the narrow and selfish interest of the ruling elite. United for survival, the peoples of the world can and must seize the initiative and proceed to work towards an alternative system of security for all to replace the existing unjust order.

Scientists, technologists and intellectuals have a special responsibility and a crucial role in the mobilization for disarmament for a just world. Thus far, they have often served as the unwitting tools of an unjust order and have lent their talents and services to be used for building and nurturing a culture based on naked power. This amounts to complicity in crimes against humanity. We appeal to them to join the peoples of the world in rejecting this culture and to turn their talents to meeting the exciting challenges which promise a rich, just and anxiety-free future.

We call upon all governments of the world to sign the proposed Treaty, and we appeal to peoples and organizations throughout the world to exert pressure for its acceptance by lobbying and organizing protests against, and resisting in every possible way, the escalation of arms and stockpiling of nuclear weapons.

The non-nuclear states have a special role to play in this regard. Only by entering this covenant will they have the necessary moral authority to lead the world towards a new order.

We appeal specially to the youth of the world to take a leading part in this movement. They should disseminate this and other similar proposals and organize campaigns of education to demilitarize the minds of the young and the old.

Towards these tasks and as a beginning, there is an urgent need to launch a global education and an action programme which may be organized by a World Commission for Disarmament and Development with units in various parts of the world. We urge the setting up of such a Commission as early as possible and appeal to all like-minded persons to come forward with ideas, funds and action programmes for translating this proposal into reality.

Economic Well-Being

INTRODUCTION

In this section we turn our attention from the war system to what might be called the poverty system. Although the war system contains an ever present threat of armed confrontation and nuclear catastrophe, global poverty poses an even more pervasive challenge to world order. This challenge arises from the daily misery and suffering of people throughout the world, including many in the richest nations. Today, more than one-quarter of humanity live in conditions of abject poverty, their lives dominated by hunger, disease, illiteracy and the absence of hope. To the modern world economy these people, being neither producers nor consumers, are marginal. Moreover, with the onrush of modernization many have been denied traditional means for providing for their own food, clothing, shelter and health. Their struggle is literally for survival itself. Of all the brutal realities of the world economic map, it is this widespread deprivation of more than a billion people that calls for the special attention of world order studies.

The world economy is characterized by large disparities in wealth both among and within nations. The misery of underdevelopment that exists in much of Asia, Africa and Latin America contrasts with the affluence of North America and Europe, where waste is abundant and where many people suffer from the problems associated with overdevelopment. In times of slow economic growth, high inflation, and declining living standards, it may seem unusual to say that people suffer from too much. Yet there is ample evidence linking our consumption to high levels of heart disease, cancer, social alienation, as well as mental illness. Overdevelopment in the industrialized world also creates enormous ecological strains. The rapid depletion of the earth's available resources and the accumulation of pollution not only adversely affect our quality of life but also impact upon development prospects elsewhere. As such, our world order approach sees the development problem applying to both overdeveloped and underdeveloped societies; both can be thought of as forms of maldevelopment.

For much of the Third World, development still remains more a dream than a reality. As a result, the conventional wisdom embodied in the "trickle down" theory of development is now increasingly being called into question. Growth, to the extent that it has been generated, has not resulted in sustainable development or in the fulfillment of basic economic needs. The emphasis on an industrial, capital-intensive, and export-oriented model of development has, in fact, been highly inappropriate for most less-developed countries. It has exacerbated economic inequalities, has created high levels of unemployment, and has destroyed once vital agricultural sectors, so that many third world countries have become food importers over the past two decades. Even in a so-called success country, such as Brazil, which enjoyed a rapid growth in GNP in the late 1960s, the living conditions for the bottom 40 percent are as miserable as ever.

On the other hand, Sri Lanka, which has eschewed the high growth model, has been successful in eliminating abject poverty. For years, Sri Lanka has allocated half its government budget to free rice rations, free education and health services, and has subsidized food and transportation. Its citizens have achieved a life expectancy typical in countries with two or three times its per capita income. The Sri Lankan experience suggests that growth and the level of national income in developing countries are only part of the answer to meeting basic human needs. A conscious and deliberate policy of distributive justice related to nutrition, health, housing, and education has been a missing link in the traditional discourse on development strategies.

The development problem is also a reflection of the deep-seated inequitable structures of the world economy itself. Most of the world's finance, technology, production, transportation, and communications are either owned or controlled by Western-based financial institutions and multinational corporations. There exists also a hierarchical division of labor in the world economy between the highly industrialized North and the mostly unindustrialized South. In recent years this division has become more complex as newly industrialized countries like Brazil, Korea, and Taiwan have begun to compete effectively in the world market. Nevertheless, the gaps between North and South still permeate the global production and distribution process, as illustrated by the following:

- *Industrial Production:* The Third World, with 70 percent of the world's population, generates less than 7 percent of global production.
- *Food Production:* In the 1930s the Third World produced a surplus of twelve million metric tons of cereals; in 1980 they had to import 88 million tons.
- *Research and Development:* The Third World possesses only 5 percent of the world's research and development capacity, with the remaining 95 percent preempted by the developed countries.
- *Single-Commodity Economy:* At least 25 developing countries currently depend on only one primary commodity for more than half their export earnings; another 13 nations rely on just two.
- *Terms of Trade:* The terms of trade of commodities versus manufactured goods deteriorated by almost one-third between the mid-1950s and the early 1970s.
- *Debt Trap:* Non-oil developing countries' external debts increased from $139 billion in 1976 to over $300 billion in early 1981.

The principal concerted challenge to this inequitable world economic order has come from the Group of 77, the Third World economic caucus that had its origin in the first meeting of the United Nations Conference on Trade and Development (UNCTAD), and which now consists of 120 less-developed countries. Coming on the heels of the successful OPEC oil embargo in 1973, the Sixth Special Session of the UN General Assembly on Raw Materials and Development was a crucial step in this challenge. The session ended with a call for the establishment of a new international economic order (NIEO) involving a "profound reorganization of economic relations between the rich and poor countries." The demands for a NIEO include improved terms of trade for the developing countries, transfer of resources and technology for development purposes, and greater control over national resources.

As part of its Second Development Decade in the 1970s, the United Nations sponsored numerous conferences on issues related to global economic resources and the North/South dialogue. Indeed, this decade may well be remembered as the period when global economic issues finally entered the agenda of world politics. Yet the concrete achievements of NIEO politics have been minimal. Despite the plethora of global bargainings and hundreds of hortatory resolutions, declarations and programs of action, global poverty and the gaps between the developed and developing countries still exist and are likely to grow still greater in years to come if present development structures and strategies are not transformed.

What is an appropriate world order approach to the problem of global poverty? The three contending approaches to world order (system maintaining, system reforming and system transforming) introduced in Part I have widely different images of the present world economic order and what should be done to resolve the poverty problem. Central to the system-maintaining approach is the conviction that the basic premises of the existing economic order can and should be preserved. The present world economic system has served the rich and powerful countries well, and therefore there is no reason to modify it. It needs only to be more efficiently managed, especially through reliance on the free and competitive free market.

This laissez-faire approach is willing to provide palliative measures to the poor on a case-by-case basis and usually through bilateral channels, which allows aid to be used for political as well as specific economic purposes. However, it resists all attempts to transfer resources from rich to poor, whether as a matter of obligation or by modification of world economic structures. Instead, it believes that the long-term economic well-being of the developing world will be secured only through its full integration into the world economy, and by increasing participation in international trade along the lines envisioned by the General Agreement on Trade and Tariffs. The notion that a developing country can capture its share of the world market through a dynamic export-oriented growth strategy deserves closer scrutiny in the light of the following structural problems of commodity trade: (1) wide price fluctuations that leave the development planning of Third World countries vulnerable to the world market; (2) increasing protectionism against exports by northern countries; (3) stagflation in the North, which reduces the demand for developing countries' exports and increases the prices of their imports at the same time; and (4) rapidly rising energy prices, especially oil, that aggravate both the industrialization and debt problems of Third World countries.

The system-reforming approach pivots around the notion of "complex interdependence," implying that certain structural modifications in the world economy may be required, but that these changes are not so fundamental as to call into question its basic organization. It focuses upon such functional goals as making the international monetary system more universal, stable, and equitable; creating international mechanisms for coordinating the supply and demand of energy and other commodities; and increasing multilateral channels of development aid to Third World countries. This emphasis on international regimes as a way of achieving greater global well-being raises some difficult questions regarding both desirability and feasibility. Who will be the manager of these global regimes? Whose interests will be served or shortchanged thereby? Will such regimes really help meet the basic needs of the world's poor, are they more likely to enhance the economic and political control of dominant elites and societies? The world order performance of the new international regimes established in recent years (such as the food regime) suggests the same credibility problem that has always plagued the United Nations: the discrepancies between legitimizing claims and pretensions and the limited capacity to realize institutional values and goals. Those who have the economic power and the technological know-how lack political will, and those who put forward normative claims lack political and economic power to bring about a fair and equitable management of complex interdependence.

Finally, the system-transforming approach shifts the focus from efficiency to equity and from national to human well-being, especially to those who are oppressed and without any representation in the present world economic order. Oriented around "world order populism," this approach takes a skeptical view of incremental reforms; instead, it strives to transform the inequitable structures of the existing world economic order as part of a protracted struggle for a more just and humane world order. It also seeks to redefine the development *problematique* by placing greater emphasis on the meeting of basic needs and distributive justice. It rejects the assumption that the benefits of economic growth will automatically be transmitted to all regions and all classes of people in the world. It examines the linkages between or among world order values, attempting to reconcile trade-offs between economic development, human rights, and environmental protection. From this comes "another development," a normative concept representing a more self-reliant participatory, equitable, and ecologically sustainable approach to development. The basic thrust of this conception of "another development" gives more weight to political and cultural factors as well as to alternative attitudes, values and life styles in mobilizing support for basic structural changes at both the domestic and international levels.

The system-transforming approach thus rejects the technical, managerial, and elite biases of both the system-maintaining and system-reforming approaches. It is also skeptical of the NIEO. It questions, in particular, who will be primary beneficiaries of the NIEO. Does it, for example, really address the problems of global poverty and basic human needs, or is it just a welfare policy for Third World elites? Does it transform or merely reinforce the worst aspects of the present world economic system? There is considerable doubt about the ability of NIEO advocates to achieve their goals without some form of struggle, given the recalcitrance of Western elites to give up their privileged position.

To date, the system-transforming approach remains an idealized norm, not a working reality. The proponents of this approach have advanced self-reliance, including collective self-reliance, as the central alternative development path for the Third World. This self-reliance approach, as mentioned above, entails major changes at the national and international levels. Thus, a serious obstacle is the resistance of dominant elites in the Third World to the transformation of domestic power structures. This is evident in NIEO politics, where the principle of individual and collective self-reliance is often confined to rhetoric and where Third World elites are preoccupied with the short-term goals of seeking both bilateral and multilateral aid. Now that even China is shifting from the self-reliant to the interdependent growth model of development in its "catching up" process, this approach has at least for the moment suffered a major setback.

The first work in this section conceptualizes economic development in terms of the attainment of middle-class style of life for the planet's four billion people, and assesses the implications of this goal in light of the demographic trends, the limits of world resources, and new scientific and technological knowledge. The novelty of Nathan Keyfitz's approach is that it accepts the peoples of the world as the basic unit of analysis. "The increase of more than 4 percent per year in the number of middle-class people who have come on the scene is too rapid in that these high consumers have to comb the world for resources," Keyfitz argues, "but on the other hand it is much too slow to satisfy the billions of people who are waiting in the wings." His prescription is a global technological fix – that is, a new technology capable of producing more with less placed in the public domain as the common possession of humankind. Is there any reason to believe that such a new world technological order is any more viable than the NIEO has been to date?

Gernot Köhler, in the second selection, offers a unique argument that the macrostructure of the global society today is similar to the apartheid structure of South African society. Köhler, like Keyfitz, views the world as a society rather than a collection of nation-states. Through this macrostructural analysis, he finds that global apartheid is more unjust in terms of distribution of wealth, power, and incidence of violence than the universally condemned system of South African apartheid. Just as apartheid policies in South Africa cannot be pursued and sustained without apartheid social structures, so the failures of the present international system to satisfy basic human needs or to reduce the inequalities that exist between center and periphery cannot be fully understood except in the context of global apartheid structure. This essay thus provides a useful framework for understanding the present global problematique and for suggesting strategies for changing it.

The article by Mahbub ul Haq probes the causes of the current derailment of

NIEO politics by delineating the major mistakes in the conceptualizations and strategies of both the North and the South. Noting that substantive differences remain to be resolved, Haq provides a set of prescriptive measures in different issue areas to get the global negotiations off center. This article presents an example of a progressive system-reforming approach to world order mentioned earlier. It proceeds from the main premise that the world economic system is becoming more complex and more interdependent, and that it is in the interests of all parties (including the Soviet bloc countries which have opted to stay on the sidelines) to participate in the reconstruction of a new global order. Change in the structures of the world economy is inevitable, Haq argues, but it is in the interests of all that we intervene to guide this change in directions that will benefit all the major groups in the global community. In this connection, it is instructive to contrast Haq's analysis of global problems, as well as his policy recommendations, with those of Köhler.

The next selection is by Fernando Henrique Cardoso, one of the most prolific and influential *dependencia* theorists. Cardoso develops a macrohistorical and macrostructural analysis of "the core of the *problematique* of another development." A major contradiction in the present world order system lies in the fact that another development is materially possible, but is blocked from realization by political and structural factors. The central value guiding another development is anchored in "a pedagogy of the oppressed." Another development displays skepticism of technological fixes; instead, it stresses such principles as self-reliance, participatory democracy, and cultural pluralism. The criteria for measuring success or failure of another development, Cardoso argues, should be based on the "*quality of life* and on *equality* in the distribution of goods and services." To enhance participatory democracy, Cardoso proposes that consumers and workers, women, ethnic and religious minorities, youth, poor peasants, shanty-town dwellers, and other social groups be made part of national delegations to international forums. How "realistic" is another development? Cardoso's system-transforming approach projects a new brand of "world order realism" premised on the belief that "it is already possible to inscribe in reality the goals we wish to attain."

The last work in this section is a third-system declaration indicting the misuse of science and technology. Adopted by a group of concerned scholars associated with the World Order Models Project, the declaration presents a vehement denunciation of the belief that science and technology are or can be value-neutral. While noting the potentials that science and technology have for human liberation and material well-being, the declaration contends that they have been used as omnipresent instruments for power and control, benefiting a small minority of economic, political and scientific elites throughout the world. That some 50 percent of all research scientists in the world are engaged in military research and development suggests the extent to which modern science and technology have been diverted from constructive service. The declaration calls for a radical reorientation of science and technology, and proclaims that they should henceforth be directed "towards the needs, skills and knowledge of the majority of the underprivileged peoples of the world."

QUESTIONS FOR DISCUSSION AND REFLECTION

Based on your reading of the works in this section, how would you define global development problems?

Of the contending development strategies advanced in both academic and policy-making circles, which one is most congenial—and which one least congenial—to the world order value of economic equity and well-being? Why?

What is your assessment of the NIEO? Specifically, what are its principal objectives, strategies, and accomplishments to date? In what sense has the NIEO failed and what have been the main obstacles to the establishment of a more just and equitable economic order?

What do you see as viable ways and means of overcoming global poverty? How can the chronic gaps between *short-term national interests* and *long-term global needs* be reconciled?

What relative position should economic well-being enjoy in the hierarchy of the world order values? Why?

What is your sense of the future development of the world economic system? Specifically, which issue—war/peace or poverty/economic well-being—is likely to dominate the agenda of world politics in the coming years and with what possible consequences for world order politics?

SELECTED BIBLIOGRAPHY

Adelman, Irma, and Cynthia T. Morris. *Economic Growth and Social Equity in Developing Countries.* Stanford, CA.: Stanford University Press, 1973.

Amin, Samir. *Unequal Development.* New York: Monthly Review Press, 1976.

Barnet, Richard. *The Lean Years.* New York: Simon & Shuster, 1980.

Bhagwati, Jagdish. *Economics and World Order: From the 1970s to the 1990s.* New York: MacMillan, 1972.

Cardoso, Fernando H., and Enzo Galetto. *Dependency and Development in Latin America.* Berkeley: University of California Press, 1979.

Development Issue Papers for the 1980s. New York: United Nations Development Programme.

Energy in the Developing Countries. Washington, D.C.: World Bank, August 1980.

Galtung, Johan, P. O'Brien, and R. Preiswerk, eds. *Self Reliance: A Strategy for Development.* London: Bogle-L'Ouverture, 1980.

Goulet, Denis. *The Cruel Choice: A New Concept in the Theory of Development.* New York: Atheneum, 1971.

Lappe, Frances M., et al. *Aid as Obstacle: Twenty Questions About Our Foreign Aid and the Hungry.* San Francisco: Institute for Food and Development Policy, 1980.

Modelski, George, ed. *Transnational Corporations and World Order.* Beverly Hills, CA.: Sage Publications, 1979.

Morris, David. *Measuring the Condition of the World's Poor: The Physical Quality of Life Index.* New York: Pergamon, 1979.

North-South: A Programme for Survival, The Report of the Independent Commission on International Development Issues Under the Chairmanship of Willy Brandt. Cambridge: M.I.T. Press, 1980.

Rifkin, Jeremy. *Entropy: A New World View*. New York: Viking, 1980.

Rothstein, Robert L. *Global Bargaining: UNCTAD and the Question for a New International Economic Order*. Princeton: Princeton University Press, 1979.

Schumacher, E.F. *Small is Beautiful: Economics as if People Mattered*. New York: Harper & Row, 1973.

Tinbergen, Jan., et al. *Reshaping the International Order*. New York: E. P. Dutton, 1976.

Tinker, I., et al., eds. *Women and World Development*. New York: Praeger, 1976.

World Development Report, 1980 (Annual). Washington, D.C.: World Bank, 1980.

20
WORLD RESOURCES AND
THE WORLD MIDDLE CLASS

Nathan Keyfitz

How much economic development is possible? Surely the planet and its materials are finite and not even all its present four billion people can live like Americans, let alone the six or eight billion that on present trends will be alive when a stationary world population is established. Indeed, there is doubt whether the 250 million people expected to populate the U.S. in the year 2000 will be able to live as Americans today. How far, then, can industrial society spread through the preindustrial world before it reaches a ceiling imposed by space, raw materials and waste disposal?

That is the wrong question to ask, if human knowledge and capacity for substitution and the resilience of economic systems are unbounded, as they may well be. In that case the right question — and certainly a more tractable and pragmatic question — is how *fast* can development progress, whether toward an ultimate limit or not? What rate of technical innovation can be attained, oriented to allow a corresponding rate of expansion of industry, and how many of the world's people will the expansion enable to enter the middle class each year?

Attainment of the middle-class style of life is what constitutes development in countries as widely separated geographically and ideologically as Brazil and the U.S.S.R. In the process peasants gain education, move to cities and adopt urban occupations and urban patterns of expenditure. Changes are involved in people themselves, in where they live, in their kind of work and in the nature of the goods they consume. These changes can be visualized in terms of a definable line, comparable to the poverty line officially drawn in the U.S., across which people aspire to move. The pertinent questions then become: How many people are moving across the line each year, what is their effect on resources, at what rate can resources be expanded by new techniques and therefore what is the size of the window through which the world's poor will climb into the middle class during the remainder of this century and beyond it?

A main issue of development for many of the people of Asia, Africa, and Latin America is how to enlarge that window into the middle class. Since, according to a generally accepted view, it is middle-class people who limit their families, the rate of movement into that class helps to determine the level at which the world population can be stabilized and that level in turn will determine the degree of well-being that can be supported by world resources. And if shortage of resources makes the opening into the middle class as it is presently constituted so narrow that the majority will never be able to pass through it, then the sooner we know this the better. The Chinese rather than the Brazilian-Russian pattern of development may be what people will have to settle for.

The questions I have raised are difficult for many reasons, including the lack of statistical information, uncertainty about the capacity of productive systems to substitute common materials for scarce ones and uncertainty about the directions in which technology will advance. Some data and some pointers are available, however.

Let us begin with population. The world population, according to the United Nations estimates I shall be following, passed the four-billion mark in 1975. It had passed the three-billion mark in 1960. Whereas the last billion was added in 15 years, the first billion had taken from the beginning (one or two million years ago) until 1825. The growth has been far faster than exponential growth at a fixed rate of increase (as with compound interest); instead the rate rose from something like an average of .001 percent per year through the millenniums of prehistory to 1.9 percent through the decade and a half from 1960 to 1975.

Apparently the rate of increase will not rise further. The same 1.9 percent, according to the UN medium variant, will hold until 1990, and by the end of the century the increase will be down to 1.6 percent per year (see Figure 1). Other estimates place the peak earlier and make the decline in rate of increase faster. Insofar as the increasing rate of increase constituted a population "explosion," we can draw relief from the fact that we are now down to "only" exponential growth. (This peaking was inevitable because of what mainly caused the rise to begin with: the decline in mortality during infancy and childhood. Mortality improvement after the reproductive ages does not affect increase much and in the long run does not affect it at all. Once the chance that a newborn infant will survive to reproduce itself gets up to about .90, the scope for further rise is limited, and whatever rise takes place will be offset by even a small decline in the birthrate.)

Those who worry about the population explosion can take some comfort in this peaking of the rate of increase, but not very much. Dropping to exponential growth still leaves the world population increasing (on the UN medium variant) by about 75 million per year now, with the annual increment rising to 100 million by the end of the century. And the absolute increase, rather than the rate, seems to be what matters. To feed the present yearly increment requires nearly 20 million tons of additional grain each year, which is more than the Canadian wheat crop and about the same as the crops of Argentina, Australia and Romania taken together. To look after the annual increment of population on even a minimum basis is going to be difficult enough; the real

FIGURE 1.

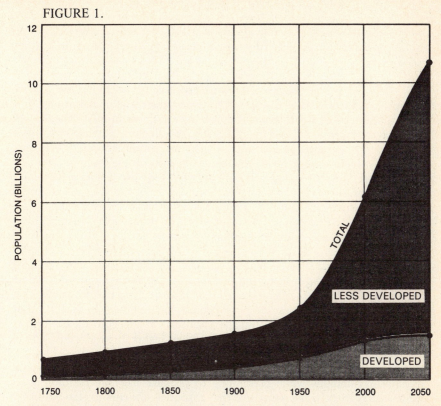

"POPULATION EXPLOSION" CURVE is the result of more-than-exponential growth; the annual rate of increase has itself been rising, most sharply in the past century, largely because of the decline in infant and childhood mortality. In this layer chart the total population (projected to the year 2050 according to the United Nations medium estimate) is given for countries currently classified by the UN as "developed" (*light color*) and "less developed" (*dark color*).

issue, however, is not how many people can live but how many can live well.

Production of most things consumed by the world's people has been increasing at a higher rate than the 1.9 percent per year of population. During the period from 1960 to 1973 meat output increased at 2.8 percent a year, newsprint at 3.7 percent, motor vehicles at 6.8 percent and energy consumption at 4.9 percent, and the rise was similar for many other commodities. These numbers can be taken to mean that on the average mankind is year by year eating better and reading more, becoming more mobile and substituting machine power for the power of human muscles. Such a conclusion would seem to be confirmed by worldwide figures on productive activity or income. For example, adding up the gross domestic products of all countries for 1970 yields a gross world product of $3,219 billion, an average of $881 per head. The total has been going up at nearly 5 percent per year in real terms, that is, after price increases. Even allowing for the 1.9 percent increase in population, we seem to be getting better off individually at about 3 percent per year. Projecting on this basis, real goods per head would double every 23 years; each generation would be twice as well off as the preceding one. To dispose of twice as much wealth as one's parents, four times as much as one's grandparents, surely cannot be regarded as unsatisfactory; the world, such figures seem to show, is moving toward affluence. That conclusion requires substantial qualification.

The division of a total number of dollars by a number of individuals to obtain an average per head has a long tradition; dividing one number by another is an innocent operation and without any necessary implication that everyone obtains the average, and yet it puts thoughts into people's minds. The first thought might be that things are not bad with $881 per head for the entire global population—a conservative conclusion. The second thought might be that things would indeed not be bad if the total was actually divided up—a radical viewpoint that has been voiced often in recent years. Income is an aspect of a way of life, however, and only a trifling part of a way of life is directly transferable.

The fallacy of redivision is encouraged by putting income into terms of money and performing arithmetical division. To say we should divide income so that everyone in the world can have his $881 is to solve a real problem with a verbal or arithmetical trick, because behind the numbers is the fact that Americans live one way and Indians another way. If, starting tomorrow, Americans were all to live like Indians, then their higher incomes would simply disappear. There would be nothing to transfer.

How much is transferable depends on the extent to which Americans could consume like Indians while continuing to produce like Americans. Simon Kuznets and others have pointed out that as soon as one tries to plan a transfer the tight bond between production and consumption frustrates the attempt. For example, the cost of travel to work is called consumption, but if people stopped traveling to work, production would fall to zero. What about the cost of holidays and entertainment, which are elements of consumption but which refresh people for further work? What about nutrition, education and health services? And what about the enjoyment of consumer goods that is the incentive to work and earn? All of these and many other parts of consumption feed back into production. Moreover, to discuss massive transfers of capital would be futile for political reasons even if it were economically practical: the declining U.S. foreign-aid budget shows how unappealing to the major donor this path to world development is.

Because the world population is heterogeneous, no style of life is in fact associated with the world average of $881. Following that average through time leads to the mistaken impression that things are getting better every year and will do so indefinitely. Even a two-way breakdown of the average is a major step toward realism.

Of the total world population of four billion estimated for 1975, 1.13 billion, or nearly 30 percent, live in developed countries. The fraction of the annual increment of population accounted for by those countries is much less, however:

only 10 million out of 75 million, or 13 percent. The annual increment in the less developed countries is more than 65 million, and it will rise to 90 million by the end of the century (again on the UN medium estimates). This division of the world into two kinds of countries, rich and poor, or more developed and less developed, has become familiar since World War II. That world 1970 product (or income) of $881 per head is in fact an average of the developed countries' $2,701 and the less developed countries' $208.

`Recent fluctuations obscure the long-term rates of increase, but suppose income for the rich and poor countries alike increased at 5 percent per year in the long term. On the population side, suppose the future increase is .5 percent per year among the developed countries and 2.5 percent per year among the less developed. Allowing for these population numbers brings the 5 percent annual gain in total product that was assumed for both down to about 4.5 percent for the developed countries and only 2.5 percent for the less developed ones.

The result is a widening gap between the two groups of countries, an exercise in the mathematics of geometric increase (see Figure 2). Think of the developed countries starting at $2,701 per capita and increasing at 4.5 percent per year in real terms; after 25 years they have risen three-fold, to a per capita income of more than $8,000 in 1995. By that time the income per head in the less developed countries has not even doubled: their $208 has risen to only $386. By the year 2020 the grandchildren of the present generation will have, in the one set of countries, more than $24,000 per head and in the other countries the still very modest $715 − one thirty-fourth as much as the rich, and not yet as much as the 1970 world average!

The calculation shows how a heterogeneous population is bound to develop a widening gap between rich and poor if per capita rates of increase are frozen. I have assumed that all national incomes increase at 5 percent per year. Overall national-income growth is not conspicuously different, on the average, for the poor and the rich countries, and so it is the differences in population growth that are decisive.

To speak of developed and less developed countries is an improvement on treating the world as being homogeneous, but it has been overtaken by the events of the past three years. Where two categories of countries once sufficed, we now find we cannot do with fewer than four.

The shifts in raw-material prices have created resource-rich countries such as Abu Dhabi and Venezuela, whose wealth is comparable to that of the developed countries, which by way of contrast can be called capital-rich. Some countries that were poor have actually been developing, including Singapore, Korea, Taiwan and Hong Kong. Finally there are the many countries that are truly poor, lacking (in relation to their population) both capital and resources. We have, then, the resource-rich countries, the capital-rich countries, the developing countries and the poor countries. Specifically identifying and classifying all cases to provide numbers for population in these groups is not easy. (Indonesia has resources but not enough so that any likely rise in prices would make its 135 million people rich.) The new categories of resource-rich and developing countries might be defined in such a way that they total 200 million

FIGURE 2.

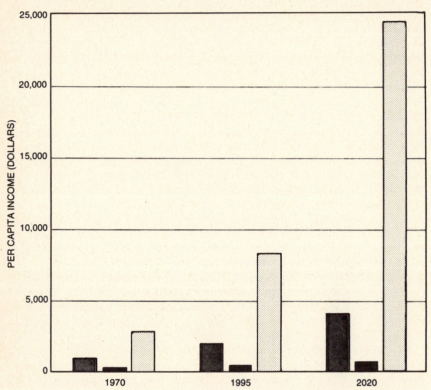

WIDENING GAP between per capita incomes in the developed and in the less developed countries is caused by the more rapid growth of population in poor countries. UN figures for the developed (*light color*) and less developed (*dark color*) countries and for the world as a whole (*gray*) were projected on the assumption that total income will continue to increase at 5 percent per year in both sets of countries but that the population of the developed countries increases at only .5 percent per year while that of less developed countries increases at 2.5 percent.

people each; the fact remains that most of the world's people are in countries that have no leverage through either control of capital or control of resources.

No country is homogeneous, however; the poorest countries contain some rich people and the richest contain some poor. Nations and their governments dominate our age so completely that individuals too easily drop out of political as well as statistical view, yet the welfare of governments is not a worthy ultimate objective; it is the people of the poor countries who deserve our concern. And so what follows will deal as directly as possible with people.

The typical poor person and the typical middle-class person are easy to visualize; the first is a peasant in Java, Nigeria, the Brazilian Northeast or elsewhere in Asia, Africa and the Americas; the second is a city dweller in San Francisco, Frankfurt, Leningrad or Tokyo with an office job that puts him well above the poverty line. There are less obvious representatives. Along with the peasant group one should count as poor the wage laborer of Calcutta or the urban unemployed of the U.S. And the middle-class group includes the unionized construction worker, the bus driver, the keypunch operator and the successful farmer in the U.S., Europe, the U.S.S.R. or Japan; that some of these are considered blue-collar is secondary to their earning a middle-class income.

In survey after survey most Americans, when they are asked where they think they belong, place themselves in the middle class. The self-classification by which most Americans tend to call themselves middle-class and Indians tend to call themselves poor accords with the distinction I have made. Most of those called middle-class in the world live in the cities of the rich countries, but some of them live in poor countries and some live in the countryside. The crucial part of the distinction is that middle-class people are in a position to make effective claim to a share of the world's resources that accords with modern living.

With an income measure of welfare, people fall on a continuum and the location of the poverty line is arbitrary. As a country grows richer its standards rise, so that the same fraction of its population may be defined as "poor" even as everyone in the country is becoming better off. In the case of the U.S., however, it has been possible to reach broad agreement on a Social Security Administration definition of poverty based on relatively objective criteria. An average urban family of four, including two children, is said to require $3,700 a year (at 1974 prices) to pay rent, buy clothing and meet basic nutritional needs, and similar levels are set for other types of household.

"Middle class" describes a style of life and can cover not only physical necessities but also such conventional needs as power lawn mowers and winter vacations in Florida. It needs to be specified separately for each culture before one can see how many people enjoy it and what the energy and resource consequences of the enjoyment are. Pending such a study I propose to call middle-class those who are above the equivalent of the U.S. poverty line, wherever they may live. Cultural differences make poverty in one country intrinsically noncomparable with poverty in another country, but they make average money incomes just as noncomparable. The effort to quantify important notions must not be prevented by some degree of qualitative difference; the fraction under the level of consumption represented by the U.S. poverty line is not the definitive way of measuring the world's poor, but it will serve for the moment. In the U.S. that fraction was 11.6 percent in 1974, an increase from 11.1 in 1973 but a decrease from 22.4 in 1959. Of the U.S. population of 210 million in 1973, some 23 million were poor; call the remaining 187 million middle-class. Let us try to find indexes that will provide a corresponding number for other countries.

Passenger cars in use might be taken as roughly proportional to the middle-class, or above-poverty, population. In the U.S. in 1973 the number of passenger cars was 101 million and in the world as a whole it was 233 million, a ratio of 2.3. Insofar as the 233 million passenger cars in the world are being driven and ridden in by a world middle class, we can multiply the U.S. middle class of 187 million by 2.3 and derive a world total of 430 million middle-class people. This number is too low, because automobiles are less a part of daily life even in other affluent countries; we know that trains continue to be used in Europe for much travel that is done in the U.S. by automobile.

Let us try telephones as the indicator. The world total in 1973 was 336 million telephones and the U.S. total was 138 million. On this index the world middle class was 187 million times 336/138, or 455 million. With electric energy as the indicator a similar calculation gives a world middle class of 580 million. Each one of these indicators is surely defective. One can nonetheless hope that their defects are more or less constant over the 20 years or so that I propose to apply them to establish a trend.

A slightly different way of doing the calculation is to take it that modern living requires about four metric tons of crude oil a year for heating, air conditioning and motoring, so that the world output in 1973, 2,774 million tons, could cover the needs of 700 million people. (The calculation is approximate because some poor people do use a little oil and large supplies go to military and other government uses.)

Averaging the several approaches gives a world middle class of 500 million for 1970. What is important is that the corresponding average number—indexed on automobiles, telephones, electric energy, oil and other items—was something like 200 million for 1950. That indicates an average increase of 4.7 percent per year in the world middle class: the workers, and their families, who are integrated into industrial society, utilize its materials as the basis of their jobs and apply their incomes to consume its product. In doing so they have an impact on resources and on the environment. Just how great is the impact of change in status from poor to middle class, particularly compared with the effect of population change?

Raw materials are used by people, and so, if all else is fixed, the drain on resources must be proportional to the number of people. If each year the world population is 1.9 percent larger than it was the year before and nothing else changes, then each year resources are claimed by 1.9 percent more people, and in the course of 37 years we shall be on the average twice as dense on the land and shall be consuming twice as much iron and other metals and twice as much crude oil. This statement is not true of pollution, where more-than-proportional effects enter. It is true of resources insofar as technology for production and patterns of consumption both remain constant.

Actually they do not remain constant; they exert effects in oppositive directions. Technology has been stretching the use of materials. We know how to put the tin on the can more thinly; we can make rubber and fabrics out of coal; we recycle aluminum. The movement, guided by price changes, is always toward less scarce materials. As income goes up, however, per capita consumption increases: more cans are used, albeit each with a thinner layer of tin. Worse still, new materials are invented—detergents, plastics, insecticides—that take a long time to reenter the cycles of nature once we are through with them. It is the net effect of these tendencies that we need to estimate.

One way to get at the net effect of increased consumption per head and of

FIGURE 3.

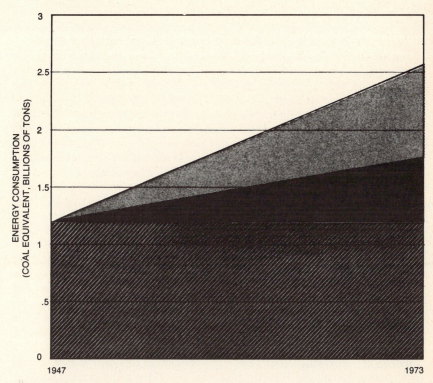

U.S. ENERGY CONSUMPTION would have increased from 1.21 billion tons of coal equivalent in 1947 to 1.77 billion tons in 1973 if it had merely kept pace with the rise in population. In fact, however, energy consumption rose to 2.55 billion tons in 1973. The increment (*light color*) due to a rise in per capita consumption stemming from affluence was larger than the increment (*dark color*) attributable to population growth. The same is true of many other materials.

technological improvements is to determine the residual change after population increase is allowed for. Let us try this for energy consumption in the U.S. in 1947 and 1973. The 1947 consumption was 1.21 billion tons of coal equivalent and the 1973 consumption was 2.55 billion. Meanwhile the population rose from 144 million to 210 million. If the larger population of 1973 had held to the same volume and patterns of consumption and production as the smaller population of 1947, it would have required 1.77 billion tons of coal equivalent. Hence of the total increase of 1.34 billion only .56 billion was due to population growth; the remainder of the increase, .78 billion, was due to affluence. Affluence was more important than population (see Figure 3). Similar calculations can be made for metals and other materials, for pollution, for the primary caloric content of food, indeed for any kind of impact that can be measured.

As an alternative way of analyzing the consumption of materials, consider that from 1950 to 1970 the part of the world population that was affluent went from 200 million to 500 million: while total population increases at 1.9 percent per year, middle-class high consumers increase at 4.7 percent. Each high consumer requires the equivalent of three-quarters of a ton of grain, whereas the poor get by on a quarter of a ton. (The consequent ratio of land use is less than three to one, because agriculture is more efficient in rich countries.) The middle-class person requires from 15 to 30 barrels of oil, whereas the poor person makes do with one barrel at most in the form of kerosene, bus fuel and fertilizer. The land and energy content of clothing may be in a rich-to-poor ratio intermediate between those for food and for transport. As a kind of average of these several ratios, suppose the middle-class person has five times as much impact on the material base as the poor person. Then the average person on the high side of the poverty line must be taken as being equivalent to five people on the low side in fuel and metals consumed. In considering impact we therefore calculate as though in 1975 the planet had not four billion people aboard but 6.4 billion. Of these, 3.4 billion were poor and three billion represented the fivefold impact of a world middle class that probably numbered 600 million.

This would make the average total impact of the small middle class on resources somewhat less than that of the large number of the poor. The middle class has been increasing at 4.7 percent per year, however, and the poor less than half as fast. At the growing edge the increase of affluence has much more effect than the increase of population; the movement of people into the middle class has more effect on materials and the environment than the increase in the number of poor people.

Indeed, it has so much effect that if the population explosion is now ending (in the sense that the world rate of increase is peaking at 1.9 percent per year and starting to decline), we now face another explosion. It arises from the arithmetic of combining two exponentials, which is to say two progressions (population growth and middle-class growth) each of which has a fixed ratio.

The effect can be expressed in stylized form by supposing the 1975 population of four billion projected forward in the ratio 1.6 every 25 years (equal to the fixed rate of 1.9 percent per year). Suppose at the same time that the middle class triples every 25 years (equivalent to a fixed 4.5 percent per year), as it did from 1950 to 1975. The poor population is the difference between the resulting numbers. If the people above the poverty line average five times the impact of those below it, then we must add five times the middle class to the number of poor for the total impact. The result is a steadily increasing rate of increase of the impact from 2.7 percent per year in 1950–1975 to 3.1 percent and then to 3.5 percent (see Figure 4). This is based on continuance of 1950–1970 rates of economic development and of population growth. Population growth will slow down, but that will not greatly reduce the impact, which in this illustration would be increasingly due to affluence. Our difficulties in maintaining the population and affluence levels of 1976 suggest that this model will not work. We cannot hope to keep tripling the middle class every 25 years. The main reason is shortage of resources.

FIGURE 4.

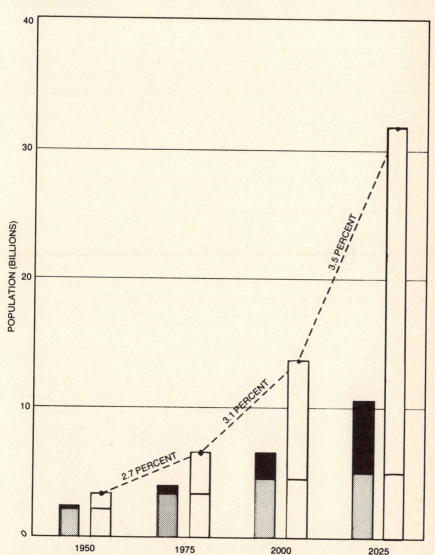

FUTURE IMPACT on world resources is affected by the growth of the middle class, whose members are assumed to consume five times as much as poor people. In population alone the middle class *(black)*, increasing at 4.5 percent per year, would eventually be larger than the poor population *(gray)*. When the middle class is multiplied by five, the resulting "consumption population" *(white)* is seen to grow at an annual rate that increases from 2.7 to 3.1 and then to 3.5 percent. World resources are already strained by the 1975 "consumption population."

Natural resources account for only about 5 percent of the value of goods and services produced in the U.S. and other developed countries. Resources are hence curiously two-sided: extracting them accounts for only a small part of the cost, yet they are the sine qua non of existence, to say nothing of progress. And particular materials do run out. England's Industrial Revolution was in part a response to a firewood crisis: cheap coal was substituted for wood, which had become scarce and very dear. In America, on the other hand, wood was cheap and labor was dear, so that houses were built of wood rather than stone, which is more labor-intensive. Now timber is dear here also, and masonry and aluminum are substituted in some products. Plastics take the place of paper in packaging. Cultivated southern pine is used for newsprint instead of the limited pine and spruce of the northern forests.

Thus history shows the resilience of the productive system, its ability to substitute commoner materials for scarce ones. Nevertheless, the extrapolation of this capacity must take account of time. Invention, innovation and capital replacement can proceed only at a certain pace. It is this pace of innovation that needs to be studied, since it sets the rate at which industrial society can spread in the face of environmental and resource limitations.

Limits to the spread of industrial society under present technology are suggested by the record of trade in raw materials over the past quarter-century. To take one example, in 1950 the production and consumption of energy were in virtual balance for the developed countries as a whole. Their deficit amounted to less than 4 percent of consumption. By 1973 production in the developed countries had nearly doubled but consumption had far outrun it and the deficit had swollen to a third of consumption.

The story for metals and other resources is not very different. No country, developed or not, has been provided by nature with a greater quantity and variety of mineral and other resources than the U.S. Yet even the U.S. had become a net importer of minerals by the 1920s, and it now imports all its platinum, mica and chromium, 96 percent of its aluminum, 85 percent of its asbestos, 77 percent of its tin and 28 percent of its iron—to select from a long list. Of course, the shortages of some of these minerals are not absolute but are a matter of price. The U.S. could produce all the aluminum it needs from domestic clay, but bauxite from Jamaica is cheaper. Having virtually exhausted the iron ore of the Mesabi Range, the U.S. resorts to lower-grade domestic taconite and to imports, in a proportion determined by prices.

The increase of more than 4 percent per year in the number of middle-class people who have come on the scene is too rapid in that these high consumers have to comb the world for resources, but on the other hand it is much too slow to satisfy the billions of people who are waiting in the wings. Whereas Europe, Japan and the U.S.S.R. have made great gains during the UN Development Decades, most of Asia and Africa are dissatisfied with their progress. Moreover, a realistic calculation would probably show a larger gap between the impact on resources of those who have raised themselves from poverty and that of those who are still poor. The weight of a middle-class person is in many respects more than five times that of a peasant. It is to keep the

FIGURE 5.

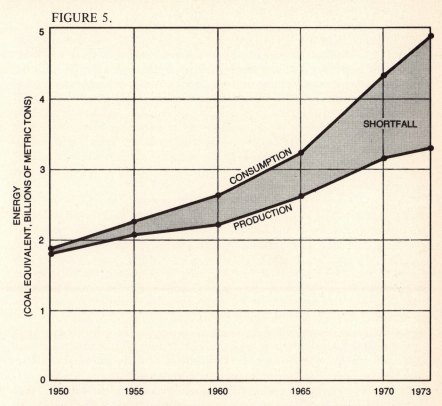

CONSUMPTION AND PRODUCTION of energy were about balanced in 1950 in the developed countries: they produced the coal, oil, gas and hydropower whose energy they consumed,
except for a small shortfall made up by imports from less developed countries. By 1973 rising
production had been outstripped by consumption; shortfall amounted to a third of consumption.

argument conservative that I suppose the ratio is five times and that the world
middle class triples every 25 years.

The combination of these two modest assumptions produces, as we have
seen, a surprisingly high measure of impact for the end of the century, by
which time the middle class, which was at 600 million in 1975, would increase
to 1.8 billion and have the effect of five times that number, or nine billion. The
total impact projected to the year 2000 is, then, that of nine billion plus 4.6
billion poor, or 13.6 billion people. This compares with an impact of 6.4 billion
for 1975, calculated in the same way. If strains are already apparent in materials
and energy, what will happen with a doubling of the rate of consumption?

The accelerating impact that appears from recognition of two categories of
people rather than one category is offset in some degree by the decline in the
impact per dollar of income once income rises beyond a certain level. People
take very high incomes in services rather than in more and more automobiles.

Moreover, the relation of impact to income varies from one culture to another, as an anthropologist would point out; an economist would add that the relation can be counted on to change as raw materials, and hence the goods made from them, become scarce and costly compared with less material-intensive forms of consumption. Although the impact on materials may taper off with increased wealth, the impact on air and water may be greater than proportional. There may be thresholds: the air may hold just so much carbon monoxide, a lake just so much fertilizer runoff, without undue effect, but beyond a certain critical point the effect may quickly rise to disaster levels. Such critical points clearly exist in renewable resources. Fishing or cutting timber up to a certain intensity does no damage at all, but continued overfishing or overcutting can destroy the fish or tree population.

The rate and direction of development of the period 1950–1970, unsatisfactory though it may be in that the absolute number of the poor would continue to increase until well into the 21st century, is still faster than can be sustained on present strategies. The resilience of the economic system, and technical innovation in particular, can be counted on to respond to needs, but only at a certain rate of speed. One can imagine sources of energy, the capacity to dispose of wastes and substitutes for metals all doubling in the century to come, but it is not easy to conceive of such a doubling in the 15 years that would keep the middle class growing at 4.7 percent per year.

To say that civilization will collapse when oil supplies are exhausted, or that we will pollute ourselves out of existence, is to deny all responsiveness and resilience to the productive system. The geologist or resource expert tends to focus on the material and technical process he knows and may be less than imaginative with regard to how a substitute might be found to deal with a shortage. On the other hand, the economist may be too imaginative; he may too readily suppose substitutes can be found for anything as it becomes scarce. The ensuing debate between pessimistic raw-material experts and optimistic economists has generated whatever knowledge we have on the subject. The middle ground to which both sides are tending is that every barrier that industrial expansion is now meeting can be surmounted by technological advance, but not in an instant. It is not a ceiling on total population and income that we have to deal with but that window. How large can the window be made?

One conclusion to be drawn from the arithmetic I did above is that a projection in terms of ratios is probably wrong in principle; in the face of natural and human limitations the pace of advance may be determined in absolute numbers rather than ratios. If, for example, pollution effects are proportional to fuel burned, then successive absolute increments in fuel consumption have the same bad effects on the fixed volume of the atmosphere. We should think not of the percent expansion of the middle class but of its absolute increase.

The calculation made in this way starts with the annual growth in world population of 75 million at the present time, gradually increasing to 100 million by the end of the century, and compares that increment with the number annually emerging into the middle class. If the latter went in a straight line from

200 million in 1950 to 500 million in 1970, then the average annual increase was 15 million. My stylized model, wherein industrial society expands through the emergence of people from the peasantry into city jobs as capital expands (while those not yet called remain at their old peasant incomes), goes back ultimately to Adam Smith. This simple application of the Smith model suggests that currently 15 million people join the middle class each year and 60 million join the poor. Even if the middle-class increment could rise to 20 million per year, the poor would still be increasing by 80 million per year at the end of the century. This at least is one reasonable extrapolation of the process of development in the post-war period. Other population estimates are lower than the UN's, but accepting them would lead to the same result: the large majority of the new generation will be poor. Therein lies the harm of rapid population growth.

The natural increase of the affluent population will create difficulties in the years ahead even though birthrates are low. Suppose the window is wide enough for 20 million to pass through it each year. Who will they be? The way the world is made, the children of the currently affluent of America, Europe and Japan will have first claim. The U.S.S.R. has found no way of preventing its elite from placing their children in the elite, and neither has the U.S. On the basis of 600 million for the middle class in 1975, a net natural-increase of .5 percent means three million children per year in excess of deaths. Apart from children who simply replace their parents or grandparents, of the 20 million net admissions each year three million would be further children of those who have already entered the middle class and 17 million would be new entrants. And these 17 million new entrants would be divided among the poor of the developed countries and those of the less developed countries, with the former having the better chance. Poor people in the poor countries sense that the odds against them and against their children are great.

All of this, it should be noted, can be seen as a critique not of development but of one particular model of development. The distinction between poor and middle-class represents the Brazilian and the Russian direction but not the Chinese. Whether because of China's special culture or the personality of Mao Tse-tung, both the specialization that equips people for middle-class jobs and the durable structures of industry and administration in which those jobs have their place have been insistently denied there. It is asserted that everyone can do everything, that people ought to take turns working as peasants, driving trucks and being scholars; people need only so much to eat, to wear and to live in, and consumerism beyond that austere minimum is vice, not virtue. Whether this view can spread among other cultures and without a regime of the same type is not clear. There is little present sign of its spreading even to India, let alone to Japan, Europe or America.

Thomas Malthus gave us a land theory of value, Karl Marx a labor theory and development economists since World War II a capital theory. Land, labor and capital are plainly all needed (and to assign priority to any one may be as much an ideological choice as a practical one), but a dynamic factor superimposed on all of them is new scientific and technical knowledge. At many points we need to know more in order even to discover the problems we face: only recently have we found out that insecticides can be dangerous poisons to organisms other than insects, and that the current worldwide rise in skin cancer may be related to depletion of the ozone layer of the upper atmosphere. Knowledge is needed even to see where the window restricting passage into the middle class is located, and only knowledge can open it wider.

Other ways of widening the window have been suggested. One is to raise the price of the raw materials on whose export some less developed countries depend for foreign exchange. Price increases such as those of the Organization of Petroleum Exporting Countries (OPEC) can have little overall effect, however, on the number of middle-class people in the world (although they have some effect on whether the newly middle-class will speak Spanish or Arabic or English). Who ultimately bears the burden of such price raises is not clear. Some of the burden is carried by poor countries that are not endowed with raw materials; when the repercussions have worked themselves out, India may find it has contributed a higher proportion of its income to Saudi Arabian opulence than the U.S. has. Certainly some U.S. fertilizer that would have gone to India before 1973 now goes to the Middle East; German chemical-plant investments are similarly diverted. The offsetting of oil price rises by French arms sales to Iran has everything to do with national power and little to do with the total distribution of poverty or even the national distribution. The main point is that only a small fraction of the world population is in resource-rich areas.

A second way to help more people escape from poverty might be for those who have already entered the middle class to moderate their consumption. In principle, if one meat eater cuts his consumption, then five grain eaters can increase theirs. If American automobiles were smaller, more metals and fuel would be available for automobiles in Zaire and Bangla Desh as well as—more immediately—fertilizer plants in those countries. If urban Americans were to live like the equally affluent Swedes, U.S. energy consumption might be halved. The trouble is that goods, as well as jobs that require materials, fit into other social activities in an interlocking scheme that is hard to change; social configurations are as solid a reality as raw materials. After two years of talking conservation, the U.S. consumes as much fossil fuel as ever. Faced with a world shortage of raw materials, every person of goodwill wants to see wasteful practices reduced, but the intrinsic limits on transfers I mentioned at the outset and the enormous inertia stored in producing and spending patterns make reduced consumption an unlikely way for the U.S. to help the poor countries.

Foreign aid and investment along conventional lines are a third possibility, but they have been disappointing. They have aided in the development of some countries (Canada is a striking example), but for various reasons the volume is inadequate to the magnitude of the problem for most of the world's population. Even where investment is solidly based in economics some intellectuals argue that it creates dependency, and the politicians of poor countries often respond by expropriation. Ironically the very mention of expropriation is expensive for the poor country because it makes investors demand a higher return.

One can say that better prices for raw materials, reduction of consumption by the rich countries and conventional foreign aid and foreign investment all ought to be pursued, but the experience of the 1950s and the 1960s shows that they will not make a decisive difference in the size of the window through which escape from poverty is sought.

What will make a decisive difference is knowledge: of how to produce amenities with less material, how to substitute materials that are common for those that are scarce, how to get desired results with less energy and how to obtain that energy from renewable sources rather than from fossil fuels. We have seen some results in the past decade. With the advent of integrated circuits, a calculator that cost $1,000 and weighed 40 pounds is now replaced by one that costs $10 and weighs a few ounces. Artificial earth satellites have lowered the cost of communication; they provide television in Indian villages and may ultimately make telephone calls around the world as cheap as local calls. Synthetic polymers have replaced cotton and wool and thus released land. The list of what is still needed is too long to itemize: efficient solar collectors, compact storage batteries to run automobiles on centrally generated power, stronger and cheaper plastics (for automobile bodies, for instance) and so on.

If the time dimension in the implementation of these inventions is crucial, then everything that is done to hasten invention will pay off for the world movement past the poverty line. There are many stages, from pure scientific investigation to the translation of science into technology, to the engineering that makes a production model out of a working prototype and finally on to parts contracting and the assembly line, and each stage takes time. The U.S., once foremost in the speed with which it could convert knowledge into the production of goods, is said to be losing this preeminence; a slowing down would have bad consequences not only for the American competitive position among industrial nations but also for the world escape from poverty. The need is not confined to scientific and engineering knowledge; prompt solutions are also required of many problems in biology and medicine, climatology and geophysics. The technical and social knowledge for birth control is of special importance; whatever the size of the window through which the poor escape into the middle class, the lowering of births will at least bring closer the day when world poverty ceases to increase in absolute amount.

Some part of American research has been directed specifically to labor-intensive devices suited to poor countries, and that line of investigation ought to be encouraged. Even after the Green Revolution, for example, poor countries still have special agricultural problems. Apart from such specific research, the U.S helps all countries when it develops knowledge that makes its own industry more efficient.

A particular preoccupation of the less developed countries is dependency; even commercial indebtedness is seen as neocolonialism. The technical evolution of the poor countries along lines suited to their own needs will be aided by American expansion of knowledge in that it will widen the choice of techniques available to them. In order that any such American contribution not create commercial indebtedness, it would be advisable to place the new knowledge and inventions in the public domain as the common possession of mankind rather than in patents on which royalties could be drawn.

Both production constraints and environmental constraints limit the growth of the world middle class. The way the U.S. can help to open the window is not through schemes for division of the existing product but by contributing knowledge that will expand the product. Solving production and environmental problems starts at home, but any genuine contribution will have value worldwide. Incentives can be devised to direct technology in environment-saving rather than environment-damaging directions. No one can forecast how much time it will take to solve any one technical problem, let alone the complex of problems, but that time—whatever it may be—will be shortened by a larger and more immediate mobilization of scientific and engineering talent.

21
GLOBAL APARTHEID

Gernot Köhler

STRUCTURAL SIMILARITIES WITH SOUTH AFRICAN APARTHEID

It would be useful for our present discussion to distinguish between apartheid as a policy and apartheid as it is practiced within specific societies. Policies of apartheid are programs or measures that aim at the creation or maintenance of racial segregation. Supporters of such policies claim that segregated development of two racial groups does not imply the dominance of one over the other. Apartheid, in this view, permits the possibility of separate but equal, or equivalent, life chances for each of the separated races. The logic of this argument apart, its validity has been disproved in fact wherever such a policy has been professedly tried. Apartheid policies just cannot be pursued and sustained except in the context of structural apartheid.

When we speak of apartheid as a structure, we refer to the social, economic, political, military, and cultural constitution of a society. Whenever a minority race dominates a majority composed of other races in a society, that society exhibits a structure of apartheid.

South Africa is a classic example of this. In South Africa, the dominance of the white minority over the black majority takes different forms—from the denial of political representation to the black majority to brutal repression to an enormous differential in living standards to many others.

Condemnation of South African apartheid has been almost universal. The UN General Assembly has condemned racism and apartheid in South Africa on numerous occasions, with majorities bordering on unanimity, despite the well-known reluctance of member-states to have the organization intervene in the domestic jurisdiction of any state. If on few issues in international politics there has been such a massive agreement, it is because policies of racial segregation, which assure the dominance of the white stratum of society, flagrantly violate the aspirations of a majority of humanity for liberation from dominance and are in sharp conflict with the norms of equality of all human beings, and because apartheid constitutes the most repugnant form of human rights violation.

Reprinted by permission from *Alternatives: A Journal of World Policy* 4, 2, 1978.

It is argued below that the apartheid structure of the global society has important similarities with that of South Africa. Indeed, the global society is a mirror reflection of South African society. One can go a step further and say that global apartheid is even more severe than South African apartheid. There seems to be no other system that is more "apart," in the sense in which apartheid is. Let us, then, look at the macrostructure of the global society.

THE STRUCTURE OF GLOBAL SOCIETY

The world is commonly seen as a multitude of countries or nation-states. World politics and world economics are commonly understood as a set of relations between sovereign nation-states. This view, though not wrong, is limited. It is true that nation-states issue passports and visas, show national flags, organize military forces, make national laws, conduct foreign policy, make trade agreements with other nation-states, and so on. World affairs can be comprehended by what nations and their governments do to each other, be it in the military, economic, cultural, or other domains. Such intergovernmental and interstate exchanges and relations today seem all-important, although their importance in relation to the activities of nongovernmental actors and in relation to supranational organizations is changing. In recent years, an increasing awareness of interdependence has led to some questioning of the manner in which the nation-state system operates. Numerous observers have become sensitive to the phenomenon of transnationalism, which implies a diminution in the sovereignty of individual states. Nevertheless, the prevailing view still is that the most useful way of understanding global politics is through the prism of the nation-state system.

Without questioning the validity of these views, we now propose an alternative—namely, to view the world as a macrosociety. This view is reinforced by pictures of the earth seen from outer space, by an increased sense of economic interdependence between countries, by the emergence of world conferences for the airing of views on diverse subjects of global interest, by intellectual endeavors and scientific models which treat the world as a single system. The notions of meeting the basic needs of four to eight billion people, establishment of minimal levels of decency with regard to civil and political liberties of all individuals and groups, notions of pollution and resource depletion and of quality of life are becoming more commonplace in the rhetoric of academics, policy-makers and knowledgeable and responsible individuals around the globe. Perhaps the most forceful illustration of this approach is a recent article by Nathan Keyfitz in which he analyzes the social structure of the world as if the globe was a single society.[1] We believe that these trends capture a part of reality not adequately comprehended by the paradigm of the nation-state system, and it is in that spirit that we wish to speculate about world society.

When we view the world society as a macrosociety, we begin to ask questions that we normally ask only with regard to national societies—e.g., is it nice to live there? What is the political system of this society? What is its economic system and how does the world society allocate its resources? How is this society stratified? What is the role of women in world society? How does world society treat its children? What are the race relations in the world society? How does the world society protect its members from murder and mass murder? How does it provide for social security? Is it a happy society? These questions are different from those dealt with in the study of international politics and international economics, if only because they relate to the world society rather than to the nation-state.

The literature that comes closest to dealing with global structure in this sense is to be found in the writings on imperialism, dependency, and center-periphery relations. These see the world society as a highly stratified macrosociety which is characterized by exploitation and relations of political, economic, military, and psychological domination and dependence between the center and the periphery of the world. This modern world system, which emerged in the fifteenth and sixteenth centuries, transcends national boundaries, cripples the economic circuits of peripheral societies, generates artificial underdevelopment, and affects both center and periphery countries in various domains other than economic.

While this mode of analysis is very valuable, it could be even more so if it stressed the important fact of racial stratification on a world scale and the attendant racist attitudes and behaviors, which are still with us although the formal empires have all but withered away. We therefore propose to use the concept of "global apartheid" for the interpretation and analysis of the present structure of world society.

As indicated above, our contention is that the structure of the world is very similar to the structure of South Africa and that both are equally appalling. The similarity manifests itself in all major dimensions of analysis—political, economic, military, cultural, psychological, social, racial, and legal. A formal definition of "global apartheid," though capturing only the skeleton of a concept, might read thus: Global apartheid is a structure of world society which combines socioeconomic and racial antagonisms in which (i) a minority of whites occupies the pole of affluence, while a majority composed of other races occupies the pole of poverty; (ii) social integration of the two groups is made extremely difficult by barriers of complexion, economic position, political boundaries, and other factors; (iii) economic development of the two groups is interdependent; (iv) the affluent white minority possesses a disproportionately large share of world society's political, economic, and military power. Global apartheid is thus a structure of extreme inequality in cultural, racial, social, political, economic, military and legal terms, as is South African apartheid.

SOME DATA ON GLOBAL APARTHEID

In South Africa, the population ratio between the nonwhite majority and the white minority is about 4.7 to 1. In the world society, about two-thirds of the population is nonwhite and one-third white. Both in South Africa and in world society, being "white" and belonging to the upper stratum tend to go together, although there are also poor whites and rich nonwhites. The upper stratum—both in South Africa and the world—is not a homogeneous group.

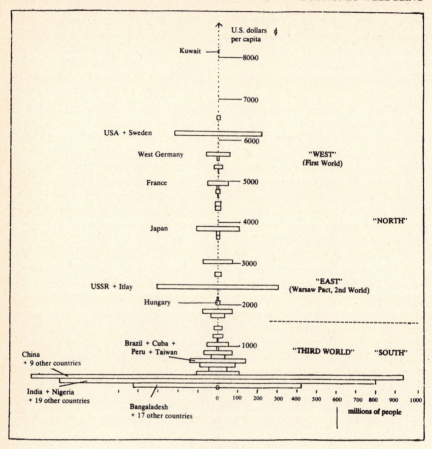

Figure 1
World income tree

Vertical axis = GNP per capita (US$) intervals of 100.
Horizontal axis = number of persons living at each income level.
Source: Ruth Leger Sivard, *World Military and Social Expenditures 1976* (Leesburg, Virg.: WMSE Publications), pp. 21–31. The grouping of data by intervals of $100.00 per capita done by the author.

There exist linguistic-ethnic-cultural cleavages within this stratum (notably, Afrikaner versus English in South Africa, and "West" versus "East" in global society). The whites in South Africa and in the world alike enjoy a higher standard of living and have more power than the nonwhites. The world income tree (Figure 1) shows the economic stratification of the world. It shows the rich countries at the top and the poor countries at the bottom according to their per capita gross national product, and countries with similar wealth are grouped together. The length of the bars shown in the figure indicates how many people belong to each income group. Figure 1 thus shows how about two-thirds of humanity live at, or close to, the bottom of the socioeconomic pyramid of the world, while one-third of humankind live in middle and top positions. The West (or, the "First World") and the East (i.e., the "Second World") occupy the top and middle ranks of this tree. They happen to be predominantly "white," Japan being the major exception. They are the upper crust of the world society in much the same way as Afrikaner and English whites in South Africa are the upper stratum of that society.

When we treat the world as a single society and compare its inequality to situations of inequality *within* certain countries, we find that *global* inequality of income is even more severe than the income inequality within national societies (Table 1). As Table 1 shows, the income inequality of the world is even worse than that of South Africa. In South Africa, the poorest 40% of the population receive only 6.2% of the national product, while the poorest 40% of the world receive an even smaller share (5.2% of the world product). At the other end of the spectrum, the richest 20% of South Africa's population take 58.0% of the income, while the richest 20% of the world take even more (71.3% of world income).

Life expectancy is also an index of global apartheid. The members of the affluent, predominantly white societies of the "North" live longer than the members of the poor, predominantly nonwhite societies of the Third World (see Figure 2). It shows that life expectancy is lowest for the poorest countries and tends to rise in proportion to a country's wealth until a certain threshold is reached. Above that threshold of wealth, life expectancy tends to change very little. The countries of the "North" enjoy a similar, high life expectancy. Eastern Europe is, in this repect, as privileged as the Western affluent societies.

It should be noted, too, that most of the world's weapons of mass destruction are owned by the white societies of the "North"—the United States, USSR, France, and England. World Wars I and II and the possibility of a future nuclear war between the United States and the Soviet Union have so much occupied the minds of some of us in the affluent countries that we fail to see that *actual* international violence (resulting from international wars and intervention) and *actual* civil violence (from revolution, riots, massacres, etc.) and actual structural violence[2] (from miserable socioeconomic conditions) are all related to global apartheid. Estimates for the year 1965 show how all three forms of large-scale violence are unequally distributed in a manner that is consistent with global apartheid (see Table 2).

Table 2 shows the enormous inequality of death and suffering from war and other forms of violence. If violence were equally distributed, the North, with 30% of the world's population, would suffer 30% of all forms of violence and the South, with 70% of world population, would suffer 70% of all violent deaths. The data indicate, however, that the South has suffered much more than "its fair share" of violent death—namely, over 90% in all categories—and that the North has had correspondingly low shares.

While comparable up-to-date estimates are not available, preliminary calculations suggest the following developments since 1965:

(a) The world total of deaths due to structural violence seems to have

320

Table 1
Income shares

	Bulgaria	USA	India	South Africa	World
Segment of population	percentages of gross national product (or gross global product) received by the three segments of population				
Top 20%	33·2	38·8	52·0	58·0	71·3
Middle 40%	40·0	41·5	32·0	35·8	23·5
Lowest 40%	26·8	19·7	16·0	6·2	5·2

Sources: 1. Roger D. Hansen, *The U.S. and World Development: Agenda for Action 1976* (New York: Praeger, 1975), pp. 148–149 for Bulgaria (1962), USA (1970), India (1964), and South Africa (1965);
2. World Bank, *Population Policies and Economic Development* (Baltimore: Johns Hopkins University Press, 1974), p. 37 for World (1971).

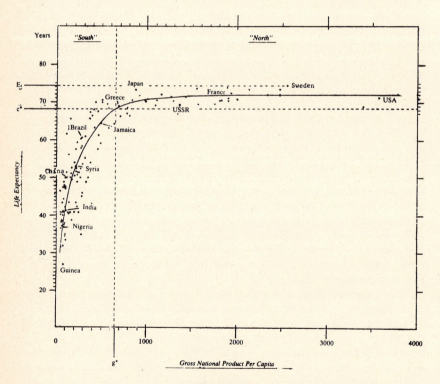

Figure 2
Relationship of life expectancy with per capita GNP

Source: Adapted from G. Köhler and N. Alcock, "An Empirical Table of Structural Violence," *Journal of Peace Research 13*, 4, 1976.

Table 2
The inequality of global violence

A. Estimated world totals, 1965. Deaths from:
international violence		11 500–23 000
civil violence		92 000
structural violence		14 000 000–18 000 000

B. Distribution of violent deaths, 1965 (World = 100% in each category)

Affluent 'North'	population	30·6%
	international violence	9·1%
	civil violence	·1%
	structural violence	4·2%
Poor 'South'	population	69·4%
	international violence	90·9%
	civil violence	99·9%
	structural violence	95·8%

Source: Gernot Köhler and Norman Alcock, "An Empirical Table of Structural Violence," *Journal of Peace Research* 4. The percentages for structural violence are based on the so-called Swedish Model.

declined slightly despite the rise in world population. It can be assumed that the distribution of fatalities between the North and South remains as unequal since 1965 as it was in 1965.

(b) The world total of deaths due to large-scale armed violence, both international and domestic, does not exhibit a steady trend but fluctuates considerably from year to year and period to period. Between 1965 and 1976, a peak was reached in 1971 when the Pakistan-Bangladesh-India war and the war in Vietnam sent the annual world total of deaths in this category to about 1.5 million or more. From 1973 to 1976, the corresponding world figure may have been around 100,000 deaths, with the inequality between the North and South remaining undisturbed.[3]

THE NEED FOR REFORM OF THE INTERNATIONAL SYSTEM

Most observers agree that the international system is currently in a phase of major changes, although there is a wide range of views both on the nature and on the most desirable direction of this transformation. In our view, the world society, structured like global apartheid, clearly requires reforms in order to make the society more suitable for living in for most of its members. Just as the world community opposes apartheid in South Africa, it should also oppose global apartheid. Ideally, reform should lead to the abolition of global apartheid. This is not merely a moral demand; for two-thirds of this world society, it is urgent and necessary to enable this multiracial majority to live a life of dignity.

For the more affluent societies of the North, the abolition of global apartheid may not seem urgent, but it is in their own interest no less than in the interest of the South to actively press for a world without apartheid. This view is dictated by political and economic prudence. As the examples of Zimbabwe (Rhodesia) and South Africa amply illustrate, the maintenance of an apartheid system is costly in political, military, social, economic, and psychological terms.

But as long as the apartheid system is not challenged from below, the self-interest of the upper stratum, defined in narrow wealth and power terms, is tied to the perpetuation of the status quo. As soon as it is effectively challenged from below, the costs of maintaining it begin to rise. When the lower stratum of the system becomes highly self-assertive and permanently "unruly" in the perspective of the predominantly white upper stratum, the self-interest of the upper stratum is no longer served by the defense of the status quo. Prudent upper-stratum statesmanship then feels inclined to doubt its usefulness in terms of the costs of maintaining apartheid. The following is a short list of such costs:

1. *Economic health.* The world economy cannot unfold its full productive potential because global apartheid impedes the productivity of the Third World and, thereby, keeps North's income from trade with the South far below what it could be. This, in turn, contributes to slow growth, inflation, and unemployment in the North.

2. *Economic security.* The affluent countries require oil, minerals and other goods from the Third World. Lack of North's responsiveness to Third World interests increases South's inclination to disrupt oil and resource flows to the North.

3. *Military security.* Deep economic conflicts in the world system contribute to the world's military instability. This is dangerous for the affluent countries in view of the fact that even those armed conflicts which are seemingly "peripheral" from the viewpoint of the North can lead to a breakdown of deterrence and to a large-scale war between the two major alliances of the North, as World War I illustrated.

4. *Liberty.* Massive poverty breeds authoritarianism of the Right or the Left. To the extent that the affluent countries cherish the world-wide presence of liberty, the lack of liberty in the world, linked to global apartheid, must be counted as a cost.

5. *Human growth.* For many people in the affluent societies who have a humanistic or spiritual orientation, the present world situation which stunts human growth and development on such a large scale is a cost.

The development of race relations in the United States provides an interesting illlustration both of the opportunities and of the difficulties encountered in the abolition of an unfair racial situation. It shows that it is quite possible that major segments of the dominant white stratum come to support desegregation policies. On the other hand, the example also shows that progress in this direction is slow and that, even after the society's attitudes and laws on race have begun to change, the problem continues in terms of class differences.

MAJOR DIMENSIONS OF REFORM

It is not enough to set out to abolish global apartheid; there ought to be a fair idea of where to go—i.e., there ought to be an image of an alternative world structure. Such an alternative would, in my opinion, have to satisfy the following criteria: (1) basic needs for all individuals are satisified and abject poverty is eradicated; (2) racial discrimination is eliminated; and (3) international and intranational income differences are significantly reduced.

For this purpose, it is necessary to make a realistic assessment of the present structure and its dynamics. As noted above, there are two competing paradigms which claim to provide an accurate view of the world: the classical nation-state paradigm and the center-periphery paradigm. It is now generally recognized that a pure nation-state paradigm does not sufficiently correctly conceptualize the enormous economic and racial stratification of the world. The center-periphery paradigm, on the other hand, though a valuable contribution to the understanding of the dynamics of the global political economy, is found to be rather constrictive when attempts are made to apply it to political and social action in all the regions of the world.

The example of South Africa is very instructive in this regard. When we apply the center-periphery analysis to the South African situation, all members of the white minority have to be considered as members of the "center," and all members of the black majority as members of the "periphery." While this interpretation seems plausible, one of its inferences does not hold for South Africa. The center-periphery analysis assumes or predicts that all members of the center have an interest in maintaining the unfair status quo. In South Africa, however, as Steve Biko pointed out, white opposition to the status quo has been at times very strong and was, on occasion, stronger than the black opposition to it.[4] The center-periphery analysis is thus—for the South African situation—not as "realistic" as one might think. I am contending that, at the global level, the center-periphery paradigm is likewise too rigid and less realistic.

At the world level, we find many members in the "center of the center," i.e., elites in the North, who oppose global apartheid and global militarism. We also find many elites in the Third World who do not behave as lackeys of the global center, as assumed or predicted by the center-periphery theory. Furthermore, the "periphery of the center," i.e., workers, housewives, employees, etc. in the countries of the North, do not unequivocally support the "center of the center" in efforts to maintain the global status quo. The activities of the lay members of churches in North America and Europe in voluntary aid to the Third World and in opposition to South African apartheid are a clear illustration of this point. Nor do the "masses" in Third World countries necessarily oppose collaboration between their leaders and Northern countries. In short, the center-periphery paradigm is partly true, but it is far from an accurate description of the reality.

If we view the world as structured on the lines of global apartheid, the role of the Northern, white opponent to global apartheid—"elite" or "mass"—makes sense. Similarly, the Southern, nonwhite moderate collaborator with the North—"elite" or "mass"—can be seen under the paradigm of global apartheid, as a shrewd politician on behalf of underdog interests or a traitor to those interests—depending on circumstances and behavior—whereas he is made out to be invariably a traitor of underdog interests in the center-periphery paradigm.

The world is thus most realistically depicted as a society which is "apart" and stratified, i.e., global apartheid, and which encompasses armed nation-states as administrative districts. Policies for world reform can mobilize support not only in the "periphery of the periphery," as center-periphery analysis assumes, but throughout the North and South, both among "elites" and "masses." As in any large-scale political movement, different sectors of the movement may support even a drastic reform movement for somewhat different reasons and on the basis of a combination of different interests.

Socioeconomic issues are obviously central to the abolition of global apartheid. At the same time other dimensions—military, political-legal, ecological, and cultural-psychological—are related to the socioeconomic issues and must undoubtedly be attended to in any attempt to abolish that system. Thus, we believe that it can be shown that the prospect of progress toward disarmament would be vastly improved by a movement directed toward abolishing global apartheid. Similarly, modification of the institutional structures at the global level (e.g., in the World Bank, international commodity markets, and others) should be enhanced to permit racial balance and fair representation of the world's multiracial majority. Thirdly, ecological considerations might be given serious attention by persons in the Third World if the movement for an ecologically sane world took recognition of the world's apartheid. Finally, in the cultural-psychological realm, we must learn cognitions and attitudes which combine positive communal and national identifications with positive attitudes toward a common world society and which entail a respect for common global concerns and interests as opposed to particularistic national interests.

TOWARD A JUST, PARTICIPATORY, PEACEFUL AND HUMANE GLOBAL SOCIETY

It is generally recognized that social theory and the major concepts of an era arise out of, and respond to, the underlying material and social conditions which have a bearing on political action and the establishment of normative order. Thus, for example, both Adam Smith and Karl Marx would probably agree that the notions of the marketplace and of class antagonism were products of empirical situations which favored the use of such concepts and the values they imply. Concepts which are able to combine a grasp of the ongoing behavioral world and provide a normative thrust become the basis, then, for determining what is considered as "knowledge," "information," and "data" about the world, and how we are to behave towards it. We have attempted to articulate the concept of global apartheid because we believe that the processes of interdependence, interpenetration, and the communicative era in which we live are making the planetary dimension of human society the most significant new prism through which to view social processes and the social organization of humanity. We believe further that the state system fails miserably in meeting the concerns and needs of this emerging global community. It is our contention that the concept of global apartheid—even in the limited form in which we have presented it here—provides us with a more comprehensive and realistic way of viewing the world, and thus enables us to suggest ways of behaving and acting in the political, economic and social realm so as to begin to realize a just, participatory, peaceful, and humane global society.

NOTES

The author is grateful to Philip Beardsley, Elise Boulding, Richard Falk, Rajni Kothari, Ali Mazrui, and especially Saul Mendlovitz for their encouragement, help and criticism. This paper is identified as LIV Paper No. 27A of the Limits to Violence Project of the Canadian Peace Research Institute.

1. Nathan Keyfitz, "World Resources and the World Middle Class," *Scientific American* 235, 1, July 1976, pp. 28–35.

2. "Structural violence" is a term used in contemporary peace research and is to be distinguished from armed violence. While armed violence is violence exerted by persons against persons with the use of arms, structural violence is violence exerted by situations, institutions, social, political and economic structures. Thus, when a person dies because he/she has no access to food, the effect is violent as far as that person is concerned, yet there is no individual actor who could be identified as the source of this violence. It is the system of food production and distribution that is to blame. The violence is thus exerted by an anonymous "structure." The measurement of the number of persons killed through structural violence uses statistics of life expectancy. By comparing the life expectancy of affluent regions with that of poor regions, one can estimate how many persons died in a poor region on account of poverty and poverty-related conditions (e.g., lack of doctors, clean water, food, etc.), which can be interpreted as "structural violence."

3. Trends in global structural and armed violence in the twentieth century are being investigated by William Beckhardt and Gernot Köhler. The research is in progress.

4. An interview with Steve Biko, conducted by Bernard Zylstra and published in the *Christian Science Monitor*, 10 November 1977, pp. 18–19, contains the following passages:

Question: What is black consciousness?

Biko: By black consciousness I mean the cultural and political revival of an oppressed people. . . . So black consciousness says: "Forget about colour!" But the reality we faced 10 to 15 years ago did not allow us to articulate this. After all, the continent was in a period of rapid decolonization, which implied a challenge to black inferiority all over Africa.

This challenge was shared by white liberals. So for quite some time the white liberals acted as the spokesmen for the blacks. . . .

Society as a whole was divided into white and black groups. This forced division had to disappear; and many nonracial groups worked toward that end. But almost every nonracial group was still largely white, notably so in the student world. . . . So we began to realize that blacks themselves had to speak out about the black predicament. . . .

At this time we were also influenced by the development of a black consciousness movement in the United States. . . .

22
NEGOTIATING THE FUTURE

Mahbub ul Haq

I

The deadlock in the U.N. Special Session in September 1980 over efforts to organize global negotiations on a New International Economic Order is not a cause for pessimism but an invitation to sober reflection. The breakdown was not just over procedures, though that was the way it appeared. The breakdown came because there are still substantive and fundamental differences between the approaches of the North and the South to these negotiations. Unless we honestly face up to these differences, a mere patch-up of procedural wrangles to revive the global negotiations will not achieve any significant results.

The first question we must face is: Why should the North—the industrialized nations—enter into any serious dialogue at all about restructuring the existing international economic order? The South—the developing nations—wishes to gain more economic power and participation in international decision-making, but why should the North willingly surrender its present privileged position? Unless there is a convincing answer to this question, North-South negotiations are likely to deteriorate into a ritual and skillful exercise in non-dialogue.

I believe that the only real answer is that change in international structures is inevitable, whether there is a dialogue or not. The real experiment involved in the North-South dialogue is whether the pace of change can be accelerated through common consent, and whether the pains of transition can be eased through orderly negotiations. It is tempting, but totally wrong, to jump from pessimism about the prospects of the North-South dialogue to pessimism about the prospects for change itself. The failure of the dialogue so far will not stem the underlying forces of change: it only means that change will continue to be disorderly and disruptive. The real case for the dialogue is that it can lead to an orderly transition and that bargains can be struck by which all sides gain, though not in equal measure.

Reprinted by permission from *Foreign Affairs*, Winter 1980/81. Copyright © 1980 by the Council of Foreign Relations, Inc.

II

What are these underlying forces of change? And why is there a certain inevitability about them? To begin with, there is an urge for liberation—"to end the tyranny of man over man" and of one nation over another. It inspired the movements of political liberation; it is fueling the desire for economic liberation now. The recent major movements in the industrialized nations—for trade unionism, civil rights, women's liberation—were inspired by the same urge for equality of opportunity. The initial casualties in this liberation movement will be national orders within the Third World, many of which are unresponsive to the needs of their own people. The current chaos and uncertainty in many developing countries are merely a prelude to that end.

But the desire for liberation, participation and equity cannot be confined within national borders. It will affect all international relations. If we add to it the strong sense of nationalism generated by political liberation of the Third World, it is clear why economic relations between rich and poor nations—whether at the level of governments, or multinational corporations, or private individuals—must proceed in a different framework than in the past.

At the same time, certain structural changes are taking place which are lending an air of urgency to the need to evolve new codes of international behavior. The demographic balance is rapidly shifting against the industrialized nations. Of the net additions to the world population in the next two decades, 90 percent will be in the Third World. The future markets and labor surplus lie in the South; the accumulating and underutilized capital in the North must come to terms with this reality. The South is also becoming rapidly urbanized. By the year 2000, about 40 cities in the South will have a population of over 15 million each, compared to 16 cities in the North. These exploding cities will provide powerful instruments of change within national orders as well as restless pressure for international migration.

Another powerful stimulus is the rising real cost of energy. The comparative advantage of industrialized nations in energy-intensive agriculture and industrial production is fast disappearing. There will have to be a major structural change in their industrial and trade patterns, environmental concerns and modes of urbanization, and in the whole conception of their life-styles. If we add to this picture the rapid emergence of China, the entry of more communist countries into the international market, the fierce competition from newly industrializing countries such as Brazil, the shifts in economic power within the industrialized bloc (particularly in favor of Japan and West Germany), and the major breakthroughs in communications, it becomes obvious why national and international orders will continue to undergo rapid changes in the next two decades.

These changes are going to be too large to be handled successfully without proper planning. In the absence of a dialogue, changes will be traumatic, abrupt and disorderly. There will be periods of unilateral actions and complete breakdown of any international rules. An orderly international dialogue is not essential for change, but it can avoid unnecessary costs which will arise otherwise, it can help balance the interests of various groups of nations, and it is the best guarantee against periodic anarchy and insanity in human affairs.

Despite the failure of the formal North-South dialogue so far, there has been a significant change in human perceptions and understanding during the 1970s. From a mindless pursuit of economic growth, there has been a gradual shift to a better understanding of the problems of poverty and the urgency of meeting basic human needs. From a period of relative indifference to the real problems and enormous potential of the Third World, the industrialized nations may at last be becoming aware of their own dependence on the developing countries and of the need to reach some form of accommodation with them. From the belligerence of the early stages of the dialogue, we may finally be entering a second phase of serious negotiations during the 1980s. While the new decade has started on a cheerless note, this may well prove to be the decade for either a major advance in North-South relations or a deep international crisis. When the outlook is so bleak, it is, perhaps, wise to analyze what could be done differently to revive hopes for progress.

III

Both North and South have made major mistakes in their approach to the negotiations for a new International Economic Order (NIEO).

First, a quick catalogue of the mistakes made by the South:

1. The objectives of the dialogue were not clearly perceived. At least two distinct schools of thought emerged. One bargained for short-term concessions; the other negotiated for long-term structural change. The first school would have been satisfied with more aid, more debt relief, more trade concessions, etc.; the second [with] dependency. The second school sought a fundamental change in prevailing market rules and a loosening of ties between North and South, including a major de-linking of trade and aid relationships. The confusion between various objectives made it difficult to pursue any consistent strategy of negotiations.

2. Many developing countries did not sufficiently realize that internal reforms were even more important than international reforms for the welfare of their people. Some of them started viewing the NIEO as a "soft" option, as an alternative to hard decisions to restructure internal order. Lack of progress on the NIEO became an alibi for explaining a variety of economic sins at home. It was also not recognized that internal reforms would have made external change merely a matter of time, as developing countries would then be speaking from a position of strength. It is also interesting to note the divergence between official and unofficial dialogue on this issue. The official dialogue has at times pretended that there was no need for internal restructuring in the Third World. The intellectual dialogue in the Third World, on the other hand, has attacked inequities of international as well as of national orders, without ignoring their logical link.

3. The Third World did very little service to its own cause by presenting the NIEO as a "demand" of the South. It should have been presented, right from the start, as a global need, since the existing economic order has not been working very well for *any* side – as is evident from problems of global inflation and monetary instability, the energy crisis, environmental concerns, commodity price fluctuations, increasing protectionism, fast-increasing armament spending and a whole range of global headaches. Furthermore, the South should have taken the interests of the North fully into account in designing any package of negotiations. This was all the more necessary since the South started with limited bargaining power; it needed the goodwill and enlightened interest of the North to "enforce" any change.

4. The South entered the dialogue without adequate preparation. Since its membership was large and diverse, it needed frequent South-South dialogues to shape a package of negotiations which would satisfy the different interests of its various constituencies. It needed to establish a basis for mutual support from some of its richer members, particularly oil-exporting and high-income countries. It badly needed a Third World secretariat to articulate and coordinate its economic proposals.

5. Finally, the South made the fatal mistake of assuming that a new order would be "given" to it by the North. It conveniently forgot that such an order will evolve mainly through its own actions, particularly in accelerating its economic development, in undertaking internal reforms, and in organizing its countervailing power to correct existing market imperfections.[1]

The mistakes of the South were, however, more than matched by those of the North:

1. The North assumed that the NIEO was essentially a demand of the Third World and, as such, no concern of its own. It adopted a strategy of filibuster in U.N. negotiating forums – finding numerous problems for every solution that the South offered, rather than trying to explore honestly a number of policy options for each problem. The only area in which it showed a keen interest was that of energy, because of the immediate crisis the North faced. But the North failed to appreciate that the energy issue was only a part of the wider global crisis of excessive demand on increasingly scarce physical resources by a handful of privileged nations.

2. The leaders from the North have been preoccupied with the immediate problems of recession, inflation and unemployment. It was felt that solutions to the short-term economic difficulties could be found without the cooperation of the South. This was a mistake. The energy issue itself should have made this clear. The existence of surplus capital goods capacity in the North in the face of unmet needs in the South should have given the Northern decision-makers some uncomfortable moments. The shifting demographic balance should have made them more conscious of potential markets in the South. But these perceptions were quite dim and seldom translated into policy. It was not realized in the North that its short-term economic problems were not temporary but part

of a long-term structural change—much the same way as this was not realized in the 1930s within the national orders until Keynesian thought and President Roosevelt's daring initiatives combined to reduce Western capitalism from its inner contradictions. The same drama is now being replayed at the global level, the economically disenfranchised now being the teeming millions in the South who lack effective demand to buy goods and services from the North.

3. Even when the North recognized the pressure for long-term structural change, there was a natural temptation to delay adjustment. Faced with shifting comparative advantage, the normal response was to protect declining industries and regions for fear of unemployment and popular unrest. Confronted with radically altered prospects of oil pricing and supply, the North postponed the more difficult conservation policies and deregulation of oil prices. Beset with mounting balance-of-payments deficits, the United States made increasing use of its international credit card and incurred more debt, thereby creating even more international liquidity and worldwide inflation. All these responses were mere temporizing. They delayed the adjustment costs, but magnified them in the process. When confronted with saving the next election or the next generation, the political leaders of the North frequently opted for the former. In such an environment, long-term changes were often mortgaged to short-term expediency. This is nothing unique in political life; but it is not the stuff of great leadership.

In many ways, both North and South have failed to understand the imperatives of the growing interdependence of mankind. The North tried to sell the old relationships of dependency to the South under the newly dusted slogan of interdependence; unfortunately, it did not recognize the practical implications of its own growing dependence on the South, or the fact that genuine interdependence is impossible without greater equality of opportunity. The South bargained for greater equality, without paying sufficient attention to the Northern interests or to the costs of sudden adjustment. The result has been a stalemate.

In this strange environment of formal motions without actual movement, the communist countries (containing one-third of mankind) have been quietly neglected by both sides. Nor have these countries themselves shown a keen interest in the North-South dialogue, opting to stay on the sidelines. In any real dialogue for a restructured world order, it would be important to obtain the active participation of them as well.

IV

The non-dialogue of the last six years has persuaded some observers that no serious discussion between North and South may be possible in the early 1980s.[2] This may well be true. It is possible that only a real international economic or political crisis will convince all sides to rush to the negotiating table—as has happened so often in human history. But to give up now on the dialogue would be a defeatist strategy. One can hope that both sides have learned some quiet lessons from the experience and mistakes of the last few years. These should be drawn upon in making a new attempt to revive the stalemated global negotiations.

A fresh approach can be made by examining the premises of the old global order in several specific fields—such as energy, food, the monetary system, resource transfers, trade, economic development, technology, multinational corporations, and international institutions. The basic strategy should be to let the analysis itself lead to the final solution rather than to start with any preconceived proposals. Four concrete questions must be posed in each case:

- What are the premises on which the old order was based?
- Are these premises still valid?
- If not, what are the new premises which should replace them?
- Will the new global order meet the legitimate interests of all sides?

We will make an attempt in the following discussion to analyze the present framework of the global order in several economic fields in this spirit.

V

The energy issue must be demystified. No reasoned dialogue on that issue has taken place so far, as it gets bogged down in side issues and peripheral controversies. Either OPEC (the Organization of Petroleum Exporting Countries) is made to feel guilty—which is hardly a brilliant strategy for soliciting its cooperation—or the industrialized nations and developing countries are asked to adjust to a new energy environment without having a clear idea of what historical and long-term forces are shaping this environment.

The energy problem can be seen in its proper perspective only if it is viewed as one of the many structural transformations that the world is going through, and if it is placed within the framework of restructuring of national and international orders which has become increasingly urgent. The energy issue arose when the world was already confronting a profound transition: concern for protecting the world environment; for eradicating absolute poverty; for developing new self-reliant styles of development in the South and a new value system in the North; for controlling the impending international monetary crisis; for the establishment of a New International Economic Order. The energy issue greatly sharpened the global perception of these other transitions by demonstrating the essential interdependence and vulnerability of all nations. It is within that broad perspective that the energy issue can be helpful as an engine of transition, so long as it is linked with other related issues.

There is a popular belief that the energy crisis (i.e., the rising real cost of energy) has "caused" the world economic crisis. This, in a way, reverses the sequence of events. The rising real cost of energy is the result of the overload of the world system, not its cause. The fast rate of increase in oil consumption in the past few decades has led to a rapid depletion of non-renewable resources. This happened because the price of oil was kept artificially low by international oil companies for a long period. Paradoxically, it was this artificially low price of oil which caused the eventual crisis by leading to an unregulated appetite for energy. If the oil price had been set not in relation to the cost of production—which was irrelevant—but the cost of alternatives, the adjustment process would not have become so abrupt and traumatic.

It is widely believed that oil prices are being kept artificially high at present through cartel-like action by OPEC: with the dismantling of OPEC, prices will crash. This is a fallacy. The current price of oil is largely determined by the forces of supply and demand as well as by the cost of alternatives. Before there are any screams of protest, let it be noted that production decisions are generally made by the national policies of OPEC members—not collectively—much the same way as the United States decides to curtail its wheat production to limit excessive supply.

In fact, many OPEC members are producing more oil (because of international considerations) than is required by their own national needs for revenue. If OPEC did not exist today, oil prices would probably stay at the same level or even rise, since it is a reasonable premise that oil production may go down in such a case, rather than increase, since many oil-producing and exporting nations may well decide to eliminate financial surpluses they do not immediately need and instead try to protect the real value of their depleting assets by keeping more of the oil in the ground.

Moreover, there is no substitute for oil on the horizon which is cheaper than oil right now. In fact, those oil-importing nations which are making costly and long-term investments in finding alternative sources of energy have a major interest by now in a relatively high price of oil which alone would justify these investments in alternatives. Finally, and most important, the real determining factor for the future price of energy may well turn out to be on the demand side: the extent to which conservation policies are pursued.

There is a widespread belief that OPEC nations are extremely rich; that they "create" enormous financial surpluses which they cannot use themselves and which put considerable pressure on the world economy; and that they are responsible for compensating oil-importing developing countries for the rise in their oil-import bills but are as yet providing inadequate financial assistance to them. Such reasoning only tries to put OPEC nations on the defensive, without either having the benefit of objective analysis or leading to any constructive results.

To begin with, most OPEC nations are not rich. They are liquid but not wealthy, though liquidity and wealth are being freely confused these days. Even including the capital-surplus nations of Saudi Arabia, Kuwait, the United Arab Emirates, Qatar, Libya and Iraq, the thirteen OPEC members had an average per capita income of less than $1,000 in 1978, only one-eighth of that in industrialized nations. Besides, most of the OPEC nations are underdeveloped, with low literacy rates, short life expectancy, unskilled labor, a low level of technology and research, little diversified development outside the oil sector, and with all the problems of a single-resource economy. OPEC nations have suddenly become financially liquid but they have yet to translate their good fortune into lasting sources of real wealth.

Second, OPEC does not "create" financial surpluses; it is the appetite of the industrialized nations for energy which does. These surpluses are "desired" by industrialized nations. If OPEC were to cut production further to eliminate present surpluses, the world economy would experience a severe slump. For OPEC nations, the economics of these surpluses is not very clear: there is a fair question whether oil in the ground will appreciate more over time than the real value of these financial surpluses. Moreover, let us also remind ourselves that these surpluses become a problem only because the world monetary system has not yet discovered either adequate market mechanisms or international intermediation through which these surpluses could be recycled to deficit countries on appropriate terms. This requires a reform of the monetary system, not of oil-pricing policies.

Finally, the capital-surplus OPEC nations have already provided over 4 percent of their gross national product (GNP) on the average during 1974-79 for concessional assistance, compared to 0.35 percent by industrialized nations—in other words, about 12 times as much as developed countries even when their per capita income is less than half that of developed countries.[3] This is truly remarkable when it is realized that OPEC assistance is being given not out of current income but out of the proceeds of oil—a depleting capital asset. Hardly any other nation in the world provides assistance by running down its capital. This is not to suggest that OPEC assistance policies are optimal, or to foreclose any further avenues of mutual collaboration between OPEC and the rest of the Third World, but only to restore some perspective on this issue.

In short, the old premises of the global energy order have all collapsed by now; new premises cannot be constructed under the dark shadow of unfounded myths and unnecesary controversies. It is possible to identify key areas for global negotiations only within such a perspective. Let me turn now to three critical questions in this field.

First, how will future oil prices be determined? Obviously they will no longer be determined by a handful of powerful oil corporations dominating the international oil market—nor by the unilateral actions of OPEC. They will be determined by a whole range of decisions and factors: OPEC national production policies; global conservation policies, particularly in the industrialized nations; investment in the expansion of oil production and other energy alternatives in the non-OPEC nations; the probable cost of future oil substitutes; the pace of growth in the world economy, etc. Until some of these unfold and have their full impact, the international community will live through a transition period when oil prices may remain volatile unless a tacit international understanding is reached.

Most present forecasts indicate a real increase in oil prices (by three to five percent a year) over the 1980s. All nations have to gain if such an increase is gradual and predictable, rather than in sudden and delayed bursts. But before any international understanding or agreement can be reached in this area, the interests of various sides will have to be identified. While oil-importing nations would like to have some agreement on the future course of oil prices, OPEC nations would probably be reluctant to enter into any such agreement without clear understandings on conservation policies in industrialized nations, protection of the real value of their financial surpluses, and assistance with the conversion of their oil revenues into real, long-term development in order to prepare their economies for a post-oil stage. It must also be recognized that OPEC alone cannot "enforce" or "guarantee" any particular oil price, since a whole range of policy decisions will influence the market, as argued above. OPEC can only reach understandings on matters within its direct control.

Second, policies for energy conservation will be an extremely crucial part of adjustment during the 1980s. Cheap oil has encouraged wasteful patterns of energy consumption and choice of inappropriate technologies. One of the problems in adjustment is that some of the decisions are frozen by now in some societies, e.g., stress on private automobiles and public highways, suburban modes of living, energy-intensive industries. Unfreezing these decisions for the future will require tremendous political and economic courage, particularly in the industrialized nations. The developing countries have as yet more options available if they review their future patterns of development and consumption styles in the light of the new energy situation. There is generally considerable room for economizing if energy prices are allowed to rise to their proper level in oil-importing nations. To a limited extent, conservation policies are already working in some of the industrialized countries, but the eventual adjustment in their patterns of consumption and development is so fundamental that it has barely begun.[4]

Third, oil-importing developing countries require substantial resources for financing larger investments in domestic energy production. These investment needs are estimated by the World Bank at around $80 billion a year (in current dollars) during 1980–90.[5] Various proposals are currently being made to provide investment resources to oil-importing developing countries for energy development, such as an energy affiliate in the World Bank to provide $5 billion a year over the next five years; expansion of the present OPEC Fund into a development agency with a capital of $20 billion; schemes for mobilization of larger private foreign investment. The total investment needs in energy are so large that there is room for all these initiatives and great merit in having diversification of channels for this purpose. What is important, however, is to ensure that these initiatives lead to additional transfers; that they reflect the changing balance of financial power in the world; and that they are based on a participatory system of management and control.

These are some of the key issues around which global negotiations can be organized in the field of energy.[6] The energy issue was analyzed at length merely to illustrate that even in a sensitive area like this, there are ways to avoid irrelevant issues and to focus on the new prices which should replace the old while meeting the legitimate interests of various nations. In the following discussion, this point is illustrated further in a few more areas under negotiation, though much more briefly.

VI

In the monetary field, just as in energy, most of the premises on which the global monetary order was built have quietly disappeared.

The Bretton Woods system after World War II was based on fixed exchange rates and the relative stability of world prices. Since the early 1970s, exchange rates have been fluctuating freely (and even violently for the dollar) and we are living with high rates of global inflation.

The International Monetary Fund (IMF) was expected to bring pressure on both deficit and surplus countries to take the necessary bitter medicine and quickly to nurse the balance of payments back to a happy equilibrium. The Fund never enjoyed much leverage with surplus countries to begin with. By now, it cannot put much pressure on the biggest deficit country—the United States. The huge financial surpluses of OPEC confronted the Fund with yet another challenge, and it has so far found no satisfactory way to recycle these surpluses to deficit countries, either in an efficient or an equitable manner, though the scale of its operations in developing countries has increased significantly in recent months. Commercial banks quickly assumed the role of recycling financial surpluses and have done a fairly good job, but only within the narrow confines of their criteria of creditworthiness and profit. About two-thirds of commercial credits have been channeled to only ten middle-income developing countries.

The United States assumed the role of a central bank; nearly 80 percent of the additional international liquidity in the last three decades was supplied by the dollar. For all practical purposes, the United States carried an international credit card which it used indiscriminately to flood the world with excess liquidity. Instead of carrying out real adjustments at home, the United States has been paying for its balance-of-payments deficits through the simple device of international deficit financing. The IMF has not been able to exercise much control over the creation of international liquidity through national reserve currencies.

The IMF was charged with the responsibility for providing balance-of-payments support to deficit countries, with reasonable policy conditionality to adjust the causes of their fundamental disequilibrium. The potential resources of the Fund have increased substantially in recent years; it can lend as much as $40 billion to developing countries from a maze of windows (called "credit facilities"). Unfortunately, there were few takers in 1979, when the IMF received more payments from developing countries than the funds it lent to them. Recently, the IMF has adjusted the policy conditionality of its lending and the scale of its operations has increased impressively. However, the critics of the Fund charge that (a) its finance is fairly short term while the adjustment problem of the developing countries is not, and (b) its policy conditionality is very tough, as it often requires that the books of a nation be balanced, irrespective of the level of economic activity and employment at which this new balance is reached.[7]

Finally, the socialist bloc still operates largely outside the framework of the

IMF. In view of the growing economic and monetary importance of this bloc, any new monetary order must seek their full participation and cooperation.

Overall, the global monetary system is in such bad shape at present that an entirely fresh start may have to be made. No marginal improvisations will suffice in the 1980s. The new premises on which the monetary order should be rebuilt are implied by the foregoing analysis and are worth recapitulating:

- National reserve currencies must be phased out of the international payments system and replaced by an international currency (modified Special Drawing Rights), to be created and managed by international jurisdiction.
- The creation of international currency should be guided by the real increase in world output and exports so as not to generate inflationary pressures.
- The distribution of this international currency should be based on present as well as potential balance-of-payments needs, including a link between international currency and development assistance.
- The IMF, or a wholly new institution, should be gradually evolved to perform the role of an International Central Bank (ICB).
- For this purpose, the ICB should include all nations (socialist bloc as well) and its management and control should be genuinely international.
- The ICB should be empowered to put as much pressure on deficit countries to adjust their balance of payments as on surplus countries, so that the present asymmetry of treatment is removed.
- The ICB should also act as the lender of last resort, to refinance short-term debts, provide a "safety net" against unforeseen liquidity crises, and play a decisive role in recycling financial surplus in collaboration with the private capital market.

These are not minor reforms; this is drastic surgery. The new monetary order can emerge step by step once an overall framework has been accepted. Major economic powers will find this degree of international discipline irksome to begin with, but they will gain a great deal in the long run from rules which are accepted by all nations. The developing countries, of course would reap enormous benefits from these reforms. Lord Keynes' vision in the 1940s would finally have been adapted to current realities—after 40 years of drift and indifferent experimentation.

VII

Before searching for a new basis for international resource transfers, it is useful to sketch out some of the implicit assumptions of the present order and what is wrong with them:

- The present resource transfers from the rich to the poor nations are totally voluntary, dependent completely on the fluctuating political will of the rich nations. The attempts by the United Nations and the Pearson Commission to enforce greater discipline in this field through the 0.7 percent-of-GNP target for Official Development Assistance (ODA) has failed miserably by now.

- Most of the present official assistance (75 percent) flows through bilateral channels rather than multilateral institutions. As such, it is greatly influenced by bilateral political relationships. For instance, only 45 percent of the bilateral official development assistance is directed toward the poorest nations that need it the most, compared to over 90 percent of ODA which flows through multilateral channels.
- The resource transfers have been in gross terms, with insufficient concern for *net* transfers. Inappropriate terms in the past have created a major debt problem, so that debt servicing reduces the gross transfers by about one-half by now.
- The international framework for resource transfers has excluded the socialist bloc, which has provided little assistance so far. New OPEC sources, while very generous, have been geographically concentrated on a few countries.
- The "aid relationship" is often viewed as a relationship of dependence, not partnership, in the Third World. Unlike the Marshall Plan, developing countries which receive assistance do not participate in the basic decisions governing such assistance.

There is no doubt that international assistance has performed a valuable role in the past. However, it is already becoming clear that a serious search must start for finding new premises for international resource transfers in the 1980s, somewhat along the following lines:

- International resource mobilization should become more "automatic" and be accepted as an international obligation toward the poor nations. International taxation can be introduced through a variety of devices: a progressive income tax on all nations, with a minimum exemption limit; introduction of a link between creation of international liquidity and development finance; indirect taxes on consumption of non-renewable resources by the rich nations; taxation of armament spending; and royalties from ocean-bed mining. The proposals are well known. What is needed during this decade is to undertake serious technical studies on them and to create a favorable political climate for the acceptance of the concept of international taxation.
- A clear distinction must be made between automatic *mobilization* and automatic *transfer* of resources. What is implied by proposals of international taxation is the former, not the latter. Once resources are raised automatically, they need to be channeled through international institutions to needy countries according to certain performance criteria—as national treasuries must determine national priorities before commit-

ting the resources they raise through taxation. In this case, the control of international institutions can become genuinely international once their resource base has become automatic and internationalized. The present awkward situation where international financial institutions are totally dependent on the goodwill of individual creditor nations will then be replaced by shared international responsibility and control.

VIII

The world food system—if we can call it that—has been influenced by three main assumptions over the last four decades:

- The comparative advantage in growing food surpluses was supposed to lie with developed countries possessing vast areas of good agricultural land and sufficient capital and technology. Thus, the United States, Canada and Australia emerged as the breadbaskets of the impoverished world. This situation is likely to change radically. Higher energy costs will shift the comparative advantage away from traditional food-exporting areas, since agricultural production has become extremely energy-intensive in these countries; in the United States it takes ten times as much energy to produce one ton of food grains as it does in India. Over the coming decades, low-income countries of Asia and Africa are expected to develop a major comparative advantage in food production.
- It has been assumed so far that developing countries need not grow all their own food, they can always import it. The food deficits of the developing countries have been increasing rapidly, from about 20 million tons in 1960 to nearly 80 million tons in 1980, and to an estimated 145 million tons in 1990.[8] Only recently has it been realized by the developing countries that, without accelerated agricultural production, there will be little stimulus for their industrialization or overall growth. Nor is there any other effective means of putting adequate purchasing power in the hands of the poorest population in the countryside. Moreover, the developing countries lack both the physical and financial capacity to import such huge food deficits, apart from the uncertainty such dependence inevitably creates. The working assumption for the next two decades has to be that developing countries would like to achieve relative self-sufficiency in food grains.[9] This means increasing the food production by four to five percent a year, compared to an average of less than three percent for the last four decades. It would require an annual investment of $30–50 billion, major agrarian reform in the Third World, and a coordinated effort by the international community to help developing countries achieve these new goals.
- Almost by default, U.S. food grain surpluses had become an unofficial guarantee against periods of unexpected crop shortfalls in the developing world. However, world grain reserves have fallen by now to only 40

days of the annual consumption requirement. Obviously, small fluctuations in world food production can play havoc with food prices and human lives in the absence of adequate reserves. A world food security system cannot be based on the present precarious assumptions. From an unofficial system, we must move now toward an agreed framework of food grain reserves over which there is multilateral, not national, control.

Thus, in the food area as well, many of the original assumptions of the global order are losing their validity. In this case, some of the adjustments can be made through national development policies and do not require an international agreement. However, accelerated food production in the developing countries and establishment of a system of world food security do require international help and collective agreement.

IX

Perhaps the main point has been amply made by now. A productive way of making a fresh start on the North-South dialogue would be to take up concrete areas of the global economic order, to examine critically the premises on which they were built in the past, and to negotiate new premises wherever the old assumptions have been eroded with the passage of time or new assumptions are required to serve the mutual interests of all nations. Such an approach would take the present dialogue away from empty rhetoric, costly filibuster, and skillfully engineered stalemate to more practical and constructive channels.

If this basic approach is accepted, it can be extended to all other areas of global economic concern—whether they be future patterns of international trade, codes for transfer of technology, environment for operation of multinationals, or management and control of international financial institutions. There is an obvious link between all these fields, but the negotiations cannot be conducted simultaneously in all areas nor can the new rules be designed in one giant step. Once it has been recognized that reconstruction of a new global order is the joint responsibility of all nations, appropriate forums can be established for concrete negotiation. The initial step is to agree on the basic approach. If the UN Global Negotiations are revived in the next few months, as they must be, they provide a unique opportunity to travel down this road.

If these global negotiations are not to repeat the sad history of the Conference on International Economic Cooperation (CIEC) negotiations in Paris in 1977, at least two mistakes must be avoided. First, all sides must approach the negotiating table in a spirit of shared responsibility and not as adversaries. Second, the negotiating agenda and format should be manageable and have something in it for all sides. The minimum agenda can consist of three items: the search for a new international energy order; fundamental monetary reforms; and more automatic mechanisms for international resource transfers.

Any enlargement of the agenda in the first instance risks dilution of negotiations and paralysis of real bargaining. Once the agenda is so limited, the best way to proceed may be to agree on some overall objectives in the UN Committee of the Whole but then break into three separate negotiating groups, each with a substantive secretariat and a concrete timetable, with the mandate to produce specific proposals (and various alternatives, if agreement is lacking) for final bargaining sessions and tactical compromises in the Committee of the Whole.

The purpose of this article is to suggest an approach, not a blueprint. It is perhaps foolhardy to be optimistic about the revival of North-South dialogue in the current, rather barren, international political environment. But great initiatives in history have often been taken not in times of affluence, but in moments of crisis.

We should take some heart from the heady (some may call it naïve) optimism of the recent Report of the Brandt Commission.[10] Whatever the critics might say, this Report marks a tremendous advance in the intellectual journey we have all made since the days of the Pearson Commission Report in 1969—from concepts of camouflaged dependency to genuine interdependence among nations; from a preoccupation with resource transfers to a concern with restructuring all international economic relations and institutions; from a quiet defense of the structure of Bretton Woods institutions to a searching analysis of the need for their future evolution.

There may be little hope that some of the concrete ideas of the Brandt Report—whether international taxation or an international currency under international control—will be implemented in the next few years or even during the decade of the 1980s. But I find great comfort in the fact that practical men and women of the world are beginning to "distill their frenzy from some academic scribbler of a few years past," as Keynes so elegantly put it in his defense of the power of ideas. If ideas are changing so rapidly, can concrete action be far behind? And why not make yet another effort to revive the presently stalled North-South dialogue? We have nothing much to lose but the present paralysis in human affairs.

X

Let me add a final word on the North-South Summit which may meet in June 1981 in Mexico, acording to present indications. History offers few such opportunities to think collectively about our global future. Careful preparations are needed from now on to realize the full potential of such a Summit meeting.

If I had a chance to brief the Summit, I would stress the essential principles, not the details; the broad architecture, not the intricate design. Political breakthroughs come from a change in political perceptions, not from detailed technocatic blueprints.

My message to the North-South Summit will be a simple one:[11]

1. Please recognize that the world's economic and political crisis is not a temporary one. It is deeply rooted in present international structures and

institutions. National actions alone will not help, unless the global structures themselves are changed, perferably through an orderly dialogue and certainly in the long term interest of all nations.

2. What is really at issue is a sharing of economic and political power, within nations as well as internationally. It will prove extemely disruptive if existing power has to be changed only through the organization of countervailing power or through unilateral national or collective actions. There is a historic opportunity for all of you to engineer an orderly change, and to minimize the costs of transition.

What is urgently needed is for the global community to finally show its readiness to assume certain global responsibilities in key areas of policy and to set in motion certain mechanisms and processes through which these responsibilities can be implemented. Such a political compact of global responsibilities should include an agreement in at least the following essential areas:

- An internationally accepted floor below absolute poverty all over the globe and a concrete framework through which this objective can be reached over the next two decades.
- An agreed system of international food security, based on additional investment for less-developed countries' national production, adequate food reserves, and emergency assistance in times of crisis.
- A global responsibility for putting in place a new international energy security system, including global understanding on energy conservation, vastly increased investment resources for energy development, and mechanisms for more predictable increases in real prices.
- Acceptance of the principle of greater automaticity in mobilization of resources to be channeled through international institutions under genuine international control.
- Acceptance of the principle that any international reserve currency should be created only under international jurisdiction and for the benefit of all nations.
- Acceptance of the global responsibility for creating adequate recycling mechanisms, particularly to ensure that adjustment in the next few years is not at the cost of either economic growth or social programs, or political survival of developing countries.
- Clear recognition of the contradictions between present levels of armaments spending, global population increase and global environment deterioration for the evolution of a new order.

I would like to suggest to the Summit that by initiating such a global Magna Carta of new premises for an old order, they will unleash forces of creativity and enterprise all over the world and provide a framework within which global negotiations can meaningfully proceed. It may even lead to a new Bretton Woods Conference to implement much of this new vision. And I should like to plead with the Summit's members that what the world badly needs today is a new vision for this ailing planet, however long it takes to implement each individual element of reform and however headstrong the incrementalism we generate, not a quick fix to get through the next six months.

NOTES

1. This aspect has been analyzed in detail in my "Beyond the Slogan of South-South Cooperation," in Khadija Haq, ed., *Dialogue for a New Order*, New York: Pergamon Press, 1980, pp. 139–52.

2. Roger D. Hansen, *Can the North-South Impasse Be Overcome?*, Development Paper 27, Overseas Development Council, November 1979.

3. For source of data, see Robert S. McNamara, Address to the Board of Governors of the World Bank, September 1980, p. 13.

4. *World Development Report 1980*, Washington: The World Bank, 1980, p. 14.

5. *Energy in the Developing Countries*, Washington: The World Bank, August 1980.

6. For a fuller discussion of these issues, see Salah Al-Shaikhly and Mahbub ul Haq, *Energy and Development: An Agenda for Dialogue*, North-South Round Table, Paper No. 2.

7. "The International Monetary System and the New International Order," in *Development Dialogue*, 1980, No. 2.

8. Willy Brandt, et al., *North-South: A Program for Survival*, Cambridge, Mass.: The MIT Press, 1980, p. 91.

9. See the final communiqué of the World Food Conference, Rome, 1974.

10. To indulge my own vanity, I would refer the reader to some of the proposals in chapters 10 and 11 of my book, *The Poverty Curtain*, New York: Columbia University Press, 1976, which find an echo in the Brandt Commission Report.

11. These suggestions are based on my concluding statement to the North-South Roundtable in Ottawa on November 16, 1980.

23
TOWARDS ANOTHER DEVELOPMENT

Fernando Henrique Cardoso

The crisis of industrial civilization—as so labelled by some—which gained prominence after the short period of challenge created by the increase in oil prices (already absorbed, according to many specialists) raised a new-old list of lamentations on the present ills and, maybe, the hopes of the future. In this list of key problems—a long one—solutions to which are known though not applied, the following could be pointed out:

- The waste of non-renewable natural resources.
- The use of technologies predatory of nature and, even worse, of labour-saving technologies in societies of high unemployment.
- Increasing environmental pollution.
- Distortions of urbanization, which are related to the more negative forms of association and behavior prevailing in mass societies (increases in criminality, drug addiction, individual insecurity, etc.).

In the countries of the periphery other problems, which in countries of the centre generally affect only the minorities, should be added to these undesired characteristics of industrial civilization:

- The growth in world population (alarming, for the disciples of the Club of Rome).
- The possible food shortage (a painful reality in some areas).
- Inadequate housing, in the same civilization which boasts of steel and glass buildings and pre-stressed concrete bridges.
- At times, even the lack of adequate clothing for the majority, contrasting with the refinements of fashion which, through instant communication, offer to the eyes of élites in South-East Asia, Andean America, the heart of Africa and every pocket of misery in the world the fascination of "alternate styles" of fashion, ranging from a "taste for

Reprinted by the Publisher's permission from *Another Development: Approaches and Strategies*. Published by the Dag Hammarskjöld Foundation, Övre Slottsgatan 2, Uppsala, Sweden.

the old" in Balmain, and Cardin's baroque fantasies, to Courrèges's "modernism," or to the false "being-at-ease" of Hechter, in a scandalous waste of imagination and mockery of the world's poverty.[1]

- The sudden jump in infant mortality rates or in the number of "plagues" (e.g., of meningitis or cholera) which, in the mirror image of the narcissist world born proudly after the Industrial Revolution, should have been buried in the darkness of the Middle Ages.
- Statistics on malnutrition and undernourishment that clash with statesmen's high-sounding words saluting the emergence over the last thirty years of countries of "medium development"—which are in fact those on the periphery—capable of embarking on a process of "dependent industrialization."
- Illiteracy, after so many "goodwill" campaigns.

This list would be long if it were to be all-encompassing, as is the list of proposed remedies. Among these, we can mention:

- The rational use of nature, emphasizing the renewable and non-polluted resources (solar energy, or water-power, for example, as opposed to petroleum).
- The combined use of intermediate and advanced technologies, in order to achieve a balance between resources of accumulated capital and available labour.
- Balanced family growth, in favour of the collective welfare (and not "instead of" economic growth), oriented by the criteria of responsible parenthood. This proposal is not as simplistic, needless to say, as zero growth rate, or as the neo-fascist theories of those attracted by the "need" to occupy empty spaces, the crooked geopolitics of those unconcerned with the quality of life in those places.
- The political reorientation of supply, benefiting producers of popular consumer goods (in general, medium and small producers), and of the more than delusive green revolutions or theories of the elastic supply capacity of foodstuffs based on the large capitalistic production unit.
- The acknowledgement that technical-industrial criteria for the definition of what is supposed to be adequate housing are also biased and that, possibly, self-help housing and direct transfer through expropriation and donation are much more effective than the so-called "self-financed" housing-fund systems, financed by regional or domestic banks.
- The quasi-monastic modesty of non-ostentatious societies, such as the Chinese, avoiding waste and luxury in life style.
- The raising of the living standards of the masses as the only real solution to health and undernourishment problems, especially those of children and mothers, demystifying the clinical, assistance or purely medical approaches, which are elitist and restricted to small segments of the population.

Comparing the world as it exists and the world as some want it to be, the sceptical conclusion may be drawn that there is nothing new in the proposals: utopias, some would say, do not penetrate the "opacity of things." Thus we reach the core of the *problématique* of another development. The "opacity of things," a "situational logic," a "web of vested interests," are roundabout ways of describing without denouncing the problem of exploitation. The problem, to use a phrase that is worn-out but still true, is the exploitation of man by man.

In this sense, even though it is true that much has been said since, say, 1945 about the ills and distortions of industrial civilization, most of it consists of half-truths, starting with the very target of criticism, industrial society, as though it existed as an entity independent of the interests of men, groups, classes, states and nations. As we move from general to more specific problems (hunger in Bangladesh or infant mortality in São Paulo, for example) it becomes apparent that it is not industrial civilization in itself which causes the problems, but rather the (often interrelated) interests of minorities in different countries, that offer the ghostly appearance of a civilization of Molochs which devours its own fruits.

Because they fail to recognize this banality—social and economic exploitation, of man by man, of one class by another, of some nations by other nations—so-called counter-élites often go round in circles, dreaming of technical solutions. The greatest example of technocratic irrationality endorsed by capitalists and socialists, industrialized and underdeveloped states can be found in the United Nations specialized agencies no less, whose all-capable and all-knowledgeable (in fact) technical programmes are, however, applied through "competent channels," i.e., governments, interest groups, different "situational logics" which, left alone, do nothing but reproduce and replace the conditions that create the problems to be fought against.

This is why sceptics insist that there is nothing new under the sun: maybe deep inside the first dominated man, the first slave, the seed already existed of a rebellious conscience and the impulse of the dialectics which would lead to the destruction of the master. If such processes do not develop it is not because they are not known or not wanted, but because they cannot. Thus, after recognizing that the basic fact that leads to the distortion of industrial societies is the existence of exploitation, and having identified the forms of domination which reflect it, another development should focus, without disguise, on the question of power.

During the nineteenth century, the same theme was already alive. At that time the dispute between "utopian" and "scientific" solutions also created profound divisions among the first universal critics of the industrial revolution, based on the exploitation of man by man. In the redeeming perspective of the greatest critics, the optimistic conviction existed that the progress of civilization and the power of conscience would combine to create the possible conditions for a new, triumphant age characterized by the renewed force of the oppressed.

A century and a half later, the culture crisis erupts in the west. The revolt appears among the children of the rich, the offspring, nauseated by the abundance of an urban-predatory civilization, at play in the universities, which isolate and bribe them with the best and by far the most histrionic means available in the arsenal of technicalities and humanistic resources. Millions of human beings finally discover the contradictions. They find out that man lives on bread and that the majority lack this same bread. They also find out that bread is not enough for those who are already filled. They then go on either to the arrogance of truth discovered ("ah, if you would only do the same as us," French students told workers in May 1968), or to complacency, that of the Berkeley drug-addicts' rebellion, that of the "naturist" communes, that of the horror of civilization, the contemporary form of the Byronic spleen. The generosity and romanticism of a whole generation was spent—almost to its exhaustion—in the counter-techniques, in the building of libertarian ghettos, in the escape through what could be viewed as a type of inverted Jansenism, which sees in the extramundane denial of the world (after becoming disillusioned with the possibility of revolutionizing it) an individual lifebuoy within an unjust social order. Hence the numerous groups of "insurgents," who never really turn into rebels, in order not to be mistaken for revolutionaries. They parade their disgust of the world, under the sign of Aquarius, through the roads of the civilization they detest, in quest of the Nepal of their dreams. The more disciplined exhibit their bald heads harmoniously complemented by white robes and bare feet, in the peripatetic groups of thousands of Zen Buddhists who cross the corner of Fifth Avenue and Central Park, announcing, by their very presence, that they no longer wish to belong to the civilization which began gaining awareness of itself in the Plaza's (ridiculous) architecture and which, all of a sudden, shook off whatever false and fanciful, though charming, it may have had of the euphoric capitalist birthday-cake style of the nineteenth century, in order to reveal, like a blade-thrust among helpless passersby, that sturdy and "logical" building in front—the General Motors building.

But the voices that echoed everywhere in favour of the "wretched of the earth" did not speak out only from the generosity of kind spirits: there were and are voices and actions coming from the ghetto (as in the Marcusian expectation-hope), of black minorities during the hot summers in Trenton, from the Algerian national liberation battlefields, from Viet-Nam, from the remaining colonies in Africa, from Cambodia and even from the spring, which many considered unnecessary and others impossible, in the streets of Prague.

Thus the outcry against the exploitation of man by man, born with industrial civilization itself, led to a beginning in the design of a new utopia—without which no meaningful action is possible—that extended, without suppressing, the vision inherited in the second half of the twentieth century from the past, the vision of the revolutionary classes, the bearers of history. For various reasons, the contemporary ideology of renewal, which may serve as a basis for another development, is more inclusive and less narrowly rationalist than the utopia of the nineteenth century, which, in the order of ideas, precedes it. It does not share so blindly the belief that through the impulse of the very development of productive forces—and thus of technology—the contradiction between private ownership of the means of production and socialization of work will lead to a new order. It adds to this basic platform of rationality an ethical-aesthetic and voluntaristic dimension, embodying the will to revolutionize the cultural matrix of contemporary civilization itself: it attempts to define another style of development.

Its elements—the "new man" of the exemplary revolutionary like Ché Guevara, the cry of Algerians under torture, Giap's people's war, the socialism of Mao's shared hardship—are prolonged contradictorily in other struggles. They are united in an unresolved amalgam—at the level of motivations, in the search for alternatives—with the almost anarchic liberalism of the French May 1968 (*"défense d'interdire"*), with the anti-racist racism of the "souls on ice" of U.S. blacks proclaimed by Sartre, with the revolted apoliticism of the missionary spirit of U.S. minorities, with feminist movements (how to combine them with socialist Islam?), and even the latent anti-bureaucracy of the Prague spring.

Utopian thought feeds on this confused and contradictory mould (but how can alternative strategies be proposed without utopias?). It arises from a collective will to assert itself which frequently looks like an individual idealistic protest: *"prends mes désirs pour la réalité car je crois en la réalité de mes désirs"* (written on the Sorbonne walls in May 1968).

It is also from this mould—although very indirectly—that the movement for the reconstruction of the international economic order is born. Instead of making a "neutral" analysis of imperialism and its power, and thus of further confirming the impossibility of change, people in the Third World, and some governments, see in the oil crisis and the OPEC union sensitive signs of a will to change which starts with what, in the logic of structures, should be the end: to obtain a fairer order among nations, even before altering the internal order within such nations.

Proposed in such terms the international liberation strategy would seem to be imbued with the same spirit as that of those who believe in the reality of desires more than in the force of reality. Nevertheless, another development does not feed only on the hydromel of utopias. A faithful reading of this will to change could also show that the internal gaps are so many and so deep in the dominating systems—created, it is true, out of the liberation struggles, by minority movements, by urban protest, etc.—that even the highest echelons of the international domination apparatus show cracks in the support structures. Perhaps this is the predominant characteristic of the way in which criticism of oppressing society is currently expressed: in struggle, in pressure from the periphery, in pressure from the societies of the centre, but also in lack of solidarity between the enlightened élites and the dominating classes. This is probably why the fight for the reconstruction of the international order and of the national structures of domination appears as a crisis of values, questioning industrial culture and civilization, as well as the basis on which they are founded. Watergate is as much an episode leading to the new order as are the wrecks that blocked the Suez canal.

If in the nineteenth-century version of utopia it was believed that the overthrow of the dominating classes by the exploited classes would automatically end alienation, inequalities and all forms of exploitation, in the twentieth-century version, the fetishism of *things* seems to be so strong that, symbolically, the utopian turns to machine-breaking, as did the English Luddites in their day. The suspicion is that with advanced technology bureaucratic control necessarily comes about and that with it, even if no private appropriation of the means of production exists, inequality and social plundering will persist which ultimately may maintain exploitation among nations, even in the socialist world.

Thus, confusedly (without necessarily having demonstrated how and why, or more important yet, through whom), the image of a new world arises—idyllic as with all strong values—in which, if nothing is there on the sixth day of creation, the knowledge at least prevails that a value hovers over it all: *equality*, capable of restoring a form of association based on the community, instead of exploiting society. It is at least known, therefore, *for whom* the new order is desired. And this is the keynote of the ideology generated by the disinherited of the affluent civilization which has marginalized the majority. With the impulse of any genuinely negating—and thus dynamic—idea, the new utopia which aims to create another style of development starts with that which the system cannot offer without falling apart. There is no technical reform capable of offering concrete equality (political, economic or social), although there are many technical reforms which may offer better health, more education or more food, conditioned to the maintenance of rigid and convenient differentiations in the appropriation of such goods by some groups. "No longer rich and poor; no longer rich nations and poor nations" is the theme that indicates that the aim is not man in the abstract, but the disinherited of the earth, the poor, the underdog.

But, how?

If the alternative strategies were to deal with final aims, only values and statements of principles would be needed. But, since another development cannot be created without political action, programmes and the reality principle are thus reintroduced; without them values and utopias remain mere hothouse flowers. Nevertheless, it is from them that the strength of the present utopia arises: contemporary industrial civilization created, in fact, the material basis for an equality with decency by increasing the minimum platforms, which are already within man's reach, technically speaking.

It is this contradiction—possibly for the first time in history—between a concrete possibility and a performance so distant from the satisfaction of the needs of all that explains the existence of a malaise even in the industrialized world, which turns every gratification into sin. *Everyone knows that the utopia of our century is materially possible.* It is not rooted only in desires, but exists as a possibility in things; if the "logic" of these does not achieve realization, it is because the desires (and interests) of some minorities do not allow it. This is why the contemporary world suffers as a torment every grain of wheat perishing on the stem. Everyone knows that the interests of some are served to the extent that this wheat is not made into bread. And yet, how the world of instant communications lives each crime committed in Lebanon, each capitulation of national dignity imposed by a banana-growing company when bribing a president, each agreement signed under pressure—be it to depose Dubček in the Kremlin, be it to oblige the confederated countries, through the Ministry of Colonies, as some call the OAS in Washington, to impose embargoes on nations which do not submit. All of this shakes and corrodes the moral fibre and the efficiency of the world order and the strength of the systems of domination. And these, in order to be efficient, cannot rely only on force; obedience requires consent, domination demands hegemony.

Thus, it is not so terrible that the definition of another development not only excites the imagination of the oppressed people, harassed by material wants, but also preoccupies the social and economic thinking of the industrialized nations. In spite of this, the ideology of development concealed until recently another aspect of reality which is now made visible: pockets of misery also exist in the industrialized countries, in which too the most coveted fruit of industrial civilization—success in increasing the gross national product—has created the problems of abundance we have listed: pollution, insecurity, impractical cities, etc. Criticism therefore springs from the situation of the blacks and Puerto Ricans in New York, of Chicanos in San Francisco, of Italians and Spaniards in Switzerland, of Algerians in Paris. And another type of criticism, which generates the urban protest in the popular classes and the fear of the city in the dominating classes, is added: in the suburbs of the rich, the scandalous neighbourhoods of rich Latin Americans, isolated in carefully built ghettos, in the modern fortresses which the luxurious apartment buildings or the large mansions are, are all those who, though theoretically consumers of the abundance civilization, in the end have to live in closed circuits of protection and boredom in order to escape their fear of the cities. Thus, the children of the rich reflect the stigma of being masters of a civilization which denies communality, which creates in fact the situation of the *homo homini lupus* that the thinkers of the eighteenth century tried to avoid through politics.

It is a civilization of poverty for the majority and fear for all.

The alternative to it, beyond the value of equality, lies in its complement, which requires freedom, of the need to *participate*. It lies in democracy, but not a democracy deferred to the quasi-mystical body of a party, or identified with a liberalism relating representativeness to the division of powers and removing all effective political stake to the summit of large state organizations, to parliament, the executive and the judiciary. Participatory democracy, which is an inherent part of another development model, starts by being more demanding and more inclusive. It turns to the new arenas in which the decisions of contemporary societies are made: the educational system, the world of labour, the organizations which control mass communication.

As the demand for equality is universal, the requisite democratic controls imply denying the authoritarianism of teaching practices which merely reproduce the established order on a larger scale. It must be education not only *for* freedom, but *in* freedom: *a pedagogy of the oppressed* with schools in which the sharing of experiences between generations allows for the emergence of new solutions and not only the codification of what is obvious from the past.

On another plane this approach leads to the search for the means to a cultural revolution. This is taking place not only in China, but also through the actions and intimation of alternatives in the U.S. counterculture, in the mobilization of teaching and work brigades in Botswana,[2] in the generalization of basic education, in never-ending university reforms and student movements. The traditional university, even in orderly societies, is in the process of becoming a museum, surrounded by living experiences of culture re-creation, which penetrate its less conspicuous openings, rejecting an education conceived merely as a conveyor-belt of the dominator's cultural matrix and as a means to impose the culture of the masters upon the dominated classes and peoples.

At the same time, in the absence of a democratic information flow, and in the face of the failure of the large organizations, public and private, to set up forums where the disciplines and the norms of efficiency of the technological civilization can be discussed, understood and agreed to by those who will suffer their effects, the world of the worker will continue to be not only alienating, but also the basis for authoritarianism, in capitalist as well as in socialist societies. This is why another development, which must be based on mass mobilization, will simultaneously be faced with the need to uproot the seeds of totalitarianism through participatory democracy, which such mobilization implies. Participatory democracy means that, before accepting any type of centralization, the what, why and for whom of general decisions will be discussed at the level of the worker, educational and political communities. In a critical review of the values inherited by contemporary societies, the idea of technical progress and rationality is not discarded, but redefined. Instead of the pseudo-rationality of the market—which in fact is the rationality of accumulation and of appropriation by a few of the results of the work of the majority—a social calculation of costs and benefits is now the aim. Instead of an increase in the product, the expansion of collective welfare is the target. This most certainly requires high accumulation and investment levels, but the orientation of investments and the forms of control over the accumulation process thus become the primary focus.

The discussion of this purpose of another development should not be confused with the debate between zero growth and "developmentalism"; with the confrontation between the insane attitude of those who say "blessed be pollution" and the naiveté of those who believe that it is better to stop producing than to contaminate the ecosystem; between those who preach the ruralization of the world and those who proclaim the virtues of urbanization at any price. In such terms, the discussion turns into a dialogue of the deaf.

When the advocates of another development insist that social rationality should prevail over pseudo-technical or instrumental rationality, they are simply reaffirming the fact that the contemporary world can count on richer and more varied alternatives; that if it is true that in order to share it is necessary to grow, it is not true that growth in itself will lead to a fair sharing of the fruits of technical progress among classes and nations.

In an effort of synthesis to express a more egalitarian style of development, requiring more participation and democratic control over decisions by those who suffer their consequences and, at the same time, substantive social rationality in the use of resources, in the use of space, in the choice of technologies and in the responsible consideration of the negative impacts which the process of economic growth may have on the environment, the term *ecodevelopment* was coined.[3] There is no place in ecodevelopment for the cynical position of those in rich countries who propose the non-development and non-pollution (therefore non-industrialization as they themselves conceive it) of the periphery. The supporters of ecodevelopment do not believe in freezing the status quo and curtailing the underdeveloped nations' chances of achieving a less needy material civilization, which would be the consequence of zero growth, but advocate instead a differentiated (thus respectful of the cultural, spatial and political characteristics of the Third World) and autonomous growth.

The concept and strategic goal which summarizes this style of development is that of *self-reliance*. This is a political category which rejects the idea that the technological advantage of the great powers is inevitable: self-reliance implies rejection of the monopoly over sophisticated technologies which is the form through which the central economies, and their dynamic sectors—the transnational corporations—seek to guarantee their domination over dependent Third World economies.

Until recently the unquestioned primacy of technology left Third World countries with almost no alternative but to copy the model of the industrial-predatory civilization in order to ensure their national integrity (or to maintain the illusion of it) and in order to carry out a process of industrial growth which would make it possible—maybe, and in the future—to increase the standard of living of their impoverished masses.

The military discovery that guerrilla forces can defeat modern armies if and when backed by the people destroyed another technocratic illusion, in the course of a historical experience stretching from the French disaster in Dien Bien Phu to the United States' defeat in Viet-Nam (which was considerably aided by the disillusionment of the cultural élites, of minorities and of young people in the United States, with the aims of the war).

Today, not only are there peoples pursuing other alternatives, but in the highly critical conscience of the more advanced techno-scientific spokesmen of the Third World countries, a conviction is being formed that:

- The technological model exhibited by the industrialized countries cannot be applied without provoking deep disturbances, if it is not accompanied by strong redefinitions of political control and its social consequences.
- Alternative viable solutions exist which require imagination, research and reorientation of investment (e.g., why maintain the same extremely expensive tradition of the Cloaca Maxima in cities of the Third World which still have no extensive sewerage systems, instead of searching for methods of eliminating residues through natural or organic techniques, for the house or neighbourhood units?).

- There are no good reasons to tie underdeveloped economies to forms of technological and economically exploitative dependence, based on trade-mark, know-how, and other contracts. These could very well be transformed into assets of the national economies, provided the Third World countries organize themselves techno-scientifically and politically to control the activities of the transnational firms in this field and to compel them to share technical knowledge.
- The cultural revolution of the Third World countries should include among its goals the development of technically qualified cadres.

People in the Third World are convinced that alternative styles of development are possible—precisely because there is a crisis of confidence over the predatory-industrializing model among the élites of the industrialized countries, and because new paths for development and for international coexistence depend on the automous action of the men and women of the Third World. Belief in self-reliance is leading Third World people through their critical spokesmen and through some governments rather to look for mutual support than to trust in the now discredited aid from the centre (particularly that linked to military or corporation interests).

On the basis of such values, leaders of the international community at the United Nations and at specialized meetings (such as that resulting in the Cocoyoc Declaration)[4] and in special forums which are being created to discuss new strategies for development (such as the Third World Forum) have started to express the aim which should guide the new international order and give consistency to another development.

Inasmuch as the concept of self-reliance implicitly acknowledges the different historical experiences of the people and defends the real contribution which the impoverished masses have to offer towards the solution of their own problems, the movement of opinion which is at present under way is modest because it is totally honest. It does not propose formulas and "models" or "aid and assistance" plans. Another development requires that within the United Nations, in governments and among the élites, the vain pretension be done away with that the final objective is already known and that it is technically possible to define the programme of aid and planning that will show the way to the wonder world.

Therefore, the starting-point is completely opposite to that which inspired the unsuccessful "development decades." In that strategy the "gaps" between industrialized and Third World countries were computed; percentages of GNP which rich countries should offer as "contributions" to poor ones were defined; and specialized bodies appointed to give financial and technical support to the plans and programmes which would be applied in the Third World in order to bring it closer to the industrialized world.

It would be unfair and uncalled-for to say that the whole of the international cooperation apparatus failed. Some relevant experiences exist—in specific programmes which actually worked. And through these programmes and actions—especially through ventures such as the United Nations Regional

Commissions—a rich exchange of opinions and experiences took place among Third World technicians and administrators and by these with institutions and individuals of the industrialized world, who were finally sensitized by the problems of the Third World countries. But as a system, international cooperation failed, inasmuch as it was carried out parallel to (and not even countering, when not favouring) international economic exploitation: reaffirming the existence of an asymmetric world order and of highly unequal national societies as well as propagating a deforming development model.

The reorganization of the world order should begin in the spirit of methodical humility which is now proposed to those wishing to cooperate in the field of international development, by some kind of collective criticism of the United Nations. This criticism should be based more on research and study of the variety of concrete experiences in dealing with critical situations faced by Third World countries than on the definition of mimetic development policies and the execution of such policies through the contemporary paraphernalia of "development plans."

An important institutional impediment in the United Nations system is to be found in the basically officious position assumed by all its bodies which, when operating in the field, are condemned to play a counterpoint to the national governments, marginalizing civil societies and giving non-governmental organizations an almost lip-service treatment. If new utopias, as we have seen, are conceived and acquire their force in social movements (feminism, anti-racial struggles, youth movements, urban protest organizations, forums for defending habitat and the environment, etc.) any international order intended to be legitimately representative within the emerging values, and any international organization wanting, in fact, to struggle shoulder to shoulder with the people (and not to act as an agency defending models to be imposed culturally on the people) should be more closely related to the roots of the national societies.

This requirement should result in a composite system at the level of the most active agencies of the international order which should provide a tribune, not only for governmental delegations, but for the voice of political minorities (they usually correspond to population majorities). Social categories such as consumers, workers (variously defined), women, ethnic and religious minorities, youth, poor peasants, shanty-town dwellers, etc. should compose country delegations. This would offer greater authenticity to international forums and would enable countries to widen the style of representation based on the values of a participatory democracy.

At the level of formal equality among nations, the scope for reforms in the system based on the ideals of another development is endless. We need only refer to the veto power and the *de facto* situations which lead to the vetoing of minorities in the specialized financial bodies (the International Monetary Fund and the World Bank, for instance) as well as in political bodies. It would be unrealistic to propose abolishing economic and strategic inequalities among nations through declarations of ideals and intentions. But it would not be so illusory to propose a counterweight system, which would aim, for example, to organize Third World delegation secretariats so as to set up and give consistency to informal groups (such as that of the 77 or of the Non-aligned) or to regional groups (such as the recently established Sistema Económico Latinoamericano—SELA), or to specific groups in countries producing raw materials—the first of which is OPEC. And it would be particularly necessary—in order to be faithful to the principle of self-reliance—that the Third World have access to organizational and financial resources, in order to give a voice to the Third World countries in the discussion of aims and experiences of development and in the easing of direct contacts and exchange of experiences between leaders and practitioners of collective social movements.

Bringing about another development in Third World countries is even harder. To begin with, it is necessary to circumscribe and demystify the very notion of Third World: the historical experiences of these countries, their relative degree of economic advance and the social and political systems existing in them are extemely varied. The language used is therefore at times highly rhetorical when it alludes to the unity of the Third World.

The new approach to development problems starts with the recognition of the diversity of points of departure and of the present phase in the historical process of the underdeveloped countries. Any pretence of imposing a unique framework on the aspirations and possibilities of these countries would repeat the same mistake made in the past, when trying to re-create in them the experience of industrialized countries. This warning is necessary and valid, since no matter how fascinating the experience of building socialist societies in countries of an agrarian-peasant economy (as in Viet-Nam or Cambodia), or in countries limited in their historical adventure owing to a relative lack of natural resources or to their colonial experience (e.g., Tanzania and Guinea now)—and also in countries with cultural experience at least as ancient and diverse as in the west (e.g., China, or Islamic countries in North Africa)—it would nevertheless be hasty and wrong to compare them, for example, to many countries in Latin America, some of which are highly urbanized, relatively industrialized and, though dependent, have almost completely assimilated western culture (e.g., Argentina, Uruguay and Chile, and to a certain extent Brazil). The roads to equality, to participatory democracy and to self-reliance in these countries follow completely different routes from those of socialist agrarianism.

Conversely, the concretization of the aims and ideals of equality, of participatory democracy, of the revitalization of regional space in response to ecodevelopment, of activating basic forces in society, and of self-reliance, in certain types of countries (for example, in rough terms, though with variations and qualifications specific to the Indian subcontinent, practially all the countries in southern Central Asia bordering the Indian Ocean down to the South East Asian extremity) would seem to have elective similarities (which in fact are structural) with the model of egalitarian and frugal socialism which starts with agrarian expropriation and has its socio-political and economic basis in the commune—in the Chinese style. This characterization obviously does not commit these countries to agrarianism (China is industrializing), and the proletarian ideal of life is not excluded. But it colours the transition process with the hues of an almost direct democracy, of an anti-bureaucratic approach and of a puritan (in fact un-urban) renewal of life styles which separates them considerably from, for example, the political life style of the Maghreb, where agrarian feudalism is added to commercial colonialism. There the weight of an urbanization is based on craftsmanship and, in the strict sense, on the manufactures deriving from the strength of the bazaar—that inheritance of the Middle Ages—and all of it is organized through a cultural tradition based on hierarchies and exclusions much more differentiating than those to be found in Asian agrarian feudalism, itself already deteriorated by centuries of submission to multiple comprador bourgeoisies. Similarly, the richness of social situations derived from the coexistence of different forms of production, reorganized by neo-colonialism, succeeded in liquidating the traditional agrarian basis of many countries of black Africa, without substituting for it an urban-industrial or urban-mercantile economy able to survive without colonialist ties. In these countries the crisis of colonial domination and the passage to a style of free, self-sustaining, egalitarian and democratic development imposes the need to reinvent a society, thus giving the imagination of the Third World a large field for experimentation.

The opportunities open to Latin American countries in this sense are much more restricted. Many of them are going through a predetermined historical experience in the urban industrial destiny of their societies and there is no longer room (in some cases, there never was) to lay the groundwork of a communitarian mould for society. Others—especially those societies in which the weight of the Andean civilizations prior to colonization is still latent—have a bigger rural problem and any alternative development strategy should take into account what one of the most important social thinkers of the continent said about his country: a revolution is either made in terms of the Indian population or is counterfeit. It goes without saying that even in these cases there is still a need to increase the technological efficiency of local economies, and we do not suggest that ruralization is all that is relevant to the historical experience of these countries. What is being considered is the definition and linking of strategic aims, which in order to be legitimate should always answer the question why and for whom and reflect the reality that the real subject of history is not individuals but social categories.

This brief outline of the varied alternatives and conditioning factors in the roads open to Third World countries in their struggle for autonomy and equality does not imply inaction or despair when confronted with such diversity. Though the roads are different the basic goals are the same. And indicators to measure performance should be devised, applied and criticized with at least as much enthusiasm as those invested in measuring economic growth. A little over two decades ago expressions such as gross national product, income per capita, import rates, etc., were unknown to most statesmen, journalists and students, in fact to people in general. With the development decades these measures of economic difference have become part of everyday language.

It is now time to reorient efforts to measure success in development by indicators centered on the *quality of life* and on *equality* in the distribution of goods and services. There has been progress in this field in the United Nations system (in the research efforts and systematizing of UNRISD for instance), as well as in individual countries. But the point has not yet been reached at which, for example, international credits are tied to the objective advance of the people's wellbeing and at which there are indicators on wellbeing as accurate as those at present measuring national solvency, the rate of inflation and the rate of growth.

Methodological instruments exist for measuring, for example, the rate of income concentration (such as the Gini coefficient), nutritional needs and minimum wage-level deficiencies. What does not yet exist—and this is an area in which the effort to attain another development should be invested—is the political will capable of transforming these indices into instruments of pressure to increase equality and improve the quality of life. It is therefore to be recommended that much effort be devoted to systematic measurement and wide publicity for the results of simple assessments to reveal, for example:

- The evolution of the rate of income concentration in each country.
- The distribution of wealth and of salaries (including a comparative analysis at an international level of lowest and highest salaries by types of firms; average, median and modal salaries among types of firms in several countries; differences between salaries paid in different countries for the same type of work, by the same transnational corporations, and so on).
- The ingredients of a basic rural and urban worker's shopping basket and the number of hours the worker uses in each country to acquire these common consumer goods.
- A "time budget" in which the way different social classes spend their energies in leisure, work, transport, health care etc., would be shown.
- The coverage of social welfare systems, to identify in particular the relative degree of differentiation (or equality) in assistance services offered to different categories in each country.
- The ways in which social welfare is financed, in order to evaluate its real effect as an instrument for income distribution and social equality, or to identify mechanisms—which are often to be found in underdeveloped countries—for transferring resources from the poor to the poorer without touching the overall distribution of wealth or the advantages of the higher-income classes.
- The mechanisms of tax systems, especially to expose such aspects as the proportion between direct and indirect taxes, etc.

The list of relevant social indicators is long and the selection strategy should concentrate on those that are the most sensitive for the measurement of social equality. Nevertheless, the critical appraisal of present development concepts does not end there: the concrete liberty of the people and participation in control over the decisions should also be included as parameters. In the search for methods to construct simple indices that can be used systematically and have assured and universal application everything remains to be done. The defence of basic liberties, both individual and social, has been left to a few institutions and organizations, generally private, and repeated denunciations made by these organizations have lost their force from repetition and because they stem from institutions which have themselves been accused many times of defending private interests or of being ideologically dependent on one particular party.

Is the time not ripe to begin through a movement springing from the Third World to create a sort of Political Conscience Court, formed by representatives of governments as well as of trade unions, universities, churches, and professions, in order to pass judgement annually—on the basis of rules agreed to and previously established by the court—on the degree of progress in political development of peoples and of governments? Instead of the models of liberty or of institutionalized oppression which the centre proposes to the periphery, should we not look for inspiration to the participatory democracy arising in the Third World for the definition of codes of civil, social and political behaviour though which the effective advances of the people could be measured in the areas of expression of thought, organization of new fields of debate and decision, of rights assured to minorities and the opposition of rejection of torture and violence?

The flaws of utopianism should not frighten those who not only wish to reform the economic and social orders but the moral order as well. It was also utopian during the Cold War and during the McCarthy period to imagine that the sit-ins, the marches, the CIA accusations and telephone tappings and the pacifist marches would—in the United States itself—lead to a major break with high-handedness that ended in Watergate and the impossibility of continuing the war in Viet-Nam.

Is it impossible to propose, and start implementing, standards for political conduct that will emerge from the dark depths of oppression in those very countries where violence and repression have been magnified into standards of national security? Such standards may finally reveal that the other development we are seeking, even if it is launched in the economic realm, opens up on to the social plane, and acquires a political dimension through the equality it proposes and through the style of participation it advocates. But another development will only be fulfilled when it finds a means of transforming the utopia into daily reality, restoring to the human experience a dimension which although moral is not unreal. The strength of this character nevertheless does not derive from the individual's proud salvation, but from the humble recognition that the expression of existence and individual integrity depend on an agreement and an action which can only be collective. The self-reliance principle, in this sense, implies a hope and belief that it is already possible to inscribe in reality the goals we wish to attain.

It is with this conviction that the reconstruction of the international order and the establishment of more egalitarian, democratic and self-reliant national societies are proposed here. These new societies are not based on the underdevelopment of the periphery and the stagnation of the centre, but on a development style which has its *raison d'être* in the social calculation of costs and benefits.

24
THE PERVERSION OF SCIENCE
AND TECHNOLOGY: AN INDICTMENT

This is an indictment of the way in which science and technology have become instruments of a global structure of inequity, exploitation and oppression. So perverted have science and technology become as instruments for power and control that we are confronted with:

- Outrageous schemes, under the guise of "appropriate technology," to feed the Third World poor on algae and garbage, while their food-producing lands are usurped by transnational corporations and local elites to grow carnations and roses for the world's rich minority;
- Biological farming in the Third World by pharmaceutical transnationals who engage in large-scale drug testing among poor populations and export blood from poor to rich societies;
- The banishment of a growing number of the First World poor from productive activity through increasingly capital-intensive technology manifested by shocking rates of unemployment;
- The employment of 50 percent of all research scientists in the world in military R&D and a significant proportion of it for developing the technology of mass destruction and repression.

We urge serious reflection and a vigorous debate on our present predicament and an active search for alternative perspectives on science and technology which relate both to the pursuit of truth and to the process of human liberation.

SCIENCE, WESTERN CULTURE AND COLONIAL EXPANSION

Something is seriously wrong. What started as a liberator of the human spirit and held the promise of "happiness and plenty" for all has resulted in inequality, exploitation, alienation and apathy. Far from being an instrument of human salvation, modern science has gone on a course that threatens survival itself.

To comprehend and cope with the multiple crises of our time, one must first

---

This statement was prepared by a group of concerned scholars at the fourteenth meeting of the World Order Models Project in Poona, India, July 2–10, 1978.

come to grips with the cultural milieu in which modern science grew and the social structure to which it has given rise. It grew in the cultural milieu of the West which put man at the centre of creation and exhorted him to use knowledge to enhance his power. Science, thus, became an instrument of "mastery" over both nature and the social order and, together with its progeny, modern technology, became the purveyor of imperial expansion, the instrument of ravaging and of manipulation of resources and the environment, of racism, of modern militarism, of fascism and of authoritarian socialism.

While the acquisitive and competitive drive of Western culture had sown the seeds of mercantilism and capitalism in the centuries before the Industrial Revolution, it was only with the availability of the enormous power released by modern science and technology that earlier restraints and the previously surviving sense of community were undermined. From that point on, capitalism acquired an expansionist thrust of new dimensions, undermining the autonomy of various societies, destroying their economies and systems of production, and turning them into vast hinterlands of commodity suppliers for what are today called developed societies. The development of such societies would not have been possible without the deliberate underdevelopment of a great many other societies.

In the course of time this capitalist thrust bent the world to its service. The result was colonialism and, following the success of national liberation movements, neo-colonialism. In fact, the neo-colonial phase, in which the penetration of the transnational corporations makes physical occupation of territory unnecessary, has led to much greater control and ravaging of the Third World, and seduction of its elites into a global structure of power, privilege and wealth. With the Third World political, bureaucratic, military, academic and communications elites accepting the superiority of Western-style "modernization" and the role of science and technology in it, there has emerged a global system of control, hegemony, exploitation and repression—all in the name of modernity and the theory of progress, all in the name of science and technology.

EXPLOITATION OF THE THIRD WORLD

To cater to the wasteful "needs" and unnecessary privileges of a rich minority of the world's people, millions of previously independent farmers and artisans are being driven from their land and displaced from their normal livelihood on a scale that makes the ravages of historical colonialism look pale in comparison. To illustrate:

- Traditional fishermen of South Asia are being forced out of their occupations by mechanized trawlers which catch shrimp and other marine delicacies for the well-nourished peoples of the industrial world. The indiscriminate fishing methods of the mechanized trawlers are leading to declining fish stocks and, thus, to a decline in protein consumption among those who have virtually no source of protein other than fish. And this is in spite of the evidence that traditional fishing activities are economically defensible, ecologically sound and employment generating.

- To feed the insatiable demands of the machines of the industrial nations and the equally insatiable desire for foreign exchange among Third World elites hungry for imported luxuries and armaments, large areas are being mined and undermined, forests destroyed, fields flooded, rivers silted, and farmers and tenants displaced from independent sources of income and livelihood.

- In the name of earning foreign exchange through tourism, where millions of poor need housing, scarce resources are being diverted to construct ten- and fifteen-storey hotels.

- By the same logic, "surplus" food and meat are being exported while children remain malnourished. Transnational corporations also contribute to infant mortality and disease by actively promoting "modern" bottle-feeding in place of "old-fashioned" breast-feeding.

- The compelling drive to sell products made possible by modern technology, regardless of whether they serve any real social need, necessitates colonization of the mind itself. High-powered advertising is used to "hook" some of the most deprived people of the world on senseless consumer goods, so that a head of family may spend a large fraction of his earnings on Coca Cola while his children starve.

PATHOLOGICAL CONSEQUENCES IN FIRST AND SECOND WORLDS

The social and psychological pathologies visited upon the First and Second Worlds through the perversion of science and technology are no less serious. These pathologies have emerged not in spite of, but because of, modern science and technology. Thus, the "civilization diseases"—mental illness, heart disease, cancer—are becoming more widely prevalent because of psychological stress and environmental pollution, both of these phenomena being particularly evident in the more highly industrialized societies. Indicators for these "civilization diseases" and criminality, to give just two examples, are inexorably increasing several percentage points each year in some industrialized countries.

Technologies which require huge capital investments and highly centralized systems of production and distribution and which rely on built-in obsolescence and wasteful consumption of non-renewable natural resources are yet another manifestation of the perversion of modern science and technology. This is reflected in the fact that huge sums are spent for research on socially and ecologically destructive nuclear technology while almost nothing is allocated for the development of renewable resources of energy.

The magnitude of structural unemployment among the poor and exploited in these countries as they are banished from productive activity through increasingly capital-intensive technology is even more alarming. Unemployment rates among young blacks in the U.S. now average 30 percent and are as high as 70 percent in some cities. The deployment of industrial robots, which are, needless to say, easier to programme and control than human workers, is already on the horizon and is likely to be operative in a number of industrialized countries by the mid-1980s, unless sharply corrective steps are taken soon.

Nowhere has this perversion of science and technology reached higher levels of obscenity than in the technology of mass destruction and repression. One particularly noteworthy aspect of this situation is that in advanced military technology, R&D activity itself provides the motive force for ever-increasing expenditures on armaments by all countries and growing arms transfers from the major powers to the Third World. When one superpower develops a more destructive weapons system to maintain its presumed advantage over its adversary, the other superpower redoubles its R&D effort to overcome that disadvantage. Other countries then clamour for these weapons to maintain their advantage over their regional adversaries. The result is both increasing appropriation of world resources by the arms race between the superpowers and growing militarization of Third World countries through massive arms exports as well as the export of technologies of repression which are used by local elites to put down movements of social and political change.

ABSURDITY OF TECHNOLOGICAL OPTIMISM

Technological optimists argue that the social pathologies generated by modern "high" technology can be overcome by more such technology. They would be players in the theatre of the absurd if they did not occupy positions of power and influence in the real world of today. Humanity must regain its sanity by reasserting the nature of scientific inquiry as the pursuit of truth, leading to technologies which liberate the many rather than facilitate control by the few.

ALTERNATIVE MODES FOR SCIENCE AND TECHNOLOGY

The scientific enterprise must henceforth be directed especially towards the needs, skills and knowledge of the majority of the underprivileged peoples of the world, especially those in the Third World. This means creative interplay between the saner elements in the prevailing paradigm of science and technology and elements resurrected from the indigenous scientific traditions of major non-Western civilizations. Efforts in this direction will enable not merely non-Western but also Western societies to acquire technologies which are highly productive as well as less destructive in their impact on the human, animal and natural world.

We do not argue for a general return to traditional science and traditional technologies in non-Western societies. These were often regressive, particularly as regards the value which must inform a global civilization: the freedom of human beings from exploitation. We seek, instead, to encourage a renewed encounter with other scientific traditions, older and also alternative, within the context of a powerful, open commitment to basic human rights, especially the right to respect and dignity. The aim, concretely, is the reduction of human drudgery, the betterment of the human material condition, the protection of all from insecurity and a genuine freedom to choose. To this end let the traditions and know-how of various civilizations be tapped and marshalled.

A CALL FOR ACTION

As we enter the final two decades of this century, the world's agenda is crowded with international events dealing with the role of science and technology in economic, social and political change: UNCTAD V, the 1979 UN Conference on Science and Technology for Development, UNIDO III and the General Assembly's Special Session on the Third Development Decade in 1980. But there seems to be little inclination among economic, political and scientific elites in either the First and Second Worlds or in the Third World to discuss the critical underlying issues which we have raised in this statement.

Unless the intellectual bankruptcy of world conferences can be arrested and reversed so that these issues are the subject of serious, open and honest debate, such conferences serve no socially redeeming purpose and are actually harmful, because they divert attention and resources from the real problems of human oppression and exploitation. We strongly urge that pressure be built from leading thinkers and scientists, grass-root movements and non-governmental organizations to see that the 1979 Conference on Science and Technology squarely faces the issues raised in this statement, accepts the need for a total reorientation of science and technology, and initiates a process of moving towards a truly liberating role for them.

Social Justice

INTRODUCTION

The protection of human rights—what we broadly refer to as social justice here—has long been relegated to a marginal status in the development of international law. This suggests the dominance of the state interest over the human interest, even in the normative domain of modern international relations. It was not until after the experience of World War II, especially the tragedy of the Holocaust, that the concept of basic human dignity entered the agenda of international politics. The inclusion of human rights principles in the UN Charter, followed by the adoption of the Universal Declaration of Human Rights in 1948, helped to establish human rights as an international as well as a domestic concern. By this time, as well, the struggle for decolonization was well under way, suggesting that a new era of greater freedom and dignity was ahead for previously subjugated peoples.

Yet, the achievement of statehood and the international recognition of human rights have not changed pre-World War II norms and practices appreciably. This period, in fact, has been marked by continuing disparities between universal demands for greater political participation on one hand, and trends toward authoritarianism of both the right and the left on the other. Throughout much of the world, civil and political freedoms have been severely curtailed, often for long periods. Torture has become an all too frequent political practice in many countries, and the increasing bureaucratization of the state, such as in Brazil, has led to new forms of society-wide repression and control. Even in the Western democracies there is concern about the viability of democratic values and practices, given the need for sufficient societal discipline to deal with the complex problems of the contemporary world (Crozier, 1975).

The present state system, with its emphasis on national sovereignty, by its very nature seems to inhibit the realization of human rights. The principles embodied in the Universal Declaration of Human Rights and in some nineteen multilateral conventions can be described best as "soft norms" implying weak compliance and even weaker enforcement mechanisms. Without appropriate international enforcement machinery, except for obligations by governments to report and explain the status of human rights in their respective territories,

365

this system must rely upon voluntary compliance. Furthermore, individual victims of government abuses, except for those in a few dozen consenting states, have no direct recourse to the international machinery that does exist, and are thus dependent upon other states to bring their cases to the international community. The system seems incapable of taking effective action, even when governments themselves share a high degree of consensus on a particular human rights problem such as South African apartheid. In sum, despite increasing juridical concern, the prevailing conception of state sovereignty still shields human rights abuses committed within the boundaries of a given state from effective international sanctions.

In addition, much of the international effort to protect human rights has been too legalistic, and in the process has ignored the underlying structural causes of human rights problems. There is a related tendency among governing elites and human rights advocates to consider only the domestic origins of human rights abuses, ignoring that governing patterns within countries are increasingly influenced by global forces. For instance, the hierarchical nature of the present world order system, with its emphasis on military and strategic alliances, has a pervasive influence on the character of governments in many regions of the world. Throughout the post-war period, both the United States and the Soviet Union have helped maintain and have on occasion even put in power repressive governments willing to serve their geostrategic interests. The United States' military and economic support of repressive states like Brazil, Indonesia, Iran under the Shah, the Philippines, and South Korea—which have acted as regional overlords of United States interests—is indicative of this process. Even under President Carter, who helped raise social justice to a new level of concern in U.S. foreign policy, the pursuit of human rights was subject to security and geostrategic interests, as the continuing support of South Korea and Iran under the Shah demonstrate.

Also, at times human rights have been an ideological and political tool, to be exploited vis-à-vis adversaries and to be soft-pedaled with allies, rather than being a serious policy goal. This inconsistent concern with human rights issues is not confined to ruling elites. Even among liberal human rights groups (who to their credit have often been more effective than governments in bringing about human rights improvements in certain countries), there is a persistent "elitist" bias. Andrei Sakharov, Kim Dae Jong, and Alicia Wesolowska elicit widespread concern, but the less visible victims of oppression—the Bangsa-Moro people in the Philippines, the Timorese people in the Indonesia-annexed territories of East Timor, to cite only two examples—are for the most part neglected. This neglect seems to be shortsighted, even from an elitist point of view, because it encourages the resort to terrorism or other forms of violence.

As pointed out in Section 4, the relationship between the war system and the denial of human rights is of central concern to world order studies. The spread of military-backed authoritarian governments that has accompanied increased world military spending is one of the most alarming features of a deteriorating global human rights picture. There are several reasons why the war system is incompatible with the widespread achievement of human well-being. It diverts enormous human and economic resources from the satisfaction of basic material needs; it reinforces and widens existing patterns of inequality and increases the need of repressive forms of governance; and it threatens the most basic of all rights: the right to survival. Thus, for world order advocates the struggle for demilitarization and for human rights overlap in significant respects.

Domestic governing structures also seem to be affected by world economic patterns and by growing ecological constraints. All developing countries face a particularly difficult task of maintaining social cohesion in the initial phases of economic and political development. This task is made more difficult by capital-intensive strategies of development linked to the world economy, which tend to create greater disparities between rich and poor, rural and urban, employed and unemployed. It is further exacerbated during periods of resource and environmental constraints and of slow growth in the world economy. Yet the claim that repression is necessary for development no longer seems empirically justified from a world order point of view. In many of the countries cited for their economic performance in the 1970s—Brazil, Chile, South Korea—the bottom 40 percent of the population is apparently worse off today than they were a decade ago. Discovering more equitable and participatory patterns of world economic development, such as those Fernando Cardoso described in Section 5, is a principal task of world order advocates, especially in periods of resource shortages.

What, then, is a just world order perspective on human rights issues? The first presentation in this section, by Fouad Ajami, sets forth such an approach. Ajami takes up the various contending conceptualizations of human rights (liberal, socialist, and third world) and draws some connections between human rights and other world order concerns, such as the war system and the new international economic order. Ajami argues persuasively that the rhetorical celebration of human rights in the early years of Jimmy Carter's presidency does not sufficiently address itself to the underlying ideological, cultural, and normative issues embedded in the very concept of global human rights. He presents a sophisticated and sensitive analysis of the Western preoccupation with political and civil liberties and with the socialist concern for collective rights, he examines the non-Western preoccupation with social and economic needs, and then exposes the inconsistencies, contradictions, and hypocrisies in the actual policies of each.

Ajami's prescriptions for a just world order concept of human rights deserve careful attention. On one hand, he rejects the antiliberty arguments from all sides on logical and normative grounds: (1) the leftist argument that liberty is an unaffordable luxury when one wants to realize socioeconomic justice; (2) the rightist argument that civil liberties threaten chaos in domestic law and order and erode national security; and (3) the pessimistic "world order" argument that the current crises can only be overcome by "iron governments." On the other hand, Ajami also rejects the arguments and efforts "to play off political freedoms against rising demands for basic economic rights." Instead, he takes an integrative approach by stressing a core set of four basic human rights: (1)

the right to survive (the right not to be subjected to the threat of nuclear annihilation); (2) the right not to be subjected to torture; (3) the right not to be subjected to apartheid; and (4) the right to food. While recognizing that no realistic concept of human rights "can ignore the conflicts between cultural relativism and universal norms," Ajami believes these rights are capable of achieving near universal consensus at this time.

Our next selection, the "Manifesto of the Alliance for Human Rights in China," suggests the universal appeal of human rights and its power to penetrate even closed societies. This manifesto also suggests that the Chinese people cannot live by bread alone, and that meeting the basic economic needs is a necessary but certainly not sufficient condition for fulfilling the yearnings of the peoples of the world. Perhaps the most remarkable aspect of the manifesto, in light of China's traditional Sinocentrism and recent isolationism from the world, is the drafters' use of the words "We are Citizens of the World." The leading spirit of the manifesto, Wei Jingsheng—electrician, publisher, and editor of the dissent journal *Tansuo* [Exploration]—was brought to trial in October 1979 on a variety of charges, and was declared guilty of "providing state secrets to a foreign journalist." He was sentenced to fifteen years in prison, marking a denouement of China's human rights movement known as the "Peking Spring."

There is no reason, however, to assume that the imprisonment of Wei Jingsheng will effectively cap the volcano of an incipient human rights movement in China. In pursuit of foreign technology, capital, ideas, and cooperation, post-Mao China has already abandoned its symbolic projection of self-reliant development, and now uses the discredited term *open door policy* in describing its attitude and posture toward trilateral countries and corporations. Given this new reality of openness toward the outside world, China has become even more penetrable to the global politics of human rights. This manifesto, like Charter 77 (the Czech manifesto presented in Section 1), raises a serious human rights problem of socialist regimes that deserves more careful analysis and prescription than it has hitherto received in world order literature.

In our third selection, Richard Falk presents a comparative analysis of the deep structural pressures and imperatives toward oppressive governance in both socialist and capitalist Third World countries. Falk considers the perplexing but crucial normative question: How do we balance the greater economic and social equity of socialist polities with the greater cultural and intellectual openness of capitalist nations? The anomalies of socialist human rights practice are explained in terms of the contradiction between the idealized *theory* of the nonstate (that the state would wither away in a Communist society) and the actual *practice* of the superstate (a bureaucratic, centralized dictatorship). This disparity, as Falk notes, has diluted much of the moral superiority associated with socialism. Yet, capitalism as a whole is seen as inappropriate for the Third World, because in failing to deal with mass poverty it creates a structural tendency for repressive rule. Given economic, social, demographic, ecological, and other structural constraints, a socialist developmental model is perceived to be preferable, though not a sufficient precondition for the realization of human rights values.

In light of the structural tendencies for oppressive governance, Falk attempts to identify an appropriate world order conception of human rights. For purposes of inquiry, reflection, and policy recommendation, he sets forth five categories of rights—(1) basic human needs; (2) basic decencies; (3) participatory rights; (4) security rights; and (5) humane governance—and suggests a matrix for evaluating the human rights performance of Third World countries during different phases of political development.

The last piece in this section is a populist Third World declaration on global human rights, adopted in Algiers on July 4, 1976. The Algiers Declaration sets forth a populist struggle theory of human rights by extending the coverage and treatment of individuals to peoples and movements. Thus, it differs from more traditional formulations of human rights as represented in the international human rights conventions. Conceptually and normatively, this declaration links human rights violations to "structural violence" among and within the nation-states. In this sense, it serves as a congenial representation of a third system approach to world order.

This declaration, however, is not without its own deficiencies. It leaves out entirely any reference to civil and political liberties and unnecessarily stresses unrestrained cultural, political, and economic nationalism. It is not clear how such a fragmented vision of struggle against social injustice can provide a viable normative foundation for building a global coalition for the rights of peoples. This accentuation of nationalism can only further fragment a human rights constituency already divided by different cultural identities and political expectations. Unless (or until) such diverse political and psychological identifications are complemented by a sense of planetary humanism, the politics of global human rights will remain an elusive quest.

QUESTIONS FOR DISCUSSION AND REFLECTION

What are the major contending approaches to "human rights" in the world today? What are the main features of a just world order concept of human rights?

Can you think of any specific "right" omitted in the contending definitions of human rights covered in the works of this section?

What kinds of human rights violations receive the most attention in the present world order system? Which receive the least attention? Why?

What are the major structural causes of human rights problems? How are the problems of militarism and economic development related to human rights?

Is the concept of global apartheid useful in describing and explaining human rights problems in the contemporary international system?

Can you think of any concrete and specific actions taken by the international community in recent years that have substantially contributed to the cause of global human rights?

How should the tension between "universalism" and "particularism" be resolved or reconciled in global human rights struggle?

SELECTED BIBLIOGRAPHY

Amnesty International Report 1979 (Annual).

Beitz, Charles. *Political Theory and International Relations*. Princeton: Princeton University Press, 1979.

Collier, David, ed. *The New Authoritarianism in Latin America*. Princeton: Princeton University Press, 1979.

Crozier, Michael, Samuel Huntington, and Joji Watanaki. *The Crisis of Democracy: Report on the Governability of Democracies to the Trilateral Commission*. New York: New York University Press, 1975.

Dominguez, Jorge, et al. *Enhancing Global Human Rights*. New York: McGraw-Hill, 1979.

Eide, Asbjorn. *Human Rights in the World Society: The Commitments, the Reality, the Future*. Pine Plains, NY: Earl M. Coleman, 1980.

Falk, Richard A. *On Human Rights*. New York: Holmes and Meier, 1981.

Henkin, Louis. *The Rights of Man Today*. Boulder, CO.: Westview Press, 1978.

McDougal, Myres, et al. *Human Rights and World Public Order: The Basic Politics of an International Law of Human Dignity*. New Haven: Yale University Press, 1980.

Moore, Barrington, Jr. *Injustice: The Social Bases of Obedience and Revolt*. White Plains, NY: M.E. Sharpe, 1978.

Nelson, Jack, and Vera Green, eds. *International Human Rights: Contemporary Issues*. Pine Plains, NY: Earl M. Coleman, 1980.

Newburg, Paula, ed. *U.S. Foreign Policy and Human Rights*. New York: New York University Press, 1981.

Rawls, John. *A Theory of Justice*. Cambridge: Harvard University Press, 1972.

Shue, Henry. *Basic Rights: Subsistence, Affluence and U.S. Foreign Policy*. Princeton: Princeton University Press, 1980.

Status of International Conventions in the Field of Human Rights in Respect of Which the Secretary-General Performs Depositary Functions: Report of the Secretary-General (Annual). UN Doc. A/35/389 (28 August 1980).

United Nations Action in the Field of Human Rights. New York: United Nations, 1980 (Sales No. E.79.XIV.6).

U.S. Department of State, *Country Reports on Human Rights Practices* (Annual).

25
HUMAN RIGHTS AND
WORLD ORDER POLITICS

Fouad Ajami

INTRODUCTION

Our concern for human rights is built upon ancient values. It looks with hope to a world in which liberty is not just a great cause but the common condition.
— U.S. Secretary of State Cyrus Vance

The question naturally arises how can all this talk about love of peace and love of man by Washington be squared with the fact that it is the United States that is creating and putting into production such a new weapon (the neutron bomb). How can one pose as a champion of human rights and at the same time brandish the neutron bomb that threatens the lives of millions of people? Washington is trying hard to do both. Its propaganda campaign about its love of man is nothing more than rhetoric around a myth.
— Soviet commentator Juri Kornilov

As long as the nuclear arms race goes on unchecked and as long as no satisfaction is given in the framework of North-South relations to the just aspirations of the developing countries, the basic requisites will be lacking so that the rights of man, in their wider and truer meaning, may be effectively respected on a global scale. The refusal to facilitate the establishment of a more just and more stable international economic order . . . is a factor which cannot be ignored or overshadowed, in the interest of respect for human rights.
— Antonio F. Azereda Da Silveiro,
Brazilian Minister of State for External Relations

Every man, woman and child has the inalienable right to be free from hunger and malnutrition.
— Declaration of the World Food Conference (November 1974),
adopted by the UN General Assembly in 1974

The passages above are a mere sample from the recent verbal celebration of the cause of human rights. They were chosen because they illustrate the

Reprinted by permission from *Alternatives: A Journal of World Policy* 3, 3, 1978.

ambiguity of the very concept itself, and because they show how states with widely differing ideological orientations and interests have come to package their own political ends in the common wrapping of human rights. Secretary Vance's statement is a standard liberal one: a plea for a world where all peoples can enjoy the same civil liberties and procedural rights which are enshrined in Western liberal constitutions and legal codes.

The Soviet and Brazilian statements indicate that societies which march to different ideological drums have other human-rights concepts of their own. The Soviets dismiss traditional Western freedoms—freedom of speech, freedom of the press, freedom of movement and assembly—as a bourgeois luxury, a mere form without any substance. The Brazilians (those presently in power, that is) give a higher priority to order than to liberty, and place greater stress on societal development than on individual rights.

Clearly, the Soviet and Brazilian statements are self-serving and somewhat defensive, coming as they do from representatives of regimes which not only violate Western liberal freedoms but ridicule them as well. The practices of both regimes have received extensive publicity of late. Soviet abuses are singled out by US opponents of détente—the Lane Kirklands, Daniel Moynihans and Henry Jacksons—who wish to reassert the differences between "free" and socialist societies. Brazilian abuses—White inquisitions in the name of order—are detailed by others who are concerned because so much violence, inequality and repression are built into the high-technology/industrial model of economic development.

However self-serving these two statements may be, they do raise questions about the "completeness" of the liberal conception of human rights, its vulnerability to charges of opportunism and self-righteousness, its capacity to speak to many forms of deprivations of human rights which are embedded in the contemporary global context. The Russian statement contrasts the actuality of the war system with the rhetoric of human rights, stating implicitly that the ability to survive without being cowed by Hobbesian notions of order or threatened by weapons of mass destruction should be recognized as a basic human right. The Brazilian statement responds to perhaps the most deepseated inconsistency in the liberal tradition by highlighting the intersection between economic rights, on the one hand, and political rights, on the other.

The fourth passage asserts a "radical" and novel right—novel, at least, on the level of the global system. Going beyond liberalism's concept of what human rights are about, this statement declares that "higher" needs—the need for liberty or freedom of expression—are meaningless and abstract unless they are underpinned by primary ones. In the words of the Declaration on the Eradication of Hunger and Malnutrition adopted by the World Food Conference, failure to honor such an "inalienable" right as the right to food "acutely jeopardizes the most fundamental principles and values associated with the right to life and human dignity as enshrined in the Universal Declaration of Human Rights."[1]

These selections should make it amply clear that the basic definition of human rights is up for grabs, and that Westerners surely hold no monopoly on it. The virtue of President Carter's campaign for human rights lies in the opportunity it presents for a genuinely global debate on the issues involved. Regardless of its motivations and shortcomings, it puts the question of human rights on the global agenda. Some causes have a way of going beyond the limits intended by those who initially embrace them. Indeed, those who raise such issues may later come to be haunted by them as others push these causes in newer and unanticipated directions, deepening and connecting them to other quests and causes. The process that follows usually becomes a test of the sincerity of the initial proponents, and of their willingness to live with the consequences of the very notions which they themselves so enthusiastically acclaimed at an earlier stage.

The human rights issue appears to be of this kind. The contrasting national, ideological and cultural emphases which mark various concepts of human rights, the practical political differences which emerge from each of these concepts, and the common omission of all prevailing approaches to human rights raise a host of questions which this essay seeks to address within a just world-order framework. Thus, this chapter has several aims:

1. To illustrate the kinds of cultural and ideological factors and sensibilities which inhere in a heterogenous world and which no discussion of human rights can afford to ignore if it is to be serious and effective.

2. To reevaluate and expand the concept of human rights, broadening it to include both political freedoms and basic economic security.

3. To expand the concept still further by connecting the question of human rights with other world-order concerns, such as militarization and peace, ways to promote humane modernization and development, and fundamental value change.

4. To suggest some appropriate steps that might be taken by global community processes in terms of this broader just world-order concept of human rights.

The first theme will run through the entire discussion; the other three will be taken up directly. One way of approaching the matters noted above is to evaluate in some depth the motivations and shortcomings of the human rights campaign espoused by the Carter Administration and adhered to by "human rights" groups in the West.

HUMAN RIGHTS IN POLITICAL TERMS

The ideological roots of Carter's foreign policy are to be found in liberal internationalism. That ideology, discredited during the Vietnam war, gained a new lease of life in the aftermath of Nixon's downfall. If Vietnam devastated the liberal internationalists—Mr. Brzezinski (1976) describes it as the Waterloo of that elite—Watergate shattered the balance-of-power world of the Nixon-Kissinger design, and rehabilitated both the pre-Vietnam elite and some of their preferences. The principal assumption of the Nixon-Kissinger policy was that foreign policy stops at the water's edge, that the way America conducts its business abroad has nothing to do with the way it orders its politics at home.[2] The Watergate revelations shattered that premise. Americans began to perceive, dimly and vaguely, that there is indeed an intimate and organic relationship between the things a country does overseas and what happens in its own domestic politics. Watergate produced in the American society an understandable desire to repudiate cynical politics; it made possible the election of Mr. Carter; once again it became respectable to moralize in politics. The politics of "realism" was discredited; it was now time for the politics of love and compassion. If yesterday America was willing to hail Brazil's concern for human rights, as Mr. Kissinger did during a visit to that country, the Carter Administration was now ready to condemn Brazilian policies. If Mr. Ford had refused to meet with Solzhenitsyn, Mr. Carter and Mr. Mondale were now willing to meet with a less celebrated Soviet dissident. Uruguay, Argentina, and Ethiopia were told that their violations of human rights were high priority concerns on Mr. Carter's agenda. Wilsonian international politics had clearly returned, expressing the certitude of liberal internationalists that diplomacy can create a world which embodies their own particular hopes and preferences.

In essence, the liberal tradition views the state as the principal threat to human well-being. But check the power of state, limit the arbitrary whims of the ruler, and individuals will prosper, goes the liberal refrain. This credo has been liberalism's undeniable contribution to the political heritage of mankind. The enemies of liberalism are on shaky grounds in trying to challenge the liberal record on that front, for no other political system has succeeded as well in checking arbitrary rulers and protecting individual citizens from the heavy hand of political power. This is really the "comparative advantage" of the liberal West (Falk, 1974). By contrast, Communist regimes in the Second World, and most regimes in the Third World, fail to buffer their subjects from the power of the state. In the Second World, the claims of the state are total, and thus overwhelm individual rights. In the Third World, military regimes, "oriental despotisms," technocracies committed to modernization, and pathological leaders inflict immense suffering on their populations. When lack of democratic "forms"—so easy to snub or take for granted—converges with political instability, rising expectations, mass poverty and enormous development tasks, the result is state terror and widespread insecurity. Western liberals are repelled by this landscape. Official terror in the Second and Third World confirms their belief in themselves, and deepens their desire to spread the "rule of law" to less "progressive" parts of the world. That is why President Carter's campaign for human rights struck such a receptive chord in the West: This is the West's message and its reassertion seemed to remind people on both sides of the Atlantic of those beliefs and institutions that distinguish the liberal West from others.

It might be well to recall that the European strand of liberalism had a very distinctive attitude to its encounters with alien and culturally different societies. The Europeans frequently spoke of their civilizing mission, of creating civilization out of non-Western barbarism. Ultimately, however, European liberalism rested on a distinction, a caste system if you will, that left most of the world beyond the pale of civilization and the liberal community. European imperialism had to be justified, and the justification was often found in the "barbarism and cruelty" of non-Western practices: in the Indian custom of Suttee (the burning of widows), in the Ottoman Empire's brutality against the Armenians and the Christians in Greater Syria, in the violence of African tribalism. If non-Westerners could be so brutal when left to themselves, then wasn't the cause of civilization better served by denying such societies the rights of autonomy and self-determination? In short, Europeans did not really believe that their liberalism was a commodity that could be exported, or their worldview which could be taught and eventually embraced by others. At most, they believed that sustained contact with European culture, institutions, and religions would tame the bestiality of non-Westerners (particularly the intelligentsia and the official classes). However, the boundaries that separated Europe from the rest of the world were forever clear and discernible to the European liberal. John Stuart Mill expressed the views of his contemporaries and of dominant European liberalism when he wrote:

> To suppose that the same international customs, and the same rule of international morality, can obtain between one civilized nation and another, and between civilized nations and barbarians, is a grave error and one which no statesman can fall into . . . Among many reasons why the same rules cannot be applicable to situations so different, the two following are among the most important. In the first place the rules of ordinary international morality imply reciprocity. In the next place, nations which are still barbarous have not gone beyond the period which it is likely to be for their benefit that they should be conquered and held in subjection by foreigners.

These European liberal prejudices also held true across the ideological aisle. In his essay on British colonialism in India, Marx observed that Britain had a double mission in India: to shatter Asiatic culture, with all its "idiocy" and "barbarism," and to lay the foundations for a modern capitalist society which, all evils notwithstanding, was preferable to Asiatic despotism. Sounding very much like any contemporary Western Liberal lamenting the abuses and brutalities of Third World Societies, he observed (Tucker, 1972):

> We must not forget that these idyllic village communities, inoffensive though they may appear, had always been the solid foundation of Oriental despotism, that they had restrained the mind within the smallest possible compass, making it the unresisting tool of superstition, enslaving it beneath traditional rules, depriving it of all grandeur and historical energies. We must not forget that barbarian egotism which, concentrating on some miserable patch of land, had quietly witnessed the ruin of empires, the perpetuation of unspeakable cruelties, the massacre of the population of large towns, with no other consideration bestowed upon them than on natural events, itself the helpless prey of any aggressor who deigned to notice it all. We must not forget that this passive sort of existence evoked on the other part in contradistinction, wild, aimless, unbounded forces of destruction and rendered murder itself a religious rite in Hindustan.

In contrast with European liberals, American liberal internationalists from Wilson and Roosevelt to Kennedy and now Carter have imbued the notion of liberty with a "timeless and abstract" quality which, in Stanley Hoffmann's words (1976–1977), reflects "America's deep conviction that the principles, practices, and institutions which have made America great can be used with similar effects elsewhere, that even when the backgrounds are profoundly different, either determined American action or satisfactory compromises will allow the survival and spread of these ideals and patterns."

All societies can be taught civilized, reasonable rules of conduct, it is assumed. Other peoples need only see the benefits of good government based on liberal virtues, and then incorporate the principles of liberty and private initiative into a modern market system. The American people themselves widely share the view that if these precepts could produce such miraculous success for Americans, they are bound to work for others as well. Woodrow Wilson's vow to teach South Americans or Filippinos how to elect good governments, his proclamation that the twentieth century was the century of the common man, his call at Versailles for the right to self-determination, stand as the clearest embodiments of American notions of human rights.

Europeans were, of course, skeptical and antagonistic to Wilson's outlook, and a somewhat similar ambivalence and skepticism can be discerned in contemporary European attitudes toward President Carter's human-rights campaign. To Europeans, such outlooks reflect that unique combination of hubris, naiveté, and the tendency to phrase material interest in moral terms that they have always associated with America. (It should be noted, however, that two recent factors now converge to check that skepticism: rejection of the *realpolitik* of the Nixon-Kissinger years, and renewed concern in Europe with both the power of the Soviet Union and the strength of local Eurocommunists.)

Other voices outside the European liberal tradition, particularly Socialist and/or Third World spokespeople, criticize North American approaches to the human rights question on far more fundamental economic grounds. Liberalism is an ideology of abundance, they say, which is therefore preoccupied only with violations committed by the *state*. It assumes that resourceful individuals and groups can provide for their own well-being as long as they are sufficiently protected from government interference. The result is insufficient attention to *societal* violations which erode the life-chances of millions of people throughout the world. If political rights constitute the "comparative advantage" of the First World's liberalism, economic rights are its Achilles' heel: it is here that liberalism is most vulnerable as an ideology of the affluent in a world seeking greater material equality. This is why liberalism, at least in its classical variety, has failed to capture the imagination of the poor within and among nations.

"On the whole," writes Kenneth Boulding in a relevant discussion of the difference between liberal and socialist thought, "political thought in the West has emphasized form: constitutions and procedures, who is to do things rather than what is to be done. Socialist thought has emphasized substance to the neglect of form . . . with the result that socialist societies have found themselves defenseless against tyranny." If socialism has been generally vulnerable to tyranny, liberalism has proven itself quite capable of living with economic inequality and injustice, particularly in the context of global politics.

The mainstream Western notion of human rights confirms the liberal obsession with forms at the expense of substance; it naturally revolves around the kind of freedoms that affluent Westerners hold dear: freedom of expression, assembly, freedom from arbitrary arrest, from torture. But precious little has been said yet concerning basic rights to at least a minimum standard of living, which would include the right to food, shelter, and work. Freedom House, a New York based organization that monitors civil and political liberties around the world and lists among its trustees Daniel P. Moynihan, Zbigniew Brzezinski, Richard Gardner, and Jacob Javits, expresses typical Western attitudes in its annual "comparative study of freedom." This survey ranks nations on a descending scale from 1 ("free") to 7 (the "least free"). By Freedom House criteria, South Africa is assigned a more favorable rating than most Third World states; much higher, for example, than Cuba, Tanzania, Algeria, Peru, and Libya. Even Transkei, a creation of South Africa, rates higher on the civil rights scale than Cuba, Algeria, and Tanzania. That South Africa can be deemed more "free" than Tanzania is testimony to the intellectual tyranny of form over substance. Looking at its own ratings, Freedom House finally articulates its own concept of "freedom" in the statement that "capitalism by itself does not assure freedom . . . but socialism by itself seems to be positively detrimental."[3] In other words, a multi-party system and a capitalist economy are more important than the provision of food, jobs, education or medical care. This survey graphically demonstrates how Western liberal notions of human rights can lead to the most ludicrous and incongruous conclusions.

It is precisely these flawed concepts of what human rights are about that have enabled the US to raise the banner of human rights at the same time that it opposes the New International Economic Order and Third World demands for a fairer distribution of global wealth. Inasmuch as economic rights are not considered basic, the US sees no contradiction whatsoever between supporting civil and political rights in the Third World, and opposing reforms in international institutions and terms of trade that *might* raise living standards in Third and Fourth World states. Indeed, one can go further and argue that there is an organic and causal relationship between the Third World's demands for a new international economic order and the American focus on human rights. Liberty becomes an answer to the Third World's demand for global equity.

Carter Administration's Human Rights Campaign

So much for the roots of the Carter policy. What of its shortcomings and traps? Three shortcomings are readily obvious: the first is the campaign's excessive self-righteousness; the second is its cold-war orientation; the third is its tendency to focus on the violations of others, and the related failure to examine Western patterns of organization which, in their own subtle ways, pose serious problems for human welfare.

Self-righteousness. / The current campaign for human rights reflects an unmistakably ethnocentric and "imperial" mentality. America is the center of the world, radiating goodness and universal norms. The rest of the world, the Third World in particular, is but a mere periphery. America calls the tune, while others are expected to follow. Foreign societies are to be measured, not by their own criteria or norms, but by America's "timeless and abstract" ones. That this kind of attitude is a recipe for disaster in an era of quite tawdry sensibilities is one problem. Another is an irony that derives from America's own failure to ratify some of the major human rights conventions. As one Congressional Report notes, "The U.S. record on ratification of human rights treaties is not good. . . . The United States, through its failure to become a party to all but a few of the human rights treaties, has become increasingly isolated from the development of international human rights law."[4] How a "latecomer" to the field of human rights can preempt the issue as its own is a question which the Carter Administration has yet to confront. It would be too much to expect the rest of the world to welcome the latest convert to the faith as the new archbishop, without voicing some strong objections and a large measure of skepticism.

U.S. self-righteousness is particularly problematic in cases involving Third World regimes. Westerners may forget—but non-Westerners should not be expected to do so—that a human-rights rhetoric of sorts was very much a part of the mythology and the ideological baggage of Western colonialism. Even when colonizing others, Europeans were fond of justifying their alien rule as a way of promoting human rights.

Since the non-Western world has for so long been on the receiving end of Western sermons and Western colonialism, and particularly because the two have been almost inseparable, it is a relatively easy matter for Third World rulers to dismiss the Western campaign for human rights as yet another form of Western interventionism motivated by the West's belief in its own "more civilized" superiority. The Third World response transcends ideological orientation: it is asserted by Fidel Castro and the Shah of Iran. Invoking the right to self-determination, drawing upon deep wells of anti-Western sentiment, reacting against years of hearing Westerners speak the language of freedom while practicing their share of aggression, Third World leaders can easily withstand the charges which emanate from the West. What is worse, because of this historical background, the "foreign connection" of local Third World dissidents can become a devastating liability. In most cases, the capacity of the dissidents to speak a local political idiom, to express their opposition to the state by appeals to their own nation's history and values, is a pre-condition of efficacy and success. A heavy dosage of Western self-righteousness can thus undercut prospects for a successful struggle against authoritarianism.

Human Rights and Cold-war Politics. / Second, it is often difficult to tell where the West's accustomed antagonism toward the Soviet Union ends and where genuine concern for human rights begins. The danger that the human-rights campaign will lose its moral credibility by resembling a pursuit of "the cold war through other means" is all too real. The image of the Soviet Union as a threat to the West has been brought back to life; if the cold war lost respectability in the age of summitry and détente, it seems to be quite in vogue again. The American President promises to "hang tough" in his negotiations with the Soviet Union and clearly strikes a receptive chord in his society. The Committee on Present Danger declares that talk of "world order politics," the devaluation of military forces, and the Third World "threat" are all nothing but suicidal nonsense. The real antagonist, the Committee argues, is the Soviet Union—a state which understands only the language of force.

The West's renewed concern with the Soviet Union at this time is a complex phenomenon; at its roots lie deeply-felt psychological needs as well as standard geo-strategic concerns. The latter, more readily apparent and frequently discussed, are easy to understand. The Soviet Union is a major rival—in fact the only power that poses a serious military threat to Western security. Consequently, the Soviet Union is also the one power whose activities can be used to reaffirm the military's position and justify its claim on resources, after a decade of disillusionment with military interventions and of growing popular demands for fewer guns and more butter.

In this context of life-threatening geopolitical rivalry, the Third World doesn't count. Concern with the Third World as a threat to the West burst on the public consciousness in 1973 and 1974, with the deployment of the oil weapon, the Third World militancy at the United Nations, and India's explosion of a nuclear device. But the Third World was not, and by a strictly military logic could not be, a serious rival. For one thing, the issues between the West and the Third World are economic in nature, and hence do not lend themselves to military solutions. Moreover, even in the event that military intervention was needed, these issues don't seem demanding enough to warrant massive budgets and technological outlays. "Police operations," such as the ones discussed in 1974 and early 1975 against the Arab oil states, are minor things; for such excursions, a small military expedition would be enough. Soviet Russia remains the principal rival if new weapons are to be developed, and if the military and those sectors of the economy and educational system that are associated with it are to retain their role as guarantors of the "survival of the West." At any rate, Russia's greater willingness to venture outside its boundaries in the aftermath of Vietnam (to intervene by proxy in Southern Africa, for example) seemed to justify a hard line against the Soviet Union, to prevent the world from interpreting the Vietnam debacle as a failure of America's will and nerve.

Profound and real as they are, such geo-strategic concerns do not, however, suffice to explain the renewed ideological assault against the Soviet Union. To comprehend that, one has to look into deeper political and civilizational factors in the West. At a time of great uncertainty and complexity, when the distinctions between "freedom" and "tyranny," or between the "free" and "Communist" worlds, are no longer so clear-cut, to yearn for the cold war is one way to recapture innocence. To go back to these "militant," "principled" days is an antidote to today's cynicism and skepticism. To return is a way for the West, especially America, to rediscover its essence, to get back in touch with the things that make it so unique. For all its considerable problems, the cold war did provide a sense of purpose, for it drew lines between philosophically and ideologically different worlds.

However, these lines have been increasingly blurred by postwar developments. Intimate alliances between America and Third World tyrants, Soviet-American détente, the cynical Nixon-Kissinger policies, and revelations about CIA activites have all helped to smother once clear distinctions. If the "West" as a cultural entity was once thought to represent unique civilizational values, that notion has now been clearly challenged at its roots.

Such disillusionment with the world of politics is only the tip of the iceberg, however; underneath lie deeper and more troubling questions sparked by a technological age. For, if the logic of the technostructure is indeed global—if, for instance, Mr. Donald Kendall of Pepsi-Cola can feel at home in Moscow, and if world-spanning multinational corporations are trans-ideological and seemingly indifferent to once deeply-held, and hotly-debated, political convictions—then surely yesterday's truths were naive and misguided.

The growing strength of Eurocommunism deepens Western malaise still further. The spectre of communist victories at the ballot box is now drawing close to home—not somewhere at the periphery of the world in poor, marginal societies, but in Italy, Spain, and France. This political development resurrects old fears of Soviet power, and revives doubts about liberal democracy's capacity to maintain itself in the face of inflation, unemployment, civil unrest, and heightened tensions between rich and poor. The relative successes of Eurocommunism tempt its electoral and ideological rivals in Europe to take once again the ideological offensive against the Soviet Union. European voters are warned that communism is still a monolithic, hostile movement, and that when the chips are down local European communists will prove more loyal to their ideology than to their nationalism.

Such are the ways that liberty has been rediscovered in the context of East-West politics. The Carter human-rights campaign thus serves to redraw ideological lines obliterated by a cynical foreign policy, by the unifying power of technology, and by the mobility of multinational corporations, all of which mock the distinction between "free enterprise" and "planned economies." A measure of simplicity is reintroduced into a world that desperately seeks it. Once again, the differences between social systems are asserted: one society punishes dissidents, while another allows a multitude of voices. Soviet dissidents themselves, notably Alexander Solzhenitsyn and Andrei Sakharov, have played a crucial role in the process of redrawing these lines. Solzhenitsyn's use of apocalyptic imagery about the decline of the West and the need for a new moral crusade turned him into an instant hero of the American Right. He spoke their language, warning that the West was "on the verge of a collapse created by its own hands;" that freedom was indivisible and must triumph over pragmatism; that détente was a flimsy thing, a mere trick played on the naive and trusting Westerners (Solzhenitsyn, 1975). Sakharov ridiculed "leftist-liberal faddishness" in the West, and the incapacity of Western intelligentsia to understand "the tragic complexity of real life." His appeals to the West were phrased in standard cold-war terms, importuning these nations to set aside their internal concerns, important as they are, in order to present a solid Western front against "totalitarianism" (Sakharov, 1975):

> I am deeply convinced that the thoughtless, frivolous pursuit of leftist-liberal fad-dishness is fraught with great dangers. On the international level, one danger is the loss of Western unity and of a clear understanding of the ever-constant global threat posed by the totalitarian nations. The West must not under any circumstances allow the weakening of its stand against totalitarianism. There is a danger for each country of slipping into state-capitalist totalitarian socialism. These two threats are of course closely related. . . . In comparison with these problems, many of the day-to-day mat-ters that are disturbing the ordinary man in the West are of slight significance. If he, his children, or his grandchildren ever live under a system even remotely resembling ours or the Chinese, they will understand—it isn't too late.

The dated rhetoric of the late 1960s was thus imbued with the authority and the moral backing of noted Soviet dissidents. If Soviet intellectuals could tell the difference between freedom and tyranny, then surely Westerners could do no less. Even Mr. Kissinger had to pay lip service to such rhetoric toward the end of his tenure. The final act of the Conference on Security and Cooperation in Europe—the so-called Helsinki Declaration—concluded in August of 1975, was a sign of things to come. Its provisions reflect a codification of the status quo in Europe that Soviet Russia wanted; the *quid pro quo* was the provisions on human rights that the West insisted upon. The "universal significance of human rights and fundamental freedoms" was acknowledged, and all par-ticipating states vowed to respect the "freedom of thought, conscience, religion or belief," to promote "the effective exercise of civil, political, economic, social, cultural and other rights and freedoms all of which derive from the inherent dignity of the human person and are essential for his free and full development."[5] In time, and particularly with a new administration in power in Washington, these standard phrases of international conferences would be brandished against the Soviet Union.

The struggle against an authoritarian Soviet bureaucracy by determined in-tellectuals and activists, and the related quest by East Europeans for greater autonomy from the tight grip of the Soviet Union, are obviously important issues. They speak to the desire for more private space, a more humane society, a more open system of governance. It is difficult not to be moved by the deter-mined and admirable effort of those who take the risk of saying "here and no more" in a society like the Soviet Union. We must hail their struggle while awaiting its slow and uncertain evolution. However, precisely because it is such a worthwhile struggle, it would be negligent and irresponsible to entangle this cause too deeply in cold-war politics or to use it cynically for the sake of "sham-ing" another state (to paraphrase Mr. Moynihan). If we respect the efforts of others, we must surely appreciate the grave and awesome problems which those efforts involve. The least we can do for such courageous dissidents (and for ourselves) is to lend their struggle the dignity and the seriousness that it merits. Anything less demeans them, ourselves, and the issues raised by this cause.

Setting One's House in Order. / The issue of human rights is not exclusively a "Southern" or a communist problem. Western discussions sound as though all is well in the house of the West, as though only in the Third World or the communist states is the effective exercise of human rights circumvented by socio-economic or political repression. While it is true that there is comparatively more direct violence in the Second and Third Worlds than in the First, the current campaign for human rights must also take cognizance of Northern violations as well. America's domestic experience with civil rights and racism affords a particularly illuminating example. It was assumed that discrimination against black Americans in housing, education, and employment was confined to the South. The generally more subtle and invidious northern (meaning the American north) abuses went largely unrecognized until the riots in the summer of 1967, because most Northerns smuggly believed that racism was an exclusively Southern problem. The same tendency can now be observed in Western pronouncements on human rights. But, rather like charity, "well ordered crusades begin at home" (Hoffman, 1976–1977), and the Western countries should embody the doctrines they preach to others in their own lives. The police is surely repressive in Brazil, but Mayor Rizzo's Philadelphia has a few grim tales of its own. The sources of human misery vary from one culture to another; each society inflicts its own version of injustice, develops its own way of not seeing the suffering of its victims, builds up its own myths to maintain the claims of the winners.

It is easy for Westerners to be outraged by endless tales of non-Western repression and brutality, and simple for them to "see" non-Western violations, but much harder to look into their own society, to puncture its myths and claims, to honestly confront the human and social costs of its own arrangements and evaluate the drift of its own history. Professor Rupert Emerson (1975) provides a sobering antidote to Western propensities to look with revulsion at Third World deviations from Western legal norms:

> Even aside from the fact that Western values have obviously no automatic applicability to other peoples, times, and climes, it would serve no useful purpose to attempt a listing of Western sins and shortcomings all of which are prominently spread on the public record, as are such virtues that the Western contribution may be held to have. . . . A staggering total of wealth has been spent and continues to be spent on wars and armaments when poverty and underdevelopment are the fate of most peoples including a substantial number of Americans. The viles of imperialism are too familiar to require elaboration, particularly at a time when anti-colonialism is a dominant global theme. The squandering of the world's limited resources and the pollution of the environment are becoming more and more evident. If the West has been the fountainhead of liberal constitutional democracy, it has also been the breeding ground of Fascism and Nazism.

President Carter's human rights campaign brings us face to face, then, with the differing and often hidden costs of social orders, especially with the capacity of some societies to conceal these costs under layers of civility and prosperity. The lesson which can be learned from critics of this campaign is that the introduction of morality and human rights into international politics cannot be controlled and selective. Other voices are destined to be heard, to add their own views and interpretations to the debate. Their motivations are sure to vary, and no doubt attempt to combine self-interest with morality. One may not agree with all of these voices, but it is folly to imagine that any one nation or outlook can single-handedly impose its own concept of order on others. Spokesmen for the Carter Administration may wish to emphasize human rights because it is, as they often put it, their "strong suit." But the rules of the international game are not set by one player alone, and no single player can constantly play his own suit. The attempt to abstract human rights from a broader, more complex agenda of problems which must be addressed is doomed to frustration—pragmatically, politically and intellectually—if only because other players (who may at times be solely interested in stalling or disrupting the game) will select some other issue as *their* "strong suit."

Professor Emerson's passage makes the kind of linkages and interconnections that adequate concepts of human rights must make: between the war system and human rights; between economic justice and equity and human rights; and between justice to one's fellow citizens and also to fellow human beings who happen to reside outside the boundaries of one's own state.

HUMAN RIGHTS IN ECONOMIC TERMS

Contrary to the Western liberal tradition, the socialist tradition has always tended to define human rights in economic rather than in political terms. The hallmark of socialist regimes, such as those in the Soviet Union and Cuba, is the attempt to establish a minimum "floor" which will guarantee a basic standard of living for all members of the society.

Right to Food. / For the poor of the world, the primacy of economic rights cannot be overemphasized. One cannot make the standard liberal arguments about equality or liberty in opposition to such rights. Indeed, the contrary argument is far more persuasive: that to satisfy these basic human needs is to give meaning to the ideal of liberty, to anchor it in socio-economic rights, and to make real the proclaimed commitment to human rights. Perhaps the most basic economic right is the right to food. As Saul Mendlovitz recently told a Congressional committee, the right to food has become part of a "new myth system" for the world community.[6] Though admittedly difficult to implement, the notion of a right to food challenges the smugness of an affluent, productive era. It asks a sophisticated, productive, enlightened community to guarantee each individual a minimum but fundamental right regardless of his or her talents, race, age, nationality. It gives the world community a way to demonstrate universal human solidarity by affirming the most elementary human right of all: the right to eat.

At present, the right to food, as Mendlovitz readily admits, is at best a moral claim; there is no machinery to enforce it, no centralized (nor even decentralized) authorities against whom such a claim can be asserted. "Realists" may say that the time to propose a right to food and other basic economic rights has not yet dawned. But one can point to their selective realism. In a cruel era, where national governing authorities seem to be on a rampage, is it time to ask them to stop torturing dissidents and begin treating political opponents with due process? The case for economic rights is no more and no less realistic than the case for civil or political rights. It is far more "realistic" to admit that these matters are decided, not on any objective grounds, but rather on grounds of sheer convenience. It is convenient for Western governments to speak of civil liberties, and troubling to confront the issue of economic rights.

For most socialist and Third World regimes, the situation is precisely the reverse. Their heads of state speak the language of egalitarianism abroad, while they defend systems of acute inequalities within their own boundaries. At the fourth session of the United Nations Conference on Trade and Development (UNCTAD), President Marcos of the Philippines was delegated to present the Manila deliberations of the Group of 77. Predictably, Marcos called for justice and interdependence, and for fairer ways of organizing interstate relations. But should we not ask why his own society embodies gross violations of the very same norms that he espouses at international conferences? For quite some time, the concern with Western dominance, combined with sympathy for the struggle of non-Westerners to break the West's hold on the rest of the world, made it tempting to look the other way where Third World violations were concerned. One did not want to play into the hands of reactionary critics of Third World regimes; the larger goal seemed worthy enough, and one did not want to deny it one's support. But to exempt the oppressed from moral judgment, or to allow their previous deprivations to provide a licence for newer and different forms of oppression, is neither morally nor politically persuasive. Unless movements for social change embody the kind of values they espouse, and unless the struggle itself constitutes the first step toward building a more decent and just social order, the entire quest is, alas, doomed to futility. A long trail of betrayed revolutions and abandoned causes bears witness to the fact that there are never solid guarantees of how any rebellion will turn out. The outcome will depend on the circumstances of history, on the quality and orientation of leadership, and on the coherence of the vision. And because that guarantee is always lacking, we must look to the particular struggle itself: its formative stage, the men and women who lead it, the ideas and visions which propel them, if we are to avoid yet another "betrayed" quest, yet another revolutionary dream that speaks the language of justice and ends up replacing one set of elites—or countries—with another.

New International Economic Order. / With OPEC's successful deployment of the oil weapon and with the Declaration of the New International Economic Order, Third World leaders began to force the attention of the international community beyond the concept of economic rights *within* nations, to the goal of greater economic equity *among* nations. The call for a new international economic order has challenged some hitherto "natural" facts of life; it has pushed the issue of equity to the forefront of world politics. Briefly, the main demands of the New International Economic Order focus on (1) inequality in the terms of trade between the raw materials of the Third World and the manufactured goods of the North; (2) access to the markets of the rich nations; (3) access to relatively cheap technology; (4) jealous assertion of national sovereignty on the part of Third World states over their resources and their right to regulate the activities of multinational corporations; (5) debt relief for debts estimated to be in the neighborhood of $160 billion; (6) a rise in official development assistance from the present 0.36 to 0.7% of the combined GNP of the rich nations. These are the specifics; the underlying ideological thrust is the attempt on the part of the Third World nations to challenge the ideology of laissez faire liberalism and the complacent belief that "the market" is capable of distributing justice and fairness.

Certainly, the ambiguities involved in the New International Economic Order should be recognized: the heavy emphasis on "state building" to the detriment of the society; an incredible obsession with acquiring the very latest weapons; fascination with imported technology; and the rise to power, in a manner all too familiar, of a group of *nouveaux riches* in states who claim to speak for the downtrodden of the world. But these ambiguities aside, and considering the alternative vision of how the rich nations want the world to look, the New International Economic Order is a landmark development.

But can its demands be met? Is the tackling of absolute poverty a "manageable" undertaking? Isn't global poverty a bottomless pit bound to tax and outrun global capacities and resources? This is the crux of the "triage" argument: that there is so much poverty and so few resources to go around that the best one can do is learn to see and hear the suffering of others without undue pain or guilt. Serious work by men like Nobel Laureates Wassily Leontief and Jan Tinbergen, as well as groups like the Overseas Development Council and the World Bank, indicates the absurdity of the triage concept, to say nothing of its callous disregard for human beings.

Some of the work surveyed is relatively precise and quite helpful. World Bank estimates contend that absolute poverty can be eliminated with an investment of $125 billion (1974 prices) stretched over a ten-year period. Food and nutrition would absorb $42 billion; education $25 billion; rural and urban water supply $28 billion; urban housing $16 billion; urban transport $8 billion; population and wealth programs $6 billion. The estimates are naturally rough and suggestive. As Roger Hansen (1977) of the Overseas Development Council notes in an analysis of the feasibility of such a strategy, Official Development Assistance by the rich countries of OECD alone could do the job over a sustained period of time in the next 15-25 years, if that aid were channeled from middle-income countries to poor ones, and if it were directed to basic human needs—i.e., literacy campaigns, rural development, and the like.

The same nexus is the centerpiece of Wassily Leontief's important study for the United Nations (1976):

> To ensure accelerated development two general conditions are necessary: first, for reaching internal changes a social, political, and institutional character in the developing countries, and second, significant changes in the world economic order. Accelerated development leading to a substantial reduction of the income gap

between the developing and developed countries can only be achieved through a combination of both these conditions. Clearly, each of them taken separately is insufficient, but when developed hand in hand, they will be able to produce the desired outcome.

The Leontief study is avowedly normative, and quite "realistic." Its aim is to reduce the 12:1 gap that now separates the rich from the poor countries, to a 7:1 ratio by the end of the century. Its aim is not utopian total equality, but a sufficient reduction in inequality to make a real difference to poor citizens of Third World societies. Its starting point is a genuine agricultural revolution in Third World societies themselves that increases agricultural production in the coming decades by an annual average of 5%. This task, the study notes, would entail land reclamation and irrigation, credit facilities, public and private investment and, above all, institutional changes that would make such a transformation possible. Land reform is an essential component of this strategy; so are "incentives towards eliminating inefficiencies in the use of land, labor, and technology."

Global changes in the terms of trade between rich and poor countries would supplement domestic agricultural reform. The report singles out the following: (a) a faster change in relative prices of primary commodities vis-à-vis manufactured goods; (b) a decrease in the dependence of developing countries in world exports of manufactured goods; (c) larger aid flows; (d) changes in flows of capital investment.

Roughly the same message is reiterated in the Tinbergen Study (1976). The two essential goals—to narrow income disparities and to abolish absolute poverty—are said to require at least three sets of measures: (i) increased transfer of resources from the industrialized to the poorer Third World countries, with particular attention to the use of these resources to directly addressing the poverty problem; (ii) increased transfer of resources from the richer and advantaged minority within most Third World countries to the poor majority; (iii) revision of development strategies of most Third World as well as some industrialized countries to pay far more attention to ensuring employment and minimal levels of *education, health, nutrition, shelter,* and *clothing*.[7]

Studies like these carry genuine hope for the future by providing the guidelines for positive politics and policies. Their conclusions leave the industrialized nations no excuse whatsoever to shrug their shoulders in defeat and write off hundreds of millions of people. While it is true that efforts to reduce inequity among nations sometimes seem to distribute money from the poor people in rich countries to the rich people in poor countries, as President Carter once put it, the studies referred to above prove that this need not be so.

MILITARISM AND THE RIGHT TO SURVIVE

When ubiquitous arms build-ups are juxtaposed with pronouncements on human rights, the contrast underlines the absurdity of, say, seeking to protect citizens from arbitrary arrest, or even to provide them with food and jobs, as long as both superpowers (and many more than anxious emulators in the Third World) continue to accumulate massive arsenals of destruction. Because one of the most fundamental of all human rights is surely the right to survive, the world can hardly fail to be skeptical about rhetorical commitments to human rights which coexist with massive military expenditures but inspire only the most timid steps toward disarmament. On this score, the American position is less than convincing, and in fact is vulnerable to precisely those Soviet and Brazilian criticisms cited at the opening of this essay.

Militarization and the denial of human righs or social justice are intimately connected in two more tangible ways. First, staggering human and economic resources are expended on the war system every year; second, military forces within a number of Third World states have recently shown a pronounced tendency, nurtured by broader global forces and trends, to assume political power. Both developments illustrate the difficulty of upholding human rights in a world system where the obsession with military power is so consuming and widespread.

The useful data assembled by Ruth Leger Sivard (1977) on world military and social expenditures depict the arms race as "a stampede, as the buying fever for newer, more powerful weapons spreads to all parts of the globe." In that race, pride of place belongs, of course, to the two superpowers, who alone have accounted for two-thirds of the global military outlays over the last fifteen years. The data show an increasing gulf between "war-oriented" and development policies. War-oriented research dwarfed other research efforts and preempted "resources that might otherwise have been invested in the technology, capital infrastructure, and human capital on which the quality as well as the rate of economic development depend."

The extent to which such expenditures of human talent as well as material resources undermine the capacity to meet basic human needs—and needs and rights can be used interchangeably here—is highlighted by Sivard's effort to show what a 5% reduction in the arms race (the sum of $17.5 billion) could do. She calculates that these same resources could alternatively be used to pay for: (1) A vaccination program to protect all infants from infectious diseases; (2) a program to extend literacy to all adults by the end of the century; (3) improved delivery of medical care to rural areas, through the use of medical auxiliaries; (4) increased aid to enable Third World nations to grow more of their own food; (5) minimum housing for the urban poor in the poorest countries; (6) food supplements for 200 million malnourished pregnant women; (8) 100 million new places in primary schools; (9) hygienic water supply systems for more than a billion people who now lack access to safe drinking water.

Hardened realists may dismiss Sivard's exercise as irrelevant to the cold world of geo-strategic interests. They may insist that welfare concerns such as these do not fall within the parameters of the game of nations. But these same so-called realists are also prone to accuse Socialist or Third World regimes of being indifferent to the "rule of law" both within their own societies and in international life. Here again, however, the problem of selective moralizing intrudes; for, by the same logic, is not the insistence that all societies embody Western

democratic norms a distortion of the cold game of nations, an introduction
into it of equally "inappropriate" demands and doctrines?

Second, a threat to human rights arises when the military seizes direct
political power, particularly in Third World states. The factors that spawn
military interventions in politics are doubtless complex. In some cases, civilian
institutions and elites have failed to govern effectively; in others, disadvantaged
minorities disproportionately represented in the military seize power in order to
overthrow established patterns of ethno-stratification (e.g., the military in Syria
is principally composed of the minority Alawite sect): in still other cases, there
is a lingering tradition of warriors or officers as wielders of political power. All
these may be strictly "domestic" factors, but they are not the only ones:
worldwide systemic factors are also involved. The global military culture which
pervades the existing international system makes it legitimate, and sometimes
seemingly essential, for officers to seize political power. Just as a legally-minded
culture aggrandizes the power of lawyers (witness the power of lawyers in the
United States), so also a world military culture, in which the two most powerful
nations are the leading disseminators of military skills and hardware, emphasizes the comparative advantage of the soldier.

Yesterday's more "liberal" international system, dominated by Western
norms and values, brought to power non-Western intellectuals who mastered
the metropolitan symbols and values. The rising power of the military in
developing societies—it is estimated that four out of every ten Third World
states are now ruled by military forces—mirrors an unmistakable trend in world
culture toward greater militarization. And whenever it has been established,
military rule has almost invariably meant greater repression, greater unwillingness to allow dissent and open politics, and a more marked contempt for life
and liberty. This holds for "leftist" Ethiopian soldiers as well as for "rightist"
Brazilian officers.

The capacity of Western societies to sustain massive military establishments
while preserving civilian control cannot be replicated in Third World contexts,
where the boundary between military and civilian sectors is increasingly blurred. For quite some time, a peculiar doctrine, subscribed to by many Western
analysts and policy-makers, dismissed the importance of the military's rising
power in Third World states. Because the military was thought to be an efficient, modern sector in this view, its ascendance to political power was thus
seen as a sign of modernization. The costs to civil liberties, human rights, and
the quality of public life were thought to be rather marginal, for it was believed
that military rulers were just like their civilian counterparts. It was never clear
why the crushing of civilian politics in the Third World, which surely would
not be so lightly taken in the West, was dismissed as of minor concern. The explanation probably lies in the presumed incapacity of Third World societies to
produce decent politics anyway, and in the lure and logic of technology, which
convinces outsiders that any sector which is modern enough to handle military
equipment can successfully perform other tasks as well. This, of course, assumes
that the task of politics is technical control, that order and hierarchy are its
central virtues, that we should welcome the men in uniform because they have

a surgical solution to the "uncertainties" and confusions of public life. By this logic, Brazil becomes the ideal model for other Third World states, because it represents a system which, as Richard Falk points out in his discussion of "brazilianization," circumvents the "risks" of politics and substitutes for it the discipline and hierarchy needed for an inegalitarian economy.[8]

The domestic conditions that propel the military to power obviously vary from one state to another. But, given a militarized world system in which the military sector has so much pull and glamor, so alarming a claim on large public expenditures, and such an edge in technological development, it will continue to be quite difficult to check the power of the military within individual states. "Atavistic" military interventions—Amin's in Uganda, among others—are not at issue here. This analysis applies, rather, to cases of the Brazilian and Indonesian type, where the military and the technocracy strike an alliance which diverts resources from social welfare to the military and from rural to urban areas—in other words, where the inspiration is a capital-intensive, high-technology vision of development. In such alliances, the military assumes the burden of "pacifying" the population, banning labor unions, and freezing wages; the technocracy is then free to remake society in its own image. The aim is "revolution from above," which requires inhibiting opposition or competition from other groups. (Hence the typical attacks on labor unions and the church.) The motivation is a desire to "catch up" with the more advanced economies, and to enter the world market under more favorable conditions, without the inconvenience of domestic dissent. In short, the military secures stability on the home front, while the technocracy improves the society's position in the global pecking order.

In standard leftist arguments, this "sub-imperial" position is always subsidiary to the main metropolitan centers of the world. But reality is not that simple, for the cases of Brazil and Iran demonstrate the existence of considerable tensions between these rising regional powers and the United States. These include tensions over nuclear ambitions, and economic tensions—manifest in negotiations over oil prices in the case of Iran, and in recent problems concerning subsidiaries of U.S.-based multinational corporations in the case of Brazil. Finally, there is the issue of human rights, which both Brazil and Iran view as a strictly internal affair on which the U.S. has no right to pass judgments based on its own standards.

In a nutshell, Brazil and Iran maintain that "development" is an awesome task which overrides traditional Western notions of liberty. In this view, self-righteous pronouncements by modern advanced nations are a way of superimposing on the "latecomers" to the world of modernization the standards, lifestyles, and values of the first-arrivals whose own atrocities—at least the more blatant ones—now lie behind them. In effect, the advanced nations are accused of changing the rules of the game after triumphing in it, by virtue of the fact that as "first-comers" to the modern world they managed to industrialize without having to meet "harsh and demanding" international standards. Historically, the argument is pretty indisputable. No foreign reporters were on the scene to cover the way American settlers dealt with the native population, no TV cameras were on hand to flash in the endless brutality of the strong toward the weak. The perpetrators of this earlier violence did not have to judge themselves by outside standards of civility and good conduct. Today, however, a world unified by communications denies societies and individuals alike the privacy enjoyed in previous centuries. Compared with the past victims of injustice, human beings no longer have to suffer in silence. If they stand up to oppression, others have an opportunity to listen and to extend a helping hand. The temptation to resist is thus enhanced, for as rebellion begins when suffering becomes a collective experience and, as Camus (1956) wrote in *The Rebel*, when the "malady experienced by a single man becomes a mass plague."

The material and ideological dikes erected by the militarized state against this kind of "collective experience" are formidable indeed. The ideology of national security, wedded to the lure of industrialization, triumphs over the cause of liberty. Even time-honored symbols of national greatness—such as the restoration of the memory of Cyrus and the backdating of the calendar in Iran—are invoked against dissidents, adding the prestige of ancient symbols to the power of the modern industrial quest. By contrast, the cause of liberty is seen as pale and ineffective, imported and inauthentic. A dominant global culture, in which lethal technology and seductive weapons occupy such a prominent place, encourages the tightening of authoritarian rule. While the sermons of outside powers may preach the virtues of liberty, "backward" states which wish to modernize in a hurry inevitably try to telescope history by leaping into the modern world as quickly as possible. A lax population must be "disciplined" if it is to acquire rapidly enough the skills needed to compete in a technocratic international order. Technology becomes a fixation, at once the source of national nightmares and national redemption. If one's neighbors somehow ascend higher on the technological ladder, the threat to the society's material interest and national psyche can be quite troubling. Hence every state must acquire its own bombs, its own breeder reactors, must trust its fate to the militarists and the technocrats, for they alone are supposed to possess the toughness, the training and the discipline to tackle the problems of the new era.

The centers of technological innovation and martial prowess, the sources of most of the world's weapons, and of the culture of weapons as well, are of course the superpowers. The United States is by far the most important entity here; it alone exports half the world's trade in arms; technologically it is, in Zbigniew Brzezinski's words (1976), the world's laboratory. Much has come out of that laboratory which has no doubt enhanced the human condition. However, the constant sophistication of weaponry, the starving of civilian technology, the emphasis on the bigger and the more centralized, are now having counterproductive effects on the genuinely positive achievements and contributions of that laboratory.

Only the most naive and patronizing would want to suggest that Third World rulers who import arms and inappropriately expensive technology are hopeless pawns, unsuspecting puppets on whom the West can dump its gadgets and goods. Far from it. Third World regimes make up their own minds; the days of blatant colonialism are gone, and gone too is the ability to blame Western imperialism for everything under the sun. But the U.S., as a global pace-setter and as a society which claims for itself such a moral mission in the world, bears a special responsibility. The example set by the U.S. as the world's most "successful" society is of considerable importance to the drift of events in that world. It is her concrete acts and choices that will ultimately sway others rather than the rhetorical commitments she makes.

We simply do not know for sure whether a serious U.S. commitment to reverse the trend toward militarization would convince other nations to arrest the growth of their own military programs. Of one thing we can be sure, however: no other nation believes that the U.S. has the right to lecture others on nuclear proliferation or the acquisition of arms, while her own military build-up proceeds without evident restraint. The U.S. may speak the language of Lockean liberty, but she certainly gives every indication of believing in a Hobbesian world.

Other nations, anxious to justify their own behavior in pursuit of their own interests, are quick to identify any gap between the moral rhetoric and amoral politics of others. Consider the following statements made by a number of world leaders to justify their own military ambitions. From the Shah of Iran we hear: "If every upstart in the region acquires atomic bombs, then Iran must have them as well." Muhammed al Quaddafi of Libya foresees the "routinization" of atomic weaponry, predicting that: "Atomic weapons will be like traditional ones, possessed by every state according to its potential. We will have our share of this new weapon." From Prime Minister Desai of India comes a justifiable attack on those who pile up their own weapons while asking others to renounce them: "I can't be a party to people having large atomic weapons in any amount and saying that others shouldn't have them."[9] These examples are not unique. Cumulatively, they reflect the pervasive militarization and the vicious logic of the state system. In particular, they indicate how difficult it is for societies at the center to convince others of the need to renounce those very things with which the major powers in the world have hitherto dominated.

The belief that technology is "value-free," with no accompanying political logic of its own, is strikingly insensitive to the established relation between technics and civilization. The important political choices of the contemporary era are dictated by the logic of deadly weapons, massive and cumbersome technology, and terrifying forms of energy. It is not easy to make the case for freedom in a techno-political order of this kind. Governments understandably anxious to avoid catastrophic errors (or who so claim, in any case) will repress their opponents because the stakes are so large. In such contexts, the language and imperatives of survival can be expected to prevail over appeals for liberty. It is in this domain that the fate of human rights will be determined. The nexus between the war system and technology is our principal trap. Its bequest is the "war society" which envelops us, making the boundaries between what is civilian and what is military increasingly difficult to detect. Robert Nisbet, an able conservative sociologist, interprets (1975) the lure of military society as a sign of political and social breakdown. Supplying its own momentum and possessing an independent ideology, militarism has managed to permeate civilian society with obviously profound and perhaps irreversible consequences:

> War and the military are without question among the very worst of the earth's afflictions, responsible for the majority of the torments, oppressions, tyrannies, and suffocations of thought the West has for long been exposed to. In military or war society anything resembling true freedom of thought, true individual initiative in the intellectual and cultural and economic areas, is made impossible—not only cut off they threaten to appear but, worse, extinguished more or less at root. Between military and civil values there is, and always has been, relentless opposition. Nothing has proved more destructive of kinship, religion and local patriotism than has war and the accompanying military mind. Basic social institutions can, on the incontestable record, survive depression, plague, famine, and catastrophe. They have countless times in history. What these and related institutions cannot survive is the transfer of their inherent functions and authorities to a body such as the military, which has . . . its own dominant values, symbols, constraints, and processes of consensus.

If Nisbet's remarks apply to the Western world, with its relatively democratic tradition and its established doctrine of civilian control over the military, they apply still more grimly to other societies. To address oneself to the issue of human rights without tackling this question is only to scratch the surface, to mistake symptoms and manifestation for deeper, more deadly realities.

TOWARD A JUST WORLD ORDER CONCEPT OF HUMAN RIGHTS

Most discussions of human rights deliberately foster the notion that political freedoms and economic rights to a significant extent represent mutually exclusive goals, and that therefore individual societies are inevitably forced to emphasize one approach at the expense of the other. This essay argues, on the contrary, that political and economic rights are merely different sides of the same coin. In fact, the passages quoted at the beginning of this chapter suggest just how counterproductive it is in practical terms, and how insensitive in cultural terms, to pursue one interpretation of human rights without the other.

Barrington Moore (1966, 1972) has written that the quest for liberal democratic politics and rights is a "long and certainly incomplete struggle to do three closely related things: (1) to check arbitrary rules, (2) to replace arbitrary rules with just and rational ones, and (3) to obtain a share for the underlying population in the making of rules." While much of this essay is critical of these liberal concepts of human rights, I nevertheless firmly believe that the accomplishments of liberalism must be maintained, and I therefore totally reject a certain fashionable argument about the irrelevance of political liberty. That argument is advanced by the left, on the ground that liberty is an unaffordable luxury when one wants to realize socio-economic justice.[10] It is advanced by the right as well on the ground that these freedoms lead to chaos when permitted in inappropriate contexts and cultures.[11] I find both arguments unpersuasive; equally unpersuasive is a still newer argument which burst on the public scene in the early 1970s, and has since won the support of numerous analysts of contemporary affairs. This is the contention that the crises of the "new world order"—overpopulation, nuclear proliferation, ecological threat—can only be surmounted by "iron governments." Robert Heilbroner (1974) expresses this sentiment when he asserts that the contemporary milieu will rally support for leaders and governments "capable of halting the descent into hell." More important, this argument is now part of the ideological baggage of rulers such as Marcos of the Philippines, the Shah of Iran, the Brazilian military. However, these arguments notwithstanding—indeed, precisely because of the very dangers these arguments cite—I believe the case for open liberal politics is as compelling as ever, and that liberty remains the best "response to the fact that we live in a world of uncertainty in which nobody can claim to have found the grail of ultimate wisdom" (Dahrendorf, 1975).

By the same token, equally unpersuasive are efforts to play off political freedoms against rising demands for basic economic rights. The fundamental thesis of this paper is that liberal freedoms, like economic freedoms, are a necessary but not a sufficient condition for building a decent social order, particularly in an age of increasing ecological scarcity.

The opposition to furthering economic rights is predictably portrayed as an appeal to liberty, and as a reaffirmation of the "trickle-down" effect. Then, too, there is the standard argument that egalitarian claims against the rich are unworkable; that equality is not of this world, that its pursuit will bring in its train the twin evils associated with egalitarian pursuits throughout history: a decline in liberty and a decline in excellence and quality. In this view, equality is a radical force that knows no limits: give them an inch and they will take a mile; satisfy the most basic aspirations and the egalitarian tide will bring down the West's liberty, destroy its productivity, and usher in a new dark age.

But this apocalyptic image does not accurately reflect the way choices present themselves in the real world. The elimination of income differentials is not the issue at stake. Inequalities will persist in any order: banish one form of inequality and another—more subtle, more difficult to detect at first—will arise. Take away private property and inequality will creep in through unequal access to state power. This has been the lesson of socialist and communist experiments the world over, and there is no use dodging it or wishing it away. The phenomenon of the "new class" in socialist orders is a sobering one; in its way, it lends credence to the conservative contention that inequality is built into the human condition.

That inequality will be with us is indisputable; the political and moral question is the degree and extent of inequality. No one advocates that Bangladesh's income be made equivalent to America's, or that Chad become another Sweden. To pose the issues on such a grand and abstract level as the desirability of human equality is to mystify them, and to suggest, in effect, that the prevailing order may as well stand by default because the alternatives to it are so difficult to visualize, let alone bring about. A more realistic approach to economic rights is to focus on changes in the present world system which can bring about an acceptable improvement in human welfare by raising living standards for the nearly one billion impoverished people—a quarter of the human race—who reside, for the most part, in the lowest income countries of the South.

Finally, I believe that a concept of human rights which is genuinely appropriate to a just world order must go even beyond the attainment of basic political and economic rights. No concept of human rights is really sufficient unless it includes the freedom to survive without constant threats of mass annihilation and freedom from racial discrimination. To put it somewhat differently, unless the cause of human rights is pursued in an integrated fashion on all these political, economic security and social fronts, more narrowly conceived attempts will inevitably fail to produce meaningful results. On the contrary, in the long run one-sided efforts will merely serve to undermine the political credibility of their proponents and/or the legitimacy of their particularistic values. This is the lesson of President Carter's human rights campaign, with its single-minded focus on political freedoms, and hence its varied reception in different parts of the world.

To integrate all these strands of the human-rights cause will be neither easy, automatic, nor without its compromises and tradeoffs, particularly within the present international system based on sovereign nation-states. The civil and political rights that concern libertarians; the economic rights that predominate in socialist thought and Third World settings; popular aspirations for demilitarization—all inevitably come up against the logic of the state system: its power as well as its limitations.

Nevertheless, there is increasing reason for optimism even within the constraints of the existing system. Save for the most diehard believers in national sovereignty—Afrikaaners who want the world to go to hell, citizens in rich countries willing to turn their backs on the poor, fanatic Third World nationalists who believe the state is the only instrument capable of dealing with the outside world—a more or less universal consensus seems to be evolving on the limits of national sovereignty, particularly where human rights are concerned.

It is ever more clear to people of every nation that the maximalist claims of the nation-state—"this is our wealth we will keep it," "these are our dissidents we will treat them as we wish"—are absurd if pursued too far. President Carter generated a great deal of enthusiasm when he claimed that any state's abuse of its citizens' rights was not solely its own concern but the concern of others too. In a different context but in the same spirit, President Julius Nyerere of Tanzania (1977) has written that "South Africa is an independent state. It is not a colony of anyone, and within the boundaries of the Republic there are no colonies to be granted independence. But its organized denial of human rights to all but 17 percent of its people on the grounds of their race makes South Africa's 'internal affairs' a matter of world concern."

Though Carter and Nyerere preside over radically different societies, and though both are trustees of the concept of national sovereignty, each is clearly recognizing limits to the rights of the state. Both assert that there comes a point at which the claims of the state run afoul of global standards; at this point, they would agree, arguments about "cultural relativity" must stop, and minimum global standards concerning human governance must come to the fore.

No realistic discussion of human rights can ignore the conflicts between cultural relativism and universal norms, between the logic of state sovereignty and the principles of a truly just world order. However, tentative guidelines do emerge from the Carter and Nyerere examples. While it would be folly to assume too great a degree of consensus on human rights (or on anything else), it does seem possible to identify a certain "core of rights," a set of global common denominators which pertain to the effective exercise of human rights at this juncture of world history. They are:

1. The right to survive; hence the concern with the war system and with nuclear weaponry.
2. The right not to be subjected to torture.
3. The condemnation of apartheid; it is accepted that other societies violate racial equality but that South Africa's blatant, officially sanctioned and codified racism is particularly intolerable.
4. The right to food.

Other rights are sure to be added, but the precepts above come close to embodying the maximum feasible consensus at this time. The first "right" is universally felt; it is a "non-negotiable" minimum. The second right, though seen in the present context of world politics as a "liberal right," clearly embodies a universal yearning. There is something particularly repugnant about torture, about one man inflicting suffering on helpless beings who cannot resist. The brutality and the cowardice of the act makes the campaign against torture both morally compelling and politically feasible at this time. At first glance, apartheid seems to be a more "particular" concern, as only the policy of a minority regime in Southern Africa. But both apartheid in South Africa and the politics of the white Rhodesians so blatantly negate the notion of human equality as to pose fundamental challenges to human capacities for justice and fairness. To eliminate apartheid is not to end all racial discrimination but to commit ourselves to doing so. It is to say that even in this cynical and unequal world, checkered as it is with all manner of racial, cultural, and economic inequalities, certain forms and degrees of inequality are simply intolerable. The fourth right, the right to food, is both very old and very new. Basic tribal units honored it, deeming it an inalienable right for all members of the community. Centuries of progress, the tendency to organize larger and larger units, to devote resources to "higher" goals—leisure, transportation, the war system—have obscured that right. Its rediscovery expresses a certain minimum commitment to the less fortunate.

To assert this set of rights at this time is to awaken the sociological and political imagination to more humane ways of governance, to suggest that even in a world riddled with differences, a certain common core of values, concerns, and rights can be discovered.

HUMAN RIGHTS AND SYSTEM CHANGE AT THE GLOBAL LEVEL

No amount of external meddling can construct just and equitable social arrangements in a particular society, create the foundation for a just state, or decree fair ways of distributing the social product. Vigorous indigenous forces must themselves promote such goals. The role of external intervention by individual states is complex. We should, of course, be fearful of intervention by individual states, for such actions are always motivated more by concern for the intervenor's perceived national interest than for the needs of citizens within other polities. At the same time, the four-point ideology of human rights suggested above can certainly be helpful if promoted by an appropriate consort of states, international organizations, and social forces.

On the political level, the possibilities for world community intervention, necessarily limited at this point, can at least provide a margin of needed help which may serve to remind dissident groups within national societies that they are not adrift or alone. Assistance to exiles, for example, is absolutely essential if humane politics are to remain alive, and if potential dissidents are to risk rebellion or oppression. It is doubtful whether outside interventions, particularly of the rhetorical type, can assume the burden of bringing down authoritarian regimes. However, when a particular system depends on outside sources of support for credit, markets or military assistance, it is clearly important to cut off these forms of external aid—if only to undermine the political legitimacy of those in power.

On the economic level, no amount of external transfer is sufficient to put countries on their feet. Ultimately, each society must determine its particular way to provide fairly for the welfare of its own citizens. World Bank estimates tell us that a mere 2% transfer of income from the upper classes in Third World societies to the bottom 40% over a 25-year period would solve the problem of absolute poverty. But given the stacked political deck in most Third World states, the prospects for redistribution on such a scale are not bright at the present time. Most governments either lack the necessary normative commitment, or else they fear that cuts in services and higher taxes will provoke enough middle and upper class dissatisfaction to topple their own regimes. The fate of Allende's experiment is a reminder of what can happen to political leaders who threaten the ways of the rich. Given the drastically skewed distribution of the political and economic resources in most Third World societies, and the state's function as a protector of upper class interests, it is unrealistic to expect the rich to underwrite massive programs of redistribution and societal services—not in the near future, at any rate.

It is here that global reforms and foreign transfers can help to promote human rights as they are broadly conceived. Though not sufficient, such transfers may be a necessary ingredient in developmental strategies which aim to meet minimum human needs. In other words, international transfers can serve as incentives for Southern elites to tackle the needs of the poor by putting new resources at their disposal and thus increasing their capacity to maneuvre and entertain new options. As skeptics will note, there is no guarantee that increased income to Southern elites—as a result of shifts in the terms of world trade, or outright foreign aid—will filter down to the poor. And in a way they are right; there is no absolute guarantee for anything of the kind. New income can be spent on the purchase of weapons or other prestige items which appeal to Third World elites obsessed with catching up with the West. New funds can be used, as in Brazil, Iran, the Philippines, and in Sadat's Egypt, to increase the relative share of the rich. Such are the tough, sobering and tragic realities of Third World states. These realities should be recognized, but they should not be allowed to justify inaction.

In the final analysis, it is up to each Third World society to deal with its own problems on its own political and economic terms, to replace uncaring, uncommitted elites with more just rulers and to construct its own preferred social order. The world community's role is to provide progressive local groups with tangible proof that they do live in a world that not only sets standards for their political conduct, but also sets minimum standards for their economic needs. Western opinion is often curiously insensitive to this kind of paradox. It thinks it is legitimate to intervene in the politics of Third World societies by lecturing them on how they should treat their dissidents, but pleads the principle of "nonintervention" when the issue of Third World poverty comes up. This is a strange contradiction: it postulates a world-order logic based on global norms in the first set of cases, but promotes the logic of national primacy in the second set. This approach postulates the existence of specific responsibilities to the world community on the one hand, but then proceeds to dilute the case for global norms when it comes to the rights of poor states. This is a "cheap" kind of world-order logic that others can easily rebel against, as indeed they have been doing of late. It demands a great deal—laws against terrorism, self-exile from the nuclear club, cooperation at the UN, "reasonable" demands when it comes to the price of raw materials, adherence to Western legal norms—but it gives very little in return. According to this logic, the mischief of Third World regimes is of "global" concern, but starvation is an "internal" matter. It is too eclectic a logic to work. States are told what they can and can't do in the name of world order, but they are not invited to participate in its construction. The architects are trained and the building blocks manufactured in the West. Other peoples are simply expected to inhabit a world made by Western architects and builders, on terms decreed by Westerners according to Western norms.

If the above logic is neither persuasive nor workable, how can others be engaged in the construction of a collective order? Clearly, that order must engage their energies, answer their needs, and demonstrate its concern for their priorities. Otherwise, non-Westerners will continue either to rebel against or to withdraw from the Western-dominated order, rejecting its laws and demands, harassing it whenever they can, or simply slipping into a marginality which breeds violence, anomie, resentment, and hate. The subculture of ghetto violence has a global equivalent. If marginalized, ignored or deprived, states too can snap the links that tie them to outside values and norms, devour their own citizens, harass others, and attack the global order at whatever strategic points may be accessible.

Rebellion is not solely a function of poverty and material deprivation; it can also be a product of affluence. The case of radical German youth demonstrates that the rich too can rebel against injustice; that the complacency of affluence, stripped of a normative commitment to something which transcends individual success and material comfort, can strain the fabric even of wealthy orders.

Material deprivation—whether suffered by its victims, or rejected by those who are better off but still repelled by poverty—does not explain all violence in contemporary life, but surely accounts for much of it. Unless that material deprivation is tackled, the underprivileged cannot be expected to believe that the dominant social order, domestic or global, really cares for them above and beyond a desire to pacify them and confine their violence within acceptable geographical limits through a perfected machinery of law and order.

If the moral incentive to enhance the life chances of over one billion human beings is not a sufficiently compelling argument for a genuine global commitment to eliminate absolute poverty, the quality of world order is a supporting rationale. Unless something is done to demonstrate that kind of commitment, the "world order" that our leaders and statesmen are constantly invoking will remain nothing more than a quest for stability, and that quest will make it difficult for the managers of order to enlist enthusiasm, tap idealism or unleash creative energy. Under the best of circumstances, stability would reign but the quality of order would deteriorate; order would have to justify itself on purely self-serving grounds.

Finally, it must be noted, there is a new consensus emerging concerning globally applicable standards of human rights. The new consensus is based on the view that the construction of a viable world order entails addressing political and economic rights and the taming of the war system; and on the view that there is growing interdependence and mutual vulnerability in the world, and that the symbols and substantive issues that persuade and move must reflect the diversity of the world system and, at the same time, basic human rights for each individual on the face of the earth.

NOTES

1. The World Food Conference Declaration on the Eradication of Hunger and Malnutrition (adopted 16 November, 1974); reproduced in *Alternatives*, I, 2–3, 337–342; reprinted in The Right-to-Food Resolution, Hearings before the Subcommittee on International Resources, Food, and Energy of the Committee on International Relations, House of Representatives, Washington, D.C.

2. I owe this observation to Professor Ali Mazrui.

3. *Freedom at Issue*, January–February 1977, Number 39, p. 12.

4. United States House of Representatives, 93rd Congress, 2nd Session, Committee on Foreign Affairs, *Human Rights in the World Community*, Government Printing Office: Washington, D.C.

5. The proceedings at Helsinki are reprinted in *Bulletin of Peace Proposals*, Number 4, 1975.

6. United States House of Representatives, 94th Congress, 2nd Session, Committee

on International Relations, *Hearings Before the Subcommittee on International Resources, Food and Energy*, Government Printing Office: Washington, D.C., June 1976, p. 117.
7. Emphasis in the original.
8. Richard A. Falk, "A World Order Perspective on Authoritarianism," unpublished paper of the World Order Models Project (WOMP).
9. Passages quoted in *The New York Times*, 29 May, 1977.
10. This recurring theme in leftist discourse is thoughtfully refuted by Michael Walzer (1970).
11. This is the position taken by George Kennan (1977).

REFERENCES

Boulding, Kenneth (1974). The shadow of the stationary state. *Daedalus*, 102, Fall, 100–101.
Brzezinski, Zbigniew (1976). America in a hostile world. *Foreign Policy*, 23, Summer, 65–96.
Camus, Albert (1956). *The Rebel*, Vintage: New York, 22.
Dahrendorf, Ralf (1975). *The New Liberty*. Stanford University Press: Stanford, 5.
Emerson, Rupert (1975). The fate of human rights in the Third World. *World Politics*, xxvii, January, 201–226.
Falk, Richard (1974). What's wrong with Henry Kissinger's foreign policy? *Alternatives*, I, 1, 79–100; also issued as Policy Memorandum No. 39 by Princeton Center of International Studies.
Hansen, Roger (1977). *The United States and World Development, Agenda for Action 1977*. Praeger: New York.
Heilbroner, Robert (1974). *An Inquiry into the Human Prospect*. Norton: New York.
Hoffman, Stanley (1976–1977). No choice, no illusions. *Foreign Policy*, 25, Winter.
Kennan, George (1977). *The Cloud of Danger*. Little, Brown & Co.: Boston, 41–46.
Leontief, Wassily (1976). *The Future of the World Economy*, United Nations: New York.
Mill, John Stuart. *Dissertations and Discussions: Political, Philosophical, and Historical, Volume 3*. William Spenser: Boston, 251–252.
Moore, Jr., Barrington (1966). *The Social Origins of Dictatorship and Democracy*. Beacon Press: Boston, 414.
Moore, Jr., Barrington (1972). *Reflections on the Causes of Human Misery*. Beacon Press: Boston.
Nisbet, Robert (1975). *Twilight of Authority*. Oxford University Press: New York, 191–192.
Nyerere, Julius (1977). America and Southern Africa. *Foreign Affairs*, 55, 4, July, 681.
Sakharov, Andrei (1975). *My Country and the World*. Vintage: New York, 89–90.
Sivard, Ruth Leger (1977). *World Military and Social Expenditures*. WSME Publications, Leesburg, Virginia.
Solzhenitsyn, Alexander (1975). *Warning to the West*. Farrar, Straus and Giroux: New York.
Tinbergen, Jan (1976). *RIO: Reshaping the International Order (A Report to the Club of Rome)*. Dutton: New York.
Tucker, Robert C. (Ed.) (1972). *The Marx-Engels Reader*. Norton: New York, 582.
Walzer, Michael (1970). *Obligations: Essays on Disobedience, War, and Citizenship*. Simon & Schuster: New York.

26
MANIFESTO OF THE ALLIANCE FOR HUMAN RIGHTS IN CHINA

The repression of dissent and the arrest of a number of human rights activists in Peking last April was not unexpected. For one thing, this repression has confirmed the general belief that the authorities in China have no time for legality in any Western sense of the word. The idea that a citizen should be entitled to civil rights, held independently from the Communist Party and the State, is nearly always dismissed as a bourgeois absurdity. The Catch-22 logic of Mao's concept of the "contradictions among the people" was manifested once again: the people do have a right to speak out freely, should fully air their views, hold serious debate on national issues, and write dazibaos (wall posters). But if they go too far, if they abuse that right, they are no longer allowed to exercise it. They become "reactionaries."

The "movement for democratic freedoms and respect for human rights" started in mid-November 1978 and lasted until April of this year, becoming known as the "Peking Spring." As part of their campaign, the activists held public meetings and organised demonstrations in the streets of Peking, as well as in the provinces. Dazibaos were put up on the Democracy Wall at Xidan Square in the centre of Peking. Unofficial publications were sold in the streets.

Among the various publications to emerge from the movement were: The Fifth April Tribune, Today, Bulletin of References for the Masses, Tribune of the People, The Alliance for Human Rights, and Tansuo ("Explorations").

Among the unknown number of those arrested were two well-known leaders of the movement: Wei Jingsheng, 29, electrician, publisher and editor of Tansuo. He is also the author of "The Fifth Modernisation" and "Qin Cheng No. 1," which describes a prison for high-level cadres in the suburb of Peking. Also detained is Ren Wanding, 35, a worker, and one of the leaders of the Alliance for Human Rights in China. Both men have been condemned by the authorities as "counter-revolutionaries," a charge that carries capital punishment.

TEXT OF THE MANIFESTO

On 1 January 1979, the Alliance for Human Rights in China formally proclaimed its constitution in Peking. Its Manifesto of Human Rights was discussed and adopted.

Reprinted from *Index on Censorship* 8, September-October, 1979.

The events of Tiananmen Square[1] which took place in 1976 were fundamentally part of the movement for Human Rights, and this struggle for human rights has a deeper and more important meaning than anything else we can strive for. It is the crucial need of our time. Because of its innovatory and original nature, the movement for Human Rights in China has gained, over the course of the year, the support and admiration of the whole world. It has helped to accelerate the setting up of diplomatic relations between China and the U.S. We proposed the following 19 points in an endeavour to achieve the Four Modernisations[2] and to promote world peace and the cause of progress:

1. The citizens demand freedom of thought and speech. We call for the release of those who have been imprisoned all over the country because of the opinions they hold. It is part of one and the same absurdity that a single person's thoughts (Mao's) are referred to in the Constitution which, together with the Party Statutes, also appoints his successor. This is a violation of the principle of freedom of thought and speech; it negates the fact that each person has a mental process individual to him; it goes against the fundamental principle of physical laws of the "diversity of matter." It represents a feudal outlook, and the people, as a whole, abhor it. The citizens demand a total elimination of idolatry and of the personality cult. Take away the crystal sarcophagus and the mausoleum, and put in their place a simple memorial. Let us solemnly celebrate the anniversary of 5 April each year.

2. The nation demands that effective guarantees be written into the Constitution whereby we have the right to criticise and judge the leaders of the Party and the State. To avoid present and future unrest, to guarantee truth and justice, to develop our productive resources, we demand the abolition of perpetual feudal power which maintains the unyielding criterion that whosoever opposes one "person" [Mao] is deemed a "counter-revolutionary." Let our society be established on the principles of true popular democracy.

3. The national minorities must be granted a real measure of autonomy. China has not only a variety of ethnic minorities but also a variety of parties, and we must take them all into account in order to develop socialism. These parties must take their place within the Representative Assembly of the Chinese people so that different political trends are given a proper platform. When this plurality is not allowed in an Assembly which purports to be the supreme organ of state power, we are in the realm of the ridiculous. It proves, above all, that the Communist party comprises the government, and that the two are inseparable. This is the very opposite of democracy. The citizens of China do not want a sham constitution.

4. We demand universal suffrage in elections for the State leadership, and local leadership, at all levels. A Citizens Committee or a Citizens Assembly must be directly elected by popular vote, and function as a permanent organ of the Assembly, taking part in all its deliberations and decisions, as well as exercising control over the government. The citizens demand that Party and State leaders be subject to legal restraints and punishment when they break the Law.

5. We ask for the following information to be made public, as a matter of right: the projected budget, and the final budget of the State; the national

revenue; the output of agriculture and industry; the military and administrative expenditure; scientific research grants; the total tax revenue; the number of civil servants and their salaries; the salaries of army personnel; the unemployment figures; the amount of social security, work insurance policy and social aid; the foreign trade balance and the amount given in economic and military aid to foreign countries (including amounts given to those parties which are not in power or are involved in an armed struggle); the effective output in each sector of the national economy; statistics on the rate of demographic growth; the number of fatal and non-fatal work accidents; the various foreign policy agreements.

6. The Assembly must no longer deliberate *in camera*. We demand that we may be allowed to freely attend its work sessions, its preliminary meetings, as well as the hearings of the Permanent Committee.

7. State ownership incorporates the means of production, and society as a whole should progressively take them over from the State. Socialisation of production requires a corresponding system of socialisation of benefits. The people must get more of the surplus. We demand to be consulted in matters such as the rate and amount of taxes that industry and agriculture pay to the State. And the State must account for the profits it makes in industry.

8. The Party has already revised its view on the theory and practice of Comrade Tito and the Yugoslav concept of Socialism. A reactionary theory inevitably entails backward productive forces. It is precisely because of the so-called theory hostile to the "road to revisionism" (*pace* the USSR) that our society had to live through a "tragi-comedy" that lasted 10 years. The national economy reached a point where it was on the verge of collapse. Zhang (Chungia) and Yao (Wenyan)[3] allege that the democracies follow the capitalist path while the Soviet Union has turned revisionist; these conceptions both stem from the same theoretical presuppositions. The great changes in domestic and foreign policies which took place in our country in recent years exemplify the theoretical and practical failure of the condemnation of the "road to revisionism" thesis. The polemics and differences that set the USSR and China at odds have already lost their *raison d'être*. The citizens demand détente. The Soviet people are a great people. Relations with the U.S. and Japan will become increasingly friendly. So must it be with the Soviet Union too.

9. Finally the citizens demand the application of the Marxist theory which ensures complete individual fulfilment in a Socialist society. The foundation of the political system of socialist countries is a development from the traditional forms of capitalism. Socialist democracy and freedom cannot survive if they turn away completely from the material benefits of capitalist civilisation.

This is an essential truth to be found in the classical texts [sic], and a vital lesson which the Chinese people have learnt from the uncertainties of the last 20 years. We must borrow from the West not only its technology but also its traditions of democracy and culture. Once the ideological shackles are broken, the breath of freedom will pass over everything. Let the Chinese people enjoy their share of the treasures of humanity. Let the generations that have suffered benefit at long last from freedom, and let the younger generations be forever spared the miseries of the past. All class prejudice and lying propaganda must be eradicated at the source.

10. Citizens must be free to ask for information and material from foreign embassies, and be able to express their opinion to foreign journalists. Everyone should have access to works of art and to films now reserved for internal use;[4] all are equally entitled to enjoy culture. We should all be given the right to foreign radio and television programmes. We demand of the State that it keeps its pledge in the Constitution to uphold a genuine right for any person to publish and print freely.

11. We call for the utter rejection of the system whereby people are allocated to work units for life. We call for the freedom to choose our jobs, to move from place to place, and to be able to dress according to our own taste. We call for the abrogation of the iniquitous regulations whereby couples are separately allocated to different places of work, thus preventing them from being able to live together. Party cadres too, demand to be free to change their postings. Persons who are bound by the State Secrets Act must be able to enjoy the freedom to love and marry the person of their choice, like other citizens. School graduates must be allowed to opt not to live in the countryside. We denounce the use of coercive administrative procedures to ensure the use of birth control and other prescriptive measures. Unemployed persons claim the right to state benefits.

12. The "educated youths" from the State Farms must be given the right to leave if they wish. They also demand an end to the inhuman treatment of which they are victims in the countryside. They claim political equality, an improvement in living conditions, and a rise in their salaries.

13. We demand a guaranteed minimum quota of wheat for the peasants.

14. We demand that the State ban the dishonest procedures used for the recruiting of different categories of personnel. Legislation must be introduced to penalise cadres who deceive people. The practice of bribe-taking must be repressed, and particularly those who receive bribes should be singled out and punished.

15. The process of modernisation must be closely fostered, and political decisions implemented. The State must improve the system whereby victims of false allegations, legal injustice, and bureaucratic mistakes can lodge complaints to appeals tribunals. There must be an extension of scope for these tribunals to deal directly with appeals submitted to them. The Law must punish persons who perjure innocent people. We demand that the State at last applies the policy decided upon immediately after the liberation in 1949 with regard to officers and soldiers of the Nationalist Party.[5]

16. The Secret Police and Party Committee members in the work units have no legal right to arrest citizens, or to launch investigations. They have no right to spy on innocent people or to be called as outside witnesses. The Secret Police force must be dismantled.

17. We demand an end to the shanty towns, the enforced cohabitation of persons of three generations under the same roof, the enforced cohabitation of young male and female adults. Tickets for entertainments should not be

distributed through (Party) organisations. There should be free access to all national and visiting exhibitions. Political control over education must cease. The examination system should impose equality for all candidates.

18. We are "Citizens of the World." We demand that our borders be opened. We want commercial and cultural exchange, and the right to export our labour force abroad. We want the freedom to leave China in order to study on a semi-study, semi-work basis. We demand to be able to travel freely, and to take care of our own prerequisites.

19. The Alliance appeals for support from the Chinese masses, and from human rights organisations throughout the world.

Founding members: Ren Wanding, Zhao Xing, Xing Guang, Li Guangli, Quan Wei, Song Yi, Li Wei, and 2 other comrades.

NOTES

1. A reference to the Tiananmen demonstration of 5 April 1976. This demonstration, which was condemned at the time by the "Gang of Four," was officially pronounced to have been a "revolutionary action" in November 1978 by the new leadership. At the time, the police dispersed the demonstrators by force.

2. The programme for the modernisation of industry, agriculture, science and technology, and the army.

3. Two members of the "Gang of Four."

4. Books, films, etc. to which only Party cadres have access.

5. The policy referred to is one of a general amnesty.

27
COMPARATIVE PROTECTION OF HUMAN RIGHTS IN CAPITALIST AND SOCIALIST THIRD WORLD COUNTRIES

Richard Falk

> *In the economic policies of the government, one finds not only the explanation for its repressive crimes, but also a greater atrocity which punishes millions of human beings with carefully planned misery. . . .*
>
> —"Open Letter" by Rodolfo Walsh to the Argentinian junta

With colonialism gone, the separate states of Africa and Asia have moved in diverse directions. The states of Latin America, despite some notable differences in terms of formal status, ethnic identity of ruling elites, and resource endowments, share sufficiently their national challenge and international difficulties to deserve to be joined with the states of Africa and Asia in a single inquiry into "the Third World." Formal independence has not, in many of these instances, brought the blessings expected. New forms of external control and influence have emerged, both more subtle and, possibly, more disruptive, perceived collectively under the vague label of "neocolonialism." Perhaps more disturbing is the degree to which Third World peoples in this period celebrated for the collapse of colonialism have found themselves yoked to new forms of internal oppression, in some instances far more terrifying and comprehensive than anything they had experienced at the hands of foreign masters.

Another source of disappointment was the American role in the decolonialization process. The United States, with its own war of independence and liberal tradition, might have exerted a benign influence on the transition to independence. Instead, geopolitics intruded to place the United States on the colonial side of the struggle, and afterwards, in the postcolonial settings of Asia and Africa and in Latin America, the United States engaged in interventionary diplomacy generally on behalf of authoritarian political solutions that were, in many instances, more inconsistent with the realization of human rights than other plausible options.

This trend toward oppressive rulership is evident in all parts of the Third World. Its perception is usually interpreted, by way of an ideological filter, as

Reprinted by permission from *Universal Human Rights* 1, April–June, 1979.

"socialist" (or "communist") or "capitalist." In both sets of cases the realities of oppression are evident, as is the characteristic tendency to enlarge the role of military influence and technique in the administration of power. Militarized politics is the most characteristic expression of oppressive rule in the Third World.

A focus on human rights represents an attempt to specify the standards of nonoppressive rule as an entitlement of all peoples, whatever their stage of development, cultural heritage, ideological persuasion, or resource base. In effect, the claims embodied in human rights take precedence over the prerogatives of state sovereignty, and acknowledge the oneness of the human family as a normative premise.

The developmental crunch in the Third World has generated a wide array of authoritarian political solutions. These solutions invariably violate prevailing conceptions of human rights, although to different degrees. The central argument of this essay is that the economic premises of authoritarian solutions are an important, although not necessarily in each instance a decisive, determinant of the degree of authoritarian severity. Socialism and capitalism, although each is manifest in a variety of forms, provide the ideological underpinnings for the principal choice between developmental options. Comparing the record of socialism and capitalism with respect to the protection of human rights seems like a useful way to consider whether there are any systemic regularities that flow from a given ideological orientation.

The choice of ideological labels raises some difficulties. It would be possible to categorize regimes by the simple "left"/"right" distinction. However, the ideological leanings of these regimes are better understood if directly identified with attitudes toward economic policy, the role of the market, of private enterprise, and of developmental priorities. Here, the affinities of Third World regimes are generally clearly drawn from "Marxist-Leninist" roots or from some adaptation of capitalism, although the latter orientation is not generally proclaimed as such. It is sometimes contended that the term "fascist" covers one or another form of authoritarian rule.[1] Some Third World governments that possess a capitalist attitude toward development disguise it for public relations reasons beneath a socialist rhetoric. Some Western ideologues prefer to call these "left" regimes "communist" rather than "socialist." The issue of nomenclature should be faced in a vigorous fashion at some point, but it is not important for the analysis that follows here.

On balance, "socialism" and "capitalism" seem like the most convenient noninflammatory ways to emphasize the links between authoritarian and development choices in the Third World.

The position taken here is that there are distinct virtues and vices attributable to capitalism and socialism in the context of Third World countries. The relative importance of these virtues and vices is difficult to assess—how does one rate, for instance, the greater economic equity of socialist systems against the greater cultural openness of capitalist systems? There is no satisfactory way to objectify such analyses. I arrive at the uncomfortable conclusion that the human rights records of both socialism and capitalism are so poor in the Third World at this point that it is quite unconvincing to insist that one approach is generically preferable to the other. This conclusion is so uncomfortable because it seems clear that only socialism has the capacity to deal with mass poverty in the short run, and surely economic deprivation is a key element of human rights. However, the transition costs of moving to socialism have turned out to be so heavy, the absence of any tradition of checks and balances or pluralist politics and culture have made the administration of power in socialist states so totalitarian, and the effectiveness of control has been so great as to make popular control over a socialist state so difficult to exert that we cannot conclude, with confidence, that a given Third World society is better off "socialist." In effect, my position is that socialism *as applied* to date in the Third World deprives it of the moral advantage associated with socialism *as theory* or as an ideological perspective.

Surely, capitalism is not attractive, in general, from a human rights viewpoint for a Third World country. Its capital-intensive approach to development does not generally improve the relative or absolute poverty of the masses. The productive process, oriented around profits and foreign exchange earnings, tends to satisfy the cravings of the rich rather than the needs of the poor. In addition, when the masses are poor and excluded from the gains of the economy, as is the case in Third World capitalist economies (with some minor exceptions having special explanations), then a *structural* tendency to repress exists. There is no way to assure long-term stability in such a societal setting except by intimidating and repressing those who are victimized by it. Thus, while socialism cannot be preferred, given its record, capitalism is a recipe for doom, unless the country is exceptionally endowed with resources, including skills and leadership abilities, and even then, as the case of Iran illustrates, the results of a capitalist orientation may be national disaster.

In effect, from an ideological perspective, socialism is the preferred system for a Third World country, but its record in practice is too poor at present to support the preference. From the viewpoint of human rights the prescriptive challenge is to reconstruct socialist practice so as to achieve greater overall protection of human rights, or alternatively, to comprehend at the level of theory the consistent betrayal in practice of socialist ideals.

Even without the developmental crunch, we would expect to encounter widespread repression in the Third World. Indeed, the integration of society by the bureaucratic state is itself coercive to a degree. In the circumstances of many Third World countries, lacking a recent tradition of political competition, the mere structure of state power creates a strong disposition toward repression, especially given the diversity of antagonistic ethnic elements contained within many Third World state boundaries. And yet, the whole point of the socialism/capitalism debate is the contention that some forms of repression are better than others in terms of the stakes, as well as the identity and proportion of winners and losers. The deep structure of oppression is important to appreciate, if only to undergird an inquiry into reasonable expectations for human rights goals. Other structural explanations of repression will be mentioned, as well. "Intermediate" structural explanations place weight on the international system, making the propensity to repress at the state level a consequence of patterns of transnational domination (e.g., imperialism, neocolonialism) at the global level. Finally, manifest structural explanations of repression place weight on the pathological makeup of those who emerge as the primary leaders of a modern state, given the competitive struggle for dominance within political elites.

This article proceeds as follows. It considers, first, the structural explanations of repression associated with statism, and refers briefly to those associated with imperialism and personal pathology. Secondly, it seeks to put the Third World human rights situation in the context of the debate between socialism and capitalism. Thirdly, it tries to identify a conception of human rights that follows from this concern, as well as from a diagnosis of Third World priorities and trends. And fourthly, it briefly illustrates the distinctive patterns of human rights failure appropriately associated with socialism and capitalism.

DEEP STRUCTURE

Simone Weil notes "What is surprising is not that oppression should make its appearance only after higher forms of economy have been reached, but that it should always accompany them."[2] In particular, socialism and capitalism as the dominant modes by which "higher forms of economy" are organized have, in this most fundamental sense, been oppressive. As Weil argues in her essay, oppression is associated with the organization of any complex social order, both through its dependence on leadership and bureaucracy to administer an unequal division of labor and by its necessary sponsorship of a dynamic of power by which only a privileged few exert control over the masses, ultimately by reliance on armed might. In this regard, the crystallization of power in the coercive state assures the persistence of oppression in this fundamental sense, and seeks to endow oppression with legitimacy. As Stanley Diamond, Marvin Harris, and Simone Weil each contend, the only instances of nonoppressive social orders are primitive forms of social organization that do not depend upon or lend themselves easily to coordination of effort and status differentiation. It is significant to note that there is virtually no support in the Third World for a destructuring of state power so as to achieve nonoppressive social orders. Gandhi's original vision of India after independence came closest, perhaps, and yet it never had much of a chance, given the overriding drive to build a modern state that could respond to domestic expectations of economic growth and modernization, as well as protect the autonomy of India against a hostile and unpredictable outside world. At this time, the deep structure of oppression is accepted by most advocates of human rights as an inevitable ingredient of modernism.

Marx clearly perceived the incompatibility between statist organization and liberation, as is evident in his celebrated prediction that the state would wither away in a communist society. However, the failure to address seriously or even to understand the tremendous resistances to the dissolution of the state in the socialist phase of societal evolution has restricted the usefulness of his deeper insight. There is an odd dichotomy in Marxist thought: in the distant postrevolutionary future we have a theory of the non-state; in the immediate postrevolutionary future we are saddled with a theory of the superstate, that is, with a legitimated dictatorship that is regarded as necessarily coercive, operates in a political vacuum, and so is not even ideologically insulated against its own intoxication with power. In country after country during this century, Marxism-Leninism in practice has led to systematic abuse of power, ossified in a variety of bureaucratic centralist governmental forms. In fairness, the ferocity of capitalist responses to socialist triumphs created an unanticipated priority for national security that inevitably hardened the state, and lent credibility to the preoccupation with internal and external enemies.

More modest than Marx, nineteenth-century liberal philosophers who set forth the creed that dominated the bourgeois state of northern Europe and North America were content with the notion of setting up a balance between different parts of government and between the state and its citizenry. Market mechanisms, as well as the sanctity of private property, were intended to create a private realm relatively secure against encroachment by government; the minimum state, rationalized by laissez-faire economics and morality, as well as by a skeptical account of human nature, was conceived to provide sufficient guidance and security for the polity without endangering the autonomy of its citizenry. Here again, however, the prescriptive vision gave way to social forces that have witnessed a steady accretion of state power as vast bureaucratic establishments have arisen, partly to assume the welfare tasks accepted by the political leadership of capitalist societies as the necessary alternative to a revolution from below. Built into the capitalist ethos is an acceptance of inequality, exploitation, and hierarchy, as well as the continuous struggle for power within and among states, necessitating a police system within the state and a war system within the global realm, realities consistent with the maintenance of oppressive structures at all levels of social intercourse.

Doing away with oppression in these fundamental senses seems tantamount to an insistence on doing away with capitalism and socialism as basic modes of social, economic, and political organization. Each of these ideological traditions is challenged on its grounds by antagonistic subtraditions that condemn the corruption of what exists in the name of capitalism and socialism as a betrayal of an underlying libertarian promise. Such libertarian critiques (ultra-individualism on the one side, anarchism on the other) call for revolutionary dissolutions of state power. These critiques are generally dismissed with scorn by mainstream opinion as lacking political credibility as well as lacking any capacity to keep order in the wider and complex social settings of the modern world. Nevertheless, the popular appeal of these radical countertraditions abides, especially in the affluent postindustrial sectors of world society, where it is increasingly understood that the reality of the modern state makes oppression inevitable.

In many African and Asian countries the challenge of state-building after formal independence unleashed dangerous ethnic antagonisms that had been bottled up or used as a divisive tactic during the colonial period. These antagonisms, combined with the drive of ruling groups to build strong states capable of standing on their own, helped produce an authoritarian "fix" in many countries. This "fix" was virtually inevitable in those states where one ethnic group captured all or most state power at the expense of others. Thus, even without the developmental crunch some strong reasons for the spread of authoritarian rule exist.

"Deep structure" also relates to the special overlapping claims of self-determination in which rival nationalities appear to seek exclusive, or at least dominant rights, within a given territorial state. The rival claims of Israeli and Palestinian self-determination, or of white and black claims in South Africa, illustrate this underlying structural situation. In such a situation, the dominant claimant must repress the subordinate or revisionist claimant so as to sustain the structure. The severity of repression reflects the actual and perceived relation of forces, as well as tactical judgments of elites as to the effects of differing techniques for exerting control. The structural basis of repression is reinforced by prevailing Hobbesian views of order that premise effectiveness on physical force and control. As a result, efforts at compromise are generally not made voluntarily, but only under pressures generated by violence. A closed loop of escalating violence is created by the action/reaction dynamics of antagonistic claimants, perhaps broken over time by exhaustion and disillusionment.

In the interim, the dominant elite is faced with a security dilemma. If it softens its approach, it makes itself feel (and quite become) more vulnerable to the destructive impulses of its rivals. If it remains hard, it unwittingly encourages its rivals to rely on brutal means and to seek total victory for itself. The structural quest for state sovereignty at the expense of an alien people seems inconsistent, at once, with either compromise or nonrepressive forms of political order.

In addition to "deep" structure there is an "intermediate" structure of transnational influences that tips the exercise of power at the state level in a repressive direction. The role of multinational corporations, arms sales and training programs, and covert operations all exert an antidemocratic interventionary influence. This feature of politics can be best understood in terms of "spheres of influence," "neocolonialism," and "imperialism," various names for patterns of domination by which rich and powerful elites in the North exert control over political life in the South. The direction of this influence is repressive in the sense that the external elites seek to maintain stability and to keep their dependable friends in power, as well as to assure access to resources, markets, and base rights. Only a dependent national elite or one isolated from nationalist consciousness would accept such an arrangement; its stability depends not so much on legitimacy as on its coercive capabilities to intimidate.

Finally, there is a structural bias toward repressive rule associated with leadership. The struggle to be primary leader in the intense political life of most Third World states seems to emphasize a commitment to nonmoderate forms of competition. The personality type that prevails in such competition tends to be acutely sensitive to the threat of displacement by others who might be equally unscrupulous. Hence, there is little toleration of oppositional activities or dissent. The leader may carry such intolerance to pathological extremes, but it is a pathology that is partially induced by the nature of the power chase in Third World polities.

These elements of deep structure are aggravated in the contemporary period by the character of military technology. The Third World, in particular, is victimized by the dangers of nuclear technology over which it has no control. Superpowers use space and oceans to establish their earth-girdling security systems, and expose the planet as a whole to enormous risks. Also, global patterns of industrialization result in disproportionate claims on energy and other earth resources by non-Third World societies. As well, dangerous environmental hazards result and are "exported" to Third World pollution sanctuaries or are "externalized" to inflict various degrees of harm on the planet as a whole. In addition, the shifting economics of productive enterprise is inducing shifts to more dangerous technologies (e.g., nuclear power). The Third World is a passive participant in the process of technological and lifestyle choice going on in the North and yet will suffer the consequences. To wit, repression as an international structure is real, even if not fully perceived.

At the same time, although deep structure conditions political prospects, it does not preclude certain forms of progress with regard to human rights.

IDEOLOGICAL AFFILIATIONS IN THE THIRD WORLD

The specific identity of a national political system can only be provisionally established by whether it is classified as "socialist" or "capitalist." Such labels may be more or less descriptive of actual patterns of organization and underlying approach to governance. Many governments in the Third World have evolved distinctive economic programs, allowing private economic initiative in some sectors, while reserving others for state ownership. Others have opted for hybrid ideological and political approaches. The declaration of Nigeria's Olusegun Obasanjo that "[n]o African country is about to embrace communism any more than we are willing to embrace capitalism" is also part of the picture.[3] Regardless of their internal development strategy most Third World governments seek to project an international image of nonalignment so as to safeguard their political independence and discourage meddling by the superpowers. Third World leaders of almost every persuasion are eager to avoid getting caught in the maelstroms of geopolitics; this preoccupation undoubtedly lay behind General Obasanjo's remark and, more widely, explains the widespread controversy in the Third World over Cuba's African presence, because whatever else, Cuba is aligned. Nevertheless, ideological orientation as capitalist or socialist does seem to have a significant bearing on the degree to which the economy and development strategy of a given society will accord priority to meeting the basic needs of its population as a whole. Despite the immense pressure from the United States, recent studies support the view that Cuba under Castro has done exceptionally well by needs criteria, even as compared to Mexico, and despite a host of other economic failures.[4]

We draw a fundamental distinction in this essay between doing away with repression and securing respect for human rights. Neither capitalism nor socialism is responsive to the fundamental challenge of the repressive state, but the enterprise of human rights is more modest, less ambitious in its goals, far less drastic in its diagnosis. The satisfaction of human rights claims does not purport to challenge the legitimacy of statist modes of organization, and in fact is endorsed by governments of all ideological persuasions. Therefore, human rights can, in principle, be realized in any state, whether rich or poor, whether organized along socialist or capitalist lines.[5] Recently, specialists in human rights, sensitive to ideological dualism in our world, have been striving to identify a set of core rights that reflect the professed values of both socialism and capitalism as operative global ideologies and not give priority to what one, but not the other, ideology regards as important.[6] Such a search for what is mutually compatible does not mean identifying the lowest common denominator acceptable to both ideologies. As "human rights" were formulated intitially as a dimension of liberal, capitalist ideology, what has been required is the elimination of those aspects of human rights that pertain *only* to capitalism (e.g., rights to property) while adding those rights that have been protected heretofore only in socialist conceptions (e.g., rights to basic human needs).

Against this background, a capitalist, liberal-democratic undertaking like that of Freedom House, which publishes its annual freedom map, is increasingly scorned as a tool for appraisal because of its ethnocentrism.[7] As Fouad Ajami persuasively argues, any approach to human rights that rates South Africa higher than Cuba or Tanzania is not worth much. Even President Carter's approach to human rights widens the conception to give lip service to "vital needs" (food, shelter, health care, and education) as one of the three areas within which to assess the human rights record of a particular country.[8] Socialist orientations, then, have attained sufficient legitimacy that even the main capitalist country incorporates their principal tenet into its conception of human rights.

Not only must the conception of human rights be broadened to take account of socialist perspectives, it must also be deepened to include international structural issues. The attempts to achieve a new international economic order are part of the struggle for human rights in the present world setting. Even the notion of "basic needs" can be regressive unless associated with the international, collective expression of economic rights (for countries, as well as for the poor in countries) prefigured in the UN Charter of the Economic Rights and Duties of States. Surely part of the squeeze on Third World societies comes from "neocolonial" patterns, as well as from distortions of international economic relationships reflecting longer term differentials of power, wealth, prestige.

It is also increasingly unacceptable to overreact to the socialist critique of Western liberalism by going to the opposite extreme of associating human rights exclusively with basic needs or economic rights, conceived of as the material bases of minimum human existence. In the development debate going on in the Third World there was a widespread tendency some years ago to repudiate the political side of the human rights agenda as formal Western liberalism that is a dispensable political luxury for most Third World societies, and to claim that the only test of satisfactory government performance is a materialistic one. On the one side are the claims of official technocrats that growth measured in terms of GNP is what counts, and on the other side are the claims of disenfranchised intellectuals that satisfaction of basic needs is the proper measure. An extension of this argument contends that human rights in the noneconomic sense are limited in their applicability to the liberal democracies of the advanced industrial countries in the North. The argument is sometimes coupled with the assertion that Third World countries have always been authoritarian, that repression is virtually predetermined by political culture, or that conditions are not yet ripe for the introduction of more moderate governing strategies. The new leader of Bolivia, General Juan Pereda Asbún, announced that he would rule over "a Bolivian-style democracy in which the armed forces ratified the popular decisions." He justified this assertion by saying that a poor country, filled with illiterate peasants, could not "have the same kind of democracy as that experienced by industrialized countries."[9] Similarly, the Shah of Iran often said, in effect, that when the people of Iran began to act like the people of Sweden, then he would begin to rule like the King of Sweden. In more recent years, as the severity of repression has increased throughout the Third World, the claim is increasingly accepted by Third World observers that nonmaterial issues relating to measures of repression are crucial to assessing a government's performance, and even its legitimacy. Now, oddly enough, it is only the capitalist exploiters who intimate the nonapplicability of noneconomic human rights criteria to their national situations.

The Cocoyoc Declaration of 1975, an important expression of recent Third World outlook, declares itself clearly:

> Development should not be limited to the satisfaction of basic needs. There are other needs, other goals, and other values. Development includes freedom of expression and impression, the right to give and receive ideas and stimulus. There is a deep social need to participate in shaping the basis of one's own existence, and to make some contribution to the fashioning of the world's future. Above all, development includes the right to work, by which we mean not simply having a job but finding self-realization in work, the right not to be alienated through production processes that use human beings simply as tools.[10]

Even China, originally exempt from criticism except from avid anticommunists, is being evaluated more recently by reference to human rights criteria additional to those associated with its programs to eradicate deep poverty and gross inequality.[11]

It would seem that socialism is *structurally* better adapted to the realization of fundamental human rights than is capitalism, especially in the setting of the Third World. In a world of resource and environmental constraint, of population pressures, and mass poverty amid rising material expectations and dissolving traditional bonds, the adoption of a socialist model of development appears to be a necessary precondition for the realization of human rights, although it is not of course sufficient. Without socialism there is no prospect of rapidly eliminating poverty, achieving relative economic equality, and imposing limited consumption on the rich. Capitalist models of development necessarily produce a privileged elite that appropriates a large proportion of the capital surplus not allocated for further development, and a substantial fraction of that elite may not even be resident in the country. Furthermore, socialist models tend to be based on national economic autonomy to a far greater extent than do capitalist models, as the roles of multinational corporations and international financial institutions are much smaller and more selective, if they exist at all. Especially in Third World country settings where securing the fruits of formal independence against outside encroachment invariably has the status of a fundamental human right of a collective character, a capitalist orientation seems disadvantageous.

Of course, in practice a given socialist Third World country (say, Cambodia) may compile a worse human rights record than a given capitalist country (say, the Ivory Coast). One political scientist recently indicted "liberal journals like the *New York Times*" for spreading the view "that any group calling itself 'socialist' must be an improvement over the 'corrupt' Lon Nol, Souvanna Phouma, and Nguyen Van Thieu." In fact, Professor Lande contends: "How relatively benign they appear in retrospect."[12] Nevertheless, the structural argument (in both its national and international aspects) holds. A capitalist-oriented polity cannot begin to achieve human rights (as these will be formulated below) unless the country happens to be endowed with exceptional wealth relative to its population, and even then the record may well be deplorable (e.g., Iran, Singapore). Of course, there are those who dispute this structural argument. Daniel Patrick Moynihan, for instance, argues that capitalist Third World regimes "commit abominations in practice; the Communist countries commit abomination in principle." He goes on: "Anyone who cares about human rights will know what type of abomination is the more destructive of those rights."[13]

Mao Tse-tung in an important speech outlining an approach to democratic centralism argued that the problems facing the Chinese government arose from only that four to five percent of the population drawn from "landlords, rich peasants, counter-revolutionaries, bad elements, and anti-Communist rightists."[14] The rest of the Chinese population, Mao went on to contend, were on the side of socialism. Of course, socialist rulers have, in practice, alienated a far greater proportion of most socialist societies, although precisely how large a proportion is difficult to assess. Nevertheless, there is, I believe, a deep insight in Mao's assertion that bears on the relative capacity of socialist and capitalist polities to realize human rights in Third World countries. There seems to be little doubt that the domestic component of "the growth dividend" in capitalist Third World countries goes predominantly to the upper ten to twenty percent of the population (as well as to external elites), widening rich/poor gaps, and in most cases deteriorating the real income of the bottom forty percent at least for a period of some decades.[15] In effect, the mass of the population suffers from a capitalist orientation toward development. This orientation can no longer be successfully legitimated by resting the claim of the rich and powerful on some traditional ground of privilege (e.g., caste, vested property rights), or by invoking "trickle down," "expanded pie" imagery. Only repression works. It is functional for a capitalist Third World country, and it generally assumes an acute form because of the depth of poverty, as well as the high ratio of poor to rich in the overall stratification of the population. For this reason, the extent of coercive authority and its duration and severity do not seem as integral for a socialist approach as for a capitalist approach in a Third World country. However, as we shall note later on, the costs of the transition to socialism seem higher in practice than those of the persistence of a capitalist social order, thereby offsetting to a significant extent the humanitarian structural advantage of socialism.

In essence, both socialism and capitalism will be repressive in most Third World contexts because of the developmental squeeze, requiring capital formation to persist under conditions of mass poverty combined with popular expectations of higher living standards. The distributional priorities of socialist states, as well as the absence of any need to produce "profits," make the squeeze, other factors being equal, both less severe and less exploitative. Again the appeal of a clean generalization gives way to some complicating realities. The capital squeeze in socialist Third World societies, although more equitably distributed in its effects, may be more severe than in capitalist societies because of the greater tendency toward self-reliance and the high priority attached to collective goals (e.g., heavy industry, defense capability).

And there is another factor. Capitalist Third World countries display a far lower capacity than do their socialist counterparts to provide jobs for their populations. The crisis of unemployment and underemployment, intensified by the introduction of profit-maximizing, discipline-minimizing capital-intensive technology, constitutes a pervasive failure on the part of capitalist Third World countries for which no relief is in sight. Even a country as relatively prosperous as Mexico now is able to provide jobs for only about half of the six hundred thousand Mexicans added each year to its work force, and this situation is not atypical for capitalist Third World countries.[16] The severity of the employment crisis is hidden to some extent by not counting the grossly underemployed (i.e., the person holding a superfluous part-time job at a tiny salary) in the ranks of the unemployed. If statistics were recalculated to count underemployed, the ranks of the unemployed in Third World capitalist countries would rise to levels between thirty and sixty percent.

There are some factors pointing in the opposite direction. Capitalist polities maintain certain realms of private freedom to a greater extent than do socialist polities. The ethos of the market, the class affinities of intellectuals and bureaucrats, the importance of sustaining ties to the liberal West all tend toward preserving, by and large, some space for cultural freedom and creativity in otherwise repressive Third World societies. Also, capitalist rulers have so far been somewhat less successful in stabilizing their repressive systems of rule than their socialist counterparts, making it easier to sustain some opposition patterns of behavior.

On balance, it still seems appropriate to argue that, except in very unusual domestic circumstances, socialism is a precondition for human rights in the

Third World, whereas capitalism assures their massive denial. At the same time, in practice the shift to socialism may entail severe transition costs that outweigh its greater equity of operation once established, and its successful domination of political and cultural space may make it virtually impossible to overcome deformations of socialism once they occur in a given concrete instance.

The international dimension of the comparison is also relevant. International capitalism as a mode of organizing the dominant global market makes its own independent, significant contributions to authoritarianism. The role of the United States as the leading imperial actor in the world system uses coercive power to advance capitalist interests, which include biasing developmental patterns in a capitalist direction, by interventionary means if necessary.[17] The Soviet imperial role in Eastern Europe reveals an analogous control process, but the Soviet role in the Third World has, up to this point, been less widely detrimental to the pursuit of human rights than has the American role. This is partly a consequence of the historical circumstance which made the protection of investment, markets, and access to raw materials a vital vested interest for the capitalist West, as exemplified by American leadership, throughout the Third World, and a rallying point of Soviet opposition.

It is possible to draw some preliminary conclusions:

(1) human rights as a focus of normative concern do not extend their reach to the wider structures of repression allegedly inherent in state power or flowing from irreconcilable claims for security and self-determination, nor do they extend to the internal effects of imperialism or of authoritarian personality types to prevail in struggles for political leadership at the state level;

(2) human rights, as a set of limits on the exercise of state power, possess historical origins associated with Western liberal ideology, including the ethos of laissez-faire capitalism, and, as such, generate an appeal that is often suspect in the Third World, although decreasingly so;

(3) reformulations of human rights are seeking to achieve sufficient universality of tone and content to engender respect and legitimacy in all parts of the world, regardless of cultural heritage or ideological orientation;

(4) an acceptable reformulation of human rights in these universal terms will necessarily be eclectic, and will include a synthesis of the equity preoccupations of socialist systems with the liberty preoccupation of capitalist systems (note that capitalist Third World dictatorships tend to preserve some kind of private economic sphere for business enterprise);

(5) nevertheless, the ideological situation is not symmetrical in the Third World, as the objective conditions of mass poverty, aroused expectations, and resource constraints make the adoption of a socialist program of development a virtual necessity except in a few isolated "special cases" (Israel, Kuwait, Taiwan, Venezuela) where affluence or external capital accumulation makes it possible (although not assured) that both the material and nonmaterial elements of fundamental human rights could be realized; therefore, capitalist systems of development should be repudiated per se on human rights grounds, although their performance relative to each other can be assessed;

(6) furthermore, neocolonialist patterns associated with superpower diplomacy, multinational corporations, and international financial institutions reinforce repressive tendencies in Third World capitalist countries to a significantly greater extent than do certain analogous international patterns associated with "socialist imperialism";

(7) no clear lines of normative preference can be persuasively drawn. On the domestic scene, transition and termination costs of socialist forms of development may seem, on balance, more severe for the population as a whole, than do the maintenance costs of capitalist forms; in the end, we are left with the requirement of assessing, at a given point in time, the foreseeable costs of alternative paths of development in the concrete circumstances of each country.

FUNDAMENTAL HUMAN RIGHTS

Having specified some ground rules, we can now clarify the content of human rights that will serve as the criteria for assessing the performance of particular governments. The most obvious starting point of inquiry is the substantial body of international law on the subject. Leaving aside the thorny question of whether and to what extent human rights norms are binding on various governments (including the extent to which the obligations imposed depend on expressions of formal sovereign consent), can we rely on the Universal Declaration of Human Rights (along with more detailed, specialized, and treaty-like instruments such as the International Covenants on Economic, Social, and Cultural Rights and on Civil and Political Rights) as an adequate description of what is to be encompassed by "human rights"? After all, the Universal Declaration is the product of intergovernmental negotiation, it has been widely endorsed and invoked as authoritative in all parts of the world, and it is an eclectic instrument that seems reasonably sensitive to the concerns of both socialist and capitalist systems. The same generalizations apply, to a lesser extent, to the subsequent international human rights treaties. There are several difficulties, however, with these "authoritative" formulations that rest on international law:

(1) the type of eclecticism embodied in the documents of international law includes whatever is *vital to either ideology* rather than what is *fundamental to both*; for instance, Article 17 of the Universal Declaration upholds the right of property, obviously inimical to socialist systems, whereas Article 23(1) affirms the right of everyone to work at a job of his or her choice, obviously inconsistent with the operational codes of capitalist systems;

(2) the rights endorsed include those that can be realized only through the dissolution of the coercive sovereign state and the abolition of the war system; for example, Article 28 of the Universal Declaration states: "Everyone is entitled to a social and international order in which the rights and freedoms set forth in this Declaration can be fully realized";

(3) the corpus of international human rights law is too diffuse in coverage to permit a focus on the most serious, pressing, or correctable violations;

(4) some important "fundamental" human rights are omitted, for example,

rights to survival associated with ecological balance and threats to use weapons of mass destruction;

(5) the normative foundations of human rights are entrusted too exclusively to mechanisms of negotiability and implementation among governments of sovereign states; the legitimacy of naturalist, communitarian, and populist assertions should also be incorporated into the basic conception;

(6) the ideological "bias" embodied in international human rights law is somewhat slanted toward the liberal ideas of capitalist society rather than toward the ideas and ideals of socialism, thereby reflecting the relevant weight of the two ideologies in the negotiating setting, and offers no proposals for rectifying the international economic order.

The Carter administration has proposed a more focused conception of human rights, loosely connected with the international legal norms mentioned above, but incorporating also features of a new global consensus that brings vital or basic needs explicitly into the orbit of human rights.[18] This conception of human rights was authoritatively set forth by the American Secretary of State, Cyrus Vance, in his 1977 Law Day address at the University of Georgia. Vance proposed the separation of human rights into three categories:

> First, there is the right to be free from governmental violation of the integrity of the person. Such violations include torture; cruel, inhuman, or degrading treatment or punishment; and arbitrary arrest or imprisonment. And they include denial of fair public trial and invasion of the home.
>
> Second, there is the right to the fulfillment of such vital needs as food, shelter, health care, and education. We recognize that the fulfillment of this right will depend, in part, upon the stage of a nation's economic development. But we also know that this right can be violated by a government's action or inaction—for example through corrupt official processes which divert resources to an elite at the expense of the needy or through indifference to the plight of the poor.
>
> Third, there is the right to enjoy civil and political liberties: freedom of thought, of religion, of assembly; freedom of speech; freedom of movement both within and outside one's own country; freedom to take part in government.[19]

As Vance observed, these rights "are all recognized" in the Universal Declaration, and yet his formulation of the American approach provides a selective focus. In actuality, the potential suspension of foreign military assistance is correlated with "gross violations of internationally recognized human rights" by legislative enactment. "Gross violations" are defined as "torture or cruel, inhuman, or degrading treatment or punishment, prolonged detention without charges and trial, and other flagrant denial of the right to life, liberty, or security of the person." The Carter administration in 1977 actually reduced aid to only three (Argentina, Uruguay, and Ethiopia) of the fifty-seven countries found guilty of gross violations.[20] It is a selective approach, omitting any reference to the Article 23 affirmation of rights associated with work or the Article 27 affirmation of rights connected with cultural and scientific activity. It provides an appealing compromise between a comprehensive approach and an emphasis on a few items that capture popular imagination at the moment. The Carter administration has consistently employed Vance's categorization in discussing human rights and has organized its annual edition of country reports (as required by congressional legislation) around this conception. As a short-hand, considered from a purely intellectual point of view, this conception facilitates communication, understanding, and mobilization, and it aptly confines its goals to the human rights enterprise of reform within the state system.

Nevertheless, the Vance conception has disadvantages. First, its formulation by American officials limits its international authoritativeness, especially in certain sectors of world society where the United States is seen as a principal violator of human rights. Secondly, it leaves out of account, as does the Universal Declaration, critical rights pertaining to ecological balance and freedom from threats of mass destruction. Thirdly, the application of the Carter approach is slanted by anticommunist domestic pressures and by the overriding geopolitical rivalry with the Soviet Union. This impression is confirmed by the concrete application of the Carter approach; for instance, Carter instructed his representatives in international financial institutions last year to vote against loans to Cuba, Cambodia, Laos, Vietnam, Angola, Mozambique, and Uganda, and other "gross violators" of human rights.[21] Fourthly, the Carter approach, as would be expected, is statist in character, resting its claims of right on what governments do.

A quite different approach to human rights is staked out by the Universal Declaration of the Rights of Peoples, adopted in Algiers on July 4, 1976 (called hereafter "The Algiers Declaration"). This declaration was the outgrowth of efforts by the Lelio Basso Foundation for the Rights of People (an Italian private institute) working in cooperation with especially qualified individuals, in a large number of countries, including representatives of National Liberation Movements.[22] The Algiers Declaration affirms the positive activity of the UN General Assembly, singling out the Universal Declaration of Human Rights and the Charter on the Economic Rights and Duties of States. The Algiers preamble makes a partisan diagnosis, attributing central responsibility for the denial of human rights to "new forms of imperialism" that have emerged in the postcolonial period "to oppress and exploit the peoples of the world":

> Imperialism, using vicious methods, with the complicity of governments that it has itself often installed, continues to dominate a part of the world. Through direct or indirect intervention, through multinational enterprises, through the manipulation of corrupt local politicians, with the assistance of military regimes based on police repression, tortures and physical extermination of opponents, through a set of practices that has become known as neo-colonialism, imperialism extends its stranglehold over many countries.

And to make its position even clearer the preamble goes on:

> May all those who, throughout the world, are fighting the great battle, at times through armed struggle, for the freedom of all peoples, find in this Declaration the assurance of the legitimacy of their struggle.[23]

The operative provisions emphasize the rights of "peoples" as distinct from "individuals"; there is a greater stress on economic liberation and on cultural autonomy. In the background of the Algiers Declaration is a preoccupation with those transnational structures of domination (and their domestic collaborators) that preclude genuine political, economic, and cultural autonomy on a national level, and that have been identified above as "intermediate" structure. The Algiers Declaration is distinctive among human rights documents by the degree of emphasis it accords to international structural factors as explanatory of violations of human rights. Article 27 of the Algiers Declaration also declares that "[t]he gravest violations of the fundamental rights of peoples, especially of their right to existence, constitute international crimes for which their perpetrators shall carry personal penal liability." Rights of resistance against internal oppression are also affirmed, including the right "in the last resort" to use force as specified in Article 28. This emphasis on criminal accountability of repressive leaders and on rights of popular resistance is also distinctive in the human rights context.

The Algiers Declaration has several advantages over the Universal Declaration or the Carter approach. First, it extends the coverage of human rights from individuals to peoples and movements. Secondly, its diagnosis and prescriptions pointedly reflect the actual content of Third World concerns, and its promulgation at Algiers gives its existence a more genuine Third World flavor, which is appropriate given the preponderance of peoples and countries in the Third World and their minimal role in earlier formulations of human rights law. Thirdly, it posits a claim that rights can be authoritatively formulated by populist initiative and do not depend upon governmental actions. Fourthly, it assesses the landscape of repression and assigns primary responsibility to the interplay between neocolonialism and struggles for control internal to the Third World, thereby linking up denial of human rights with capitalist dynamics. Fifthly, it introduces ideas of popular rights of resistance and enforcement, and of criminal responsibility, into the corpus of human rights law.

The Algiers Declaration also has several disadvantages, or, more aptly, limitations. First, it is incomplete without incorporation of the traditional corpus of human rights, and yet it never sufficiently clarifies its connections with it. Secondly, the legitimacy of a populist norm-generating procedure is highly controversial, and its claims are ignored or dismissed by most governments and many private groups. Thirdly, the content of analysis and prescription is unbalanced to the extent that it virtually overlooks abuses to the rights of peoples emanating from socialist origins. Fourthly, as with other approaches considered, it fails to depict rights relating to environment and to threats of mass extermination.[24] Fifthly, the auspices of the Algiers Declaration are relatively obscure, and funds at its disposal sparse, as compared to principal governments or even the United Nations, and therefore its position on human rights remains relatively unknown.

Various attempts have been made by individuals to focus the human rights struggle by proposing specific formulations. Moynihan, in the course of attacking Carter's approach to human rights for its tendency to avoid the central ideological struggle, argues on behalf of an antitotalitarian focus, as the priority element in any adequate conception of human rights. Partisanship is the hallmark of Moynihan's approach, and he resents Carter's attempt to equate the pursuit of economic goals with antitotalitarian ones. Moynihan believes that the socialist countries, led by Soviet armed might, "are the most powerful opponents of liberty on earth," professing "the only major political doctrine that challenges human rights *in principle*." For this reason, Moynihan believes that overriding attention should be given to the plight of the "billion-and-a-half" persons who "live in totalitarian Marxist states."[25] Moynihan regards the struggle against socialist forms of totalitarianism as being a matter of survival rather than moral preference: "*Human rights has nothing to do with our innocence or guilt as a civilization. It has to do with our survival*." He views the Vietnam defeat in this light, as a setback in the struggle to halt the expansion of totalitarianism; "it did not end the expansion of totalitarianism, nor yet the need to resist. If anything, it added enormously to the importance of ideological resistance, and this precisely is the role of 'Human Rights in Foreign Policy.'" For this reason, he connects the American response to the Third World with the willingness of specific governments to join in on the correct side of this struggle: "*The new nations must be made to understand that our commitment to them depends on their ceasing to be agents of the totalitarian attack on democracy*."[26]

Moynihan's approach, although substantively almost opposite from that taken in this paper, is notable in at least one respect. It links the conception of human rights to a value-oriented, explicit politics that is appropriately centered on the ideological tension between capitalism and socialism.

However, such a politicized approach has serious drawbacks. First of all, it chooses sides on a basis that is unconvincing, especially with respect to the well-being of Third World people; it overlooks the achievement of socialist societies in reducing dramatically the incidence of poverty and gross income disparities. Secondly, by mobilizing human rights constituencies around an avowedly anti-Soviet interpretation of the central global struggle, it tends to increase international tensions, thereby contributing to an arms race mentality and quite possibly increasing the risk of general welfare without doing anything appreciable to help human rights in the target societies. Thirdly, Moynihan's approach is completely insensitive about the degree to which American initiatives, direct and covert, have contributed to the rise of totalitarianism in the Third World, or about the seriousness of human rights violations at home, or elsewhere in the capitalist First World. Fourthly, this self-righteous, militantly anticommunist emphasis is extremely unpopular with public opinion in most parts of the world and, thereby, does not possess any capacity to mobilize wider international support for human rights concerns.

Another quite different approach has been advocated by Peter Berger. Berger argues strongly that much of the debate on human rights is flawed by its failure to draw a clear distinction between ethnocentric and "fundamental" human rights; only the latter are sufficiently legitimated by underlying cultural values to support an international stature. It is necessary, Berger argues, to reject those claims of right that owe their origins to Western values, and, in effect, to ignore even those rights incorporated in international legal instruments that cannot pass the test of cultural resonance. Therefore, Berger excludes from the fundamental category of human rights those associated with either "political democracy" or "economic rights," contending that these are distinctively Western. Berger restricts the scope of human rights as international claims to those "grossest cases" of abuse that infringe the minimal views of decency embodied in every major world cultural tradition:

> Genocide; the massacre of large numbers of innocent people by their own government or by alien conquerors; the deliberate abandonment of entire sections of a population to starvation; the systematic use of terror (including torture) as government policy; the expulsion of large numbers of people from their homes; enslavement through various forms of forced labor; the forced separation of families (including the taking away of children from their parents by actions of government); the deliberate desecration of religious symbols and persecution of those adhering to them; the destruction of institutions that embody ethnic identity.

According to Berger, "in condemning *these* as violations of human rights, we can call upon a consensus far wider than that of Western civilization. That consensus emerges from all the major world cultures—especially in their religious foundations."[27]

Peter Berger's approach has several attractions. First, it anchors the international affirmation of human rights in a universal consensus that allegedly has identifiable indigenous roots in each principal world culture. Secondly, rooting human rights in values rather than norms premises the basis for collective international action on more promising grounds when it comes to mobilizing genuine support. Thirdly, the concreteness of Berger's list of specific abuses has a mobilizing potential that the more abstract designations each lack, and yet it appears to lack the partisanship that mars Moynihan's approach.

Berger's approach is not, however, on balance, very appealing. First, by placing an overriding emphasis on tradition-based cultural values, Berger's "consensus" seems to reject critical elements of an operational consensus emergent in the Third World outlook, especially its emphasis on basic needs, on economic rights and duties of states, and on the campaign against apartheid; as a consequence, contrary to what Berger claims, his approach *appears* to stress only those concerns that currently agitate the West, and possesses the very partisan character it is so preoccupied with avoiding. Secondly, the Berger list omits some critical universal dangers, including those associated with threats of mass destruction and ecological decay, that seem important to include in a contemporary conception of human rights, regardless of whether they pass the cultural resonance test. Thirdly, the Berger list of fundamental human rights makes no assessment of responsibility as between socialism and capitalism for their abridgement, purporting to rest human rights on a basis that transcends this central, ideological fissure, and therefore deprives the domain of human rights of a principal moral and political rationale; in this regard, cultural consensus as the central tenet of legitimated human rights is insensitive to their potential role on behalf of reformist claims in the international political system. Fourthly, Berger's approach overlooks international factors (e.g., "neocolonialism," interventionary diplomacy) that cause, or at least reinforce, various repressive tendencies, and therefore avoids making structural prescriptions as human rights correctives.

A quite different attempt at a human rights focus is that of Fouad Ajami. He orients his analysis toward the debate about human rights initiated by Carter's approach. He contends that "flawed concepts of human rights" allow the United States to be a human rights champion while at the same time opposing "the New International Economic Order and Third World demands for a fairer distribution of global wealth."[28] Ajami also criticizes Third World leaders who "speak the language of egalitarianism abroad, while they defend systems of acute inequalities within their own boundaries." He regards militarized politics at home as almost invariably leading to severe denials of humane politics, a characterization, he contends, that holds for "'leftist' Ethiopian soldiers as well as for 'rightist' Brazilian officers."[29] In the spirit of the Algiers Declaration, yet with less partisanship, Ajami's approach to human rights seeks to attribute responsibility for their decline to an interlocked series of domestic and international factors. As a consequence, the political roots of repressive rule give direction to Ajami's views as to what needs to be done.

Perhaps the most original, challenging feature of Ajami's approach is to place emphasis on the link between the war system and human rights. He argues that matters of survival (rather than liberty, or even equity) provide the "domain" within which "the fate of human rights will be determined"; "the nexus of the war system and technology is our principal trap." Against this background Ajami affirms an eclectic conception of human rights that seeks to encompass principal sensitivities involving liberty, equity, and survival without enumerating a long shopping list of human rights issues. Ajami emphasizes four sets of concerns that embody "the maximum feasible consensus at this time":

1. The right to survive; hence the concern with the war system and nuclear weaponry.
2. The right not to be subjected to torture.
3. The condemnation of apartheid; it is accepted that other societies violate racial equality but that South Africa's blatant, officially sanctioned and codified racism is particularly intolerable.
4. The right to food.[30]

The Ajami approach is attractive for several reasons. First, it is encompassing and universalistic, yet focused. Secondly, it is sensitive to the main areas of perceived abuse and danger. Thirdly, it stakes out a progressive position, and yet criticizes all sectors of international society without seeking refuge in legalism or moralism. Fourthly, it regards militarization, nuclear weaponry, and threats of mass destruction as core human rights issues. Fifthly, it formulates human rights issues in language that can be translated into political action and goals.

Although I find these positive features generally persuasive, a few reservations about the Ajami approach do exist. Firstly, there is no effort to ground its proposals in the Universal Declaration and other legitimating instruments, although this could easily be done. Secondly, the approach does not focus directly on the link between neocolonial features of the international system and national development impacts on the national level, although the stress on the New International Economic Order (NIEO) could be so interpreted. Thirdly, it doesn't relate the struggle between capitalist and socialist models of development to the prospects for human rights, especially in relation to the rapid alleviation of mass misery in the poor societies of the Third World. Fourthly, its short list of four human rights goals places an emphasis too insufficient on restraining state power to allow it to have a wide appeal at this time.

Jorge Dominguez has attempted to combine the focus of a short list with the coverage of a comprehensive conception. He grounds the content of human rights in the norms of the Universal Declaration on Human Rights, yet he offers an orientation that identifies the most serious violations: "At the top of the hierarchy I would place concern for any identifiable government action that reduces a people's right to life and health. Attention would be focused not only on political massacres, arbitrary action by governments, but also on governments whose identifiable actions aggravate famines and epidemics."[31] The Dominguez image of priority rights is much less crystallized than is the Ajami short list; as such, it leaves more room for interpretative differences. It does encourage an observer to concentrate on specific accomplishments and failures in a given country and, as such, is far more amenable to social science observations or to acceptance by human rights nongovernmental organizations than is the Ajami list. Ajami's list, on the other hand, is more useful for mobilizing change-oriented constituencies, as it is much more responsive to political agendas that dominate international policy-making arenas.

My purpose is intermediate between those of Dominguez and Ajami. I seek a theoretically sound framework for comparison, yet one that yields an understanding that can relate easily to policy debates. At the core of my approach, as has been outlined above, is the conviction that socialism and capitalism are the fundamental approaches to Third World actualities, and that these actualities center on choices of developmental strategy. In the background of developmental choices are some wider issues of world order that also should be brought into the human rights framework, including those relating to cultural autonomy, the war system, and overburdening of the environment.

The content of human rights is obviously controversial. My proposal of five categories draws inspiration from the approaches discussed here. It does not restrict its image of human rights to norms legitimated by intergovernmental consent or, even, by United Nations consensus. Populist initiatives (e.g., Algiers Declarations) can also achieve legitimacy. To focus inquiry, reflection, and policy recommendation, five categories of rights are set forth as a proposal to delimit the subject matter of human rights:

1. *Basic human needs*: the rights of individuals and groups to food, housing,

health, and education; the duty of governments to satisfy these rights, taking into account resource constraints and natural disasters (e.g., drought, flood);

2. *Basic decencies*: the rights of individuals and groups to be protected against genocide, torture, arbitrary arrest, detention, and execution, or their threat; the duty of peoples and governments and their officials to establish an atmosphere wherein these rights can be securely realized, including the protection of the society against paragovernmental violence of various kinds (e.g., "death squads"), taking into account constraints on governmental capabilities and the threats and tactics relied upon by enemies of the state;

3. *Participatory rights*: the rights of individuals and groups to participate in the processes that control their lives, including choice of political leadership, of job, of place of residence, of cultural activity and orientation; the duty of peoples and governments to uphold these rights in ways that provide individuals and groups with opportunities to lead meaningful lives, including the freedom to participate in procedures for the shaping and execution of norms;

4. *Security rights*: the rights of individuals and groups (including those of unborn generations) to be reasonably secure about their prospects of minimal physical well-being and survival; the duty of governments and peoples to uphold this right by working to achieve sustainable forms of national and ecological security;

5. *Humane governance*: the rights of individuals and groups to live in societies and a world that realizes the rights depicted in 1-4; the duty of individuals, groups, governments, and institutions to work toward this end.

Categories 1-3 are fairly standard. Category 4 speaks to the special circumstances created by nuclear weaponry and other military technology, as well as to the situation created by the scale and character of global industrialization; these concerns are a consequence of what has taken place in non-Third World sectors of world society, yet their effects on the Third World are potentially massive. Category 5 is a kind of world order imperative that implies an inability to achieve human rights in 1-4 without transforming the political order that now exists; as such, it extends the boundaries of human rights beyond those set by the state system with its operative code of sovereignty that limits attention to carefully depicted national territorial limits.

This approach does not purport to achieve a rigorous conception of what is a "right," how "rights" inhere in unborn individuals or in relation to protection from policies that risk nuclear war or environmental harm. A theory of right that rests upon the emerging reality of planetary citizenship needs to be developed as an intellectual foundation for the approach advocated here.

Such an approach loses the specificity of a more legally grounded conception of human rights that assesses whether a claim is a right by whether it is potentially justiciable according to some constituted judicial or administrative procedure. The broader approach is less directed at issues of enforceability than of appraisal, the standards relevant for assessment of how far a given polity realizes the elements, as set forth, of humane governance.

It is also important, especially given the focus of socialism versus capitalism, to have some way of capturing phases of the cycle of political development. To simplify matters, three phases seem crucial: initiation, maintenance, and termination. These phases direct attention at essential aspects of ideologically diverse developmental experiences:

1. *Initiation Phase*: the inception of a political system as socialist or capitalist, and its secure establishment as the stable, dominant order. Here, in general, the initiation costs tend to vary with the degree of societal discontinuity, as well as with the relation of internal forces. Capitalist developmental forms are more continuous with colonialist or dependent status than are socialist forms. Soviet and Chinese initiation costs entailed millions of casualties. The initiation phase may also include a period of civil strife that can involve great suffering and loss of life. The Indochina War, carried on against the French, and then against the Americans, should be understood, in part, as a struggle between socialist and capitalist developmental orientations. Outside capitalist forces greatly magnified the transition costs to socialism in Indochina.

At the same time, the initiation costs in Cambodia, relatively more severe than in either Vietnam or Laos, suggest that factors other than ideological orientation broadly conceived can be significant. The prevailing attitude about the construction of socialism in the aftermath of a devastating internal war is a significant variable in the initiation phase. The behavior of outsiders, especially their adherence to norms of nonintervention, is likely to exert a strong influence on the construction of human rights in the initiation phase. Also significant is the "openness" of the society, its readiness to engage in diplomatic, economic, and cultural contacts with outsiders across ideological battlelines. In this regard, Vietnam seems particularly "open," possibly because it seeks to avoid being squeezed between rival socialist superpowers.

If capitalist developmental forms are reestablished, even after interludes of "soft" socialism, as in Indonesia (1965) or Chile (1973), the initiation costs are also likely to be quite severe, suggesting that the degree of discontinuity may be more telling than ideological identity.

Initiation costs are sometimes minimized by allowing "enemies" to emigrate, especially if their destination is distant. However, if exile communities continue an armed opposition, under the protective cover of a foreign state, then the initiation costs can be high and the phase extended for a longer period. Cuba experienced this pattern, being confronted by enemy exiles given encouragement, protection, resources, military training and equipment, and a political presence by a hostile neighboring superpower, the United States. Naturally, such a climate hardened internal security requirements in Cuba, and may have helped generate an internal security apparatus that would otherwise have evolved differently and played a lesser role. Also, we must assume that the extent of Stalinization of Cuban socialism reflected to some degree the extent of the Soviet presence, which was itself largely a reaction against American antisocialist hostility.

Thus, we can say that socialist orientations are generally more discontinuous with the socioeconomic structure of a given country, and hence most likely to stimulate an all-or-nothing struggle. This discontinuity is reinforced by the greater tendency for foreign capitalist states, especially the United States, to support the internal capitalist faction by funds, arms, and advice. As a conse-quence, heavy start-up or initiation costs are associated with the transition to socialism, although most of these costs may be incurred during the armed strug-gle phase which included an anticolonial rationale. Once socialism is estab-lished, then the reestablishment of capitalism will also tend to induce heavy costs during its initiation phase.

Comparing initiation costs of the new order with the maintenance costs associated with the old one is difficult. One observer, for instance, reports thirty thousand deaths in connection with the initiation costs of the Ethiopian socialist regime as of mid-1977, whereas maintenance costs for its predecessor included two hundred thousand victims of the 1972 famine, many of whom might have survived if the ruling elite at the time had acknowledged and com-petently responded to the problem.[32]

2. *Maintenance Phase*: the maintenance of a stable socialist or capitalist order after it has secured control over the apparatus of state power. Here, no issue of discontinuity is present, although a given political form, whether socialist or capitalist, evolves along a broadly varied path. In this regard, even ultra-stable political systems are experimental, especially in their efforts to generate satisfac-tory economic policy. Also, political elites factionalize and struggle, at least within limits, for dominance, especially at times of economic crisis and of leadership succession.

In general, after the initiation phase, socialist systems seem stable in the maintenance phase. The programmatic commitments to equity and the elimination of poverty, as well as the capacity to find jobs for virtually everyone and to orient productive output around needs, lead to a condition of mass ac-quiescence (or subservience). Extreme self-reliance (Cambodia during famine, China after earthquake) suggests that socialist governments may not acknowl-edge disasters even sufficiently to receive outside help that could mitigate the suffering.

Capitalist maintenance is more problematic. The capitalist approach necessarily slights the well-being of the masses and runs contrary to the Marxist economic and ethical consensus dominant among intellectuals and students in the Third World. Because capitalism emerged often with the help and support of "liberal" Western outlooks, extreme repression was not undertaken, meaning that an opposition persists, and is likely to grow, in the maintenance stage. For these reasons, governments like those in South Korea, Iran, and the Philip-pines have to sustain high levels of active repression throughout the course of their existence. The class politics of capitalist development means that the masses must be kept actively disorganized and their leaders intimidated.

At the same time, the pluralist character of a capitalist system, with its private business and cultural sphere, its nominal consumer and intellectual diversity, makes it easier for an opposition to stay alive and flourish. The totalness of socialist control makes it less necessary to repress, yet the control itself is a form of repression. Cuba and Yugoslavia have shown some limited capacity, especially at certain stages, to combine cultural pluralism with a socialist approach to development.

In general, socialism seems to do better in the maintenance phase with economic rights and with those human rights concerned with the avoidance of extreme abuse of the person, while capitalism seems to do better with respect to preserving some cultural and political space for oppositional tendencies and general creativity.

3. *Termination Phase*: the period during which a political system is discarded and replaced by another. The termination phase is analogous to the initiation phase, calling attention to the dynamics of a transition. Whereas "initiation" is located in time as postcolonial (or post-1945), "termination" is viewed as a subsequent phenomenon in which socialism replaces capitalism or vice versa. Also, initiation refers to the birth process, once a particular elite is established in power, while termination refers to the death throes of a particular system.

The essence of termination is the process of getting rid of an abusive or weak regime. We assume that withdrawal of popular consent, via electoral politics, is rarely sufficient, especially in the case of a socialist governing elite. Experience suggests that it is virtually impossible to get rid of socialist regimes once they have managed to get into the maintenance phase and have adopted a "hard" orientation toward the retention of state power. Outside intervention, as in Iran (1953) or Guatemala (1954) can topple a "soft" socialist or socialist-inclined government rather easily.

By contrast, "soft" capitalist governments cannot survive, and have been steadily superseded by harder ones. The evolution of capitalist governance in South Korea, the Philippines, and Iran is exemplary. With the elaboration of bureaucratic structure, internal security systems, and a militarized form of politics, the "hard" capitalist regimes are also becoming very difficult to terminate, even when exceedingly unpopular.

What is true, however, is that oppositional forces remain active, coherent, in struggle in capitalist instances of authoritarian rule. Enough "space" is maintained because of pluralist pretensions and realities; degrees of factional disagreement as to how much repression is necessary also tend to produce periods of reduced repression. Unlike a socialist conception of total control by the state as integral to class rule, the capitalist conception relates repressive rule more closely to functional necessity; as such, it is more reactive, although its bureaucratic structures have a life of their own.

As yet, we have no experience with the termination of "hard" socialist regimes. The attempts of Eastern European governments to evolve in moderate directions and to break away from Soviet domination suggest the phenomenon. The perception is blurred by the heavy element of Soviet imperial presence, blocking termination initiatives. Also, the Soviet imperial issue establishes a legitimated basis for oppositional tendencies except in the most Stalinized of socialist systems.

The approach advocated, then, would suggest the matrix shown in Figure 1. A given government could, then, on the basis of available data be rated on a scale of 1–5 for each category in each phase; lack of data would be indicated by the notation "i.d." (insufficient data); nonapplicability of instance by notation "n.a." (not applicable).

FIGURE 1.

Phases of governance / Categories of human rights	Initiating Phase	Maintenance Phase	Termination Phase
Basic human needs			
Basic decencies			
Participatory rights			
Security rights			
Humane governance			

SOME REMARKS ON APPRAISAL

Of course, the criteria set forth are difficult to apply. Requisite data are either unavailable or uneven. What data exist are difficult to use in any systematic and objective way. It is an immense task to make a careful appraisal for all Third World countries, requiring a staff of specialists. At the same time, one of the purposes of the framework is to propose an orientation for data collection and evaluation projects.

Obviously, a comparison of countries should be as objective as possible, making it desirable to operationalize criteria of appraisal. At the same time, qualitative considerations are often decisive. For instance, a human rights comparison that overlooked Kathleen Gough's finding that workers in a Vietnamese community are far more satisfied with their lives than workers in an Indian community at a similar socioeconomic level would be deficient.[33] So would one that did not assess the relative degree of cultural vitality operative in a given polity.

At this stage, the evidence available enables only crude forms of comparison with respect to the relative achievement of human rights in particular states at particular times. It heightens sensitivity about broad Third World patterns and trends. One way to proceed is to try out exemplary case studies of national profiles of ideological prototypes: for instance, to describe Brazil, Iran, and South Korea for capitalist variants, and to describe China, Cuba, and North Korea for socialist variants. The hypothesis is that these cases would reveal, in addition to their critical, distinctive features, a patterning of developmental dynamics and human rights that would be more or less played out in other country examples. Such a hypothesis is central to the view that ideological orientation is associated with certain structural patterns. This hypothesis need not be deterministic: variations would emerge (due to resources, quality of leadership), pressures may vary (due to mass consciousness, safety valves for opponents, geographical position, attitudes by external governments), policies may reflect diverse antecedent conditions (due to land tenure arrangements, ethnic diversity and structure, prior degree of industrialization, reliance on foreign skills and capital). Nevertheless, the fundamental argument remains: Authoritarian solutions seem virtually unavoidable in most Third World countries over the period of the next decade or so, although their degree and form of severity will vary greatly. In general, socialist forms of authoritarianism are to be preferred to their capitalist counterparts because of a combination of domestic and international factors that have been indicated above, but not unreservedly.

NOTES

1. See A. James Gregor, *The Fascist Persuasion in Radical Politics* (Princeton University Press, 1974); Eqbal Ahmad refers to authoritarian/capitalist regimes as partaking of "developmental fascism"; for a useful review of the question of labeling see Herbert Feith, "Repressive-Developmentalist Regimes in Asia: The Search for Hope," World Order Models Project discussion paper, Poona, India, July 1978.

2. Simone Weil, "Analysis of Oppression," in George A. Panichas, ed., *The Simone Weil Reader* (David McKay Co., Inc., 1977), p. 131.

3. Quoted from the *Boston Globe*, 25 July 1978, p. 6.

4. For careful, well-documented comparison see Jorge Dominguez's contribution to the forthcoming 1980's volume on human rights, Jorge I. Dominguez, Nigel S. Rodley, Bryce Wood, and Richard A. Falk, eds., *Enhancing Global Human Rights* (New York: McGraw-Hill, The 1980's Project, 1979).

5. See Eric Lane, "Demanding Human Rights: A Change in World Legal Order," *Hofstra Law Review* 6, no. 2 (1978): 269–95; H. Lauterpacht, *International Law and Human Rights* (1950), on links between Westphalian system and the realization of human rights.

6. For discussion see Dominguez, *Enhancing Global Human Rights*; Fouad Ajami, "Human Rights and World Order Politics," Working Paper no. 4, World Order Models Project, 1978, pp. 1–33; Peter Berger, "Are Human Rights Universal?" *Commentary* 64, no. 3 (Sept. 1977), pp. 60–63.

7. See also careful categorization of forms of repression in Ernest Duff and John Mc-Camant, *Violence and Repression in Latin America* (Free Pres, 1976), esp. pp. 24–55.

8. Cyrus Vance, "Human Rights and Foreign Policy," *Department of State Bulletin*, vol. 76, 23 May 1977, pp. 505–508; see also manner in which country reports on human rights are organized—"Country Reports on Human Rights Practices," Report of State Department to Congress, 3 February 1978.

9. Quoted from the *New York Times*, 25 July 1978, p. A3.

10. For convenient text see *Development Dialogue*, no. 2 (1974): 88–96; note that rights affirmed here extend beyond what it is reasonable to achieve within the state system.

11. See for example Simon Leys, *Chinese Shadows* (Penguin, 1978); also Donald Zagoria, "China by Daylight," *Dissent* 22 (Spring 1975): 135–47; Susan Shirk, "Human Rights: What About China?" *Foreign Policy*, no. 29 (1977–78):109–127; Jerome A. Cohen, "Human Rights in China: U.S. Should Press Issues, But Not As Barrier to Ties," *Washington Post*, 23 April 1978, p. D2.

12. See Carl H. Lande, "Letter to the Editor," *New York Times*, 25 July 1978, p. A14.

13. D. P. Moynihan, "The Politics of Human Rights," *Commentary* 63, no. 4 (April 1977), p. 24.

14. Mao Tse-tung, "Talk at Enlarged Workers Conference of January 30, 1962," released and printed in *Peking Review*, no. 27 (7 July 1978): 13.

15. See for example Irma Adelman, "Development Economics: A Reassessment of Goals," *American Economic Review* 65 (1975): 302–309.

16. See Philip Russell, "On Mexico," *New York Times*, 20 July 1978, p. 21.

17. See R. J. Barnet, *Intervention and Revolution*, rev. ed. (New American Library, 1972); F. Schurmann, *The Logic of World Power* (Pantheon, 1972).

18. For creative assessment see Lane, "Demanding Human Rights."

19. See Vance, "Human Rights and Foreign Policy," p. 505.

20. See Lane, "Demanding Human Rights," p. 270.

21. *New York Times*, 30 July 1978, sec. 4, p. 4.

22. For discussion and evaluation of Algiers Declaration see Antonio Cassesse and Edmond Jouve, eds., *Pour un droit des peuples* (Paris: Berger-Levrault, 1978).

23. For convenient text see Universal Declaration of the Rights of Peoples, 4 July 1976 (Paris: François Maspero, 1977).

24. Algiers Declaration should be read in conjunction with Delhi Declaration on Disarmament and Development, May 1978, also a populist Third World-oriented initiative.

25. Moynihan, "The Politics of Human Rights," p. 24.

26. Ibid., p. 25.

27. Berger, "Are Human Rights Universal?", p. 62; note that Carter's middle category of "vital needs" is not embraced by Berger's notion of "grossest cases."

28. See Ajami, "Human Rights and World Order Politics," p. 8.

29. Ibid., pp. 16, 21 respectively; cf. David H. Bayley's more agnostic view of the military in power in *Public Liberties in the New States* (Rand McNally, 1964), p. 3.

30. See Ajami, "Human Rights and World Order Politics," pp. 25, 28–29 respectively.

31. See Dominguez, *Enhancing Global Human Rights*.

32. An observer, "Revolution in Ethiopia," *Monthly Review* 29, no. 3 (July/August 1977): 46–60.

33. See Kathleen Gough, "The Green Revolution in South India and North Vietnam," *Bulletin of Concerned Asian Scholars* 10 (Jan.-Mar. 1978): 13–23.

28
UNIVERSAL DECLARATION
OF THE RIGHTS OF PEOPLES

An international conference of jurists, politicians, sociologists, and economists, meeting from 1 July to 4 July, 1976 in the Palais des Nations in Algiers, prepared, discussed and approved a declaration which "consecrates the rights of self-determination, of protection of the environment, of control of natural resources, and of the protection of minorities." The text is given below.

PREAMBLE

We live at a time of great hopes and deep despair;
—a time of conflicts and contradictions;
—a time when liberation struggles have succeeded in arousing the peoples of the world against the domestic and international structures of imperialism and in overturning colonial systems;
—a time of struggle and victory in which new ideals of justice among and within nations have been adopted;
—a time when the General Assembly of the United Nations has given increasing expression, from the Universal Declaration of Human Rights to the Charter on the Economic Rights and Duties of States, to the quest for a new international, political and economic order.

But this is also a time of frustration and defeat, as new forms of imperialism evolve to oppress and exploit the peoples of the world.

Imperialism, using vicious methods, with the complicity of governments that it has itself often installed, continues to dominate a part of the world. Through direct or indirect intervention, through multinational enterprises, through manipulation of corrupt local politicians, with the assistance of military regimes based on police repression, torture and physical extermination of opponents, through a set of practices that has become known as neo-colonialism, imperialism extends its stranglehold over many peoples.

Aware of expressing the aspirations of our era, we met in Algiers to proclaim that all the peoples of the world have an equal right to liberty, the right to free themselves from any foreign interference and to choose their own government,

Reprinted by permission from IODC (International Documentation Center) *Bulletin 47*, September 1976.

the right, if they are under subjection, to fight for their liberation and the right to benefit from other peoples' assistance in their struggle.

Convinced that the effective respect for human rights necessarily implies respect for the rights of peoples, we have adopted the Universal Declaration of the Rights of Peoples.

May all those who, throughout the world, are fighting the great battle, at times through armed struggle, for the freedom of all peoples, find in this Declaration the assurance of the legitimacy of their struggle.

ARTICLES

1. Every people has the right to existence.
2. Every people has the right to the respect of its national and cultural identity.
3. Every people has the right to retain peaceful possession of its territory and to return to it if it is expelled.
4. None shall be subjected, because of his national or cultural identity, to massacre, torture, persecution, deportation, expulsion or living conditions such as may compromise the identity or integrity of the people to which he belongs.
5. Every people has an imprescriptible and inalienable right to self-determination. It shall determine its political status freely and without any foreign interference.
6. Every people has the right to break free from any colonial or foreign domination, whether direct or indirect, and from any racist regime.
7. Every people has the right to have a democratic government representing all the citizens without distinction as to race, sex, belief or colour, and capable of ensuring effective respect for the human rights and fundamental freedoms for all.
8. Every people has an exclusive right over its natural wealth and resources. It has the right to recover them if they have been despoiled, as well as any unjustly paid indemnities.
9. Scientific and technical progress being part of the common heritage of mankind, every people has the right to participate in it.
10. Every people has the right to a fair evaluation of its labor and to equal and just terms in international trade.
11. Every people has the right to choose its own economic and social system and pursue its own path to economic development freely and without any foreign interference.
12. The economic rights set forth above shall be exercised in a spirit of solidarity amongst the peoples of the world and with due regard for their respective interests.
13. Every people has the right to speak its own language and preserve and develop its own culture, thereby contributing to the enrichment of the culture of mankind.
14. Every people has the right to its artistic, historical and cultural wealth.

15. Every people has the right not to have an alien culture imposed upon it.

16. Every people has the right to the conservation, protection and improvement of its environment.

17. Every people has the right to make use of the common heritage of mankind, such as the high seas, the sea-bed, and outer space.

18. In the exercise of the preceding rights every people shall take account of the necessity for coordinating the requirements of its economic development with solidarity amongst all the peoples of the world.

19. When a people constitutes a minority within a State it has the right to respect for its identity, traditions, language and cultural heritage.

20. The members of a minority shall enjoy without discrimination the same rights as the other citizens of the State and shall participate on an equal footing with them in public life.

21. These rights shall be exercised with due respect for the legitimate interests of the community as a whole and cannot authorise impairing the territorial integrity and political unity of the State, provided the State acts in accordance with all the principles set forth in this Declaration.

22. Any disregard for the provisions of this Declaration constitutes a breach of obligations towards the international community as a whole.

23. Any prejudice resulting from disregard for this Declaration must be totally compensated by whoever caused it.

24. Any enrichment to the detriment of the people in violation of the provisions of this Declaration shall give rise to the restitution of profits thus obtained. The same shall be applied to all excessive profits on investments of foreign origin.

25. Any unequal treaties, agreements or contracts concluded in disregard of the fundamental rights of peoples shall have no effect.

26. External financial charges which become excessive and unbearable for the people shall cease to be due.

27. The gravest violations of the fundamental rights of peoples, especially of their right to existence, constitute international crimes for which their perpetrators shall carry personal penal liability.

28. Any people whose fundamental rights are seriously disregarded has the right to enforce them, especially by political or trade union struggle and even, in the last resort, by the use of force.

29. Liberation movements shall have access to international organizations and their combatants are entitled to the protection of the humanitarian law of war.

30. The re-establishment of fundamental rights of peoples, when they are seriously disregarded, is a duty incumbent upon all members of the international community.

Ecological Balance

INTRODUCTION

Throughout history, human populations have had to live within the ecological limits imposed by the territories they have inhabited. If these limits were exceeded, the very capacity of the system to sustain human life was threatened. It is only in the last decade that we have come to realize that the planet itself has a certain finite carrying capacity, which we may be rapidly approaching. The ecological crisis that we face as a result presents a critical challenge to our adaptability. Are we willing and able to change our social values, habits, and institutions sufficiently in time to arrest this ecological deterioration?

The ecological problematique is complicated and multifaceted. It is a function of many factors, including expanding populations, increasing industrialization and urbanization, higher per capita levels of consumption, and wasteful and wanton economic practices. We are concerned here with its two major dimensions: the depletion of the earth's resources, including the land, air, water and minerals required for a life of dignity; and the accumulation of pollution, which threatens not only the quality of the air we breathe and of the water we drink but which also, over time, threatens the life-carrying capacities of our oceans, lakes and lands.

Our world order approach considers the ecological problematique to be deeply rooted in the prevailing modern industrial worldview, and in the dominant moral and ethical precepts that underlie it. Derived largely from Judeo-Christian theology and medieval political philosophy, which sees humanity as the center of the universe, this worldview has a highly destructive attitude toward nature: Nature exists only to be conquered for humankind's pleasure and profit. Human progress is measured in terms of material growth and expansion. In recent decades this idea has gained near universal acceptance as more and more nations have come to imitate the industrial development model of the West.

The ecological problem also seems to be compounded by the nature of the state system, which functions not by the logic of ecological balance, but by the logic of social Darwinism. Separate national states, each attempting to maximize its own immediate economic gains, violate the common good and decrease the global community's productive capacity. Moreover, national boundaries are defied by most environmental problems today; many, such as ozone depletion, the buildup of carbon dioxide in the atmosphere, and oceanic pollution, are literally global in scope. Yet the competitive nature of the international system inhibits the development of global mechanisms for the effective control of even the most common environmental problems, such as air and water pollution.

The response of the international community to the environmental crisis has in fact been slow. It was not until the 1960s that a general concern for the human environment and for the "limits to growth" began to enter public consciousness. The publication of Rachel Carson's *Silent Spring* in 1962 was an important catalyst for the development of the environmental movement. By 1965, it became known that relentless commercial exploitation of the blue whale had finally brought to the edge of extinction the largest animal ever to inhabit the planet. Two years later, in 1967, the grounded Liberian supertanker *Torrey Canyon* spilled some 120,000 tons of heavy crude oil onto British and French coastlines, vividly dramatizing the planet's ecological crisis.

Nevertheless, the protection of the human environment did not become a world order issue until the 1970s. The United Nations Conference on the Human Environment, held in Stockholm, June 5–16, 1972, marked the official entry of environmental issues onto the agenda of global politics. The 1970s witnessed numerous UN-sponsored global conferences on environmental and related issues, but it is difficult to find hard evidence of any *substantive* breakthroughs. We are still faced with the question of how a fragmented international order can come to terms with ecological deterioration. A recent study of how the international community has responded to marine pollution suggests a high degree of dependency on "eco-disaster" to catalyze international political action (M'Gonigle and Zacher, 1979: 259). This study also concludes that the wealthy industrialized capitalist countries of Western Europe and the United States and Japan—the primary consumers of global resources and the main polluters of the human environment today—have dominated the politics of oil pollution control, but that their policies and strategies are guided predominantly by *economic interests*, not by ecological concerns. The minor influence of the Soviet bloc is a corollary of its *commercial and economic isolation* in the global economy. The weakness of the developing countries, too, follows from their *economic dependence* on the developed industrialized countries (M'Gonigle and Zacher, 1979: 348).

Ecological problems increasingly intersect with other world order concerns. The growing scarcity of resources, for example, contributes to stagnation and inflation in the world economy, places greater strains on societies to meet basic needs, and tends to promote increased international conflict. The proper normative relationship between ecological balance and other world order values, especially economic well-being, remains a controversial question. The Limits to Growth message, contained in the Club of Rome's First Report, has been vehemently criticized as a form of "class politics" (Galtung, 1977). Third World developmentalists also have viewed the environmental movement with mistrust, suspecting it to be another Western ploy to deny them a more just role in the world economy. To reconcile this tension between extreme environmentalists in the West and extreme developmentalists in the Third World, we need to ask what percentage of the global population consumes what percentage of the global resources, for what purposes, and with what ecological consequences. Surely, the differential impact of the rich and the poor on the world's environment must be taken into account. Ecological deterioration, as Nathan Keyfitz notes in Section 5, is not just a function of population, but more importantly of per capita consumption.

Theoretically, the world order values of economic well-being and ecological balance can be mutually complementary. Human maladaptive behavior toward the environment also has a deleterious impact on the resource base necessary to achieve economic well-being. At present, for example, between 50,000 and 70,000 square kilometers of useful land go out of production each year, with over 9 million square kilometers being desertified *as a result of human activities*. Desertification is estimated to cost about $15.6 billion a year in lost agricultural production. This symbiotic relationship between environmental and socioeconomic goals is becoming increasingly recognized by world order advocates, and is leading to the formulation of new development strategies that are ecologically sustainable as well as more economically and politically just (Kothari, 1980).

Our first presentation in this section, by Dennis Pirages, makes a strong case for an ecopolitical theory of international relations. There is now an impending ecopolitical revolution, Pirages argues, whose epistemological and normative implications are comparable to those of the earlier agricultural and industrial revolutions. Highlighting all the anomalies and dilemmas, as well as the irrelevance of the prevailing realist school, Pirages advances an ecopolitical paradigm as an alternative "model of reality" for describing, explaining, and projecting shifts in world politics. Because of its planetary scope, survivalist ethics, functional approach, and futurist time dimension, this ecopolitical paradigm is congenial to world order studies.

Pirages' holistic ecopolitical paradigm, however, poses two difficult world order questions. At the normative level, ecopolitics must be assessed by the extent to which it can be reconciled with the global imperative of meeting basic human needs. There is always the danger that ecological constraints will be used as a justification for writing off portions of humanity. Until the normative ambiguities between the values of ecological balance and economic well-being are reconciled, global ecopolitics will be incapable of engaging the support and commitment of the oppressed peoples of the world. At the empirical level, the year 1980 witnessed a renewal of geopolitical struggle that calls into question Pirages' assertion that "the focus of international political conflict has now shifted from an East-West to a North-South direction." The accelerated nuclear arms race, the revival of a Cold War atmosphere, the revision of nuclear doctrine in a more destabilizing direction, and the impending new cycle of interventionary and counter-interventionary coercive diplomacy in the domain of global ecopolitics (resource war), all suggest that the declaration of the demise of the East-West conflict was premature.

In our next selection, William Ophuls considers ecological issues in both their comparative and international contexts. What are the major similarities and differences in the approaches adopted by key global actors? Ophuls extends his analysis to the international arena, delineating the tragedy of the commons as the operational logic of the international politics of scarcity. Ophuls argues that the dynamic of the tragedy of the commons works even more intensely in the anarchical international society than it does in any domestic society. He concludes with a strong argument for world government, but recognizes at the same time that "the very ecological scarcity that makes a world government ever more necessary has also made it much more difficult of achievement."

The third selection, "Who Owns the Ozone?", by Norman Cousins, broadens the concept of "crimes against humanity" by extending it to the human transgression of the life-protecting ozone in the stratosphere. This essay also makes a linkage between the two world order values of peace and ecological balance. The environmental consequences of the war system are a neglected domain of world order studies. The nuclear arms race, for example, not only threatens the existence of humankind, it also squanders natural resources even without the outbreak of war. Ozone depletion is just one among many environmental hazards caused by the continuing arms race. We have little knowledge about the amounts of radioactive isotopes that silently pollute the human environment in the course of researching, testing, manufacturing, and deploying nuclear weapons. We are not fully aware of the potentially disastrous consequences of novel military plans that call for geophysical and environmental warfare far beyond the use of fire and defoliants. "Even with optimistic expectations regarding future refinements in technique," concluded a recent study by the Stockholm International Peace Research Institute (1977: 61), "the outcome of geophysical modifications for hostile purposes is likely to be unpredictable in magnitude, spatial confinement, side effects and duration."

Our next selection is taken from *The Global 2000 Report to the President*, the most comprehensive set of projections developed by U.S. Government agencies on "what will happen to population, resources, and environment if present policies continue." Dr. Mostafa Tolba, Executive Director of the United Nations Environment Programme, has characterized this report as "perhaps one of the most significant publications of this most worrying decade, [the] 1970s." The report shows a depressing picture of the planet in the year 2000: if present trends and policies continue, the world will be more crowded, more polluted, more inequitable; conflict-prone and filled with tension; less stable ecologically and more vulnerable to irreversible disruption or disaster. Can the opportunity costs (which inevitably result from denying ecological reality and refusing to adapt behavior to reality) be anything less than the "global tragedy of the commons" alluded to by Ophuls? *The Global 2000 Report* issued a public warning:

"The adverse effects of many of the trends discussed in this Study will not be fully evident until the year 2000 or later; yet the actions that are necessary to change the trends cannot be postponed without foreclosing important options."

The Dai Dong Declaration on the Environment, the final selection in this section, is a third system challenge to the less holistic second-system approach as symbolized by the United Nations Conference on the Human Environment. It calls not only for basic changes in our political, economic, and social structures, but also for changes in our individual life styles to assure human survival in a way that facilitates human fulfillment. This implies a global social learning process involving material self-restraint for individuals and groups, particularly those in the advanced industrialized countries. The most powerful message of this third-system declaration is that the environment should not be abstracted as an isolated or independent value in order to prevent the rise of ecological colonialism—that is, ecological standards should not deny to the poor the wealth-producing technology that has enabled the rich and powerful to attain their positions of dominance. The declaration conceptually and normatively links ecological balance with peace, economic well-being, and human dignity. In short, the declaration poses a challenge to the dominant mainstream ecological thinking along institutional and technological lines.

Whether changes wrought by demographic, technological, and economic pressures are affecting the environment in ways beyond present and projected means of coping with them remains an unanswered—and perhaps unanswerable—question. What is certain is that the role of inextricable linkages among technology, demography, geography or environment, and global politics has become an important domain in world order studies. Harold and Margaret Sprout (1965, 1971) have made a path-breaking contribution toward the development of various hypotheses for explaining person-milieu relationships in the study of international relations. As some of the works in this section show, the ecological perspective entered the agenda of global politics only in the last decade. Does this coming of a global politics of ecology imply subordinating our short-term national interests to the consideration of long-term global costs and consequences? In the final analysis, the impending ecological struggle at local, national, regional, and global levels centers on the adaptability of human behavior to live in dynamic harmony with the basic principles of nature.

QUESTIONS FOR DISCUSSION AND REFLECTION

What are the assumptions and arguments of "extreme developmentalists" and "extreme environmentalists?" Where do you stand in this ecodevelopmental dialogue, and why?

Based on your reading of this section, what kind of "state of the globe report" on the human environment would you submit? Who are the main polluters?

Who are the chief victims of pollution? Who are the main users of the world's resources? Is this fair? When does use of resources become waste?

What is your perception of the role, fitness, and prospect of different nation-states as managers of the environmental crisis? Compare and contrast the value premises of socialism and capitalism as they relate to the environment. In terms of practical policies, do you see any difference between the socialist and capitalist approaches to the environmental crisis?

How would you rate the world order performance of the international community on the environmental crisis? What do you see as main obstacles in the present world order system in responding more effectively to the ecological crisis, and what sorts of transition strategies (that are both desirable and feasible) can you suggest?

To what extent must modern industrial civilization be modified to meet the ecological challenge? Will major changes in our lifestyles be required?

SELECTED BIBLIOGRAPHY

Brown, Lester. *The Twenty-Ninth Day: Accommodating Human Needs and Numbers to the Earth's Resources.* New York: Norton, 1978.

Carson, Rachel. *Silent Spring.* Boston: Houghton Mifflin, 1962.

Cole, H.S D., Christopher Freeman, et al. *Models of Doom: A Critique of the Limits to Growth.* New York: Universe Books, 1975.

Commoner, Barry. *The Closing Circle.* New York: Bantam Books, 1974.

Daly, Herman E., ed. *Toward A Steady-State Economy.* San Francisco: W. H. Freeman, 1973.

Deutsch, Karl W., ed. *Ecosocial Systems and Ecopolitics.* Paris: UNESCO, 1977.

Enloe, Cynthia H. *The Politics of Pollution in a Comparative Perspective: Ecology and Power in Four Nations.* New York: David McKay, 1975.

Galtung, Johan. "Limits to Growth and Class Politics." *Journal of Peace Research.* 10, 1973:101–14.

Hardin, Garrett. *The Limits of Altruism: An Ecologist's View of Survival.* Bloomington, IN: Indiana University Press, 1977.

Kothari, Rajni. "Environment and Alternative Development." *Alternatives: A Journal of World Policy.* Vol. 5, No. 4 (1980).

Lovins, Amory B. *Soft Energy Paths.* New York: Ballinger, 1977.

Meadows, Donella, et al. *The Limits to Growth.* 2nd edition. Washington, D.C.: Potomac Associates, 1974.

M'Gonigle, R. Michael, and Mark W. Zacher. *Pollution, Politics and International Regimes.* Berkeley, CA: University of California Press, 1979.

Ophuls, William. *Ecology and the Politics of Scarcity.* San Francisco: W. H. Freeman, 1977.

Orr, David W., and Marvis S. Sorros, eds. *The Global Predicament: Ecological Perspectives on World Order.* Chapel Hill, NC: University of North Carolina Press, 1979.

Schneider, Jan. *World Public Order of the Environment: Towards an International Ecological Law and Organization.* Toronto: University of Toronto Press, 1979.

Sprout, Harold, and Margaret Sprout. *The Ecological Perspective on Human Affairs, with Special Reference to International Politics.* Princeton: Princeton University Press, 1965.

———. *Toward a Politics of the Planet Earth*. New York: Van Nostrand Reinhold Co., 1971.

Stockholm International Peace Research Institute. *Weapons of Mass Destruction and the Environment*. London: Taylor & Francis, 1977.

Todd, Nancy, ed. *The Book of the New Alchemists*. New York: Dutton, 1977.

The Trilateral Commission. "Energy: Managing the Transition." The Triangle Papers 17.

United Nations Environment Programme. *Report of the Governing Council* (Annual). GAOR, Supplement 25.

29
THE ORIGINS OF ECOPOLITICS

Dennis Pirages

THE IMPENDING REVOLUTION

The last quarter of the twentieth century marks the beginning of a fundamental shift in human history as the world's rapidly growing human population encounters environmental limits to growth on a global scale. Since ancient times, the world's population has been dutifully following a biological imperative and the biblical admonition to increase and multiply. In the year 8000 B.C., there were only about 5 million people on the earth, a much smaller population than that of contemporary New York. For the next ten thousand years, population increased slowly. This slow pace of growth resulted in a world population of about 500 million in A.D. 1650. Thus, world population doubled only six or seven times during this entire ten-thousand-year period. Then, something happened to trigger enormous population growth. World population doubled from 500 million to 1 billion in only two hundred years, between 1650 and 1850, and then it doubled again in the eighty-year-period between 1850 and 1930. At present, there are more than 4 billion human beings, and this number is expected to double once again in only thirty-six years.[1]

When humanity greets the year 2000, then, there will be more than 6 billion human beings to jointly celebrate (or lament) the occasion. And each one of them will be a much greater burden on the earth's natural resources than they are at present if current economic development plans are followed. This explosion of population and consumption is unparalleled in human history, and the burden that it places and will place on human institutions and natural resources is staggering.

This impending revolution will not be the first time that human beings have changed their impact on the environment. Two previous revolutions in human history also dramatically altered the nature of the human environment. The first, the Agricultural Revolution, began around the year 8000 B.C. It was driven by the domestication of plants and animals, which in turn provided better diets, more energy, and a more secure source of food for human beings than existed in the preceding hunting and gathering societies. The growth of agriculture was closely paralleled by a slow expansion of a more secure and sedentary human population, which no longer depended on the hunt for food.

The second great revolution, the Industrial Revolution, began to gather momentum in the fifteenth and sixteenth centuries and culminated in the rapid advance of technology characteristic of the twentieth-century. The Industrial Revolution enhanced human productivity by harnessing energy derived from fossil fuels to do tasks previously performed by human beings and beasts of burden. It produced increasing abundance through the large-scale exploitation of many nonrenewable natural resources, and this abundance has, in turn, helped cause the contemporary population and consumption explosion.

There are many indications that the coming decades mark the beginning of a third great revolutionary period in human history. Unlike the previous revolutions, which were growth-oriented and given impetus by new technologies and greater abundance, there is as yet no positive guiding vision of economic abundance to facilitate the impending transformation. The nature of the transformation is now unclear but, from the present perspective, it appears that the rapid growth of population and per capita consumption, and the related institutions dependent upon growth, cannot much longer endure within the closed ecological system represented by planet Earth. The curves of population growth and increased consumption, which slope sharply upward, cannot continue to go up further since eventually there would be standing room only on the planet's surface.[2]

The causes and the consequences of this third great revolution and its impact on international relations are the subjects of the chapters that follow. Just as the Agricultural Revolution made possible highly organized warfare and empires, and just as the Industrial Revolution made possible an international system, colonialism, and two world wars, the third great revolution is once again transforming the nature of society as well as the nature of international relations.

The impending revolution has already given birth to a new set of perceptions and new rules of behavior in international relations. These new perceptions and rules can be summed up by the term "global ecopolitics." Global ecopolitics involves the use of environmental issues, control over natural resources, scarcity arguments, and related concerns of social justice to overturn the international political hierarchy and related system of rules established during the period of industrial expansion. Along with this partial erosion of the old international power hierarchy, the focus of international political conflict has now shifted from an East-West to a North-South direction. The consensus that has bound existing international alliances together in the industrial world is also changing as alliance concerns shift from military matters to economic issues and the problem of maintaining cheap access to the commodities that are the essential building blocks of industrial societies. Finally, even the language of international relations has begun to change, and terms such as "exponential growth," "resource depletion," "energy gap," and "never to be developed countries" are replacing terms that were more common to analysts of past decades.

Recent international conferences on population, environment, water, and food have been dealing with the moral aspects of current ecopolitical issues. These include life and death questions of whether nations should be permitted to maintain high rates of population growth, whether foreign assistance should be offered to nations having no birth control policies, whether food should be sold only to those who can buy it, and whether moral obligations exist to provide food to the starving. The right of some industrialized countries to increase consumption at the expense of global environmental integrity also has been challenged. Control over natural resources and their use as an economic and political weapon has become a critical bargaining chip in the recent ecopolitics. And the usefulness of the old energy- and resource-intensive model of industrial development to contemporary less developed countries is being questioned by less developed countries, as are the advantages of trading with the highly industrialized nations.

The Changing World View

In his work on scientific revolutions, Thomas Kuhn has used the word *paradigm* to describe the model of reality that is internalized when people become socialized as members of scientific communities. Research in these scientific communities is based on shared paradigms—a collective understanding of facts, rules of scientific inquiry, and shared standards. Paradigms endure in the sciences because when they are intially established they have enough intellectual power to attract some adherents from competing models of reality, and they also raise interesting scientific problems yet to be solved by scientists working within the paradigm.[3]

Scientific paradigms have occasionally changed throughout the history of science. Perhaps the best example of a paradigm shift, or complete change in perception of reality, is the Copernican revolution in astronomy. Prior to the Copernican revolution, astronomers invested a great deal of time and effort in shoring up the Ptolemaic paradigm which placed the earth at the center of the universe. As astronomy became a more precise science, many measurements could be fit into the Ptolemaic model only with great difficulty. These "anomalies" began to mount up, and they led to extremely complex explanations of planetary behavior. Eventually, the anomalies became so obvious that a new view of the solar system, one that placed the sun at the center, provided the model for scientific revolution in astronomy—a revolution that also affected humanity's view of its place in the universe.

A paradigm, then, guides scientists in choosing research topics, in searching for data, and in interpreting results. It is like a pair of glasses that clarifies a fuzzy world of empirical data for the researcher. It also defines the "is" and "ought" of a profession, the problems that are worthy of solution, and suggests methods by which they can be solved. A paradigm also insulates a scientific community from problems and anomalies that may be important but are not amenable to solution within the framework provided by it.[4] Paradigms remain dominant within the social system of science for long periods because disciplinary reward structures encourage conformity to the established scientific norms. In other words, a good scientist accepts the "givens" of his profession, doesn't rock the boat, and is rewarded with cash, power, and scientific prestige.

On a much larger scale, shared paradigms not only guide scientific research but help members of all societies define social, economic, and political reality. The collection of norms, beliefs, values, habits, and survival rules that provides a frame of reference for members of a society is called a dominant social paradigm (DSP). A dominant social paradigm, then, is the predominant world view, model, or frame of reference through which individuals or, collectively, a society gives meaning to the world in which persons live. A DSP defines the nature of both the physical and social world, indicates problems in need of solutions, and outlines the range of acceptable solutions to these problems. It also defines the "is" and the "ought" in society, or rules of social survival and social ethics.[5] Throughout most of history, ethical codes or rules of survival have been embedded in organized religions, which helped to pass social paradigms from generation to generation.

A DSP represents a mental image of reality that forms social expectations. Thus, social paradigms are essential for social stability. Dominant social paradigms are passed from generation to generation through socialization and education processes. In normal times they change only very slowly in response to experience with the real world; a world that historically has changed very slowly. But during periods of major social upheaval, characterized by mounting social anomalies caused by discontinuities between what people perceive to be the case and what they think it ought to be, there can be rapid and very dramatic changes in the DSP. During these periods, the *perceived* nature of physical and social worlds, the problems seen to be in need of solution, and the values and ethics guiding human behavior may be completely transformed in a very short period of time.

Each of the two previous great revolutions in human history was defined by major shifts in the existing social paradigm. The components of the dominant social paradigm in most hunting and gathering societies did not have much in common with the dominant paradigm that evolved along with the Agricultural Revolution. And the dominant social paradigm of industrial societies shares little with the dominant social paradigm of agrarian ones. The third great revolution in human history will foster a predominant view of the world that is as different from the present DSP as the industrial one was from its agrarian predecessor.

Shifts in dominant social paradigms result from social anomalies or dilemmas, conditions for which the prevailing DSP cannot provide an explanation. These shifts can be minor or major, rapid or slow, objectively destructive or constructive, depending upon the rate at which anomalies accumulate and the incentives that individuals have to alter their views of the world. Minor shifts in components of dominant social paradigms have not been infrequent occurrences, especially since the beginning of the Industrial Revolution. But major, rapid, and thorough transformations of basic world views have been rare. In the case of the Agricultural Revolution, diffusion of new agricultural technologies was very gradual, as were the ensuing changes in norms, values, beliefs, and survival rules. During the Industrial Revolution, by contrast, the changes in norms, values, ethics, and survival rules were very rapid, and industrial technologies and related changes in dominant social paradigms were diffused throughout most of the world in only a two or three hundred year period.[6]

In the early stages of a paradigm shift, it is not easy to detect the changes that are taking place. That a transition is now imminent might not immediately be obvious to many persons, because early in a revolutionary period most are still very much captive of the old way of looking at things. But evidence is beginning to mount that a period of transformation of great consequence has now begun. It is similar to the previous revolutions in that it will result in an entirely new way of looking at the world and a new set of values, ethics, and survival rules.

Willis Harman has suggested that there are four key dilemmas (anomalies) within the DSP of industrial societies that may not be resolvable without a system transformation. He labels these *the growth dilemma* (we need continued growth but can't live with its consequences), *the control dilemma* (we need more guidance over technological innovation but shun centralized control), *the distribution dilemma* (rich individuals and rich nations find it too costly to share wealth with the poor but failure to do so can lead to disaster), and *the work roles dilemma* (society cannot provide enough legitimate roles to keep up with expectations being instilled in the young). He links these dilemmas that are intrinsic to the present DSP with a "new scarcity." The old scarcity involved shortages of things that were required to meet basic human needs. These old shortages could be overcome by improving technology and using more territory—traditional economic solutions. The new shortages, however, result from approaching planetary limits to growth.[7]

There is a long list of interrelated new scarcity problems that are now beginning to slow growth on a planetary scale and shake some of the fundamental assumptions in the present social paradigm. Central to all of them is the dwindling global supply of petroleum and natural gas. In 1974, the world found out what it is like to cope with energy shortages and higher prices. On that occasion, scarcity was brought on by the actions of a cartel of energy exporters. But several studies indicate that projected energy shortages in the latter years of the 1980s and early years of the 1990s might well result from lack of reserves and capacity rather than from any contrived scarcity.[8]

There is also a growing global water shortage, which represents another potential limit to growth. Additional potential shortages exist in food production, production of nonfuel minerals, and in the ability of natural waste disposal systems to absorb pollution created by industrial progress.[9] Energy lies at the center of all these new scarcity problems, however, because if abundant energy is available it can help ameliorate the other problems.

There are many other aspects to the argument that a new revolution is imminent. In *The End of Progress*, Edward Renshaw has argued that a law of diminishing returns governs many of the processes responsible for progress within the industrial paradigm. Speed in transportation, for example, has been pushed to a point where it is no longer economically practical to move faster, especially given higher prices for fuels. This results from a rapidly rising cost curve for moving things faster. In many cases, each additional mile per hour now costs more than any related increase in human productivity. Similar relationships operate in automation and increased scale of production and distribution. Huge, automated, multinational corporations have, in many cases, reached the point of diminishing returns in the scale of their centralized international operations. Increasing transportation costs now make decentralization and duplication of facilities a preferable alternative. And an unemployed pool of laborers numbering as high as one-third of the work force in many less developed countries makes labor-intensive rather than energy-intensive growth a preferred development strategy for the future.[10]

There is a continuing debate over the meaning of these new scarcities for the future quality of life on a planetary scale. One side in the debate claims that the resilience of industrial society will lead to new technological innovations and energy alternatives that will solve new scarcity problems.[11] At the other extreme, there are many who see conservation, a more frugal lifestyle, and new social institutions as essential to maintaining a minimally acceptable quality of life.[12] The significance of the debate is not that one side or the other will be proved wrong. Regardless of which vision of the future turns out to be more correct, the present dominant social paradigm in industrial societies will be transformed as the rapid growth associated with fossil fuels either comes to an end or assumes a radically different shape.

There are many different levels on which—and areas in which—paradigms and paradigm shifts may be studied. In the physical sciences, for example, there is one general paradigm that dominates most scientific inquiry. Within this paradigm, assumptions are made that physical events are predictable, that there are physical laws that can be discovered by human efforts, that a set of rules called scientific method best guides inquiry, and that deductive reasoning leads to accumulation of knowledge within the paradigm. The more general scientific paradigm, however, is very complex, and there are many different subparadigms representing different segments of the physical world. Thus, astronomy, physics, and biology each have their own paradigms containing rules of inquiry very similar to those governing all science but with a content and perspective that are discipline-specific. A paradigm shift can occur in any discipline, and the effect on the general scientific paradigm can be greater or lesser depending upon its linkage with the discipline.

Similar complexities are found in dominant social paradigms. Just as there are subparadigms that are component parts of the scientific paradigm, there are also subparadigms applicable to different areas of social life and social inquiry. People share certain perspectives and beliefs about the economy, politics, and social life, as well as about other nations and international affairs.[13] A revolutionary shift in the DSP affects all of these subparadigms, but a shift in a subparadigm can take place and have a greater or lesser effect on the DSP depending upon how integral it is to the entire predominant way of looking at things.

This book focuses upon changes in that subparadigm of the DSP called international relations. This is the part of the DSP that deals with relations among actors in the international system. These actors may be individuals, groups, subnational units, nations, international nongovernmental organizations such as multinational corporations, or international organizations. The old dominant paradigm in international relations contains a view of international reality, defines issues that divide and unite actors within the international system, and provides a frame of reference through which actors can interpret the flow of international events.

The dominant paradigm in international relations is changing in response both to changes in dominant social paradigms and to the realities governing relations among actors in the international system. The Agricultural Revolution was responsible for the birth of something resembling an international system as well as the creation of small empires. The Industrial Revolution gave birth to the European state system in international affairs, more communication among nations, colonialism, world wars, and interdependence, as well as supporting ethics and ideologies. The third great revolution is creating an ecopolitical paradigm in international relations based upon recognition of the finite nature of the planet and the inextricable interdependence of the states making up its territory. Concepts, scholarly purposes, research agendas, and methods of inquiry are now changing in response to perceived inadequacies in previous ways of looking at the world.

Harman has suggested three types of conditions that indicate that a transformation in a paradigm is imperative: (1) the complex of problems, dilemmas, and discontinuities is so great that a change in basic values is required for their resolution, (2) the presence of "lead indicators" is increasingly noted, (3) a competitive paradigm or model can be identified.[14] Each of these conditions can be found in contemporary international affairs. There can be little doubt that the related issues of increased energy prices, high rates of malnutrition or even starvation in many areas of the world, inequities in international trade, failure to meet development targets, unemployment, economic recession, and political instability provide an exceptional challenge to accepted views of global economic and political progress. While these conditions may have existed to a lesser or greater extent throughout history, they now are *perceived* by political leaders as pressing issues, and these leaders are attempting to do something about them. It is also easy to find related lead indicators that reveal an international system undergoing a transformation. Global inflation, commodity speculation, growing insecurity over access to natural resources, collapse of respected banks, and in some cases a near economic collapse of nations, fear of the future, and a growing sense of alienation could be cited as on the basic list of lead indicators. And there is an emerging paradigm, offered by leaders of less developed countries in the guise of a new international economic order, which promises to remedy present social and political ills. Just as an expansionist perspective dominated international affairs during the Industrial Revolution, an ecopolitical paradigm will emerge to make order of the apparent chaos accompanying this third great revolution.

AN ECOLOGICAL PERSPECTIVE

In order to understand the dynamics behind the emergence of ecopolitics, it is necessary to understand some basic principles of ecology. *Homo sapiens* is governed by the same physical laws that regulate the growth and development of all other species. And theories explaining how populations of human beings act in relation to other populations are thus best anchored in basic ecological principles that govern interactions among all types of populations.

For much of human history, populations of *Homo sapiens* were directly involved in life and death struggles with populations of many other species. But human creativity as revealed in technological developments has enabled human beings to triumph over other species and escape the extinction that might have occurred in "hand to hand" combat with other carnivores. First the Agricultural and then the Industrial revolutions improved the human competitive position until now human beings perceive themselves, within the industrial paradigm, to be dominant over nature. If necessary, mountains can be moved, rivers redirected, and climates altered to overcome natural barriers to human progress. In the face of all of the contrary evidence inherent in the rise and fall of great empires, this human dominance perspective sees an industrial future of growth without limits.

This dominance perspective was molded by an extended period of technological advance and geographical expansion of the horizons of Western European industrializing nations. The fifteenth and sixteenth centuries marked the beginning of a geographical expansion by virtue of Western European colonization of distant lands that culminated in vast empires that persisted well into the twentieth century. In the United States, abundance was promoted by the westward push of the frontier beginning in the eighteenth century and culminating in Alaska in the twentieth century. In both Western Europe and the United States, a technological revolution made existing land and resources much more productive on a per capita basis with each passing decade. Human populations expanded rapidly in this atmosphere of increasing abundance but food production and manufacturing were more than able to keep up.

In the last quarter of the twentieth century, however, this abundance and human dominance perspective is being shaken by the specter of new scarcities. This is in no small part due to the absence of new frontiers. Only the Antarctic and Arctic remain to be colonized, and they promise little relief for growing and restive populations. Attempts to circumvent the new scarcity by creating a new "frontier" in the form of space colonies are taken seriously mostly by a small coterie of science fiction buffs, avant-garde social scientists, and vested interests in the aerospace industry.[15] It is in this context that the concerns of demographers and ecologists become relevant to international relations theory.[16]

Populations and Interaction

Populations are central to analysis in building ecological theory. For an ecologist or biologist, a population is technically a group of individuals of the same species. In this general sense, the human population of the world could be said to number approximately 4 billion. But this is not a very valuable way to use the concept. There are subpopulations of almost all species, closely knit groups that interact almost exclusively with each other and almost never with other members of the species. Biologists and ecologists compromise by further restricting the definition of population to a "dynamic system of interacting individuals . . . that are potentially capable of interbreeding with each other."[17] By this definition, the preindustrial world was inhabited by thousands of human populations. Similarly, since almost all human beings are now linked into a global communication system and at least have the potential to interbreed, it could be said that there is now just one population of human beings and that they are all citizens of the world.

Obviously, people generally do not perceive themselves to be citizens of the world but of populations living within various geographical units called countries. Theoretically, every human being—or every white-tailed deer—in the world could, through some conceivable set of circumstances, mate with any other human being—or white-tailed deer—on the planet. But the likelihood of certain persons or deer interbreeding varies according to physical and social distance. Thus, the possiblity that a Canadian Eskimo and a Nigerian Ibo would interbreed is almost zero, while the likelihood that a single male and female on Manhattan would do so is very much greater. In defining the boundaries of a population, it is critical to examine the *comparative frequency of interaction*. But when dealing with human populations, as opposed to other species, it is important to keep in mind that interactions can be of a face-to-face nature as well as mediated through mass communications.

Although this application of the formal definition of population to human beings in national units might upset some biologists and ecologists, it is an extremely useful way to begin to understand what an ecological perspective on relations among actors in the contemporary international system can offer. If all of the direct and mediated communications of all of the people of the world could somehow be mapped, it would be clear that there are some clusters of human beings that interact much more frequently than others. These clusters usually are demarcated by the boundaries of nation states. "Peoples are marked off from each other by communication barriers, by 'marked gaps' in the efficiency of communication."[18] In other words, nationality is determined by social communication and economic intercourse among people. People who identify themselves as members of a national population feel that their fortunes "covary" with those of other people within the national population.[19]

An analysis of these interaction patterns would reveal sharp discontinuities representing national boundaries, but also significant differences in interactions among people within national boundaries. This simply means that countries vary in the extent to which all segments of the population have been integrated effectively into national life. While there are certainly difficulties in dealing with marginal or minority populations within nations, the vast majority of the human race can be identified as belonging to national populations through their communication patterns.

Such interacting populations have been the basic units of identification for human beings since the earliest recorded human history. While the principle of in-group identification is at least as old as culture itself, the size of the population units with which individuals identify has increased along with communications capabilities. The size of early political empires was constrained by horse-dependent transportation and primitive communication networks. Preindustrial Europe, for example, consisted of many small populations loosely knit into larger confederations. Relations between centralizing political leaders of the larger confederation and those of smaller groups in the periphery varied over time in relation to the aggressiveness, power, skill, wealth, and communications capabilities possessed by the core. The technological, economic, and social factors responsible for the unification of contemporary large industrial nations have been well documented elsewhere.[20] The important point here is that the Industrial Revolution as a source of military, transportation, and communications technology aided the transformation of loosely knit confederations into contemporary, integrated nation states.

Populations and Resources

Whether small principalities or large nation-states, territorial units in isolation have a limited capability to sustain human populations because they are endowed with limited quantities of natural resources. Human populations, just as those of other species, have always pressed against the limitations inherent in the natural resource endowment found within their geographical territory. These natural factors regulating populations have been historically manifest to human beings as tragic "unnatural" events, such as famine and plague, which may well have been related to periodic changes in climate. During periods of relatively favorable crop-growing weather, human populations have grown and flourished only to be cut back during ensuing less favorable decades.[21]

A number of natural resources are essential to the activities of all populations. To an ecologist, "a resource is anything needed by an organism, population, or ecosystem which, by its increasing availability up to an optimal or sufficient level, allows an increasing rate of energy conversion."[22] An abundance of resources in relation to demands guarantees the growth of consumption and expansion of numbers within a population. One of the most basic of ecological principals, Von Liebig's law of the minimum, holds that the life of an individual or the size of a population is limited by the resource necessary for survival that is in shortest supply (see Figure 1). Thus, even though a population may have plenty of space into which it can expand, lack of available water or other resources can inhibit such expansion.

Paul and Anne Ehrlich have categorized six types of resources essential to the

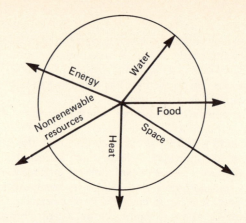

FIGURE 1   *Von Liebig's Law and Resource Space. The arrows represent relative quantities of resources. According to Von Liebig's law, this population can expand only to fill the circle, since water is the resource in shortest supply. This population has more food, space, heat, energy, and nonrenewable resources than are necessary to sustain its present level.*

survival of human populations.[23] These include energy, nonrenewable resources, water, food, space, and heat. When taken in combination, these essential resources found on any piece of territory can be called a "resource space" available for expansion of population and consumption. All natural populations tend to expand nearly to fill this available resource space until their expansion is halted by the resource in shortest supply.

The amount of available resource space, then, limits the carrying capacity of any piece of territory. *Natural carrying capacity* is defined by ecologists as the maximum total biomass (the dry weight of all living flora and fauna) that can be supported by any given piece of territory within the constraints of current solar income (sunlight). The mixture of flora and fauna grown within these limits can, of course, affect the maximum dry weight that can be supported. Natural carrying capacity is related to the ability to get energy from food, which is a function of the fertility of the soil, temperature, rainfall, and amount of sunlight available. Under hunting and gathering conditions, the natural carrying capacity of a piece of land sets constraints on the number of human beings that the land can support. A given human population can expand to its maximum size within these constraints by eliminating the competition for available food, by using great skill and new technologies in husbanding needed resources, or by consuming only enough food per capita to meet minimal human needs.

Natural carrying capacity represents a useful point of departure in analyzing the loads that human populations put on existing national territories. It seems obvious, for example, that the human population of Bangladesh is pressing much closer to the limits of natural carrying capacity than is the population of Australia. But, on the other hand, it is not so clear that Bangladesh is closer to these limits than is a country like the Netherlands, a highly industrialized nation that must import considerable quantities of raw materials from other national territories. The key to this distinction lies in the fact that *Homo sapiens* is unique in his use of trade and advanced technologies to enhance the natural carrying capacity of inhabited territories. The food available to a population of deer is determined by natural constraints: sunlight, temperature, and rainfall patterns. The deer have no choice but to rely upon the vagaries of weather, and their numbers are limited accordingly. Human beings, by contrast, use various kinds of institutions and technologies to increase carrying capacity and thereby more effectively use resources.

The two most important sets of technological developments that permitted the world's human population to increase were the domestication of plants and animals during the Agricultural Revolution and the discovery and utilization of energy in fossil fuels on large scale during the Industrial Revolution. In the first case, the technologies developed within the constraints of current solar income, and related population increases could be sustained indefinitely. In the latter case, however, many of the new technologies were dependent on finite supplies of fossil fuels and the related expanded populations will not be able to exist within the constraints of perpetually renewable current solar income once these supplies of fossil fuels disappear.

Trade is the other main method by which national populations change the carrying capacity of their territory. National populations do not live in complete isolation in the contemporary international system. Resources abundant in one country might be scarce in another and vice versa. Through mutually beneficial exchanges of resources and products, cooperating nations can increase their carrying capacity and hence their populations. The advantages of trade are obvious, but there are also drawbacks. Relying on a trade partner (Country A) for a resource whose lack has previously checked population growth in Country B makes Country B vulnerable to the machinations of Country A. If Country A decides to cut off trade in the essential resource, the population of Country B could collapse back to its original level.

The contemporary international trade system is much more complex than this simple example indicates, however. Returning to the example of the Netherlands and Bangladesh, the population of the Netherlands is sustained by a complex trade network whose tentacles reach to the far corners of the globe to secure the dozens of essential resources not found on Dutch soil. The Netherlands is the second largest importer of protein in the world and imports almost all of its cotton, iron ore, bauxite, copper, gold, nickel, tin, zinc, phosphate fertilizers, and a host of other important commodities.[24] In this respect, the population of Bangladesh could be said to be existing much closer to the constraints of natural carrying capacity. If the world trade system were suddenly to disintegrate, the Netherlands would suffer an economic and demographic catastrophe of great magnitude, while Bangladesh would escape with minor economic damage.

A more useful formulation of the carrying capacity concept as it relates to human populations in a complex industrial world takes into account existing levels of technological sophistication as well as the position of a country in the world trade system. *Current carrying capacity* is the total biomass (or human equivalent) that can be supported by national territorial units given existing levels of technology, a reasonable degree of autarky (self-sufficiency) in essential natural resources, and a reasonably balanced trade profile. Although the current carrying capacity is very difficult to define precisely and measure, it is an essential concept to use in building ecopolitical theory in international relations.

Technological sophistication is the primary determinant of current carrying capacity. Some nations are technologically more developed than others, and the extent of these differences can be at least crudely measured. Higher levels of technological development indicate greater ability to manipulate the natural environment in order to sustain larger numbers of people at higher levels of consumption. More highly developed countries can use existing resources more efficiently. In countries that are less developed, current carrying capacity is usually very close to natural carrying capacity. But in industrially developed countries, there is a large gap between the two. The less developed countries, of course, seek to enhance their current carrying capacity through industrial growth, but this is not easily accomplished. Increasing current carrying capacity through industrialization requires capital, long lead times, and creation of an appropriate technologically sophisticated infrastructure.

A second determinant of current carrying capacity is the domestic natural resource base. Highly industrialized economies require large amounts of energy and a diverse assortment of natural resources. If these are available domestically, current carrying capacity will be restricted only by technological sophistication in using them. But if large quantities of natural resources must be imported, this dependency can act as a brake on growth. Joseph Nye and Robert Keohane have made a useful distinction between the *sensitivity* and the *vulnerability* of one country to the actions of others. This distinction is very helpful in understanding the problems of countries that support populations well in excess of both natural and current carrying capacity. Countries are sensitive to the actions of others when they are in a position of mutual dependence by choice. The United States and Japan are now very sensitive to each other because of existing trade patterns. But this sensitivity could be reduced in either country through deliberate policies designed to redirect the flow of trade to other parts of the world. Vulnerability exists where there are no readily available alternatives to the situation in which a country finds itself. Thus, Japan is extremely vulnerable to the nations in the Organization of Petroleum Exporting Countries (OPEC). A rapid increase in oil prices or a cutoff of exports from the Middle East would have grave consequences for the Japanese economy, since there are no readily available alternative sources of petroleum.[25]

Thus, it is possible for countries to live beyond both their natural and current carrying capacity. But the further beyond current carrying capacity a country strays, the more vulnerable it becomes to the actions of others, although there are strategies for reducing this vulnerability. The primary strategy is to maintain a variety of suppliers and export markets. There is, however, no way to eliminate entirely vulnerability based upon natural resource imports essential to populations living well beyond current carrying capacity.

Any list of countries in which populations could be considered to be living well beyond current carrying capacity and thus vulnerable to the actions of other countries would undoubtedly be headed by Japan. The Japanese import large quantities of food and almost all of the fuels and minerals used by Japanese industry. They pay for these imports by exporting manufactured goods, largely to markets in Western Europe and the United States. Thus, Japan is doubly vulnerable, being dependent on a small list of exporters for essential natural resources and on a limited number of export markets from which Japan must earn foreign currency to pay for mineral and fuel imports.

There is a third kind of carrying capacity, ultimate carrying capacity, which is a hypothetical figure about which only conjectures can be made. It is defined as the biomass or human population that could be sustained by a country or by the planet as a whole given the most optimal development and implementation of new technologies. But no one knows what new technologies can reliably be expected to exist in the future, so this concept is not a very useful one in policy making.

These concepts of natural carrying capacity, current carrying capacity, and ultimate carrying capacity help explain why there are recurring controversies over how many people can or should be sustained on the earth. Some claim that the human population and consumption levels are already too large and will soon collapse, while others claim that 20 or 30 billion persons could ultimately live on the planet's surface.[26] Both sides could be right. It is clear that more than 4 billion people cannot be sustained by the earth's natural carrying capacity, although those 4 billion *can* be sustained at present standards of living given present levels of technological development—at least until reserves of fossil fuels are exhausted. Given certain optimistic assumptions about future technological innovations, it would not be impossible to double or even quadruple the earth's population and sustain it at high standards of living, but it makes much more sense when planning national population policies to begin with technologies that do exist rather than conjecture about those that might exist.

In summary, then, nations are composed of interacting populations of human beings who make different levels and types of demands on the natural resource base of the relevant geographical territory. Each national unit has a natural carrying capacity that limits the biomass that can survive within the constraints of solar energy. Current carrying capacity denotes the biomass that can be supported by present-day technologies combined with a reasonable degree of autarky in natural resources. The number of human beings that can be sustained at present within the limits of current carrying capacity is a function of their basic physical needs; their *perceived* wants, which result from existing systems of stratification; and competition for scarce resources with other species on the same territory. The pressures generated by population growth and technological developments within nations give rise to the interactions among nations that can be explained by ecopolitical theory.

The Global Population Explosion

World population and demand for natural resources have exploded as a result of the social impact of industrial technology. The world population grows exponentially and now doubles very rapidly. Exponential growth occurs when quantities increase by a percentage of the base over a unit of time. In a bank savings account, for example, an annual rate of interest is paid on the amount of money in the account, the base, which is steadily increasing because of interest payments. If there is $100 in the account and interest is paid at the rate of 6 percent per year, at the end of the year there is about $106 in the account. During the second year, interest is paid on the full $106, the expanded base, that exists at the beginning of the year rather than only on the $100, and so on. World population growth is the most important example of the dynamics of exponential growth. If each family in the world were to have four children, and if each of these children were to produce four more offspring, it is easy to see how rapidly the world population base could increase. Fortunately, not all families have four children, and world population is now growing at an exponential rate of 2 percent per year.

The best way to contrast exponential growth with the more familiar linear variety is to think of two gamblers agreeing to flip a coin in an attempt to build their fortunes. A gambler who understands the dynamics of exponential growth might suggest to his opponent that he will give the opponent one dollar for each time the coin turns up heads and ask "only" that his opponent give him a nickel for the first tail, double for the second tail, and so on. Under normal conditions, by the twelfth toss the clever player is making $1.60 for each tail while the linear thinker gets only one dollar for each head!

A quantity that is growing in an exponential manner will double its base in a number of time units that is determined by the percentage increase per time unit. Because of the mathematics of compound interest formulas, an approximation of this doubling time can be obtained by dividing the percentage increase per unit of time into the number 70. Thus, a country exhibiting an annual increase of 3 percent in population growth will double its population every twenty-three years. Consumption of a mineral for which demand is increasing at 5 percent each year doubles every fourteen years.

At present, the world population is doubling every thirty-five or thirty-six years. This means that if present trends continue, the earth's 4 billion persons will be 8 billion in number shortly after the year 2015. Another doubling could then be expected by the year 2050. In the sixteenth through the nineteenth centuries, much of the world's growth in population took place in Europe and the United States. But the twentieth century has been the century of non-European population growth. The impact of the Industrial Revolution on the less developed world has been very uneven, leading to discontinuities in established patterns of population growth in less developed countries. At present, the external manifestations of industrialization—factory smokestacks, automobiles, television sets, Coca-Cola bottles, and so on—are obvious around the world, exported by the industrial countries along with the life-prolonging technologies that have accompanied industrialization. But these advances in diet, sanitation, medicine, and hygiene have not been accompanied by changes in reproductive behavior, which is governed by the traditional values of the impacted populations.

Available data illustrate the unevenness of world population growth and demonstrate that there is a very close relationship between levels of industrial development and rates of population growth. In highly industrialized Western Europe, the rate of population growth is presently only about .1 percent per year, meaning that populations in this region will double only every 700 years at present rates of growth. In the USSR, a relative latecomer to industrialization, the population is growing at about 1 percent annually. In Latin America, by contrast, population is growing at an annual rate of 2.7 percent. In Africa, the figure is 2.6 percent, and in Asia, it is 2 percent. Individual countries show even more pronounced differences. For example, Finland, Luxembourg, and East Germany have almost reached zero population growth. By contrast, Kenya, Rhodesia, Iraq, Jordan, the Philippines, Thailand, Honduras, Nicaragua, and the Dominican Republic are all growing at the rate of 3.3 percent or better annually. Just keeping up with population growth requires that these latter countries double industrial and agricultural production every 20 years, an almost impossible feat. . . .

In 1970, there were 1.1 billion persons (30 percent of the world's population) living in industrial countries and 2.6 billion persons (70 percent of the world's population) living in less developed countries. If present rates of population growth are maintained until the year 2020, there will be only 1.6 billion persons (11 percent) in the industrial world and 12.7 billion persons (89 percent) in the less developed world, a population shift of great ecopolitical significance. Then, inhabitants of the highly industrialized countries will represent a tiny minority of the world's population. . . .

With the exception of the World War I period, there has been an almost steady increase in rates of population growth, until 1975, when a slight decrease was noted. The world birthrate remained nearly constant at 35 per 1,000 persons over this period of time until the most recent decade, when it tapered off to about 30 per thousand. But due to improved methods of life extension, the death rate has been steadily plummeting from 30 per thousand persons at the turn of the century to only 13 per thousand persons at present. And this is the factor responsible for the contemporary rapid growth of world population.

The process that explains the uneven patterns of world population growth is called the *demographic transition*. The demographic transition is best described as being composed of three stages. In the first stage, characteristic of preindustrial societies, populations are in equilibrium as high birthrates are matched by high death rates. Pronatalist norms and values are predominant and are effectively enforced by a variety of social sanctions and economic incentives. The second stage of the demographic transition is characterized by declining mortality as life-prolonging technologies become available. Thus, populations grew rapidly in Europe from 1650 to 1900 because of declining mortality and are now growing in the world's less developed countries. During the second stage of this transition, death rates tumble but conformity with rigid pronatalist norms maintains high birthrates.

Industrialized Western Europe and the United States have now passed into stage three of the demographic transition, which occurs when pronatalist norms, values, and attitudes begin to crumble and are replaced by industrial values and population equilibrium. Parents come to understand that each child born will probably survive and become an adult, which is definitely not the case in the preindustrial setting. The economic value of children also declines along with urbanization. As people move from rural areas, where children are an asset as farm laborers, to urban areas, where large numbers of unemployed children are an economic burden, birthrates drop. Furthermore, the economic cost of educating and raising children compares unfavorably with the washing machines, televisions, or automobiles that can be purchased instead. For these and a number of other reasons, the birthrate has historically fallen at advanced levels of industrialization.[27]

In order for a country to move into stage three of the transition, however, norms and values governing reproduction must change in response to new physical realities. It can take three or more generations for a substantial transformation of these values to take place, and different cultures are characterized by different susceptibility to these industrial values. Before fertility rates will change, potential parents must: (1) find it socially and morally acceptable to assess the costs and benefits of having more children, (2) perceive having children to be less desirable than not having them, (3) have effective techniques for preventing unwanted births available to them.[28]

At the present time in much of the less developed world, pronatalist norms and values still govern reproductive behavior. Economic progress is painfully slow, and there is little incentive to rural populations to have less children, despite the birth control devices lavished on most of the less developed world by foreign aid programs. In many less developed countries, it is now questionable whether economic and social conditions will ever be conducive to movement into this third stage of demographic transition.[29]

In summary, then, contemporary world population is growing exponentially at about 2 percent each year. This growth is very unevenly distributed. The third stage of the demographic transition has been completed in most industrial countries, and norms and values governing reproductive behavior have changed in response to the economic imperatives of industrialization. The location of the most vigorous present population growth is the less developed countries, where life-prolonging technologies have been introduced while birthrates remain high. Because of great difficulties in changing the syndrome of norms and values anchored in large families and because of the large number of young people in the populations of the less developed countries, populations will continue to grow there for the foreseeable future. Worldwide, if the number of children per family remains the same as it is at the present, there will be at least

12 billion people on the earth around the year 2020. Even if by some miracle all families in the world cut back to two-child families by the year 1990, there would still be nearly 6 billion mouths to feed by the year 2020, and the political and economic pressures rising from the resource demands of this population will shape the content of the emerging ecopolitical paradigm.

THE GREAT TRANSITION: EXPANSION TO ECOPOLITICS

The International Politics of Expansion

The dynamics that underlie an ecopolitical theory of international relations have always been important in determining interactions among nations. But at present these dynamics are becoming much more obvious. For example, in retrospect it is apparent that technology, energy, agriculture, and related factors that determine current carrying capacity have also been important in shaping world economic and political history. The course of human history has been marked by repeated clashes among national populations, the rise and fall of great civilizations, and the expansion and contraction of empires. Historians, political scientists, climatologists, and demographers are now suggesting that an increasing number of historical conflicts, periods of imperialism, and shifts in political and economic organization can be attributed to factors that changed the carrying capacity or population of the relevant political units.[30]

The evolution of the human race has been characterized by expansion and growth. The growth that took place in the days when most human beings lived by hunting and gathering came about at the expense of other species. The more recent and substantial population growth has been sparked by the technologies inherent in the Agricultural and Industrial revolutions. The Agricultural Revolution was based on the domestication of plants and animals, a big step forward over the hunting and gathering societies that previously provided subsistence. Agriculture was accompanied by related social innovations, including settlement in permanent villages, a more complex division of labor within exchange economies, new forms of social and political organization, and eventually organized conquest on a much larger scale. Agriculture also led to a jump in the human population, since abundance of food energy and the predictability associated with regular harvests permitted greater numbers to survive. The productivity of lands brought under cultivation was dramatically increased *within* the energy budget provided by current solar income.

The Industrial Revolution fostered a much greater increase in the number of human beings and also created an international politics of vigorous expansion. Unlike the technologies of the Agricultural Revolution, which increased carrying capacity within the constraints of current solar income, the technologies of the Industrial Revolution increased carrying capacity by tapping into stored solar income found in fossil fuels. This fossil fuel subsidy, the amount of useful energy derived from fossil fuels in excess of the energy used to get them, and related new technologies have expanded current carrying capacity very dramatically, replacing work done by human and animal energy with work done by mechanical equipment. It has been during the Industrial Revolution that many national populations have begun living well beyond the natural carrying capacity of the land.

Thus, historically there has been a slow acceleration of growth in population, in the development of new technologies, in the variety and per capita demands for resources, and in contacts among national populations. But, it has only been during the last three hundred years that extremely rapid and destabilizing growth has become one of the main factors shaping relations among nations. During this period, the population of the world increased eight fold, consumption of fossil fuels increased from almost nothing to current levels of nearly 7 billion metric tons of coal equivalent annually, the quantity and variety of non-fuel minerals used skyrocketed, the size and power of national units grew rapidly, and the frequency and intensity of interaction among national populations greatly increased. The three-hundred-year period between 1650 and 1950 produced not only an industrial revolution but an international political and economic order based on rapid, technology-inspired growth and expansion of national territory.

The historical roots of this economic and political expansion can be traced back to twelfth- and thirteenth-century Europe and an outward surge that accompanied the feeble beginnings of industrialization. Immanuel Wallerstein identifies two major outward thrusts from Western European nations that followed on the heels of innovations in transport and communications.[31] The first occurred between the eleventh and mid-thirteenth centuries. It was marked by the reconquest of Spain from the Moors, the recapture of Sardinia and Corsica by Christians, territorial acquisitions associated with the Crusades, and an English expansion into Wales, Scotland, and Ireland.[32] The second, and better known, outward thrust was the Atlantic expansion of the fifteenth and sixteenth centuries, which was motivated by gold, spices, fuel, and food staples needed in Western European nations.

According to Wallerstein, the pressure for the second outward expansion came mainly from a combination of scarcity and greed.[33] The fourteenth century was not a happy time for the European nobility. Opportunities for internal growth declined as even marginal lands, areas not really fit for optimal production, were planted and harvested to increase income. There are indications that changes in climate also cut deeply into agricultural productivity. Furthermore, a series of small wars made increased taxes a necessity and further cut into the lifestyle of the nobility. Given declining economic growth prospects, rising conspicuous consumption among the nobility, and a need for improved diets for expanding populations, one obvious course of action was a major push outward to the less explored portions of the world.

The Portuguese were the first actively to acquire colonies, a fact that can be largely explained by lack of other expansion opportunities. They were soon followed by the Dutch, British, and eventually other European powers and Japan in securing distant territories. Many of the Atlantic islands thus colonized became sources of wood, cereals, and sugar for European populations pressing close to then-current carrying capacity. The American colonies became sources of lumber, silver, gold, and tobacco. This wave of expansion finally carried European armies into even the most remote corners of Africa and Asia.

During this period of expansion, growing populations, new technologies, and increasing standards of living caused most European countries to move well beyond natural carrying capacity, and there could be no return to the current solar income energy systems. These countries financed growth through technological innovation and used the fossil fuel subsidy to build industrial economies. But they also turned outward, and through trade and conquest began to acquire larger portions of their natural resource needs from colonial empires. At first, this was expansion by choice, moving outward to colonize lands that were capable of providing luxury agricultural commodities. Subsequently, however, the colonizers became locked into an international economy in which a steady stream of raw materials from a colonial empire became essential to their physical and economic well-being. This dependence was particularly pronounced in Spain, where a steady flow of gold from the New World supported lavish lifestyles that could not be sustained when the flow of gold dried up.

This second wave of European expansion was related to technological advances, population growth, rising expectations, and insufficient domestic opportunities. The more industrialized the European nations became, the greater the quantity and variety of resources that were needed to meet domestic demands. Nazli Choucri and Robert North have used the term "lateral pressures" to refer to the dynamics of foreign expansion that resulted from growth pressures within a confined geographical territory: "When demands are unmet and existing capabilities are insufficient to satisfy them, new capabilities may have to be developed. . . . Moreover, if national capabilities cannot be attained at a reasonable cost within national boundaries, they may be sought beyond."[34] Lateral pressures can take several forms. Expansion of trade is one option for a country that possesses natural resources or industrial commodities of value in the international marketplace. Political confederation or formation of common markets is another possible response. Acquisition of colonies is a third option for countries with sufficient military power. The method a country uses to get needed resources beyond its boundaries is determined by domestic economic and military capabilities, technological sophistication, geographic location, and the power, friendliness, and resources of neighboring states.[35]

Thus, much Western European growth associated with the Industrial Revolution led to and was supported by an international expansion that augmented current carrying capacity through colonization of most of the non-European world. There are now more than 165 national populations having sovereignty over their territory; the majority of these countries were colonial possessions as little as two decades ago. At the beginning of World War II, colonial possessions occupied nearly one-third of the world's population and land area, and these possessions were used largely to meet the resource needs of colonial powers. European countries—Great Britian, the Netherlands, France, Belgium, Portugal, Italy, and Spain—with a combined population of 200 million persons, controlled over 700 million people in their colonies. Japan controlled over 60 million people, and the United States about 15 million.[36]

The underlying dynamics of this global expansion are clear in retrospect, but at the time, the colonizers were neither aware of nor honest about their motives. Some justified lateral expansion in the name of religion: bringing Christianity to heathens in Africa and Asia. Others rationalized these pursuits as necessary exploration and discovery. Still others found justifications in commercial and mercantile imperatives. Colonies were taken to be part of a natural state of affairs and essential to economic progress. At the time of the expansion, there were very few moral inhibitions about taking territories from relatively defenseless inhabitants. Might made right, and the pressures for expansion could be halted only by counterforce from another expanding power.

The Industrial Revolution, then, gave birth to an expansionist international politics accompanied by lateral pressures that forced an outward expansion in trade and development of networks of colonies. National populations and their per capita demands for natural resources soon exceeded the capacity of existing territory. Resource deficits were made up by imports from colonies. Over time, the dependence of colonizers on their colonial empires continued to rise, and they strayed further from their natural carrying capacity. The independence movement of the post-World War II period came as an economic as well as a political shock to these countries, which had come to count on colonies as sources of natural resources. The colonial powers were ill prepared to cope with the independence movements is either a military or an economic sense, since they had depleted their strength in the protracted combat of World War II. And now they must devise new strategies for obtaining natural resources that were once imported from colonies.

The Foundations of Ecopolitics

The international relations of the Industrial Revolution and the period of growth and abundance associated with it are currently being transformed into an international relations of limited opportunities. A central factor in this transition is *perceived* new scarcities. "Ecopolitics" is the term that describes the cluster of economic, ecological, and ethical issues that accompanies these changes in perspective in international relations. Ecopolitics is emerging from a new assessment of remaining resource-intensive growth possibilities in a finite world.

In order to assess better the nature of this transition, it is important to address some of the key questions that have interested scholars in international relations. There are at least four key questions that can be distilled out of the long list of candidates that help describe the nature of the emerging ecopolitics:

1. What are the key issues in international politics that form the basis for unity and division among various actors in the system?

2. Who are the significant actors in the international system, what is the nature of the international system, and what is the nature of the prevailing codes of conduct among major actors?

3. How is power used in relations among actors in the international system and what are its sources?

4. What is the level of interdependence in the international system?

Ecopolitics represents the emergence of broader ecological, ethical, and economic issues and conflicts in international politics as a partial substitute for the narrower military power issues typical of the international politics of the industrial era. Bergsten, Nye, and Keohane have found this new international politics to involve the politicization of economic issues as well as changes in the utility of force and economic power for most states.[37] This changing context for international politics now involves a new ecological way of seeing things that stresses international politics as a "system of relationships among interdependent, earth-related communities that share with one another an increasingly crowded planet that offers finite and exhaustible quantities of basic essentials of human well-being and existence."[38]

Serious ecopolitical issues were not totally absent within the old international politics. It is a fact that those states in a position to set the international agenda of key issues were not interested in or motivated to discuss them. Thus, many ecopolitical issues that are now coming to dominate international negotiations were then not considered worthy of discussion. Peter Bachrach and Morton Baratz have pointed out that one important aspect of the exercise of power is the ability to keep certain issues from coming to public attention.[39] In international politics, as in other political arenas, dominant forces are often able to mute political conflict by keeping countless potential issues from being placed on agendas. It was a consensus among the major powers that kept these ecopolitical issues from surfacing on international agendas.

It is a clear sign of the growing power of the presently less developed countries that they have been able to shatter this old consensus and thrust the relevant "nondecisions," issues that have previously never been openly debated, onto the agenda of international negotiations. Within the old and established paradigm there was a large consensus, and routine international relations predominated. At present, this consensus is crumbling and, as aspects of the old paradigm are questioned, a new international politics is beginning.[40]

There are many reasons why consensus sometimes breaks down. New actors with different views can obtain a position of power in a relevant political system. Shifts in power relationships can occur among old system members. Or the social and physical environments can generate problems that cannot be solved by old methods. There is an element of all three in the rise of ecopolitics. For example, the advance of technology combined with natural resource limitations has made access to and control over petroleum and natural gas an important issue in contemporary international politics. Two decades ago, control of the world energy industry was firmly in the hands of multinational corporations based in the industrially developed countries, and this situation was quietly accepted within the then-existing consensus. Since then, oil power has elevated Saudi Arabia, Iran, Kuwait—and OPEC collectively—into a much more powerful position in the international system. And dependence on foreign oil and natural gas has differentially weakened the position of formerly powerful industrial nations.

Periods when an existing consensus is called into question in social life are accompanied by changes in morals, as old values and ethics are questioned. Thus, changing definitions of human rights are a central theme in ecopolitics. During the period of rapid industrial expansion and overt colonialism, there was little concern over individual rights of people in conquered territories or even over the rights of other countries. But human rights issues that were formerly settled by benign neglect have now become matters of international debate. Rights to minimal diets, the morality of large income gaps between rich and poor nations—and between the rich and poor within those nations—rights to work, just wages, racism, colonialism, neocolonialism, and several other moral issues that were largely ignored in the old international consensus now occupy center stage in international politics. In some respects, the "is" of *realpolitic* is being replaced slowly by the "ought" of ecopolitics. This does not mean that all leaders of all nations have suddenly become moralists. It does mean, however, that ethical considerations are now being interjected into the new international politics and could become much more significant as determinants of international behavior.

Finally, a growing realization that all states and individuals share a finite ecosphere* and that there are limits to the burdens that can be imposed on that ecosphere has given impetus to new issues of both an economic and a moral nature. Publication of *The Limits to Growth* in 1972 rekindled the debate over growth prospects that began in the eighteenth century with the Reverend Thomas Malthus.[41] But this time the debate is taking place on a planetary scale. Many subsequent studies have further refined the growth debate and focused on the morality of great differences in consumption between rich and poor nations.[42] Irrespective of the accuracy of the world models involved, in political affairs empirical reality is often overshadowed by perceptions of this reality. These perceptions, in turn, are often conditioned by rhetoric instead of fact. The new array of ecopolitical issues has been given a tremendous boost by the limits to growth thesis, and leaders of less developed countries have seized upon it as a potentially powerful moral argument for major programs of global wealth redistribution.

NOTES

*"Ecosphere" is a term used to refer to the global ecosystem, the complex sum of many smaller interrelated ecosystems. An ecosystem is a community of flora and fauna combined with its nonliving physical environment.

1. See Paul Ehrlich and Anne Ehrlich, *Population, Resources, Environment* (San Francisco: W. H. Freeman, 1971), pp. 6–7. See also Paul Ehrlich, Anne Ehrlich, and John Holdren, *Ecoscience* (San Francisco: W. H. Freeman, 1977), chap. 4.

2. See the discussion of exponential curves and "deflection points" in Jonas Salk, *The Survival of the Wisest* (New York: Harper & Row, 1973), chap. 3.

3. Thomas Kuhn, *The Structure of Scientific Revolutions* (Chicago: University of Chicago Press, 1962), chap. 2.

4. Ibid., chap. 4.

5. See Dennis Pirages and Paul Ehrlich, *Ark II: Social Response to Environmental Imperatives* (San Francisco: W. H. Freeman, 1974), p. 43.

6. The impact of the Industrial Revolution on the shaping of the present dominant social paradigm is discussed in Karl Polanyi, *The Great Transformation* (Boston: Beacon Press, 1957).

7. Willis Harman, "The Coming Transformation," *The Futurist* (February 1977). See also Willis Harman, *An Incomplete Guide to the Future* (San Francisco: San Franciso Book Co., 1976), chap. 2.

8. See, for example, Organization for Economic Cooperation and Development, *World Energy Outlook* (Paris, 1977); Central Intelligence Agency, *International Energy Situation: Outlook to 1985* (Washington, D.C., April 1977); and Carroll Wilson, *Energy: Global Prospects 1985–2000* (Cambridge, Mass.: MIT Press, 1977).

9. See Donella Meadows et al., *The Limits to Growth* (New York: Universe Books 1972), and Ehrlich and Ehrlich, *Population, Resources, Environment*, chaps. 4–7.

10. Edward Renshaw, *The End of Progress* (North Scituate, Mass.: Duxbury Press, 1976).

11. The best examples of the "technological optimist" position are offered by Herman Kahn, William Brown, and Leon Martel, *The Next 200 Years* (New York: William Morrow, 1976), and Wilfred Beckerman, *In Defence of Economic Growth* (London: Jonathan Cape, 1974).

12. See William Ophuls, *Ecology and the Politics of Scarcity* (San Francisco: W. H. Freeman, 1977), and Herman Daly, ed., *Toward a Steady-State Economy* (San Francisco: W. H. Freeman, 1973).

13. An early attempt to gauge these perceptions of other nations is found in William Buchanan and Hadly Cantril, *How Nations See Each Other* (Westport, Conn.: Greenwood Press, 1972).

14. Harman, "The Coming Transformation," *The Futurist* (April 1977).

15. See Gerard O'Neill, "Space Colonies and Energy Supply to the Earth," *Science* (December 5, 1975), and Jack Salmon, "Politics of Scarcity vs. Technological Optimism: A Possible Reconciliation?" *International Studies Quarterly* (December 1977).

16. See, for example, Harold Sprout and Margaret Sprout, *Toward a Politics of the Planet Earth* (New York: Van Nostrand Reinhold, 1971), and Nazli Choucri, *Population Dynamics and International Violence* (Lexington, Mass.: D. C. Heath, 1974).

17. Kenneth Watt, *Principles of Environmental Science* (New York: McGraw-Hill, 1973), p. 1.

18. Karl Deutsch, *Nationalism and Social Communication* (Cambridge, Mass.: MIT Press, 1953), p. 100.

19. Karl Deutsch, "Communication Theory and Political Integration," in Philip Jacob and James Toscano, eds., *The Integration of Political Communities* (Philadelphia: J. B. Lippincott, 1964).

20. See Barrington Moore, *Social Origins of Dictatorship and Democracy* (Boston: Beacon Press, 1966), and Charles Tilley, ed., *The Formation of National States in Western Europe* (Princeton: Princeton University Press, 1975).

21. The influence of weather and plagues on human populations is documented in William McNeill, *Plagues and Peoples* (Garden City, N.Y.: Anchor Press, 1976).

22. Watt, *Principles of Environmental Science*, p. 20.

23. Ehrlich and Ehrlich, *Population, Resources, Environment*, p. 59.

24. Paul Ehrlich and John Holdren, "The Impact of Population Growth," *Science* (March 26, 1971).

25. Robert Keohane and Joseph Nye, *Power and Interdependence* (Boston: Little, Brown, 1977), pp. 12–13.

26. See S. Fred Singer, Ed., *Is There an Optimum Level of Population?* (New York: McGraw-Hill, 1971).

27. Thomas Espenshade, *The Value and Cost of Children* (Washington, D.C.: Population Reference Bureau, April 1977). See also Michael Teitelbaum, "Relevance of Demographic Transition Theory for Developing Countries," *Science* (May 1975), and Jay Weinstein, *Demographic Transition and Social Change* (Morristown, N.J.: General Learning Press, 1976).

28. Ansley Coale, *Proceedings of the IUSSP International Population Conference* (Liege, Belgium: 1973), p. 65.

29. See S. E. Beaver, *Demographic Transition: Theory Reinterpreted* (Lexington, Mass.: D.C. Heath, 1975); Robert Cassen, "Population and Development: A Survey," *World Development* (October-November 1976); and Timothy King, *Population Policies and Economic Development* (Baltimore: Johns Hopkins University Press, 1974).

30. See Immanuel Wallerstein, *The Modern World System* (New York: Academic Press, 1974), pp. 33–37; Stephen Schneider, *The Genesis Strategy* (New York: Plenum Press, 1976); and McNeill, *Plagues and Peoples*.

31. Wallerstein, *The Modern World System*, pp. 38–39.

32. Archibald Lewis, "The Closing of the European Frontier," *Speculum* (October 1958).

33. Wallerstein, *The Modern World System*, pp. 39–48.

34. Nazli Choucri and Robert North, *Nations in Conflict* (San Francisco: W. H. Freeman, 1975), p. 16.

35. Ibid., p. 15.

36. David Finlay and Thomas Hovet, Jr., *7304: International Relations on the Planet Earth* (New York: Harper & Row, 1975), pp. 22–23.

37. C. Fred Bergsten, Robert Keohane, and Joseph Nye, Jr., "International Economics and International Politics: A Framework for Analysis," in C. Fred Bergsten and Lawrence Krause, eds., *World Politics and International Economics* (Washington, D.C.: Brookings Institution, 1975), pp. 6–7.

38. Sprout and Sprout, *Toward a Politics of the Planet Earth*, p. 14.

39. Peter Bachrach and Morton Baratz, "Decisions and Non-Decisions: An Analytical Framework," *The American Political Science Review* (September 1963).

40. For more detail on nondecisions and stability, see Dennis Pirages, *Managing Political Conflict* (New York: Praeger, 1976), pp. 81–88.

41. Malthus's original work, *An Essay on the Principle of Population as It Affects the Future Improvement of Society with Remarks on the Speculations of M. Goodwin, M. Condorcet and other writers*, was published anonymously in 1798.

42. See Mihajlo Mesarovic and Eduard Pestel, *Mankind at the Turning Point* (New York: E. P. Dutton, 1974), and Jan Tinbergen et al., *Reshaping the International Order* (New York: E. P. Dutton, 1976).

30
ECOLOGICAL SCARCITY AND
INTERNATIONAL POLITICS

William Ophuls

THE COMPARATIVE PERSPECTIVE

The United States [may be] the most extreme version of modern industrial civilization, [but] the peculiarities of the American form of this civilization ought not to be allowed to obscure the wider implications of [an] analysis. Some problems may be uniquely American, but most are universal in one form or another. Let us therefore extend the analysis to other nations and then to the international political arena. We shall find that the basic political dynamics and dilemmas of ecological scarcity . . . remain unchanged. Furthermore, much of the specific analysis of American institutions . . . can in fact be applied, with appropriate modifications, to all developed and even many so-called developing countries, capitalist and communist alike, as well as to the world in general. The crisis of ecological scarcity is thus a planetary crisis.

For brevity's sake, the Western European nations can be treated as a bloc: as the depressing sameness of their reports to the United Nations Conference on the Human Environment at Stockholm in 1972 clearly indicated (UNIPUB 1972 catalogs these), Europe's environmental problems are essentially the same in character and magnitude as those of the United States, and its governments seem to exhibit the same degree of capacity to deal with them. In certain respects, due to the greater density of population and industrial development, Europe's pollution problems are worse than our own; the contamination of the Baltic and Mediterranean Seas and of the Rhine River, heavy oil spillage from tankers and refineries (soon to be increased as the North Sea's oil and gas resources are fully exploited), and the "acid rains" that fall on Scandinavia are only some of the most notorious examples. With respect to resources, Western Europe's predicament is clearly much worse. Even taking due account of the temporary respite that development of North Sea gas and oil will bring, Europe's long-term dependence on external sources of energy is far greater than our own; for example, Europe has nothing resembling America's vast coal reserves. Similarly, European mineral resources are almost negligible compared

Reprinted from *Ecology and the Politics of Scarcity* by William Ophuls. San Francisco: W. H. Freeman & Co., 1977.

to actual and potential demand. Perhaps more critically, Western Europe as a whole is a major net importer of food and fiber, and the dependence of many European countries, like Denmark and the Netherlands, on food imports is overwhelming (both to feed the populace and, ironically, to sustain energy-intensive agricultural systems that are mainstays of their economies). Thus Western Europe is even more overextended ecologically in relation to its own resources than the United States. For us Americans, a major disruption of world trade would cause painful retrenchment, to be sure, but there would be little danger of starvation, and domestic energy would be available in sufficient quantity to keep the economy limping along. Europe does not enjoy such luxury. World trade must continue along established lines or economic collapse threatens—but, as we shall see later in this chapter, recent and impending changes in the terms of trade create the specter of just such a collapse.

Nor do the Western European nations appear to have any greater prospect of coping politically with ecological scarcity than the United States. All share the same basic growth-oriented world view. All have followed the path blazed by the United States toward high mass consumption and, to a somewhat lesser extent, high energy use. All are mass democracies in which political parties compete for favor largely on the basis of how well they can satisfy the material aspirations of the citizenry. In short, having travelled the same basic path in roughly the same manner for the last 250 years, we Westerners have wound up in approximately the same place.

Nevertheless, just as there are some differences in the nature and degree of ecological scarcity, so too there are some significant differences in the potential for political adaptation. For one thing, Europe has had to contend with ecological scarcity in numerous ways even during an era of unparalleled abundance. Not possessing the same cornucopia of found wealth, for example, Europe has never been as profligate with its resources as the United States. For instance, Europeans manage to achieve roughly comparable living standards while using only about half as much energy per capita as Americans. Also, Europeans practice sustained-yield forestry, control land use quite stringently by U.S. standards, and so on. Thus, both because of necessity and because of a generally less doctrinaire attachment to the principles of laissez faire, there exists in Europe a much greater willingness to accept planning and social controls. Moreover, at least in some quarters, disenchantment with bourgeois acquisition as a way of life has grown markedly. In general, therefore, European nations may cope somewhat better with ecological scarcity than the United States, despite the greater physical challenges they will face.

Japan

While in terms of ecological scarcity the situation of Japan is much more desperate than that of Europe, it possesses countervailing political and social advantages over Europe. With about half the U.S. population, a land about the size of Montana that is mostly mountainous and poorly endowed with mineral and energy resources, and the third largest economy in the world, Japan is a very tight little island indeed. Prevented from gaining by military means a position of power, respect, and economic security in the international community, the Japanese entered the great postwar international GNP stakes determined to win economically what could not be won by force of arms. They "aped" (their own word) the acquisitive ethic and mass-democratic institutions of the West so effectively that they achieved economic growth of unprecedented intensity and rapidity. This extraordinary "success" has earned them notorious pollution problems, like the mercury poisoning that killed or paralyzed almost 700 people and affected at least 8,000 more, and a level of dependence on foreign trade and foreign sources of raw materials and fuels that makes them extremely vulnerable to international turmoil and resource scarcities, whether due to natural exhaustion or to artificial restriction by cartels. Japan thus faces ecological scarcity in an extreme form. A serious interruption of oil supplies from the Persian Gulf, a substantial decline in the fish catch, the inability or unwillingness of the United States to continue to supply vast quantities of food—these and numerous other potential threats could have severe consequences for Japan, which has totally committed itself to the modern way of industrial life and to living far beyond its ecological means.

Beginning in the early 1970's, and especially after the energy crisis of 1973–1974, the Japanese awoke to the fact that they were headed for an ecological precipice. The Japanese government cracked down on pollution with progressively greater severity and has recently moved to conserve energy and control growth in general. An awkward problem for Japanese political leaders, largely drawn from the business-oriented, conservative Liberal-Democratic Party (LDP), which has ruled throughout the postwar era, is that the powerful economic interests that are the LDP's main source of support, financial and otherwise, are also the chief polluters and main beneficiaries of growth. On the other hand, there are a number of positive factors. Having lived on a tight little island for centuries, the Japanese have a highly developed sense of community and a tradition of self-sacrifice for the common good. The phenomenal success of the postwar Japanese birth-control effort is an indication of how readily this communal ethic can be mobilized to achieve ends desired by leaders. In addition, a latent Shinto-Buddhist respect for nature, the remnants of a feudal code of values that despised wealth, and a tradition of government intervention in all areas of economic and social life (as in the birth-control effort, which included the vigorous promotion of abortion almost thirty years ago) will all assist Japan's leaders as they try to come to terms with an extreme form of ecological scarcity.

The Soviet Union

The Soviet Union is the most interesting and revealing comparative case.[1] Because it is the leading non-market industrialized nation it should seemingly be exempt, if not from the basic political dynamics of scarcity, at least from most of the failings of American market economics and politics. . . . In fact, however, the U.S.S.R. has severe and growing environmental problems and has so far demonstrated no greater capacity to deal with them than the United States and other market-oriented democracies. In brief, the imperatives of the industrial production system common to East and West have brought about a convergence of environmental ills that call into question the basic premises of the industrial system—and therefore of many features of the political institutions rooted in that system, whether those institutions are nominally capitalist or communist.

That the Soviet Union has serious environmental problems has been extensively documented (Goldman 1972; Pryde 1972) and is not denied by Soviet spokesmen. With the sole exception of problems related to the mass use of private automobiles, which has not yet reached a significant level, Soviet pollution problems are in almost all respects identical with those found throughout the industrialized world. Nor, despite a relatively favorable position compared to Europe and America, is the U.S.S.R. exempt from ecological scarcity with respect to resources. For example, sizable grain purchases in recent years have made it evident that the Soviet Union's agricultural situation is problematic, even if the prospect of Malthusian starvation is remote. Also, the Soviet Union's apparent abundance of domestic energy resources may be illusory, at least in part. One recent study (Slocum 1974) points out that these resources are not readily exploitable, for they lie for the most part in remote and environmentally forbidding regions; also, they may be less substantial than rough estimates had indicated; in addition, they must be seen in the context not of Soviet needs alone, but also of the increasing demands of the COMECON countries of Eastern Europe; finally, they can probably not be fully exploited without advanced Western technology and even Western capital (at a time when the West confronts a potential capital shortage of its own).

Even as they acknowledge that environmental problems exist, Soviet spokesmen almost uniformly deny the reality of the limits to growth (Fyodorov 1973; Kiseleva 1974). The basis for their optimism appears to be the fundamental Marxist axiom that the problems of mankind have their origin in the structure of social relationships, specifically the social relationships surrounding the means of production; nature as such presents no obstacles that cannot be overcome by appropriate social arrangements and the wonders of scientific-technological productivity unleashed by the bourgeois revolution. Furthermore, say the spokesmen, since the Soviet system is not held in thrall by selfish market interests, it will easily be able to deal with any environmental problems that do crop up, whereas pollution and other environmental ills in the West are seen as serious emerging "contradictions" (inherent self-destructive forces) that capitalist nations will not be able to overcome.

Less partial observers paint quite a different picture. First, because the ideology of growth and belief in the power of technology are even more strongly entrenched in the U.S.S.R. than in the West, abandoning or even compromising growth in production for the sake of environmental protection or resource conservation is a much more heretical concept. For one thing, the Marxist utopia depends for its achievement on the abolition of material scarcity, so that to abandon growth is tantamount to abandoning a utopian promise that has inspired the whole society. Worse, this cherished utopian goal is used to justify many features of Soviet life that seem to conflict with basic Marxist principles. Soviet leaders, for example, explain the use of differential rewards (as opposed to the true communist principle of "to each according to his needs") as a necessary expedient to help build the requisite material and productive base for a utopia of abundance; more important, the "proletarian dictatorship" and "democratic centralism" exercised by the Communist Party are also rationalized with this brand of logic. The loss of such convenient justifications could thus cause awkward political repercussions.

Second, largely as a result of this fundamental ideological bias toward material expansion (but also because of security consciousness), the primacy of narrow economic concerns in policy matters is almost total, and fixation on production to the virtual exclusion of all else makes the Soviet elite very resistant to more than token concern for the environment.

Third, although they are employed by the state rather than private corporations, Soviet economic managers compete with other managers within the basic framework of the national plan, and their reluctance to spend money on nonproductive pollution control, their willingness to shove the external costs of production off on others, their desire to win promotions by overproducing the quota, and so forth, all make them behave just like capitalist managers with respect to the environment. Moreover, in the Soviet Union the economic managers have far greater political power than their Western counterparts. In one respect, the tragic logic of the commons operates even more viciously in the U.S.S.R.: because not only air and water, but virtually all natural resources, are (thanks to state ownership) treated as free or semi-free goods, there is an even greater tendency on the part of economic managers to use land, energy, and mineral resources wastefully.

Fourth, because government decisions are made in private council by leaders who put production and the vested interests of the state economic bureaucracy first, those concerned about the problems of growth have little opportunity to influence policy as it is being formed; they can only point out the adverse consequences of past policies. However, articles critical of Soviet environmental policy seem to be appearing in the press more frequently; perhaps this indicates that environmental and conservationist concerns are being communicated to Soviet decison makers more effectively than in the past.

Finally, although there has been some public discussion of the wisdom of continued pronatalism, the Soviet government continues to encourage population growth in a variety of direct and indirect ways.[2]

In short, Soviet economic and political institutions seem designed to produce environmental deterioration and resource depletion just as inexorably as their American counterparts. The essential reason has been sardonically stated by a leading expert on Soviet environmental policy: "The replacement of private greed by public greed is not much of an improvement" (Goldman 1970). The nature of political institutions through which the "greed" for material growth is translated into economic output appears to make relatively little difference: in fact, if they are very strongly committed to growth, highly centralized and effective governments may wreak more and faster havoc on the environment than even the most laissez-faire government. (This calls socialism into question as an answer to environmental problems.) Conversely, of course, once Soviet leaders are forced by ecological scarcity to cease trying to abolish scarcity by indefinite material growth, then party rule, Soviet law, and the power of state planning institutions (along with the Soviet Union's relative wealth of resources) will be great assets in making a rapid and relatively turmoil-free transition to a steady-state economy. However, abandoning the utopian goal of total abundance would remove much of the regime's moral legitimacy, and the longer-term political consequences of this loss of legitimacy could be grave indeed. In the long run, therefore, the Soviet Union may face a profound challenge to its political viability.

The Third World

The developing or less-developed[3] countries (LDCs) constituting the so-called Third World of course differ greatly from each other in many important respects, but for the purposes of this analysis, little is lost by considering them together. In brief, most LDCs, and especially the group of exceptionally poor countries now sometimes called "the Fourth World," are not sufficiently developed to experience neo-Malthusian ecological scarcity. Instead, they confront ecological scarcity in its crudest Malthusian form: too many people, too little food. . . . Almost everywhere the difficulties seem greatly to exceed the capacity of current governments in the LDCs to cope with them. Even now, for example, many governments cannot assure all their citizens enough food to maintain life, and the future prospects are grim. However, there are some interesting exceptions to this general picture.

The LDCs run the gamut from virtual non-development to what is usually called semi-development, in which considerable industrialization and modernization coexist with continued backwardness, especially in rural areas. In general, countries moving toward semi-development seem to follow established models. Mexico and Brazil, for example, have followed a basically American path, so that Mexico City has a smog problem rivaling that of Los Angeles, and Brazil's treatment of its undeveloped wealth, especially such fragile and irreplaceable resources as the Amazon rain forest, epitomizes frontier economics at its most heedless. On the other hand, Taiwan and South Korea have proceeded more or less along the lines laid down by Japan and are beginning to encounter many of the same problems. In the same way, the countries (now mostly beyond the stage of semi-development) that have travelled the Soviet path experience the same kinds of environmental problems and suffer from similar political liabilities in coping with them. In general, then, development by any path eventually brings environmental problems and creates awkward political dilemmas.

China

The one major exception to this generalization is China (and perhaps Tanzania, which has taken a similar approach to economic development). The Chinese have stressed national self-reliance instead of dependence on foreign trade and technology, decentralization and local self-sufficiency, "appropriate" technology that is cheap and suitable for small-scale use, cadres with practical technical skills instead of highly specialized and expensive training, labor-intensive instead of capital-intensive modes of production, careful husbandry of resources and fanatical vigilance against waste, and some degree of ecological restoration (for example, the reforestation of mountains denuded since ancient times).

However, it remains to be seen whether these principles will continue to guide Chinese development. It seems likely that they have prevailed so far because hard-headed Chinese planners, from Mao on down, have seen that they are the most efficient means of achieving rapid, self-generated economic growth under current Chinese conditions. The Chinese leaders have clear ambitions for industrial and military might, as well as for substantially higher living standards for their people, so that once current policies have built the requisite infrastructure for industrial power, one suspects that development will proceed along somewhat different lines. This impression is reinforced by Chinese spokesmen's tireless reiteration of the basic Marxist principle that only social relations are problematic and that nature itself presents no obstacles that cannot be conquered with technology and appropriate social organization. Above all, as in Marxist philosophy in general, there seems to be no criterion of developmental sufficiency—How much development is enough?—in Maoist philosophy; yet, as we know, this is indispensable for a steady-state economy. Thus China's current ecological virtue appears to be mostly circumstantial, rather than truly principled, and the higher levels of output in prospect seem certain to generate the same array of environmental problems that developed nations now confront.

Finally, it must be noted that the undeniable achievements of the Chinese, including the ecological virtues enumerated above, have only been made possible by a degree of social regimentation that is irreconcilable with Western concepts of individual liberty. The disturbing question that has run throughout this entire analysis therefore reemerges with stark clarity: Can a steady-state society come about or be maintained except through some such regimentation?

THE INTERNATIONAL STATE OF NATURE

The International Macrocosm

If in the various national microcosms constituting the world political community the basic dynamics of ecological scarcity apply virtually across the board, in the macrocosm of international politics they operate even more strongly. Just as within each individual nation, the tragic logic of the commons brings about the overexploitation of common property resources like the oceans and the atmosphere. Also, the pressures toward inequality, oppression, and conflict are even more intense within the world political community, for it is a community in name only, and the already marked cleavage between rich and poor threatens to become even greater. Without even the semblance of a world government, such problems depend for their solution on the good will and purely voluntary cooperation of nearly 150 sovereign states—a prospect that does not inspire optimism. Let us examine these issues in more detail, to see how ecological scarcity aggravates the already very difficult problems of international politics.

The Global Tragedy of the Commons

The tragic logic of the commons operates universally, and its effects are readily visible internationally—in the growing pollution of international rivers, seas, and now even the oceans; in the overfishing that has caused a marked decline in the fish catch, as well as the near extinction of the great whales; and in the impending scramble for seabed resources by maritime miners or other exploiters. There is no way to confine environmental insults or the effects of ecological degradation within national borders; river basins, airsheds, and oceans are intrinsically international. Even seemingly local environmental disruption inevitably has some impact on the quality of regional and, eventually, global ecosystems. Just as within each nation, the aggregation of individual desires and actions overloads the international commons. But, like individuals, states tend to turn a blind eye to this, for they profit by the increased production while others bear most or all of the cost, or they lose by self-restraint while others receive most or all of the benefit. Thus, Britain gets the factory output, while Scandinavia suffers the ecological effects of "acid rain"; the French and Germans use the Rhine for waste disposal even though this leaves the river little more than a reeking sewer by the time it reaches fellow European Economic Community member Holland downstream.

However, if the problems are basically the same everywhere, the political implications of the tragedy of the commons are much more serious in the international arena. It has long been recognized that international politics is the epitome of the Hobbesian state of nature: despite all the progress over the centuries toward the rule of international law, sovereign states, unlike the citizens within each state, acknowledge no law or authority higher than their own self-interest; they are therefore free to do as they please, subject only to gross prudential restraints, no matter what the cost to the world community. Brazil, for example, has made it plain that it will brook no outside interference with its development of the Amazon, and well-meaning ecological advice is castigated as "scientific colonialism" (Castro 1972). Also, despite strong pressures from the international community, the U.S.S.R. and Japan have openly frustrated the effort to conserve whale stock—both at the negotiating table and at sea. In international relations, therefore, the dynamic of the tragedy of the commons is even stronger than within any given nation state, which, being a real political community, has at least the theoretical capacity to make binding, authoritative decisions on resource conservation and ecological protection. By contrast, international agreements are reached and enforced by the purely voluntary cooperation of sovereign nation states existing in a state of nature. The likelihood of forestalling by such means the operation of the tragedy of the commons is extremely remote. Worse, just as any individual is nearly helpless to alter the outcome by his own actions (and even risks serious loss if he refuses to participate in the exploitation of the commons), so too, in the absence of international authority or enforceable agreement, nations have little choice but to contribute to the tragedy by their own actions. This would be true even if each individual state was striving to achieve a domestic steady-state economy, for unless one assumes agreement on a largely autarkic world, states would still compete with each other internationally to maximize the resources available to them. Ecological scarcity thus intensifies the fundamental problem of international politics—the achievement of world order—by adding further to the pre-existing difficulties of a state of nature. Without some kind of international governmental machinery with authority and coercive power over sovereign states sufficient to oblige them to keep within the bounds of the ecological common interest of all on the planet, the world must suffer the ever greater environmental ills ordained by the global tragedy of the commons.

The Struggle Between Rich and Poor

Ecological scarcity also aggravates very seriously the already intense struggle between rich and poor. As is well known, the world today . . . is sharply polarized between the developed, industrialized "haves," all affluent in a greater or lesser degree and all getting more affluent all the time, and the underdeveloped or developing "have nots," all relatively and absolutely impoverished and with few exceptions tending to fall relatively ever farther behind despite their often feverish efforts to grow. The degree of the inequality is also well known: the United States, with only 6 percent of the world's population, consumes about 30 percent of the total energy production of the world and comparable amounts of other resources, and the rest of the "haves," although only about half as prodigal as the United States, still consume resources far out of proportion to their population; conversely, per capita consumption of resources in the Third World ranges from one-tenth to one-hundredth that in the "have" countries. To make matters worse, the resources that the "haves" enjoy in inordinate amounts are largely and increasingly imported from the Third World; thus economic inequality and what might be called ecological colonialism have become intertwined. In view of this extreme and long-standing inequality (which moreover has its roots in an imperialist past), it is hardly surprising that the Third World thirsts avidly for development or that it has become increasingly intolerant of those features of the current world order it perceives as obstacles to becoming as rich and powerful as the developed world.

Alas, the emergence of ecological scarcity appears to have sounded the death knell for the aspirations of the LDCs. Even assuming, contrary to fact, that there were sufficient mineral and energy resources to make it possible, universal industrialization would impose intolerable stress on world ecosystems. In short, the current model of development, which assumes that all countries will eventually become heavily industrialized mass-consumption societies, is doomed to failure.[4] Naturally, this conclusion is totally unacceptable to the modernizing elites of the Third World; their political power is generally founded on the promise of development. Even more important, simply halting growth would freeze the current pattern of inequality, leaving the "have nots" as the peasants of the world community in perpetuity. Thus an end to growth and development would be acceptable to the Third World only in combination with a radical redistribution of the world's wealth and a total restructuring of the world's economy to guarantee the maintenance of economic justice. Yet it seems absolutely clear that the rich have not the slightest intention of alleviating the plight of the poor if it entails the sacrifice of their own living standards. Ecological scarcity thus greatly increases the probability of naked confrontation between rich and poor.[5]

Who Are Now the "Haves" and "Have Nots"?

An important new element has been injected into this struggle. The great resource hunger of the developed and even some parts of the developing world has begun to transfer power and wealth to those who have resources to sell, especially critical resources like petroleum. As a result, the geopolitics of the world has already been decisively altered.

This process can be expected to continue. The power and wealth of the major oil producers is bound to increase over the next two decades, despite North Sea and Alaskan oil and regardless of whether the Organization of Petroleum Exporting Countries (OPEC) manages to maintain its current degree of unity.

Some believe that oil is a special case and that the prospect of OPEC-type cartels for other resources is dim (Banks 1974; Mikesell 1974). While these assessments may be correct, it seems inevitable that in the long run an era of "commodity power" must emerge. The hunger of the industrialized nations for resources is likely to increase, even if there is no substantial growth in output to generate increased demand for raw materials, because the domestic mineral and energy resources of the developed countries have begun to be exhausted. Even the United States, for example, already imports 100 percent of its platinum, mica, chromium, and strontium; over 90 percent of its manganese, aluminum, tantalum, and cobalt; and 50 percent or more of twelve additional key minerals (Wade 1974). However, the developed countries seem determined to keep growing, and assuming even modest further growth in industrial output, their dependence on Third World supplies is bound to increase markedly in the next few decades.[6] Thus, whatever the short-term prospects for the success of budding cartels in copper, phosphates, and other minerals, the clear overall longterm trend is toward a seller's market in basic resources and therefore toward "commodity power," even if this power grows more slowly and is manifested in a less extreme form than that of OPEC.[7]

Thus, the basic long-standing division of the world into rich and poor in terms of GNP per capita is about to be overlaid with another rich-poor polarization, in terms of resources, that will both moderate and intensify the basic split. Although there are many complex interdependencies in world trade—for example, U.S. food exports are just as critical to many countries as their mineral exports are to us—it is already clear that the resource-rich Third World nations stand to gain greater wealth and power at the expense of the "haves." Already, for example, through nationalization and forced purchase the OPEC nations have largely wrested control of drilling and pumping operations from the Western oil companies; their expansion into other areas of the oil business is only a question of time. Thus, although most of the earlier fears of imminent economic takeover have proven to be unfounded, a substantial transfer of real wealth is certain to occur in the next few decades. In addition, as is already evident, the newly resource-rich are not likely to settle for mere commercial gains. They have long-standing political grievances against other nations—most especially the developed nations—that they will try to remedy with their new power. Israel's future, for example, has suddenly become much cloudier.

Other problems abound. For example, international financial and monetary institutions, established for a simpler world of indefinite growth and a clear demarcation between "haves" and "have nots," are creaking under the unprecedented strain of the rapid shift in economic and geopolitical realities. In addition, poor countries without major resources of their own will suffer—indeed, already have suffered—major setbacks to their prospects for development. This is true not only of the hopelessly poor Fourth World, but also of countries whose development programs have already acquired some momentum. In India, for example, the quadrupled price of energy has dealt an all but mortal blow to the energy-intensive Green Revolution, on which so many of the country's hopes for development were pinned.

In sum, world geopolitics and economics are in for a radical reordering. Western economic development has involved a net transfer of resources, wealth, and power from the current "have nots" to the "haves," creating the cleavage between the two that now divides the world. In particular, the enormous postwar growth in output and consumption experienced by the industrialized nations was largely fueled by the bonanza of cheap oil that they were able to extract from relatively powerless client states in the Middle East. The success of the oil cartel is a signal that, from now on, wealth and power will begin to flow in the opposite direction. But only the relatively few "have nots" who possess significant amounts of resources will gain; the plight of the rest of the poor is more abject than before. Thus the old polarization between rich and poor seems likely to be replaced by a threefold division into the rich, the hopelessly poor, and the nouveaux riches—and such a major change in the international order is bound to create tension.

Conflict or Cooperation?

The overall effect of ecological scarcity in the international arena is to intensify the competitive dynamics of the preexisting international tragedy of the commons, so that increased commercial, diplomatic, and ultimately military confrontation over dwindling resources is more likely. At the same time the poor, having had their revolutionary hopes and rising aspirations crushed, will have little to lose but their chains. Also, to many of the declining "haves," ill-equipped to adapt to an era of "commodity power" and economic warfare, the grip of the nouveaux riches on essential resources will seem an intolerable stranglehold to be broken at all costs. Thus the disappearance of ecological abundance seems bound to make international politics even more tension ridden and potentially violent than it already is. Indeed, the pressures of ecological scarcity may embroil the world in hopeless strife, so that long before ecological collapse occurs by virtue of the physical limitations of the earth, the current world order will have been destroyed by turmoil and war — a truly horrible prospect, given the profoundly anti-ecological character of modern warfare.

Some, on the other hand, hope or believe that ecological scarcity will have just the opposite effect — because the problems will become so overwhelming and so evidently insoluble without total international cooperation, nation states will discard their outmoded national sovereignty and place themselves under some form of planetary government that will regulate the global commons for the benefit of all humankind and begin the essential process of gradual economic redistribution. In effect, states will be driven by their own vital national interests — seen to include ecological as well as traditional economic, political, and military factors — to embrace the ultimate interdependence needed to solve ecological problems (Shields and Ott 1974). According to this hypothesis, the very direness of the outcome if cooperation does not prevail may ensure that it will.

Unfortunately, the accumulating evidence tends to support the conflictual rather than the cooperative hypothesis. Faced with the new power of the oil barons, the first impulse of the United States was to try to go it alone in "Project Independence," while Japan, France, and others maneuvered individually to ensure their own future supplies, torpedoing the solidarity of the consuming countries confronting OPEC. Canada has served notice on the United States that it intends to end America's ecological colonialism; henceforth, the resources of Canada will be saved for its own use. Thus, the rich seem readier to follow "beggar thy neighbor" policies than to cooperate among themselves. Sympathy for the plight of the poor is even less evident. Some talk about expanding still further the scale of ecological colonialism; a West German research group has even put forward a scheme for the diversion of East Africa's Niger River to supply Europe with heat for energy (Anon. 1974). For others, continued interdependence of any kind with the poor is seen as so problematic and so full of threats to the sovereign independence and high living standards of the rich that the only sensible course is autarkic self-sufficiency.

Naturally, there has been considerable talk about cooperative international action to deal with the problems of ecological scarcity, but little or no momentum toward greater cooperation has developed. In fact, all the talk may have served chiefly to heighten further the tensions within the world community.

An Upsurge of Conference Diplomacy

By the late 1960's some of the alarming global implications of pollution and general ecological degradation had become widely apparent, and preparations began for a major international conference at Stockholm in 1972. Depending on one's point of view, the Stockholm Conference — to give it its proper title, the United Nations Conference on the Human Environment — was either a major diplomatic success or an abysmal failure. On the positive side, the elaborate preparations for the conference (each country had to make a detailed inventory of its environmental problems), the intense publicity given the over two years of preliminary negotiations, and the conference itself fostered a very high level of environmental awareness around the globe. Virtually ignored by diplomats in 1969, the environmental crisis had by 1972 rocketed right up alongside nuclear weapons and economic development as one of the big issues of international politics. The second major achievement of the Stockholm Conference was the establishment of the United Nations Environment Program (UNEP) to monitor the state of the world environment and to provide liaison and coordination between nation states and among the multitude of governmental and non-governmental organizations concerned with environmental matters. Finally, a few preliminary agreements covering certain less controversial and less critical ecological problems, like setting aside land for national parks and suppressing trade in endangered species, were reached either at the conference or immediately thereafter.

Despite these acknowledged achievements, environmentalists were by and large rather unhappy with the conduct and outcome of the conference. They were especially disillusioned, for example, by the way in which the original ecological purity of the conference's agenda was rapidly watered down by pressures from Third World countries, who made it plain that they would have nothing to do with the conference unless, in effect, underdevelopment was converted into a form of pollution. Moreover, a great part of the proceedings was devoted not to the problems on the agenda, but to the kind of "have" versus "have not" debate discussed above, and routine ideological posturing on political issues like "colonialism" consumed additional time. Also, cold-war politics refused to take a vacation; for example, the U.S.S.R. boycotted the conference because East Germany was not given full voting status. Thus the perhaps naively idealistic hope of many that the ecological issue would at last force quarrelsome and self-seeking sovereign nation states to put aside stale old grudges, recognize their common predicament, and act in concert to improve the human condition was completely dashed.

Worse, some of the features of the current world order most objectionable from an ecological point of view were actually reaffirmed at Stockholm—namely, the absolute right of sovereign countries to develop their own domestic resources without regard to the potential external ecological costs to the world community, and the unrestricted freedom to breed guaranteed by the Universal Declaration of Human Rights. In addition, established international institutions, like the World Health Organization and the Food and Agriculture Organization, extended distinctly lukewarm cooperation to the organizers of the conference, both because of bureaucratic jealousy and because of fear that environmental concerns would force them to alter or abandon programs, like all-out support for the Green Revolution and the eradication of malaria with DDT, that are a large part of their raison d'être. As a result, the Secretariat of UNEP was given little real power and only a minimum of resources to perform its coordinating and monitoring functions. Also, the headquarters of UNEP were eventually established in Nairobi, and although this has had the very positive effect of keeping the Third World interested in UNEP and its programs, it has definitely hampered the expansion and effectiveness of the global environmental monitoring and liaison that was to be UNEP's prime responsibility.

Since 1972, there have been more environmentally oriented conferences—principally the UN World Population Conference in 1974, the UN World Food Conference in 1974, and a series of UN Law of the Sea Conferences from 1974 to the present. However, there has been little progress since Stockholm. The World Population Conference somehow managed to end "without producing explicit agreement that there was a world population problem" (Walsh 1974). The World Food Conference produced few concrete achievements and left crucial problems on its agenda unsolved. The Law of the Sea Conferences have promoted progress toward a global consensus that seems likely to become the basis of an international treaty once future negotiating meetings dispose of some of the still unsettled issues. Unfortunately, the basis of this emerging consensus is an agreement to carve the oceans into national zones of exploitation, instead of making them into the common heritage of mankind; thus, as at Stockholm, the principle of national sovereignty has been even further entrenched.

The forces that prevented Stockholm from fulfilling its promise were even more strongly in evidence at these and other post-Stockholm international meetings directly or indirectly concerned with environmental issues. First, the spirit of militant nationalism that has animated so much of the history of the postwar world has not abated. Thus states insist on the absolute and sovereign right of self-determination in use of resources, population policy, and development in general, regardless of the wider consequences. Second, the demand by Third World countries for economic development has, if anything, increased in intensity, and whatever seems to stand in the way, like ecological considerations, gets rather short shrift. Third, largely because their prospects for development are so dim, Third World countries have begun to press even harder for fundamental reform of the world system (a "new international economic order"); thus every discussion of environmental issues like food and population is inevitably converted by Third World spokesmen into a discussion of international economic justice as well, which enormously complicates the process of negotiation. In short, environmental issues have become pawns in the larger diplomatic and political struggle between the nations.

In addition, diplomats, like national leaders, have attempted to handle the issues of ecological scarcity not as part of a larger problematique, but piecemeal, so that their interaction with other problems is all but ignored. For example, the World Food Conference was solely concerned with the problem of feeding the hungry and gave virtually no attention to the eventual ecological consequences of growing more food or subsidizing further overpopulation with radically increased food aid. To some extent, therefore, the successes of international conferences that simply try to solve one small piece of the larger problem are as much to be feared as their failures.

If one wished to be optimistic, one could conclude that the world community has taken the first halting attitudinal and institutional steps toward meeting the challenges of ecological scarcity. A more realistic assessment would be that little has been accomplished so far and that major impediments to further progress loom large. One might even be forced to conclude, more pessimistically, that the world political community as presently constituted is simply incapable of coping with the challenges of ecological scarcity, at least within any reasonable time.

Planetary Government or the War of All Against All

In short, the planet confronts the same problems as the United States, but in a greatly intensified form. Even before the emergence of ecological scarcity, the world's difficulties and their starkly Hobbesian implications were grave enough. Some saw the "revolution of rising expectations" pushing the world toward a situation in which wants greatly exceeded the capacity to meet them, provoking Hobbesian turmoil and violence (Spengler 1969). Also, ever since Hiroshima the world has lived in a state of highly armed peace with a nuclear Sword of Damocles dangling over its head. We have all learned to live with the bomb, and the hair suspending the nuclear Sword has indeed held, although for how much longer no one can say. Now the world must live under the blade of another Sword of Damocles, slower to fall but equally deadly. Unfortunately, the hair holding this environmental Sword has come loose; pollution and other environmental problems will not obligingly postpone their impact while diplomats haggle, so the Sword is already slicing down toward our unprotected heads. There is thus no way for the world community to put the environmental issue out of mind and go on about its business, as it has done with the bomb. The crisis of ecological scarcity is a Sword that must be parried, squarely and soon.

Thus the already strong rationale for a world government with enough coercive power over fractious nation states to achieve what reasonable men would regard as the planetary common interest has become overwhelming. Yet we must recognize that the very ecological scarcity that makes a world government ever more necessary has also made it much more difficult of achievement. The clear danger is that, instead of promoting world cooperation, ecological scarcity will simply intensify the Hobbesian war of all against all and cause armed peace to be replaced by overt international strife.

NOTES

1. Almost everything in this section of the essay applies equally to other socialist countries within the Soviet economic orbit.

2. The question of population limitation in the U.S.S.R. is complicated by its connection with the politically delicate "nationality" issue.

3. Lacking any reasonable alternative, I employ these well-established but, it seems to me, culturally biased terms in their narrow economic sense. Bhutan, a country that

preserves the ancient and admirable Tibetan culture in virtually all of its traditional richness, is scarcely undeveloped, fanatical modernizers to the contrary notwithstanding.

4. The ecologically viable alternative . . . is a locally self-sufficient, semi-developed, steady-state society based on renewable or "income" resources, like photosynthesis and solar energy. As indicated above, only Tanzania seems currently to be taking this path as a matter of principle. Others find themselves unable to see such apparent frugality as a realistic option. All the pressures are toward "efficiency," standardization, centralization, and large scale. Also, since semi-development is workable only with a reasonable population and most LDCs are heavily overpopulated, choosing this option implies a willingness to use harsh measures or cause widespread suffering; it is not surprising that most leaders prefer to continue in the illusory hope of achieving heavy industrialization. In addition, the lust for status and prestige, the desire for military power, and many other less than noble motives are also prevalent, and the frugal modesty of semi-developed self-sufficiency can do little to satisfy them.

5. In the short run, growing environmental pressures and restrictions in the developed countries will probably result in the export of polluting industries to some of the less industrialized LDCs, who will for the most part be delighted to accept ecological degradation along with economic benefits. However, only a few favored countries will benefit significantly. Moreover, without continued growth in the now industrialized nations, the growth prospects of the Third World are dim; our growth is essential to theirs (Boserup 1975; Quigg 1974). Thus, although the basic rich-poor polarization will be moderated by many complex interdependencies, there is no escaping the basic opposition of interests created by ecological scarcity.

6. Naturally, there will be short-term exceptions. Europe, for example, may become relatively independent of Middle Eastern oil supplies during the peak years of North Sea oil production. But respite from the overall trend toward increasing dependence will be transitory and limited to particular commodities.

7. However, OPEC-like cartels in other resources might be preferable to a disorganized seller's market. Cartels can be bargained with and integrated into the normal diplomatic machinery, so that the drastic price fluctuations and outright interruptions of supply that cause extreme economic distress are avoided. But the price of stability is higher prices for commodities and increased political power for cartel members.

REFERENCES

Anon. 1974. "Take Water and Heat from the Third World," *New Scientist* 62:549.

Banks, Fred. 1974. "Copper is not Oil," *New Scientist* 63:255–57.

Boserup, Mogens. 1975. "Sharing is a Myth," *Development Forum* 3(2):1–2.

Castro, Joao A. de A. 1972. "Environment and Development: The Case of the Developing Countries," *International Organization* 26:401–416.

Fyodorov, Yevyevgeny. 1973. "Against the Limits of Growth," *New Scientist* 57:431–32. (Abridged from Kommunist 14).

Goldman, Marshall I. 1970. "The Convergence of Environmental Disruption," *Science* 170:37–42.

Goldman, Marshall I. 1972. *The Spoils of Progress: Environmental Pollution in the Soviet Union.* Cambridge, MA: MIT Press.

Kiseleva, Galina. 1974. "A Soviet View: The Earth and Population," *Development Forum* 2(4):9.

Mikesell, Raymond F. 1974. "More Third World Cartels Ahead?" *Challenge* 17(5):24–31.

Pryder, Philip R. 1972. *Conservation in the Soviet Union.* New York: Cambridge University Press.

Quigg, Philip W. 1974. "The Consumption Dilemma," *World Environment Newsletter* in S.R./World, Nov. 2, p. 49.

Shields, Linda P., and Marvin C. Ott. 1974. "Environmental Decay and International Politics: The Uses of Sovereignty," *Environmental Affairs* 3:743–767.

Spengler, Joseph J. 1969. "Return to Thomas Hobbes?" *South Atlantic Quarterly* 68:443–453.

Wade, Nicholaus. 1974. "Raw Materials: U.S. Grows More Vulnerable to Third World Cartels," *Science* 183:185–86.

Walsh, John. 1974. "UN Conferences: Topping Any Agenda is the Question of Development," *Science* 185:1143–44, 1192–1193.

31
WHO OWNS THE OZONE?

Norman Cousins

The ozone in the stratosphere is no less vital in sustaining life than the oxygen in the atmosphere. The ozone shield protects living things against the destructive effects of ultraviolet rays. In particular, ozone prevents the sun's rays from tearing apart protein molecules in plant and animal life.

We now fear that the test explosions of thermonuclear bombs by the United States and the Soviet Union in 1960 and 1961 punctured the stratosphere, resulting in a 4 percent loss of ozone. The loss may be irreversible. The disclosure comes from Dr. Fred C. Iklé, director of the Arms Control and Disarmament Agency.

No figures have been released, assuming they are available, about the effects on the ozone of nuclear testing by France and the People's Republic of China. Both countries have persisted with nuclear explosions despite world-wide protests. If the human race had 96 percent of its life-supporting ozone left after the United States and Soviet Union got through with it, how much is left now? Ninety percent? Eighty percent? How much would be left after a full-scale nuclear war?

Dr. Iklé has explained that the heat produced by a nuclear explosion results in the formation of nitric oxides. As the atomic cloud rises, the nitric oxide molecules destroy the ozone molecules. The resultant loss of ozone could create all sorts of havoc with the delicate and intricate chain of life on earth.

Much remains to be known. No one yet has any definite knowledge about the critical limits; that is, precisely how much ozone is necessary to sustain human life. Dr. Iklé says that too many punctures could "destroy critical links of the intricate food chain of plants and animals, and thus shatter the ecological structure that permits man to remain alive on this planet."

Meanwhile, one thing is obvious. The nuclear tests of 1960 and 1961 represented no more than one or two percent of the total megatonnage of nuclear power now stockpiled by the United States, the Soviet Union, China, France, Great Britain, and India. The existing nuclear stores, if used, would create more than enough nitric oxide to obliterate the ozone.

Under these circumstances, even the possession of nuclear explosives is an

Reprinted by permission from *Saturday Review/World*, editorial by Norman Cousins, October 5, 1974.

explicit crime against humanity and should clearly be recognized as such by world public opinion. The notion that these ozone-altering weapons are essential for national security makes no sense unless we take the view that the right to wage nuclear war is more important than human rights, more important than the need to preserve the human habitat, more important than the future of civilization, more important than our obligations to generations to come.

Justifying the nuclear-arms race on the basis of national security is no more rational than justifying a race to drill the largest holes in the opposite ends of a lifeboat. In a very real sense, all the peoples in the world today are adrift in such a lifeboat. The Americans are at one end, the Russians at the other, the rest of the world's people in between. The fact of a common peril has yet to penetrate the minds of the boat's occupants. The only chance for survival is through recognition of a common destiny. Yet the leaders are seized by the idea that they can safeguard their own sections of the same boat by threatening to drill larger holes in the enemy's section than the enemy can drill in theirs.

The prime failure of modern society is that it has neither the philosophy nor the institutions to deal with crimes against humanity itself. Public fear and indignation are aroused by palpable things—a woman assaulted in a doorway, the hijacking of a plane, the terrorist bombing of a school bus, Watergates. But the conversion of masses of men into killers, the disfiguration of human values on a mammoth scale by governments themselves, the diversion of natural resources and human energies into the means of senseless total destruction, the assault on the conditions of life, the puncturing of the ozone layer—these are towering crimes. The failure to see them as such is a danger in itself.

The governments persist in their policies despite the fact that no nation can wage nuclear war against another without also going to war against the human race. Even the preparation for such a conflict is tantamount to an act of war against the species. Yet there is no institution in this world that can pull the nations back from the brink, that can define crimes against humanity and act against the criminals, that is capable of making and carrying out moral judgments, or that can uphold the rights of the next generation.

No need on earth today compares in urgency or size with the need to create such an institution. The United Nations is the closest we have come to it, but the curious notion persists that a world organization can only reflect, and not transcend, world differences. The main business of the United Nations is human survival. Any lesser concept perpetuates the present insanity.

32
THE GLOBAL 2000 REPORT
TO THE PRESIDENT:
ENTERING THE TWENTY-FIRST CENTURY

The world in 2000 will be different from the world today in important ways. There will be more people. For every two persons on the earth in 1975 there will be three in 2000. The number of poor will have increased. Four-fifths of the world's population will live in less developed countries. Furthermore, in terms of persons per year added to the world, population growth will be 40 percent *higher* in 2000 than in 1975.[1]

The gap between the richest and the poorest will have increased. By every measure of material welfare the study provides—per capita GNP and consumption of food, energy, and minerals—the gap will widen. For example, the gap between the GNP per capita in the LDCs and the industrialized countries is projected to grow from about $4,000 in 1975 to about $7,900 in 2000.[2] Great disparities within countries are also expected to continue.

There will be fewer resources to go around. While on a worldwide average there was about four-tenths of a hectare of arable land per person in 1975, there will be only about one-quarter hectare per person in 2000[3] (see Figure 1). By 2000 nearly 1,000 billion barrels of the world's total original petroleum resource of approximately 2,000 billion barrels will have been consumed. Over just the 1975–2000 period, the world's remaining petroleum resources per capita can be expected to decline by at least 50 percent.[4] Over the same period world per capita water supplies will decline by 35 percent because of greater population alone; increasing competing demands will put further pressure on available water supplies.[5] The world's per capita growing stock of wood is projected to be 47 percent lower in 2000 than in 1978.[6]

The environment will have lost important life-supporting capabilities. By 2000, 40 percent of the forests still remaining in the LDCs in 1978 will have been razed.[7] The atmospheric concentration of carbon dioxide will be nearly one-third higher than preindustrial levels.[8] Soil erosion will have removed, on the average, several inches of soil from croplands all over the world. Desertification (including salinization) may have claimed a significant fraction of the world's rangeland and cropland. Over little more than two decades, 15–20 per-

Reprinted from *The Global 2000 Report to the President: Entering the Twenty-First Century*, Volume One. Prepared by the Council on Environmental Quality and the Department of State. Based on material in Chapter 13, "Closing the Loops," pp. 390–431.

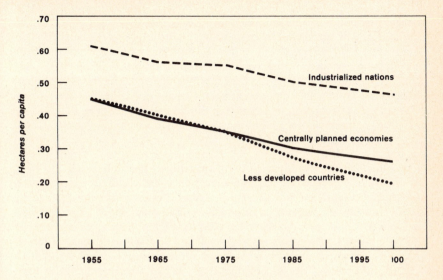

Figure 1   Arable land per capita, 1955, 1975, 2000.

cent of the earth's total species of plants and animals will have become extinct—a loss of at least 500,000 species.[9]

Prices will be higher. The price of many of the most vital resources is projected to rise in real terms—that is, over and above inflation. In order to meet projected demand, a 100 percent increase in the real price of food will be required.[10] To keep energy demand in line with anticipated supplies, the real price of energy is assumed to rise more than 150 percent over the 1975–2000 period.[11] Supplies of water, agricultural land, forest products, and many traditional marine fish species are projected to decline relative to growing demand at current prices,[12] which suggests that real price rises will occur in these sectors too. Collectively, the projections suggest that resource-based inflationary pressures will continue and intensify, especially in nations that are poor in resources or are rapidly depleting their resources.

The world will be more vulnerable both to natural disaster and to disruptions from human causes. Most nations are likely to be still more dependent on foreign sources of energy in 2000 than they are today.[13] Food production will be more vulnerable to disruptions of fossil fuel energy supplies and to weather fluctuations as cultivation expands to more marginal areas. The loss of diverse germ plasm in local strains and wild progenitors of food crops, together with the increase of monoculture, could lead to greater risks of massive crop failures.[14] Larger numbers of people will be vulnerable to higher food prices or even famine when adverse weather occurs.[15] The world will be more vulnerable to the disruptive effects of war. The tensions that could lead to war will have multiplied. The potential for conflict over fresh water alone is underscored by the fact that out of 200 of the world's major river basins, 148 are shared by two countries and 52 are shared by three to ten countries. Long standing conflicts over shared rivers such as the Plata (Brazil, Argentina), Euphrates (Syria, Iraq), or Ganges (Bangladesh, India) could easily intensify.[16]

Finally, it must be emphasized that if public policy continues generally unchanged the world will be different as a result of lost opportunities. The adverse effects of many of the trends discussed in this [chapter] will not be fully evident until 2000 or later; yet the actions that are necessary to change the trends cannot be postponed without foreclosing important options. The opportunity to stabilize the world's population below 10 billion, for example, is slipping away; Robert McNamara, President of the World Bank, has noted that for every decade of delay in reaching replacement fertility, the world's ultimately stabilized population will be about 11 percent greater.[17] Similar losses of opportunity accompany delayed perceptions or action in other areas. If energy policies and decisions are based on yesterday's (or even today's) oil prices, the opportunity to wisely invest scarce capital resources will be lost as a consequence of undervaluing conservation and efficiency. If agricultural research continues to focus on increasing yields through practices that are highly energy-intensive, both energy resources and the time needed to develop alternative practices will be lost.

The full effects of rising concentrations of carbon dioxide, depletion of stratospheric ozone, deterioration of soils, increasing introduction of complex persistent toxic chemicals into the environment, and massive extinction of species may not occur until well after 2000. Yet once such global environmental problems are in motion they are very difficult to reverse. In fact, few if any of the problems addressed in the Global 2000 Study are amenable to quick technological or policy fixes; rather, they are inextricably mixed with the world's most perplexing social and economic problems.

Perhaps the most troubling problems are those in which population growth and poverty lead to serious long-term declines in the productivity of renewable natural resource systems. In some areas the capacity of renewable resource systems to support human populations is already being seriously damaged by efforts of present populations to meet desperate immediate needs, and the damage threatens to become worse.[18]

Examples of serious deterioration of the earth's most basic resources can already be found today in scattered places in all nations, including the industrialized countries and the better-endowed LDCs. For instance, erosion of agricultural soil and salinization of highly productive irrigated farmland is increasingly evident in the United States,[19] and extensive deforestation, with more or less permanent soil degradation, has occurred in Brazil, Venezuela, and Colombia.[20] But problems related to the decline of the earth's carrying capacity are most immediate, severe, and tragic in those regions of the earth containing the poorest LDCs.

Sub-Saharan Africa faces the problem of exhaustion of its resource base in an acute form. Many causes and effects have come together there to produce excessive demands on the environment, leading to expansion of the desert.

Overgrazing, fuelwood gathering, and destructive cropping practices are the principal immediate causes of a series of transitions from open woodland, to scrub, to fragile semiarid range, to worthless weeds and bare earth. Matters are made worse when people are forced by scarcity of fuelwood to burn animal dung and crop wastes. The soil, deprived of organic matter, loses fertility and the ability to hold water—and the desert expands. In Bangladesh, Pakistan, and large parts of India, efforts by growing numbers of people to meet their basic needs are damaging the very cropland, pasture, forests, and water supplies on which they must depend for a livelihood.[21] To restore the lands and soils would require decades—if not centuries—*after* the existing pressures on the land have diminished. But the pressures are growing, not diminishing.

There are no quick or easy solutions, particularly in those regions where population pressure is already leading to a reduction of the carrying capacity of the land. In such regions a complex of social and economic factors (including very low incomes, inequitable land tenure, limited or no educational opportunities, a lack of nonagricultural jobs, and economic pressures toward higher fertility) underlies the decline in the land's carrying capacity. Furthermore, it is generally believed that social and economic conditions must improve before fertility levels will decline to replacement levels. Thus a vicious circle of causality may be at work. Environmental deterioration caused by large populations creates living conditions that make reductions in fertility difficult to achieve; all the while, continuing population growth increases further the pressures on the environment and land.[22]

The declines in carrying capacity already being observed in scattered areas around the world point to a phenomenon that could easily be much more widespread by 2000. In fact, the best evidence now available—even allowing for the many beneficial effects of technological developments and adoptions—suggests that by 2000 the world's human population may be within only a few generations of reaching the entire planet's carrying capacity.

The Global 2000 Study does not estimate the earth's carrying capacity, but it does provide a basis for evaluating an earlier estimate published in the U.S. National Academy of Sciences' report, *Resources and Man*. In this 1969 report, the Academy concluded that a world population of 10 billion "is close to (if not above) the maximum that an *intensively managed* world might hope to support with some degree of comfort and individual choice." The Academy also concluded that even with the sacrifice of individual freedom and choice and even with chronic near starvation for the great majority, the human population of the world is unlikely to ever exceed 30 billion.[23]

Nothing in the Global 2000 Study counters the Academy's conclusions. If anything, data gathered over the past decade suggest the Academy may have underestimated the extent of some problems, especially deforestation and the loss and deterioration of soils.[24]

At present and projected growth rates, the world's population would rapidly approach the Academy's figures. If the fertility and mortality rates projected for 2000 were to continue unchanged into the twenty-first century, the world's population would reach 10 billion by 2030. Thus anyone with a present life expectancy of an additional 50 years could expect to see the world population reach 10 billion. This same rate of growth would produce a population of nearly 30 billion before the end of the twenty-first century.[25]

Here it must be emphasized that, unlike most of the Global 2000 Study projections, the population projections assume extensive policy changes and developments to reduce fertility rates. Without the assumed policy changes, the projected rate of population growth would be still more rapid.

Unfortunately population growth may be slowed for reasons other than declining birth rates. As the world's populations exceed and reduce the land's carrying capacity in widening areas, the trends of the last century or two toward improved health and longer life may come to a halt. Hunger and disease may claim more lives—especially lives of babies and young children. More of those surviving infancy may be mentally and physically handicapped by childhood malnutrition.

The time for action to prevent this outcome is running out. Unless nations collectively and individually take bold and imaginative steps toward improved social and economic conditions, reduced fertility, better management of resources, and protection of the environment, the world must expect a troubled entry into the twenty-first century.

NOTES

Unless otherwise indicated, the following chapter citations refer to the various chapters of *The Global 2000 Report to the President: Entering the Twenty-First Century*, vol. 2, *Technical Report*, Washington: Government Printing Office, 1980.

1. *The Global 2000 Report to the President: Entering the Twenty-First Century*, vol. 2, *Technical Report*. Washington, D.C.: U.S. Government Printing Office, 1980. Chapter 2.
2. Ibid., Chapter 3.
3. Ibid., Chapter 6.
4. Ibid., Ch. 10; "Energy Projections and the Environment," Ch. 13.
5. Ibid., Ch. 9.
6. Ibid., Ch. 8.
7. Ibid.; "Forestry Projections and the Environment," Ch. 13.
8. Ibid., Ch. 4; "Climate Projections and the Environment," Ch. 13.
9. Ibid., "Food and Agriculture Projections and the Environment," "Forestry Projections and the Environment," and "Closing the Loops," Ch. 13.
10. Ibid., Ch. 6.
11. Ibid., extrapolating from Ch. 10, which assumes a 5 percent per year increase over the 1980–1990 period.
12. Ibid., Ch. 6–9.
13. Ibid., Ch. 10 and 11.
14. Ibid., Ch. 6; "Food and Agriculture Projections and the Environment," Ch. 13.
15. Ibid., Ch. 4; "Climate Projections and the Environment," Ch. 13.
16. Ibid., Ch. 9.
17. Robert S. McNamara, President, World Bank, "Address to the Board of Governors," Belgrade, Oct. 2, 1979, pp. 9, 10.
18. *The Global 2000 Report*, Ch. 13.

19. Ibid., "Food and Agriculture Projections and the Environment," Ch. 13.

20. Ibid., "Forestry Projections and the Environment," Ch. 13, and Peter Freeman, personal communication, 1980, based on field observations in 1973.

21. Ibid., "Population Projections and the Environment," "Food and Agriculture Projections and the Environment," "Forestry Projections and the Environment," and "Water Projections and the Environment," Ch. 13.

22. Ibid., "Population Projections and the Environment," and "Closing the Loops," Ch. 13; Erik Eckholm, *The Dispossessed of the Earth: Land Reform and Sustainable Development*, Washington: Worldwatch Institute, June 1979.

23. National Academy of Sciences, Committee on Resources and Man, *Resources and Man*, San Francisco: Freeman, 1969, p. 5; *The Global 2000 Report*, "Closing the Loops," Ch. 13.

24. *The Global 2000 Report*, "Closing the Loops," Ch. 13.

25. Projection by the U.S. Bureau of the Census communicated in a personal letter, Feb. 26, 1980, from Dr. Samuel Baum, Chief, International Demographic Data Center. This letter and projection are presented in vol. 3 of the *Global 2000 Report to the President*, Population section.

33
THE DAI DONG DECLARATION: INDEPENDENT DECLARATION ON THE ENVIRONMENT

Dai Dong's Independent Conference met on June 1–6, 1972, at the Graninge Stiftsgard, a small retreat center situated on the beautiful but polluted Baltic, a dozen miles from Stockholm.

The thirty-one participants represented 24 countries, several racial and religious backgrounds, differing political beliefs. They ranged in age from the early twenties to the late sixties. With such diversity, easy accommodation and agreement were neither possible nor expected.

But the purpose of the conference was not only to write a declaration but to produce a highly visible alternative to the United Nations Conference on the Human Environment which, meeting a week later in Stockholm, was expected to—and in fact, was—dominated by the special interests of powerful nations and the ruling elites of smaller countries.

Visibility was quickly achieved: from its opening day, the Dai Dong conference drew headlines in both the Stockholm and the world press, and was the source of constant radio and television stories and interviews.

Agreement on a Declaration was not easy. No one at the Independent Conference spoke for the "establishment." Everyone recognized the economic and political roots of the environmental crisis. There was a unanimous belief that the world's people really are one family with common interests and in common peril.

But centuries of oppression and exploitation are not easily forgotten either by the victims or those who have benefited, no matter how indirectly or unwillingly, from oppression. There was disagreement, sometimes heated, especially on matters of national sovereignty, population, and violent revolution.

Yet in the end, the Declaration was written and signed by all of the conference participants. Paradoxically, it represents both a compromise and a consensus. A few days later, Alfred Hassler, at the invitation of Secretary-General Maurice Strong, read the document before an early plenary session of the United Nations Conference.

There is no way to document what influence the Dai Dong conference and the publicity that surrounded it had upon the UN Conference and the UN Declaration, although there is reason to believe that the influence was considerable. But the real importance of the Independent Conference and its Declaration is that they represent a phase in an ongoing examination of the issues—a debate that must be continued in hundreds of such meetings, among thousands of people.

DECLARATION

Human beings live as a part of a complex natural system with aspects of interdependence which have only recently become dramatically evident. They are also a part of complex social, economic and political systems which they themselves have created, usually without an appreciation of the unpredictable and sometimes disastrous effects of such systems on the life-giving capabilities of nature. These systems, moreover, contain faults and imbalances which prevent them from responding equally to the needs of all people, but provide a minority with a surfeit of goods, while leaving the greater part of the world's people in poverty and despair.

The interaction between the social and natural systems on this planet has in our time resulted in an environmental crisis which, although it can be traced largely to the economic practices of the industrial nations, affects every person on Earth. The awareness of the environmental crisis has come at a time when the deprived nations and the poor and deprived people in all nations are struggling for power to control their own destinies and asserting their right to full participation in national and world affairs. The survival of humanity demands that the condition of the natural environment and the needs of human beings be considered as interrelated parts of the same problem. This will require profound changes in our political, economic and social structures on the one hand and our individual life-styles on the other, with the aim not only one of survival, but of survival with the maximum possibility of human fulfilment. It will also require massive programs of education to enable people to understand the interrelatedness of the world's problems, and the kinds of changes that need to be made. In such endeavors, certain guiding principles must be followed:

1. *Human survival depends upon the life activities of uncounted thousands of species of plants, animals and micro-organisms, and upon intricate physical and chemical reactions in the atmosphere, oceans, fresh water, and on the land.* The vastness and complexity of this interdependence have recently become evident with increasing human intervention into the life-giving processes of our planet. All life is dependent on the transactions of matter and energy carried out in Earth's ecosystems. It is these transactions which we are altering, even before we fully comprehend them. The people of the world must come to understand them, to preserve them and, when altering them, to do it with care and wisdom.

2. *There is a fundamental conflict between traditional concepts of economic growth and the preservation of the environment.* During the last century, uncontrolled continuous growth in the industrial production of environmentally harmful substances and products in some regions of the world has produced dangerous amounts of pollution and has been responsible for an inordinate waste of resources. At the same time, an increasing concentration of economic power

and industrial activity has led to a centralization within a few nations of the benefits from the use of the Earth's natural resources, and the international political influence that is derived from the control of these resources. It has become clear that a more rational distribution of industrial power is necessary if the global problems of environment and society are to be solved. Such a redistribution would achieve at the same time a more equal apportionment of economic and political benefits among nations and individuals.

3. *The exploitation of Third World national and regional resources by foreign corporations, with a consequent outflow of profits from the exploited regions, has resulted in a vast and growing economic disparity among nations and a monopoly of industrialized countries over production, energy, technology, information and political power.* Complementary to this is the flooding of developing countries with surplus goods and capital, with a resultant distortion of their economies, and the deformation of their environments into monocultures in the interest of further enriching the industrial states. The foreign investments, economic development and technological practices of such industrial states must be curbed and altered by the basic claim of a region's people to control of its resources. Use of these resources, however, should not be dictated by the accidents of geography, but must be allocated in such ways as to serve the needs of the world's people in this and future generations. The authority of any region's people over resources and environment must include the obligation to recognize that the environment is an indivisible whole, not subject to political barriers. The environment must be protected from avoidable pollution, destruction and exploitation from all sources.

4. *It is obvious that human population growth cannot continue indefinitely in a finite environment with finite resources. At the same time, population is one of a number of factors, no one of which in the long run is the most important or the most decisive in affecting the human environment.* In fact, the question of population is intrinsically inseparable from the question of access to resources. A true improvement in the living conditions of the people of developing countries would go further in stabilizing population growth than programs of population control. Population is not a single problem, but one which has a complex interrelationship with the social, economic and natural environments of human beings. Population size may be too small or too large at any particular time depending on the availability of natural resources and the stresses on the environment. The ecological principle regarding the role of population is equally applicable to human and animal populations. However, in human populations social organization is such as to change or modify this principle.

On a global scale, the population problems of the developing countries have coincided with the colonial expansions of the last two centuries, and the exclusion of Third World populations from full access to their own resources. This process of economic exploitation still continues in spite of the nominal independence of various former colonies and dependencies. Meanwhile the alliance between economic elites in the developing countries and industrial interests in the metropolitan countries makes it impossible for the people of the Third World to use their resources to fulfil their own needs. The redistribution of resource use on a global level is an unconditional prerequisite for correcting this historic process.

As long as resources are wasted, as they manifestly are, it is deceptive to describe population growth as if this were the source of all evils. There is obviously a confusion in many people's minds between overcrowding and population, but the fact that some urban areas grow like cancers should not serve as a pretext to divert attention from the real task of our generation, which is to achieve proper management of resources and space. Those nations that are mainly responsible for this state of affairs have certainly no right to recommend population-stabilizing policies to the world's hungry people.

It should be noted that, for economically developed countries, the combination of an increase in industrial consumption per capita with a stable population, or of stable consumption per capita with a growing population, will both lead to further resource depletion and pollution. This need not be true if the appropriate socio-economic changes that will lead to an ecologically sound production and consumption pattern are made.

5. *Economic development of any kind will require technology.* Much conventional technology and many of its proliferating products have proved ecologically harmful. We cannot reject technology *per se* but must restructure and reorient it. Ecologically sound technologies will minimize stresses to the environment. A rapid development of the new approach should be complemented by a technology review and surveillance system to assure that any new technology is ecologically compatible and will be used for human survival and fulfilment. It is not enough to add anti-pollution devices to existing technologies, although this might well be the initial stage of phasing out present polluting technologies.

6. *The culture of the industrial nations reflects their political and economic ideology, and is based on an ever-increasing accumulation of material goods and an uncritical reliance on technology to solve humanity's problems.* This ideology, in which the ethical element is a forgotten dimension, is spreading throughout the world; its acceptance will not only cause individual and national disappointment and frustration, but will make rational economic and environmental policies impossible to carry out. An increase in economic well-being will help deprived countries preserve their own cultural and spiritual heritages, but many people in industrial countries, faced with a reduction in their material possessions, will need to find new definitions of progress in values compatible with environmental and social well-being.

7. *Among the most critical problems that constitute an existing and accelerating threat to human survival is war.* Even apart from the colossal cost in human suffering that all forms of war entail, arms expenditures place an overwhelming economic burden on rich and poor nations alike, and an equally heavy burden on the environment. Military technology, being such a large part of industrial activity, particularly in economically developed countries, is a major cause of global pollution and resource depletion. Thus, war and preparation for war are both directly related to environmental problems. With nuclear proliferation, both civil and military, the environmental hazard has become increasingly critical, arms control more difficult, and nuclear war more probable. The

enormous sums consumed in military expenditures must be applied directly to the task of resource redistribution and environmental improvement. As long as we tolerate the waste and the destructiveness of war itself, we cannot achieve the stable environment on which the survival of all of us depends.

Yet the determination to abolish war must be accompanied by a recognition of the right of peoples to struggle, and the certainty that they will struggle, to liberate themselves from national and international systems that oppress them. Those who most earnestly seek an end to war must affirm their solidarity with their fellow humans engaged in such a struggle, while simultaneously insisting on the need to develop effective non-violent methods of solving the social and international conflicts of a world in danger of an annihilating war.

PART THREE

TOWARD JUST WORLDS

Alternative Images
of the Future

INTRODUCTION

World order inquiry is concerned not only with the accurate depiction and explanation of current international behavior, but also with establishing a framework of thought and action for shaping the future in a more just and humane direction. Such a concern necessarily entails the use of futures research, futures modeling, and the like. Of relevance to world order inquiry is both *probable* world modeling (i.e., the linear projection of empirical demographic, economic, and social trends) and *preferred* world modeling (i.e., the imaging or construction of alternative frameworks of world order, sometimes called "relevant utopias," capable of realizing world order values).

The imaging of alternative world futures is especially important because of the sociopsychological relationship that exists between world order and futures studies. This relationship might be formulated for our purposes as follows: what we feel, believe, think, expect or wish shapes not only our present behavior but also the kinds of futures we will transmit and posterity will inherit. This idea has been expressed in a variety of ways. Anatol Rapoport (1964: 30) noted that "probabilities which we assign to events become reflections of our preferences rather than of our knowledge." In a similar vein, Kenneth Boulding (1956: 6,11) has argued that our behavior depends on "the subjective knowledge structure" of individuals and organizations, which consists "not only of images of 'fact' but also images of 'value.'" According to W. I. Thomas (1928: 572), an important American sociologist, "if men define situations as real, they are real in their consequences." This proposition, in the words of a leading contemporary sociologist, has now become "a theorem basic to the social sciences" (Merton, 1949: 179). For our analytical purposes, we accept the reality of "image" (some might prefer the use of such other terms as worldview or dominant social paradigm) in relation to its cognitive, evaluative, and prescriptive roles. Such a concept of image can help link world order and future studies.

Five hundred years ago, well-informed Europeans had the image of a world in which the earth was flat. They therefore believed it was impossible (utopian) to sail west to get to Asia, which was thought to lie overland to the east. Earlier, the planet earth was also believed to be the center of the entire universe. As a consequence, scientists were unable and unwilling to acquire knowledge about gravitational forces that might be overcome to achieve a variety of technological breakthroughs, including aerial flight. Such an image of self and of the outside world contributed to the fragmentation of human identity. Contrast this medieval image of physical reality with the space-age image of earth as seen from Apollo 8, described by the astronaut Frank Borman:

> The view of the earth from the moon fascinated me—a small disk, 240,000 miles away. It was hard to think that that little thing held so many problems, so many frustrations. Raging nationalistic interests, famines, wars, pestilence don't show from that distance. I'm convinced that some wayward stranger in a spacecraft, coming from some other part of the heavens, could look at earth and never know that it was inhabited at all. But the same wayward stranger would certainly know instinctively that if the earth were inhabited, then the destinies of all who lived on it must inevitably be interwoven and joined. We are one hunk of ground, water, air, clouds, floating around in space. From out there it really is "one world."

An image can constrain the reform of "social reality" in harmful ways. For centuries, slavery was "imagined" as an integral part of the natural social order; hence, it was utopian to think of its abolishment. It is clear that the image holds a powerful grip on how we establish the outer limits and possibilities of our social behavior. Our future is not prefigured. Self-determination and self-realization depend upon our uses of freedom. Everything we do or do not do works its way into the shaping of our future. Whether or not we realize it, tomorrow is always present in our image of today. The sense of the future is part of the "is" because we have developed a sense of cultural expectation that certain things or events are supposed to recur in a wave-like continuous motion. Historically, radical social and scientific thinking always embodied alternative images of the future and alternative possibilities of human destiny in the image of the existing reality. But radicalism (or a radical vision of the future) should not be equated with utopianism (the impossible). What the dominant elites oppose or do not want to change is often characterized as utopianism. Contrary to the public image of hard-nosed realism, the Pentagon is the most avid consumer of "utopian" future thinking. Its entire military R&D program is based on "planned obsolescence," and every new weapons system is based on an alternative image of future warfare. And the notion that more weapons will bring more security is one of the most dangerous utopian ideas ever given influential currency.

It is also clear that an image can be maladaptive, lagging behind the development of objective social or scientific realities. As Pirages pointed out in Chapter 29, there are moments when the image (or what he calls dominant social paradigm), for a variety of reasons, is overwhelmed by a massive assault. When this occurs, the image or dominant paradigm is supplanted by an alternative paradigm. One illustration is the shift from Newtonian physics, dominated by mechanical energy, to Einstein's theory of relativity of time and position with respect to the motion of atoms. Is there a comparable emergent ecological revolution involving a basic shift in our dominant social paradigm from an industrial to an ecological axis, as Pirages asserts? The assertion of such a prospect should be accepted as much as an assertion of fact or trend as of value. It can also be understood as an interpretation of objective social reality seen and evaluated by a subjective knowledge structure. The study of the future of human society is not, and perhaps can never be, a hard science. It should be regarded instead as a branch of normative studies whose goal is to specify sociohistorical reality in an expanded time framework and to design purposive images of plausible preferred futures.

Every image of the future is implicitly or explicitly biased. There is simply no escape from this because there is no such thing as a value-free social paradigm. Our effort to link world order and future studies does not purport to offer a value-free paradigm. Indeed, the value premises and value goals of each paradigm are highlighted and critically assessed by reference to the normative, holistic, and future-oriented criteria of world order modelling. What are some of the major value assumptions and biases underlying various types of futures research?

Perhaps the most prevalent assumption on which so much of mainstream futures research is conducted rests on system-continuity. The system-continuity assumption expresses itself in the extrapolation from the past to forecast or project possible alternative futures. This was the dominant assumption for *The Year 2000: A Framework for Speculation* by Herman Kahn and Anthony Wiener. Even *The Global 2000 Report*, the most ambitious and comprehensive projections ever developed by U.S. Government agencies to interpret the societal significance of what will happen to population, resources, and environment, is based on the assumption of system continuity and of the continuity of "present policies." In its essence, the report projects "continued economic growth in most areas, continued population growth everywhere, reduced energy growth, an increasingly tight and expensive food situation, increasing water problems, and growing environmental stress" (*The Global 2000 Report*, Vol I: 43).

In contrast, note what happens when the system-continuity assumption is rejected in a global future modelling. The Latin American World Model (also called the Bariloche Global Model), developed as a Third World reaction to the Club of Rome projections in *The Limits to Growth*, is a helpful illustration. Instead of projecting the future based on the present policies and trends, this model asks: "How can global resources best be used to meet basic human needs for all people?" The model is based on a system-change orientation—an egalitarian, nonexploitative, wisely managed world society that avoids environmental degradation and reaches optimistic "if . . . then" conclusions about the potential for positive change (Herrera, 1976).

The competing images of the future in our times are particularly susceptible to the imperatives of demographic and technological revolutions. Malthusian demographic pessimists and Kahnian technological optimists, to borrow the Chinese metaphor, "sleep in the same bed but have different dreams." In the alternative image of the future held by technological optimists there is no need for or likelihood of system transformation. On the other hand, according to the crystal ball of Robert Heilbroner, convulsive system change will be forced upon us by the pressure of events rather than by our conscious choice or purposive image of the future—by system catastrophe rather than by human calculation.

Our image of the future is also biased and limited by historical and cultural space and time. As with the prisoners in Plato's allegory of the cave, our heads, too, are chained by national and cultural prejudices and present preoccupations in such a way that we can only see our own shadows and project our own torments. We are all prisoners of our culture and historical time space. Why has global future modelling come into being as an almost exclusively Western preoccupation? Why has this intellectual enterprise been subsidized largely by industrial and corporate interests? Why has this come about at the time of resource depletion and scarcity? Why has the Third World been so negative in its reaction to global modelling?

Like the U.S. reaction to the Sputnik satellite of the Soviet Union, global modelling arose in part as a scientific and technological managerial response to an increasing sense of concern and fear that Western economic hegemony was in jeopardy. Partly for this reason Third World students of world affairs have been suspicious about mainstream global modelling and futurism. World order forms of global modelling have attempted to avoid this bias, but it remains questionable whether they have succeeded. As made evident in Cole's synoptic evaluation in this section, much of future modelling exercises rely upon computer technology and involve narrowing the scope of inquiry to a relatively small number of quantifiable variables; almost no attention is devoted by these models to specific human wants or basic human needs, nor to the psychological, cultural, and spiritual dimensions of the world in which we live. In short, the world order challenge of futures research is not to plunge into this mode of intellectual exercise blindfolded, but, first of all, to liberate ourselves to the extent possible from the cultural, historical, and technological biases that define the outer parameters of our dominant social paradigm. An alternative image of a more just and humane world order calls for an alternative way of visioning the future.

In this section we present two articles that we believe provide a comprehensive survey of futures research and images of world order. In the first selection, Sam Cole provides a summary and evaluation of 17 separate studies of the future. Because they are summaries, skillfully done to be sure, they should be examined carefully in order to understand the implications of the images presented. The reader should look at the various images in terms of the assumptions and propositions concerning resources, technology, and development strategy, and the capacity of the present system to sustain itself. What values and worldviews underlie the methodology and theory in constructing these alternative images of the future? Who are the optimists and who are the pessimists with regard to the future of human society? What are the crucial differences in assumptions, approaches, and findings separating the optimistic futurists from the pessimistic ones? How does each of the futurists represented in Cole's piece relate to world order studies or to the realization of world order values? For those concerned with achieving a just world order it is necessary to enhance their understanding of the outer limits and possibilities that the present and projected technologies and resource reserves offer. Technological and resource constraints have to be linked to the present and projected normative and structural constraints in world politics in order to establish a "realistic" frame of reference to sketch out preferred futures.

The second selection employs an explicit world order framework. Rather than using futures methodology, Richard Falk sets out seven images of the world with a number of variations, and asks us to look at these images from the viewpoint of their workability and potential for realizing world order values. In doing so he returns us to a central question of world order inquiry: who will hold power and exercise authority? At the same time, Falk challenges us to ponder the question of the extent to which incremental reforms of the present system are capable of providing the changes required to realize world order values. In projecting a range of images from a corporate-dominated world system to world government, he opens up a variety of options for alternative forms of governance, within which he suggests but does not specify the nature of the domestic structures of governance in different regions of the globe, and what their impact is likely to be on the global polity.

QUESTIONS FOR DISCUSSION AND REFLECTION

Based on your reading of this section, what is *your* dominant social paradigm? What is *your* image of the future? Whose paradigm or whose image of the future in this chapter comes closest to yours?

Has your exposure to world order and future studies altered your image of the future?

Of the contending future studies, which one is most useful—and which one least useful—to world order studies?

Do you believe that our images of the future are a factor shaping our behavior and institutions?

What is your response to the rhetorical question raised by Robert Heilbroner, "What has posterity ever done for me?"

What do you think will be the most powerful forces shaping the future? Will it be technology, carrying capacity of biosphere, demographic pressure, human values and beliefs, social habits or institutions, or hegemonic rivalry of the superpowers?

SELECTED BIBLIOGRAPHY

Bell, Daniel. *The Coming of Post-Industrial Society: A Venture Into Social Forecasting.* New York: Basic Books, 1973.

Beres, L. R., and Harry R. Targ. *Constructing Alternative World Futures: Reordering the Planet*. Cambridge, MA: Schenkman Publishing Co., 1977.

Boulding, Kenneth E. *The Image*. Ann Arbor, MI: University of Michigan Press, 1956.

Brzezinski, Zbigniew. *Between Two Ages: America's Role in the Technetronic Era*. New York: Viking, 1970.

Fuller, Buckminster. *Utopia or Oblivion*. New York: Bantam Books, 1969.

Harman, Willis W. *An Incomplete Guide to the Future*. Stanford, CA: Stanford Alumni Association, 1976.

Heilbroner, Robert L. *An Inquiry Into the Human Prospect*. New York: W. W. Norton, 1974.

Henderson, Hazel. *Creating Alternative Futures*. New York: Berkey Publishing, 1978.

Herrera, Amilcar O., et al. *Catastrophe or New Society? A Latin American World Model*. Ottawa, Canada: International Development Research Center, 1976.

Jungk, Robert, and Johan Galtung, eds. *Mankind 2000*. London: Allen and Unwin, 1970.

Kahn, Herman, et al. *The Next 200 Years*. New York: William Morrow and Co., 1976.

Leontief, Wassily, et al. *The Future of the World Economy*. New York: Oxford University Press, 1977.

Mead, Margaret. *World Enough: Rethinking the Future*. Boston: Little Brown, 1976.

Merton, Robert K. *Social Theory and Social Structure: Toward the Codification of Theory and Research*. Glencoe, IL: Free Press, 1949.

Nozick, Robert. *Anarchy, State and Utopia*. New York: Basic Books, 1974.

Ornauer, H., et al. *Images of the World in the Year 2000: A Comparative Ten Nation Study*. Atlantic Highlands, NJ: Humanities Press, 1976.

Thomas, W. I. *The Child in America*. New York: Knopf, 1928.

Toffler, Alvin, ed. *The Futurists*. New York: Random House, 1972.

Wager, Warren. *Building the City of Man: Outlines of a World Civilization*. New York: Grossman Publishers, 1971.

34
THE GLOBAL FUTURES DEBATE, 1965–1976

Sam Cole

INTRODUCTION

In the last few years a series of long-term global forecasts has caught the attention of the media and the public. Many have called for dramatic new thinking about the possibilities for the long-term future, and for a reorientation of present trends in world development. The purpose of this chapter . . . is to compare the content and prescriptions of some of these forecasts, to set out some of the assumptions upon which they are based, and to distil from such comparison whatever guidance they have to offer for our own approach to thinking about the future.

Since this book is concerned with long-term alternatives for development, and in particular the availability of natural resources of all kinds, we shall first examine forecasts in terms of global ecological constraints. We shall not be comprehensive, but shall try to show a wide range of views, and to give some idea of the recent debate about them. The authors considered and their major work are listed in Table 1. Most of them have had much publicity, some have achieved notoriety, and some are believed to have an influence on government policies.

The futures debate of the last decade has taken place against a background of rapidly changing national and world affairs. The late 1960s and early 1970s was a period of economic growth slipping into recession and inflation. Problems of alienation and environment became major issues, reflecting for some people a more general disillusion with industrial society. Many people argue that there has been a shift in the global balance of power. The humiliation of the United States in South East Asia, and the successful attempt by the OPEC group of countries to reverse terms of trade for a major commodity have added weight to calls for a new international economic order. Forecasters have certainly been influenced by these events, but it is far less clear in what way their prognoses have influenced the course of affairs.

During the decade there have also been important international conferences

Reprinted with permission from *World Futures: The Great Debate* edited by Christopher Freeman and Marie Jahoda, Universe Books, New York, 1978.

505

TABLE 1   *Major Authors Considered*

Kahn and Wiener	USA	(1967)	*The Year 2000 – A Framework for Speculation on the Next Thirty-Three Years*
Spengler	USA	(1966)	'The Economist and the Population Question'
Ehrlich	USA	(1970)	*Population, Resources, Environment – Issues in Human Ecology*
Forrester	USA	(1971)	*World Dynamics*
Meadows *et al.*	USA	(1972)	*The Limits to Growth* – A report for the Club of Rome's Project on the Predicament of Mankind
Heilbroner	USA	(1974) (1976)	*An Inquiry into the Human Prospect Business Civilisation in Decline*
Dumont	France	(1974)	*Utopia or Else*
Schumacher	UK	(1973)	*Small is Beautiful – A Study of Economics as if People Mattered*
Mesarovic and Pestel	USA/W. Ger.	(1974)	*Mankind at the Turning Point* – The Second Report to the Club of Rome
Leontief *et al.*	USA	(1976)	*The Future of the World Economy*
Kaya *et al.*	Japan	(1974)	'Global Constraints and A New Vision for Development'
Herrera *et al.* (Bariloche Foundation)	Argentina	(1976)	*Catastrophe or New Society?*
Tinbergen	Netherlands	(1976)	*Reshaping the International Order (RIO) – A Report to the Club of Rome*
Modrzhinskaya and Stephanyan	USSR	(1973)	*The Future of Society – A Critique of Modern Bourgeois Philosophical and Socio-Political Conceptions*
Kosolapov	USSR	(1976)	*Mankind and the Year 2000*
Kahn, Brown and Martel	USA	(1976)	*The Next 200 Years*
Galtung	Norway	(1977)	*Self-Reliance: Concepts, Theory and Rationale*

on a range of global issues, several of which are under the auspices of the United Nations: the Human Environment (UNEP, Stockholm, 1972), Population (UN, Bucharest, 1974), Food and Agriculture (F.A.O., Rome, 1975), the North-South Conference for International Economic Cooperation (Paris, 1975), the Habitat Conference on Human Settlements (Vancouver, 1976), the Conference on the Law of the Sea (UN, New York, 1976) and Trade and Development (UNCTAD IV, Nairobi, 1976). The topics of these conferences in fact indicate the major agenda of the futures debate. Most futures studies have something to say about each of these issues, although the focus of the debate has shifted systematically and parallels these conferences.

Several forecasters, such as the Hudson Institute, have had direct access to, and are employed by, government. One group, the Club of Rome, has even included cabinet ministers among its membership, and has brought together leaders including heads of state from several nations to discuss long-term issues. The extent to which these discussions have extended the horizons of their day-to-day actions is debatable. Other forecasters, such as Paul Ehrlich, have gained spectacular coverage by the media, and the sales of works such as *The Limits to Growth* reached several million in more than a dozen languages.

Many modern forecasts are variations or extensions of the Malthusian view that there is a tendency for population to outstrip food supply. Works such as *The Limits to Growth* and the writing of Robert Heilbroner and the Ehrlichs take this view. Many other forecasters, notably Herman Kahn and his colleagues, most Soviet writers and the Latin American Bariloche group, claim explicitly to be non-Malthusian. However, they do forecast or speculate about an end to demographic and economic growth. Underlying the prognoses and the suggestions about change there are often very different socio-political views and very different assumptions about the nature of physical resource constraints and technological change.

One new aspect of the world futures debate is the application of computer models to the analysis of global trends. Several of the authors we discuss have constructed world models, arguing that the complex and interacting nature of the modern world makes such a device for analysis essential. But there is controversy about this; we hope to identify in our discussion how and where the models have made a specific contribution to the debate about the future.

Each of the current views of the future that we present has its precursor in the nineteenth century or before. The humanist view of the prospect for improvement in human nature and social structures goes back at least to Thomas More and Francis Bacon. The technological optimist's view is aptly summed up by Charles Babbage, the progenitor of the modern computer: "the dominion of mind over the material world advances with an ever accelerating force." Babbage's views (in 1832) have a familiar ring. He sees technology not merely as a means for expanding production, but as a creative response to future problems. He foresees, for example, an energy crisis—"power is not without limit and the coal mines of the world may be ultimately exhausted"—and proposes some strikingly modern-sounding technological solutions: tide power for driving machinery, geothermal energy, the liquification of natural gas. The pessimistic neo-Malthusian outlook and its critique have strong nineteenth-century counterparts. The comparison of the first edition of Malthus' *Essay on Population* with *The Limits to Growth* is a familiar one.

For the present, however, we shall consider only contemporary works on the future, presenting them in more or less their original order of publication and indicating where appropriate more recent modifications in the views expressed by their authors.

FUTURES OF CONTINUED GROWTH – A WESTERN VIEW

Until the end of the 1960s, the most popular forecasts of the postwar period reflected a desire for economic growth and a certain technological optimism, expressed by writers such as Arthur C. Clarke (1964), Colin Clarke (1970), Buckminster Fuller (1972), and by Herman Kahn himself.

We start our review with the best-known of the futurologists – Herman Kahn. We return later to his most recent book and the way in which his views have been influenced by the intervening futures debate. In *The Year 2000 – A Framework for Speculation on the Next Thirty-Three Years*, published in 1967, Herman Kahn and his co-author Anthony Wiener "sketch out constraints on social choice." Before this in 1960, through a book entitled *On Thermonuclear War*, Kahn had aroused both fear and respect from many quarters for thinking about the unthinkable in relation to atomic weapons.

In *The Year 2000* the authors emphasised problems rather than solutions but, compared with others whom we consider later, Kahn and Wiener perceived relatively few major problems. "The most crucial issue of our study is that economic trends will proceed more or less smoothly through the next thirty years and beyond," and "capacities for and commitment to economic development and control over our external and internal environment are increasingly seeming without foreseeable limit" (p. 116). Contrary to the fears of some other authors, Kahn and Wiener argue the "quite plausible" view that "despite much current anxiety about thermonuclear war generally we are entering a period of general political and economic stability at least so far as the frontiers and economies of most of the world nations are concerned" (p. 128). In the main, therefore, in *The Year 2000* and later works, Kahn and his various colleagues see the world entering *la belle époque*.

The Year 2000 describes a set of "plausible," fairly detailed, alternative "scenarios" of the future. A variety of global politico-economic situations is considered, ranging from fast growing "development oriented integrated worlds," to less appealing "destruction dominated worlds culminating in all-out nuclear war," culled from Kahn's writing *On Thermonuclear War*. Kahn and Wiener's original work is now over ten years old, and its "dated" nature has already become evident in some of the detailed predictions. *The Year 2000* did not predict such international and domestic political issues as the ecological movement, the oil crisis or the 1970s' recession.

The idea of scenarios as employed in the book is to outline possible mechanisms whereby these varied but "hypothetical" futures might occur. In *The Year 2000* these are centered around a so-called "surprise free" or "standard world," which is obtained by projecting a set of "multifold trends." These forecasts are based on the idea that "the basic trends of Western society, most of which can be traced back to the twelfth or eleventh centuries, can be seen as part of a common, complex trend of interacting elements" (p. 6). Kahn and Wiener pay considerable attention to justifying these trends and the underlying idea of "continuity" in world affairs, although they caution that any day may witness some "historic turning point."

The numerical projections are, in fact, largely exponential extrapolations of recent economic and demographic trends with modest growth rate adjustments to account for the peculiarities of particular nations. Because of the model of development they use, developing nations are assumed to follow the stages of growth of already industrialised nations. Although their "surprise free" projections in *The Year 2000* give a world in which all societies become more wealthy, notwithstanding changes in the relative international economic pecking order, it is essentially a picture of the world status quo maintained. It is also a world in which Western technology and Western social forms are adopted by developing nations.

Like other authors who see levels of economic development beyond those that industrial societies have already attained as desirable, Kahn and Wiener tend to concentrate on what this life might be like. They provide a number of illustrations, almost entirely confined to the U.S.A. "The upper middle classes" in the America of the year 2000 might "in many ways be emulating the life style of the landed gentry of the previous century, such as emphasising education, travel, cultural values, expensive residencies, lavish entertainments, and a mannered and cultivated style of life" (p. 207).

Kahn and Wiener's book has the reputation of being technologically optimistic. Through a list of "very likely" technical innovations they indicate further the kind of benefits that economic growth as it is currently proceeding is likely to bring; for example, "general and substantial increases in life expectancy, postponement of ageing and limited rejuvenation" and , more exotically, "physically non-harmful methods of over-indulging." They list a range of devices that "most people would consider as (largely) unambiguous examples of progress or human benefit" (p. 52). They observe that their "optimistic" projections derive from the increased rate at which new technology is being developed (p. 122).

Despite fabulously high income levels and the achievement of "post-industrial society" by several major powers, Kahn and Wiener foresee large variations of income. Except for the "voluntary poor," most "relatively poor" people would be "amply subsidised." They dub even this society as "alienation amid affluence" (p. 193). Unlike some other authors, Kahn and Wiener see much alienation as essentially containable and unlikely to bring about major social changes.

When we come to consider Kahn and Wiener's discussion of possibilities for world economic and institutional reform, the nature of their optimism is again made clear. They observe that although many violent scenarios are "realistic," few people believe that anything but peaceful scenarios (natural revolution, aided evolution and negotiation) can be "used to play an important role in reforming the system." Yet, "it is the mechanisms of low-level violence of crises and small wars that are most likely to be involved in systematic change." These will occur, they say, whether we like it or not, and we should be prepared to exploit these mechanisms of transition. Repeating the thinking of *On Thermonuclear War*, they argue that it might be better to accept a greater amount of "low-level violence" in order to "deal better with high levels of violence" (p. 385). The issues of distribution, they say, "provide one reason for believing that a world government could only be created out of war or crisis—an emergency that provided an appropriate combination of the motivations of fear and opportunity" (p. 382).

The threat of war seems, in the opinion of Kahn and Wiener, to be confined largely to the developing nations. The disparity between the rich and poor worlds, even if it gives rise to radical political movements, "probably does not imply any serious confrontation in the twentieth century, for the underdeveloped countries even in concert are unlikely to possess the resources . . . to wage serious military campaigns against one or more developed countries" (p. 365). A picture of "international anarchy . . . ignores entirely the self-regulative mechanisms and rules of behaviour that can arise and be maintained in informal organisations" (p. 363).

Throughout the book, Kahn and Wiener are less certain about the fate of poorer nations: "Whether satisfaction in their absolute progress or envy and resentment of increasing discrepancies between rich and poor will be the dominant reaction of the people of the less developed world depends of course on many economic, political and cultural factors." While the improvements in living standards compared with their parents will be clear to many people, "the increasing discrepancies between their lives and those of the industrialised societies will be brought inescapably to the attention of even the most primitive and isolated communities by cheap and improved worldwide communication and transportation" (p. 142). There can, they say, "be little doubt that problems of development constitute a serious economic and moral concern" (p. 364).

Despite their reputed optimism about technological change, Kahn and Wiener point out that more "controversial issues" are raised by the arrival of some of the technical innovations that they list as very likely before the year 2000. These are issues of "accelerated nuclear proliferation; or loss of privacy; of excessive governmental and/or private power over individuals; of dangerously vulnerable, deceptive and dependable over-centralisation; of decisions becoming necessary that are too large, complex, important, uncertain or comprehensive to be left to mere mortals whether private or public; of new capabilities that are so inherently dangerous that they are likely to be disastrously abused; of too rapid or cataclysmic change for smooth adjustment and so on" (p. 116).

Indeed, in some scenarios in The Year 2000, Kahn and Wiener briefly point to the dangers that are central to the neo-Malthusian authors to be discussed next: "Finally we question whether man's unremitting Faustian striving may ultimately remake his natural conditions—environmental, social and psychological—so far as to begin to dehumanise himself or to degrade his political or ecological situation in some very costly or irrevocable manner" (p. 117). Once more we see the less optimistic side of Kahn and Wiener's forecasts. Even though they hint at the very things that concern authors such as the Ehrlichs, Meadows and Heilbroner, and indeed often appear to be describing the *same* futures as these authors, they simply refuse to be overawed by the magnitude of the problems posed. The standards Kahn and Wiener set for the resolution of major problems are surely lower than those of other futurists, and so their pessimism about achieving them is also less.

Despite their numerous caveats, Kahn and Wiener's work gives the impression of inevitability about the underlying trends they describe. In addition to theories of "continuity," there is an impressive display of facts and figures and the whole document is backed up by the reputation of the Hudson Institute. As Marien has observed (*Futurist*, 1973), "for better or worse Herman Kahn heads nearly everyone's list of futurists and *The Year 2000* tops nearly everyone's list of contemporary professional books on the future." According to Wiener, the work reflects a "more or less Western capitalist ideology." Soviet commentators, for example Arab-Ogly, view Kahn's work as a "premeditated attempt to influence public opinion rather than a serious attempt at prediction" (1975). Indeed Western commentators too, such as Shonfield and de Jouvenel, have shared this opinion. Dumont, an author we consider later, sees Kahn's brand of optimism and inevitability as "semi-lunatic!" True or not, as Marien points out, Kahn warrants very serious consideration – "the Hudson Institute view of the future has actually influenced both government and corporate policy in the United States and presumably will continue to do so."

CHALLENGES TO GROWTH – THE MALTHUSIAN SPECTRE

During the late 1960s the concern about rising populations and environmental deterioration increased. The neo-Malthusian prospect, outlined by Julian Huxley at the United Nations as early as 1948, was repeated by several authors. In direct contrast to Kahn's *la belle époque* or the works of Marxist writers, they give the impression that the world is rushing blindly towards catastrophe. There will be an inevitable clash between exponential population growth and a finite environment. Like Malthus himself, they often place great emphasis on the need for moral reform, and their views about the nature of the crisis, and the ways to avoid it, inevitably reflect their underlying political and economic values.

An influential restatement of the Malthusian position was given by the American economist Joseph Spengler in his 1965 presidential address to the American Economic Association, in a paper entitled "The Economist and the Population Question." In more recent work, but without serious modification of his original thesis, Spengler has extended his analysis and data base. In the book *Population Change, Modernisation and Welfare* (1974) he provides a more detailed theoretical justification of the modern Malthusian position.[1]

Spengler's projections and recommendations are directed particularly at the poor countries and indicate to him a long-run prospect that is "definitely Malthusian." "Population cannot cross the boundaries imposed by physical limits." In setting out the reasons for the failure of Malthus' projections, Spengler, in contrast to Kahn, emphasises that poor nations lack the same opportunities to repeat the historic development of the rich countries. Even if aid were given, without skills and without capital there is little chance of it being used properly, since these countries have not yet reached the conditions for economic "take-off" (p. 19).

In Spengler's view, economic measures such as carefully designed taxes on population and on wasteful consumption would serve to correct Malthusian trends. Strict population control and "prudence" are the key. One dollar spent on population control is worth a hundred spent on aid (p. 16). If only population growth could be brought under control, other problems could be solved, and economic growth would proceed. What is needed is a restructuring of "relevant penalty-reward structures" and of the "motivational milieu" in developing countries. Rapid increases in urban employment would permit application of labour-saving agricultural methods. High personal investment and advanced technologies introduced from abroad but adapted to local needs are central to his economic strategy. At the international level he advocates restructuring of international exchange rates to encourage trade in raw materials and agricultural products. Spengler sees many of the same barriers to advancement as Kahn and Wiener, but he is considerably less hopeful that they can be overcome. Nevertheless, he does not appear to be as pessimistic as other authors (such as Heilbroner), whose population and resource assumptions are very similar.

Eco-catastrophe

Compared with some other neo-Malthusian authors, Spengler's pessimism about the future is restrained. With the publications of Anne and Paul Ehrlich the idea of eco-catastrophe was born. Passionate television appearances made Paul Ehrlich for a time a focal point of a strong environmental movement. In their book *Population, Resources, Environment* published in 1970 and in their more popularised works *The Population Bomb* (1971) and *How to be a Survivor* (1971), the Ehrlichs argue that the world is *already* over-populated and, in the industrial countries at least, "overdeveloped" in terms of the world's ecological resources. In their view the ecosystem is already in jeopardy, and for ecological reasons the planet simply cannot stand the kind of industrialisation imagined by Kahn or even Spengler (p. 62). Unlike Kahn and Wiener's book, which concentrates much more on case studies of possible *future* situations, the Ehrlichs detail a large number of areas in the recent past in which things have gone wrong, and use these to exemplify specific objections to various "optimistic" schemes that have been proposed.

The Ehrlichs consider it possible that the "capacity of the planet to support human life has already been permanently impaired." "Spaceship Earth" is now filled to capacity or beyond and is running out of control (p. 3). As population growth especially continues there is the possibility of lethal plagues, nuclear war . . . even driving the human race to extinction (p. 332). The kind of technological optimism expounded by Kahn and Wiener is based on ignorance about environmental and other issues.

For the Ehrlichs, "de-development" of the industrial regions rather than growth is needed. Taking a radically different view from Kahn and Wiener, the Ehrlichs propose that in the "over-developed countries" economic growth rates should be reversed in order to "bring our economic system (especially patterns of consumption) into line with the realities of ecology and the world resource situation" (p. 323). The Ehrlichs summarise their view of the current situation as follows: "By making the fundamental error of basing our standard of progress on expansion of the GNP, we have created a vast industrial complex and great mental, moral and aesthetic poverty. Our cities are disaster areas, our air is often unbreathable, our people increasingly regimented and our spirit increasingly dominatable" (p. 304). There must be a massive campaign to de-develop the United States: "Once the United States has clearly started on the path of cleaning up its own mess it can then turn its attention to the problems of the development of the other developed countries; population control and ecologically feasible semi-development of the under-developed countries" (p. 323).

Opponents of economic growth such as the Ehrlichs are not criticising only the Western model of development; they explicitly include the Soviet Union's aspirations for development: "A major cause of humanity's current plight . . . lies not in the economic differences between the super powers . . . but in the economic attitudes that they have in common" (p. 279). Dramatic measures must be taken to effect some level of redistribution of the wealth of the world, and they advocate "unprecedented aid"; the figure mentioned is twenty per cent of rich nations' GNP over a fifteen-year period (p. 302). But unlike Kahn and Spengler, the pattern of development cannot be a Western "consumist" one. They observe that the "most impressive of the many reasons why under-developed countries cannot and should not be industrialised along the developed country lines" are the environmental ones of pollution and thermal limits. Most pressing is "ecologically sensible agricultural development . . . that is for semi-development" (p. 300). "They must design a low consumption economy of stability and in which there is a much more equitable distribution of wealth than in the present one" (p. 323). In the Ehrlichs' view, even if the measures advocated by Spengler could be introduced, the environment would not be capable of supporting them.

The difference between the measures advocated by the Ehrlichs and those advocated by Spengler lies largely in their emphasis on governmental and collective moral reform towards a conservationist ethic. For the Ehrlichs, "the basic solutions involve dramatic and rapid changes in human attitudes, especially those relating to productive behaviour, economic growth, technology, the environment and conflict resolution" (p. 322). Religion, the conservation movement, education, the legal system, must all be used to bring about changes. "The world cannot in its present critical state be saved by merely tearing down old institutions even if rational plans existed. We simply do not have the time. Either we succeed by bending old institutions or we will succumb to disaster" (p. 324).

Despite their plea for massive redistribution, the Ehrlichs often appear to be overawed by the magnitude of their own prescriptions. Indeed, their position is frequently ambiguous: "For some very poor nations there may already be no hope." In their more pessimistic passages the Ehrlichs advise us to "prepare for the worst" and suggest that a policy of "triage" may be called for. This involves writing off all nations that are felt to be beyond "realistic help"; those that belong to the tragic category that is "so far behind in the population-food game that there is no hope that our food aid could see them through to self-sufficiency." The Ehrlichs say India might be a candidate for triage, and that if experts who advocate it are right "this would be preferable to thoughtless dispersal of limited food reserves without regard for their long range effects" (p. 310). Thus, the Ehrlichs consider the extreme alternatives: altruism and despair. Frightened by their own image of the world, they retreat into despair.

The Limits to Growth

Those who were not convinced by detailed documentation of the state of the environment and the earth's limited potential in the Ehrlichs' book might well have been moved by an even more dramatic Malthusian prediction issuing from a computer: world population growth and industrialisation in the face of finite natural resources would bring about starvation, ecological disaster and an abrupt decline of population. Ignoring Kahn and Wiener's region by region extrapolation, this was the message of Jay Forrester in *World Dynamics* (1971). Forrester's computer model essentially described five interlinked "global sub-systems": population, natural resources, capital, agricultural and pollution. The fact that it came from a computer made Forrester's a dramatic and original forecast. His authoritative-looking graphical output made front page reading in the international press. Surprisingly, however, virtually no empirical evidence was given to substantiate the numbers he had inserted in his model (Cole, Freeman, Pavitt and Jahoda, 1973).

The book contained an important idea, which was expressed by earlier Malthusian authors such as the Ehrlichs but not spelt out so clearly—that of the mutually reinforcing nature of events. Forrester's claim is that attempts to solve one problem will only exacerbate another. For example, attempts at population control would be inherently self-defeating since the consequent rise in living standards would promote industrialisation and this, he argues, is ecologically even more disturbing than population growth (p. 11). By the same token, attempts to improve diet by improved agricultural technology would be defeated for precisely the reasons indicated by Malthus. Forrester dubs this decline "overshoot and collapse." Only a package of population, resource and environmental policies directed towards some kind of equilibrium society would suffice, for even the most optimistic expectations for technology do not permit continuing growth. We may now be living in the "golden age." It may be unwise for poor countries to attempt to industrialise, and the rich-poor gap may well be closed by an unwilling fall in the living standards of industrial nations (p. 12). Redistribution apart, Forrester shares a view with the Ehrlichs: "the wealthy nations must move back a generation in the production of material wealth." Without this, international strife over environmental rights could pull average world-wide standards back a century.

Forrester poses the question, "what will happen when the resource supplying countries begin to withhold resources because they foresee the day when their own demand will require the available supplies? Pressures from impending short-ages are already appearing . . . will a new era of international conflict grow out of pressures from resources shortage?" (p. 70). Elsewhere (Laszlo, 1973) he has suggested that "the present accelerating pace of international trade is a device to allow growth to continue until the entire world simultaneously approaches shortages of all traded goods." This interdependence is used as a partial justification for the global averaging used in the *World Dynamics* model, but it is also used to support some arguments for "triage." To avoid being affected by collapse in the least able poor nations, industrialised countries should as far as possible disassociate themselves economically and politically from them.

Forrester's criticisms of "contemporary capitalism" are certainly less am-biguous than the Ehrlichs'. His specific recommendations for action oppose the more altruistic of the measures advocated by the Ehrlichs. Forrester would con-sider their proposals on aid quite unrealistic. He argues instead that humanitarian impulses, as embodied in health services, food aid or attempts at industrialisation, are counterproductive (p. 124). Elsewhere he repeats his asser-tion that "development aid is a disservice to most countries because it attempts to establish a non-sustainable future" (*Futurist*, 1976). He advocates the reversal of such policies in order to bring about "rising pressures" by rising populations. Forrester argues that attempts to solve problems of physical shortage arising from Malthusian limits by technology only without paying attention to popula-tion increase would merely "transfer the pressures to the social area, resulting in such symptoms as loss of confidence in government, kidnappings, aircraft hi-jackings, revolutions and war." "By solving the problem of physical limits without controlling population and industrial growth, we essentially say we will accept major atomic war as a solution to the growth problem; when put that way I doubt that it is a good trade." He argues that we should "equalise pressures"—"tolerate some hunger, some energy shortage and some revolutions." Only with "effective arbitration," presumably through interna-tional regulation, can war and violence over resources be averted (p. 125). He excuses the lack of discussion of these issues: "Only broad aspects of the world system are discussed here, not the difficulties of implementing the changes that will be necessary if the present course of human events is to be altered" (p. ix).

Forrester's computerised intervention in the debate gave significant impetus to the Malthusian cause, being cited, for example, in "Blueprint for Survival" (*The Ecologist*, 1972), a document insisting on the need for the United Kingdom to set course for equilibrium and to halve its population. In more recent articles (e.g., *Futurist*, 1976) Forrester has modified his original position to some extent, preferring to assert that the world is currently passing through the turning point in its logistic growth, and so could be heading towards the equilibrium state, rather than into "overshoot and collapse."

Forrester's appearance in the world futures debate was stimulated by an inter-national group of businessmen, civil servants, academics and (more recently) politicians—the Club of Rome. This group was and still is concerned to bring to the attention of the world's leaders the nature of the so-called "World Prob-lematique" (i.e., the interrelated issues of population growth, environment and moral decline), and has sponsored several of the studies described in this review. Its members hit on the idea of using a computer to advertise their cause. In the words of their spokesman and chief executive Aurelio Peccei, "What we needed was a vehicle to move the hearts and minds of men out of their ingrained habits" (Gillette, 1972). Despite its impact, Forrester's *World Dynamics* was originally intended as an exploratory venture in this direction.

Under the auspices of the Club of Rome, Forrester's model was developed further by Dennis Meadows and his team of system dynamicists. The result was that Forrester's impressionistic and starkly Malthusian forecast was almost immediately "confirmed" by this apparently more authoritative and more widely publicised study, *The Limits to Growth*. Unlike Forrester, the Meadows' team initially express some concern in *The Limits to Growth* about world regional differences and demonstrate by simple extrapolation that present trends in population and GNP for particular nations lead to a phenomenally large income gap between rich and poor.

Using a more elaborate version of Forrester's computer model, but still with variables globally averaged, the authors of *The Limits to Growth* conclude that "if the present growth trends in world population, industrialisation, pollution, food production and resource depletion continue unchanged, limits to growth on the planet will be reached some time within the next one hundred years. The most probable result will be a rather sudden and uncontrollable decline in both population and industrial capacity within the next one hundred years" (p. 23). In fact, the current trends lead to a collapse of the world economy and of world population *before* the year 2000. Surprisingly, the assumed growth rate of the world economy in the model up to the point of collapse seems considerably higher than Kahn's forecasts or extrapolations.

The Meadows remark that in their model "discontinuous events such as wars and epidemics" have been ignored. These would bring an end to growth "even sooner" than the model actually indicates, and so the model is, in fact, "biased to allow growth to continue longer than it probably can in the real world" (p. 126). The Meadows' team are more emphatic than Forrester about the need for urgency in tackling the "World Problematique." To delay thirty years makes the problem insoluble even with the solutions they suggest.

The principal difference from Forrester's results lies in the greater stress placed on the need for "ecological and economic stability." In this state, as with Forrester, world population and capital would be deliberately held constant at something less than twice the present levels. The Meadows stress the urgency of the present predicament; like the Ehrlichs they view an end to growth as something to strive for. They argue that income redistribution is more likely in this new "equilibrium society," but with the Malthusian sting that redistribution becomes "social suicide" if populations get too large and the "average amount" available is not enough to maintain life (p. 178).

The Meadows' team have almost nothing to say about what should or might happen to poor nations relative to the rich nations under the policy of no growth. "There is, of course, no assurance that humanity's moral resources would be sufficient to solve the problem of income redistribution even in an equilibrium state" (p. 179). However, they say, there is "even less assurance" in the present state of growth. Even so, they cite without comment and with apparent approval the seemingly contradictory remark that "the stationary state would make fewer demands on our environmental resources, but much greater demands on our moral resources" (p. 179).

The Meadows are at pains to distinguish an "equilibrium" society from a "stationary," unchanging society. An equilibrium with zero population or capital growth would not be seen as an "end to human development." Technological change would permit increased consumption. "The possibilities within an equilibrium state are almost endless," although it would require some sacrifices. They are as unforthcoming as Forrester about how this state would be achieved. At their most explicit they speak in *The Limits to Growth* of global society and "controlled, orderly transition from growth to global equilibrium" (p. 184), of "managing" the transition (p. 180), "if the world's people decide to strive . . ." towards this goal (p. 24).

Equilibrium would require trading of certain human freedoms such as "producing unlimited numbers of children or consuming uncontrolled amounts of resources, for other freedoms such as relief from pollution and crowding and the threat of collapse of the world system" (p. 179). Elsewhere Meadows is reported as giving some idea of what he means by coordinated management: "really outstanding companies . . . tend to have small leadership, maybe one guy, able to diffuse throughout the organisation a concept of goals and values. He pushes these down, not decisions. He guides people in a fashion much more co-ordinated than you would have with central planning. We have the capability to achieve that" (Rothschild, 1975).

For many people the debate about the future is the *Limits to Growth* debate. The use of the computer, big interdisciplinary research teams and evangelical television presentations helped to reinforce ideas already set out by Ehrlich, Spengler and others. Much as Kahn, *The Limits to Growth* has been a stimulus for other forecasters, some also sponsored by the Club of Rome. Despite their efforts to publicise the dramatic nature and urgency of the prescriptions of *The Limits to Growth* (Gillette, 1972), the Club of Rome prefer to view the work as a first hesitant step towards a new understanding of our world (King, 1974).

The Culmination of Despair

The most fatalistic of the present-day Malthusians is Robert Heilbroner. In his works "The Human Prospect"[2] and "Growth and Survival" he accepts with some qualification the basic resource-limited future of *The Limits to Growth*: "Under any and all assumptions, one irrefutable conclusion remains. The industrial growth process, so central to economic and social life of capitalism and Western socialism alike, will be forced to slow down, in all likelihood within a generation or two, and will probably have to give way to decline thereafter" (p. 32). LIke the Ehrlichs and Meadows, Heilbroner argues that environmental constraints and the enormous population growth in poor countries will drive beyond present misery to a "grim Malthusian outcome," but he rejects the viability of their "solutions" and goes beyond them to describe the mechanisms of social and economic breakdown and societies' attempts to survive these disasters. He is "more sanguine" about possibilities for technological change than the Meadows and sees polemics against economic growth as futile; "only a major disaster will slow the pace of growth." He argues that there is no hope of meeting the challenges of the future without paying a "fearful price."

In his descriptions of future conditions in poor countries Heilbroner provides a stark contrast to Kahn's visions of the post-industrial society. "The descent of large portions of the under-developed world into a condition of steadily worsening social disorder, marked by shorter life expectancies, further stunting of physical and mental capacities, political apathy intermingled with riots and pillaging when crops fail . . . ruled by dictatorial governments serving the interests of a small economic and military upper class and presiding over the rotting countryside with mixed resignation, indifference, and despair. This condition could continue for a considerable period, effectively removing these areas from the concern of the rest of the world, and consigning the billions of their inhabitants to a human state comparable to that which we now glimpse in the worst regions of India or Pakistan." The "intolerable social strains" that resource shortages will bring are thus made quite explicit (p. 23).

Because of the increasing rich-poor gap, "nuclear blackmail and wars of redistribution" must be anticipated. But he expresses doubt whether even the wealth of the industrial nations could solve the food problems of the poor. "We are entering a period in which rapid population growth, the presence of obliterative weapons and dwindling resources will bring international tension to dangerous levels for an extended period" (p. 32).

Heilbroner describes the kind of institutions required to bring the escalating effects of environmental constraints under control. He argues that many of the "economic and social problems lie outside the accustomed instruments of policy making" (p. 21). In fact, he says, "only two outcomes are imaginable"—anarchy or totalitarianism (p. 23). Nevertheless, preferring totalitarianism to anarchy, Heilbroner suggests the occurrence of quite dramatic institutional changes. Only authoritarian regimes are likely to be able to cope with problems arising from the central environmental issues of the future: "To solve the problems of pollution . . . assuredly the extension of public control far beyond anything experienced in the West, socialist or capitalist . . ." is needed. "If the issue for mankind is survival, such governments [capable of rallying obedience far more effectively than would be possible in a democratic setting] may be unavoidable, even necessary" (p. 31). This advocacy of "strong government," which he says appears to play into the hands of those who applaud "orderliness of authoritarian or dictatorial government," is justified because the "weakest part" of the humanitarian outlook is that it is unable and unwilling to come to grips with certain "obdurate human characteristics." Current institutions have failed and there is a loss of confidence in industrial societies, geared to material improvement, which have "failed to satisfy the human spirit" (p. 22).

Heilbroner's major concern is how to cope with inevitable economic decline. Although in the longer term he looks to the same kind of changes in values as other Malthusian authors, he feels obliged to distinguish between "temporary" and "longer term" solutions. To meet the challenge he foresees, Heilbroner rebuffs "appeals to our collective foresight, such as the exhortations of the Club of Rome" or the "Blueprint for Survival" (1972). He says the "challenge to survival still lies sufficiently far in the future, and the inertial momentum of the present industrial order is still so great that no substantial voluntary diminution of growth, much less a planned reorganisation of society, is today even remotely imaginable" (p. 33).

In his most recent work, *Business Civilisation in Decline* (1976), Heilbroner again emphasises that "the unavoidable curtailment of growth thus threatens the viability of capitalism by removing the primary source of the profits" (i.e., expansion) (p. 108). Not only Western society is threatened; "the curtailment of the future must bear on every form of civilisation . . . most important by far is apt to be the growing tension between poor nations and rich ones" (p. 106).

LIVING WITH LIMITS

Other authors have also taken the thesis set out by Meadows et al. as a point of departure for their own discussion. René Dumont, with his book *Utopia or Else . . .* (1974), is quite typical of authors who for many years have been concerned with the plight of poor countries, and he uses the opportunity of debate about world-wide development and possible ecological disaster to restate his position. E. F. Schumacher, similarly, uses the futures debate to further his own critique of present patterns of development. Dumont rejects Kahn's "unthinking optimism," and accepts much of *The Limits to Growth*. He concludes that there is no possibility of poor countries reaching the standards of living realised in the United States: "the rich countries' hopes of surviving rest solely on the continued poverty of the rest of mankind" (p. 14). Like the Ehrlichs, Dumont is exceedingly critical of the wasteful consumption in rich countries, which, he says, can only continue to take place at the expense of the poor. Ultimately this situation "will incite these nations to launch a series of dangerous revolts" (p. 6). "By the time the under-developed nations are eventually in a position to build up their own heavy industries from their own resources they will already have been robbed of their best minerals and oils. This will mean they can never become even remotely competitive and their expansion will be dreadfully restricted." He castigates "Western profligacy" and insists that rich countries should direct their production to helping less-developed nations. In view of their high levels of consumption, he sees a major task as reducing population growth in rich countries (p. 66). Armaments and the private motor car must be abolished. Dumont points out that his diet of austerity for rich nations does "not in any way imply that production should be brought to a halt." Rich countries must expect to manufacture increasing amounts of industrial equipment and provide increasing quantities of fertiliser, at least until the developing countries can provide for themselves.

Although Dumont accepts the importance of aid and other assistance from

rich to poor nations (the figure mentioned is five per cent of rich country incomes), he insists that rich countries cease to "burden" and "dominate" poor
countries; thus aid must be *given*. But most important in Dumont's scheme is
that poor countries should achieve independence; as a first stage, agricultural
independence.

Dumont considers that "Revolts are inevitable in dominated countries" (p.
81). He believes that "this new world is not and never will be a rational structure; it will be an arena of confrontation and struggle" (p. 97). "A common
front on behalf of the condemned people of this earth" with the "dual aim of
less inequality and improved chances of survival" should operate on a world
scale (p. 141). However, poor nations should "put their faith in a neutralist,
non-aligned foreign policy" (p. 83). Nevertheless, he sees ultimate institutional
cooperation at a world level.

Schumacher shares many sympathies with Dumont, particularly concerning
the situation of poor nations and the underlying themes of *The Limits to
Growth*. But while he views Herman Kahn type optimists as "the blind leading
the blind," he is equally unsympathetic to the "doom watching pessimists" and
especially to Heilbroner (*Futurist*, 1974). In *Small is Beautiful* (1973) Schumacher
describes in some detail his concern with the nature of modern technology. It is
too large, and as it grows it requires more and more simply for its own
maintenance: "The most striking thing about modern industry is that it requires so much and accomplishes so little" (p. 97).

According to Schumacher, a principal reason why in many parts of the world
the poor are becoming poorer is the "negative demonstration effect" of modern
technology. The established processes of foreign aid, which cause sophisticated
technologies to be introduced into unsophisticated environments, are counterproductive. The essential problem facing mankind, he says, is the choice of
scale. Although somewhat less pessimistic about resource limitations than
many authors, Schumacher argues that growth must stop. In any case, there is
little evidence, he argues, that growth is conducive to world peace. "Only by
reduction in needs can one promote a genuine reduction in those tensions
which are ultimate causes of strife and war" (*Futurist*, 1974).

THE "SECOND GENERATION" MODELS

Although *The Limits to Growth* computer models and the world-wide publicity they received provided a powerful stimulus to the futures debate, both the
techniques and the underlying theories were subjected to strong criticism. On
the technical level the shortcomings of the models and the unreality of many of
the aggregative assumptions were exposed. As a result a "second generation" of
models attempted to eradicate some of the more obvious weaknesses and
errors. At the same time, others attempted to use the technique of computer
simulation modelling for very different purposes and came up with conclusions
diametrically opposed to those of *The Limits to Growth*.

The new models all attempt to tackle the question of international trade and,
with the exception of the Latin American model, they all explore futures in

which global development is fostered largely by expanded international trade. Unlike *The Limits to Growth* these world models treat the world as a set of interacting regions.

Strategy for Survival

Mankind at the Turning Point by Mihajlo Mesarovic and Eduard Pestel (1974a) outlines the content of a global computer model far grander than that of the Meadows' team. The original Forrester model had only 40 equations, the Meadows model had 200, but that of Mesarovic and Pestel is claimed to have 100,000 (p. 34). Like *The Limits to Growth* this model received considerable support and publicity from the Club of Rome. The major theme is the interconnectedness of world events and the need for global solutions. It also emphasises the possibility of impending disaster and reflects the "conviction that the world will have to face a cluster of crises of unprecedented type and magnitude which might very well appear before the end of the century and possibly more overwhelming thereafter in ever faster succession" (Mesarovic and Pestel, 1974b).

Mesarovic and Pestel are more concerned than the authors of *The Limits to Growth* with the questions of income redistribution on a global scale. Although they pay homage to the long-term problems arising from resource and environmental constraints and particularly the potential dangers arising from the "Faustian bargain" of nuclear power, they are also less pessimistic than the Meadows team about global resources. They merely declare that "long-term availability cannot be taken for granted" and that "now the world is again approaching an era of scarcity" (p. 85).

Their so-called Strategy for Survival model assumes (contrary to *The Limits to Growth*) that some effective population policies will be introduced. Even with a slowing down of population growth, and without setting severe resource constraints, a widening gap between rich and poor worlds is predicted, most seriously for the region they described as South and South East Asia, which would lead to "collapses" at a regional level "possibly long before the middle of the next century" (p. 122).

Mesarovic and Pestel argue that in the "emerging world system" there is the "world-wide dependence on a common stock of raw materials, problems in providing energy, and food supply, sharing of the common physical environment on land, sea and air. . . ." This creates a high level of interdependence, which causes a "disturbance" of the normal states of affairs in any part of the world to spread quickly elsewhere (p. 18).

Like Heilbroner and Schumacher they see the widening rich-poor gap threatening world political stability. International political polarisation with the threat of nuclear war, in their opinion, "makes closing the gap a question of the survival of the world system as such." They observe that "desperadoes" and "nuclear blackmail" will "paralyse further orderly development" (p. 69). "For each region its turn would come in due time." Like Forrester, they see the possibility of progressive collapse across regions. The oil and food crises should not be viewed as temporary; they are early manifestations of a long-term global development crisis.

Mesarovic and Pestel argue that since the problems of the world are inter-related they require a "global approach." There is "no more urgent task than to guide the world system to a path of organic growth" (p. 196). The closest they come to a definition of this is "functional inter-dependence between constituent parts in the sense that none of them is self-contained but rather has to fulfil a role assigned through historical evolution" (p. 5). "Co-ordinated global cooperation" is its most important facet—it would, for example, avoid the possibility that "undesirable growth of any one part [of the system] threatens not only that part but the whole as well." But unlike Forrester, who sees trade as a mechanism for encouraging global collapse, Mesarovic and Pestel see it as essential to build up the export potential of poor countries and especially South Asia, for the solution of the world food problems. Attempts at self-sufficiency are likely to lead to "disastrous results."

In economic terms, Mesarovic and Pestel envisage a "world-wide diversifica-tion of industry leading to a true global economic system." "Balanced develop-ment" in all regions would take account not only of national conditions (factors of production) but, just as important, of long-term, world-wide interests. It is essential to build up the economic base of poor countries; apart from food com-modities, only investment aid that provides the right kind of "intermediate technology" (p. 66) should be given to developing regions. They estimate the cost of aid if an attempt were made to reach the income targets suggested by the Tinbergen Committee for the Second United Nations Development Decade. This would reduce average income differentials with rich countries to a max-imum of 5 to 1 for the poorer regions such as Tropical Africa and Southern Asia, and to about 3 to 1 for Latin America (Codoni, 1974).

The economic transfers required would, they argue, not be possible with prevailing international economic arrangements. They call for social and in-stitutional reforms and repeatedly emphasise that in "the urgent quest for peace" evolution through cooperation rather than confrontation is essential. It would *not*, they emphasise, involve "globalism" in the sense that favours unifor-mity; not "a monolithic world system, one language, one structure, one govern-ment, etc." Like the Meadows, they do not attempt to spell out in detail what it would involve, only what it would foster, namely, "world consciousness." They do not make global Malthusian resource assumptions and, surprisingly, given their exhortations about the "oncoming age of scarcity" (p. 147), the world growth rates implied by Mesarovic and Pestel's computer results are much closer to those of Kahn and Wiener than to those of Meadows and Forrester. Thus, with "domino effect" collapses averted, these authors appear to foresee relatively high economic growth for some time to come.

The United Nations World Input-Output Model

The world input-output model constructed by Nobel Laureate Wassily Leon-tief forms part of the United Nations study on the impact of prospective en-vironmental issues and policies on the international development strategy initiated in 1973. The objective of the study was to investigate the interrela-tionships between future economic growth and environmental issues: "One question specifically asked by the study was whether the existing and other development targets were consistent with resource availability and geographic distribution" and whether "to the extent that some resources are limited . . . desired growth rates [should] be modified" (Leontief et al., 1976, p. 3). But, unlike *The Limits to Growth*, The United Nations model is concerned more with the closing of the income gap between rich and poor countries than with the possibilities of world economic growth.

According to the authors, a scenario based on current trends "turns out to be rather pessimistic" (p. 72). Furthermore, scenarios based on the recommendations for the Second United Nations Development Decade do not provide for a sufficiently rapid closing of the gap, when population increases are taken into account. Instead, the authors examine the implications of scenarios in which the growth rates are set to reduce the income gap between poor and rich countries by about half by the year 2000, from the present average of 12 to 1 to 7 to 1.

The model is claimed to provide detailed results by region and by sector of the "conditions of growth" needed to achieve these targets. The results appear to contradict those of *The Limits to Growth*. The authors argue that "mineral resource endowment is generally adequate to support world economic development at relatively high rates, but that these resources will probably become more expensive to extract, as the century moves towards its conclusion" (p. 25). On questions of environmental pollution they are more optimistic: "though pollution is a grave problem for humanity it is a technologically manageable problem" (pp. 31, 49). They estimate that the costs of control are in the region of 1.5 to 2 per cent of gross domestic product.

The study concludes that "No insurmountable barriers exist within this century to accelerated development of the developing regions . . . the principal limits to sustained economic growth and accelerated development are political, social and institutional in character" (p. 48). However, no prescription is given in the work for these changes. The implications of the assumptions about technology in the model are not discussed either, except for a brief mention of need for redistribution. Thus, the limits to growth imposed by mineral resources, agriculture and environment can be overcome. But the achievement of targets is dependent on significant changes in current economic relations between the rich and poor nations. The study stresses the need for a "steady increase" in investment in poor countries: "Accelerated development is only possible under the condition that from 30 to 35% and in some cases up to 40% of their gross product is used for capital investment" (p. 49). The study discusses what restructuring of developing country economies might be needed: "Accelerated development in the developing regions would lead to a continuous and significant share in the developing regions' world gross product and industrial production" (p. 50). Growth in developing countries would therefore in part come through a "brisk expansion" of international trade. In this context they emphasise the importance of reducing the balance of payments deficit of developing countries. This would be done by stabilising commodity markets, stimulating export of manufactures from the developing countries and increasing financial transfers (p. 51).

Global Constraints and a New Vision for Development[3]

Like other global modelling studies, "A New Vision for Development" is a reaction to *The Limits to Growth*. The Japanese work team of the Club of Rome, led by Yoichi Kaya, argue for an international order based on a modified international division of labour, which would provide for both the immediate problems of poor nations and their longer-term development needs. "The approaching limits of our earth however compete for our attention with another equally, if not more serious problem, the poverty and inadequate economic growth rate of the developing nations. In these nations of Asia, Africa, and Central and South America, where over half the world's people live, development is made extremely difficult by rapid population growth, chronic malnutrition and often by an unstable political order" (p. 277). The authors continue: "Furthermore, if we look some distance into the future we can easily see that the developing nations will run into another impasse when their manufactured goods begin to compete with those of the advanced nations of the world market."

They set out to devise a "New Plan for Development" based on a world-wide redistribution of industry to help the developing nations (p. 371). They calculate the pattern of investment world-wide that would lead to a maximum rate of increase in poor nations' gross products. The authors argue that their industrial redistribution plan is "actually a form of indirect foreign aid whereby the advanced countries co-operate to facilitate the development of the less wealthy nations" (p. 386). The Japanese work team suggest a "new type of international division of industry . . . light industry should be promoted in Asia, and agricultural industry in Middle and South America as well as in North America and Oceania" (p. 279). In addition, "relatively high capital effective types of industry could be, with suitable restrictions, transferred from the advanced to the developing nations" (p. 278).

Redistribution of industry is seen as especially important because, the authors argue, "if economic self-sufficiency should be overly emphasised then only the regions with adequate natural resources would actually attain this goal" (p. 385). The idea of "encouraging self-development through expansion of agriculture and mining industries comes from a mistakenly exaggerated idea of the richness of natural resources in the developing nations" (p. 372). They are, thus, against isolationist strategies such as those suggested by some authors and conclude that a policy of economic self-sufficiency is unfavourable, for if each nation should strive to maintain self-sufficiency the plan would be largely ineffective. This plan would impose sacrifices especially on Japan and Western Europe among the developed nations, and on all of the developing nations (p. 386).

Beyond Underdevelopment and Dependence – Basic Needs

For the Latin American Bariloche group, led by Amilcar Herrera, current trends clearly lead to a widening gap between rich and poor nations. The catastrophe predicted by "some models in vogue" (an oblique reference to *The*

Limits to Growth) is already a reality for much of mankind. It is not necessary to wait a hundred years to perceive it, nor to build a model to show it. Global aggregation and focusing on relatively distant issues causes attention to be drawn from more pressing and important problems.

The Bariloche team, like Mesarovic and Pestel, concern themselves with world-wide redistribution, but they also place great emphasis on redistribution *within* regions. While they emphasise the need to account for ecological limits, they take a "non-Malthusian" stance and argue that present-day Malthusians only support the interests of rich countries. In their opinion socio-political factors rather than the resource limitations—stressed, for example, by Forrester and Dumont—stop backward societies developing in the same fashion as the presently developed nations. Resources will not be exhausted in a "historically significant time-scale."

Like Dumont, however, they believe that the consumption patterns of populations in rich countries and the cities in poor nations are irrational and destructive. They share both the Ehrlichs' and Heilbroner's view that the ideology of growth is strongly built into Western forms of capitalism and socialism. Indeed, pollution and environmental deterioration arising from this could provoke ecological collapse. Bariloche see the widening rich-poor gap and destructive patterns of consumption as having socio-political origins. The result of failing to rectify these obstacles to development could be "almost as catastrophic as any Malthusian scarcity." According to Bariloche the problem for the Third World countries "consists essentially of finding new principles such as 'eco-development' to avoid dangers which now confront industrialised countries."

Their model describes a world society in which consumption is divided evenly within four regions: Latin America, Asia, Africa and the rich world. Using the model, the authors claim to demonstate the material viability of an "ideal" society. They demonstrate how each of the major world regions can develop to a maximum, non-ecologically-destructive level. Where this differs dramatically from *The Limits to Growth* equilibrium state is that it would be "an egalitarian society, at both the national and international levels . . . [with] . . . inalienable rights regarding the satisfaction of basic needs—nutrition, housing, health—that are essential for complete and active participation. . . ." (Herrera et al., 1976, p. 25). The model is designed around this concept.

Unlike most other modellers, the Bariloche group stresses the importance of "autarky." The satisfaction of the basic needs is achieved in all regions with the use of almost exclusively local economic resources. This does not exclude trade, which remains at about the current proportion of regional product. Each world region is treated as an economic unit, which "pre-supposes total collaboration between the countries forming it" (p. 44). Differences between socialist and capitalist countries are not made explicit in the mathematical model (p. 43) and all countries are assumed to "follow the same policy after 1980."

The Latin American team thus appear to be examining quite a different international economic order from that proposed elsewhere. The authors argue that basic needs can be met within thirty years, except for Asia where the "food sector fails." The solution advocated by the authors is an effective population policy and the use of non-conventional foodstuffs. They examine a scenario that assumes "international solidarity" and that the developed region devotes two per cent of income to aid exclusively Africa and Asia, a scenario not dissimilar to that advocated by Mesarovic and Pestel. For Africa this does not affect the time period within which basic needs are satisfied, and for Asia it makes "very little difference" (p. 101). Assuming that the present distribution of income is maintained does, however, appear to have a much greater impact on the results: "At the very best [it] delays the goals of a liberated humanity, free from suffering and misery, by at least two generations. It also implies need to devote between three and five times more material resources to the achievement of the desired objective, thus multiplying the pressure on the environment" (p. 106).

The significant contributions of the Bariloche model therefore are the concept of "basic needs" (which now appears to be rapidly entering the vocabulary of international organisations; I.L.O., 1977), and the demonstration that an egalitarian society requires far fewer resources to satisfy basic needs than does an inegalitarian one. The assumptions about trade are, however, formally and quantitatively little different from those of Mesarovic and Pestel or Leontief.

In *Self Reliance: Concepts, Theory and Rationale* (1977),[4] Johan Galtung has presented many political and social ideas similar to those used in the Bariloche study. He argues that the spread of Western thought through culture and science, of socio-economic practice through capitalism, and of military-political practice through colonialism has meant that the "world-encompassing centre-periphery formation [is] built as a program into Western civilisation" (p. 1). He argues that the Third World cannot become self-reliant by imitating the First and Second Worlds. The hierarchical interactions of the present structure of the world economy must be broken up, and replaced instead by cooperation between countries in the same socio-economic position. He is in favour not of anarchy, of the world divided into small, local communities, but of a world where more power, initiative and higher levels of needs-satisfaction are found at what is now the periphery.

Self-reliance takes the form of using local factors—local creativity, raw materials, land and capital, which too often the centre has drained away (p. 5). Galtung argues (p. 19) that there is a problem in delineating self-reliant regions; it should be sought at many levels, local, national or collective (sub-regional, regional or Third World) but, if this does not work, some type of "limited co-operation" with the developed countries might be sought. Self-reliant countries must be able to produce for basic needs, so that food dependency, in particular, cannot be used as a weapon in a crisis. Galtung also suggests (p. 15) that a self-reliant country would better be able to withstand military pressure, since, because of its localised structure, it could offer paramilitary and guerrilla-type resistance, as well as non-military forms of resistance, even after an occupation has taken place. Because of the inevitable external pressure that Galtung considers would be placed on poor countries, he argues that self-reliance as a doctrine is more in the field of "psychopolitics" than in the field of economics.

The International Order

The most recent of the published studies sponsored by the Club of Rome is entitled *Reshaping the International Order* (RIO). The project team, which includes many members of the Club of Rome, was led by Nobel Laureate Jan Tinbergen, who also chaired the "Tinbergen Committee" (see Codoni, 1974), which was responsible for the national development targets advocated for the UN Second Development Decade (and considered in the Mesarovic and Pestel and the Leontief studies). The RIO report was "promoted" by the results of the UN General Assembly Sixth Special Session, 1974, to work towards the establishment of a new international economic order (Tinbergen, 1976, p. 4). With this study the Club of Rome appears to be refining a position hinted at in the study by Mesarovic and Pestel, and the Club of Rome's "World Problematique."

According to the Tinbergen study, Vietnam, OPEC, inflation, economic instability, growing alienation and threats to basic values, all engendered by pressures to consume more, make it clear that the "cornucopia of economic growth" is turning into a "Pandora's Box" (p. 12). In Tinbergen's view a "sudden and historically important change" took place in 1973 when the OPEC initiative took the Third World from "deference to defiance" (p. 13). Consequently, he argues, the world's problems have increased substantively, and the world has become more complex politically, with the appearance of many new powers of importance and strength in the neutral and third worlds (p. 43). The rich and poor have unparalleled problems that cannot be solved independently (p. 21).

On physical resources the authors appear less pessimistic than either of the two other major Club of Rome studies, *The Limits to Growth* and *Mankind at the Turning Point*: "Fears expressed in recent years concerning the exhaustion of natural resources may well be exaggerated" (p. 37). Although technologies can be developed that will help solve problems of exploitation, extraction, substitution and environmental degradation, failure to recognise that maldistribution is an important aspect of the "environmental crisis" might prove "disastrous for all" (p. 33).

The authors call for a new international order in which "a life of dignity and well-being becomes an inalienable right of all" (p. 4). But they say any new world order cannot be based on an exclusive philosophy of economic growth and material riches. In fact, poor countries should reject the aspiration for a Western style of life: "no sane person could seriously envisage a world in which the world's poor live like today's affluent minority . . . to believe it is possible is an illusion, to attempt to construct it would be madness" (p. 74). Thus, although the book argues that resource constraints are apparently less severe than Mesarovic and Pestel fear, economic growth possiblities are in fact more limited.

Unlike the other Club of Rome projects considered so far, the RIO study does not employ a computer model, but goes well beyond their previous analysis of economic, technological and institutional factors. Tinbergen argues that, although in the post-war period political realities have changed, these have not been reflected sufficiently in international institutions. An equitable order entails changes in the distribution of power (p. 105). Like Dumont, the Bariloche team and Galtung he argues that dependency relationships of poor countries must be reduced through "new-style self-reliant development"—they should exercise full sovereignty over the exploitation of their own resources and play a larger part in their processing (p. 179).

The industrial countries are vulnerable to the collective pressures of the poor, whose greatest power is in their solidarity (p. 37). There should be greater collective bargaining through the United Nations, more resource cartels and more trade between the Third World countries themselves (p. 180). But, by the same token, the "humble wheatsheaf" could be destined to become a powerful weapon of economic warfare against the Third World countries (p. 31) unless they achieve greater self-sufficiency in basic foods (p. 179).

In Tinbergen's view, both industrial and poor countries must develop the industries in which they have a comparative advantage, and not attempt to protect inefficient industries (p. 112). On this point his argument bears similarities to the Japanese Club of Rome study on the international division of labour. The greatest disparity between industrial and poor countries is in the field of scientific research and development. Because multinational firms excel in both technological and marketing knowledge, a major problem is to reconcile the interests of "transnationals" in security of investment with the independence and development objectives of developing countries (p. 40). As matters stand, international firms tend to accentuate rather than reduce income inequalities in poor societies (p. 4). Tinbergen hints at the threat posed by the "sky-rocketing" expenditure on armaments (p. 76) which employs, he says, almost half the world's scientific and technological manpower. The problem is not simply to shift from a war to peace economy, "but from a war to a peace mentality" (p. 26).

SOVIET VIEWS OF GROWTH

Soviet futures literature is often highly critical of Western "bourgeois futurology." Marxist writers are especially cynical about Kahn's efforts, but neo-Malthusian writers are similarly denounced.

Most Soviet futures literature spells out in considerable detail the Marxist theory that forms the basic framework for thinking about the development of society. Western futures literature, in contrast, usually leaves the underlying theory implicit or, as in the case of Kahn and Wiener, constructs a theoretical position based on long-standing "multifold trends." However, like Kahn, the society of the future envisaged by the Soviet authors is claimed to be non-utopian—it is the result of a "natural-historical" transition from capitalism.

It is evident that the Eastern European debate about the future responds to the debate in the West—about environmental issues for example—although it is less clear where the various nuances within the Soviet debate arise. According to Modrzhinskaya (1973) the catastrophes viewed by neo-Malthusian authors are seen merely as the material manifestations of a basic, essentially political problem: the whole course of social development shows us that imperialism alone is guilty of the fact that the mass of the population in the Asian, African and Latin American countries is forced to live in poverty. The downfall of the capitalist system is needed; notions of post-industrial social improvement are mere reformism: "the future under capitalism can only be gloomy." Thus, Modrzhinskaya quotes Lenin in advocating whole-hearted "development of the revolutionary movement . . . in every country without exception" (p. 346). However, there may be some catastrophes and setbacks as intimated through another quotation from Lenin: "It is undialectical, unscientific and theoretically wrong to regard the course of world history as smooth and always in a forward direction, without occasional gigantic leaps back" (p. 260). But these are essentially only incidents on the road to socialism.

In the main, Soviet forecasters do not make detailed global forecasts of the kind described here for other authors. Like Kahn and Wiener, Modrzhinskaya sees the main line of progress as economic growth. Citing Lenin, she states "Marxists regard the development of productive forces as the main and supreme criterion of progress" (p. 257).

Although Modrzhinskaya's estimates of *current* known reserves of raw materials and energy are very similar to those used by the Meadows' team and other Malthusians, her faith in mankind's ingenuity to extend these resources is far greater: "Over the last twenty to thirty years the pace of scientific and technological development has acquired quite exceptional hitherto unprecedented proportions, and it is difficult to imagine with what tremendous speed man's prospects for mastering the forces of nature will develop in the future" (p. 336).

Modrzhinskaya has total confidence in the scientific and technological revolution: "Soviet scientists . . . categorically reject all theories of future energy shortage and raw materials shortage" (p. 315). The basis for the long-term energy forecast is the exploitation of nuclear technologies: "simple calculations show that there is enough deuterium as a fuel on earth to last for hundreds of millions of years." With limitless energy come limitless resources: "All in all, the earth's crust for 16 kilometres below the surface contains trillions (10^{17-18}) of tons of different metals. This makes it difficult even to envisage a level of production at which mankind would begin to experience a shortage of metals" (p. 317). In agricultural production man will be equally successful, eventually "turning the deserts into flowering orchards" (p. 332). Modrzhinskaya argues that scientists now recognise the dangers posed by environmental factors, and sets out future tasks ranging from the transformation of the deserts to the damming of the Bering Strait in order to conquer the Arctic permafrost.

V. Kosolapov[5] timetables the progress of science and technology in his book *Mankind and the Year 2000* (1976). Like Modrzhinskaya he believes that technology will be "ecologised" and will, wherever possible, improve the ecological equilibrium (p. 208). There are many similarities with Kahn and Wiener in the breakthroughs he expects: by the turn of the century land transport will travel at 500 km/hour and passenger aircraft at 12-15,000 km/hour; by 2030 rail transport will be established on the moon (p. 179); construction technology will have developed from the application in 1970 of the mass-produced composite materials to the use of "biological principles in the manufacture of materials" (p. 161); nuclear, cybernetic and automated technologies will be applied in all areas of development; by the end of the twentieth century there will have been a tenfold increase in the level of scientific research. Economically viable weather control techniques will be available for individual areas and atomic power stations will be the main suppliers of electricity (p. 210).

The lifestyles that these technological breakthroughs will provide are described by Modrzhinskaya. For the Soviet Union, she says, there will be "a considerable rise in the material and cultural standards of the whole people" (p. 352). Towns will be planned so that the "majority of inhabitants will have to walk only 100 to 150 metres (2–7 minutes) from their flat to work, school and the shops. . . ." (p. 328). In some towns, people will live in "ultra-high blocks of 200–300 storeys and higher . . . to leave more room for sun, greenery, fresh air and water." Kosolapov expands on this view of the future. Housework will be fully automated by the year 1990, and by 2005 tourist trips to the moon will be in operation (p. 211). Most industries are expected to become highly or totally automated: transport will be operated, as a rule, without direct human participation, with the help of electronic devices such as automatic pilots and autodrivers.

Despite the similarity to Kahn and Wiener in the degree of technological optimism displayed and similarities in the lifestyles described, the Soviet writers' future is more strongly normative. We are told the progress of knowledge "is creating a totally real scientific and technological basis for producing any degree of prosperity for *all* people in the world." A major "prospective achievement of a socialist world order" would be "truly human, highly moral relations between peoples and nations, total abolition of all forms and traces of social oppression and social inequality." But Modrzhinskaya argues, "it is impossible to switch distribution according to needs if there is no full abundance" (p. 358).

Thus, in Eastern European authors' views, changes in technology would bring about social reforms. As a Rumanian forecaster, Manescu, explains: "the gap between high and low incomes, between the earnings of the various social categories will grow smaller as a result of the process of social homogenization, of training and qualification, of gradual disappearance of the essential differences between physical and intellectual work" (Nicolescu, 1974, p. 28).

Ultimately, the aim of the society would be a transformation into a "creative collective engaged predominantly in mental work" (Kosolapov, 1976, p. 211). Here, again, there is a difference in emphasis between the futures posed by Kahn and those of Soviet authors. In Kahn's world, "intellectuals" may achieve little satisfaction; in Kosalapov's world, cultural life is centred on educational activities and scientific achievements of all kinds. By 1983 advanced countries will spend up to 8–10 per cent of income on education; by 2020 this figure would rise to 10–13 per cent. In this respect, the future presented by the Soviet authors resembles Bell's (1974) post-industrial society more than the populist version put forward by Kahn and Wiener.

Similarly, Kosolapov claims that by the year 2000 international agreements would "guarantee a stable living standard for everyone on the basis of the advance in the level of production" (p. 211). Progress will be limited not by scientific and technological possibilities, nor by labour and financial resources, but by the social structure, in particular the contradictions of the capitalist system, the danger of wars and colonialism. Indeed, most of the Third World countries given by Kahn as examples of "successful" development would be counted by Modrzhinskaya as "colonies" still dominated by the capitalist world.

Although all Eastern European forecasters take a Marxist perspective as the basis for their forecasting activities, there are differences in emphasis. Kosolapov appears to take a less conflict-ridden view of the future of international relations, although still arguing for the transformation of capitalist societies and the disappearance of colonialist and racialist regimes. In his view the next decades will be marked by a continued détente in international relations. Global measures will be implemented first to limit the arms race and then to reduce armaments. The production of nuclear weapons will be discontinued. Of the saving in military spending, "a considerable part" will be channelled in aid to Third World countries (p. 208). By the year 2000 "national economies will become integral parts of a world-wide system of economic relations." It must be assumed that Kosolapov means that trade will be fully internationalised—"finally the future society will develop into a global association of people engaged in creative labour" (p. 209).

THE FULL CIRCLE

This review began with a summary of Kahn and Wiener's book *The Year 2000* (1967). Much of the influential futures literature that has emerged in the intervening decade has been very critical of Kahn's approach as overcomplacent in terms of both overall possibilities for growth and its distribution. Kahn has responded to the neo-Malthusians in a highly critical manner. Like other authors, however, over the years he has modified his position.

His latest book, *The Next 200 Years* (1976), written with Brown and Martel, is presented so as to counteract the pessimism of the neo-Malthusians. Disasters, they say, are not impossible but "any limits to growth are more likely to arise from psychological, cultural or social limits to demand, or from incompetency, bad luck and/or monopolistic practices interfering with supply rather than from fundamental physical limits on available resources" (p. 181). Further, far from being despondent about the situation of the poor nations, Kahn and his colleagues assert: "Prospects are good and getting better for the coping nations, . . . [some] developing countries . . . will help drive the world's economic growth in the twenty first century. For the non-coping nations the immediate prospects are not good, but our projection is that over the long-term they will gradually join the ranks of the coping nations" (p. 213). Indeed, they argue, "without growth the disparities among nations so regretted today would probably never be overcome" (p. 9).

The basic "theory" underlying the predictions of *The Year 2000* was that of continuity of the "long-term multifold trend" and exponential extrapolation (to 2020) of economic and demographic trends. In *The Next 200 Years* the idea of the multifold trend is retained, at least to explain cultural and political tendencies in the world at large (p. 180). For economic and demographic trends the theory is modified more dramatically: "The basic assumption underlying our 400 year earth-centered scenario is that the rates of world population and economic growth are now close to their historic highs and will soon begin to slow until finally, roughly 100–200 years from now, they will level off in a more or less natural and comfortable way" (p. 26). "In much the same way that the agricultural revolution spread round the world, the Industrial Revolution has been spreading and causing a permanent change in the quality of human life. However, instead of lasting 10,000 years, this second diffusion process is likely to be largely completed within a total span of about 400 years or roughly by the late twenty second century" (p. 20). The slowing of growth rates will already be apparent by the year 2000: "Barring extreme mismanagement or bad luck, the period 1976–1985 should be characterised by the highest average rate of world economic growth in history, perhaps 6%, although by 1985 or soon thereafter the slowdown of the upper half of the distorted S-shaped curve should begin to be felt" (p. 188). Kahn and his colleagues are at pains to stress therefore that "a reduced level of *demand* rather than inadequate supply will drive the transition" (p. 50).

In *The Next 200 Years* the authors are far more thorough in their analysis of natural resources and technological possibilities (p. 85). *The Year 2000* led to Dumont's (almost correct) rebuke that he could find only one mention of agriculture in the whole volume.[6] In *The Next 200 Years* the authors attempt to demonstrate in some detail that there is not *one*, but several plausible technological routes that would satisfy expected demand for food, raw materials and energy whilst preserving a satisfactory environment.

Despite the long-term tendency for demand to decline at the higher levels of income, the authors observe that for a long time to come poverty will remain. The "relatively successful portion (about half) of the Third World should attain about $2000 per head by the year 2000 and a still desperately poor group, mostly concentrated in the Indian sub-continent but including limited parts of Latin America and Africa . . . could (with reasonable policies) average about $200 per head by the year 2000" (p. 195). "In particular we believe that large income gaps between nations could persist for centuries, even though there will be some tendency to narrow" (p. 208).

The very existence of this gap offers the greatest hope to developing nations. "The task ahead for America and for the developed world is to help raise the capacity of these [developing] nations' institutions to exploit the gaps whose very existence can accelerate their growth" (p. 214).

The authors see the United States as responsible for world economic growth, and are not enthusiastic about the activities of zero growth advocates. In complete contrast to the exhortations of Dumont, Heilbroner and especially the Ehrlichs, they say Americans have a duty to be rich. The diffusion of growth is seen by the authors of *The Next 200 Years* as a "more or less natural and comfortable process" but nevertheless they say "there are lots of wiggles and reversals in the basic trends" (p. 185). Quoting Kuznets, the authors point out that "Difficulties and the problems lie in the limited capacity of the institutions of the underdeveloped countries—political, legal, cultural and economic—to channel activity so as to exploit the advantage of economic backwardness" (p. 214).

Before the end of the century they expect to see internationally "the end of the post–World War II system politically, economically and financially" (p. 189), leading to a "unified but multipolar, partially competitive, mostly global and technological economy" (p. 191). This will exhibit "Increasing worldwide unity in technology, private industry, commercial and financial institutions, but relatively little unity in international legal and political institutions" (p. 192). "Despite much hostility, [there will be] a continuing, even growing, importance of multinational corporations as innovators and diffusers of economic activity and as engines of rapid growth" (p. 191).

The growth centres will be the United States and Japan especially, but a new developed bloc comprising mainly the Comecon, O.E.C.D. and Persian Gulf nations will emerge (p. 194). The threat of war and direct military intervention seems to be somewhat reduced as compared with Kahn's previous work. "In comparison with any earlier period the developing nations are relatively safe from military threats by the developed world" (p. 46). Nevertheless, the authors say, "a war involving the widespread use of nuclear weapons . . . as we contemplate the tasks ahead, . . . is probably the 'single biggest danger'" (p. 219).

Their detailed recommendations, they say, "run counter to the major conclusions of the Club of Rome's second report [Mesarovic and Pestel, 1974a] which emphasises the importance of global interdependence and stresses the necessity of solving problems in a 'global context' by 'global concerted action.' We believe that this goes in exactly the wrong direction, and that the organic interdependence it suggests would ensure that a dislocation anywhere would be a dislocation everywhere. We prefer redundancy, flexibility and a degree of 'disconnectedness.' If India, for example, goes under we want to be able to save her, not go down with her" (p. 216).

CONCLUSIONS

Thus, the future debate has become vast in scope. It has also become confused in nature. Different authors use the same words to express different ideas, often adapting their language to the jargon of the day: expressions such as "radical institutional and social change," "appropriate technology," "self-reliance," or "the new international economic order" each encompass a wide range of meanings, depending on who uses them.

To some extent this is inevitable, given the complexity of the problems and the diverse national and disciplinary origins of the participants in the debate. The Bariloche group explicitly take up a stance favourable to the Third World in general, and to Latin America in particular. The report of the Japanese Club of Rome reflects a strong national interest when, for example, it criticises the doctrine of self-sufficiency, or "American and Australian Monroeism" (Kaya and Suzuki, 1974, p. 386). Throughout the debate Kahn champions the U.S.A. and Modrzhinskaya the U.S.S.R.

Some futures writers have strong commitments to particular disciplines and methods. Ecology has had such a strong influence on neo-Malthusian writers that it has been described as the new "dismal science." At the same time, advocacy of systems-analytic methods has on occasions been as evangelical as the policies prescribed. It can be argued that Forrester used the spectacular and controversial results of *World Dynamics* to highlight his own simulation technique, as he did in his earlier *Urban Dynamics* (1969). Forrester, Mesarovic and Pestel and, less forcefully, Leontief, all recommend their own preferred method whilst pointing to the unsatisfactory features of others. Each, in effect, argues that the world is "extraordinarily complex," that its main tendencies are beyond the comprehension of the unaided human mind. Only a holistic (i.e., integrated) analysis is adequate, and this requires systems models. Meadows links holism to Eastern philosophy and the ecological unity of humanity and nature. High technology methods of analysis are thereby justified on the basis of notions of natural harmony and simplicity.

The inadequacy of empirical data increases the possibilities for arriving at different assertions about trends in one and the same phenomenon. Even where data exist, futures writers have often been very cavalier about empirical evidence.

But whatever the differences, limitations or imperfections in their work, all the futures writers of the past ten years share common concerns very similar to those of the classical economists of the late eighteenth and first half of the nineteenth century. Adam Smith, Thomas Malthus, David Ricardo, John Stuart Mill and Karl Marx each had his personal foibles, and they differed amongst themselves on many fundamental issues. Yet they were all concerned with long-term trends in a modernising and industrialising society; with the possibilities of, and constraints on, economic growth offered by natural resources, investment, population and technical change; with the effects of economic growth on income distribution, patterns of living and the quality of life; and with debate about the appropriate objectives, policies, institutions and structures of power for the changing society.

Like the classical economists, today's futurologists all calculate that world economic growth and population growth must or will eventually stop. But they differ enormously about when and at what level this will or should happen. They also differ about the desirable and feasible distribution of the world's future wealth and about the institutions, political systems and styles of life in a better future world. These differences are fundamental to the debate and their origins can be traced back to differences of opinion in three problem areas: resources and technical change; the desirable political objectives and norms for society; and the economic, social and political processes whereby society evolves and changes.

NOTES

I am indebted to Jay Gershuny and Ian Miles for help with this chapter.

1. The contrast with the population debate of the 1930s is interesting (see Pohlman, 1973). Spengler has in fact been active in the debate about population since the early 1930s when he was concerned with under-population in industrial nations rather than over-population in the developing nations. In *The Birth Rate—Potential Dynamite* (1932) Spengler observes that "Among the white peoples living in countries where industrialisation has made its greatest advances . . . at present not enough children are being born to replace the existing population. Only in the agricultural white nations, among the Asiatic peoples and in Egypt do we find a high birth rate and a steady increase in the population. . . . Will the birth rate continue to decline? Will the swarming peoples of Latin America, Africa and the Orient crush the low-birth rate nations?" To combat this decline Spengler argued, "let the state offer to pay to couples whatever wage is necessary to induce these couples to undertake the work of producing, rearing and educating the desired number of children."

2. The version of "The Human Prospect" cited here appeared originally in the *New York Review of Books* (Jan. 1974). It was later published with some modification as a book. "Growth and Survival" originally appeared in *Foreign Affairs* (1972) as a review of *The Limits to Growth*. Heilbroner's conclusions about an end to growth in the industrialised world are a far cry from his writings of the early 1960s. In *The Making of Economic Society* (1962) he considers that there is "every reason to believe that the present trend of technological advance will be maintained. . . . By 1980 or by the year 2000—a work week of 30 hours or even 20 hours is by no means unimaginable" (p. 234).

3. The most easily accessible English translation available is in the journal *Technological Forecasting and Social Change*, Vol. 6, Nos. 3 and 4, 1974.

4. Our commentary is based on a draft.

5. The work of this author appears to be based on the preliminary findings of the long-range development plan covering the period 1976—1990 set up in 1972 by the Central Committee of the CPSU and the USSR Council of Ministers (p. 44).

6. Kahn and Wiener remark in *The Year 2000* that they have "left out such important things as food, agriculture, new non-nuclear power sources, new methods of transportation, new materials and so on" (p. 116).

REFERENCES

In this selection, page references refer to the first named book for each author.

E. Arab-Ogly, *In the Forecaster's Maze*. Moscow: Progress Publishers (1975).
D. Bell, *The Coming of Post Industrial Society*. London: Heinemann (1974).
C. Clark, *Starvation or Plenty?* London: Secker and Warburg (1970).
A. C. Clarke, *Profiles of the Future*. London: Pan (1964).
R. Codoni, *The International Division of Labour in View of the Second Development Decade*. Zurich: Center for Economic Research, Swiss Federal Institute of Technology (1974) (Research monographs new series Vol. 10).
R. Dumont, *Utopia or Else. . . .* London: Deutsch (1974).
A. and P. R. Ehrlich, *Population, Resources, Environment—Issues in Human Ecology*. San Francisco: Freeman (1970).
P. R. Ehrlich and R. Harriman, *How to be a Survivor*. London: Pan/Ballantine (1971).

P. R. Ehrlich, *The Population Bomb*. London: Pan (1971).

J. W. Forrester, *Urban Dynamics*. Cambridge, Mass.: M.I.T. (1969).

J. W. Forrester, *World Dynamics*. Cambridge, Mass.: Wright-Allen (1971).

J. W. Forrester, "Population vs. Standard of Living—The Trade Off that Nations Must Decide," *Futurist* Vol. X, No. 5, October 1976.

R. Buckminster Fuller, *Utopia or Oblivion: The Prospect for Humanity*. Harmondsworth, Penguin Books (1972).

J. Galtung, *Self-Reliance: Concepts, Theory and Rationale*. Oslo: University of Oslo (1977), Paper No. 35.

R. Gillette, "The Limits to Growth: Hard Sell for a Computer View of Doomsday," *Science*, Washington, D.C. (March 1972) p. 1088.

R. L. Heilbroner, "Growth and Survival," *Foreign Affairs*, New York (1972) p. 139.

R. L. Heilbroner, *An Inquiry into the Human Prospect*. New York Review of Books (24 January 1974) p. 21, and New York: Norton (1974).

R. L. Heilbroner, *Business Civilisation in Decline*. London: Boyars (1976).

A. Herrera et al., *Catastrophe or New Society?* Ottawa. I.D.R.C. (1976).

H. Kahn, *On Thermonuclear War*. Princeton: Princeton University Press (1960).

H. Kahn and A. J. Wiener, *The Year 2000*. London: Macmillan (1967).

H. Kahn, W. Brown, and L. Martel, *The Next 200 Years*. New York: Morrow (1976).

Y. Kaya and Y. Suzuki, "Global Constraints and a New Vision for Development," *Technological Forecasting and Social Change* (1974) Vol. 6, Nos. 3 and 4, p. 277 and p. 371.

Y. Kaya et al. *On the Future Japan and the World—A Model Approach*. Tokyo: Japan Techno-Economics Society (1973).

A. King, "The Club of Rome Today," *Simulation in the Service of Society*. August 1974.

V. Kosolapov, *Mankind and the Year 2000*. Moscow: Progress Publishers (1976).

W. Leontief et al. *The Future of the World Economy*, Preliminary Report. New York: United Nations (1976).

D. Meadows et al., *The Limits to Growth*. New York: Universe Books (1972), and London: Pan Books (1974).

M. Mesarovic and E. Pestel, *Mankind at the Turning Point*. New York: Dutton/Readers Digest Press (1974a).

Y. Modrzhinskaya and C. Stephanyan, *The Future of Society*. Moscow: Progress Publishers (1973).

E. Rothschild, "How Doomed Are We?" *New York Review of Books* (26 June 1975) p. 31.

E. F. Schumacher, *Small is Beautiful—A Study of Economics as if People Mattered*. London: Blond and Briggs (1973).

E. F. Schumacher, "Economics Should Begin with People not Goods," *Futurist*, Washington, D.C. (December 1974) p. 274.

J. Spengler, *Population Change, Modernisation and Welfare*. Englewood Cliffs, N.J.: Prentice Hall (1974).

J. Tinbergen, *Reshaping the International Order—A Report to the Club of Rome*. New York: Dutton (1976).

35
WHAT NEW SYSTEM OF WORLD ORDER?

Richard Falk

The world-order consensus fashionable among world leaders presupposes the persistence and adequacy of the state system. Constructive efforts at world-order reform will, in this gradualist view, be directed towards making the state system operate in a more moderate fashion rather than in transforming it into something quite different. Moderation is associated with clamping down on conflict among principal states, making their relations less likely to degenerate into periods of crisis and confrontation as well as outbreaks of war. To assure moderation it is desirable to evolve a framework for communication and cooperation, an atmosphere in which the existence and legitimacy of rivals is confirmed, and an international mood conducive to the compromise of disputes and rivalries. The Nixon-Kissinger efforts to bring "a generation of peace" are premised on establishing an international framework in which these forms of moderation could flourish. The attainment of moderation in the world-order system would clearly be desirable provided that it does not prevent attempts to overcome more fundamental frailties and inadequacies.

There is nothing objectionable in seeking to avoid destructive forms of great-power rivalry. However, there are serious inadequacies associated with regarding moderation of statecraft as a world-order solution rather than a stopgap. First of all, moderation of conflictual behavior tends to produce toleration of poverty, repression, and environmental decay as well as acquiescence in extreme forms of inequality. Second, the ethics of moderation are extensions of statist logic under altered international circumstances where a more direct protection of world-community interests is necessary; as such, laissez-faire patterns of behavior and maximization of state power and wealth continue to flourish. Third, moderate views of world order, by their stress on the sufficiency of traditional great-power diplomacy, tend to diminish, if not altogether displace, visions of planetary unity derived from the Apollo mission, of human solidarity derived from the prophets of world culture, or of ecological and nuclear vulnerability on a global scale associated with interdependence and the absence of a central guidance mechanism.

The human species may be better prepared for transition to a new system of

From Saul Mendlovitz, ed., *On the Creation of a Just World Order*. Reprinted by permission of the Free Press, a Division of Macmillan Publishing Co., Inc.

world order than is generally evident, especially to those accustomed to thinking about change in the short time horizons of power wielders. Teilhard de
Chardin and Sri Aurobindo, among others, have discerned a shift in human
sentiment toward solidarity and altruism, and we believe that this shift is one
significant feature of our generally bleak modern situation. Just as the collapse
of colonialism was comprehensible only after it happened, so might the collapse
or displacement of the state system become visible only when we get a chance
to look backward. The call for a world order more responsive to bioethical requirements—species survival, including habitability of the planet—represents a
new impulse in human history, itself a hopeful sign.

We believe it necessary to delimit the contours of a relevant utopia before
urging any specific lines of action in the present situation. Our preferred system
of world order therefore precedes *in analysis* our conception of transition, even
though the transition process is earlier *in time*. It is like deciding where one
wants to go before selecting the route or mode of conveyance; it is not only a
question of choosing effective means to reach preferred ends. There may be
other motivations as well. We may need to reach our destination by a certain
time, or we may have only limited money at our disposal, or we may have a
phobia about heights or tunnels, or we may be willing to take longer or pay
more if the route is scenic or the mode private and comfortable. Means and
ends are not neatly separable in world-order thinking or action, despite the importance of concentrating both on a model of an alternative system and on
transition tactics and strategies.

In world-order speculation we also, as a traveller with a tight schedule and a
fixed budget and some keen curiosities, have constraints and biases that condition our approach. To orient the approach, we enumerate those biases that
seem relevant:

- We should like to bring the new system into being by the year 2000 or
  shortly thereafter.
- We should like to reach our destination without relying on violence or
  intimidation.
- We should like to make the shifts in organization and priorities result
  from preference rather than necessity.

On a more concrete level such a world-order budget places a premium on
limiting expectations. We cannot hope to achieve all our goals by the year
2000, assuming survival without catastrophe until then, even if developments
are very favorable. We might however reach a world-order destination that
overcomes the worst features of the present situation and initiates a process of
change that builds momentum in the direction of further positive
developments.

The first leg of the journey is long and difficult, beset with dangers, uncertainties, and adversaries; the odds of getting through do not seem high. World-
order expectations involve a comprehensive response to rising danger and
deepening decay in the present context. Our concerns can be enumerated:

- The planet is too crowded and is getting more so.
- The war system is too destructive, risky, and costly and is getting more so.
- An increasingly large number of people live at or below the level of subsistence.
- Pressure on the basic ecosystem of the planet is serious and growing, as is the more tangible pollution of air, water, and land.
- Governing groups in many societies are repressing their own people in an intolerable manner.
- Human and material resources of the planet are wasted and depleted in a shortsighted way, and at increasing rates.
- Technologies are not adequately managed to assure planetary and human benefit.

On the basis of these concerns we seek by the end of the century a world system that:

- achieves and moves beyond the norm of zero population growth;
- moves toward dismantling the war system, including putting into effect a plan for drastic disarmament;
- moves toward a world economic system in which each individual is assured the right to the minimum requirements of body, mind, and spirit and in which food, clothing, housing, education, health, and work are regarded as collective as well as personal responsibilities;
- moves toward an integrated and coherent system of dynamic equilibrium so far as human impacts on the biosphere are concerned;
- achieves and moves beyond a minimum bioethical code based on human survival, planetary habitability, and species diversity;
- moves toward a conservation policy that is sensitive to the life chances of future human generations and protective of natural wonders and species diversity;
- achieves an effective system of global oversight on the side-effects of technological innovation.

Although these objectives are extremely ambitious, they are mainly designed to plug leaks and improve man's prospects of survival. These reforms are designed to overcome the worst features and tendencies of the present world system and stabilize the results without discouraging further world-order reform. We expect the shape of the relevant utopia for the first generation of reformers of the twenty-first century, assuming prior realization of WOMP goals, will involve liberating people from various sorts of bondage—work, mores, anxieties—so that more and more of them can participate more fully in a life of dignity, joy, and creativity that mobilizes the full energies of self-development. Putting this sense of potentiality differently, we believe that on the average human beings are now able to make use of 5 percent or so of their potential for development and that our preferred world-order system might reasonably expect to raise the average to 20 percent or so, but the challenge and opportunity will remain immense after our initial program of world order reform has been completed. In this first phase, WOMP/USA is seeking to deal only with the establishment of *minimum preconditions* for tolerable human existence, free from high risks of catastrophe and misery.

Our focus is on the *organizational framework* of collective human existence. We believe it will be necessary to modify the present structure of world order, but that it will be possible only after a considerable effort of persuasion, planning, and mobilization in the principal parts of the planet. One ingredient of this effort involves the design of the sort of organizational framework that will realize our minimum goals and support the continuing pursuit of the objectives of personal development.

To economize on space and focus response we shall rely on some visual representations of design structures for new world-order systems. The rationale of our preferred system will become clearer in the exposition of the transition strategy in the next section [of the original source book], but at least its principal properties may be indicated at this point in the discussion.

We begin with several general considerations:

- First, conventional world-order thinking has tended to proceed on the basis of a stark alternative between virtual anarchy and virtual world government. We seek to explore the *numerous* intermediate world-order *options*, as well as the many variants of world government and anarchy.
- Second, our design of a system is put forward as a tentative sketch that will be frequently revised as the world-order building process unfolds. It is therefore misleading and trivial to make highly detailed institutional proposals, which would exhibit *the fallacy of premature specification.*
- Third, our design of a preferred world system is not confined to *external linkages* of principal actors but also encompasses the *internal linkages* of national governments to substructures and to the population as a whole, thereby reflecting the hypothesis that a progrssive world order is not reconcilable with regressive systems of domestic order, at least in principal societies.
- Fourth, our design is intended to convey a sense of *organizational pattern* rather than embody *precise measurements* of relative actor roles and capability.
- Fifth, preferred organizational solutions will involve simultaneous dialectical movements towards *centralization* and *decentralization* of authority within and among states.

We shall now consider these types of systems: the existing system; a five-power world; a regional system; a transnational functional system; a world-government system; a world-empire system; and a WOMP/USA central guidance system.

Our purpose is to depict the principal alternative futures of the world-order system. This presentation emphasizes the form and distribution of capability and authority among principal bureaucratic actors. The description of various status patterns for actors in different systems is as yet a primitive mapping technique, involving highly selective and imprecise features of the overall context. Nevertheless, we believe that such visual displays of power/authority patterns encourage thinking about a range of constructive world-order alternatives. First of all, comparative features are stressed. Second, the variability of any type of world-order solution—the array of world structural arrangements—is easily grasped. Third, more sophisticated mapping can gradually provide visual analogues to configurative analysis of the political setting.

1. *The Existing System.* Figure 1 displays the basic interplay of actors in the existing international system. The predominance of state actors is readily apparent, as is the emergent role of regional and universal functional actors. Such actors would not have been represented at all on a comparable display of actors in 1900, when colonial clusters would have been prominent. Only the rather insignificant Portuguese colonial cluster remains at present, although a fuller display that attempted to depict hegemonic relations or spheres of influence might suggest a new series of neocolonial clusters of significance. Also omitted in Figure 1 are alliance clusters, which have considerable importance in creating patterns of cooperative behavior in the war/peace area as well as in establishing alignment and interaction patterns embracing the whole spectrum of transnational relations.

Nevertheless, the statist character of this system is apparent, as are the hegemonic and condominium potentialities arising from the inequality of state actors and the predominance of the two superpowers; this predominance is especially apparent in relation to military affairs. Figure 1 makes no effort to consider variations in internal political arrangements as a factor in the capacity of state actors to realize WOMP values.

Figure 2 represents a crude attempt to take account of the internal political arrangements of state actors in the present system of world order. The smaller the diameter of the internal black circle the more directly the prevailing governing perspective is regarded as committed to the promotion of WOMP values, and vice versa. The size of the inner black circle expresses the degree of militarization (size of military budget, military budget as proportion of national budget and of GNP), the extent of social privation (proportion of population at subsistence level or below, provision of basic life necessities), the extent of political privation (number of political prisoners, protection of civil liberties, existence of an active opposition movement), and the extent of ecological privation (extent of pollution, responsiveness to ecological consequences of policy).

Our contention is that the values around which existing governmental centers of power and authority are organized directly correlate with their capacity and willingness to participate in a peaceful transition to a more beneficial arrangement of world-order values. Simplistic views as to the responsiveness of national actors to WOMP values are bound to be misleading. We recognize that a given government might have a good record on social welfare and a poor one on political liberty or peacemindedness. We also recognize that a domestic disposition toward or away from WOMP values does not *necessarily*

$S_{1(1970's)}$

Figure 2. Existing world order system: internal dimensions.

correlate with attitudes towards the direction and preferred character of world-order reform, but we believe the following propositions are generally accurate: that the value priorities of domestic governments are relevant to prospects for world-order change and that there is a tendency for attitudes toward world-order reform to reflect domestic value priorities. Thus Figure 2 augments Figure 1 by contending not only that states dominate the existing world-order system but that their distinctive influence significantly reflects their domestic orientation towards the four WOMP values.

2. *The Five-Power Variant of the Existing World Order System.* Figure 3 represents an effort to display the Nixon-Kissinger (-Brezhnev?) world-order design based on the contained or moderated competition of five principal actors (the U.S.A., the U.S.S.R., China, Japan, and Western Europe). This model of world order is premised on maximizing certain oligopolistic tendencies

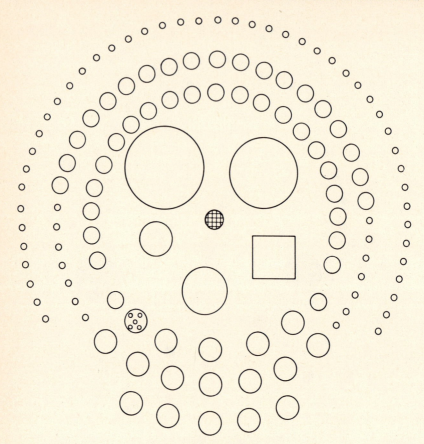

Figure 3. Nixon-Kissinger design.

in the existing system. It attempts to diminish the destructive risks of rivalry, to adapt to an emergent condition of multipolarity in economic and security affairs, and to simplify the procedures for mainstream cooperation in a world of increasing complexity and interdependence.

The five-power variant of the existing system is basically an intergovernmental managerial notion without contemplated normative reforms. The main world-order objectives are to eliminate destructive forms of political and military rivalry by encouraging moderate relations among existing centers of power and wealth. Ideological differences are respected and minimized; a condition of efficient global management is ideological tolerance. Supranationalism is diminished in status and role beneath even current levels, although particular functional tasks may be assigned to specialized institutions under the effective control of principal government actors.

The agenda of world-order issues does not accord priority to values of social welfare or political dignity. A five-power scheme is fully compatible with toleration of high levels of poverty and repression within the system as a whole. Even violence outside the framework of great-power relations is acceptable, and no major emphasis is placed on peacekeeping or nonproliferation of weapons. Environmental quality is a fit object of inter-actor cooperation, but again it is presumed to be manageable if dealt with by cooperative undertakings of the dominant international actors.

The five-power design is in significant respects an improvement on the cold-war years, provided it does not encourage an era of complacency and does not itself degenerate into a two-power condominium arrangement. SALT and the Brezhnev-Nixon Declaration of Principles design also fail to affirm ideals of human solidarity or to seek ways of overcoming the immense inequities and miseries endured at present by such a high proportion of the human race. This five-power conception also tends to underestimate the ecological constraints and risks arising from continuing patterns of uncurtailed economic growth in a decentralized world system. Finally, principal actors excluded from significant management of world-order concerns, such as India, Brazil, Nigeria, and Indonesia, may be led to organize rival groupings. A concert of principal actors that denies participation to many other important actors in the global arena is likely to provoke reactions of bitterness and opposition.

3. *Regionalist Modification of the Existing World Order System.* There are definite potentialities—functional and political—for developing stronger regional actors, both as an offset to the degree of fragmentation associated with the state system and as a protection against the sort of homogenizing centralization associated with a direct move toward world government. The progress of regionalist approaches in Western Europe is irreversible in many respects and provides an example to the rest of the world of the possibility of reconciling national autonomy with rather advanced forms of regional integration with respect to economic and security sectors. In Latin America, Eastern Europe, the Middle East, and Africa it is possible to envision considerable regionalization or subregionalization of national activity over the next three decades. There are major obstacles in each region to embarking on a regional or subregional course, but there are also major incentives relating to efficiency and bargaining leverage vis-à-vis other major actors.

The basic appeal of regionalism over the short run is that it appears to safeguard two principal goals of the foreign policy of weaker and poorer countries: first, it improves the capabilities for national development by taking better advantage of the international division of labor arising from varying national capabilities; second, it gives poorer and weaker governments a better chance to defend themselves against interventionary pressures mounted from outside the region and provides an increased prospect of access to and participation in various world decisional contexts such as world monetary policy, ocean resources, and skyjacking regulation.

As such, regionalism has considerable appeal as a world order halfway house. It seems more feasible in the near term as a step beyond state sovereignty that can be used to dilute nationalist sentiments during a period when global

$S_{2(Reg.)}$

Figure 4. Regional actor system.

loyalties need to grow stronger. Also such regional tendencies could overcome some inequalities of the existing system without requiring the principal state actors to alter their formal role in any way.

Figure 4 illustrates a regional plan for world order. This plan is one of many variations on the fundamental notion that regional actors could become very important centers of decision and control by the end of the century. The basic assumption of this model is that functional, global, and large state actors are all diminished in their respective roles during the period of regional build-up. The emergent system depicted in Figure 4 might evolve into a Nixon-Kissinger concert of principal actors (see Figure 3), but with regional actors playing a much more significant role.

Further, the structural visions of world-order reforms developed by WOMP/USA are expressive of normative priorities arising from the affirmation of four world-order values. Thus we would associate the outcomes of transition depicted in Figure 4 as a consequence of the impact of WOMP values. As will become clear when we discuss the transition process, changes in prevailing patterns of political consciousness are preconditions for structural modifications.

As a matter of emphasis we believe the world-order reforms implicit in Figure 4 are neither plausible nor responsive enough to the agenda of challenges to warrant primary emphasis at this time. From a problem-solving, value-realizing perspective the regional growth model is far more attractive than the Nixon-Kissinger five-power model, although its attainability is more dubious. Regionalist developments to date, most ambitiously exhibited in EEC, constitute a mixture of world-order reform and a tactical statist program to achieve national priorities in competition with the two superstates. There is no prospect that regionalist movements, even if much more successful than now seems possible, could provide the kind of central guidance mechanisms needed to administer the resource base of the world, to cope with the intricacies of economic and technological interdependence, or to give a sense of direction to the emergent world culture. Regionalist solutions also overlook decentralizing and transnationalizing tendencies that may become as important for solving problems and realizing values as centralizing tendencies.

In sum, the regional alternative has an important place in thinking about reform of the present world-order system, but it does not seem to offer the most promising solution to present problems.

4. Transnational Corporate Modifications of the Existing World-Order System. Figures 5 and 6 suggest the potential significance of multinational corporate actors as reshapers of the world system. Managers of large corporate operations increasingly portray themselves as the new globalists, ardently expressing their commitment to a world without boundaries and to a labor and consumer market of maximum scope. Whether such transnational corporate ambitions are compatible with the interests of major governmental actors remains to be seen.

In Figure 5 we envision the continuing displacement of state actors by multinational corporate actors oriented toward WOMP values of social and political responsibility. In Figure 6 we envision a somewhat comparable growth of multinational corporate power but project this growth as essentially an extension of statist logic rather than as a constructive response to it. These polar variations are presented to stimulate reflection about the uncertain impact of multinational corporate activity on the world-order system. Such simplified alternatives are in fact unlikely to develop. The picture is likely to be more mixed and far more complicated. Nevertheless, it is important at this stage of

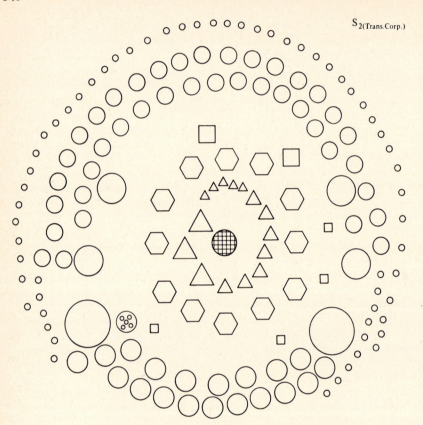

$S_{2(Trans.Corp.)}$

Figure 5. Transnational corporate system.

primitive mapping to take account of multinational corporations as actors in the world-order system and to explore their positive and negative relations with the specific program for world-order reform endorsed by WOMP.

Establishment of large production plants by Pepsi-Cola and Fiat in the Soviet Union is a significant indicator of the ability of multinational corporate actors to penetrate the socialist sector of the world system. No comparable penetrations have been made by international institutional actors. It may be that governmental actors, even of diverse ideology, find it easier to reconcile themselves to the *division* of functions implicit in the world-order reform patterns depicted in Figures 5 and 6 than to the *transfer* of functions implicit in Figures 4, 7, 8, 10, and 11. In this regard, the normatively positive image depicted in Figure 5 would be helped by the formation of comparable socialist economic units which establish bases of operation in leading capitalist societies. Such intermingling might lead to new social and economic orientations for corporate actors. In this regard the recent movement by shareholders to press

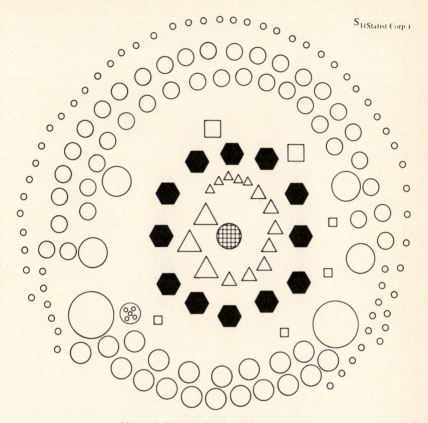

Figure 6. Transnational corporate system.

corporate management to promote social goals alongside growth and profitability goals should be of extreme interest to world-order specialists. In many institutional settings, investment codes are emerging around debates about transnational issues that bear directly on WOMP's concern with peace and justice. For example, the numerous church and university inquiries into the propriety of holding investments in firms doing business in Namibia are indicative of this new trend to bring noneconomic interests to bear in corporate settings. The controversial Polaroid experiment in South Africa represents a corporate effort to satisfy some of these normative demands and signifies the acceptance of their legitimacy. It is time that world-order analysts appreciated the extent to which the corporate arena is relevant to their concerns.

5. *Functionalist Modifications in the World-Order System.* Figure 7 portrays a world-order solution premised on the growth of global and regional functional actors, that is, intergovernmental actors like the World Health Organization or the Food and Agricultural Organization concerned with a specific subject. The

$S_{2(Funct.)}$

Figure 7. Functionalist system.

basic reform premise is that the most viable compromise between existing realities and future needs and preferences can be achieved by accenting the role of functionalism. Technical competence is concentrated in specialized actors, flexibly allocated among regional or global actors as problems, needs and opportunities for institutional development dictate. Political competence is left virtually as it is at the state level. Figure 7 is one example of a *type* of world-order solution that could be varied in proportion in many ways. This solution is attractive because it achieves a balance between the centralizing requirements of problem-solving and the decentralizing goals associated with protecting and enhancing zones of diversity and autonomy on the level of group and individual action.

Is this reconciliation plausible? Would not functional actors of such importance acquire political roles as well? Would state actors allow their roles to be eroded and bypassed? Would a functional network possess sufficient coordinating capabilities to meet the needs of the planet? If such coordinating capability existed, would the world solution then resemble a weak variant of world government (see Figure 8)?

These questions cannot be understood fully in the framework of the early 1970s. The world-order solution we project presupposes the experience of a transition process that achieves value reorientations generally supporting the

Figure 8. World government.

WOMP program of world-order reform. As we suggest in Figures 10 and 11, our own recommendation is for a compromise between the functionalist line of development (Figure 7) and the world-government line of development (Figure 8).

6. *The World Government Modification of the Existing World Order System.* Figure 8 depicts an intermediate form of world government in which there has been a substantial centralization of political power and authority combined with a drastic reduction in the status and capability of state actors. In this conception of world government, regional and global functional actors play a much more important role than they do in the existing world-order system (compare Figure 1).

A world-government solution to the challenges of world order seems to be

Figure 9. World empire.

the most logical response to the torments of war and interstate rivalry, although there are important reasons for skepticism. Further, deep-seated ethical and religious affirmations of human unity seem to support a movement toward political unification. There has been an historical tendency toward larger units in human affairs, although the cyclical build-up and collapse of empires suggests a process more complex than the steady increase in the size of units dominating the international scene. Indeed, it is plausible to interpret recent patterns of political behavior, especially the activity of numerous militant separatist movements, as leading to a period of fragmentation of existing states into units that are ethnically and psychologically more meaningful than larger ones for most of their inhabitants.

Figure 10. Preference model.

Finally, the technology of today relating to communication, transportation, and information creates the possibility (and fear) of an efficient global administrative apparatus, not necessarily one based on hierarchical concepts of organization.[1]

In the decade or so ahead it seems unlikely that any kind of world government can get started. National governments are not disposed to cede their present array of capabilities and roles to a central world actor. Change-oriented groups and individuals engaged in opposing the policies and pretensions of national bureaucracies are unlikely to be attracted in the near future to a project for a superbureaucratic arrangement for the entire planet. A governmental solution to the world-order crisis of the present period is only likely to engender meaningful levels of support in post-catastrophe contexts—after World War III or as a reaction to a fundamental ecological failure. WOMP emphasizes planned, nontraumatic transition potentialities and will not investigate seriously world-government possibilities arising from traumatic transition scenarios.

$S_{2(WOMP/USA)}$

Figure 11. Preference model: internal dimensions.

7. *World Empire or World State Modifications of the Present World-Order System.* In Figure 9 we illustrate the culmination, in organizational terms, of imperial tendencies in the existing world-order system. The present system of rival, unequal states would be supplanted by the complete triumph of a single center of state power. In contrast to the situation shown in Figure 8, concentration of power is achieved by coercion rather than contract. Such a process of transition can be envisioned only as a consequence of World War III or as a sequel to a series of successful infiltrations of principal domestic power structures by members of a global integration movement. In either instance such an imperial solution is neither likely nor desirable, nor would it be likely to persist even if established.

An imperial organization of the planet is likely to require violence and manipulation to maintain itself, and to embody great inequality between the ruling centers of decision and control and the subordinate societies. An imperial or statist solution to the world-order crisis is likely to represent from a WOMP normative outlook a worsening of the existing system. It is true that the failure of planned transition . . . to proceed at a satisfactory rate may induce desperation or catastrophe, which would make an imperial strategy more attractive and necessary. If adjustment to pressures in the existing system is delayed too long or the magnitude of the pressures is underestimated the very urgency of the situation may make it almost inevitable that central management will be "arranged" by the strongest concentration of power-wielders. It is possible to envisage a conspiracy to create a world empire constituted by the leaders of the two or three most powerful governments.

As matters now stand, however, we present Figure 9 mainly to suggest what might happen to the global system in the event that planned transition fails to proceed at sufficient speed.

8. *Preferred World Alternatives to the Existing World-Order System.* Figures 10 and 11 provide a structural image of a preferred world-order system that could be brought into being by a planned transition process sometime around the year 2000. Figure 10 emphasizes the new arrangement of power/authority relations, and Figure 11 emphasizes correlative domestic reorientations of state actors. Both sets of transformation are conditioned by the dominant influence of WOMP values. Without the dominance of this influence in domains of consciousness and aspiration, no process of planned transition could take place.

In Figure 12 we indicate the table of organization for the central guidance system that is entrusted with general functions of coordination and oversight. The specific allocation of institutional roles is discussed elsewhere, but it should be emphasized that the degree of bureaucratic complexity apparent in the diagram does not entail either a highly bureaucratized or hierarchical arrangement of functions and powers.[2] Instead, the high degree of differentiation among institutions seeks to combine considerations of efficiency arising from specialization with the diffusion of authority designed to invigorate a network of checks and balances within the central guidance framework. The institutional arrangement seeks to embody the value priorities underlying proposals for world-order reform as put forward by WOMP/USA.

The basic conception of our preference model is that considerations of what is possible by 2000 suggests a dual emphasis on macrofunctional potentialities and on the trade-off between global managerial build-ups and partial dismantling of national bureaucracies. In essence we anticipate the centralized administration of many realms of human activity—health, environmental protection, money, business operations, ocean and space use, disarmament, disaster relief, peace-keeping and peaceful settlement, and resource conservation. These superagencies will enjoy competence only in relation to their functional domain. Augmented international political institutions less tied to the state system will attempt to assure that normative priorities are upheld and that various functional activities are coordinated. As is any other political mechanism, it will be vulnerable to whatever deficiences exist with regard to the intensity and clarity of the underlying consensus shaped around WOMP values during the transition process.

Constitutional mechanisms will attempt to mediate between concerns for efficiency and dignity. There will be checks and balances, as wide a participation

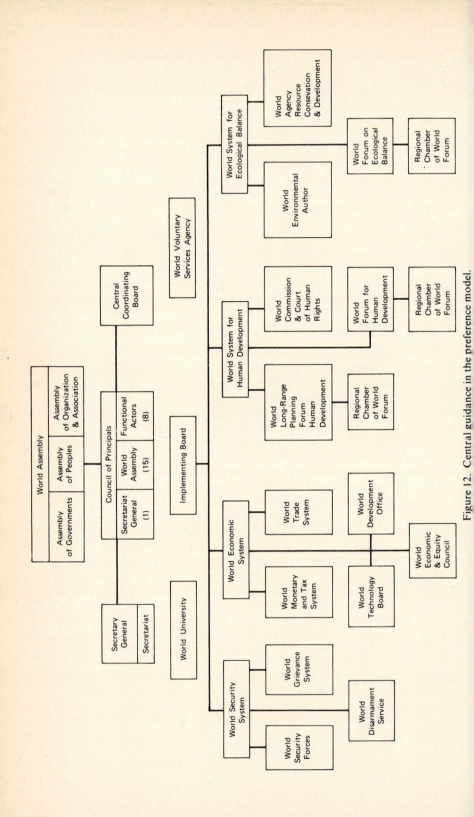

Figure 12. Central guidance in the preference model.

in decisional processes as feasible, procedural opportunities for review, a code of restraints designed to safeguard diversity, autonomy, and creativity, and a minimization of the bureaucratic role.[3]

The WOMP/USA preference model also allocates authority between the global and regional levels to a considerable extent. This allocation reflects a commitment to diversify control arrangements, to limit centralizing tendencies to real functional requirements, and to offset the decline of the state system in as balanced a fashion as possible. Part of the offset and balance would also be achieved by transnational economic activity organized in a progressive way, as portrayed in Figure 5. Indeed Figure 10 is a synthetic model drawing on features implicit in Figures 4, 5, 7, and 8.

Figure 11 carries forward our fundamental stress on domestic reorientation as a precondition of global transformation. The diminished inner circles reflect the increasing influence of WOMP values on the internal organization of states. As will become evident in the discussion of our transition proposals, this domestic reorientation will be a major undertaking early in the transition process, especially by highly industrialized states; such reorientation of domestic arrangements will proceed unevenly throughout the world system, and the process will go on long after the preferred world order comes into being. The ideal toward which we proceed at all levels of social organization is a minimum degree of coercion and bureaucratization and a maximum degree of spontaneous solidarity, participation, and discipline.

Finally, Figure 10 is not a terminal model. If achieved it will become the system that will in turn stimulate twenty-first century world-order reformers to express new preference models and transition strategies. No world-order solution is acceptable unless it encourages a continuous search for ways to transcend new limits; the dignity of man depends on the provisionality of political and social arrangements, on their imperfectibility, except in the imagination. We reject all closed systems of world order as candidates for preference models.

In conclusion, Figures 1 to 12 are offered as images to encourage and orient world-order analysis. Their role is to give visual expression to the notion of comparative systems of order. We believe such mapping operations can be developed with far greater precision in the future. Our goal is to make the idea of alternative futures as vivid as possible in the course of outlining a world-order solution responsive to our value preferences.

NOTES

1. In this regard the forthcoming work of Ervin Laszlo is especially promising. Professor Laszlo uses a cybernetic orientation to design world-order models with normative objectives similar to WOMP. See Laszlo, *The Systems View of the World* (New York: Braziller, 1972); but especially Laszlo, *Norms for the Future: An Application of Systems Philosophy to the Study of World Order* (New York: Braziller, 1974).

2. Such nonhierarchical patterns of organization become increasingly possible as a result of modern information technology, which is capable of both decentralizing decisional activity and coordinating widely scattered inputs into an over-all decisional process.

3. These principles of constitutional restraint are crucial to the normative acceptability of our preference model. They are elaborated in Chapter IV of the full WOMP/USA document.

Orientations to Transition

INTRODUCTION

Throughout this book we have been gradually constructing the image of a desirable world by reference to the world order values of peace, economic well-being, social justice and ecological balance. We have also been attempting to understand why the present world order system fails to realize these values, and in what directions present trends are taking us. Our concern now turns to the problem of transition, by which we mean how do we get from where we are to where we want to be. This concern necessarily entails an understanding of how social change occurs at various levels of human interaction.

The studies of the future presented in the last section suggest that major changes in the world system are likely to occur over the next two decades. Shifting demographic factors along with technological innovations and ecological constraints are creating enormous pressures for modifications in wealth, social patterns and even governing structures. A wide array of future worlds is possible and while substantial change is inevitable, the character and content of the future remain uncertain. Human choice and intervention in political and social process, which studies of the future cannot adequately take into account, will contribute to the shape of global society over the next two decades.

The study of transition, social change and human intervention is an underdeveloped aspect of world order studies. Early conceptions of global reform tended to ignore the problem of transition. Some reform-oriented authors placed their faith in rationality, expecting the persuasiveness of their proposals to generate by itself a politics of acceptance. Their approach was to design a better system of world order and then argue for its adoption. This orientation toward transition assumed that existing elites would be moved by the reasonableness of the argument or by the general ethical attractiveness of the new system.

A similar but somewhat more realistic approach to transition involved putting forth a timetable for the realization of certain intermediate goals: a 10% reduction in military spending in 5 years; the establishment of an international tribunal in 10 years, and so on. Such an approach, while suggestive to the extent that it established certain intermediate target goals, tended to ignore inquiry into what kind of social and political action was necessary. Both approaches tended to be utopian because they did not come to grips with politics, let alone with the possibility that confrontation and outright struggle may be essential to transform present structures of power and interest in desirable directions.

An adequate conception of transition, therefore, must be grounded in political reality. It must connect analysis of what is projected as preferred with an inquiry into the actors and social forces that might make such an outcome materialize within a certain historical context. In this section, we deal with some orientations to a transition process conceived of in this way. We do not attempt to provide here a comprehensive theory of social change or a concrete program of social action. Rather, our purpose is to provide a range of perspectives, which together will provide a basis for a framework of inquiry into the transition process.

Orientations to transition are necessarily influenced by existential circumstances. As several of the contributions to this section suggest, change is usually brought about by the exertions and struggles of those who suffer from the existing order and become conscious of their suffering and form a political will to overcome it by acting in concert with other similar victims. To what extent an individual or group perceives itself to be oppressed is one element in determining its willingness to engage in political and social action to change the present order. An awareness of one's own oppression, as well as the conviction of its moral unacceptability, is a precondition to change. Awareness and discussion are also important to achieving a general climate more receptive to demands for change as well as building wider support for a transition movement.

Mere enlightenment, however widespread, is unlikely to be a sufficient condition for change. It is in the realm of political and social struggle that structural changes in the present international system are likely to be determined. Again, one's existential circumstances affect what form the struggle takes. Steve Biko's struggle in South Africa, for example, was naturally against the oppressive apparatus of apartheid. The peasant in Brazil, on the other hand, is concerned primarily with the multinational corporation that has usurped his or her means of livelihood; for citizens living near nuclear reactors in the U.S., it is natural to demonstrate against those local nuclear power installations that directly threaten personal health and well-being. Furthermore, one's life circumstances dictate the extent to which one is capable of assuming responsibility for change throughout the globe. Certainly, a middle class student at a university in the United States or Western Europe has more opportunity and resources to devote to transnational action than does a Korean citizen in opposition to an authoritarian regime, let alone an impoverished Sahalian peasant or a Kampuchean boat person.

With this understanding, it is possible to see that there will be a multitude of actors, groups, and organizations differently motivated, acting in distinct ways, for diverse goals, and in various arenas, all of which may be relevant to the struggle for a just world order. There will be many agendas as well as many tactics for change, including electoral politics, social activist movements, civil disobedience, spiritual transformative initiatives, and armed struggle. Action will occur at all levels of social organization, particularly at the local and national levels, and will undoubtedly involve struggles to change domestic structures in all societies—East European and Third World as well as Western. Many of the political struggles that may be central to improving human well-being are already under way. Others, such as the disarmament movement, are only in their formative stages, and there are others that are yet to be born; consciousness of oppression has not yet been sufficiently stirred.

An important world order task involves identifying all these forces, assessing how they are related, and encouraging roles for them that are mutually supportive of world order values. Some overriding cohesive vision also seems necessary. There needs to be a recognition that there are some crucial interests common to the people of this planet regardless of where they live or their social class or their race, religion or gender. A new myth of human unity and solidarity might help give rise to this sense of global identity. Such a global identity seems necessary if humankind as a whole is to benefit from disparate political struggles.

We recognize that much transnational political struggle in the near future will directly or indirectly be aimed against the West, against its domination of others, against its privileged position. This suggests a special responsibility for those of us living in Western society. The manner in which we as a society respond to challenges on the world scene, given our destructive capabilities, may prove decisive for the future of the planet as a whole. Will we react belligerently, clinging by military means to our privileged position as long as possible, or will we work hard to build something new, some new type of society more humanly grounded, that does not need to dominate and control others?

An important part of the world order struggle involves the imaging of viable alternatives. Envisioning new institutions, whether they be self-reliant communities, appropriate technology industries, human service organizations, or global mechanisms of accountability, poses a challenge to existing institutions and structures. It is thus a form of struggle as well.

New institutions imply new social values, habits, and patterns of behavior involving deep cultural change and even new lifestyles. This development of alternative patterns of behavior throughout the globe will undoubtedly be informed by local and historical traditions; simultaneously, however, these diverse forms must all join in the interpenetrative process through which a form of global culture will emerge. The relationship between authenticity of one's own unit and a sense of global identity, then, becomes one of the crucial foci in the transition process. In sum, transition is a two-fold process: one of confronting and breaking down outmoded structures, and one of building new forms of cooperation, new economic arrangements, new political institutions, and congenial cultural units at local, national and global levels.

The first paper in this section is by the Indian scholar Rajni Kothari. In a provocative analysis of the present international system, Kothari argues that

Western industrial civilization has penetrated the entire planet, but due to its own internal contradictions and the forces set in motion by decolonization, the hegemonic influence of the West is declining. In his view, the world is going through a major transformation that involves a redistribution of wealth, power, and privilege in favor of Third World states, especially those that themselves are undergoing major domestic changes to meet their population's basic human needs, and which simultaneously practice individual and collective self-reliance. Kothari emphasizes the necessity for a grand global coalition in which progressive governments of the Third World join activist reformers and radical social movements in the North. He suggests the manner in which India, China, and the Soviet Union might play a progressive role in this coalition, although he notes the difficulties these societies might have in providing world order leadership. Kothari's analysis, like Hedley Bull's in Section 2, raises the issue of whether it is possible to implement a policy for a just world order through the nation-state system. Kothari believes that the state system is a necessary framework for action at this stage of history. It should be noted that Kothari ascribes a key role to intellectuals in the transition process, because they are capable of transcending their particular cultural roots; nevertheless, he is wary of calls for world order and globalism that derive from Western society.

The second selection, by Johan Galtung, is an excerpt from his recent book *The True Worlds.* He approaches the problem of transition by emphasizing that both an actor and a structural perspective are necessary for understanding the manner in which individuals and groups may successfully intervene in ongoing social, political, economic, and cultural processes to bring about desired change. Like Kothari, Galtung argues that Western hegemony has penetrated the globe, fragmenting previously existing political and cultural units. The best way to fight Western domination, Galtung contends, is not through counter penetration but by becoming more autonomous. His normative orientation to transition is a thoroughgoing attitude of self-reliance, by which he means faith in one's self and reliance on one's own resources first. Since self-reliance is to Galtung an open-ended concept, he does not spell out in operational detail how it might work. But he does suggest that self-reliance should be pursued at all levels—local, national, and regional—and that it entails greater cooperation and interaction among similarly situated units. Finally, he lays out some guidelines for both peace and development activists and encourages individuals and groups to initiate and participate in transformational projects within their own existential circumstances.

War, a traditional preoccupation of world order inquiry, is the subject of the next essay, by Richard Falk. As the title of that work suggests, however, Falk broadens the traditional approach to war considerably by dealing with militarization, a concept that comprehends international conflict, hegemonic domination, and internal repression. This orientation resembles in some respects the framework developed by Dieter Senghaas in Section 4. Delegitimating and reversing current trends toward militarism must be considered a central part of any transition process. As suggested in Section 4, militarism is intrinsically related to problems of poverty, underdevelopment, repression, and the escalation of large-scale violence in many parts of the world. Moreover, as long as military force remains a legitimate instrument of statist elites, peaceful change in domestic societies, as well as in the international system, remains highly problematic. Recognizing this, Falk explores and attempts to identify "creative space" in the struggle against militarization. Taking into account the political structures and restraints of different polities, the author examines normative initiatives that challenge the root assumptions of militarization and that can be linked to actual social forces working for principled demilitarization.

Falk utilizes the concept of "third system" in his approach to these problems. He argues that, at the present time, the First System (the state system and its support infrastructure) is supportive of the underlying logic of militarization, and that the Second System (the UN and regional international institutes) is mainly a dependency of the First System and unable to implement demilitarization initiatives. The Third System (represented by people acting individually and collectively through voluntary institutions) can promote at this stage normative initiatives of consequence for demilitarization. Normative initiatives relevant to demilitarization undertaken in the Third System can aid in mobilizing effective opposition to militarization in all three systems by altering the normative climate, thereby producing new "creative space" for political innovation. Finally, Falk provides examples of some promising Third System normative initiatives at the global, regional, sovereign state, and individual levels.

George Lakey's "Manifesto for a Nonviolent Revolution," our last selection, suggests the importance of local struggle to global transformation. Lakey envisions "a new society" that is egalitarian, participatory, nonviolent, and ecologically responsible, and that comprehends a just world order. In this selection, Lakey presents a concrete statement for a strategy of revolution. Recognizing that many people feel uncertain and even impotent to act usefully to promote a just world order, he suggests five stages for the development of a movement from a small band of agitators to a mass struggle movement capable of fundamental change: 1) conscientization; 2) building organization; 3) confrontation; 4) mass noncooperation; and 5) parallel government. Whether this conception of movement development is the most helpful is a matter of conjecture. It does, however, suggest ways in which persons may become active during the transition period.

Lakey has been extensively involved in political and social activism on both local and global issues. He was a member of the group who sailed the Phoenix, a 50-foot sloop, to deliver medical supplies to both North and South Vietnam in 1967–1968. In 1972 he was a founding member of the Movement for a New Society, which now consists of a network of some 30 communities of citizens who have chosen to live in the problem areas of urban centers throughout the United States. Lakey, who has taught at Haverford College and the University of Pennsylvania, is also very much aware of the need for combining research and scholarship with struggle and transition projects. As a nonviolent activist, he recognizes why oppressed people turn to direct violence as a means to transform intolerable oppressive conditions. He makes the plea, however, that before resorting to violence, all nonviolent alternatives be explored. Finally, he argues that a movement for a new society and a just world order must necessarily be transnational.

QUESTIONS FOR DISCUSSION AND REFLECTION

What structures do you consider to be the most formidable obstacles to a just world order? What kinds of actions do you think might be taken to overcome these structures?

Do you believe that Western society is one of the major obstacles in achieving a just world order? If not, what are the major stumbling blocks?

What problems do you feel must be treated at the "global" level in order to achieve a just world order? Specifically, what does this mean in terms of participation by what kind of actors, in what kind of organizations, dealing with what kind of struggle?

What do you understand by the term "local" in referring to local/global relationships? If it is territorial, how do you know the perimeters of the territory? To what extent do you believe the movement for a just world order must rely upon "local" movements for transformation?

What sort of activism is it reasonable to expect of third system individuals and organizations in Eastern Europe? In various authoritarian states of the Third World?

How would you define the term "self-reliance?" Are there any groups, units, or political, social, or cultural organizations that you can identify as presently being self-reliant? How significant do you believe self-reliance is in the transition for achieving a just world order?

To what extent do you feel violence is necessary to achieve desired world order goals in the world? Are there nonviolent techniques that might be used instead of violence?

Do you believe that an activist nonviolent attitude can lead to a series of political and social projects and programs that would promote transformation toward a just world order? Specifically, where would you initiate such programs?

To what extent do you think legal processes might be useful in bringing about desired change anywhere in the world? Can legal processes be combined with social movement activities such as the way in which civil rights activism in the streets of the United States combined with suits brought in U.S. courts?

Are you a member or participant in any political or social activist organization? How might it relate to a social movement for a just world order? What other political, social, cultural, or religious organizations do you know that could be involved in a movement for a just world order? What kinds of programs do they promote? What more might they do? Do you know any organizations that are transnational in composition and have transnational targets or goals? How effective are they?

SELECTED BIBLIOGRAPHY

Coover, Deacon, Essex, and Moore. *Resource Manual for a Living Revolution.* Philadelphia: Movement for a New Society, 1978.

Dellinger, David. *More Power Than We Know.* New York: Doubleday, 1971.

Ferguson, M. A. *The Aquarian Conspiracy: Personal and Social Transformation in the 1980's.* Los Angeles: J. P. Tarcher, 1980.

Freire, Paulo. *Pedagogy of the Oppressed.* New York: Herder & Herder, 1970.

Gurr, Ted Robert. *Why Men Rebel.* Princeton: Princeton University Press, 1970.

Lakey, George. *Strategy for a Living Revolution.* San Francisco: W. H. Freeman, 1973.

Laszlo, Ervin. *Goals for Mankind: A Report to the Club of Rome on the Horizons of Global Community.* New York: Free Press, 1977.

Satin, Mark. *New Age Politics: Healing Self and Society.* New York: Dell, 1980.

Sharp, Gene. *Social Power and Political Freedom.* Boston: Porter Sargent, 1980.

36
TOWARDS A JUST WORLD

Rajni Kothari

INTRODUCTION

We seem to be on the threshold of a new epoch in world history. It is not certain that it will be crossed in a manner that will lead to a sane and humane world and not to one that is sinister, and inimical to, the dignity and autonomy of diverse human entities. Crossing it so that the first kind of world is ensured calls for a vision based on a firm grasp of the historical process—with its unfolding dialectic and future possibilities—and a capacity to intervene so as to translate such possibilities into reality. Above all, it will call for the forging of a coalition for change that spans various regions and political systems and is able to identify specific issues around which interventions can be initiated, and one, too, that is capable of conceiving relevant strategies for moving toward the envisioned future, and then enlisting a set of actors that would generate the necessary interventions from a variety of locations and vantage points. This essay deals with these various components of a design for an alternative future.

There is bound to be a great deal of resistance to such a process of change. There exists a powerful constellation of interests with a wide-ranging structure and still occupying a dominant position in access to resources and institutions that would oppose any basic change in the existing arrangement of human affairs. Such resistance is in many ways unrealistic in that it reflects an insensitivity to the far-reaching historical process that is already under way, but it is wholly understandable; for this constellation has so much at stake in the prevailing order with its deeply ingrained structure of interests and a widely shared *mystique*. Both the alignment of interests and the mystique have acquired tremendous power and can evoke a great deal of sentiment and loyalty for the prevailing order. It is an order that has not only been a going concern for some time now; it is also rooted in a phenomenal unfoldment of history in the last two hundred years before which the whole of earlier human history appears far too fragmentary, diffuse and without an immanent thrust or purpose.

Reprinted by permission from *Alternatives: A Journal of World Policy* 5, 1, 1979.

THE PROCESS OF 200-YEAR HISTORY

The last two hundred years, beginning with the Industrial Revolution in the West, and its colonial expansion throughout the globe, have been marked by a fundamental civilizational drive, informed by a clear doctrine based on the European enlightenment, the theory of progress, and the idea of secular history. Arising from a dualism between the secular and the spiritual, the idea was subsequently legitimized by the conquest of a larger and larger domain of man's nature and territory through a materialist interpretation of science and technology. This doctrine released tremendous energy and led, among other things, to a superiority in armaments and the art of warfare which proved critical in extending the frontiers of Western civilization and its normative framework to cover almost the entire globe.

This entailed a new conception of universalism. The old universalistic conceptions—found in China, India, the ancient Greece and Turkey, in the thinking of the Buddha and the Zoroastrian teachers—were all, despite their considerable diversities, based on the transcendence of the immediate, the local and the temporal through the cultivation of the mind and a search for comprehension and meaning in an admittedly mysterious and complex reality, and led to a moderation and containment of selfish and expansionist drives in the human personality. By contrast, the modernist conception of universalism that emerged in the West was based on the expansion of a local civilization and on dominance over the rest of the world, legitimized by a belief in the manifest destiny that was peculiar to Judeo-Christian religiosity in the post-medieval age.

The Western imperial thrust that was stimulated by modern technology and the accompanying economic expansion as well as by a psychological urge arising from a conviction of racial superiority was, in turn, supported and spurred on by the balance of power in Europe. It thus extended the competitive ethos of the growth of capital and territory at home to the exploration, acquisition and consolidation of colonial empires abroad. The result was global domination by European state power and its economic infrastructure. Indeed, modern European imperialism represents the first major effort at unifying the entire globe under the dominion of a single regional centre. Though the rise of Prussia and Bismarck's clever manipulation of the Congress of Vienna system produced internal crises within this edifice (which eventually led to two world wars and the shift of the locus of imperial power from continental Europe to the United States), the basic momentum generated by superior technology and superior armaments—and, of course, by cultural penetration during and after the colonial period—still persists and has, if anything, made Western domination a far deeper reality than ever before.

Inner Contradictions

And yet, it was from the very dynamics of this revolutionary upheaval and the enormous historical drive from one regional centre out into the whole world that its dialectic also emerged. This has given rise to entirely new forces that have already begun to erode the stability of the prevailing structure of world power and threaten to put an end to the era of Western domination. Such a dialectic was inherent in the Europe-based world model. Any system which is based on expansion, domination and forced homogenization (unlike one that is based on restraint, harmony and respect for diversity) must give rise to inner contradictions and imbalances. In the European case, the dialectic developed along three lines:

1. States system. First, the states system, based on a "balance of power" which was itself unstable and lasted only until the rise of national consciousness in central and eastern Europe, generated an altogether new dynamic, and the highly uneven growth of imperialism abroad upset the balance of forces within Europe. The rise of Germany, Italy and resurgent nationalisms in the Eastern backwaters of the European establishment gave a jolt to the states system then prevailing and, in the end, weakened its staying power. The October Revolution in Russia undermined its *raison d'être* and ushered in a new era of world politics. The anti-colonial heritage of America and its growing economic might further, and in a way decisively, contributed to this.

2. Economic imperialism. Second, the acquisitive and competitive ethos of European secular culture and a narrowly economic impulse to universalism produced a scramble for material advancement of a highly parochial kind, both in the outlying empires and at home. Economic universalism provided the spur to modern imperialism which went on a rampage and turned the colonies, over which they had acquired political dominion, into captive production centres providing raw materials and indentured labour – and slaves and serfs – and captive markets for European manufactured goods (whose production rose at fantastic rates, thanks to the miracles of technological growth). In the process, they undermined indigenous industrial traditions and implanted in their place a totally new economic model.

Two results followed from such a design of exploitative imperialism, one abroad and the other at home. With the collapse of the local economy and the introduction of minimum necessary health and education facilities of the modern type (for ensuring cheap colonial labour), there accumulated in the colonies a huge back-log of adult population for whom there was no economic function. Providing the barest minimum of livelihood and security for them became a massive burden either on the colonial exchequer (as, for instance, in India) or on the coercive machinery of the colonial state (as in most parts of Africa). Meanwhile, there emerged a local entrepreneurial class (whose interests conflicted directly with the colonials) and a local educated class (which received the Western doctrines of liberalism, nationalism and socialism positively and used them against the colonials). The rising cost of administering the colonies and the nationalist awakening of the bourgeoisie and the intelligentsia in the vast land masses of Africa and Asia together turned the "glorious" empires into eyesores which led the imperialists into a protracted process of negotiations aimed at conceding independence but retaining economic and indirect political control.

At home, the easy availability of cheap and plentiful raw materials and new sources of energy and transportation – from each of which, incidentally, European business made huge fortunes – prompted the adoption of a new industrial culture, applying more and more capital and labour-saving technology and transforming a slow-moving industrial revolution into an economy of affluence. This led to another remarkable result for the West: the containment of class conflicts by extending the benefits of imperialism to the labouring classes at home. This was given the name of welfare state. The Marxist scenario of revolutionary upheaval in the centres of capitalism failed to materialize largely because of this.[1]

On the other hand, thanks to the availability of cheap and plentiful raw materials from the colonies and incredibly expanding markets for consumer goods, largely at home but also abroad, it became possible to introduce capital-intensive and labour-displacing technology without affecting employment at home, except for temporary setbacks occasioned by the trade cycle. The Westerner went over with gusto to the new culture of affluence – indeed, he encouraged it by aggressive salesmanship – cutting across class boundaries. It was much later that he realized how dependent he had become on the erstwhile colonies. By this time the age of imperialism had drawn to a close and a new mode of Western domination, based on technology and armaments, had begun.

3. *Clash of ideologies*. Contributing very significantly to these emerging countervailing forces was the third mode of the European dialectic: the dialectic of ideas. Building in part on earlier traditions of emotional protest and romantic revulsion against the capitalist mode of material civilization, there took place the Marxist rebellion in the Western thought process. This marked the great watershed of modern history. Though philosophically firmly rooted in the Western secular mode of thought, Marx provided a vision of the future and a method of getting there that had a special appeal to oppressed people everywhere. Indeed, in course of time the new doctrine and philosophy travelled abroad and found converts in non-Western settings. It facilitated the emergence of new modes of organizing state power – in the Soviet land mass, in Eastern Europe, in China, in Cuba, in Vietnam, and in many an emergent polity struggling against the racial and economic vestiges of colonialism – based on an alternative model of civil society which, in course of time, produced a different kind of world altogether. But this was still in respect more of the internal structure of national societies than of relations between them, though undoubtedly it changed the latter too. The change occurred in three important ways: first, by bringing more than a third of mankind under the communist ideological spectrum; second, by lending substantial support to national elites committed to put an end to dependence on the West; and, third, by a partial and often discreet but nonetheless growing convergence of efforts between the socialist countries and the countries of the Third World. All three processes are still under way.

Together, the three modes of historical dialectic described above – in the central fulcrum of power, in the underlying economic structures, and in the normative-ideological superstructure – have released forces that have been slowly converging to bring about a qualitative transformation in the world system.

The Tolling of the Bell for the Western Era

The main import of this transformation is to be seen in the modification and gradual erosion of the West-dominated world system. The rise of Germany, a child of the nationalist creed born in the European cradle and heir to the anti-revolutionary creed of the European Alliance, undermined the fine balance on which the European states system was based. The Russian Revolution dealt a more serious blow at a deeper level by projecting an alternative social order as well as a polar alternative in world politics. The end of World War II saw both the rise of Soviet power in world affairs and the rise of a new wave of nationalism in Asia and Africa putting an end to empires and challenging the hegemonistic designs of the old world order. The spread of communism to Eastern Europe and China made it a "spectre" that really began to "haunt" the West, which, with the shift of the locus of power from the European cultural zone to America, lost its earlier poise and restraint and collided with the new world forces, ending in the Vietnam debacle.

Alongside all this, anti-colonialism has been transformed from a broad political front for national liberation movements into a global trade union of Third World countries struggling to change the global distribution of resources and restructure the world economic and technological order. This is already producing some important modifications in inter-regional balances. Despite the frustrations of the North-South dialogue, and despite the tactical "convergence" represented by the US-USSR détente, the world seems to be moving decisively towards a diffuse and diversified structure.

Meanwhile, the supreme confidence in the rightness of the Western path has been shaken in the West itself. The ecological crisis and the "limits to growth" debate, the precipitous decline in the legitimacy of the doctrine of economic growth (which has only served to globalize the European class conflict by shoving it off to other regions), deep doubts about the philosophical premises of modern science, and the steady uncovering of the racist tendency in the Western psyche—all have led to a fundamental questioning of values and assumptions held to be valid for so long. Such questioning, now spreading beyond intellectual circles, has set in motion a process of psychological erosion, a basic decline in the legitimacy of institutions, a growth in fundamental dissent from the basic postulates of Western civilization, culminating in the search for an alternative framework of ordering human relations. This uneasy period in world history is characterized by a combination of a slowly evolving crisis of confidence in the prevailing system and a growing sense of some impending transformations in it.

Such a general consciousness of historical mutation (at the moment perhaps confined to the thinking strata) is also buttressed by concrete evidence of transformation along several dimensions: a fast changing economic scenario of major world regions; far-reaching demographic changes, not just in the population size but also in respect of a radical restructuring of age compositions and of large movements of population across regions; a fundamental reorientation in technological balances and their impact on human ecology and the biosphere; an equally fundamental reorientation in energy needs and in the availability and distribution of material resources; new directions in the diffusion of military and political power; and powerful new cultural configurations and encounters.

There is as yet no certainty, however, where the totality of these changes (and the larger transformation involved in their mutual intertwining) will lead the world. They could conceivably lead to a world that feels more peaceful and secure as a result of becoming more decentralized and just, following a period of negotiated settlement of major sources of conflict and informed by mature statesmanship at regional and global levels. But it could also lead to a world racked by increasing turbulence, a greater sense of insecurity among the major centres of power—and hence to a further tightening of the structures of domination and domestic repression—producing in their wake an intensification of the arms race and militarization of regimes, encouraging regional conflagrations, and setting the stage for an eventual global holocaust.

RESPONSES TO THE IMPENDING CHANGE

Needless to say, almost all those concerned would like to avoid the latter scenario, or, at any rate, extreme manifestations of it. But there seems to be little agreement on how to avoid it. There is some, though by no means universal, agreement that the age of a relatively homogeneous and stable world based on domination from one regional centre—the West—is coming to an end and that a new framework of relations between major regions of the world has become necessary. But there seems to be hardly any consensus on the nature of the new framework. The dominant Western powers themselves look at it in one way; the newly emerging powers—namely, the countries of the Third World—look at it in quite a different way. The Soviet Union's view of it is different from both and, in turn, affects the perspective of other important powers—above all, of China. The Soviet Union's view is conditioned by two opposite pulls: its stake in maintaining the bipolar system of world management and security, and, in the process, containing China; and its desire to bend large sections of the non-Western world into enabling it to increase its influence in world affairs, and hence its position in the bipolar system. In a fundamental way, however, the Third World, China, and the Soviet Union and its allies are, in their very different ways, pitched against the Western alliance.

We shall examine the Soviet position and its points of convergence and divergence from the Third World later in this paper. More critical from our point of view, however, is the Western response to the changing world situation. This is so because the world as we know it today was shaped by it in a fundamental way, because it is still the more dominant of various world centres, because it still happens to be the nerve-center of global communications, technology and strategic doctrine, and because it is the pace-setter of things, given its preponderant position in access to the world economic surplus. The manner in which it responds to present and emerging changes in the world scene can thus prove decisive for the future of the world.

Western Response

Creation of a "World Order." / The Western response consists of a combination of two modes of expression, one in rhetoric (which in itself is suggestive and, in fact, *could* represent a shift in thinking), the other in Realpolitik, i.e., in terms of policies designed to preserve the status quo through minimal adjustments to a changing situation.

The new rhetoric is couched in the language of "world order," consisting of three main dimensions: a common "Trilateral" front between the US, Western Europe and Japan, providing the inner core of stability in a fast changing world; involvement of the more powerful among the Third World countries in a system of global management and sharing of power and prosperity; and, of course, continuation of detente with the Soviet Union as a necessary condition for the pursuit of both Trilateralism and partnership with the Third World (and, indeed, of more ambitious aims like undercutting Soviet influence in Third World regions and penetrating the Soviet zone of power in Eastern Europe and elsewhere). It is a language that appears to shift the emphasis from bipolar hegemony over the world for the pursuit of national interest to one that thinks in terms of a "world order" based on recognition of a changing reality, and to enter into a partnership with major countries in the Third World to bring such a "world order" about.

It is important to grasp the thinking underlying this new language of global management. In part it is a continuation of, and in part a shift from, the earlier Nixon-Kissinger approach of a three-power concert (US, USSR, China, with Western Europe and Japan thrown in as US partners) through which the tensions of the world are sought to be managed, defused or simply held at bay. It continues the old approach in that it is still a managerial response to a changing structure of world power. At the same time, it represents a shift from the earlier approach in that it is not sanguine about the Soviet Union's intentions, and also in that it relies less on the capacity of the US to topple uncomfortable regimes abroad or on the doctrine of limited wars (both having been shattered by the Vietnam war) and more on other means to protect Western interests. It is thus more realistic about the potential power of the Third World, and that is why it seeks to co-opt major centres instead of simply trying to quarantine the centre powers from the "peripheries" of the world.

The rhetoric of world order is meant to further this new approach to maintain the status quo. Incidentally, it may be mentioned that the new language has sought to gain legitimacy from a radically different and far more idealistic school of thinking in the US which is committed to world order. The latter has been urging an end to the nation-state system and, with it, the arms race, the utilization of world resources and technology for the fulfilment of basic needs of all human beings, the promotion of social justice and the generation of an ecologically balanced process of development—and global governance for undertaking these tasks. It is interesting to note how, in a period of imperial retreat, new legitimization is sought from dissident sources, how the paranoid strains in national culture converge with idealistic strains in the same culture to produce an apparently new ideology in the defence of old interests.

Underlying both the concert-of-powers approach of Nixon and Kissinger and the "world-order" approach of Carter and Brzezinski is a historic reality which neither of them could ignore. This is the signal of the end of American dominance which had followed the collapse of European imperialism. By the end of the sixties, the US lost its strategic monopoly. Soon thereafter came the end of American dominance over world capitalism, heralded by the rise of Japanese and European economic power and the decline of the dollar. The capacity of the US to intervene in the Third World whenever a government or a movement (or a leader) was found uncomfortable — and, if necessary, to topple either — also came to an end with the Vietnam debacle. Vietnam put an end to the doctrine of limited wars in which the US could directly engage to maintain hegemony; henceforth the job had to be done by collaborators round the world. Finally, Vietnam undermined national consensus *within* the US which was so necessary to pursue a forward foreign policy. The need thus arose of finding a new basis for national acceptance of America's world role.

The response to such a retreat on so many fronts came in two stages. The first was conceived by Henry Kissinger who brilliantly drew upon the American cultural mix of doing good to the world and remaining on top of it. "Stability with peace" was the watchword of the Kissinger policy. It was a policy of containing not so much communism as the Soviet Union itself and, as part of that strategy, an opening up to China, on the one hand, and pacification of the Middle East, on the other (the US becoming the chief arbiter in Middle East affairs). Having succeeded in turning East-West ideological rivalry into a straight game of power, which spanned across ideological divisions (with Washington being the main balancer of a new concert of powers), Kissinger could afford to ignore the sensibilities of the Third World. Indeed, he dealt with it rather contemptuously (as with India during the Bangladesh crisis and, later, with Chile) and generally had no qualms in supporting repressive regimes and subverting democratic ones in the developing world.

Kissinger's moves proved too short-lived, however, and could not stand either the longer-term effects of OPEC, the tumultuous developments in Africa (starting with Angola), or even in the Middle East, when Israel failed to play Sparta to Rome or when the Shah of Iran displayed ambitions to get bigger than his boots. Meanwhile, Kissinger had alienated Japan, alarmed his West European allies, and he paid no attention to arresting the decline of US economic power — a process that had been under way for more than a decade — in cooperation with US allies.

By the time the Carter administration came to power, the rhetoric of peace and stability appeared unworkable, the Soviet Union having been found too difficult to manage within the concert-of-powers concept. On the other hand, the assertion of the Third World, following OPEC, and the shift in economic power to Western Europe, Japan and West Asia meant that the rest of the world could not be taken for granted, either. The conditions for continuing US primacy had drastically altered.

The Kissinger approach showed clearly how, faced by a fast changing global reality, the "Number One" nation of the world was desperately trying to follow old goals by manipulating new situations. Under Carter and his Trilateral advisers, who never gave up the ambition of continuing to be "Number One," three major tactical shifts are noticeable. Some of these shifts had, in fact, started under Ford and found expression in Kissinger's statements towards the end of his tenure as Secretary of State.

First, peace has ceased to be the principal watchword, and its place has been taken by human rights. Second, the politics of detente is slowly giving place to a frank espousal of the politics of antagonistic collaboration—accepting a common interest in limiting superpower confrontation in the battlefield, but also accepting superpower competition in regional power balances. Third, there is the policy of regional flanks for both strategic and economic purposes, under which certain selected countries in different regions are armed to the teeth. These are countries in which the multinationals have invested their huge capital—Brazil, Chile, Iran (till recently), Saudi Arabia, Zaire, South Korea, Indonesia. It is this convergence of strategic and economic interests and their global reach through a worldwide military-industrial complex (in which several ruling elites act as surrogates of an imperial power in pursuit of a global design in return for their becoming regional overlords) that constitutes the new *Pax Americana.*

New Corporatism. / Such a package of response under the rhetoric of "world order" to the transformation taking place in the world represents a doctrine of global management and provides the framework for Realpolitik. This Realpolitik is, in some ways, far more pervasive in its approach to world power than was the policy of global encirclement through military pacts during the Cold War, or even Kissinger's policy of stridently playing Metternich through a global oligarchy of powers. In one way, it is the first truly global convergence of elites based on a conscious role for world capitalism, on the one hand, and a frightening willingness to use military means to defend Western interests, on the other.

The vision of "world order" that informs such a strategy is one of a corporate world society consisting of (a) a global network of economic enterprises set up by multinational corporations in command of high technology, enormous funds for R&D and an array of experts and managers produced in the techno-centres of the world and "transferred" to its peripheries (sought to be integrated into a "world economy" by making them dependent on that technology); (b) a states system monitored by supranational centres and administered by regional overlords who would provide order and stability in their respective regions and hold the "forces of chaos and revolution" at bay; (c) a corresponding structure of strategic and military power for providing regimes of security in the various regions; (d) a globally co-ordinated network of intelligence agencies that would safeguard the interests of this corporate structure of political and economic power; and (e) a system of information and communication media that spreads a "culture" of thought and behaviour that facilitates structures of domination and undermines local autonomy and diversity. The basic thrust of this world order comes from a comprehensive cultural process of homogenization of human aspirations, based on standardized inputs of education, technology, management and coercion, and co-ordinated through a vertical structure of governance that would envelop all the regions of the world. It is an order that would enable all nations (which prove their eligibility through co-operation rather than confrontation with the West) to partake of the "peace and plenty" which modern technology has made possible and which the West has already achieved.

Behind such an all-encompassing thrust to "order" the world—a world that is fast slipping from under conventional means of control and manipulation—lies a deep sense of fear and anxiety. It derives from the perception of a growing economic challenge from the South and of the possibility of a decline in living standards in the West despite its technological, military and strategic superiority. This perception was at its strongest immediately following the economic ascendancy of the OPEC, which stimulated a measure of confidence among the Third World elites (who tended to close ranks despite the immediate economic hardship that the rise in oil prices caused to most non-oil-producing Third World countries, especially those of the so-called "Fourth World"). Since then it has evaporated to some extent, thanks largely to the co-optive capacities of Western capitalism, which we shall presently discuss, but it still exists and, as we shall show later, is likely to produce more menacing forms.

Militarization and Global Dominance. / The manner in which the Western powers have dealt with the economic challenge of the Third World provides yet another instance of the remarkable staying power of the prevailing "system" and its periodic rejuvenation by shifting the means employed to achieve the same old goals. The crisis posed by the "challenge from the South," following the solidarity of the members of OPEC and the consequent stimulation of a wider solidarity among Third World countries, produced considerable nervousness in the advanced capitalist countries. They found themselves "dependent" on the developing world—incidentally, equally suddenly making them conscious of the fact that we now lived in an age of "interdependence." The same crisis also underlined the crucial importance of military and strategic power, which was presumed to have been of no avail in dealing with the group of OPEC but which, in fact, got a new lease of life.

This has happened because, in pacifying the sources of challenge from the South, the technological and military power of the North has played a very major role in several ways. One was the oft-mentioned induction of petro-dollars into the financial institutions and investment trusts of the West. Another was the sustained and painstaking diplomatic effort by Mr. Kissinger on the Arab-Israeli front, which made the United States the arbiter of the Middle East conflict and prepared the ground for amity in place of hostility in the relations between the US and the Arab countries. But equally important, perhaps even more important, for understanding the world order conceived in Washington was the unprecedented spurt in arms sales to the Middle East, its growing militarization, and the transport of not just military hardware but a large number of military personnel, ancillary industrial installations, and training and consulting infrastructures as well. There has also been a large-scale export of Western technology and the culture of conspicuous consumption that goes with it.

The economic challenge that 1973 posed has thus been met by deploying the military and technological power of the highly industrialized countries in the *nouveau riche* societies. And the new sense of power and autonomy that was generated in the wake of the new-found riches has been channelled into the acquisition of new symbols and artifacts of national grandeur that once again have made these countries dependent states. The same processes have been at work in meeting the challenge of the ascendant countries in Latin America, Africa, and Southeast Asia. In all these regions diplomatic manoeuvres, economic penetration through multinationals, political subversion of uncomfortable regimes, and hard-headed economic bargaining for maintaining favourable terms of trade for the dominant nations (in the face of increases in oil and commodity prices) have been employed; but it is the induction of armaments, with the concomitant culture of militarization, that has ensured the perpetuation of the global status quo. As this kind of penetration spreads wider and becomes systemic to the structure of global management, the dominant role of military power in the design of the states system is likely to increase.

New Threat Perceptions. / Yet, despite the success of the United States and other Western industrialized countries in containing the economic and political consequences of OPEC after 1973, concern and anxiety still prevail in the establishment circles in these countries over the growing "challenge from the South" which, in the coming decades, might pose a threat to the maintenance and continuous rise in the living standards of their people, upset the balance on which the present system of power relations rests, and ultimately erode the long-established supremacy of the West in world affairs.

Such a perception of threat (reflecting the long-standing habit of dominating and conceiving of domination as the only way of managing an unequal and divided world) springs from the fear of emerging shifts in global magnitudes and relationships which might produce a scenario of uncertainty and conflict in the years and decades to come. The indicators of such a perception are:

(a) the "menace" of population growth;

(b) the growing demand from other regions of the world for a greater share in world resources, a large proportion of which is located in the developing regions;

(c) the quickening of industrial growth in these regions and the effect of this—and of comparative advantage in production costs—competition for the world market;

(d) the diffusion of sophisticated technology to these regions and their acquisition of nuclear power;

(e) the unprecedented level of "mobilization" in these regions consequent on the growth of middle-class nationalism, of education, and of large cities;

(f) the consequent pressure of all these on the environment and on the availability of agricultural, forest and fossil surpluses so necessary for keeping the wheels of industry moving in the developed world and for preserving its present life-style;

(g) the inevitable growth in competition for scarce resources in the wake of all this within and between societies; and

(h) the serious strains which the cumulative impact of these developments entail for "stability" everywhere and the possibility of a breakdown of the existing "world order."

Such a perception of threat, and the need to evolve contingency plans against it, are clearly set forth in a recent report by the Rand Corporation.[2] While the focus of the report is on strategic doctrine, it prognosticates an economic and political conflict between the industrialized North and the developing South. It is representative of many other statements emanating from the United States since 1973. According to this prognosis, the conflict between the North and the South goes far beyond the impact of the fourfold rise in oil prices and is an "expression of a much deeper conflict" based on "the political mobilization of the Third World, following several centuries of Western dominance." Consequently, it views the demand for "New International Economic Order" (NIEO) as essentially a political demand, "aiming at a major modification of the power relations between the former colonial powers, which are at present the most advanced industrial societies, and the former colonies, which are still in the early stages of modernization and industrialization." Instead of viewing this as a natural culmination of a long historical process, the Rand report, like many other expressions of Western response to the rise of the Third World, views it as something that must somehow be resisted. And the reason it advances for such resistance is couched in demagogic overtones characteristic of so much of American diplomatese ever since the Sixth Special Session of the UN General Assembly: the American people expect their government to protect their economic position. "Nations, like individuals, do not divest themselves voluntarily of their accumulated wealth and of their sources of income merely in response to moral appeals," it says, and then goes on to add that "the American people will probably expect their government to negotiate from a position of strength."

The American argument that the Third World demand for NIEO is expressed in economic terms but is, in essence, a design at changing power relations can be turned against the US. It would run like this: in the garb of maintaining its standard of living, the US is seeking to preserve its political and strategic hegemony.

In reality, however, the specious economic argument by the US is a clever subterfuge for a deeper design—namely, the maintenance of supremacy in global power relations and, hence necessarily, in the global structure of strategic and military balances. The Rand report states this quite bluntly:

> As a superpower cast by history in a role of world leadership, the United States would be expected to use its military force to prevent the total collapse of the world order or, at least, to protect specific interests of American citizens in the absence of an international rule of law.
>
> Such contingencies might generate military requirements without precedent in the experience of American military planners, who may not yet fully comprehend the significance of events that are already happening, such as the intersection between the old East-West conflict, the new North-South conflict, and the accelerating consequences of planetary mismanagement.
>
> More attention may have to be devoted to the development of doctrine, plans, weapons, and force structures in anticipation of possible uses of military force in some novel crisis situations. The American people may demand that its national interests be protected by all available means if global turbulence prevails in the 1980s.
>
> The military posture implications of such a situation are not self-evident. If a harsh international environment were to develop in the 1980s, additional military capabilities might be required besides the forces directly dedicated to Soviet and other well-understood contingencies.

DEEP SCHISM: DISMAL PROSPECTS

The Rand report is perhaps no more than an exercise in contingency planning as well as in the development of US strategic doctrine. The reason for citing it here is that the political analysis on which it is based is shared fairly widely in the West and underlies the grand strategy of erecting a "world order" that provides the main ideological thrust of US foreign policy. If such be the perception of threat from the rise of the countries of the Third World after a long period of suppression and tutelage, and if such be the calculated response to it, one can see the depth of the schism facing humanity. No amount of world order rhetoric can hide the reality of this schism.

Such a "world order" militates, not only against the values of peace and human dignity, but also against the crying need to concentrate all efforts and resources on urgent tasks facing humanity: providing human beings everywhere with basic necessities; discovering new sources of energy and new forms of technology; preserving the environment, the sea-beds and the outer space from destruction in the race for political and technological hegemony; and many others. Given the pursuit of hegemony in a world undergoing rapid transformation, and given its inevitable stress on militarization of the globe as a means of restoring dependency relationships, the prospects facing humanity seem to be dismal.

Particularly dim are the prospects of peace and harmony in such a world. This is not simply a function of the spread of military culture round the world, though no doubt such a culture militates against an atmosphere of peace and harmony. The roots of a peaceless world lie deeper: in the socio-political structure of the world. For "peace"—unless it emanates from, and is rooted in, a social structure widely seen to be just and fair—can be highly stultifying and repressive of the forces of change and reconstruction. Those strongly entrenched in a given social and political order have always wanted peace so that the "order" they preside over may endure and remain unchallenged. Those not so entrenched, including both the newly-ascendant and the as-yet deprived, want peace on the basis of justice and a share in power and decision-making. For, in their view, a structure of inequity and exploitation is the primary source of conflict and violence.

These observations apply as much to the international order as to the national and regional ones. It is a characteristic of the world we live in that the structure of inequity extends to both socio-economic and politico-strategic dimensions. It is a situation of cumulative inequity in which a fantastic command over instruments of violence and military power supports both a system of economic and political domination globally and a framework of privileged elites and repressive regimes locally. The basic design of the "world order" that is sought to be organized includes both these dimensions. Indeed, neither could endure without the other. Each needs the other desperately; for both of them feel threatened with erosion in the wake of fundamental changes. Their hope is that they could somehow stem the tide through a process of convergence at the top.

TOWARDS A POLITICS OF TRANSFORMATION

What are the prospects of restructuring the world economic and political order in the face of what we have described as a situation of cumulative inequity? Are the developing countries doomed to a permanent state of dependence—economic, political and military and, hence, also in respect of distribution of natural resources, sources of energy, and technology, as well as in respect of their own culture and identity? The prospects of an alternative world system based on the twin principles of justice and nonviolence will depend crucially on the answers to these questions.

Working Out the Dialectic

The answers to these questions will depend very much on the capacity of both newly enfranchised states—still emerging from a colonial past and still struggling to achieve an independence based on national autonomy and economic self-reliance—and independent groups and movements in these as well as other societies to engage in a concerted effort against the "world order" pictured above. There should be no illusion about this being an easy process in any way. Those who believe that just because modern communications and technology have produced the conditions of a more integrated world, such a world will in fact come about, and those who romantically look for a "world community" in the middle of all the tensions and divisions are simply living in a world of make-believe. Any conception of a new world system, if it is to be realistically conceived, must be based on a perception of the conflicts that are inherent in the situation and the struggle that lies ahead.

On the other hand, those who throw their hands up in despair or feel overwhelmed by the forces of strife and evil that abound seem to underrate the dialectic that these very forces are already generating, a dialectic that will unfold more steadily and continuously as the growing awareness of both the inequity and the instability of the present system leads to a determined intervention in the historical process. There is little ground for complacency in the present situation, but there is no cause for fatalism either.

Even the process of erecting a "world order" according to the perceptions and prescriptions of Western strategists must contend with several opposite tendencies. For what is being sought after is a global system of privilege and power, based on co-opting the elites of the Third World in a global corporate structure through transfer of technology and armaments. The "interdependent" order thus erected will be expected to suppress forces of anarchy and revolution round the world. This is basically a highly defensive and, in some ways, a desperate model seeking to preserve a system that has become vulnerable and unstable and is beset with contradictions.

Identifying Contradictions

First of all, note has to be taken of the fact that at the heart of this system there is tension between the old-fashioned ideologues, keen to maintain Western supremacy by rallying to the cause of regimes like Rhodesia, South Africa and Israel, and pragmatic liberals willing to abandon these and to come to terms with the new facts of international life to make the best of it. The nature of American domestic politics, on the one hand, and the nature of the Palestinian question, on the other, as well as the close linkage between American security interests in the Indian Ocean and the white regime in South Africa generate compulsions that do not afflict other Western nations. This gives rise to tension within the Western world itself. Added to this is the growing divergence between the United States and other major centres of world capitalism, Japan and Western Europe, referred to earlier. The dominant position of US economic power in the world has declined with the rising cost of maintaining its imperial role. The defeat in Vietnam, the devaluation of the dollar in 1971, and the growing challenge from Japan and Western Europe seriously undermined the system created by the United States, and its capacity to influence the actions of others has suffered a steep decline. The divergence has grown further with the assertion of the Third World following the OPEC action in 1973.

Second, there is tension between the imperial core of the new "interdependent" order and the new elites that are sought to be accommodated in it. Thus even "stooges" have been keen to maintain an independent stance. The Shah of Iran, for example, saw great advantage in maintaining close links with other Asian and Third World powers; even the age-old rivalry between Iran and Iraq was undergoing some imaginative rethinking and readjustment. Similarly, the Saudis, traditional opponents of the Palestinians, have been under pressure for accepting the claims of the latter. The Saudis are certainly more conservative and keen on the American connection, but other oil-producing centres have shown greater independence and will not allow the Saudis to stray too far away from the OPEC establishment. In fact, the Saudis are engaged in a role that is at once conservative and progressive. While seeking to preserve what remains of the old international order, they have also been forging an Islamic front that is aimed—in part, of course—against the liberals and the leftists in the Arab world but essentially against Israel, the outpost of the West in West Asia and an ally of the US. Iran itself, armed to the hilt by the US, actually turned out to be increasingly less pliable to Western influence even under the Shah. Even so, the Shah was still seen as an agent of reaction and was swept off by one of the most dramatic populist revolutions of our time. It was a revolution that would perhaps have more far-reaching consequences internationally than domestically. Just as Vietnam put an end to the doctrine of limited wars, Iran may well put an end to the doctrine of collaborative imperialism.

Third, there is growing pressure from the Third World intellectuals and significant segments of even the ruling elites for a closing of ranks among the governments of the Third World. Several factors are contributing to this. The non-oil-producing and poorer among the Third World societies have shown considerable capacity for solidarity despite hardship. This is beginning to bring returns in the shape of a series of bilateral pacts and the creation of special funds. Some South and Southeast Asian countries have been enabled to export man-power and manufacturing and machine goods.

Again, despite the recycling of petro-dollars into Western investments and arms sales, a massive shift in capital and financial resources has taken place within the oil-producing societies and their neighbourhoods (in West Asia, Southeast Asia, West Africa and Latin America). This will have many consequences. The growth of welfare states in hitherto feudal and hierarchical societies, the pressure for greater equality within these states involving structural changes hitherto unheard of, the anomaly between a globally progressive position and a domestically elitist and repressive policy, and in all this the example and the role of technologically, educationally and politically advanced countries within the Third World—all are producing a new structure of collaboration covering various aspects of national and regional development. There seems to be a growing and widely shared sentiment against multinationals and against the West, especially America. Combined with the growth of democratic movements in these countries, all this is likely to add up to a growing ferment in the very societies on whose cooperation the Western-dominated "world order" is supposed to be based.

In fact, the whole concept of order and stability depending on a structure of management supported by the induction of the newly powerful into a pre-existing order is no longer valid, apart from being offensive to basic values and the dignity of diverse entities. The concept underrates two major movements that are gaining in power and momentum. One is the counter-assertion of national sovereignty and autonomy of hitherto suppressed and exploited societies. This constitutes the next phase in the revolution of the states system. The other is the growing delegitimization of the basic institutions and assumptions of social order that grew out of Western industrial capitalism and technology. The transformations that are inherent in the present historical stage can be steered towards a new order only by recognizing both these forces and moving towards a new political structure of the world based on the autonomy of diverse nations and a just social order based on a noncapitalist path of techno-economic development.

What we face, then, is a combination of objective changes in the world situation providing the conditions for a transformation in the existing arrangements and the emergence of a conscious desire for such transformation among many people round the world. The subjective factor is as important as the objective one. There is, on the one hand, a struggle between two opposite and powerful tendencies, one seeking to alter the framework of political and economic power, the other resisting such change by accommodating the more powerful among the new forces and, through such accommodation, trying to defeat the forces of revolutionary change. There is, on the other hand, a struggle going on in the minds of men, between an assertion of the utility of prevailing structures and the search for an alternative framework of human organization based on a new scale of values and priorities. There is a search, too, for new conceptions of development, power, technology and human destiny.

Movement for Change

It is from this combination of struggle for a new order that is already on and the emerging search for an alternative framework of ideas and institutions that can provide the ongoing struggle with a sense of direction and purpose that a new historical epoch is likely to emerge. As was mentioned earlier, it is going to be a difficult and tortuous struggle. The conditions may be propitious, but the process is by no means assured. It calls for a widespread movement for change—in the developing countries, in the centres of industrial and military power, in the various world bodies, and in the framework of public opinion, attitudes and beliefs at various levels. Such a movement will have to encompass both the basic perception of the human condition in our time and the strategies for redesigning it. It will involve both an intellectual effort, aimed at reorienting basic concepts and interpretations of the objective reality, and a political effort, aimed at altering the framework of objective reality itself.

Furthermore, such a movement will have to be directed principally at two major components of the present scenario of tension between and within societies and, of course, cumulative injustice: (1) the arms race and the militarization of regimes and social structures; and (2) the structure of economic exploitation and political domination. The battle for demilitarization and an equitable and just order must first be fought and won in the minds of men. Without it, whatever gains may be made will be illusory, or ephemeral, or both. Demilitarization of the mind is a necessary prerequisite of demilitarization of regions and regimes. Without it, there will be no guarantee that even if some de-escalation of the arms race took place, it would not soon be reversed. Similarly, the struggle for economic equity and political autonomy must be waged at the level of consciousness and normative perception as well as in concrete situations of encounters of power and resources. Without it, there will be no guarantee that even if a just social order was created, it would not soon be toppled. Perceptions of reality more often than not shape reality; they must undergo a profound change if changes in reality are to be successfully carried out and are to endure.

It should be realized that the power of the status quo has always been largely derived from its capacity to control subjective perceptions, beliefs and myths, and to induce in those who oppose it a feeling that the situation is hopeless, that the course of history is set, and that any attempt to change its course will only invite backlash and repression from those in control of institutions and channels of information and communication. A closer look at the historical situation will, however, show that it is the fear of change that terrifies those who preside at the status quo, especially when they know that it is becoming unstable and precarious. To prevent the upsetting of their apple-cart, they try to transmit their own fear of change among their opponents. It is for those who are opposed to the existing system to perceive the objective forces at work, canalize the discontent with the existing arrangements into a movement for change, inspire confidence in their ranks by building an oppositional movement based on a conception of an alternative future, and forge a coalition of interests opposed to the status quo with a view to engaging in a sustained intervention in the historical process.

Vision of an Alternative Future

The elements of an alternative perspective, proposed as a model for the future, are fairly well known and have been the subject of a great deal of writing and discussion in the last several years. It is a perspective based on the realization of a set of values. Important among these are minimization of violence and elimination of the war system; maximization of justice and equity in economic arrangements at both national and international levels; a decentralized and participant political structure, operating at various levels, with sufficient provision for the rights of individuals, minorities, dissidents and diverse social and national units; and a model of technology and development that is in keeping with an integral view of the natural environment and an equally integral view of human diversities and the distinctiveness of cultures.

Underlying this value-predisposition is a non-manipulative view of knowledge and of science. Integral to it is a view of prosperity and well-being that is non-acquisitive and that is restrained by a control of personal gratification and sensual desires, and an approach to power that ensures the widest possible sharing between, and participation of, diverse units, and unequivocally rejects the view of politics as a zero-sum game.

When we conceive of contemporary historical change as emanating from the end of Western domination, we have in mind more than a mere shift in the regional balance of power. The end of the era of Western dominance must also mean an end of the dominant Western world-view based on the theory of progress and the ethic of individualism. It also means the abandonment of the related assumptions of the relationship between knowledge and power, on the ends of economic activity, and on the structure and management of politics and the nature of the state. Here, too, the basic point is not simply that the dominant Western paradigm, and the *praxis* based on it, violates the values stated above; it is also that they have ceased to be workable and are no longer valid.

There is need to move to a different approach to both the general theoretical paradigm of man-in-society and the *praxis* based on it. Such a paradigm and *praxis* should provide for not just a more preferred structure of reality, but also for one that is conceptually more valid and, on simply pragmatic grounds, more stable and durable. The global movement for a just world discussed above thus becomes a comprehensive movement for change towards such a world, a movement that will provide a transition to a new kind of world system, a transition totally different from the one that is being forged by the Trilateralists in the US and other regions and their tactical collaborators in the socialist countries. Hence, the conception of this being an oppositional movement based on an alternative perspective.

A New Coalition

This brings us to the central issue in the transition to an alternative future—namely, forging a coalition of interests opposed to the status quo. For the notion of a global movement is meaningless unless it takes into account the great divisions and the appalling disparities that characterize the present states system. There is, therefore, need both to support the struggle of the under-privileged and exploited stratum of the states system against the privileged and the exploiting stratum and to accept the fact of different and often opposite strategies adopted by differentially positioned groups of actors.

To think of globalism in a passive way (as simply emanating from the communications and technological revolutions that have a global reach, or as something forced by a perilous arms race that has a global sweep and hence calls for a global solution), or in terms of other pessimistic scenarios (such as "limits to growth" because of a worsening relationship between population and resources and the consequent spectre of hunger and malnutrition) is an exercise in wishful thinking and is symptomatic of loss of will to face the real issues. And to plead, on the basis of such scenarios of the future, for global management of human affairs through co-operation and "interdependence" (among the existing states and their ruling elites) is to acquiesce in a foreclosure of all attempts to change the world order of the purveyors of the status quo. It is to accept defeat even before the battle for a structural transformation of the system has been joined.

The projected model of globalism and "world order" seeks to perpetuate international hegemonies, class exploitation within and between nations, and structures of governance that are repressive and inhumane. Such an order is designed to ward off movements from below of exploited classes, peoples and nations and the assertion of their rights, including the right of national sovereignty and "collective self-reliance" by countries whose economies and polities are affected by an international structure of domination and exploitation. Without such a combative self-assertion by exploited nations, *tied closely to movements for structural change within nations*, globalism and world orderism will remain a recipe for management of the globe through an oligarchy of governing elites. We must reject such a diabolical conception of globalism.

As pointed out earlier in this paper, even the idealistic and extremely well-meaning proponents of globalism and world order have unwittingly contributed to such a conception. Their view of nationalism and assertion of state power as inherently inimical to the attainment of a just and peaceful world does not take enough cognizance either of the deep divisions and antagonisms that characterize the present world or of the necessity of first dealing with them. Their enthusiastic support of the newfangled diversionary slogan of "fulfilment of basic needs of the poor" and their near-contempt (unspoken, of course) for the political elites of the Third World have also served to legitimize a managerial and apolitical perspective on the world and its problems. We must reject both their analyses and prescriptions.

Instead, consciously and as an essential part of conceptualizing the *world problematique*, we should recognize the basic contradictions and historical antagonisms of the present world system and seek to make them the basis of a creative dialectic. We need to recognize, for instance, that movements of national self-determination and regional self-reliance in the Third World are necessary preconditions for a more just and humane world. And we need to recognize this as part of differential situations obtaining in different parts of the world, and consequent conflicts of interest between different national and regional groupings—the new setting of class conflict according to many.

The perception that the transformation of our time arises from the disintegration of the nation-state system is, of course, not without an element of truth in it. But it is a perception that needs to be informed by another and deeper perception—namely, that the crisis we face is a crisis in the states system evolved in, and radiated from, Europe and that the challenge we face is one of moving towards a new states system, at once more diffuse and participant and more co-operation-based and integrated. But it is not possible to move towards such a world without first going through the dialectic based on the counter-assertion of national and regional identities and solidarities through a new coalition of power comprising hitherto submerged political and economic entities, both in the Third World and elsewhere. As was stated in an important document of the World Order Models Project (WOMP):[3]

> The perspective on nationalism should be dependent on the context: what is to be urged or discouraged in a Northern industrial context obviously differs from the things that should be sought or avoided in Southern Africa, the Middle East, or South Asia. We are not for or against nationalism *per se*; it depends on its given roles in each context separately considered. State power may thwart equality in one part of the world and conceivably promote and protect it in another. What is true of nationalism and statism also applies to a variety of other "isms" and "movements": liberalism, feminism, peace movement, ecology movement. We cannot generalize beyond context, nor beyond the specific relation between means and ends necessary to bring a just world system into being. Very often difficult tradeoffs have to be made, and the perspective of one group may fail to impress another dominated by wholly different priorities, but there is no substitute for a politics that begins with the actual

needs and aspirations of peoples in their various world situations. Unless this kind of messy politics with a variety of agendas is accepted as the basis for a transition movement, all efforts are bound to be parochial and futile. It is necessary to build from the interplay of diversities and linkages that are very much the essence of the contemporary world system. Those who defend the status quo seem able to put together that kind of coalition politics; progressive peoples and groups should surely be able to match capacity. Unless they do, the prospects for humane change will remain dubious indeed.[4]

A Strategy of Intervention

What should be the various components of such coalition politics, based on the "interplay of diversity and linkages," together producing the movement for transition to a just world? Who are to be the principal agents of change? Who will work on what agenda? From what sites and at which levels of world reality will they work?

These questions take us beyond the *diagnosis* of human problematique in our time (without which, of course, not much is possible) into "what is to be done," by whom, and how? There is little doubt that the forces of change at work in our time shall, given the will and confidence and a perspective of history, transform the world.

Indicators of such change are many, and they cover a large spectrum of sociopolitical space. Among these are: (a) the growing sense of power in the Third World following decolonization made particularly salient by the economic challenge of OPEC and related phenomena; (b) the gathering crisis in global power relations, emanating from the last phase of national liberation movements, and the grim battle for the values of freedom and dignity in large parts of Africa and the Middle East; (c) the disenchantment of the intelligentsia, the youth and the unemployed round the world with the established order; (d) militant movements of civil disobedience and nonviolent action against nuclear power and the thoughtless arms race; (e) the growing sentiment against the power and high technology of the multinationals, which undermine cultural diversity and indigenous traditions of freedom and self-reliance; (f) the alternatives movement at the grass roots of several societies affecting life-styles, institutional frameworks and cultural assumptions underlying the Western scientific and technological paradigm; (g) the secessionist movements in the North and the movements for civil and political rights of peoples and against authoritarian and collaborative regimes in the South; (h) the growing realization, in the UN bodies, on the part of independently inclined countries within both capitalist and socialist worlds as well as a growing number of international civil servants, of the imperative, on the one hand, to heed the just demands of the Third World and, on the other hand, to arrest the global spread of militarization and the technology of repression; and (i) the permeation of all this into the thinking of influential non-officials, religious leaders and the mass media in the imperial and metropolitan centres themselves.

There is little doubt that, while these forces of change are at work, powerful interests and entrenched elites are engaged in resisting any major reordering of power relations and patterns of economic and cultural domination. If the clash between these opposite tendencies is not to result in massive violence and repression, and if the world is to move towards a genuine alternative to the present states system and its technological and cultural apparatus, it is essential to devise a strategy of intervention that forces the status quo to yield to the forces of transformation in a manner that is less catastrophic and more constructive. This is not impossible, given the demonstrable defensiveness of the upholders of status quo, but it does call for a set of interventions from a variety of sites, resulting in a new coalition of interests and a *politics* that involves a large number of actors occupying strategic positions in various regions and at various levels. It is necessary that the interventions be based on an assessment of the unfolding historical process, and that they seek to strengthen certain processes (different in different parts of the world) which are already under way but which may not yet be seen as complementary to each other and as part of a common endeavour. It is necessary to consciously perceive them as components of an overall strategy of intervention in the working of history and incorporate them in the movement for change.

Third World Initiatives

The main spur to such a movement must without doubt come from the peoples of the Third World who have borne the brunt of more than two hundred years of virtually planned underdevelopment (planned by others) and are today victims of a global system of inequity and exploitation. The task facing these countries today is to actualize their known opportunities for throwing off the incubus of history. It is by now obvious that these opportunities cannot be utilized, much less optimized, unless the countries and regions of the Third World close ranks, lend a helping hand to each other, and deal unitedly with the threat of pre-emptive measures held out by the status quo powers.

Individually, most of these countries are vulnerable; collectively, they can be formidable. These countries constitute a majority of nation-states—representing a majority of the human race—and are in a position to command weight and respect in international forums. Also, between themselves the countries of the Third World encompass a wide range of capabilities, actual and potential, both in the domain of modern knowledge and its application and in the domain of traditional know-hows, models and technologies some of which are quite rich and sophisticated and have been evolved over centuries to deal with basic needs of human collectivities.

Somehow, the considerable scope for co-operation, joint exercises, collaborative research in alternative models, and the pooling of political visions and economic opportunities has not been explored. The notion that "beggars" can't help each other is based not only on a colonized psyche that looks with indifference and even disdain at one's own and other Third World societies and peoples and with awe and deference at the Western and the socialist world. It is based also on ignorance of both the great diversity in levels of development between the countries of the Third World (some of these countries even suffer from surpluses which they do not know how to handle) and the rather limited scope of, and considerable frustration in, developing profitable economic relations with the industrialized world.

Even some of the proponents of the "New International Economic Order" (NIEO) seem to suffer from the hang-over of the colonial mind, still seeking transfers of technology as well as greater allocations of aid from the industrialized countries. They put too little emphasis on pursuing lines of co-operation among the Third World societies. (The Group of 77 itself suffers grievously from such an orientation.) It is only when the pursuit of a new international order is based primarily on mutual co-operation and the sense of Third World solidarity, and collective self-reliance that it generates, that the global structure of dependence and inequity can be ended, new paths of development based on new thinking developed, and a new confidence generated within the Third World. And once this happens, the elites of the Third World can feel more secure and, instead of turning their countries into military fortresses in a vast desert of economic misery and underdevelopment, direct their energies to discovering latent resources that lie beneath their lands and oceans, utilize their immense man-power for their economic betterment, and eventually find their rightful place and standing in the world by dint of their own strength.

Domestic Transformation

Crucial to this whole effort is the ability of Third World countries to attend to their internal problems, to move rapidly toward economic policies that will raise levels of satisfaction, to develop durable political structures that can provide a sense of integral wholeness to diverse entities of language, tribe and religion without in any way undermining them, and to contain sources of turmoil and turbulence by evolving appropriate decentralized structures of participation. There is a close linkage between success on these fronts internally and success in achieving autonomy externally.

The concept of dependencia in explaining the present plight of the developing countries has been an important contribution of Latin American and African intellectuals to development theory. But it is necessary not to overstretch this concept. There is a serious danger of its being used as a total explanation of all Third World ills, and its being made into rationalization for inaction. Such an attitude is widely prevalent among Third World intellectuals who are prone to pass the responsibility for improving the state of their societies to the metropolitan centres. In a deep sense this is a survival of the colonial psychology. For the fact of the matter is that, historical analysis notwithstanding, "they" can do little to improve the lot of the people in the Third World. The issue of autonomy cannot be resolved that way. It can be resolved by positive self-assertion in one's own arena, internal transformations inspired by fresh and indigenous thinking, integration of efforts between similarly placed countries and, overarching all this, struggle with external sources of exploitation and underdevelopment.

Indeed, quite a large part of the struggle for equity and basic human rights by deprived groups will need to be waged in domestic political and economic settings. A "new international order" is not possible without reordering domestic societies. This reordering is bound to affect the global framework of power. It will open up opportunities of undermining the present structures of dominance and dependence and defeating the new design of global management (we have seen that a crucial element of the proposed corporate world structure is the co-optation of dominant elites from the socialist and Third World societies). It will make it possible for Third World societies to move out of a uniform conception and a fixed paradigm of human development, born out of the age of European enlightenment and expanding outwards. As this happens, nations will begin to value alternative world-views and alternative paradigms of science and technology and civilizational perspectives, and, instead, draw upon them for the benefit of the world as a whole.

It seems that we are already at such a turning-point in history. There are several indicators of this: the awakening of consciousness and an emerging sense of potency among the powerless of the world; the rising tide of democratic aspirations in hierarchically structured societies; the spontaneous revulsion of millions of peoples against authoritarian regimes claiming their legitimacy in the name of "progress" and "modernization"—all or several of them exemplified by the sweeping defeat of Indira Gandhi in India in 1977 and by the Iranian Revolution against the powerful Shah in 1979. One consequence of such an awakening at the grass-roots of societies is a fundamental delegitimization of age-old institutions, symbols and myths. Another is the emerging awareness of the existence of like-minded peoples in neighbouring countries and even more distant parts of the world, and of opportunities for forging new modes of co-operation for building a more humane world. This *has* to happen first domestically in a few centres and then, by the weight of example and demonstrated capacities for change and aggregation of new experiences, in the world at large. In any event, the reordering of the international order and the existing states system will depend crucially on fundamental transformations in the domestic social, economic and political structures of Third World countries.

A very large number of these societies carry the burden of enormous excretions of the historical process, large pools of stagnant and oppressive social structures, and, in many cases, *indigenous* traditions of centralization, militarism and structural violence. All these have received a new lease on life from the contemporary global conditions of scarcity and plunder and exploitation as well as from the intense rivalry for local status and power in the face of new ideologies of social transformation and human dignity. Without in any way succumbing to cultural and technological invasions from outside, there is need to put one's own house in order and to operationalize the values one stands for in regional and international forums in one's own local setting.

Indeed, this is the only real setting available to one for initiating any movement for change, including a global movement. In this lies the true source of legitimacy for waging a larger movement at other levels. The rhetoric of confrontation that at present envelops the reality of a deep sense of inferiority and frustration in the Third World will then give place to a dignified and responsible posture that is derived from real strength gained through common effort aimed at undoing the deep dualism of the present world. This will also make it possible to identify areas of common interest between the Third World and the rest of the world, giving rise to a new structure of international co-operation.

GLOBAL ALLIANCE FOR A NEW INTERNATIONAL ORDER

The rationale for such co-operation is already being articulated on grounds other than a romantic or a manipulative predisposition towards globalism. The re-emergence of the spectre of scarcity in the Western world, the realization of "inverse dependence" of the West on raw-material producing nations (and the uncovering of the West's vulnerability), the perception that shortages of essential resources and maladies like unemployment and chronic inflation—even hunger—are global in scope and reflect a basic crisis in technological capitalism, and, above all, the widespread consensus on the danger of a limitless arms race arising out of relentless competition for global and regional hegemonies—all are leading to a growing sense of crisis, not only among sensitive thinkers of the West, but also in larger currents of public opinion and influential political groups in the Western world.

As such a sense of crisis spreads, it should be possible to drive home the point that extremes of inequity are not only morally indefensible but politically unwise, and that if a global class war is to be avoided it is necessary to accept the compelling logic of the spokesmen of, and for, the Third World for restructuring the international economic and political order. It is a logic that should make sense first of all to those in the Western countries who have waged, and are waging, a struggle for equity at home. There is already evidence of the growth of a new kind of global humanism in some of these countries—Scandinavia, the Netherlands and other smaller European countries—where the voices of reason and compassion and the values of equity and justice have struck roots in domestic policy-making and can therefore be extended to the formulation of foreign policy as well. These countries also supply a number of devoted individuals working in UN agencies, international organizations involved in North-South economic relations, and in a variety of nongovernmental organizations (NGOs). In a number of other countries, too, there are sizeable and fairly influential groups that are pressing for a positive relationship with the Third World—in the new regimes of Spain, Portugal and Greece, in the UK and Canada, and even France, though here the reasons are more complex.

It is necessary to both deepen and broaden this humanism (which still tends to be conceived in static forms such as foreign aid and technology transfer) into the forging of a political alignment that springs from a clearer understanding of a common stake in moving towards a new world order, and that is alive to the need for sustained co-operation to achieve that end. A majority of the countries of Europe—not merely in Western but also in Eastern Europe—can contribute a lot to such a consummation, if they choose to move away from being passive partners of the two military giants that have held the whole world to

ransom for a quarter century to being active partners with the great civilizations of the South, with whom they have in the long run much more in common than with these giants.

As such a new alignment takes shape, the importance of military power will
be reduced, and it may become possible to move towards global disarmament.
The real danger to the world arises less from diffusion of power, at which
Western strategists seem to be worried, than from its immense concentration—and that, too, in a largely physical form. The diffusion also has its dangers so long as it is largely physical and military. As the diffusion spreads along
economic, technological and social dimensions, and finds its moorings in a
widely shared set of values, it should pave the way for greater confidence at all
levels and, on that basis, a greater and more genuine sense of common destiny.

Reordering the World Compass

What was implicit in the foregoing should be made explicit here. The
mobilization of international support for deconcentration and diffusion of
power in the world arena, and the concomitant changes in the techno-
economic structures of the world, should necessarily extend to the communist
world. Here, too, with the break-down of the old monolith and the emergence
of a more plural structure (as in the Western world), there is a growing concern
with the reordering of world economic and political relations. There is need
now to enlist this latent support in the communist world for active partnership
in the new alignment for global change. The point that needs to be driven
home with respect to these countries is that their commitment to socialist
transformation needs to be once again affirmed in global terms. This will involve a shift in the old doctrine of a world revolution by taking cognizance of
the regionalization of global class conflict. It entails moving towards a more
eclectic strategy of global change so that it is sensitive to the aspirations of the
Third World. It involves their active participation in the North-South debate,
in international economic institutions, and in the non-aligned movement. The
role of Yugoslavia in this respect is, of course, critical and widely recognized.
But it should not be difficult to persuade countries as far removed in their
respective ideological stances on the East-West conflict as Rumania and Cuba
to support the movement for a new international order. Indeed, the political
isolation of the two countries, and others like them, on the East-West axis can
be broken by their more open involvement in the North-South axis. This will
contribute significantly to global change.

Of particular importance in this respect is the role of China. Thanks partly to
its preoccupation with the Soviet Union and partly to its search for a place in
the global framework of technological and military power (a framework that
was first laid out by the West and then accepted by the Soviet Union), China
poses the danger of playing a counter-revolutionary role in the global struggle
for a more just and equitable world order. It is necessary that the quite considerable links that countries of the Third World have with China should be
utilized to make China resume its revolutionary role in the North-South

dimension of world politics, even if it is forced to join forces with the US and other Western countries in the East-West conflict.

Significant Actors

In this process of channelling elements in the East-West conflict for reordering the techno-economic and political power relations along the North-South axis, an important role will have to be played by the emerging power centres in the Third World itself. The major centres of wealth and power in the Middle East and other important members of the OPEC, new regional groupings (such as the ASEAN bloc of countries, provided they act in close co-operation with Vietnam, on the one hand, and India, on the other), and countries like India are all capable of exercising leverage in restructuring global and regional balances, especially in respect of trade and commodity flows, production of basic necessities and raw materials, competition for markets, as well as in respect of military and strategic matters.

Several factors have combined to enable India in particular to move out of its rather limited role as a regional power and take on a global role: its pivotal position in the non-aligned movement, its consistent support of liberation movements in Africa, its network of economic and technical co-operation in Asia and Africa, its potential for making an imaginative use of its scientific, industrial and nuclear capabilities, and its political and moral stance in the United Nations and on issues like disarmament and human rights. In the years to come, it can re-establish close ties with China, respond to revolutionary and democratic movements in the Persian gulf region, and, along with China, try to draw Japan into Asian economic reconstruction.

The issue before the emerging centres of economic and political power in the Third World is this: are they going to be co-opted in the world order of status quo, or are they going to align themselves with the forces of change and revolution? Intellectuals of these regions and leaders of various progressive movements (anti-poverty movements, human-rights movements, alternative-technology movements) should see to it that they choose the latter, not the former.

Penetrating the Centre

If the alliance for change laid out above takes effect, it should be possible to influence the thinking and action even at the heart of the present system. A combination of the centrifugal pulls at the monoliths over which they preside with their reduced capacity to co-opt regional powers can well make the superpowers themselves see reason in the demands for reordering existing economic and political relations along both the North-South and the East-West axes of the world compass.

The Soviet Union has been deflected, over the last two decades, from playing its role as a revolutionary world power, thanks largely to its excessive fear of the technological and military superiority of the West. True, it still continues to support liberation movements in the Third World; true, also, that it has, on balance, aligned itself with the Third World on many issues. But, at the same time, it has been indifferent to the prevailing inequitable world order, and at least on two critical dimensions—the struggle for a new economic order and the Third World stance on the questions of nuclear proliferation and global disarmament—it has supported the status quo position. It has also occasionally used some Third World countries as pawns in its global power game. In consequence, detente between the two superpowers has turned out to be a device for freezing the North-South divide. It is necessary that pressure be mounted on the Soviet Union by Third World countries whose friendship it needs badly—India, Vietnam, Angola, the liberation fronts in Zimbabwe, Namibia and South Africa, and, above all, Cuba—for enlisting its support on behalf of the pro-changers in the North-South conflict.

Even in the United States and among its allies there is scope for building public opinion against the status quo as well as against policies designed to undermine the forces of change that are emerging in various parts of the world. The fact that these are liberal democracies does not guarantee that such public opinion will necessarily influence official policies. The capacity of bourgeois governments to manipulate their peoples—and the peoples of other nations—through corporate structures of economic and technological power and communications media is well known. Yet, in a plural polity there is a possibility of influencing opinion at various levels and instilling some realism in official and semi-official thinking.

Thus, the very fact that the powers that be in the US and in other Western democracies find it necessary to employ the rhetoric of "reconstructing the world order" and to keep in check their capacity to mount a backlash against the economically powerful or the ideologically left-wing regimes in the Third World suggests that they no longer take Western pre-eminence for granted. The fact that military strategists in the West are anxious about the growing diffusion of technological and strategic power into the Third World regions lends support to the inference. The task before the Third World influential centres, before China, and politically visible dissident groups and movements within the US and Western Europe is to strengthen the more liberal and globally sensitive lobbies in the US. The voice of the global alliance for change must ultimately penetrate the very apex of the present world order. There should be no illusion about this being an easy task. But if the present structures of inequity are to be shaken, and if the frightening concentration of military and strategic power is to be brought to an end, there is no escape from extending the movement for a just world to the United States itself.

Catalysts of Change

In delineating the various components of the politics of global transformation, we have deliberately focused attention so far on the reordering of the states system. For, despite the growing realization among the leaders of opinion round the world of the necessity of change, and despite a significantly positive shift in subjective predispositions and preferences of large segments of the global population that may come about through the cumulative influence of various movements of change, a just world order will remain in the realm of utopia. It is only when an impact has been made on the world political processes such that it leads to the emergence of a new coalition of interests powerful enough to reorder the *structure* of authority and power in the world that a just order will have moved from the realm of utopia to the realm of action.

There is little doubt that the efficacy of movements for change depends crucially on a proper understanding of the forces of change that are already at work. Much depends, too, on a coherent theory of intervention for translating potentiality into reality. For, while no historical change ever comes about by merely wishing it (because it is determined by specific changes in the structure of reality), its precise direction, as also the extent of human suffering involved in it, depends very much on a conscious intervention by a set of actors informed by a clear perspective and a clear vision and possessed of a vibrant sensibility to the hard choices involved in the intervention.

In fact, the movement for intervention in the global structure will have to be thought of as a *process* involving constant interaction between ideational and activist work, between opinion catalysts and mass mobilizers and political decision-makers, between the paradigm of thought and the paradigm of action. This is the way all major structural changes and cultural transformations have come about.

The role of the intelligentsia in this process is indeed crucial. It is in this stratum of society that identities transcending individual, group, class and national interests are to be found—identities that are conscious of the conflicts generated by the historical process, of the irrationality and injustice of the status quo, and of the necessity of change.

Needless to say, not all intellectuals have developed the capacity of transcending the boundaries of narrow interests for the sake of more global communities of interest. As a matter of fact, a very large number of highly educated people with a middle class background, including a wide array of scientists and professionals, are employed for defending the prevailing institutional order, perfecting the instruments of domination, and for providing expertise to repressive regimes, military establishments, multinational corporations and international institutions designed to perpetuate the status quo. And yet, it is from the intellectual and scientific community that new ideas about ordering society based on a holistic perspective on the human condition, integrating diverse trends into a comprehensive framework of analysis and action can emerge. The need for intellectuals to do so is urgent now as never before. They should use their demonstrated capacity to rise above narrow class and sectional interests at the service of larger causes in different domains—anti-colonial, civil rights, anti-war and environment movements, the struggle for emancipation of workers and peasants and the poor in general, women's rights movement in the West, integrationist movements at national and regional levels in the Third World. They will thus provide a new cultural orientation for a comprehensive global movement for a just world.

Once such a coalition of the various movements of ideas is joined in terms of a larger community of interest and acquires an identity (provided, of course, that it has a clear and candid perception of the conflicts that are inherent in the situation and that must be dealt with and resolved through a set of policy initiatives and action profiles), it should not be difficult to relate the same to the emergent coalition of power for moving towards a new international political and economic order. Intellectuals have a major role to play in catalysing this process.

The catalytic role of the intellectual and scientific community spelt out above is more or less in line with what was delineated in earlier periods by men as diverse as Marx (with his conception of de-classing and his definition of the task of philosophers as world changers), Mannheim (with his idea of "freefloating intelligentsia" engaged in a global movement for "fundamental democratization"), and Gandhi (with his indictment of the middle classes for their over-intellectualization and his call to them to find their salvation through identifying with the struggling masses). At the same time, it is necessary to insist once again that mere enlightenment and commitment to change are insufficient conditions for change, and are often likely to lead to idealistic images of the future which, because they are not grounded in real confrontations, may turn out to be either wholly utopian or, as argued earlier in respect of the advocates of world order, may play in the hands of the strategists of a new imperial design.

The point is to link the domain of ideas, with its normative and didactic interventions, to the domain of action in which various movements for transformation are already engaged. This will serve to bring to the latter a sense of the larger struggle for a more equitable and just world. The role of the intellectual in history is a modest one, though no doubt critical. It is limited to catalysing possibilities that are latent in the situational reality, making them part of the stream of consciousness, and propelling interventions in the light of such consciousness by those whose vocation it is to act and intervene.

Let us then locate the intellectual task in the framework of the ongoing movements for change. There is no space here to discuss any of these in detail, and all we can do is to identify important movement groups in different parts and at various levels that have some relevance to the global movement for a just world.

MOVEMENTS FOR CHANGE: THEIR TASKS

There is already evidence of the globalization of concern on major issues that divide the world and cry for consensus on the actions needed to compose the differences and conflicts so that national and international bodies can work towards a common framework of policy and action. This is suggested by the series of world conferences on environment, population, food, water, habitat, law of the sea, desertification, employment, science and technology, status of women and condition of the child, besides the special sessions of the UN General Assembly on a new international economic order, disarmament, and a new international development strategy for the 1980s. The task is to move from endless debate on vital issues—which can, and do in fact, often become a device for defusing energy and blocking the forces for change from gaining momentum—to consciously relating informed opinion and action to various movements for change and making them part of a more comprehensive movement for a just world.

Peace, Disarmament and Anti-militarism

There exists a widespread peace movement, especially in the North (in both the Western world and Eastern Europe as well as in Japan and Australasia). There is also a growing movement in these countries, including non-violent non-co-operation, against nuclear power both in its military and in its civilian forms. To these should be joined the activities of a wide variety of groups concerned with the growing militarization of the Third World. This militarization has serious implications for regional peace and solidarity, autonomy of these regions falling prey to a new dependency based on wholesale transfers of arms and military technology, and, above all, for the growth of repressive regimes in the Third World bolstered by the strategists of world hegemony who are seeking to meet the challenge of the Third World by introducing or strengthening the virus of militarism and fantasies of regional hegemony.

There is a tendency among Third World intellectual and political leaders to think of disarmament as a problem for the rich countries alone, and to take a back seat in negotiations on it. Nothing could suit the superpowers and their allies better. Because their domination over the world power structure depends crucially on the perpetuation of the world military order, they are keen to co-opt new centres of power into it. This is what accounts for the relative unpreparedness of Third World governments at the time of the UN Special Session on Disarmament in 1978, for which they had been long clamouring, and for their failure to wrest any commitments from the superpowers. It is essential to coalesce the movement for global peace and disarmament, the movement against nuclearization in the Western and Eastern segments of the North, and the struggle against militarism in the Third World, and then to relate them all to the more generic movement for a just world.

Equity and Justice

We have in this chapter dwelt at length on the emerging struggle for greater equity in distribution of resources, control over techno-economic relations, and the institutional framework for a new international order. We would only like to add that there is a close interrelationship between the spectre of militarism and the spectre of poverty and inequity. War and militarism cannot be wiped out in an unjust world, one in which large-scale technology and ostentatious consumption standards of one segment of the world make even moderate rates of development and minimum standards of living in another segment unrealizable. Meanwhile, the bottling up of global resources in a mad race for military and technological prowess *within* the North makes both peace and the eradication of poverty on a global scale equally unrealizable. It is essential, therefore, to link the movements for disarmament and demilitarization to the movements for economic justice and technological reform.

Alternatives in Development

Such a perspective on a common struggle for peace and justice at the level of the macro structures of the world should find a very large constituency of support across the world's regions in thousands of groups operating at micro levels and the grass-roots of society. All of these want to move away from the murderous course on which the new corporatism – based, as pointed out early in this paper, on new conceptions of statism, technological capitalism, global militarism and transnational intelligence networks – is set. Literally hundreds of thousands of the world's youth, scientists, ecologists and plain seekers of a more humane quality of life are engaged in fascinating experiments with new sources of energy, more wholesome technology, recycling of resources, austere life-styles and a conception of community that is at once global and mindful of cultural diversity and individual freedom. Equally important are the experiments, again being pursued all over the world, in alternative modes of education, systems of health and housing, and the planning of human space and ecosystems of town and country.

Alternatives in development should not be perceived as just a path to be followed by Third World societies alone because of their different factor combinations. They must be perceived rather as a movement that has a world-wide relevance, given the fact that it has grown out of the excesses to which modern man has pushed technology and the science of economics all over the world. Without such a universal perspective, there is little chance of the movement succeeding. For Third World countries will refuse to be treated as "second class citizens" of the world and will predictably engage in the suicidal path of "catching up" with the so-called "developed" world, in the process joining the race to hasten the collapse of the biosphere, the demise of the integrity of diverse cultures – and ultimately of civilization itself.

There is need, therefore, for *a new social contract* between world regions in which, while the essential infrastructures of agrarian and industrial productivity and devices that put an end to human drudgery are to be widely shared, there is also an agreement on limits to the more wasteful, socially inequitable and environmentally hazardous techno-systems and consumer life-styles. Once such a social contract is arrived at, the various micro experiments will cease to be movements of marginalized or dissident groups; they will begin to contribute to the larger stream of consciousness concerned with creating a more humane world. In a world torn by massive inequity and the war system, it is difficult to appreciate the fundamental search in which the grass-roots experimenters are engaged; they are seeking to find answers to the serious problems of the present to avoid a horrendous future, a future that is more likely than not to visit us fairly soon unless the movements for disarmament and development and the new international order build into their agenda a concern with science and technology, the environment, and life-styles. It is only with such convergence that the more comprehensive movement for a just world can acquire momentum and depth.

Socio-economic Movements and the NIEO

It would be a serious mistake to think of the movement for a just world in terms of strict rationality, as something that everyone will agree with if only they saw reason—in short, as an essentially managerial and technical exercise. It is important to remember that all such movements are essentially political, that they span major areas of conflict in which the purveyors of the status quo will seek to prevent any major transformation of the present order. This applies as much, and perhaps even more, to alternative conceptions of technology, life-style, education and health and systems of planning, especially if they are not limited to the Third World and are designed to coalesce with the struggle for a new international order. Thus, it is interesting to note that the establishment in the Western world became highly receptive to the basic needs approach to development only after they saw the demand for a new international order gaining ground and challenging the existing states system and corporate power. They would likewise be willing to go along with the self-reliance school in the Third World; for it, like the basic needs school, leaves the global structure of power and resources largely unaffected. For the same reason, they would support "intermediate" or "appropriate" technology for the Third World.

Hence the need to conceive of the alternatives movement as an essential part of a global movement for a just world. And the same applies to the basic needs and self-reliance schools of thought. While these concepts are of great value in correcting domestic imbalances and inequities and states of economic dependence—we have argued early in this section that this is the crucial arena for any movement of change—they should not be allowed to be used for perpetuating global dualism and quarantining the South from the cosy affluence and political stability of the North. All such movements—alternatives in development, basic needs, self-reliance—should be seen as parts of the global struggle for justice, never in isolation.

Sectoral Movements

By the same token, it is necessary to build into the larger framework of the movement various movements of an earlier vintage which seem to have lost relevance of late but which are essential to any struggle for equity and justice. The most important among these is the struggle of the working class, but no less important are the youth movements in various parts of the world, the peasant movements, the movements of minorities in multi-racial and multi-ethnic societies, and the movement for women's rights in urban industrialized societies. Now many of these movements are in danger of being co-opted by the managers of the status quo. Trade unions are found to be militant opponents of the rights of the unemployed—the immigrants and the rural poor who are outside the organized sector; they seem to have lost their earlier militancy and have acquired a stake in the capitalist order. Their short-term calculations have cut them adrift from the global struggle against poverty and injustice. The same applies, though in different forms, to the youth, civil rights and women's movements for greater equality within the national settings of capitalist societies. Although, no doubt, in each more global perspectives have been held out by some enlightened advocates of the cause, especially by those who also happen to participate in transnational interactions, all are, more often than not, highly ethno-centric in their perceptions; and all have failed to detach themselves from the highly competitive ethos of Western egalitarianism which militates against a truly global perspective.

It is essential to mobilize these powerful unionist strains in Western capitalism by invoking new symbols for their militancy and by disabusing them of the misleading calculus they have been led to believe in. According to the Marxist analysis, for instance, the proportionate share in national income and wealth of the working classes in Western Europe has remained more or less static despite the rapid strides made by these societies, that the increase in their absolute living standards has been largely at the expense of the world's poor and unemployed (including those at home), and that the real beneficiaries of both domestic increase in productivity and international transfers have been the world's middle classes—against whom they should be waging their battles. Behind the domination of the global middle class are the multinational corporations that have spread technologies making at once for a sprawling tertiary sector (not least in poor societies) and for massive unemployment, in the process stimulating in the working classes of affluent societies the craving for a middle class life-style—and the fine gradations of socio-economic status that go with it—instead of finding common cause with the underprivileged and unorganized masses of the world.

It is necessary to raise the consciousness of the working classes, as of the industrial youth, the mechanized peasantry and the middle class women, in the West to these facts so that they become, in course of time, sensitive to these and other perceptions. Their various movements must not be allowed to be deflected from the basic struggle for restructuring world economic and political relations. A clear prerequisite of this is for them to show a willingness to accept moderation in life-styles and to accept, too, that beyond a point a higher living standard is not worth striving for. This will not be easy, given the differentials in living standards, but it must be insisted upon in any drive for mobilizing the unionized elements of the industrialized countries into the global movement for a just world.

These tasks appear more formidable than they actually will be in the years and decades to come. For, failing a new global contract across the regions, and social classes within regions, there is little doubt that a fierce struggle for world resources will inevitably ensue. The Third World countries may have to go through a lot of turmoil, but the affluent world will suffer no less from increasing recession, unemployment and inflation, which together will put an end to the optimism of the last few decades and give rise to strife among social classes, ethnic groups and subnational identities. The true dimensions of conflict will then dawn on the less privileged strata in the affluent world, and on the working classes in general, forcing them to find a common cause with the struggle of the Third World and oppressed people everywhere. It is to be hoped that they do not wait till the zero hour when there will be a total breakdown of the old order amidst large-scale violence and chaos. It is to be hoped that much before that the rising consciousness round the world of the ills of the present world order and the widely felt need to close ranks to deal with them will permeate them so that they make a positive contribution to a world-wide movement for a just world.

Human Rights

Perhaps the most potent source of change in the world, and one that may push the myriad struggles for a just world into a truly global movement, will come from an altogether different source: the rising tide of the movement for democratic rights in various regions of the world involving large masses of people (reference to which was made above under "domestic transformation"). Modernization of societies has produced deep schisms everywhere, leading to massive discontent and alienation and a decline in the legitimacy of constitutional authority. Through a curious dialectic, though, the doctrine of modernity has implanted in people two powerful drives. One is the assertion of indigenous cultural identities. The other is a quest for equality and, as an aspect of this, social and spatial mobility, cutting at the roots of both traditional and modern hierarchies and discrimination on grounds of race, class, caste, language, sex and age. It is a new combination—exemplified so vividly in the high drama of the Iranian Revolution—that is likely to provide a more human and holistic anchor of culture and civilization to the various movements of economic and political change.

The movement for "human rights" has to be conceived in the broadest possible sense and taken out of the politics of detente and other Machiavellian uses to which it is being currently put. It should include in its span democratic upsurge against authoritarian rulers. It should include movements for civil rights and "reverse discrimination" of ethnic and religious minorities, caste groups and subnational entities, including secessionist movements in blatantly unequal unions of nationalities. It should include class-based movements for democratic participation, within and across nations. The divisive tendencies planted by multinational corporations must be countered by the growth of multinational trade unions and fraternal movements for economic rights of the exploited classes. Above all, the struggle of the poor and the unorganized millions round the world for economic survival, for the right to work, and for security and job tenure must be included in the movement for human rights if it is to have any meaning for humanity as a whole. And, last but not least, it should include the increasing search for cultural authenticity and human dignity in a variety of ethno-religious settings.

CONCLUSION

We have in this paper provided the elements of an emergent coalition of ideas, interests and institutional initiatives towards global transformation—emergent but by no means already there, as yet more potential than real, but at the same time embedded in the dialectic of history. We have deliberately not dwelt on the kind of international and global institutions that would emerge out of such transformation, for we are interested less in providing a model for the future than in outlining a process of intervention for moving towards a world in which violence, inequity, exploitation and technological tyranny can be minimized. This process of intervention—by the diverse movements for change which, taken together, can provide the politics of a global transformation—will throw up the structures and institutions that are immanent in the specific historical situation.

It must be admitted, as was made clear earlier in this chapter, that the politics of global transformation cannot be consummated except by the intervention in the states system itself by governmental and political elites. But it is our view that this is too important a matter to be left to governments alone. Governments generally act when the force of opinion and the weight of political pressure force them in certain directions. Our conception of a new coalition of interests engaging in the politics of global transformation is thus based on an interpenetration of both governmental and non-governmental actors. The span of the latter ranges from intellectuals to movement groups operating at the grass-roots, to the peoples of the world themselves.

NOTES

1. It was not an accident that the Western countries which had failed to benefit from economic imperialism—Germany, Italy, Spain and Portugal—failed to develop a democratic polity and were able to preserve capitalist economies and avert revolutions only through resort to fascism.

2. The report is based on a study conducted by the Rand Corporation for the US Department of Defense. It is entitled *Military Implications of a Possible World Order Crisis in the 1980s: A Project Air Force Report Prepared for the United States Air Force.*

3. An association of individuals and institutions throughout the globe engaged in research, education, dialogue, and action aimed at promoting a just world order embodying the values of peace, economic well-being, social justice and ecological balance. The author belongs to the core group of WOMP.

4. *Montreal Statement*, presented to the meeting of WOMP scholars held at Montreal in 1975.

37
SELF-RELIANCE: AN OVERRIDING STRATEGY FOR TRANSITION

Johan Galtung

Typically, proposals for transition focus on what should be done and why it should be done—but not on who should do it, how and when and where. What is missing is the actor-designation (whether of *actual* or *potential* actors); a clear image of the *transition path*, including the first steps; and some idea of the *concrete context*. This is not to say that proposals that fall short of these criteria are worthless, even when the receiver remains anonymous and "somebody should do something" is the whole message. A proposal of that kind is like a cry, more or less well articulated, often despairing, and should perhaps be considered incomplete rather than wrong. The declaratory part, the preamble so to speak, is there; but the proposal falls short because the operational part is missing. Without the operational part the proposal becomes a vision only; with nothing but the operational part, the proposal becomes a bureaucratic directive to designated people to do something without informing them of the goal and the rationale for their action. It is in the combination of the vision and the directive that the possibility of developing good action proposals lies.

Since our focus is on the designation of actual and potential actors let me first say a few words about *how* and *when*. Transition paths can be worked out by using the scenario technique as a heuristic device. One assumes that the goal has been arrived at, and one asks "What happened before that, and before that again?" Paths into the future can be mapped out this way as soon as they become linked to the present, to here and now. That carries directly into the third missing element in most peace proposals: *when* and *where* to start, the concrete context for action. The scenario is useful only if it becomes a program with a *specific point of departure*. A rigid program is probably worse than no program at all, but a concrete program stimulates thinking and action much more than a distant vision. What matters is to have a direction in which to start.

The basic problem is who shall do it: the actor-designation. To designate an actor is to scan the social horizon to find the material for one. Two scanning devices seem particularly significant, building on the role of consciousness and

From *The True Worlds: A Transnational Perspective*. Reprinted by permission of The Free Press, a Division of Macmillan Publishing Co. Inc., New York, 1980.

organization in the theory of revolutions: (1) *motivation*—who are the actors who might be motivated to implement a proposal? (2) *capability*—who are the actors who might be capable of implementing the proposal?

If we assume that progressive action proposals in general involve a basic change in the status quo because it is intolerable, filled with direct and structural violence, then it follows that the most capable actors usually will not be highly motivated. They may prefer remaining on top of an unpeaceful status quo to an uncertain position in a possibly more peaceful future. Similarly, the most highly motivated actors may not be among the most capable, leading to the prediction that the status quo will prevail. But if this is the case today, then it was probably also true yesterday and before that. And yet, the world is changing all the time. Some changes do not depend on motivation and capability, as they are not the outcomes of volition. Also, there are actors who are both motivated and capable of positive change, often because they align themselves with the nonplanned changes and because new consciousness formation and mobilization take place. There is no reason to assume that the world has come to rest in a state of peacelessness.

The sources of *motivation* can conveniently be divided into the classical push and pull forces, depending on whether the emphasis is on why one should get away from here or on what one should try to build for the future. In both cases I am thinking of conscious forces.

The *push forces* from the present may be seen in terms of absolute or relative deprivation, leading to a state of despair from which forces for change are spontaneously generated. For a sense of absolute deprivation to develop it is not enough that basic needs—material and/or nonmaterial—are left unsatisfied; they also have to be seen as satisfiable, for example, by changing social structures. Relative deprivation may come about by comparing one's own low position in the structure with somebody else's high up or may arise in an actor high on literacy, knowledge, and education but low on power and wealth (whether the actor is a country or a person).[1] It may be rooted in time, as when improvement of conditions has led to rising expectations that are suddenly frustrated. It may be located in space, for instance, in a demonstration effect between countries.

Social disequilibria, frustrated expectations, and demonstration effects become like blockbusters working on the human mind, at a private level as well as at a collective level. They may propel the individual into self-centered action to improve his own lot; and if he is sufficiently self-seeking the motivation will peter out with the solution of his own personal problem. But it may also lead to more genuine political consciousness and group action, not only as a coordination of individual desires, but also because needs of groups and classes of individuals and countries are reflected. Political man and woman are capable of solidarity, of collective identification beyond private goals.

Then there are the *pull forces*, the images of the future, the visions of what could be done. Who are the visionaries? Of course, they are largely the people and countries motivated to get away from the present. The visionaries are often the people who have insight without power, and there is usually antagonism between them and the people with power but devoid of insight.

Let us then turn to *capability*. That capability or power is not necessarily translated into basic action is seen clearly in the field of arms races. Countless conferences are being held involving precisely the top actors in the military-political-industrial complex, yet the result is negligible—certainly not for lack of power, but for lack of motivation. On the other hand, there are such actors as those scientists who keep the systems going by developing new weapons systems so that the arms race may jump from one phase to the next, in what looks like a stable interplay between qualitative changes in the machinery of destruction.

But what looks stable is in reality a highly unstable equilibrium, supported only as long as scientists cooperate with the system. The moment they withdraw from weapons research and development, the system will change dramatically. *Capability in this case lies in the ability to upset an unstable equilibrium*, turning the apparently static nature of the system into a dynamic force. What holds for scientists also holds for underprivileged and exploited people and countries: solidary mass action is needed to upset the system. *There is political space.*

Many people have thought throughout history that the major key to upsetting an intolerable but unstable equilibrium is to eradicate one particular person, for instance through tyrannicide. The assumption has been that the vicious circle can be eliminated by eliminating one or a few persons. This analysis leaves out the other side of the equation: it is not only that the evil person creates the evil system; it is also that the wrong structure calls for the evil person, and he who understands this fully can quickly fill the vacuum created by the bullet or the poison pellet. Change has to have structure as its target, not merely persons. And the structure is upheld by everybody in it. There is always some complicity on the part of the victims, some element of cooperation with the tyrannic person or country, and that cooperation *can* be withdrawn.[2]

A second key to capability lies in long-term trends. Thus, today in some countries the right of the government to enroll its citizens into armies and the duty of these citizens to fight and die in wars are increasingly being questioned, not only in words (as always), but in deeds of protest and withdrawal.[3] This is particularly clear in the United States and in the Bundesrepublik. If this is a trend the forces upholding it and resisting it should be analyzed. If one believes the results to be productive, the analysis would focus on how the support can be strengthened and the resistance weakened. But, needless to say, more important trends in the world today are directed against structural violence in the form of peoples' wars and national wars of liberation, in the whole trend of events that so far have culminated with the OPEC 1973 action and the fall of Saigon on 30 April 1975.[4]

In other words actor-designation would build on a social analysis not only to find who would be motivated but also to find who would be capable of upsetting malignant, but unstable equilibria and/or of supporting benign trends. In both cases, the forces concerned have to be so strong that counterstrategies, even repressive terror, cannot easily wipe them out. If those who are motivated are incapable and those who are capable are unmotivated, a peace proposal will have to proceed one step further: how can motivation be increased at the strategic points in society? How can those who are motivated develop latent capabilities? For instance, how can scientists cooperating with "defense establishments" be motivated to see their activity in another light, and how can they turn that motivation into action? How can impoverished peasants organize and throw off the yoke on their shoulders?

Scanning the society with this program in mind will usually bring out some suggestions as to potential actors. Who they are, and how many, depends on one's social theory. At this point an important point should be made about social theories: actors will differ in degree of motivation and capability, *but a social theory that designates only a limited category of the inhabitants of society as the carriers of the new (and better) times to come is a dangerous theory, regardless of how well it may have corresponded with facts in the past.* Whether favoring industrial workers (Marx, Lenin), peasants (Mao), or students (Marcuse), any designation that focuses on one group of people is almost bound to introduce a new vertical distinction in society between those designated to be the *force motrice* of history and those not. The former are predestined to become an elite, the others become at best spectators, at worst suspect.[5] One cannot designate a chosen group (or people) without implicitly rejecting others. *Moreover, everything this new elite does is by definition progressive.* The net result of such theories is only that a new *Herrschaft* is constituted, often as capable of direct and structural violence as any *Herrschaft* it was set up to overthrow. In other words, a theory of that kind, for example gambling on professionals (liberal version) or the proletariat (Marxist version), is an instrument of marginalization, introducing a distinction between first-class and second-class people. Consequently, it cannot be a peace theory.

The answer to this dilemma is not to abandon actor-designation and return to the peace proposals without any address, and, for that reason, also without a market. Nor is the answer to assume that *everybody* should feel called upon and capable of doing everything; that would be an expression of historical, and structural, blindness. Motivation and capability are differentially distributed; and even if propaganda and other ways of raising consciousness (e.g., confrontation) can affect the former, only concrete social action, organization and mobilization can affect the latter.

Hence, the answer lies rather *in having tasks for everybody*, in giving unifying participation to everybody, perhaps not of equal immediate significance, but of direct relevance. Any theory that systematically leaves out groups, *a priori*, is from this point of view bad theory. Good theory should not designate enemies, nor should it relegate some into apathy and elevate others into elite positions by virtue of their "role in history." As far as humanly possible peace proposals should be directed against the peacelessness in social structures, not against fellow human beings. Strategies for change should be inclusive, not exclusive—if there are enemies they should designate themselves through their action, not be outlawed by some theory. For this reason dogmatic, linear or nonlinear, theories of history (written History) may become very dangerous tools of oppression.

Liberal theory has a tendency to overdesignate elites as actors; Marxist theory has a tendency to overdesignate the proletariat (or the elite with proletariat origin). As usual the stand taken here will be a combination of the views embedded in the actor-oriented and structure-oriented perspectives respectively. New social forms, with more freedom and equity and less violence do not come into being by themselves; they are not the result of automatic processes. Human choice and will enter, but I have tried to point out that abstract values and goals are not enough: values and goals have to be internalized in actors who are strategically located. The liberal emphasis on *values* is necessary but not sufficient because it does not locate actual and potential actors in the social structure. Correspondingly, the Marxist emphasis on *contradictions* is necessary because each social contradiction can be translated into a motivation for change (through perception of absolute or relative deprivation), but it is not sufficient. To stimulate all kinds of contradictions toward "maturity" through consciousness formation and mobilization may lead to much dynamism, but not necessarily in the same direction and not necessarily in the right direction. Some overall direction is needed, in the sense of both coordination and goal setting. Sometimes this comes about through the dictatorship exercised by a group, a class, or a party; sometimes it is the outcome of a natural or social catastrophe, for example, a world war or imperialist plunder crystallizing society; sometimes both reasons operate.

To summarize: the point of departure is the social structure—locally, domestically, globally. Within the social structure contradictions arise that I have referred to many times as verticalities—basically in the form of exploitation supported by penetration, fragmentation, and marginalization.[6] Each structure divides people into exploiters and exploited. But as human beings participate in several structures one man may be an exploited worker in one structure and an exploiting middle-aged husband in another. In the global and domestic structures not only people but *peoples* may be exploited.

The set of exploited peoples everywhere (the Lapps in northern Norway, the Catholics in Ulster, the American Indians, women, peoples in Latin America, Africa, and Asia) *is the Third World.*[7] Thus, the Third World is a structural concept, not a geographical one. It is not what was left after the Old World had conquered the New World in North America, nor what is left when one subtracts developed capitalist and socialist countries, nor what is left when one subtracts superpowers and the other industrialized countries (the Chinese concept). The Third World has its pockets in the Old World and in the New; the latter have their pockets in Latin America, Africa, and Asia.

In general, structural reasoning leads to more complex maps of social reality than classroom geographical maps are able to reflect. Moreover, contradictions are multiple; there is no single overriding contradiction (e.g., capitalism) that contains the key to the elimination of all the others. As no single contradiction contains the essence of all the others, there is no single exploited class that constitutes the single answer to the question of actor-designation either (e.g., the industrial proletariat).[8] With a multiple theory of contradictions there is also a multiple theory of actors who can be carriers of new values: the exploited everywhere; the Third World in the sense given, particularly the rural masses; women; the very young and the very old; all those who are made into clients under the tutelage of bureaucrats and professionals—perhaps intellectuals in general—not to mention pupils and students; and certainly also industrial workers.[9]

Whether because of Marx himself or dogmatic Marxists, great damage has been done by those who insist on one singular, overriding contradiction and one singular, overriding actor for progressive social change. My view here is more like what I perceive to be the Chinese view: contradictions are multiple, even unlimited in number, and will always be with us. But in each concrete case—with specific answers to the questions of *where* and *when*—there is usually one contradiction that is more important than the others and should be attacked *first*. However, and significantly, in deciding which contradiction is most important I would look at *how much* it impedes the satisfaction of *how basic* needs for *how many*; not at some theory about possible linkages between one contradiction and others. It is on that basis I arrive at the conclusion that capitalist imperialism is contradiction number one[10] in the world today and consequently that its destruction and elimination is a positive act needed to build something different—to let one hundred, one thousand, ten thousand flowers of alternative systems emerge and blossom—not on the basis of a theory of history.

SELF-RELIANCE: THE OVERRIDING STRATEGY

There is a need for one overriding strategic concept, and the one that comes closest is, in my view, the idea of *self-reliance*. One tremendous advantage with the term "self-reliance" is its open-endedness. The term has a certain nucleus of content, but it is up to all of us to give it more precise connotations (certainly the only self-reliant way of going about defining the term "self-reliance"). The following is one suggestion, one effort to fill it with content, even to build some kind of ideology around it.

Roland Berger has this to say about the Chinese origin of the idea:[11]

> In his August 1945 speech Mao Tse-tung used the phrase "tzu li keng sheng" which literally translated is "regeneration through our own efforts." This more accurately conveys the true meaning of the policy than the term "self-reliance." "Regeneration through our own efforts" also makes it clear that this is a policy radically different from "self-sufficiency" or "autarchy." It is in fact the mass line applied on the economic front and stems directly from Mao Tse-tung's consistent emphasis that "the people, and the people alone, are the motive force in the making of world history" and that "the masses have boundless creative power."

Although nothing in what follows is contrary to what has just been said it would be less than self-reliant to give to the Chinese any kind of monopoly of this precious idea. After all the idea of local self-reliance, in the sense of the small community relying on its own forces, is as old as humanity itself: This was the normal form of human existence. Then something happened: the world-encompassing center-periphery formation built as a program into Western civilization[12] (with the West in the center, of course), put into (1) *cultural practice through the spread of Christianity and later on Western science and other forms of Western thought*, into (2) *socioeconomic practice through capitalism*, and into (3) *military-political practice through colonialism*—all wrapped together in the imperialism of the nineteenth century and the first half of the twentieth century and the neoimperialism of our part of the twentieth century.[13] The neoimperialist experience informs us that center-periphery formation is a much deeper phenomenon than political-military colonialism. *One* basic theoretical assumption is that its roots lie in the economic infrastructure, for example, in the centralizing networks and economic cycles spun by the transnational corporations. *Another* assumption, to which I myself subscribe, working backward with the given list (and working backward in history), is that the roots are cultural-civilizational, and of a double nature. On one hand, *one* civilization in the world, the Western one, not only considers itself the center of the world (as is natural) but also universally valid, the center from which messages of all forms radiate to a periphery eager to receive the Western truth in material and nonmaterial forms. On the other hand, because of a number of geographical and historical circumstances the rest of the world has to a large extent let itself be impressed by the West and has to some extent accepted a position in the Periphery in exchange for some of the Center products, material and nonmaterial, that the Center has considered not only its right, but its duty to distribute all over the world. In other words, I postulate an element of Periphery complicity in the form of a submissiveness it is up to the Periphery to withdraw. In this factor a basic source of change is located.

This analysis serves to place self-reliance in a historical context. Self-reliance is not merely an abstract recipe, a way of organizing the economy with heavy emphasis on the use of local factors, but a highly concrete fight against any kind of center-periphery formation with the ultimate goal of arriving at a world where "each part is a center."[14] As the essence of center-periphery formation is vertical division of labor, with exchanges across a gap in level of processing where trade is concerned, a gap in level of knowledge where science is concerned, a gap in level of initiative where politics is concerned, and so on—the difference between the sender and the receiver, the leader and the led—the basic idea of self-reliance is to get out of this type of relationship. Three supporting mechanisms (of exploitation) have to be attacked—penetration, fragmentation, and marginalization—which leads one straight into the practice of self-reliance as a way of fighting center-periphery formation.

Penetration, or dependency (the Latin American *dependencia*), is essentially a power relation: it means that what happens in the periphery is a consequence of causes located in the center. Thus, it gives broader scope to "power" than is usually given in actor-oriented analysis where the "cause" referred to has to be somebody's *intent* to exercise power; it also takes in the type of power that is built into a structure. Because power of any type can be seen as being one or more of three kinds:[15] normative-ideological, remunerative, and *punitive* (persuasion, carrot, and stick power, to put it simply), the fight against penetration also has to have three ingredients. To withstand normative-ideological power emanating from some kind of center, *self-confidence* and self-respect (the Latin American *dignidad*) are needed—a faith in one's own values and culture and civilization, in both the traditional way *and* in the ability to create new culture. To withstand remunerative power absolute self-sufficiency or autarchy is not needed. On closer analysis it is clearly seen that the point is *to be able to produce for basic needs, particularly food, so that in a crisis food cannot be used as a weapon.* Another aspect would combine the fights against cultural, ideological, and remunerative penetration in the struggle for independent taste formation, being less susceptible to "tastes" generated from the center and satisfiable with center goods only. Finally, to withstand coercive power a certain *fearlessness* is needed, both as an attitude and as a structure of defense, as an attitude and practice of invulnerability.

Thus, with the focus on such expressions as "self-confidence," "*ability* to be self-sufficient," and "fearlessness" and "invulnerability," it is clear that self-reliance as a doctrine is located more in the field of psychopolitics than in the field of economics. It would be a gross misunderstanding to reduce it to a formula for economic relations alone, although that would be in line with the economism of our times and with the assumption that the root of center-periphery relations is in the economic infrastructure alone. More particularly, self-reliance is not a new way of "bridging the gap," of "catching up" in the sense of equalizing GNP per capita or some similar measure. There are at least two good reasons that such a goal is not compatible with the idea of self-reliance: It means taking over the *goal structure* of other societies, which then become models to imitate; and it probably also means taking over the *means* used by the rich industrialized Western countries, including center-periphery formation within and between countries. The Third World does not become self-reliant by imitating the First and Second worlds, nor by exploiting some kind of Fourth World; the Fourth World, by exploiting the Fifth World (whatever that might be), and so on.[16] Self-reliance cannot be attained at the expense of the self-reliance of others; it implies the autonomy to set one's own goals and realize them as far as possible through one's own efforts, using one's own factors.

In general terms the way to fight penetration is not through counterpenetration, trying to do to the Center what the Center has always done to the Periphery (persuasion, threats, and promises), but through becoming autonomous. There is much evidence to indicate that this is best done in a process of struggle; that the struggle itself generates patterns of attitude and behavior and new structures that not only serve to break down ties of penetration but also to build true self-reliance.[17] Much of the success of the Chinese revolution was no doubt due to their ability and opportunity to combine liberation with positive self-reliance during the long years of struggle. Whether this type of experience is a necessary condition for true self-reliance later is another question, however. The Chinese, Vietnamese, and partly the Cuban experiences seem to indicate that it may be closer to a sufficient condition.

The dual character of self-reliance—breaking up old relations in order to build new ones—comes out equally clearly in the efforts to counteract fragmentation and marginalization. The point is to break up the Center monopoly, or near-monopoly, on *interaction* by initiating new patterns of cooperation and to break up the Center near-monopoly on *organizations* by creating new organizations. These are both active, outward-oriented aspects of self-reliance, showing clearly how different it is from self-sufficiency as a concept. The point is not to avoid interaction but to interact according to the criterion of self-reliance, which means in such a way that no new center-periphery relationship emerges. In practice this means a preference for horizontal interaction—particularly trade—with others at the same level—"level" meaning something like "degree of peripherization" rather than the highly misleading GNP per capita. The dual nature consists in using the same horizontal organizations of people, districts, countries, even regions in the same position relative to dominance from the center as solidarity organizations in the struggle against the present pattern *and* as the ties out of which a more equitable future world can be built.[18]

So much for the general *concept* of self-reliance as a pattern of regeneration through one's own efforts, of fighting dominance by starting to rely on oneself, meaning individual self and the collective Self of others in the same position. But concretely what is the *practice* of self-reliance? Two principles seem to be at work here in addition to everything said before: the *principle of participation* and the *principle of concentric circles*. These principles are crucial as guidelines, but like all such principles become ridiculous when they generate into dogmas.

Self-reliance is a dynamic movement *from* the periphery, at all levels—individual, local, national, regional. It is not something done *for* the periphery; basically, it is something done *by* the periphery. Thus, control over the economic machinery of a country by national, and even by local, state, or private capitalists in order to produce for the satisfaction of basic needs is not self-reliance. It may be to "serve the people," but it is not to "trust the people"—to use the Chinese jargon. Self-reliance ultimately means that the society is organized in such a way that the masses arrive at self-fulfillment through self-reliance—in participation with others in the same situation. Obviously this points directly to a decentralized society, e.g., in the form of the 70,000 (or so) Chinese People's Communes with their subdivisions (brigades and teams), and sufficient autonomy locally to permit participation down at the grassroot level.[19]

Hence self-reliance should ideally be seen as something originating in the antipode to the metropoles in the Center: the vast rural lands in which the larger part of the world population still lives. Concretely it takes the form of using local factors—local creativity, raw materials, land, and capital. Often the center has drained away so much of the conventional raw materials and the local capital that the task is to find forms that stimulate local creativity. This should not be confused with labor: intensive forms of production which may constitute a solution where there is scarcity of capital and excess of labor. Such factor substitution is entirely compatible with centralized management and manipulation, professionalism, and bureaucratization. Rather, the point would be to opt for those forms of production that permit local grassroots initiative and innovation yielding results compatible with local conditions, tastes, and culture. The point would be that the loss in efficiency caused by sometimes reinventing something already invented elsewhere is more than offset by the gain in self-confidence in accepting the challenge of being the innovator. To be the able recipient of a technology developed elsewhere casts the person/community/country/region in the role of the good pupil, a role that is very difficult to unlearn and the very opposite of being self-confident.[20]

The basic economic principle, then, would be to use local factors and produce for local consumption. Before producing anything, however, the basic question during times of crisis should always be asked: "Do we need this product?" The argument that it can be used for *exchange* even if we do not need it for any use presupposes that there are other communities that are not based on self-reliance, as capitalism assumes that there will always be a periphery somewhere that can serve as a "market." Moreover, only with the masses in command is there a sufficient guarantee that first priority will be given to production for the satisfaction of the basic needs of those most in need, emphasizing use-value over exchange-value.[21]

If the answer is "Yes, we need this product," the task would be to try to produce it from local factors rather than to get it in exchange for some factor held to be available in excess quantities (labor, raw materials) or in exchange for some locally produced product. In so thinking, and acting, there is no doubt that self-reliance is profoundly anticapitalist, for capitalism is based on mobility of factors and products in world-encompassing cycles. Capitalism generates trade, which in turn is good for the traders.[22] If it had also been good for development all over the world that would have shown up already, for there has been an enormous increase in world trade during the last centuries. Hence the theory is that self-reliance will serve the purpose of development better, for reasons to be given.

But what happens if the product needed cannot be produced locally, from local factors, in a federation of villages with no industrial experience or base in the conventional sense? One does what people do in times of crisis; one finds some new ways of using raw materials to get the product nevertheless (the Cuban use of sugar cane as general raw material for a vast variety of products), or one changes the product so that it still serves the purpose but makes better use of local factors (the Chinese use of hydroelectric energy for tractors in some regions).

However, there are obvious limits to local efforts, given the asymmetries in the world economic geography, which are numerous indeed—the most important one probably being the asymmetry of water distribution. Canals can be dug by people rather than by machines, but pumps are among the best devices made by man, and one should not necessarily wait until the industrial base for making pumps has been developed. The problem is *where* to go to get the pumps when they are indispensable and cannot be produced locally. This is where the principle of concentric circles enters: start the search for a partner in this type of cooperation with another community at the same level in the same district; if that does not work, have the district cooperate with another district in the same province; if that does not work, have the province search for another province in the same country; if that does not work, cooperate with another country in the same subregion (meaning Grupo Andino, ASEAN, West or East African communities, etc.); if that does not work, try for Third World cooperation; and ultimately, if that does not work either, try some type of limited cooperation with the "developed" countries.

In a simplified version this leads to three levels of self-reliance: local self-reliance, national self-reliance, and collective (subregional, regional, Third World) self-reliance. The relations among these three levels pose important problems to be studied. Thus, far from being antithetical to trade and exchange and cooperation a consistent policy of self-reliance may even increase the exchange level in the world because it will engender much more cooperation between neighbors in geographical and social space. The point is not to cut out trade but to *redirect* it and *recompose* it by giving preference to cooperation with those in the same position, preferring the neighbor to the more distant possibility, cooperation to exchange, and intrasector to intersector trade. Working outward from oneself and oneSelf, in a set of oceanic circles as Gandhi might have said,[23] is just the opposite of the prevalent pattern today that links the periphery of the Periphery to the center of the Center through a series of costly middlemen with obvious vested interests and power to fight for the status quo, including the intellectual power to rationalize the status quo through concepts like comparative advantages.[24]

PEACE ROLES OLD AND NEW

We now have a general theory of progressive action and an effort to encapsulate the transition strategy into one concept: *self-reliance*, at the local, domestic, and global levels. But we are concrete human beings, not abstract structures or paper plans. How do we act? What do we do here and now? The following provides some reflections on how one works concretely for peace-development-self-reliance. I have chosen to present them in six points, not particularly well systematized, for a reason that will be spelled out in the first point.

[1] *History is a process, not a structure.* There are many ways of stating this simple and important point. Human action unfolds itself in time. Whatever we do today is a part of the stream of history. We are not starting the work for a better future today, nor will that job be completed in a generation's time, by the year 2000, or at some other goal point. We are continuing what others have done before us, not as a transition from X to Y but as very small parts of something more gigantic. We shall always be underway. Goals formulated in this book and similar goals are neither fixed nor constant; they are parts of the stream of history and will change as we go along. Hence, let us not overdramatize. Humankind has been working at the job of improving its existence for a couple of million years and will continue to do so for some time. We shall do our part,

but it would be an expression of "time centrism"[25] to assume that the major turning point of history is just around the corner.

[2] *Consciousness is a key dimension.* In the world today there is no scarcity of action. No doubt much will be gained when more people can become more active, liberated from the shackles of insecurity, poverty, repression, and alienation. But a much more active world is not necessarily a much better world, for the simple reason that action may be in the wrong direction; one individual's increased activity may be canceled by his neighbor. There must be some guiding, crystallizing element, and that is what I have referred to as consciousness. Think of what countries have been able to do by mobilizing their inhabitants in times of war and times of peace, crystallizing and aligning their action through some shared consciousness. Today we might react negatively to much of that because of its parochialism and its dedication to such abstract goals as nation building, but as a historical force it has ranked and still ranks among the strongest in human history.

Hence, the basic need right now is the cultivation of a global consciousness that I have tried to identify with a dedication to the human race, concretely in terms of the needs for security, economic well-being, freedom, and identity within the limits set by our ecology. One little point to be added gives this goal teeth and substance: to satisfy the human needs of everybody, yes — *but starting with those most in need.* [26] If we have limited resources, as we do, we must start building security for and with the least secure, start raising the level of economic well-being for the most miserable among us, start relieving the repression of the most repressed, start giving more meaning to those who have the most alienating, boring type of existence. We others can wait. Even if we do not wait, we have no right to proceed in such a way as to deprive others of the resources for their need satisfaction. In short, all the work done today to bring into being a global consciousness based on identification with human beings everywhere, thereby crystallizing and aligning human action, is work for peace and development.[27]

[3] *All levels of action are relevant.* Look at the key dimensions of our existence, at space and time; there is "here and now" and there is "the whole world in the future." Some people are best at the micro-level, some are most effective at the macro-level; one does not exclude the other. The concept of local self-reliance makes the localism of the here and now much more relevant, not as an experiment to be replicated at higher levels, not as a training ground, but simply because it *is* development; it is not "only" local. "Local" is where people live. To bring about a modestly decent family life is difficult enough — and yet there are few places where security, well-being, freedom, and identity can so effectively be realized. To ensure that the domestic and global structures in which these small units are embedded do not make such a life impossible, the struggle for higher levels of self-reliance is a necessary condition. Human beings have limitations; nobody should blame anyone else for not being able to be active at all levels and in all the right directions at one time. Mutual respect among those who at least do not counteract human self-reliance anywhere is itself a positive force, because less energy is lost in unnecessary struggle and a basis is laid for

solidarity, for example, among the leaders of progressive countries in the First, Second, and Third worlds; progressive mass movements; and ordinary, decent people everywhere. There is also the level of time: some people act now, others plan for the future, acting on paper. Obviously, these activities are equally complementary. Action can be concrete and it can be abstract; the former alone leads to actionism, the latter alone to abstractions. The two have to be tied together as they often are in political movements. The basic components for action are there but require much more clarity about the goals.

[4] *Avoid vertical division of labor.* If all action compatible with a very minimal ideology based on human need satisfaction everywhere, starting with those most in need, is positive, then none should by definition be seen as more important or prestigious than others. Intellectuals who work with large chunks of space and time, with visions of the whole world in the future, are indispensable, as is the mother who embraces her newborn child and in the single act of giving her breast provides security, well-being, freedom, and identity all in one. But the former should not be given too much more power or prestige just because they are less numerous, have more education, and are less substitutable relative to more people (the mother is also insubstitutable, but in a very limited circle). More particularly, patterns should be avoided whereby the intellectuals only make grand designs or serve as catalysts or as the staff of look-out institutions, then step aside, leaving the hard job to the masses, later reappearing as ministers of planning. There is room both for the professionals and for the populists, for elite persons and for masses in our contemporary vertical society; and the latter should not be the tools of the former. The tremendous dedication to promote human self-reliance and self-realization found at all levels of human society every day should be given much more prominence, lest progress become identified with making plans and models of progress.

[5] *Actor-oriented and structure-oriented peace roles are both relevant.* No doubt the old peace roles were predominantly actor-oriented: the often lonely, particularly devoted and capable individual who could negotiate and mediate; the statesman who could navigate in troubled waters. Out of this came the obvious idea of trying to cultivate the skills of such people by codifying what goes into successful peacekeeping, peacemaking, and peacebuilding. The same occurred for development: entrepreneurial skills were analyzed, schools of management created, experts trained by bilateral and multilateral aid agencies back in the 1950s and 1960s. The approach is usually structure-blind, based on the assumption that the structure is capable of carrying peace and development further if only the right individuals with the right training are given the opportunity at the right point in space and time. In a professionalizing society all such efforts were seen as natural.[28]

But the slogan on which this was based only serves to highlight the problem of this section: "peace as a profession." For here we immediately run into the four characteristics of structural violence. He who has a profession is already a member of a caste with a monopoly on the exercise of that profession. And all the others are fragmented clients whose consciousness is penetrated precisely because the professional is regarded as the only person with *competence*, presumably not only knowing better but also knowing what constitutes knowledge. In every concrete work situation the professional will have the important and challenging tasks, while other people will be used as assistants. Thus, every profession is in and by itself some form of structural violence. Not all are equally peaceless: there are those with more and there are those with less structural violence built into them. Among the most violent one could mention the U.S. Air Force: On big posters at the Nouasseur base in the neighborhood of Casablanca one could read, written with very big characters, "Peace Is Our Profession." When that is the interpretation of "peace as a profession," it does not seem to be worth having.[29]

One important aspect of the idea of "structural violence" is perhaps that by means of this concept a social net is constructed whereby birds of many feathers can be caught and kept, not only the good old scapegoats such as "capitalists" but, for instance, also us, the intellectuals. With this concept an instrument is created whereby intellectuals, including peace researchers, can be seen as carriers of violence, just as much as any other professional always claiming that "I know . . ." He is in a neomonopoly position to give answers and to formulate the acceptable questions. Can one define peace-strategic roles that are compatible with such an expanded concept of peace, and really distribute democratically the tasks of peace? The following is a short list of four roles—not definitions, not even examples, but rather illustrations to make the point more clear.

(a) *Citizens' initiatives.* First are the citizens' initiatives. Hans Eckehard Bahr and others at the Bochum University have written important books about this theme, such as *Politisierung des Alltags.*[30] Citizens' initiative constitutes some kind of proof of the falsehood of a sharp dichotomy between evolution and revolution: these initiatives transcend that dichotomy. As we are always living under the pressure of false dichotomies, what makes this a false one? It is almost always assumed that the revolutionary process takes place at the level of the nation-state: one can imagine a revolution in Germany, but not in Niedersachsen. A revolution in Rheinland-Pfalz even sounds like a semantic impossibility. The problem however, is not "Federal Republic versus Rheinland-Pfalz," not a question of size or territory.

Rather, the point is that we have come to know other forms of revolution. Since 1968 there have been revolutions at the micro-level, in the schools, in the prisons, in the hospitals, in universities, at institutes—for instance, at the International Peace Research Institute in Oslo. Thus, when the definition of structural violence was applied to our own institute one saw more clearly how there is a small caste of researchers who fragment assistants and secretaries, even to the point of penetration and exploitation. What does one do then? One might try such efforts as equalization of salaries, giving for instance to a secretary with seven years' professional experience exactly the same salary as to a Ph.D. with seven years' "experience"—which in the latter case means "experience in university life, combined with studies." One may try to have researchers do more typing and let the secretaries participate more in research. Some experiences have accumulated, and perhaps a certain creativity has developed, but not too much progress has been made. Maybe one can say only that we have seen clearly how the concepts of "violence," "revolution," "peace," and so on have to be developed in such a way that they also focus the attention on oneself, not only to be traps in which to snare others—but that is already something.

Citizens' initiatives can be seen as a plurality of revolutions at the micro-level: they are concerned with city blocks and wards, with factories and institutes, with organizations in general, and also with the family. When in a small family father and mother say to their two-year-old child, "What would you like to have for dinner today? There are two possibilities," instead of saying "Here is your food!" then that has something to do with the opposite of marginalization, which is participation, and also with solidarity, autonomy, and equality. In fact, a large quantity of micro-revolutions is not incompatible with a bigger revolution (but may be a condition or a consequence of that one), nor is it incompatible with general evolution. All such dichotomies tend to be false, for they are almost never dichotomies but trichotomies or polychotomies, and there are almost always possibilities of combination, there is always a *tertium*.

By means of such citizens' initiatives a fight against structural violence is launched, experience is gained, autonomy is realized, peace is created. Broad masses in the population learn *that*, and to some extent *how*, peace can be made. And the important point in this connection is not that structural violence is dangerous because it may one day express itself in direct violence. That was the old problem formulation, the one that also has found its place in the charter of the United Nations. The point is that structural violence *is* peacelessness, *is* violence, which makes a fight against structural violence active peace politics regardless of the level at which it is carried out. The method of fighting is in itself a fight against structural violence: through active participation people are no longer objects of conflict, but subjects of conflict.[31]

And when that has happened, we would no longer live in a society where there is a clear division of labor between the subjects and the objects of a conflict. Thus, small children are in general shown only the glossy surface of social life. It is almost always true, particularly in middle-class families, that the family as a whole and the parents in general present themselves to others, in everyday life, in a conflict-free state: conflicts are something one deals with when the children are not present. One saves the children from the conflict, keeping them unconscious and at a distance, so that they grow up with a very limited possibility of conflict participation. When they achieve school age, conflicts are also taken away from them and processed as raw material by teachers, parents, and organizations, always insisting that the children are not mature enough for participation in this process. Then they become about eighteen years old and they get into conflict, but by this stage the possibilities of their understanding conflict through their own experience have been so curtailed that their conflict resolution repertory for that reason is very limited. As a conclusion they become highly manipulable, as objects rather than subjects.[32]

The most significant point about citizens' initiatives, hence, is precisely the collection of *own* experience. A person who comes from the outside, a "third party" saying "Here I am, I know quite a lot about conflict, and you seem to have a very interesting one, let me solve it for you!" is, structurally speaking, a thief, for he takes away from others a possibility for personal, and thereby social, growth. At this point one could actually mention, at the international level, how Finland—although it certainly is a country very much to be admired—has developed a high capacity in the import of other nations' conflict as raw material for processing in Helsinki. Just as efforts to solve conflicts have such important spin-off effects as the booming hotel industry in Geneva there is also a conflict-resolution industry in the Finnish foreign office with obvious consequences for its qualitative and quantitative growth.[33]

One might speculate a little bit about the conditions of success for such citizens' initiatives. Concretely they usually take the form of *action*, even of *confrontation*. But these are phenomena that have to take place in time and space, not abstractions like paper solutions and verbal theories. Preferably, time and space should be defined in such a way as to have immediate relevance for the issue. Thus, if the issue is the devastation of an old quarter of a town with highly unprofitable but also highly stimulating, soothing, inspiring houses, *time* could mean when the issue is debated in the city parliament or when the bulldozers are about to start working. *Space* could be outside the city parliament or in front of the bulldozers. In either case it is quite clear how the correct choice of time and space facilitates communication to the opposite party, to the neutrals if there are any, and to one's own side. The abstract action with no inherent time and space link to the issues is very often a kick in the air: the empty demonstration gathering at some square frequently used for that purpose and at a good demonstration hour—for instance, right after schools and working places are closing down for the day. Such demonstrations tend to be ritualized citizen action, not instrumental.[34]

One obvious problem in connection with citizens' initiatives is that the *international* calendar of events is so removed from citizens' lives. A foreign minister has his diary studded with significant events, but the entries in the citizens' diary are more likely to deal with birthdays, parties, and other events of daily life. Hence, what is more than anything else needed in this field is some kind of convergence between the diaries, some way in which citizens' daily lives have an immediate link to international affairs. My experience so far is that one important way to achieve this is the referendum on international policy, for instance, the referendum that took place in Norway on Norwegian entry into the European Community—possibly the most mobilizing political event in modern Norwegian political history.[35] Again, it is obvious that too many such events will also have a ritualizing effect.[36]

(b) *Noncooperation*. The second possibility is, under certain circumstances, to refuse to participate in certain social positions with a particularly pronounced component of violence. It would not be a bad idea if a list of transnational corporations were estabished, so that one could clearly see which of them (according to the four criteria of structural violence given above) are responsible for most of the structural violence in the world. One could then appeal to everybody who wants a position in an organization of this type to abstain from that move, by pointing to the twenty or so corporations on top of the list.

Similarly, there are governments with whom it is important not to cooperate, and within these governments there are some ministries that are worse than others.[37]

In short, it is important nowadays that governments be not regarded as sacrosanct. Actually, one should regard them only as groups within our societies, with no mystical source of legitimacy above the ability to do a good job, not only for one's own population but the world in general. This legitimacy has to be proven over and over again because it should be doubted every day, as we saw so clearly in the Watergate affair in the United States. Of course, the Watergate scandal was only an expession or an idiom in which a much deeper scandal could be expressed, something built into the very structure of that gigantic society. But it was useful to expose misdeeds at that point, particularly because the roots of the scandal were so deep, although it probably mystified the deeper scandal.

(c) *Increased transparency*. Any good journalist and social critic sees it as his task to make the workings of society more transparent for the citizens living in it. However, much more dramatic forms than analysis—and that is what peace research usually limits itself to—can be found, and one might think particularly of Daniel Ellsberg. As a matter of fact, there are interesting parallels between Ellsberg and Ossietzky: neither of them functioned as a spy or an agent for a foreign power, Ellsberg even defined himself as a "spy for humanity."[38]

But before that Ellsberg was certainly an exponent of the "peace is our profession" ethos in the sense of the U.S. Air Force. He participated in the formulation of equations and diagrams with military input and military output; the destruction potential and the destruction made, particularly in terms of people killed; for instance, measured in megabodies, one million dead. (The Vietnam wars had perhaps brought it so far as to two megabodies, all together.) Ellsberg was a part of this monstrous death factory, as were other intellectuals in Boston, at Harvard University or the Massachusetts Institute of Technology; he was a "specialist" like the others. They conceived of themselves as first-rate intellectuals fighting against a fifth-rate power, only to see later that they were fifth-rate intellectuals engaged in a fight against a first-rate power.

They worked on the increments of the variables and expressed the relation in curves, using their expertise about military input and megabody output, and estabished an upper limit, the famous "unacceptable damage" for the military output. But then they experienced that this limit was a very different one in a society with total mobilization of the creativity of the total population, something quite different from the analogue they had consciously or unconsciously been using, contemporary American society. This came as a shock to Ellsberg—one could even express it biblically by invoking the analogy of Saul on the road to Damascus—the conversion was total and now he is, as he says himself, a different human being.

So, how would it be if instead of *megabodies* one made use of a *megadan* ("Dan" for Daniel Ellsberg)? That would be one million people in foreign offices, in defense ministries, in the transnational corporations, in each and every organization that somehow disposes over the means of structural and direct violence, implementing them and improving them. At times of crisis they would publish secrets, as Daniel Ellsberg did for the Vietnam conflict with the Pentagon Papers. For these papers were made secret not in order to protect or promote humanity but in order to protect the United States and more particularly its government, not to mention its president. Most secret documents are of that kind.

Thus, Ellsberg's role was a new peace-strategic role; and mobilization of all the Ellsbergs of the world would be a rewarding as well as an important task. With that mobilization the monopoly of governments on secrets would be threatened, which would by and large be a most positive and significant contribution to peace. Thus, if the Norwegian Nobel Peace Prize Committee had had as much courage as it had in the year 1935/36 when Carl von Ossietzky was given the Nobel Peace Prize, then Ellsberg would undoubtedly have been the recipient of that prize.[39]

(d) *Toward new science and technology.* Fourth, there is much work to do in the field of new technologies and new branches of science. Consider that so many scientists in one major country in the Western world, believing in humanity and Christianity, were made use of for the Vietnam war. Research at the Massachusetts Institute of Technology was to a large extent financed by the Pentagon, but it is more general than that: there was an almost incredible intellectual mobilization for the war we today know extremely well, a war about which we probably know most of what there is to know. What strikes one as horrifying is the compatibility, even identity between war and science—the way in which one has come to conclude that there is something in modern science that in and by itself makes it disposed for war.[40]

In our model of science the vertical division of labor is already built into the structure. This leads to the question of whether this is a good social model at all. It promotes a small elite that designates itself as scientific, regarding others as clients, as students who understand little and whose consciousness it has a right, even a duty to help form. This is the problem not only for peace research, but for any science; and it is not enough to engage in popularization, since that is only a form of paternalism. Another solution would be to develop scientific concepts less based on division of labor so that everybody is included, everybody can participate.[41]

Such attempts were made in Maoist China; in our vertical society not even efforts are made in that direction. Not only should science and technology be geared toward the satisfaction of basic material needs for food, clothes, shelter, health, and education for all—starting with those most in need—but efforts should be made to generate forms of research whereby everybody can participate as a producer of knowledge.

[6] *Peace action has to be generated spontaneously.* At this point I stop. It is not for me to produce endless catalogs suggesting praxis for other people to engage in. The task is to do it, to seek activation, to be active. And there is no substitute for the form of activation that springs out of one's own consciousness, triggered by the injustice of a social situation, tempered by the fear that it will get worse rather than better, motivated by a vision of an achievable,

viable alternative—and crystallizing into plans for action in solidarity with others in the same situation. In the process, experience is gained, tested against one's assumptions, and the unity of research and action that is so desirable so brought about—in this our difficult and wonderful world.

NOTES

References to *Essays* are to Johan Galtung, *Essays in Peace Research*, 5 vols. (Copenhagen: Ejlers, 1975–1980) (Atlantic Highlands, N.J.: Humanities Press).

1. This combination, or any similar high-low combination, is known as rank disequilibrium. For a general theory of its implications, see, for instance, Galtung, "The Dynamics of Rank Conflict," *Essays* III, 6.

2. This is the basic insight on which Gandhian forms of resistance are based.

3. Thus in Germany as much as 10 percent of the age class has been registered as COs.

4. Rereading this I wonder why I did not write "liberation of Saigon." There is a reason though: there was little in terms of a spontaneous uprising inside Saigon. In the longer time perspective what happens may prove to be liberalizing also for that particular part of the Vietnamese that inhabited the Saigon I know from a study there in January 1968. In the short run the "fall of Saigon" is probably a more correct term.

5. I have dealt with these themes at some length in "East-West Security and Cooperation: A Skeptical Contribution," *Essays* V, 2, and *Journal of Peace Research* (1975), pp. 165–78, and "Deductive Thinking and Political Practice: An Essay on Teutonic Intellectual Style," *Papers on Methodology* (Copenhagen: Ejlers, 1979).

6. For details, see Johan Galtung, *The True Worlds: A Transitional Perspective* (New York: The Free Press, 1980), section 4.2.

7. In other words, this is an effort to define the Third World more in terms of people rather than countries—in line with the basic theme of this book.

8. For this is the basic thing we could learn from China. See Galtung and Fumiko Nishimura, *Learning from the Chinese People* (Oslo, 1975).

9. It is high time to start thinking in terms of the alliances among all these types of topdogs, particularly the very powerful technocratic alliance between bureaucrats, capitalists, and professionals/researchers on which the dominant structure in modern society to a large extent is based.

10. I do not agree with the Chinese idea that "social imperialism" is worse than "capitalist imperialism": the latter affects more people in more countries and in terms of even more basic needs. The former may affect the Chinese more, however.

11. Roland Berger, "Self-reliance, Past and Present," *Eastern Horizon* IX, no. 3, pp. 8–24. See also Ashok Parthasarathi, "The Role of Self-reliance in Alternative Strategies for Development," a paper prepared for the Twenty-fifth Pugwash Conference (Madras, 13–19 January 1976), with a summary by the secretary-general of Pugwash. One particular aspect of self-reliance is analyzed in Surendra J. Patel, "Collective Self-reliance of Developing Countries," Background Paper no. 8, WFUNA Annual Summer School. Also see the Cocoyoc Declaration of 1974 for the general philosophy of self-reliance. I have chosen not to try to reflect the recent changes in China after the death of Mao Tsetung and the demise of the so-called Gang of Four as I am not at all convinced that the new course will be long lasting. Rather, it is probably in a zig-zag pattern oscillating between distribution-oriented and growth-oriented policies that the key to Chinese development strategy can be found, and this is quite consistent with the self-reliance policy of "walking on two legs." That mistakes may be made and that struggle takes place

would be normal in human affairs. However this may be, more time is needed to see more clearly what the social meaning of all this is, and in the meantime there will always be much to learn from recent Chinese history.

12. This is a basic theme of the Trends in Western Civilization research program of the Chair in Conflict and Peace Research, University of Oslo.

13. The standard term is "neocolonialism," but the phenomenon is broader in scope; it is actually imperialism no longer supported by military-political colonialism in the classical sense.

14. From the Cocoyoc Declaration: "The ideal we need is a harmonized cooperative world in which each part is a center, living at the expense of nobody else, in partnership with nature and in solidarity with future generations."

15. Power is then seen as a *relation* between a sender and a receiver, not as something existing in the sender alone. The latter would be power potential.

16. Extreme care should be taken in using concepts like the "fourth world" that are usually introduced to indicate divisiveness inside the Third World. On the other hand there is no reason to conceal that dominance relations also develop inside the Third World. If one should talk meaningfully about the "fourth world," however, it would probably make much more sense to see it as located within all Third World countries—the vast periphery of the Periphery—than to see it as a group of countries such as the twenty-five designated as the least-developed countries.

17. This is probably a contingent relation, though. It is hardly absolutely necessary, but that it is not absolutely sufficient is seen from the Algerian case today, and probably also from the Soviet case. In both cases a tremendous struggle preceded independence and transition to socialism, but the systems can hardly be characterized as self-reliant.

18. Thus, the UNCTAD 77 is certainly more than an organization for global articulation and collective bargaining; it is also a setting within which new cooperative structures are emerging.

19. This is developed in some detail in Galtung and Nishimura, *Learning from the Chinese People*, chap. 4.

20. At this point a Western preoccupation with the loss of efficiency in multiple innovation, or reinnovation, enters. Great efforts are exercised to avoid this through "coordination and documentation." Without denying the value of that approach in some fields it should be noticed how this serves the function of reinforcing the Center as Center because it has the largest capability (e.g., in pure R&D, science and technology terms) for creating new science and technology.

21. However, no absolute dogmatic position about producing only for use, never for exchange will be taken here. When one produces for the use of others there is always an exchange element present that makes it hard to draw an absolute borderline. But the concept of production for socially beneficial goals, including the satisfaction of basic material needs of oneself and others, might be seen as a basic ingredient in self-reliance as a concept.

22. This is probably one of the few absolutely safe statements one can make about capitalism, from which it follows that capitalist patterns will be maintained not necessarily only by countries with a dominant private sector but by countries that base their economies to a large extent on trade, whether most of the economy is in the private or the public sector.

23. Gandhi may be seen as one of the ideologists and practitioners of self-reliance, through the *sarvodaya* concept at the (local level) and *swadeshi* concept (at the national level) inside a pattern of local capitalism, but of the type normatively regulated through what Gandhi referred to as the "horizontal" aspects of caste, the trade union aspects.

24. The concept is probably, as Myrdal has argued, meaningful for countries at the

same level of development, making exchanges of products at roughly speaking the same level of processing, thus balancing the externalities and keeping terms of trade relatively stable.

25. Again an aspect of Western civilization: *here*, in the West, is the center of the world; *now*, right now, is the center of time.

26. In a sense this may be seen to be the most important point in the Christian ethic, translated into economic practice in the economic systems of socialism, but easily perverted into something far more materialistic than originally intended.

27. The Cocoyoc Declaration is a typical effort to produce ideology of that type.

28. An example was the International Peace Academy, which started operating in 1970 with sessions in Vienna—originally as a broad forum for the development and exchange of information and views on all kinds of matter related to peace, later turning more narrow, focusing on peacekeeping only in a professionalizing manner.

29. Peace should never be professionalized, for when that happens a closed group is formed, a guild, a caste, with high technical competence but increasingly removed from the people they are supposed to serve. Technical efficiency, command of the means, becomes more important than the ends: the well-being of everybody. This is particularly clearly seen in the unquestioning way in which military men develop such horrendous doctrines as countervalue strategies whereby masses of fellow human beings are held as hostages, possibly to be exterminated in a nuclear holocaust.

30. Luchterhand, 1972.

31. This is the major theme in Galtung, "Conflict as a Way of Life," *Essays* III, 15.

32. For a further exploration of that theme, see Galtung, "Schooling and Future Society," *Papers*, no. 7, Chair in Conflict and Peace Research, University of Oslo.

33. Thus, an expansion program of considerable magnitude was initiated by that foreign office in 1971 when it became clear that they were to play a major role in the all-European process.

34. This is particularly true to the extent that the authorities learn patterns of dealing with them: treat them with respect, permitting or even encouraging the demonstration process, and then pay no attention to them whatsoever.

35. The referendum was held in September 1972 and was a very close race (53 percent against, 47 percent in favor) as an indication of how heated the political debate had been.

36. I am thinking here of the Swiss referenda, often having very low rates of participation but giving the population a chance to pronounce themselves on details of policy-making not found in other countries.

37. Working along such lines is an integral part of the World Indicators Program, Chair of Conflict and Peace Research, University of Oslo.

38. That does not mean that they were accepted as such by their contemporaries who tried to see them as spies for "the enemy"—not only to blackmail them but also, partly, because this was the only alternative to loyalty and apathy known to the authorities in either case.

39. Lacking that courage, it instead gave the prize to Henry Kissinger, and later to Eisaku Sato and to Menachem Begin and Anwar Sadat, leading to a major depreciation of the value of that prize.

40. This point is repeatedly made by Herbert Marcuse.

41. See Galtung, "Social Structure and Science Structure," chapter 1 in *Methodology and Ideology* (Copenhagen: Ejlers, 1977).

customers. Such *tactical demilitarization*, the essence of arms control as a perspective on the war system, involves tinkering with the geopolitical setting, making it marginally safer, cheaper, or more manageable. At best, arms control achieves temporary relief from the dangers and burdens of unregulated militarization; it may also involve an effort by military elites to concentrate spending on particular types of weaponry or to discourage rivals from specific arms development. *But tactical demilitarization, whatever its guise, offers no challenge by governments to the fundamental role of military power and violence or their linkage to the international structures of fragmentation and hierarchy.*

The focus here is upon *principled demilitarization* that sets as its goal the abolition of war and defense establishments, and conceives of its task as the initiation of a political process that moves toward that goal. Preconditions for achieving the goals of demilitarization are the substantial erosion of fragmentation and hierarchy in the world order system. In their stead, demilitarization proposes the goals of *coherence* and *equality*, structures by which planetary concerns are protected by institutions of a global identity and relations among actors based upon mutuality and respect.

With this outlook, the policy question is a matter of identifying the location of *creative space* for innovation within the world political system. In effect, demilitarization is a political process, that is, a struggle to carry out a radically revisionist program. As such, it is bound to encounter resistance from the main institutional actors of the state system and its prominent supportive organizations (including multinational corporations, international financial institutions and private banks). In this respect, even international institutions, such as the United Nations, should be understood primarily as extensions of the state system, being dependent on voluntary financial contributions from leading governments, lacking even a fully autonomous enclave of territorial space outside the jurisdiction of sovereign states, and having no independent enforcement capabilities. Militarization is thus firmly entrenched, and because the technology of war evolves so rapidly with such disquieting potential, it is exceedingly difficult to gain any official support for principled demilitarization. This reality is made even more formidable because of the confusion caused by assimilating some aspects of tactical demilitarization into the overall militarization process itself via arms control, peace rhetoric and nominal statist support for human rights. Semantic confusion is inevitable, as antagonistic social forces accord lip service to the same values and goals. As a consequence, world public opinion has grown skeptical about professions of faith in peace and justice.

An initial effort is needed to cut through the mystifying language used by most power-wielders to confuse and distort policy prospects. First, is the misleading contention that existing elites, even in the superpowers, would welcome a trustworthy path of demilitarization. Secondly, is the derivative claim that demilitarization is not feasible because of the specific qualities of the enemy, or because of the way the world is structured, or even because of the inherent characteristics of human nature. Thirdly, is the fatalistic belief that it is necessary, in the sense of being unavoidable, "to live with" militarization, minimizing its risks and costs to the extent possible. Fourthly, is the view that constructive action should not attempt more than to contain the velocity and some wasteful or menacing features of the militarization process. And fifthly is the general claim that prudent militarization as a permanent posture will succeed at least in preventing general nuclear warfare and will keep the peace among the advanced industrial countries.

This ideological underpinning of militarization enjoys the overwhelming support of entrenched elites in the North, including the Northeast or Soviet sphere of influence. Militarization also seems to be accepted, as well, although accompanied by varying degrees of distress, by the leadership of international institutions. A credible demilitarizing challenge, then, will have to come from the popular sector, perhaps activating certain currently subdued voices within prevailing structures of political power. On an ideological level, the challenge of principled demilitarization will have to be clear about its goals, its strategies, and its vision of the future. In essence, such an image of demilitarization implies moving toward the realization of a world order system in which collective violence is minimized, economic well-being of all people is assured, social and political standards of justice realized, and ecological quality restored and protected. To attain these ends in a coherent form requires several decades of concerted effort, presupposes struggle, and implies the restructuring of power, wealth, and authority at all levels of social organization. The vision of restructuring at least implies a diminished role for states in the dominant sector of world society: a selective destructuring of state power, combined with the emergence of carefully constrained central guidance capabilities to express the underlying *unity* of planetary life and to protect effectively the general human interest in a sustainable environment and an undiminished stock of renewable resources. At the same time, by destructuring state power, the underlying diversity of planetary life would also be assured, thereby accomplishing an entirely novel blend of centralization and decentralization in the world order system.

Thus, our starting point is the search for creative space in an atmosphere dominated by the dynamic of persisting, indeed intensifying, militarization. In this atmosphere any fundamental challenge is ignored if possible, and repressed as necessary. To mount a challenge at this stage is primarily a matter of political education, piercing through the pacifying mystique of militarization as an inevitable feature of the human condition. The setting is adverse, and yet there are some positive signs. For one thing, nuclear weapons have revealed the horror of war to a new extent and their spread to a variety of governments makes it seem unlikely that nuclear peace can be maintained indefinitely. Secondly, state leaders are increasingly faced with a series of non-military problems that they are unable to solve within the constraints of the present world order system, and their capability for effective and humane governance seems to be steadily declining. Thirdly, the diffusion of power by means of decolonialization, by the spread of military and economic prowess, and by the growth of Third World solidarity has posed a threat to the *hierarchical* arrangement of geo-political relations in the world. Fourthly, the growth of interdependence — economically, ecologically and culturally — has exposed the inadequacy of this *fragmented* and *adversary* structure of secular power and authority in the world. As a consequence of these four developments, the legitimacy of militarization is being eroded in the short run by the economic squeeze, in the longer run by its genocidal style of risk-taking. In effect, powerful social and historical forces are undermining militarization at its apparent point of maximum momentum, but this subversive process is slow, uncertain in its effects and non-linear in its path (there are numerous regressions with the possibility always present of a decisive regression by way of World War III).

Therefore, the active, explicit challenge of demilitarization requires a feeling for how, when and whether to intervene in the social/political dynamic surrounding the role of war. Above all else, meeting this challenge requires clarity about non-creative or sterile space that reinforces the dynamic of militarization while pretending to oppose it. To expect institutions in the dominant sectors to shift to demilitarization by the serious espousal of genuine disarmament proposals is one familiar instance of meaningless gesture. Similarly, to suppose that arms control agreements will lead in the direction of disarmament is another venture in sterile space—although such agreements may be valuable as short-term managerial instruments, reinforcing tendencies toward prudent militarization. To explore and identify creative space in the struggle against militarization is the purpose of this paper. The proposal of particular normative initiatives needs to take account of the political structure that exists in different polities. Under this framework of constraints, we seek those normative initiatives that both enhance *understanding* and promote *realization* of world order values.

THREE SYSTEMS OF POLITICS

Basic to this line of analysis is the primacy of *the third system* for the work of *principled demilitarization* given the present global political situation.

For purposes of clarification, the three systems of political action can be distinguished:

The First System. The system of power comprised by the governing structures of territorial states; in short, the state system, including its supporting infrastructure of corporations, banks, media; a system that is *hierarchical, fragmented,* and in which war and violence are accepted as discretionary options for power-wielders and in which armies, weapons, police, and military doctrines play a crucial role within and among states.

The Second System. The system of power comprised by the United Nations, and to a lesser extent by regional international institutions; this extension of the First System enjoys a verbal mandate that remains nominal, a mere promise of substantial achievement; a system that is supposed to mitigate hierarchy and fragmentation; as well, it repudiates the discretionary option of states to make war or use force to advance their particular ends; states, as members, are the primary actors in Second System arenas.

The Third System. The system of power represented by people acting individually or collectively through voluntary institutions and associations, including churches and labor unions; a system oriented around challenging the domestic manifestations of militarization, and subject to regulation and repression by the First System on "law and order" grounds; the Third System is the main bearer of new values, demands, visions, although its proposals may be coopted or subverted to varying degrees by the First System, or even on occasion, the Second.[1]

The idea of *normative initiative* is one of changing the terms of permissible action, by placing a boundary, or at least an inhibition, on what is discretionary. The international law of war represents a normative initiative of the First System. The prohibition of force except for purposes of self-defense in the Charter of the United Nations is a normative initiative of the Second System. The campaign against torture conducted by Amnesty International is a normative initiative of the Third System.

In essence, the argument here is that as matters now stand the First System has been increasingly mobilized on behalf of the logic of militarization; this process has spread around the world by way of arms transfers, sales, and the development of indigenous war-making and repressive capabilities. The Northern sector of the First System has also relied upon militarization to maintain favorable aspects of *international hierarchy*, especially in relation to the Southern sector. Finally, governing structures in all sectors have embraced militarization to maintain *intranational hierarchy*, organized along class, ethnic, religious, and regional lines.

These generalizations stand up despite the concessions made by the First System to demands for demilitarization, especially in the aftermath of World Wars I and II: for instance, the creation of the Second System (League of Nations superseded by the United Nations), the advocacy and proposal of general and complete disarmament, and the renunciation of war as an instrument of foreign policy by way of an international treaty (Pact of Paris, 1928).

The Second System is a creation and dependency of the First System. Yet, it has a normative logic and even a limited institutional momentum of its own. The Charter of the United Nations establishes a tension between statism (sovereign equality) and supranationalism (global community activity). The normative mission of the United Nations ("to save succeeding generations from the scourge of war . . .") is tantamount to a call for demilitarization. Yet, the Second System remains dependent upon the First System, although subject to varying orientations depending on shifting internal coalitions among member governments. The Security Council and the General Assembly are its most important organs. Membership consists of states represented by political appointees who act under instructions from their governments. The Security Council, alone empowered to make decisions binding on Members, even partially incorporates the hierarchical feature (in the name of "realism") of the First System in the form of permanent Members enjoying a right of veto. Furthermore, the professional staff of the United Nations is financially dependent upon contributions made by member states, especially a few rich and powerful ones. And despite the promise of the Charter, no effort has been made to endow the United Nations with autonomous peacekeeping capabilities.[2]

The capacity of the Second System for demilitarizing initiatives, then, is neutralized by its dependence on the First System; it is insufficiently *autonomous* to pose a structural threat to militarization. Nevertheless, the Second System has made some helpful contributions to demilitarization, especially through the General Assembly on North-South issues of hierarchy: support for decolonialization, for the new international economic order, for human rights, for the prohibition of nuclear weapons, and for environmental protection are notable in this regard. The General Assembly has also endorsed normative initiatives helpful and relevant to the struggle for demilitarization: the Universal Declaration of Human Rights, the Covenants of Human Rights, the Nuremberg Principles, and the call for a global effort in the area of disarmament.

These notable achievements have to be linked to social forces, however, in order to transform behavior. Movements for national liberation and OPEC have implemented Second System normative initiatives with structural consequences, whereas endorsements of the Nuremberg Principles and prohibition of nuclear weapons have not had any impact, as yet, because they have not been connected with a political process capable of altering behavior. Their significance is mainly latent or potential, possibly symbolic, as tools or catalysts available for the appropriate movement. We can illustrate this question of potency by reference to the anti-apartheid campaign waged so vehemently in the Second System. The normative initiative represented by the so-called anti-apartheid norm means little by itself, until coupled to resistance struggles or intervention threats. Then, however, by shifting the balance of legitimacy to the anti-apartheid side, it alters the status of First System rules of the game in a significant manner, validating normally "illegal" anti-regime intervention and invalidating normally "legal" pro-regime intervention, or at least shifting perceptions of crucial First System actors on matters of validity.

The Second System can be directed toward a demilitarizing orientation by several developments:

- any evolution that accords its institutional elements greater autonomy, thereby making it more likely to lend weight to its natural mission which is to dismantle the war system, to put peace on a secure footing, to promote equality and dignity at the expense of hierarchy;
- a repudiation by critical First System actors of the militarizing path, thereby using the Second System as a strategic political arena;
- a growth of a Third System movement around the goals of demilitarization that regards the Second System as a strategic political arena;
- a broadening by Third World countries of their attack upon the adverse effects of the First System hierarchy to include its military dimensions.

The importance of the Second System for demilitarization is therefore considerable, even if its role remains largely latent and symbolic, awaiting catalytic stimulus from without.

The Third System is segmented as a result of the degree of control exercised over political space by the territorial governments that constitute the First System. There is no free space where people could promote demilitarization without interference from the First System. Indeed, the First System sets the rules of the game for the Third System. These rules are confusing because they are not uniform. The diversity reflects the different strategies of governance and dominant political ideologies that control the definitions of the rights of people within any given sovereign state. In theory, each government purports to represent and protect the overall interest of its people, yet it continues overwhelmingly to resist pressures for fair and representative governance by falling back upon the logic of militarization (that is, law and order, security through military strength). Also, the First System overwhelmingly controls the dissemination of information and the educational process, assuring that the public is assaulted by militarizing propaganda from cradle to grave. Again the segmented character of the First System results in different degrees of control.

As does the Second System, the Third System suffers from a lack of *autonomy*, thereby greatly restricting its role in promoting demilitarization. In overtly repressive polities, this pressure on the Third System is direct, as well as indirect as through propaganda. In more liberal polities, this pressure is mainly indirect, although the boundaries of dissent are policed; to date it has successfully relied upon various forms of mystification and pacification to obtain support for the policies of militarization from a large majority of the population.

There are, however, certain tendencies that are threatening the credibility of First System domination over the Third System. The potency of popular discontent has been evident throughout this entire historical period. The outcome of the Algerian and Indochina Wars of Independence suggested the limits of transnational First System military superiority. Gandhi's movement against colonial rule in India, Khomeini's movement against tyranny in Iran, both revealed the power of non-violent mass movements when highly mobilized.

On the level of legitimacy, the First System has weakened its claim to unrestricted authority by acknowledging the validity of certain normative restraints: international law; United Nations; specifically, human rights, including the Nuremberg obligation. In the Soviet Union, for instance, dissenters have long invoked the human rights commitments made by the Soviet government as the basis of their attack upon certain features of domestic hierarchy; in 1980, Polish strikers insisted, among their other grievances, that the Polish government abide by the conventions of the International Labor Organizations.

Because of the carnage of past wars and the danger of future wars, the First System is on the defensive. It concedes at a verbal level the legitimacy of demilitarization. This concession is reinforced by virtually universal moral and legal normative orders. This normative foundation provides solid footing for Third System activities, including challenges directed at the First System.

One formidable constraint on the Third System is the tendency of the popular sector to restrict itself to territorial goals, that is, to reform only the national governing process in specified ways. To the extent that Third System goals are directed against various expressions of *hierarchy* within the national polity, it is important to emphasize the linkages that exist to global hierarchical structures. Beyond this, and more difficult to convince Third System activists about is the importance of overcoming on a global scale specific types of *fragmentation*. Those that tie a state into the path of militarization are of especial relevance, exposing ordinary people to the hazards of nuclear and other types of war, as well as to the waste of precious resources through military expenditures and to the insertion of military elites into the governing process thereby tending to erode the protection of human rights at home. As well, economic, ecological and cultural interdependence create a Third System stake in the operation of the global system. In particular, there appears to be a shared human commitment, as a matter of species identity, in the avoidance of irreversible catastrophe by way of mass war, environmental decay, or depletion of natural resources. Furthermore, the popular sector has an interest in impartial limitation of territorial power through effective procedures for enforcing human rights, that is, on the balance between assuring *autonomy* vis-à-vis *international patterns of hierarchy* and providing *global community* protection vis-à-vis *intranational patterns of hierarchy*. A Third System movement for demilitarization depends on the emergence of a planetary consciousness that is alive to the interlinked dimensions of militarization and understands that autonomous liberation on a national scale is only partially attainable and not fully sustainable without reinforcing transformation of the state and statism. A transnational series of Third System initiatives alive to the global dimension of militarization is the most hopeful prospect in the years ahead. Part of the process of encouraging such a development is within the realm of Third System normative dimensions where obvious interconnections exist between the domestic demand for reform and its dependence upon corresponding shifts in global policy.

Of particular importance are *normative initiatives* relevant to demilitarization that can be undertaken in the Third System; that is, initiatives that challenge the root assumptions of militarization by insisting upon certain norms of procedures and substance that rest upon some adequate moral/legal foundation. For this reason, movement to prohibit the use, threat or even the possession of nuclear weapons is of significance beyond the effort to constrain governmental discretion. The intention of such initiatives is to mobilize effective opposition to militarization in all three systems by altering the normative climate. Such a new climate would create new creative space within both the First and Second Systems enabling demilitarizing moves to win backing.

Normative initiatives are not the only important activities of the Third System with respect to demilitarization. The movement against nuclear power in the Third System Northwest is questioning domestic hierarchy in some critical respects. Its wider implications extend from a concern with safety of the nuclear fuel cycle, to the safety of any nuclear activity, including those related to military purposes. Comparable issues of safety in mining plant operation, waste disposal, and transporting and safeguarding of fissionable materials exist in the military nuclear sector, and perhaps are even compounded by secrecy and the absence of public scrutiny. By discrediting nuclear power, the Third

System will go a long way toward agitating Third System concern about nuclear weapons, and even about traditional (militarized) conceptions of national security. This anti-nuclear movement, important as it is for demilitarization politics, nevertheless falls outside the main focus of this paper, since it is not an initiative whose dominant motivation is to establish or enforce a norm.

As is obvious, there are positive and negative feedback relations among the three systems. At present, the main strategy is to alter the orientations of First System leaders by building pressure directly upward from the Third System, as well as by way of the Second System. As segments of the First System shift toward a comprehensive demilitarization orientation, the political current of energy works its way back down via the Second System to other segments of the Third System, and then back up again to new segments of the First System. In this regard, it is necessary to view the three systems as interconnected and flowing parts of a unitary evolving global political system.

The political opportunities (and challenges) also cross system boundaries. It is easy to contemplate, for instance, the formation of a pro-demilitarization coalition joining activist social forces in the Third System Northwest, with the leaders of segments of the First System South, and with elements of the Second System. A global demilitarization movement, then, is likely to partake of all three systems to some extent.

NORMATIVE INITIATIVES IN THE THIRD SYSTEM AND DEMILITARIZATION

There are several reasons why normative initiatives are an attractive focus for demilitarization. For one thing, every government in the First System, no matter how repressive, acknowledges its accountability to moral/legal norms; hence, a universal basis for seeking adherence to these norms exists. This is especially important for Third System activity, as it is often constrained by the boundaries of First System tolerance; that is, since the entire world (except for high seas and Antarctica) is divided into territorial states each Third System arena is governed to some degree by a First System actor.

Secondly, the ambiguity of authoritative norms, including the distinction between what *is* forbidden and what *ought to be* forbidden, creates "space" for prescriptive politics in most First System settings. This ambiguity extends to questions of what is binding by reference to international law upon a particular First System actor (e.g., are the Nuremberg Principles binding because declared and endorsed by the General Assembly and by an array of international law experts?). The point is that Third System activists committed to demilitarization can act *as if* the Nuremberg Principles *are* binding, and thereby raise questions of accountability in many First and Second System settings.

Thirdly, a normative dimension for demilitarization emphasizes two possible grounds for an overall challenge: it vindicates the right of resistance against illegitimate political authority at the First System level and suggests the possibility that a comparable right of resistance should be postulated at the Second System level, that is, to the mode and manner by which global interests are protected.

The locus of normative concern in the Third System needs also to be explained. The First System is the principal source of authoritative norms because of its dominance of the international legal order, but it is unwilling and incapable of implementing those norms supportive of demilitarization (e.g., prohibitions on aggressive war, nuclear weapons, abuses of human rights). The Second System keeps these norms alive in the public imagination because its credibility depends on some expression of minimal concern about the dangers confronting human society; yet it is paralyzed politically as a result of its dependence on the First System. Hence, it is only among elements of the Third System that there is a clear commitment to the enforcement of demilitarization norms by securing First System adherence. Even in the Third System, misinformation, hostile propaganda, pacifications, intimidation, and reactionary priorities confuse most people about their real stake in demilitarization. Also, different First System settings condition Third System priorities and openings. Human rights concerns seem paramount for those First System settings where the domestic hierarchy is most oppressive. More global (Second System) concerns may be more permissible in these settings even if felt to be less vital, although any attempt to insist that one's own government take demilitarizing initiatives because of a normative obligation to do so is likely to encounter stiff opposition.

The problems facing the Third System are different in the North and South. The center of militarization is in the North, as divided between the Northwest (USA-dominated) and the Northeast (USSR-dominated). The liberal orientation of the governing process in the Northwest allows explicit concentration on the demilitarizing imperative of their own First System actors as a matter of first priority. Such a priority seems sensible both because the repressive features of the Northeast are generally resistant to external pressure and because First System actors in the Northwest pretend to be already committed to demilitarization. This pretense can be exposed for what it is, partly by normative initiatives in the Third System Northwest (e.g., a demand for disarmament, an insistence on the illegality of nuclear weapons, a claim that the sort of threats to use nuclear weapons contained in strategic doctrine are themselves instances of "crimes against humanity"). This exposure can arouse public indignation, as well as demonstrate the need for imaginative normative initiatives that operate beyond the boundaries of conventional politics.

The ideological orientation of the governing process in the Northeast also has implications for the Third System. It creates a natural umbrella for demilitarizing concerns, although First System apologists in the Northeast blame the Northwest, that is, the main capitalist sector of the First System, for militarist tendencies in the world. Secrecy and control of information in the Northeast also make it more difficult to mount useful Third System campaigns on demilitarizing themes, except as proposals by relatively isolated intellectual dissenters (e.g., Sakharov) whose impact seems to be largely transnational. Issues of human rights (domestic non-economic hierarchy) enjoy a manifest demilitarizing priority in the Third System Northeast-USSR. Such realities expose the absence of "creative space," and reveal a reliance by First System actors to protect the human interests of their own citizenries. For the non-Soviet portion of the Third System Northeast, special questions of international hierarchy (that is, Soviet domination) are added to issues of intranational hierarchy. Struggling against these repressive features will not necessarily contribute directly to the global demilitarization process, except by opening up space in which the pursuit of normative concerns is accepted as legitimate activity for citizens.

In the South, the weight of militarization is partly felt in the North-South hierarchical structure, especially to the extent that the militarizing tendency is associated both with international dependency and intranational repressiveness. The Iranian Revolution against the Pahlavi dynasty illustrated a Third System movement of extraordinary force animated by opposition to these two interlocking aspects of hierarchy. The main normative element in the Iranian revolutionary process was the stress on human rights, including gestures of solidarity, especially in the Third System Northwest. It remains unclear what will be the character of the Islamic Republic as a First System actor, but it seems probable both that its anti-dependency posture will have a short-term major demilitarizing significance (cancellation of arms purchases, refusal to supply oil beyond Iranian capital requirements, support for liberation movements) for Iran, although not necessarily for the region, and that its governing process will generate a new agenda of human rights concerns.

In general, the Third System in the South is concerned with opposing the continued hierarchy dominated by the North; the anti-colonial struggle goes on in the period of formal independence of the states in the South. To the extent that international hierarchy is linked with domestic hierarchy, as when outside actors from the North help keep a First System elite in power, then the struggle for human rights at home is also a struggle against the militarization of the planet as a structure. Unlike the North where the First System actors are the main agents and beneficiaries of militarization, in the South the First System actors are, at best, subordinate links in the system, having been to sharply varying degrees socialized into "the military habit." Indeed, acquisition of weapons, even nuclear weapons, in the South is ambiguous, as it can be seen positively as a necessary step to achieve autonomy for a given state or region, and possibly to shock the North into some denuclearizing initiatives of its own.[3] Partly for these reasons, normative initiatives emanating from the Third System of the South are directed mainly at First System actors in the North, thereby attributing responsibility for global militarization (e.g., normative demands to renounce nuclear weaponry and strategy) mainly to those few states, especially the two superpowers.

SPECIFIC PROPOSALS

Which Third System normative initiatives have most promise when it comes to demilitarization remains to be considered. A long list could be compiled. What follows is illustrative and tactical, suggesting the kind of proposals that seem most appropriate and the ones that have the most promise.

Global Scale

The most significant Third System normative initiative at the global system level may be the projection of credible images of a comprehensive demilitarization process. This effort needs to be centered in the Third System, consisting of various individuals and groups linked together by collaborative arrangements, perhaps with the informal backing of some progressive First System actors. It is normative to the extent that demilitarization is a way of specifying what is preferable, that is, what would be normative for the politics of the future. The academic foundations for such an outlook are being developed under various rubrics: world order studies, future studies, peace studies, utopography, macro-history, dialectics of the future, "soft" science fiction. Its essential feature is a conviction in the possibility and necessity of an encompassing transformation of the present orientation of First System elites so as to combat the increasingly severe militarization of the planet. What is needed in the Third System is the dissemination of these images beyond the community of academic intellectuals in forms that are accessible to people in various circumstances of consciousness and literacy. Furthermore, a transnational consensus-building process around the issue of what demilitarization implies and reliance on various means to promote its goals in different areas, depending especially on First System constraints varying from country to country. Although image-forming is principally a Third System initiative, it would be helpful to have strategies for promoting demilitarization advocated from within the First and Second Systems.

The second area of normative initiative on a global scale would involve generating pressure for all varieties of denuclearization, especially in the military domain. On no issue is the global and human interest more evident than in the delegitimation of nuclear weaponry. Normative consensus would contribute to this result by placing a stigma upon the reliance on nuclear weapons and strategy. Illustrative of such directions of initiative are the issuance of two non-governmental declarations, each informed by the ethos of denuclearization: the 1978 Delhi Declaration for a Just World[4] and the 1980 Lisbon Declaration on Denuclearization for a Just World: the Failure of Non-Proliferation.[5] Both documents, drafted and endorsed by concerned citizens from around the world, express in unambiguous terms their conviction that any threat or use of nuclear weapons would be a crime against humanity. The Delhi Declaration even insists that the mere possession of nuclear weapons is a crime against humanity; the Lisbon Declaration also regards possession as criminal but not until a time definite has been formally established by the joint initiative of non-nuclear states. The Third System consensus on the menace of nuclear weaponry is an important element in a global movement for denuclearization. In the Northwest, the struggle against nuclear power, as unsafe and authoritarian in implication, combines certain elements of resistance to *intranational hierarchy* — anti-democratic structures — with opposition to the war system as the fundamental expression of *international hierarchy*.

A third area for normative initiative concerns direct opposition to militarization tendencies. Here again the circumstances of a given national setting suggest the specific form of struggle. The domestic arenas of the two super-powers are obviously critical, both very different from one another. In the United States, movements against draft registration, opposition to specific weapons systems (MX, Trident), and opposition to specific arms transfers (e.g., to repressive regimes) and to increases in defense spending are important. In the Soviet Union, national security policy as such seems beyond citizen scrutiny, but calls for more consumer goods and denunciations by dissenters of interventionary uses of Soviet military power work in a demilitarizing direction. The basic demilitarizing imperative in the Soviet Union, however, is the struggle for human rights, which is in its essence a demand for domestic demilitarization. If this struggle were to enjoy success, the demilitarizing effects would exert influence on the Soviet approach to international security.

Throughout the world, also, it would be helpful to promote the efficacy of non-violent approaches to conflict.[6] India, with its rich Gandhian legacy, is especially situated, although not by its own recent defense policy, to gain a global hearing for non-violent politics. Academic efforts to discover and highlight non-violent, pacificist, and altruistic elements in the various great cultures of the world would help to convey the understanding, so needed at present, that non-violence has universal roots and many practical successes. To be serious about the abolition of war as a social institution implies putting something in the place of violence; necessarily, then images of non-violent polities of varying dimensions must be fed to the political imagination of peoples throughout the world seeking relief from an apocalyptic war destiny.

Regional Scale

Regional enactments of global scale initiatives are obviously appropriate. Beyond this, regional and sub-regional efforts to decouple their security systems from the menace of war would be beneficial. In this regard, nuclear-free zones, intra-regional peacekeeping and disarmament moves, and general efforts to insulate Third World regions from superpower competition and ex-colonial intervention are beneficial moves in the appropriate direction.

Sovereign State Scale

Normative initiatives directed at the governing process in sovereign states are of great importance at this stage of history. One important line of effort would be to restrict force structures and military doctrines to defensive conceptions of the use of military power. Admittedly, the defensive/offensive distinction is difficult to draw as so much depends on intention and context, yet the insistence that international force be used defensively, if at all, is vital as the experience with private violence within states suggests. The struggles for governmental accountability in the use of force as an instrument of foreign policy is one direction, sanctioned by Nuremberg. Keeping governments within a framework of law, subject to interpretation by an independent judiciary, is also obviously relevant. Again, demilitarizing priorities will be diverse, even contradictory, from setting to setting. For instance, the demilitarizing priority in South Africa may require Front Line states to augment their war-fighting capabilities in the short run or a Third World beleaguered state such as Manley's Jamaica might do well to increase its defense budget as an inhibition against intervention.

As suggested, especially in anti-imperial context, certain apparent contradictions exist. Short-term belligerence may be required as a foundation for lasting peace; at the extreme, additional proliferation of nuclear weapons capabilities may be a precondition for denuclearization.

Individual Scale

What one does with one's own life is a primary political statement. The shift from militarized to demilitarized allegiances will be expressed, in the first instance by what people do with their lives. Refusal by scientists and engineers to design weapons, or at least weapons related to mass destruction or offensive use, is one dimension; refusal to engage in secret research on security issues; tax refusal; draft resistance; more radical forms of civil disobedience—pouring blood on the gates of the Pentagon, blocking the completion of a Trident submarine base—illustrate the range of undertakings.

In the liberal democracies, where citizens' rights are formally protected, the idea of a Nuremberg obligation to resist crimes of state is crucial. If individuals in sufficient number manifest this kind of higher loyalty, then a powerful movement against endowing governments with the option of discretionary violence and war-making will begin to take shape.

CONCLUSION

We need to monitor developments in the world from a demilitarizing perspective. This requires a sophisticated frame of reference, alive to struggles against domestic tyranny and injustice and against forms of imperialism, as well as preoccupied with the avoidance of warfare, especially beyond the nuclear threshold. The tactics of demilitarization cannot normally—beyond the issue of nuclear weapons threat or use—be expressed in too universalistic terms. Finally, the First System seems generally implicated in the ongoing dynamics of militarization, the Second System seems stalemated by a tension between its impotence and its mandate, and the Third System, alone at present, seems able to sustain normative initiatives of consequence that move in a demilitarizing direction.

NOTES

1. In some formulations, for instance that of the International Foundation for Development Alternatives (IFDA), the Second System is associated with the market and market forces such as corporations and banks, while all governmental institutions, including intergovernmental mechanisms—for instance, the United Nations—are assimilated into the First System. For world order purposes, however, the tripartite division of systems, as presented in the text, seems better adapted for inquiry and analysis.

2. But see article by Robert C. Johansen and Saul H. Mendlovitz, "The Role of Enforcement of Law on the Establishment of a New International Order: A Proposal for a Transnational Police Force," *Alternatives*, 6, 2, 1980, pp. 307–337.

3. For a fuller statement of this position, see Ali A. Mazrui, *The African Condition* (Cambridge: Cambridge University Press, 1980).

4. *Disarmament for a Just World: Declaration of Principles, Proposal for a Treaty, and Call for Action*, issued on the occasion of the International Workshop on Disarmament, 27–31 March 1978, New Delhi. For text, see *Alternatives IV*, 1, 1978, pp. 155–160.

5. *Declaration for a Just World: The Failure of Non-Proliferation*, Draft prepared by a group of concerned scholars to be presented at the Lisbon Conference of the World Order Models Project, 13–20 July 1980. The final text appears in *Alternatives* 6, 3, 1980, pp. 491–496.

6. See Glenn D. Paige, "Normative Politics for Disarmament," *Alternatives*, 6, 2, 1980, pp. 287–305.

39
A MANIFESTO FOR
NONVIOLENT REVOLUTION

George Lakey

How can we live at home on planet Earth?

As individuals we often feel our lack of power to affect the course of events or even our own environment. We sense the untapped potential in ourselves, the dimensions which go unrealized. We struggle to find meaning in a world of tarnished symbols and impoverished cultures. We long to assert control over our lives, to resist the heavy intervention of state and corporation in our plans and dreams. We sometimes lack the confidence to celebrate life in the atmosphere of violence and pollution which surrounds us. Giving up on altering our lives, some of us try at least to alter our consciousness through drugs. Turning ourselves and others into objects, we experiment with sensation. We are cynical early, and blame ourselves, and wonder that we cannot love with a full heart.

The human race groans under the oppressions of colonialism, war, racism, totalitarianism, and sexism. Corporate capitalism abuses the poor and exploits the workers, while expanding its power through the multinational corporations. The environment is choked. National states play power games which defraud their citizens and prevent the emergence of world community.

What shall we do?

Rejecting the optimistic gradualism of reformists and the despair of tired radicals, we now declare ourselves for nonviolent revolution. We intend that someday all of humanity will live on Earth as brothers and sisters. We issue this manifesto as guidance in the next decades to ourselves and others who choose not to escape, who want to recover their personhood by participating in loving communities, who realize that struggle is central to recovering our humanity, and who want that struggle to reflect in its very style a commitment to life.

The manifesto includes a vision of a new society—its economy and ecology, its forms of conflict, its global dimensions. The manifesto also proposes a framework for strategy of struggle and change, which is presented here.

Reprinted with permission from *A Manifesto for Nonviolent Revolution*. Philadelphia, PA: Movement for a New Society, 1976.

STRATEGY FOR REVOLUTION

A person may be clear in his or her analysis of the present order, may have a bold projection of a new society, but still be uncertain about what course to take in getting from here to there. Should I devote myself to building counter-institutions, or to shooting practice, or to protest demonstrations? Should I organize among students, workers, the unemployed, or the "solid citizens?"

Decisions on what to do are often taken on impulse or because of movement fashions; a particular tactic like occupying buildings may be taken up because it meets the psychological mood of the moment. Serious long-run struggle cannot be waged on such a basis, however. Mood and fashion are too much at the mercy of repression. Rosa Luxemburg may have been exaggerating when she said that we shall lose every battle except the last, but the basic point is sound; the struggle will be long and hard and our actions cannot be evaluated only by short-run psychological satisfactions.

Further, struggle by impulse is undemocratic. Wide popular participation in decisions about struggle can only come through wide discussion, which requires time, which requires planning ahead. Leaving strategic decisions to the crisis point means delegating power to a central committee or to the demagogue who is most skilled at manipulation of mood and fashion.

Tactics—actions at particular moments—often must be improvised as best they can, and leaders have their role at such times. *Strategy*—a general plan which links the actions into a cumulative development of movement power, and which provides means for evaluating tactics—is too important to be left to the leaders.

Creating a Strategy

The most effective strategy is specific to the historic situation. The Chinese Communist Party, for example, began with a strategy borrowed from Europe and tried to organize the industrial proletariat. Only when Mao Tse-Tung devised a strategy for the Chinese situation, emphasizing peasants rather than workers and the countryside rather than the city, did the struggle have more chance for success.

In the Belgian socialists' struggle for universal suffrage there was a period of flirtation with a violent strategy imported from the French revolutionary tradition. Only when the workers turned away from the romance of the barricades and, through wide discussion, decided on a disciplined general strike, did the campaign achieve its goal.

Strategies gain in power as they gain in specific relation to the situation. Every situation, however dismal it may seem, has some leverage points. (Even in Hitler's concentration camps inmates organized resistance movements.) The hopeful, creative revolutionist will find those leverage points and develop a plan for struggle.

A Revolutionary Process

The need to develop a specific strategy does not prevent learning from others' experience. The experience of struggle movements in many countries can be analyzed into a framework which may guide us past mistakes and point us to opportunities.

One way to honor those who have suffered in the struggles for justice is to take their experience seriously.

Our framework emphasizes the development of the movement itself, since we see the movement's growth carrying some of the seeds of the new society in its very style of organization and action. Of course the major conditions for struggle are provided by vast social forces beyond intentional control: by economic conditions, by ecological tensions, by declining legitimacy of old institutions, by the rise of hope in new possibilities, and so on. The movement's task is to make this struggle effective, by constantly increasing its ability to grow, to renew itself, to practice its values in its internal life, to plan the new society.

Our framework has five stages for development of a movement from a small band of agitators to a mass struggle movement making fundamental change: (1) conscientization, (2) building organization, (3) confrontation, (4) mass non-cooperation, (5) parallel government.

Conscientization. / Why are things going wrong in my life? Why am I so powerless? Do those who decide have my best interests at heart? Why are so many of us in my situation?

More and more persons ask these sorts of questions as conditions deteriorate. People begin to see their problem with a critical awareness of the larger world. They develop a *collective* consciousness, for workers, women, blacks are not exploited as individuals but as a class. People must develop a sense of their personal destiny as interwoven with that of a collectivity before they will act together.

In this stage agitators should develop a political consciousness which translates private troubles into public issues and connects individuals to others in a community of the oppressed. This requires an analysis which makes the social structure transparent, and which helps people understand the dynamics of domination.

A negative movement can stop there. It can point out injustice, analyze inequality, and make a virtue out of everlasting protest. A positive movement goes on to create visions of a new society, identifying itself with aspiration as well as anger.

Having an analysis and a vision are still not enough, however, because the pervasive feeling of impotence which oppressed people have cannot be strongly countered without a strategy for change. When people realize the *how* as well as the *why* of revolution, they are most likely to move.

The tactics used in the stage of conscientization are commonly pamphleteering, speeches, study groups, newspapers, conferences, and so on. The particular methods of education must, of course, be geared to the culture of the people.

Innovation is also necessary to methodology, especially where the existing methods encourage elitism in the movement. New methods of education are being invented, for example by Paolo Freire who coined the term "conscientization" and emphasizes reflective action through indirect methods of developing group awareness over time.

The nonviolent training movement is also developing methods for political education: strategy games, scenario-writing, utopia-gallery, role-play, case study are a few. By means of *participatory* methods of learning skills and knowledge, the agitators show by their very style that this is a democratic movement, rooted in the people's understanding rather than in the oratory of the leaders.

In many countries the stage of politicization is already well advanced, but there is also a sense in which it is never finished. Movement agitators should work in ever-widening circles, realizing that long after the nucleus of the movement is at an advanced stage of revolutionary development, some sectors of the population have still only a vague idea of the sources of their discontent. By expanding the area of work agitators also learn more, since there is a reservoir of knowledge and awareness which is held in many people who on a superficial level seem unpolitical. Only the sectarians take a missionary view of their educational work: that they have all the truth and need only to proclaim it. Genuine education is *interaction*; a democratic movement wants all the insight it can get, even from those who might carelessly be labelled "enemies."

Building Organization — Stage Two. / An individual can agitate, but only the people can make a revolution. An individual can exemplify certain values, but only a group can begin to live the patterns of a new social order. Just as the wise farmer does not rest with sowing the seed, but returns to care for the young plants, so the wise agitator becomes an organizer, preparing healthy social environments for the growth of revolutionary spirit.

A basic tension exists in organizing for the new society. The organizational forms can reflect so literally the radical vision that they become the end instead of the means to social change; the revolutionists can isolate themselves into sects of the righteous. On the other hand, the organizational forms of the movement might fit so well into the prevailing culture that they reflect the racism, sexism, authoritarianism, and other patterns which need to be eliminated. Such old wineskins can hardly hold the new wine of the radical vision; the contradiction between stated values and actual practices becomes too strong to contain.

Although the particular organizing patterns may vary from place to place, we propose a basic principle: the means must be consistent with the goals. An egalitarian society will not be built by an authoritarian movement; a community of trust will not be built by the competition of rival leaders; the self-reliant power of the people will not be uncovered by tight bureaucracies.

Consistency of means and ends does not mean the *collapsing* of ends into means; the utopian community as an end in itself is in many situations irrelevant to social change. The community as a base-camp for revolution, on the other hand, provides an important alternative to the narrow style of revolutionary parties. It provides a way of living the revolution as well as waging it. It provides a training ground where movement people can undergo those personal changes which we need to become strong and clear-sighted.

Counter-institutions, or a constructive program, can provide another opportunity for innovation in organization. Can the new society be organized in egalitarian ways? Can consensus decision-making be widely applied? Which functions can be decentralized and which not? Some of these questions can be explored by the movement so that, when it comes time for actual transfers of power from the old regime (stage five), there is a reservoir of movement experience available.

Counter-institutions can provide needed services which are provided expensively or inadequately in most countries. They are a powerful form of propaganda because they demonstrate that movement activists are practical and respond to material needs, and that our style is fundamentally constructive even though we know we must struggle for change.

It is true that counter-institutions lend themselves easily to abuse as charities, substituting "service to the people" for "power to the people." Charity cannot lead to fundamental change; it is part and parcel of the system of inequality. Charity does not mobilize people for change; it continues their dependence on do-gooders. The constructive program becomes mere charity unless it is linked (as it was for Gandhi) to a mass struggle movement for fundamental change.

Only a mass movement can bring about the new society, because only a mass movement has the power to do it. Further, mass participation is necessary because freedom cannot be given by a few to the many; freedom by its nature requires active seeking. On the other hand, human liberation involves a heightened sense of individual confidence and worth rather than a loss of identity through submergence in the crowd.

We propose that the basic building block of mass movements be the small affinity group. Small groups can support the individual, experiment with simplified and shared lifestyles, work as a team within the larger movement. They can arise from already existing friendships or ties of workplace or religion. They can grow as cells grow, by division, and can proliferate rapidly when conditions are ripe. Unlike communes, they do not necessarily involve common living, yet they have a commitment to each other as persons and therefore provide a good movement context for individual growth.

Affinity groups as the fundamental units of the mass movement meet the dilemma of collectivism versus individualism. Unlike some of the old communist cells, their style is not secret or conspiratorial, therefore they cannot hold individuals to them rigidly with implicit threats. On the other hand, there is sufficient community to help the individual overcome his or her excessive attachment to self. The solidarity which enables people to withstand the terror of repression is even more likely in teams than in an unstructured mass facing waterhoses or bullets. Studies of combatants in battlefield conditions have shown that the solidarity of the small unit is crucial in conquering fear and withstanding attack. Fear, of course, is the central weapon of repression. In a movement of small groups we may hold hands against repression and continue to struggle.

Under some circumstances it may be necessary to work within reformist organizations. Frequently, however, radical caucuses can be organized within those organizations to help them see the need for fundamental change. The masses of people will not turn to basic structural change if they feel that reforms will alleviate conditions sufficiently. If the analysis of this manifesto is correct, reforms will not be sufficient; fundamental change is necessary.

In a democratic movement our slogan is: "No radical change without radical consciousness"—we do not believe in revolution behind the backs of the people. Reformist organizations will rarely allow radical analysis and vision to be projected through their channels, and so it is necessary to create new organizations which can respond radically to challenges of history. At this early stage, clarity is often more important than acceptability.

There are some reforms which, if they can be achieved, involve such a shift in power relations that they can fairly be called "revolutionary reforms." Analysis of the political economy suggests what these struggle points are, and gives important goals for the next stage of revolutionary development, confrontation.

Confrontation—Stage Three. / Unfortunately, the pen is weaker than the sword. Time and again the truth about injustice has been known widely, with pamphlets and tracts easily available, yet most people remain passive. Mass mobilization for the new society will not develop from the first stage of politicization alone; the reality of evil must be dramatized.

In the past this dynamic has often been at work: the Russian Bloody Sunday in 1905, which sparked a massive insurrection against the tyranny of the Czar; the Amritsar Massacre in India in 1919, which spurred the first national civil disobedience against British imperialism; Alabama's repression of Birmingham blacks in 1963, which mobilized radicals and liberals in America for legislation against racism.

The best form of confrontation for dramatizing injustice is a campaign over a period of time, rather than a one- or two-day witness. Usually a campaign will educate more people than a single event, and educate them more deeply.

The first step is to select a campaign goal which is consistent with radical analysis, such as a revolutionary reform. Second, reduce the problem and solution to picture form, so that no words are necessary in order to explain what the confrontation is about. The picture should show the gap between a widely-held value and the particular injustice. Third, take group action which paints that picture in vivid colors. The campaign should build to a crisis, in which the authorities are put in a dilemma: if they allow the demonstration to go on, fine, because the action is dramatically pointing up the situation of injustice. If they repress the demonstration, all right, because their repression further reveals the violence on which the regime rests.

The "dilemma demonstration" is much different from mere provocation. In provocation, the immediate goal is to bring down repression on the heads of the demonstrators. In a dilemma demonstration the campaigners genuinely want to do their action: block an ammunition ship, wear a black sash, etc. The demonstrators are not disappointed if the authorities use unexpected good sense and allow the demonstration to continue. But repression is also acceptable, since voluntary suffering further dramatizes the situation and erodes the legitimacy of the unjust authority.

Violence by the government is an inevitable result of radical social change work in most societies. It cannot be avoided, because injustice needs violence for its defense; when inequality is challenged, those on top resort again and again to violence.

The strategic question is: how can that violence work against the government itself, rather than against us? The government's own force can work against itself, as in jiu-jitsu, when it is met indirectly. Instead of pitting guns against repressive violence, meeting the opponent on his superior ground, the movement responds nonviolently. This has two effects: it begins the process of demoralization among the troops and police which may accelerate in later stages, and it discredits the government in the eyes of the masses.

Voluntary suffering is dynamic when we can stand it without fleeing. For most people that will require the preparation of conscientization and of organization. By changing our ideas about ourselves and our social world, and by developing a strategy we have confidence in, and by training in direct action tactics, we can get ready for open struggle. By joining others in small struggle communities we develop the solidarity necessary to face government terror.

Picture, then, movement groups waging campaigns of a month to several years duration, engaging first in propaganda of the world, then in training and mobilization of allies, and finally in propaganda of the deed. Confrontations lead to achievement of immediate goals in some cases, repression in others. Counter-institutions provide support; radical caucuses agitate for support within the trade unions and the professions.

These political dramas pierce the myths and rationalizations which cover up oppression and force the violence of the status quo out into the open.

In the meantime, some movement agitators are working in new circles on conscientization, widening the revolutionary process in the population. Gaining fresh impetus from the spotlight which is trained on injustice by the campaigners, organizers are helping newly aware people find each other and the network of solidarity so necessary for struggle.

The tempo of the revolutionary process depends largely on history: economic conditions, ecological strains, political rigidities, cultural development. In some societies it may happen very quickly, in some more slowly. Confrontation remains at the head of the movement until large numbers of people are ready for noncooperation.

Mass Noncooperation—Stage Four. / By saying "no" when the regime depends on our saying "yes," we unlearn the habits of submission on which every oppressive system rests. The all-out civilian insurrection touched off by government repression, as in the Russian rising of 1905, provides a heady moment in which people defy the regime, but it is not enough. More than a moment—or even a year—is required to change those deep-rooted habits of inferiority. There must be a succession of battles, a long march, a continuing exposure to the nature of power and authority. Else we will never learn to stand erect during the intervals between euphoria and rage.

Movements may therefore want to plan organized, long-term and selective forms of mass noncooperation. All-out campaigns for total change at this point are unrealistic because they cannot be sustained, even after careful organizational and political preparation. Noncooperation should usually be focussed on clearly defined, limited goals, which if achieved would be revolutionary reforms. The specific demands help to rally the people (not everyone is moved by goals which seem vague and far away). When the immediate goals are achieved morale is heightened. Those who thought they were powerless find that they have achieved something. The skeptics who thought that struggle is useless may see their mistake.

The economy is often the part of the oppressive system most vulnerable to noncooperation, and repression may be particularly severe in response to economic direct action. Therefore it is important that the organization and preparation to this point have been done well.

Quite a variety of economic tactics exist to express noncooperation, for example: the three-day general strike, boycotts, the declaration of holidays almost constantly, go-slows, rent refusal, full strikes in specific industries of great importance to the oppressive system.

For the population at large, political noncooperation can involve mass civil disobedience, boycott of elections, draft resistance, student political strikes, tax refusal. Legislators can resign in protest, boycott the sessions, or attend the sessions and obstruct the proceedings. Workers in the state bureaucracy have many opportunities to noncooperate and give useful information to the movement.

The tactics of intervention can come strongly into play at this point. In intervention people put their bodies in the place where the business of the old order goes on, in such a way as to disrupt it. Sit-ins, occupations, obstruction are major forms of intervention. In addition to their ability physically to dislocate the status quo, they can have strong symbolic overtones by "acting out the future in the present," that is, by imagining how a facility can be used in the new society and then proceeding to use it in that way. Such a tactic leaves the burden on the authorities to try to return the situation to the previous condition; if they fail, a piece of the new society has been planted.

Machiavelli long ago noted the impossible position of a government which sees the people's compliance dissolve; he said that the prince "who has the public as a whole for his enemy can never make himself secure; and the greater his cruelty, the weaker does his regime become."

One tangible measure of weakness is the demoralization of police and soldiers. As Lenin discovered from the experience of the 1905 rising, soldiers are more likely to become ineffective and even desert if they are *not* shot at in a revolutionary situation. The guiding aim of the movement should be to win people over, not to win over people. When that basically open, friendly spirit is maintained even toward the agents of repression, a decisive break is made with the cycle of violence and counter-violence which so often in the past has distorted struggles for justice.

The counter-institutions and other forms of organization planted in the second stage need to grow rapidly in this period, both to generate concrete demands for which we launch noncooperation campaigns, and to provide the alternatives which keep nay-sayers from becoming nihilists. The small affinity groups, the radical caucuses, and other forms of movement organization must by this stage develop strong coordinating links; sustained mass action requires unity.

In some societies four stages of revolutionary process may be sufficient to produce fundamental change. A series of revolutionary reforms forced by mass noncooperation may decisively shift the distribution of power and the basis of the economy. The change of this depends very much on the global context.

In most societies, however, mass noncooperation for specific goals will finally reach a wall of such resistance that an all-out struggle will occur, out of which a transfer of power may come. The noncooperation will need to be generalized and intensified, with direct intervention such as occupations stepped up. In a number of historic cases ruthless dictators have been overthrown by the social dislocation of all-out mass noncooperation. The next stage, parallel government, is the stage of final transfer of power.

Parallel Government—Stage Five. / In this stage the ordinary functions of governmental authority are taken over by the revolutionary movement. The people pay taxes to the movement instead of the government. The movement organizes essential services such as traffic regulation, garbage collection, and the like.

The counter-institutions become part of the unfolding new order as people transfer allegiance from those institutions which have discredited themselves by their failure to change. This stage is, therefore, linked directly to the second stage of organization-building which, of course, never stopped.

We are clearly not proposing that a mass party, governed by a central committee, confronts the rulers in a final tussle for control of the apparatus of the state. Even less are we suggesting that a small, professional revolutionary elite stage a coup d' etat. Our concept is that the old order is attacked and changed on *many* levels by many groups, that is, that the people themselves take control of the institutions which shape their lives. The radical caucuses within trade unions and professions play a major role here, for they provide the expertise necessary to re-organize institutions for the new society.

In this populist model of transfer of power, coordination springs from association of the caucuses, affinity groups, neighborhood councils, unions. Because outlining the features of the new society already began in stage one, with involvement by ever-widening circles of the people, the revolutionary program will have a great deal of consensus behind it.

The military state withers away in the very process of revolution, its legitimate functions taken over by people's institutions. Redistribution of power is not postponed until after economic functions are reorganized; in stage five the workers occupy and begin to operate their own factories according to plans already widely discussed rather than wait for a directive from a party or state bureaucrat.

Repression would by this stage be very mixed. In a popular, nonviolent revolution there would be the full range of sympathetic response from the soldiers, from inefficiency to mutiny. Prior fraternization would also be producing disloyalty among the police. On the other hand, some of the police and army might remain loyal to the old regime and reactionary groups would certainly act on their own as they saw the government's ability to maintain order crumbling. There might, therefore, be pockets of extreme brutality while large areas experienced a peaceful transfer of power.

Historians have remarked on how little violence has accompanied the actual transfer of power in a number of revolutions, the Russian, for example. Widespread violent repression is even less likely with the use of the framework we propose, because the people would be prepared to respond nonviolently to provocation and to hasten the desertion of the soldiers.

The dissolution of the power of the military state and giant corporations into democratic people's institutions is a short-hand way of marking when the revolution has occurred, but their's is a broader view of the sweep of radical change. We look at revolution as a continuing development, not completed when the people's institutions take authority. We realize that authoritarianism, greed, ignorance, and fear will continue to shape institutions and will need to be attacked again and again.

The nonviolent revolutionary process arms the people against distorted institutions, however, through the widespread application of pacific militancy. The people learn in struggle how to use the power of truth. We have confidence in the future because of the consistency of our means: we can *wage* the revolution, and *live* it, and *defend* it, through nonviolence. We need not hope against experience that figs will grow from thistles, that a life-centered society will grow from widespread killing. The same determination, freedom from fear, and ability to love which liberates the individual will bring humankind to higher levels of evolution.

Revolution and Human Growth

The revolutionary process we propose could be compared to an individual's successful re-orientation of a destructive relationship with another person. First, awareness comes: unhappiness, an idea that things could be better, a realization of the dynamics of the relationship. Second, the individual mobilizes him or herself: priorities shift, inner resources are called on, relations with other persons may be strengthened. Third, confrontation: communication becomes more honest through conflict; new patterns of relationship are suggested. Fourth, noncooperation: the most oppressive of the old patterns are broken by refusal to participate; the destructive games stop because one person will no longer play. Fifth, new patterns are strongly asserted and accepted by the other person. (The new patterns may be a joint creation in some respects, developing from the dialogue and conflict of the two.)

Of course there is nothing inevitable about this ordering of things: sullen noncooperation may precede open confrontation, for example. There is nothing at all inevitable about our strategic framework. But there is some logic in the framework of stages from the viewpoint of human liberation. This becomes clearer when we retrace the steps.

The new society is more likely to ensue from parallel government than from capture of the state apparatus because the parallel institutions are grown from the bottom up, through the course of the revolutionary struggle. These institutions have the resources of people who have been changing themselves (rather than the civil servants of the old state) and organizational innovation (rather than bureaucracy). This is not to say that civil servants and corporate managers have no use in the new society, but only that re-training and personal change will in many cases be necessary, and this should be led by those who have committed themselves to innovation rather than to maintaining the old order.

Even the mass society of industrialized nations is undermined by the revolutionary process. The movement's internal organization is not one of mass politics, with a few leaders vying for control of the party apparatus while the movement rank and file serve as an audience, but instead is based on small action groups and communities. The movement itself becomes a liberated zone in which the values of the revolution are practiced.

Mass noncooperation (the fourth stage) should come before parallel government because the habits of submission which maintain the old order must be unlearned, personal independence must be declared, before new, cooperative relationships of governance can be firmly rooted. Unless that growth point is reached, it is all too easy for the passive compliance of the old order to become passive compliance to the new society, which would be a contradiction in terms. The new society is participative in its nature; it cannot be built on the mere acquiesence of people still needing the towering authority of the state.

Mass noncooperation is not likely, however, until the issues are clarified and dramatized. There will likely be a series of disasters (mass starvation, depressions, wars, ecological breakdowns) in the next decades which will erode the foundations of the present order, yet we should not wait for them to provide the revolutionary dynamic. We want people to work for change before the worst disasters occur in order to minimize the suffering. By creating crises through showing the contradiction between positive values and present injustice, we can raise the level of consciousness without disasters.

Further, disasters can be ambiguous: a war can strengthen the state, as well as weaken it; ecological breakdown can be blamed on the consumers instead of on the industrialists, and so on. We need to counter the official rationalizations with our own definitions of the situation, and do that dramatically and clearly. Confrontation can do that.

When the masses of people see for themselves what the stakes are, they are ready to refuse cooperation. Therefore it is sensible for mass noncooperation to follow the third stage, confrontation.

One major problem of the confrontation stage, however, is the violence which is meted out to the movement. Repression is never easy to stand up against; solidarity, however, makes an enormous difference. Terror works best against people who feel alone. Logically, therefore, organization (the second stage) should come before confrontation. Another reason why organization-building should begin early in the revolutionary process is because the development of skills, experimenting with new working styles, and making of milieus for personal change are all essential for later stages in the struggle.

Organization, however, is a hollow shell if it is not rooted in the changing perceptions of its members. Radical groups cannot be catalyzed without a new consciousness, at least not if they are to be democratic. Motivation for pro-tracted struggle, although often beginning in vague feelings of impotence and alienation, needs growth and positive development to support revolutionary organization. And so the revolutionary process begins with conscientization.

Growth is not only for "the people"—it is most important for those who take the initiative in the revolutionary process. Such individuals should consider what growth means in terms of their functions: in the first stage, agitators; in the second, organizers; in the third, actionists; in the fourth, campaign developers; in the fifth, coordinators.

Since the revolutionary process begins again and again in ever-widening circles, agitators are needed in some sections of the population even while other sections are engaging in mass noncooperation. The gifted agitator might be tempted to "freeze" into his or her role, forever searching for new people to educate. An organizer might spurn action and continue to specialize in building organization. This tendency of specialization of roles may discourage personal growth on the part of leaders. It also casts a shadow over the develop-ment of the movement as a whole, because coordination is more difficult when people do not have a "feel" for the variety of tasks which must be done. The leader who balks at personal change needs to realize the hollowness of her or his appeal for drastic change in the social patterns and life styles of others.

On Wars of Liberation

People are not free when they are subjected to violence. Therefore the strug-gle against violence must be seen in the context of a revolutionary effort to liberate humanity. We know that violence takes many forms, and that in addi-tion to the direct violence of guns and bombs, there is the silent violence of disease, hunger, and the dehumanization of men and women caught up in ex-ploitative systems.

With a reticence that comes from our knowledge that we do not have answers to many of the problems of revolution, we must say that men should not organize violence against one another, whether in revolution, in civil war, or in wars between nations. If it is argued that our position is utopian and that people can turn to nonviolence only after the revolution, we reply that unless we hold firmly to nonviolence now, the day will never come when all of us learn to live without violence. The roots of the future are here and now, in our lives and actions.

But our unwavering commitment to nonviolence does not mean that we are hostile to the revolutionary movements of our time, even though on certain fundamental issues we may disagree with some of them. It is impossible for us to be morally neutral, for example, in the struggle between the people of Vietnam and the American government, any more than we were able to be morally neutral 12 years ago in the struggle between the people of Hungary and the Soviet Union. We do not support the violent *means* used by the NLF and Hanoi, but we do support their *objective* in seeding the liberation of Vietnam from foreign domination.

We particularly emphasize our support for our friends in the Buddhist move-ment, who at great risk, and with little support from world opinion, have sought to achieve self-determination without using violence. It is particularly important for pacifists to maintain close contact with those elements in the revolutionary movements which quietly hold to nonviolence.

We do not romanticize nonviolent action and know better than anyone else its setbacks. But we ask our friends who feel they have no choice but to use violent means for liberation not to overlook the problems they face. The violence of revolution destroys the innocent just as surely as does the violence of the oppressor. Nor is the use of violence a guarantee of victory for the revolu-tion. Most guerrilla struggles have been defeated by the guardians of the status quo; Malaya, Greece, Bolivia, the Philippines, Guatemala are a few of the places where guerrillas have been defeated. In Spain there have been organized appeals for violent action against Franco for the past twenty years, and yet Franco still holds power.

A violent revolution creates a violent structure in which, having killed one's enemies, it is all too easy to kill one's friends for holding "wrong positions." Having once taken up weapons it is difficult to lay them down. If it is argued that a nonviolent revolution is too slow a method, and that violence more swiftly brings justice and freedom, we point to Vietnam where a violent strug-gle has raged for 26 years and where millions of people have been killed, and the revolution has not yet been won.

Certainly we are not saying that there is a nonviolent revolutionary answer in every situation. There has never been a nonviolent revolution in history, in the sense we mean it in this manifesto. We acknowledge our own limitations: we have sometimes been guilty of inaction when struggle was necessary, of neglecting our homework when study was imperative, of narrowness when peace was utterly dependent on social change.

The challenge we make to our nonpacifist friends in the liberation movements is to develop the outline of a nonviolent strategy for revolution before rejecting it out of hand. If you see violence only as a last resort, then first put time and energy into the next-to-the-last resort. If you see yourselves as practical people choosing among alternative courses, then *create* a nonviolent strategy so your choice will have meaning. The framework in this manifesto will help, but only someone immersed in a situation can create a strategy which can be concretely examined.

We remind all pacifists and all sections of the War Resisters International that the greatest single contribution we can make to the liberation movements is not by becoming entangled in the debate over whether or not such movements should use violence, but by actively working to bring an end to colonialism and imperialism by attacking its centers of power.

One of the basic reasons why we hold to nonviolence, even when it seems to have failed or when it cannot offer a ready answer, is because the nonviolent revolution does not seek the liberation simply of a class or race or nation. It seeks the liberation of humankind. It is our experience that violence shifts the burden of suffering from one group to another, that it liberates one group but imprisons another, that it destroys one authoritarian structure but creates another.

We salute those people who are using nonviolent action in their struggle despite the current trends and pressures towards violence. We also salute our sisters and brothers in the various liberation movements. We will work with them when it is possible, but without yielding up our belief that the foundation of the future must be laid in the present, that a society without violence must begin with revolutionists who will not use violence.

Why the Movement Must Become Transnational. / The basic problems facing people today transcend the nation in which they live. Poverty cannot be understood without seeing the economic empires which create a world-wide division of labor, with world-wide maldistribution of benefits. War cannot be understood without seeing the arms races and the big power rivalries. Racism is not confined to national boundaries, nor is sexism. Pollution is a global problem, and the depletion of resources will leave us all bereft no matter what country we live in.

This means that radical social change cannot occur neighborhood-by-neighborhood, or even country by country. The critical points of decision are shifting to the international context and power must be challenged where it is. A revolutionary movement must be based at the grass roots or it is not a people's movement, but if it remains at the local level only, it raises hopes only to disappoint them.

At the same time, this powerful dynamic pushing social affairs beyond the nation-state creates conditions in which it is finally possible to organize a *transnational movement.* We can ourselves go beyond the loose associations of national groups (*inter*nationals) to associations which reflect the new world society of the future.

Not only does our analysis lead us to a transnational perspective, but also our vision of a new society. However much has been accomplished by the radical movements of China and Sweden, for example, they still show in some of their dealings with other countries a betrayal of their own socialist principles. No country can exist in a vacuum and no revolution can be made in one. If the global context is not changed drastically, it will limit the achievements of the national revolution.

The ecological challenge especially shows the declining viability of nation-states. Humankind must reorganize to deal with global problems. If the new society of the future is a global society, our movements should reflect that now.

Our strategy also requires a transnational perspective. We need each other across national lines to exert powerful leverage for change. Some trade unions are already discovering that the multinational corporations cannot always be confronted by workers in one country alone; the unions must combine across national lines to be able to tackle the giants of modern capitalism.

Activists in various countries have much to teach each other. Even though conditions vary widely, sharing hard-won experience and analysis will lead to a more mature movement. Our own nationalism will probably only be outgrown through encounter with others.

The War Resisters International intends to play its part in encouraging a transnational movement for nonviolent revolution. We are encouraged by the increase of direct action projects organized across national lines, by the growth of consciousness of pacific militancy and the development of nonviolent training, by the increasing solidarity of war resisters everywhere, by the celebration of life and love in the midst of hardship and distress, and by the recognition in our movement that "the struggle against war will never be effective until it forms an integral part in the struggle for a new society."